MEMOIRS AND REFLECTIONS

MEMOIRS AND
REFLECTIONS

ROY McMURTRY

Published for The Osgoode Society for Canadian Legal History by
University of Toronto Press
Toronto Buffalo London

ISBN 978-1-4426-4830-2

∞

Printed on acid-free, 100% post-consumer recycled paper
with vegetable-based inks.

Publication cataloguing information is available from
Library and Archives Canada.

University of Toronto Press acknowledges the financial assistance to its
publishing program of the Canada Council for the Arts and the
Ontario Arts Council.

University of Toronto Press acknowledges the financial support of the
Government of Canada through the Canada Book Fund for its
publishing activities.

To my wife, Ria, and our family,
who have been the bedrock of my life

Contents

Part Three: Attorney General of Ontario

Part Four: At the Court of St James and Home Again

Part Five: Sixteen Years as a Judge

Part Six: Retirement

Illustrations follow pages 178 and 410

Foreword

THE OSGOODE SOCIETY
FOR CANADIAN LEGAL HISTORY

Few people have had a career as extensive, varied, and transformative as R. Roy McMurtry. In the public positions he held – reforming attorney general of Ontario, architect of the agreement that brought about the patriation of the Canadian Constitution, high commissioner to the United Kingdom, and chief justice of Ontario – he made immense contributions to Canadian law, politics, and life. Throughout, he has been a champion of anti-racism and human rights and an inspiring leader and motivator of others. Roy McMurtry also founded the Osgoode Society more than thirty years ago, and for that reason, among many others, we are delighted to be able to publish his *Memoirs and Reflections*.

This volume covers all the principal activities of his career enumerated above and, in addition, encompasses his law practice, his work on various commissions of inquiry, and his reflections on family, sport, and art. The memoirs are both an account of his life in public service and a portrait of a remarkably talented, humane, modest, humorous, and optimistic individual deeply concerned about his community and his country.

The purpose of the Osgoode Society for Canadian Legal History is to encourage research and writing in the history of Canadian law. The Society, which was incorporated in 1979 and is registered as a charity, was founded at the initiative of the Honourable R. Roy McMurtry and officials of the Law Society of Upper Canada. The Society seeks to stimulate the study of legal history in Canada by supporting research-

ers, collecting oral histories, and publishing volumes that contribute
to legal-historical scholarship in Canada. It has published ninety-two
books on the courts, the judiciary, and the legal profession, as well
as on the history of crime and punishment, women and law, law and
economy, the legal treatment of ethnic minorities, and famous cases
and significant trials in all areas of the law.

Current directors of the Osgoode Society for Canadian Legal History
are Robert Armstrong, Kenneth Binks, Susan Binnie, David Chernos,
Thomas G. Conway, J. Douglas Ewart, Violet French, Martin Fried-
land, John Gerretsen, Philip Girard, William Kaplan, C. Ian Kyer,
Virginia MacLean, Patricia McMahon, Roy McMurtry, Dana Peebles,
Paul Perell, Jim Phillips, Paul Reinhardt, Joel Richler, William Ross,
Paul Schabas, Robert Sharpe, Lorne Sossin, Mary Stokes, and Michael
Tulloch.

The annual report and information about membership may be obtained by writing to the Osgoode Society for Canadian Legal History,
Osgoode Hall, 130 Queen Street West, Toronto, Ontario, M5H 2N6.
Telephone: 416-947-3321. E-mail: mmacfarl@lsuc.on.ca. Website: www.
osgoodesociety.ca.

Jim Phillips
Editor-in-Chief

Acknowledgments

I would like to begin by expressing my deep gratitude to my out-standing and renowned editor Rosemary Shipton, who has been an invaluable guide throughout the writing of this memoir. Jim Phillips, the Editor-in-Chief of the Osgoode Society, has also been incredibly encouraging about the project and of great assistance.

In addition, I want to thank the readers, both anonymous and those identified, who shared their expertise with me and commented gener-ously on the text. Among the ones I know by name are Justice Robert Sharpe, Justice Rosalie Abella, Justice Robert Armstrong, Alison War-ner, Professor Martin Friedland, William Kaplan, Ian Kyer, and Paul Schabas.

I am also most appreciative of the assistance of my cousin An-drew McMurtry and my mother's sister, Genevieve Williamson, with respect to our early family history. Genevieve, a former librarian at Dartmouth, is, at the age of ninety-three, still a great life force and in-spiration.

At Gowlings, I would like to express my appreciation to Mary Thomson, chair of the litigation department, for all her encouragement in writing these memoirs. I also want to thank my assistants Deborah Pritchard and Judy Bew, for their great patience and perseverance over a number of years in overcoming the major challenge of deciphering my scribblings. To them and to my former assistant Cathy Lanni at the Court of Appeal, I express my appreciation and affection.

In recent years I prepared two major reports for the government of Ontario on the Roots of Youth Violence in Ontario and, in the context of the G20 meetings in Toronto in 2010, on the *Public Works Protection Act*. I would like to thank my Gowlings' partner Lynn Mahoney for her valuable assistance in creating both these reports.

It is simply not possible in the space available to express my appreciation to the many individuals who have played an important and supportive role in my life. I am confident, however, that they all know who they are, and I thank them sincerely for everything they have done for me.

Finally, I would like to thank Len Husband and Wayne Herrington of the University of Toronto Press for their enthusiasm and assistance. I also wish to acknowledge copy editor John St. James and indexer Gillian Watts for their contributions to this book.

PART ONE

Getting Established

1

The McMurtry Family Tree

I have always been of two minds when it comes to reading lengthy family histories at the beginning of memoirs or biographies. Though the narratives of the ancestors can be interesting in themselves, I generally prefer to get quickly into the protagonist's own life, with just a brief overview of the background story. In my own case, however, our family cherished the stories from the past and recounted them often. As a result, the exploits of many of my forebears in work and sport and the ideals they held about politics, humanity, and poetry had a direct influence on me and on the choices I made in my own life and career, so I feel compelled to recount in this first chapter the colourful family stories on which I grew up.

Our family papers and remembrances have been gathered together in a history written by my cousin Andrew McMurtry. They record that, about 1820, soon after my great-great-grandfather James McMurtry married his fiancée, Nancy Wilson, they left County Derry in the province of Ulster, Ireland, for Canada. The McMurtry family originally came from Scotland, according to *Greater Toronto and the Men Who Made It*, but had held property in Ireland probably since the 1600s. The young couple settled in the Ottawa Valley in March Township, an area originally opened up by English soldiers who had received land grants of riverside properties for their service to the Crown during the Napoleonic wars and the War of 1812. At that time the timber on the land was especially valuable to most of the residents because the lumber camps provided seasonal work for the men once the crops were harvested.

My great-grandfather George McMurtry was James and Nancy's second son. He established his own tannery business and also manufactured shoes, boots, and harnesses for the many timber crews that came through South March. His brother David opened the McMurtry General Store in the town. They were smart to go into business. A local history, *March Past*, describes what life was like there in the 1850s: "Tradesman in March benefited enormously from the lumber industry in the Ottawa Valley. Imagine the scene as [up to] four hundred men, with three hundred teams of horses, passed through March Corners during the winter months, sleeping overnight at many of the hotels, seeking repairs of their equipment from the blacksmiths or purchasing new footwear at McMurtry's Tannery."

George married Mary Younghusband, whose father, John, had emigrated to Canada from England in 1828 and who shared a common lineage with the explorer and mystic Sir Francis Younghusband. In 1863 George McMurtry became a councillor for March Township – the first family member to be a publicly elected official in Canada. He supported the Reform Party, in opposition to the Conservatives, whose principal personality in Canada West was John A. Macdonald. George McMurtry favoured universal public education. He proposed that a public school be built in South March, and three years later there were no fewer than eight such schools in the township. He also suggested an important resolution that required the auditors to circulate copies of the local budget, giving the residents an early taste of a more open and accountable government.

George and Mary's sixth and youngest child, my grandfather William James McMurtry, was born in 1866. Three years later his father died, but the official cause of his death remains unknown. According to a record kept at the time, the priest at their Anglican church was "using opium and couldn't see straight to keep accurate records."

William McMurtry left home at the age of sixteen in search of work in the lumber companies. He was a hardy young fellow, "able to compete with any man in the Ottawa Valley in a canoe and any French or Indian woodsman in the winter months," as one journalist described him. "He could do anything with a paddle and anything on snow shoes." He was clearly well known for his courage and hard work and regarded as a fearless and natural leader of men. When he was only nineteen he was made the "woods boss" for a large lumber company. One newspaper article about him records that "the rugged lumbering world was startled when the young man became a successful camp boss, which meant driving his crews in the bush, leading his loggers on dangerous river drives and taking on all comers without Queensbury rules when the lumberjacks were paid off and carousel bent." His duties also often involved carrying the camp's cash payroll by canoe from Ottawa to the camps with just a shotgun for protection.

After five years in this position, William had saved a significant sum of money, and he decided to "trade in his Mackinaw for a sack suit" and look for other adventures. First he married Lillian Lucy Waters, who was the same age as he and the daughter of Charles Thomson Waters, an Ottawa journalist and writer of popular satirical poems, and Pauline Foubert, a francophone whose ancestor Jean Baptiste de Foubert had arrived from Paris in 1775 and founded the town of Foubertville (now known as Buckingham, Quebec). Stories about Lillian's ancestors became a significant part of the McMurtry family saga – particularly those detailing her grandfather, Charles Waters.

Charles Waters was born in Vermont and, between 1834 and 1836, he served as the Reform Party member for Prescott in the Legislative Assembly of Upper Canada. His parents, Abel and Sarah Waters, arrived in Canada in 1783 as United Empire Loyalists, though the family had been in New England since 1639, when the first Waters ancestor had arrived from London. Abel Waters led a party of one hundred loyalists from Portland, Maine, and they settled near Trois-Rivières in Quebec. After a brutally cold winter, Abel and Sarah moved to New Carlisle, where Abel, having been a junior officer with the King's American Dragoons, was entitled to a grant of 300 acres. They didn't settle down, however, and in 1787 the family returned to the United States, where Abel became involved in political activities in the generally progressive Republic of Vermont. In addition to being a town moderator and a justice of the peace, he was elected on four occasions to the General Assembly of Vermont. On January 10, 1791, he was one of the 105 delegates who voted in favour of Vermont becoming the nineteenth state of the United States of America. However, by 1803 Abel and Sarah were back in Canada, where they settled in Longueuil.

Their son, Charles, my great-great-grandfather, continued the family's interest in politics. He served first as a magistrate, a coroner, and a lieutenant in the Prescott Militia, before becoming a Reform member of the Legislative Assembly. With his background in Vermont, where there was a complete separation of church and state, he opposed the close relationship between the church and the state in both French Canada and English Canada.

Among the multitude of injustices stemming from the Conservatives' collaboration with the Church of England, Charles Waters was most upset by the Clergy Reserves. These lands had been set apart in Upper and Lower Canada under the *Constitutional Act, 1791* "for the support and maintenance of the Protestant Clergy" – in other words, the Church of England. As an inspector of Clergy Reserves, Charles had witnessed the problems they caused for settlers unable to link communities with a direct road because of unused reserves blocking the way. During the 1835 session of the Upper Canada Legislative Assembly, when he chaired the House Committee on Clergy Reserves Reform, he introduced legislation that would have sold the lands reserved for the Church of England in Upper Canada and used the money to fund a public education system. The legislation was adopted by the Legislative Assembly but vetoed in the unelected Legislative Council.

These sympathies brought him into contact with some increasingly radical Reformers led by William Lyon Mackenzie. Unidentified sources record that "Waters thought of ... Mackenzie as one of his closest friends." The conflict between the Conservatives and the Reformers steadily escalated after the 1836 election, when the Conservative faction was returned to power with the support of the radically anti-Catholic Orange Order. Both Waters and Mackenzie were defeated. Immediately, Mackenzie became even more radical and spoke openly of armed rebellion. At the same time, the Reformers in Lower Canada were more strongly anti-British than those in Upper Canada. Having endured decades of English repression, Irish Catholics joined with French Catholics at a meeting led by Louis-Joseph Papineau at Saint-Charles, Quebec. The "Patriotes," as they were known, had not prepared effectively for an armed rebellion, and they were defeated during battles at Saint-Denis, Saint-Eustache, and Saint-Benoît. Papineau made his way to the United States, but, before he left, according to our family history, he stopped at Vankleek Hill in Ontario to meet with his friend Charles Waters. A substantial award of $4,000 had been offered for information that would lead to his capture, but Waters courageously hid Papineau until he could make his escape across the border undetected.

Meanwhile, Mackenzie decided to take advantage of the fact that, with the soldiers sent to quell the rebellion in Lower Canada, the city of Toronto was largely unguarded. On December 6, 1837, he called for his supporters to arm and assemble at Montgomery Tavern. Believing he would gain spontaneous support, Mackenzie led an expedition down Yonge Street. As the force neared Toronto, however, it was easily dispersed by a few shots. Mackenzie fled to the United States.

Charles Waters had already decided not to participate in an armed struggle and, rather, to take the constitutional path. He formed a society called the Young Men's Political Association. Still, as a Reform member of the Legislative Assembly, he came under the immediate suspicion of local Conservatives. Soon after Papineau had departed, word of the rebellion in Toronto reached Vankleek Hill, and Waters's home was surrounded by a vigilante mob ready to set it alight. According to a *History of Prescott*, "Waters' home was raided and thoroughly searched, but the soldiers found nothing more dangerous than the constitution of the Young Men's Political Association."

The failed Rebellion of 1837 actually accelerated the speed of reform and helped to create the foundation and structure of Canada's future federal parliamentary system of responsible government. The British dispatched Lord Durham to settle the volatile situation, and his 1838 report recommended such reforms as a parliamentary system with extended control over local affairs and the union of Upper and Lower Canada into one province called Canada. Before long, the union led to the historically important partnership between Sir Louis-Hippolyte LaFontaine and the anglophone reformer Robert Baldwin, who in 1842 became co–prime ministers of the new province of Canada.

Charles Waters wrote to Baldwin, congratulating him and expressing his pleasure over the probable formation of a new nation on the broad principles of the British Constitution. In 1843 Waters was appointed as an inspector of Clergy Reserves for the Ottawa District, though as a member of the Legislature he had earlier recommended that the reserves be sold off to fund public elementary schools and improved road access.

The Conservatives won the 1844 election, and our collection of family papers and cuttings includes a number of letters written by Charles Waters to Robert Baldwin lamenting the changed political atmosphere. One of January 29, 1845, states in part: "What machinations … what traitors they are and who could have believed that the individuals could have proved themselves to be such … but it is so. We must make the best of it, good may yet come of it." And on March 10, 1845, he wrote, "What a deplorable and degraded condition we are in" and expressed his hope that "order and justice will triumph over oppression and corruption."

In 1849 the Reformers were returned to government, and the second Baldwin–LaFontaine ministry was formed. Both English and French became official languages throughout their mandate. Amnesty was granted to William Lyon Mackenzie and his exiled rebels. In 1850, when township councils were created, Charles Waters was unanimously elected as the first clerk of the Township of West Hawkesbury.

After Mackenzie returned to Canada, he renewed his correspondence with Waters. In a letter dated October 2, 1850, Waters expressed his view that Canada must move towards nationhood: "Canada can never be in a state of permanent prosperity so long as she remains a Colony, upon this subject my mind has never changed." When Mackenzie was elected to the Legislature, Waters wrote to him on May 5, 1851: "Permit an old and unflinching Reformer of the Old School to congratulate you on your triumph in the Haldimand Election over a list of enemies of every shade." The letter went on to express Waters's continuing concern about the Clergy Reserves: "That a body of men whether of the administration or of the Legislative Assembly could be found out of the Old Conservative Family Compact to have been so degraded and so cringing and subservient as to unite the Imperial authorities, the bishops and the denomination that have for so many years devoured and fattened on the profits of those Reserves so wrongfully and corruptly surrendered … the want of those very reserves to educate our youth and whilst our provincial debt and abominable and unheard of extravagance absorbs our revenue." The Clergy Reserves were finally abolished in 1854.

The last letter in our collection from Waters to Mackenzie was particularly complimentary to the old rebel.

You have never swayed or turned your coat or back upon the principles (and patriotism). You deserve much better …

As for myself, I am getting old (in my 70th year). Fortune has not been a favourite of mine, yet, I am not bought or sold or wavering.

He expressed his concern about the "slavery question and serious difficulties within the borders of that great Republic." The letter concluded: "Pray let me hear from you if you can spare a moment and may the Lord bless you and your dear family."

Charles Waters died in Quebec City on September 9, 1865. His opposition to the Conservatives had caused him problems in business and employment generally, but his long commitment to parliamentary and other positive reforms is still a matter of great pride for our family.

On May 17, 1866, Charles Waters's son, also named Charles, and daughter-in-law Pauline Foubert welcomed my paternal grandmother, Lillian Foubert Waters, into their family in Cumberland, Ontario. This younger Charles spent his working life as a journalist and poet before his early death at the age of fifty. Regrettably, most of his writing, which was scheduled to be published, has disappeared. Lillian in turn became a successful poet, and much of her work was published in Canada and the United States.

* * *

There is no documented family history of the courtship of my grandfather William James McMurtry and Lillian Foubert Waters. They were married in 1889, and their wedding is recorded at Christ Church in Ottawa. By that time the Ottawa Valley was no longer the hub of a booming lumber industry. However, Sir John A. Macdonald's National Policy of protection for Canadian industries was beginning to produce positive results, and William sensed that there were opportunities to move from the raw lumber business into manufacturing. After living briefly in Mattawa, William and Lillian moved to Toronto in 1890. There he co-founded the Gold Medal Spring Company. A few years later he bought out his partner and changed the company name to the Gold Medal Furniture Manufacturing Company, producing a wide range of home and office furniture. He was very successful and became a founding member of the Canadian Manufacturers' Association. Despite his and his wife's Reform ancestry, in deference to John A. he became a lifelong federal Conservative.

Photographs of Lillian McMurtry show her to be a beautiful woman with the heavy-lidded eyes I later inherited. She is remembered as a very spiritual person, sensitive, caring, and devoted to her poetry. She had a particular concern about the less fortunate, and many of her poems refer to "the fall of helpless ones" or the need to "uplift the burden, share with them the best." She gave birth to four sons between 1895 and 1904: Claude in 1895, Bruce in 1898, Roland Roy (my father) in 1901, and Warren (Teddy) in 1904. She fed them a steady diet of novels and romantic adventure stories. These tales were extended into real life every time her brothers, Abel and Harold, came to visit. Abel was a long-time missionary in Africa, and Harold worked in the Yukon during the gold-rush days.

Not long after William and Lillian arrived in Toronto, they bought a home at 98 Jameson Avenue in the Parkdale area, which had become a prosperous neighbourhood. The property included a large Victorian home with a balcony supported by five white pillars, horse stables in the back, and separate servants' quarters. The family would travel by horse and buggy or simply on horseback. As the McMurtry furniture business prospered, my grandfather built a factory on Dupont Street just east of Dufferin. He also opened furniture factories in Winnipeg, Montreal, and Uxbridge. During the First World War he converted his furniture company into a manufacturer of military equipment, producing cots, waterproof ammunition boxes, and other items for the Canadian and British armies. In the 1920s he created the Radio-Phonograph Company, which became a pioneer Canadian manufacturer in this new area. But he lost a patent dispute to Standard Radio over the production of battery-powered radios, and that in effect destroyed this venture. Then he lost much of his fortune during the Great Depression in the early 1930s.

Lillian and William McMurtry must have been an interesting couple. We always called them Grandmère and Grandpère, in recognition of Lillian's francophone mother. William was a product of the rough-and-tumble logging industry, while Lillian, though a Protestant, had enjoyed a formal education at a convent. She was a talented pianist and writer and was active in many intellectual associations. She was often invited to write guest columns for the *Toronto Star* and the *Globe*. My grandpère was renowned for his toughness, hard work, and, as I have learned over the years, his integrity.

Their eldest son, Claude, served as a British officer in the First World War from November 1915 on and "celebrated" his twentieth birthday at Ypres in Belgium. Later he was moved to the Somme and participated in continual fighting for the next two years, witnessing many of the horrible massacres in that tragic war. Bruce, the next son, obtained an officer's commission in the 116th Battalion of the Canadian Infantry so he could join the Canadian Expeditionary Force, but he was injured during training and never saw action on the Western Front. It was one of his great disappointments in life. Lillian's principal contribution to the war effort was the writing of patriotic songs and poems.

For my father, the most memorable event during the war was a newspaper report of him playing most of a football game for St Andrew's College, his secondary school, with a broken arm. When Claude returned from the war, he inspired my father in 1919 to follow his example and enrol at the Royal Military College in Kingston. Later, when Claude was an honoured guest at his former college, Dad was a student there. He became the heavyweight boxing champion of RMC, just as Claude had been the welterweight champion. It was often said that William McMurtry's skill with his fists was encouraged in all his four sons.

One of my favourite entries in Lillian's journal is her description of the Georges Carpentier–Jack Dempsey match in 1921 for the world heavyweight championship in New Jersey. She was in Paris with William at the time, and the match there was described as the "battle of the century" by boxing enthusiasts:

Every preparation that the people of Paris could devise had been made to make the expected victory of their beloved Carpentier one of all-night rejoicing with incomparable brilliancy.

All day the city was tense with subdued yet obvious excitement full of joyous anticipation of a glorious all-night carnival of joy. Your dad thinks about two million people were out on the squares and boulevards. All the newspapers officiated that the signal of victory would be a green flare for Dempsey and a glorious red flare for Carpentier.

Ah what descriptive powers one would need to describe the scene when the green flare suddenly shot up. The words "Dempsey is the victor" swept across the bulletin board.

It was tragic! The faces of men and women went absolutely white. In a table near us sat two splendid young chaps, one almost Bruce's double. Both grew deadly pale and without a word lit up cigarettes with a calmness (yet trembling hands) that spoke volumes. For moments not one sound came from the great sorrow-stricken throng.

Just plain silence in which the bowed heads suggested the moment of benediction at a church service. Paris was stunned. To see all of Paris rejoicing must be the highlight of brilliancy. To see Paris defeated is to see something sublime.

The fourth McMurtry brother, Warren, known as Teddy, also attended St Andrew's College, which by then had moved from its location in Rosedale to Aurora, thirty miles north of Toronto. There he gained a reputation as an outstanding athlete. Teddy decided to join the family business rather than go to university, and he soon rose from salesman to sales manager. His wife, whom I remember as Trudy, was a graduate of Havergal College in Toronto and of Boston University.

Although my father did not see a great deal of his brothers, I remember Uncle Ted as a gregarious individual who loved a little "rough and tumble" with his nephews.

My Uncle Bruce was in charge of the Toronto plant of the Gold Medal Furniture Company. He had read widely about industrial relations and had personally witnessed the havoc caused by the general strike in Winnipeg in 1919. In 1925, under his direction, Gold Medal implemented what was described in trade journals as "the most progressive industrial relations profit-sharing program known at the time." The program directed that 50 per cent of the net profits were to be divided among the employees and, in addition, 10 per cent should be placed in a charity fund. The employees were given joint control of the Toronto plant through a committee they elected. It met with management every week and had regular access to the company's accounts. A large clubroom was also provided at the factory for the employees.

Bruce married Kathleen Marie Fallis in March 1931. She became a widow at a young age, when Bruce died at forty. He was committed to the "horsey set" – a good rider who owned his own horse and belonged to the Eglinton Hunt Club. He also loved a good party during the roaring twenties, along with all his wealthy friends. Unfortunately, the challenges faced by the Gold Medal Company in the early 1930s only worsened his own increasing depression, and he developed a serious addiction to alcohol. His widow, our Aunt Kay, remained an important and much-loved member of our family for many years.

My father took a different route from his three brothers and went into law. He was called to the Ontario bar in 1926. The following year, the Gold Medal Company faced a serious challenge when an American Company, Gold Medal Camp Furniture Manufacturing Company of Racine, Wisconsin, challenged our Canadian company's entitlement to the trademark "gold medal" name. My father successfully represented the family company all the way to the Supreme Court of Canada. It was a wonderfully happy victory, although Dad advised me when I became a lawyer never to act for relatives!

When he was twenty-nine, my father married Doris Elizebeth Belcher, who was only seventeen at the time. They had met on the tennis courts at Britannia, a popular summer resort on the Lake of Bays near Huntsville, Ontario. Dad was there with his closest friend, Parker Denovan, a fellow lawyer. He immediately told Parker he had just met his future wife. Parker took no notice, as he had heard similar romantic sentiments from Dad before. It was a whirlwind courtship, however, and the happy couple were married a year later on September 3, 1930. I was their first child, arriving on May 31, 1932. Stories of the Belcher ancestors were another huge influence on my life, so again I will digress into a little more detail about them.

* * *

My mother's father, Walter Rashleigh Belcher, had immigrated to Canada from Ireland in 1906. He came from an old and well-known Anglo-Irish family in Bandon, County Cork, which had arrived in Ireland from Gloucestershire about 1610. Bandon, a Protestant enclave in the heart of Catholic Ireland, is situated in the western part of County Cork in the Province of Munster. The Belcher family produced six generations of doctors, including Walter's father, Dr John Belcher, a military physician, whose tomb I located in 1970 during my first visit to Ireland. The family also produced a number of Church of Ireland clergy, whom Walter described as "a sort of junior branch of the Church of England." My grandfather also often carried a news clipping that outlined the story of his great-granduncle Captain Robert Tresillian Belcher, who fought in the Battle of Waterloo and was honourably mentioned by the Duke of Wellington in his report on the famous battle.

My Irish-born grandfather had a quiet but highly developed sense of humour. In the delightful short history of Bandon he wrote, he concluded on a nostalgic note:

That mournful country – A charming peasantry upon a fruitful sod fighting like devils for conciliation and hating each other for the love of God.

Poor dear old Ireland, I can truthfully say, With all thy faults I love thee still.

In Walter Belcher's words, the family was "hard-up." One of his brothers died as a soldier in the South African War, and a second brother settled in Canada in 1896 and eventually became a deputy commissioner of the North-West Mounted Police, the predecessor of the RCMP. His own son also attained this position. Walter Belcher seems not to have liked lawyers during his years in Ireland. He refers to his only prosperous relatives, an uncle and his son, both solicitors, as "Blaze (angry) George" and "Shifty Bob," respectively.

Walter's father died when he was sixteen years old, leaving "a very moderate amount of insurance and an immoderate amount of debt." As the oldest male left, my grandfather was obliged to take on the responsibility of supporting his family, and he got a position as a junior teller in a bank. Before leaving for Canada, he had worked in several banks, including one in the town of Dunmanway in Cork for some years.

After he passed the examination sponsored by the Institute of Bankers in Ireland, he was accepted by the Hong Kong and Shanghai Banking Corporation. The job had a strict age requirement, however, and Walter was six months too old. He decided to travel to London, where he successfully applied for a banking job in Canada: he left from Liverpool on July 12, 1906, and arrived in Montreal one week later. Before leaving Dunmanway, as he described in his memoir, "there occurred one of the most pleasing events of my life, the presentation of a very handsome and valuable gold watch by the people of the Town." As his oldest grandchild, I inherited the watch, which remains a treasured possession.

My grandfather reported to his new employer the Bank of British North America in Montreal and was assigned to a branch office in Fredericton, New Brunswick. Two years later he was transferred to a branch in Toronto. There he met Doris May Baines, and they were married on April 15, 1912. She was a distant relative of Elizabeth Johnson Baines, the wife of Colonel John By, who in 1826 was contracted to build the Rideau Canal and went on to found the city of Bytown, now Ottawa. Shortly thereafter, Walter was sent to be manager of a small branch of the bank in the west end of Toronto. My mother, Doris Elizebeth, was born in 1913, and her sister, Genevieve, in 1920. In the fall of 1918 Walter's bank was amalgamated with the Bank of Montreal, and for many years he worked as a branch manager. In 1922, when he took over the branch in Niagara Falls, my mother was enrolled at Loretto Abbey. She always had happy memories of the dedicated nuns at that school.

My mother's maternal grandparents were William Banks Baines and Helen Digby Wyatt, who married in 1883. Both their families had been very active in Toronto society in business, sailing, and the Anglican Church. William had a series of jobs in the Baines family companies, particularly in the brokerage and insurance businesses, though his last position was with the Ontario Department of Lands, Forests and Mines.

In 1916 my grandmother Belcher's brother Egerton Baines, who had joined the army and gone overseas, was involved in an attack at Ypres in Belgium. He was killed while commanding a group of soldiers who were laying barbed-wire obstacles. His body was never found. In 1917 a memorial plaque was dedicated in the Church of St George the Martyr, where four generations of the Toronto Baines family had worshipped.

In 1932, the year of my birth, Walter Belcher was appointed as the Bank of Montreal manager in Kingston, where he worked until his retirement in 1945. He continued to live there until his death in 1965. I was very close to my grandmother Belcher, and she had a positive influence on me in my younger years. She had a strong religious faith and subscribed to a Christian weekly publication, *The Daily Word*, which she regularly sent to me, particularly during my boarding-school years at St Andrew's College. "Ga," as she was known to her four grandsons, truly believed that religious faith could accomplish good results. The combination of *The Daily Word* and the daily chapel services at St Andrew's created a strong religious faith in me during my teenage years.

* * *

My grandmother Lillian Waters McMurtry passed away in 1934, and her death was the subject of many obituaries, one of which stated in part:

A writer of international distinction and a member of an illustrious pioneer Canadian family passed away in the person of Lillian Waters McMurtry, the gifted poet, whose work is familiar to thousands of Canadian readers …

Of United Empire Loyalist stock and four generations of Canadians, the late Mrs. McMurtry was the daughter of Pauline Foubert and Charles Tomlinson Waters, who also was a well-known writer and son of Charles Waters, one-time member of parliament for Prescott and Russell (and friend of Papineau and Mackenzie), and the great-granddaughter of Abel Waters, who led a number of Loyalists from Portland Maine to L'Original at the beginning of the nineteenth century.

The family patriotic tradition continued when Canada entered the Second World War. Once again the Gold Medal Company dedicated much of its production to the war effort. At the same time, my Uncle Claude attempted to re-enlist, and he wrote letters seeking support to senior military associates in both Canada and Britain – all without success. My own father was ineligible for military service because the rheumatic fever he suffered shortly after his marriage had affected his heart.

After the death of his wife, Lillian, my grandfather William McMurtry married Margaret Taylor Otto, and he had a modest home built in Weston, just outside Toronto. My father took us to visit regularly on weekends, and my brothers and I enjoyed exploring the nearby forest. When William died in 1946 at the age of eighty-one, the historian and journalist Kim Beattie wrote an obituary in the magazine published by the Canadian Manufacturers' Association:

They are the truly great, but unfortunately their solid contributions to the national life, and their inestimable value to Canada, are seldom realized until their honest counsel, wise experience and steadfast personalities are suddenly missing. Such an unsung Canadian great was William James McMurtry, founder of the Gold Medal Furniture Manufacturing Company, Ltd., who died at his home in Weston, near Toronto, last October 18 in his eighty-second year.

For years the extensive group of Canadian furniture manufacturers had considered William J. McMurtry as a leader and a dean; but now he is seen to have been much more. He was one of the stalwarts of all Canadian industry. He had always held the respect of the Canadian business world, and he was known everywhere in it, but now a review of his life revealed him as an inspiring, far-sighted leader of the Dominion's commerce, and one of the most confident in its future.

If there was a key to the character of the late furniture manufacturer, it lies perhaps in a medley of strong qualities – calm, sound judgement, unswaying insistence on honest products, backed by indomitable will. Nothing but such a combination could have seen "Gold Medal" furniture survive the storm of 1926 and the depression of the 1930's. And if there was ever a tribute revealing of an employer's worth, it was in the men gone old and gray in his service, who mustered at William J. McMurtry's funeral. Had he seen it that would have been held far more precious than all the printed eulogies announcing his death.

The Gold Medal Furniture Manufacturing Company was left equally to WJ's sons Claude and Teddy. Unfortunately, without the moderating influence of their father, the brothers disagreed constantly as the strain of being business partners stretched their already competitive relationship to the breaking point. In 1957 they decided to go their separate ways in business, though they continued to operate out of the same factory on Dupont Street. Claude's company, C.A. McMurtry Furniture, prospered for some time, but neither of the founder's children was interested in joining the firm. Teddy's business was less successful. The original building remained a well-known Toronto landmark until it was destroyed by fire in 1996, long after both brothers had passed on. The property had been sold much earlier to condominium developers, who at the time of the fire were marketing the "McMurtry Lofts."

Although my father did not remain close to his brothers, we cousins all got along quite well. On this note, I'll leave my ancestors behind and move on to my own story.

2

School and Sports

My childhood years were personally idyllic and untroubled by the harsh realities of the larger world, which included the Great Depression. Born in 1932, I was the first of four sons for my parents, Elizebeth and Roy McMurtry, followed by my brothers William (Bill), John, and Robert (Bob).

My earliest memories are of trains speeding by just below the porch of my parents' home on the Old Bridle Path in Toronto when I was not yet two years old. My next recollection is being served with a "summons" by a member of the Toronto Police Department in my playpen when I was about three years old, after we moved to Glenayr Road in Forest Hill. As my father expanded his law practice, he had become the first legal counsel to the newly formed Toronto Police Association in 1930. In my later years as a lawyer when I became familiar with police department politics, I often wondered how he balanced his role as legal adviser to the police association with his friendship with General Dennis (Deny) Draper, the Toronto police chief, who was one of my godfathers. Draper was regarded as a somewhat pompous and militaristic martinet, and given the present uneasy relationship between police unions and police chiefs, a friend of the chief would be a most unlikely choice as legal counsel for any police union. Years later I followed suit in my own practice, acting as legal counsel to the Metropolitan Toronto Police Department and representing police chiefs and other rank-and-file officers in public inquiries and trials, both civil and criminal.

I remember a tearful separation from my mother when she first deposited me in kindergarten in 1937 at the Forest Hill Village School on Spadina Road. Then, early on in my school days, I was bitterly disappointed when I was relegated to the "stick" section of our musical rhythm "band." I desperately wanted to play a tambourine or a triangle, and my mother's oft-repeated observation that "life is not always fair" failed to console me. The wider world seldom intervened in our sheltered existence. The arrival of my brother Bill, just before my second birthday, interrupted my brief reign as the centre of the universe, but the birth of the younger two, John and Bob, seven and nine years my junior, were exciting events. My most poignant memories concern my infatuations with several attractive female teachers during my early school years, particularly my appropriately named grade 1 teacher Jean Care.

The Glenayr Road home was comfortable but not ostentatious. I shared one bedroom with Bill, and my younger brothers shared another. Bill and I were constant companions in our early years and, once John and Bob were old enough to join us in ball games and shinny ice hockey, we became close with them too. Our parents constantly emphasized the importance of family loyalty to us, and I have no recollection of any sibling rivalry whatsoever. When we were children, the live-in maid occupied the fourth bedroom on the second floor. My mother did most of the cooking, and we boys formed the washing-up brigade. My dad was no handyman, so did little around the house. Every day milkmen and bakers delivered dairy products and bread on our street from horse-drawn wagons. They were a fascinating sight to urban children and a significant presence in our neighbourhood. I still feel tinges of guilt, however, when I remember how I and some other kids once frightened a horse onto a neighbour's meticulously manicured lawn. It was not a pretty sight. This house remained my base until I finished university and married in 1957. It was quite the "legal" street, and a number of my father's highly respected law colleagues also lived there, including John Robinette, Edson Haines, John Pickup, a former chief justice of Ontario, and the parents of my long-time legal and political colleague Eddie Goodman.

In contrast to my father's strong, competitive, and emotional personality, my mother was gentle and calm. Having married at seventeen, she had not gone on to university, though she was very intelligent and enjoyed learning about things. Later in life she enrolled at York University and, over about fifteen years, earned her bachelor of arts. The degree gave her confidence to volunteer in schools helping children in special education classes. She was quite religious, and every Sunday took us to Sunday School at our Anglican church, Grace Church on the Hill. Dad was not a church goer, so he stayed at home. They were affectionate and caring parents, and we boys always knew that we were loved. Occasionally our parents played bridge with friends, but for the most part they restricted their social life to family gatherings. My father's favourite recreation was Saturday night hockey games at Maple Leaf Gardens. No doubt my mother attended more sporting events than she bargained for when she married my dad!

My father had been called to the bar of Ontario in 1926, and over the years he had a variety of partners or shared office space with long-term colleagues. His litigation practice was largely related to civil actions, particularly in insurance law involving aviation and the construction of the original subway system. Occasionally he conducted criminal defences, and he often talked about them over dinner with the family. He was very much a gentleman of the old school in his relationships with his legal colleagues, but very aggressive in the actual trials. He certainly enjoyed the drama of the courtroom and was fond of repeating Chief Justice William Riddell's well-known statement that "a trial is not a tea party." In fact, his former juniors and law students later liked to tell me about the processions he led on his way to any trial. "We were made to feel like we were going to war," they said. At the same time, he believed strongly in Shakespeare's sage advice: "As advocates do, strive mightily but eat and drink as friends."

I saw my father in court only once, when I was eighteen, in a much-publicized criminal trial involving two former sportsmen who, shortly before their arrest, had been named athletes of the half-century in their respective sports in Canada. One of the accused, Dalton, was represented by the renowned criminal defence counsel G. Arthur Martin, who was generally regarded as the dean of Canadian defence lawyers. Dad represented the co-accused, Ecclestone. They were charged with stealing and selling electronic equipment. The two defence counsel demonstrated a dramatically different style in court, with Martin's low-key approach juxtaposed against my father's forceful attack, yet each in his own way was very effective. Both the accused were acquitted, notwithstanding what appeared to be a strong case for the prosecution.

My father's hard-line advocacy in this trial both in his cross-examination of witnesses and in his address to the jury was fuelled to some extent by his belief that important police evidence had been significantly changed between the preliminary inquiry and the actual trial. Given the high-profile nature of the trial, the determination of the prosecution to obtain convictions was hardly surprising. Dad's hostility towards the police witnesses was not a reflection of his general attitude to the police force as a whole. I remember in particular the way he interrupted the closing address to the jury by Crown prosecutor Henry Bull, QC – a formidable, aggressive, and effective advocate. Later I learned that an interjection at this point in a trial is considered most inappropriate.

I don't know why my father broke this code, but I vividly recall the language he used. He alleged that Mr Bull was employing vicious "Russian-like tactics" in his conduct of the prosecution – and at a time in the Cold War when Communist Russia was regarded by Westerners as the epitome of evil. Such language in a courtroom today would likely result in a new trial on any Crown appeal. However, the incident did not appear to be of particular concern to the presiding judge, and the trial continued. The Crown did not appeal the acquittal of the accused. Henry Bull never forgave my father for this incident, but he became a friend and mentor of mine after my call to the bar. Possibly he was compensating for his well-known dislike of my dad by assisting me in the early years of my career.

Despite his success, my father instilled in us boys that he found his greatest satisfaction in pro bono work, helping poor people who had been treated unfairly by fate. In addition, he strongly opposed any form of racial or religious discrimination. At the time he began his law career, anti-Semitism was prevalent in society and remained so for many years to come. Jewish lawyers and doctors, for example, found it extremely difficult to be accepted by major Toronto law firms and teaching hospitals. Dad always described anti-Semitism as one of the world's greatest evils, and he never hesitated to speak out against it. He was also a friend and close colleague of B.J. Spencer Pitt, who, as one of the few black lawyers in Ontario in those years, suffered cruel discrimination at times. Spencer Pitt often retained Dad to act as counsel on his behalf in the Ontario Court of Appeal and the Supreme Court of Canada. My father told us about their first trip to Ottawa together when they were appearing before the Supreme Court and Pitt was denied access to the Château Laurier. Dad intervened decisively, and on that occasion and on all their subsequent visits, they were provided with one of the most comfortable suites in the hotel.

My father usually worked at home on his cases in the evenings so he could interact with his family – and by example and precept he had a huge influence on us. He regaled us with stories about King Arthur and the Knights of the Round Table, imbuing us with the idea that we could make a difference in life and, because we could, we must. He was a keen athlete himself, and liking the blend of cooperation and competition in team sports, he urged all his sons to participate in as many as we could manage. We continually played street games of football, baseball, and hockey. Eddie Goodman in his autobiography wrote of the McMurtry brothers "living" on his parents' garage roof, while John Robinette often spoke about our footballs bouncing around his front garden. It was generally agreed that the McMurtry boys' activities did little for property values on this otherwise quiet and elegant street.

Although athletic activities were an important part of our lives, the vast array of organized sports that became available in later years did not then exist. We became particularly interested in football and hockey, our father's favourite sports, and we also played baseball, basketball, and lacrosse. On special occasions Dad took us to a hockey game at Maple Leaf Gardens, a football game at Varsity Stadium, or a Toronto Maple Leaf Triple A baseball game at the Fleet Street stadium near the Toronto waterfront. He was a most exuberant sports fan and rarely resisted the opportunity to express his views in uninhibited terms. Sometimes I was embarrassed by his enthusiastic and vocal partisanship. At the same time, although he seldom missed the opportunity to encourage his sons in their athletic activities, to compete and win, he never criticized us. He would have been appalled by the many "hockey moms and dads" who pollute hockey arenas across Canada today with their diatribes – which are often directed at their own children.

Memories of our summer vacations are particularly vivid – long, lazy, hazy summer days at a rented cottage near Jackson's Point on Lake Simcoe and, later, at a cottage my parents purchased on Stoney Lake. One day I built a go-cart for my brother Bill. We also fished together on the Black River for pails of sunfish, and occasionally we went on longer expeditions with our local handyman. My father, although an expert canoeist, showed little interest in fishing, and I never developed any serious interest in that sport. I've always been envious, though, of the special companionship that activity brings, particularly between fathers and their children. Our summers also included visits to the cottage belonging to my mother's parents near Kingston. It was during one of those visits in September 1939 that Canada entered the Second World War, and I heard my parents and grandparents solemnly discussing the newspaper headlines. Earlier that summer I had excitedly waved a flag, together with thousands of other schoolchildren, during the visit of King George VI and Queen Elizabeth to Toronto.

My father attempted to enlist in the Canadian Army, but was rejected because his earlier attack of rheumatic fever had damaged a heart valve. I remember his daily comments on the progress of the war, and particularly his scepticism about the political leadership in Ottawa. He was also one of the legal counsel in a commission investigating the inadequate footwear being manufactured for the Canadian military. However, the most traumatic moment of the war for my parents was when Bill Wood, the junior lawyer in my father's office, was killed in battle in Italy in 1943. He was a particular favourite, and Dad regarded him almost as a son. Following his death, Dad sank into a profound and long depression. In the many memorial-day services I have attended at Osgoode Hall, the reciting of the name William Ballentine Wood always stirs memories of those sad days.

Dad came to the conclusion that it was Prime Minister Mackenzie King's reluctance to impose conscription that had led to the inadequate reinforcements of the Canadian Army in Italy and the death of Bill Wood. I recall a breakfast harangue related to Mr King which ended by my father stating that he was going to take the next train to Ottawa and shoot the prime minister. My mother had learned to allow these eruptions to pass in silence, and I don't recall the subject being raised again. Nevertheless, it was clear Dad was not a supporter of the federal Liberal Party, and he sometimes helped Progressive Conservative candidates both federally and provincially at election time. On the whole, though, he had a healthy scepticism about politics, and he never encouraged me to become active in any particular political party.

My father was much more interested in talking about law than about politics, and I never did learn much about his own political philosophy. I regret that political discussions never formed part of our conversations, as I would have liked to probe the range of his political beliefs in greater detail. True to his Irish ancestry, he was more inclined to articulate what he was against than what he supported. He never considered running for elective office, and when my brother Bill and I entered law, he cautioned us against the distractions that could be caused by any preoccupation with the world of politics. "The law is a very jealous mistress" was one of his favourite sayings, and in his view, a serious lawyer had little time for anything beyond his family and his profession. He believed strongly, however, that service to the less-fortunate members of the community was a duty for everyone who had been privileged by a good education and a strong family background. Still, I have no doubt that if my father had lived longer, he would have become very enthusiastic about my own political career.

It was not until the end of the Second World War that I became aware of the enormity of the horrors related to that monstrous conflict. While there was no shortage of atrocities during those tragic years, the revelation of the Holocaust was particularly shocking. Information about this human depravity shook the foundations of my world and made a profound impact on me. We had many Jewish neighbours and schoolmates in our area, and the murder of millions solely because of their race and religion shattered my illusions about the innate sense of humanity in the world. At the age of thirteen, I had always been sheltered from cruel realities, including the virulence of anti-Semitism in Canadian society itself.

I still recall the news of the death of Franklin Delano Roosevelt and the uncertainty surrounding the elevation of Harry Truman to replace him. My father liked to take a winter holiday in Florida, and his Republican friends in the United States contemptuously dismissed Truman as "a failed haberdasher" because of his earlier unsuccessful clothing store in St Louis, Missouri, following the First World War. I also remember some Republican businessmen who regularly visited the Ontario lake country and dismissed FDR as a dangerous socialist president. I believe this early exposure to the visceral divisions in American politics helped to develop a lifelong suspicion towards the Republican Party in me. In any event, I came to respect Truman as one of the most important and courageous presidents in US history.

During the summer of 1945 I got my first "job," working for a month on a farm near Garden Hill, Ontario. The farmer, one of Dad's friends, believed that "lazy, hazy summers" for boys should include some manual labour. My days began at sunrise with milking, followed by feeding chickens and gathering eggs before stooking hay in the broiling sun. It was all an interesting and challenging contrast to the relaxing summers I had earlier enjoyed with the family. There was no financial compensation, and my principal reward was riding bareback through the forest on my favourite "western pony." For a thirteen-year-old, it was a romantic adventure, and ever since, I have enjoyed the fragrance of new-mown hay as well as the less-appealing barnyard odours.

The end of the war marked the beginning of my final year in elementary school. I was an indifferent student, more interested in sport both as a participant and a spectator. Fortunately my teacher, Donald Graham, had been an assistant coach of the University of Toronto football Varsity Blues, and he encouraged a commitment to both studies and sport. In 1945 he coached the Forest Hill Village School 100-pound football team – a group that included a number of people who have remained friends, such as lawyers Herb Solway and Lionel Schipper and hotel magnate Isadore Sharpe. Given that my weight has not dipped below 200 pounds in more than fifty years, it has not been easy to convince family and friends that I ever played for a football team where the maximum weight was 100 pounds. Graham was a gifted teacher, leader, and motivator and a tremendous role model – for many years I too wanted to become a teacher. He went on to become director of education for the Forest Hill schools.

That autumn of 1945 my father arranged for me to be a trainer's assistant, or "water boy," on game days for the first post-war Toronto Argonaut football team. He had played briefly for the Argos after the First World War, and his former coach was then an Argo director and team doctor. At that time the Canadian Football League was called the Canadian Rugby Union, with two separate leagues in the East and the West, and the champion of each league competed for the Grey Cup. The Eastern League comprised the Toronto Argonauts, the Hamilton Tigers, the Ottawa Rough Riders, and the Montreal Hornets. The Hamilton Tigers later merged with the Hamilton Wildcats (a team in the other football league, the Ontario Rugby Football Union, or ORFU) to become the Hamilton Tiger Cats, and the Montreal Hornets evolved into the Montreal Alouettes. The Western League was also made up of four teams – the Winnipeg Blue Bombers, the Calgary Stampeders, the Edmonton Eskimos, and the Regina Roughriders (who later became the Saskatchewan Roughriders).

The ORFU included the Toronto Balmy Beach, the Toronto Indians, the Sarnia Imperials, and the Hamilton Wildcats. The winner of the ORFU league was entitled to play a semi-final game on alternating years with the Eastern and Western League champions. The ORFU winner never made it to the Grey Cup after 1945, and the right of that league to challenge for the Grey Cup was eliminated when the Balmy Beach team almost upset the Winnipeg Blue Bombers in 1950. The near upset would have meant that two Eastern teams would have challenged for the Grey Cup, destroying the East-West rivalry that had long made the Grey Cup one of the major Canadian national sporting events.

It is interesting to reflect on the interest in Canadian football which existed in Toronto in 1945. As well as the Toronto Argos, the Balmy Beach, and the Toronto Indian teams, there was the University of Toronto Varsity Blues, which had also challenged for and won the Grey Cup in earlier years. Football was a major sport in Toronto high schools, and many community junior leagues competed at a level between high school and university. In any event, it was exhilarating for a thirteen-year-old to enter the dressing room of the fabled Toronto Argonaut football team. The coach was Ted Morris, who was still attired in his Second World War naval uniform. The senior trainer was George Stockwell, whose son Bill and grandson Chris both went on to have significant careers in municipal and provincial politics.

The members of the Argo team were heroic figures to me, and it was a great privilege to attend to the minor chores of distributing uniforms and towels and to carry a bucket of water out onto the field during a game. The 1945 Argos defeated the Winnipeg Blue Bombers 35–0 to win the Grey Cup. The stars of the team were Joe Krol at quarterback and Royal Copeland as a running back and pass receiver. The Krol-to-Copeland forward-pass combination was to dominate the league for several years as the Argos also won the Grey Cup in 1946 and 1947.

The Old Varsity Stadium had a roof over the western stands, and spectators were often distracted by the pigeon droppings from the many nests in the roof beams. Notwithstanding these minor irritants, the Argos had a tremendously enthusiastic following in 1945 and for several more decades. My nostalgia for those years was strengthened when I became the chairman and chief executive officer of the Canadian Football League in 1989, although by then the league was engaged in a struggle for its very survival.

My father regarded football as the greatest of all team sports, and certainly my 1945 adventures with the Argos and the Forest Hill Village school 100-pound football team began a lifelong interest in the game. Then, over the summer, my somewhat erratic academic career persuaded my parents that a more structured and disciplined school setting would benefit their eldest son. I did not for a moment doubt their wisdom and accepted the transaction, though with a degree of apprehension. In September 1946 I was enrolled in St Andrew's College in Aurora, Ontario, where I spent my remaining high-school years. My father had attended the same school years earlier when it was located in the Rosedale area of Toronto. Fortunately, autographed photographs from Joe Krol and Royal Copeland followed me to the school and provided me with a modest degree of celebrity as I embarked on the challenge of a completely new environment.

* * *

I was quite apprehensive about leaving the sanctuary of a close-knit family for the foreign world of a boarding school. I had never even attended a summer camp and, apart from the time I'd spent working on the farm, had never lived away from home. However, I had great confidence in my parents' wisdom and accepted their decision with a modest degree of enthusiasm.

The world has utterly changed for teenagers today compared to the generally conformist attitudes of my generation. We spent our youth living through a worldwide depression and war, followed by growing tensions with the Communist bloc. The desire for security and stability was a dominant factor in our Western culture, leaving little room for youthful rebellion. We were also considerably less worldly than those who later grew up in the age of television and the "global village."

The all-male boarding-school environment of 1946 was highly structured and had little contact with the outside world other than occasional parental visits and athletic competitions with other schools. We were allowed only one weekend visit home every term as well as the holidays at Christmas and Easter. We attended classes six days a week, with Saturday classes ending at 1 pm. Each day commenced with a chapel service, although St Andrew's College was a non-denominational school. Participation in organized sport, including boxing, was compulsory unless a student had been given a medical exemption. The entire school population numbered only 230 students in my entering year, yet we fielded eight football teams that participated in interschool competition. Membership in the school cadet corps was also obligatory except for the members of the junior elementary school. The whole system was based on British public school traditions, and we wore our uniform with jackets and ties to every class and every meal.

The majority of the students came from Ontario and Quebec, though some hailed from Peru, Mexico, Bermuda, and Trinidad, including many whose families had enjoyed a long association with the college. Some of the South American students arrived speaking only Spanish. In this environment, we had to adapt to survive, and there was little opportunity to march to our own drummers. It was not a mindless conformity but simply a willingness to participate in a broad variety of school activities – including team sports, music, and drama. The school provided a valuable learning experience in getting along with other students, particularly for shy students like me. There may have been a few unhappy boys, but all told it was a congenial atmosphere.

"New boys" in the upper school were expected to perform a few services for the senior students, such as making beds. I don't recall any bullying in the dormitories. Despite the medieval appearance and horror stories that abound about this tradition, my own experience of these routine chores was altogether positive. It even enabled me to become friends with a few students who were in grade 13, something that otherwise would have been very difficult for a grade 10 student. These friendships gave me a level of confidence which helped me to enjoy my boarding-school adventure. I was perhaps fortunate in meeting with particularly supportive senior students. In any event, this minor serf tradition has appropriately long since been abandoned in most boarding schools.

The small school population enabled most students to get to know one another, and any sign of anti-social behaviour was generally not well received. Everyone seemed to appreciate the peril of taking himself too seriously, though inevitably there were cliques. However, the entire school spirit was characterized by mutual support rather than confrontation.

Our teachers were a disparate group in age, character, and academic qualifications. Many of them spent their entire careers at St Andrew's College – three of my teachers, for instance, had taught my father thirty years earlier. Unlike the situation today, where the staff in independent schools are qualified teachers, most of our masters had no teaching certificates, though they were usually university graduates. Some were lifelong bachelors, and others were married without children. Several of my teachers resembled Mr Chips, the title character in the famous film set in a British boarding school, in the way they became "institutions" themselves. They generally combined both stern disciplinary techniques with warmth and humour. Other masters, for one reason or another, failed to earn the respect of their students: they proved to be singularly inept as teachers, could not keep discipline, or were unable to connect. Young boys can be cruel on occasion and make the lives of such masters quite miserable – with the result that these men usually had but brief careers at the school.

In 1946, a year after the end of the war, male teachers were in particularly short supply, and salary levels were modest. We had no female teachers at the school during my years there. One of our teachers, as an example, was a graduate in classics from Cambridge University. After he arrived in Canada and applied to teach at St Andrew's, our headmaster, Kenneth Ketchum, liked him, but the school needed a physics teacher, not another classicist. When Ketchum learned that the young man had served as a radar officer in the navy, he decided that the experience qualified him to teach high-school physics. I remember "Radar," as we called him, as a very nice person, but his teaching career at the school was not a success. Headmaster Ketchum, in contrast, came from a distinguished family of educators. He was clearly dedicated to his responsibilities and appeared to know every one of the students.

In those years, the application of a bamboo cane to a lad's backside was a routine form of discipline. The recipient of a "caning," however, most often regarded it as a badge of honour. On the few occasions when I was the target, I never experienced any sense of humiliation; rather, it was an event to boast about to my peers. I don't recall any sadistic intent on the part of any of the masters as they administered the punishment. Sometimes, in fact, the caning was delivered with a degree of humour, or, when a sterner demeanour was required, as a necessary but unfortunate responsibility. On one occasion when around one hundred boys were disciplined after defying our headmaster and taking part in a Hallowe'en torch parade into the town of Aurora, those who had not participated were most reluctant to admit that they had been "spared the rod!" that evening.

My most unforgettable teacher was Thomas Dunston Barnabus Tudball, the long-time housemaster of the college's middle-school Flavelle House. "Tuddy," as he was known to generations of "Andreans," was one of those masters who had taught my father. Born in England, he had been a victim of a gas attack during the First World War – a misfortune that contributed to his unpredictable moods. His frequent bursts of anger often ended with an unexpectedly humorous remark. Nevertheless, no student wanted to incur his wrath, which could result in writing out hundreds of repetitive lines: "Only the nightingale opens its mouth solely for the emitting of sound" was one of his favourites. Although a strict disciplinarian, Tuddy never gave the impression that he disliked the boys he punished and he never lost our respect. His unpredictable tantrums also provided a bond among his students, as any one of us could be a target for disapproval at any given time. We were quite accustomed to being scolded in terms such as "You are an impudent, impertinent, insolent young man and you are going to run around the quadrangle until you drop." Tuddy seldom smiled, but there was often a twinkle in his eyes.

As residents of Flavelle House, we were expected to keep our rooms tidy and clean – to the point of not allowing dust to accumulate on the tops of the doorframes. The rooms in our residence were usually shared by three students, and every day brought a detailed inspection. Tuddy often assigned himself that task and, once done, he posted notices on the bulletin board which documented any lapses in the maintenance of our rooms.

The school placed great emphasis on participation in both team sports and individual sports, such as track and field, swimming, and boxing. Until my graduating year, I was one of the smallest persons in my class, and I did not demonstrate notable talent or accomplishment in any sport, even though I was enthusiastic about football, hockey, cricket, and boxing. I became very competitive, however. The teams I played on were not particularly successful on the scoreboard, but the pleasure of being a member of an athletic team continued well into my adult life. Following my graduation from university and from law school, I continued to play lacrosse, rugby, and, in particular, hockey until past the age of fifty.

In my experience, organized sport has served many people very well. While certainly not a prerequisite for success, it can be an invaluable tool for individual development. The lessons in cooperation, the breaking down of class and cultural barriers, and the self-respect developed by a degree of achievement can help to prepare young people to navigate the daily challenges of life. Though certainly an exaggeration, there is truth in the reputed statement of the famous Notre Dame football coach Knute Rockne that "there is more character developed on the one yard line than anywhere else in life."

During my high-school years, the thought of entering politics never crossed my mind, and it was only later that I learned that St Andrew's College had, in fact, been a breeding ground for Newfoundland politicians. My contemporaries included John Crosbie, who was to become a major political force in both provincial and federal politics, and Frank Moores, who later served as a federal member of parliament and as the premier of Newfoundland. The Crosbie family had long been at the centre of Newfoundland politics and commerce, and the Moores family had major fishing interests, headed by Frank's father, the legendary Captain Cyrus Moores. The captain was a major force in the fishing industry and much admired by coastal communities for his fairness and decency – even though it was often speculated that there might be a number of little Cy Moores scattered around the outports. A few years after leaving St Andrew's, I played a significant role in Frank Moores's entry into the political arena (chapter 9). While still at the college, John Crosbie was clearly engaged by the fierce debates that were raging in Newfoundland about whether Newfoundland should join the Canadian confederation. His father, Chesley Crosbie, was a leader of the "no" forces. For John, the very mention of Joey Smallwood would provoke colourful, uncomplimentary language. John went on to a brilliant academic career at Queen's and Dalhousie universities, followed, in the unpredictable nature of politics, by serving for a time in Smallwood's Cabinet and entering the federal arena as a strong Canadian nationalist. In 2008 the Harper government appointed him as lieutenant governor of Newfoundland and Labrador.

My four years at St Andrew's College were a very positive experience. In my final year I was appointed a prefect – a recognition of respect that came with some lowly disciplinary duties such as hall monitor. The compulsory study hours assisted me in developing greater academic discipline. History and English literature were my favourite subjects, and I began to think about a career in teaching them at the secondary-school level, along with coaching football and hockey teams. I believed that, in my boarding-school environment, I had been well served by the combination of academic and athletic pursuits.

When I left St Andrew's College shortly after my eighteenth birthday in 1950, I was certainly an unworldly teenager. I was also a stranger to the temptations of alcohol, and, for me, girls were distant and exotic. I had grown up in a family of four boys without any sisters or female cousins, and I had been educated in a male-only environment. I had not travelled, and almost the entire world was foreign territory to me. However, immediately after my provincial senior matriculation examinations, I went to Bermuda as a member of a cricket team made up of athletes from Upper Canada College, Ridley College, Trinity College School, and St Andrew's College. My excitement and anticipation before the trip helped me through the intense preparation required for the grade 13 province-wide examinations. Before that, my only trip outside southern Ontario had been to Detroit with my father to attend a Leafs / Red Wings playoff game. The cricket tour of Bermuda was a memorable and somewhat boisterous adventure, and the remainder of that summer, spent painting summer cottages, was definitely an anticlimax.

3

Student Days at the University of Toronto

I decided to enrol at the University of Toronto, mainly because I wanted to live at home with my parents and my three younger brothers. During my four years at St Andrew's College, time with my family had been limited to summers, the occasional weekend, and the Christmas and Easter vacations. A less-structured life at home had great appeal after the rigours and discipline of boarding school.

I had greatly admired some of my high-school teachers, and a career as a teacher and coach continued to appeal to me. In particular I enjoyed studying history, and the four-year Honours Modern History program offered by the university looked interesting. The History Department in 1950 was led by some of Canada's most distinguished historians – Donald Creighton, Frank Underhill, and Maurice Careless, among others.

I applied to Trinity College, the Anglican college within the University of Toronto, primarily because my mother had intended to go there before marriage to my father derailed her plan. I didn't even investigate what the other colleges had to offer. Trinity was also the favourite choice among graduates from the independent, or "private," schools, so I remained in the same rather narrow and privileged culture as in my previous years. Nevertheless, Trinity turned out to be a happy choice. Its grey stone architecture, built around a quadrangle and influenced by Oxford and Cambridge colleges, remains an attractive facility, and the size of its student body, only four or five hundred at the time, meant that I got to know almost everyone. Although I did not live in residence, I soon made many friends. I relished my new collegial life along with the personal freedom I enjoyed.

I had to enrol in six courses in my first year of the Honours History program, and I selected history, English, French, political science, economics, and, as required by Trinity, religious knowledge. These courses continued on through my university career, although I took more than one history course every year. Certainly writing essays and researching in the library became a large part of my academic life. I was no model student in my first two years, distracted as I was by a busy social and athletic schedule, but I became far more serious in my third and fourth years. I appreciated having those well-known historians among my professors. Underhill was a dynamic and provocative instructor, while Careless, though in the early stage of his career, was already an excellent teacher.

Shortly after my arrival on the campus, I became involved in the intercollegiate football program. Most team members at that time played both offence and defence, and I was a linebacker and a guard. My teammates came from every faculty and college, and football gave me the opportunity to meet a broad cross-section of the student body. I was, in fact, the only Trinity man on the team. After the Second World War, intercollegiate football again became a major sports attraction in Toronto. A renovated Varsity Stadium opened in 1950 with seats for almost 25,000 spectators. During my four years at the university, at least 20,000 spectators attended every home Varsity Blues football game. Sports writers from the three Toronto newspapers also came to every football practice and reported on the fortunes of the Blues on a daily basis. The scores of Varsity Blues and Toronto Argos games were the main headline of the late Saturday edition of the *Toronto Telegram*. Many young athletes made it their goal to be selected as a member of this top campus team.

In the fifties, there were two University of Toronto intercollegiate football teams – a senior and an intermediate team. In earlier years there had also been a junior team. Any male student enrolled in a course of more than three years was required to play on the intermediate or "Baby Blues" team during first year. The competition to make the senior team was ferocious, and two or three hundred aspiring football players would try out for the intermediate team as the first step towards the Varsity Blues. In early September the university Athletic Department operated a two-week football camp at Lake Couchiching, near Orillia, where about fifty players were invited to train and compete for a position on that fabled team.

During my university years, the four major Canadian intercollegiate football teams were the University of Western Ontario Mustangs, the Queen's University Golden Gaels, the McGill University Redmen, and the University of Toronto Varsity Blues. The rivalries were intense, and it was not uncommon for thousands of students from each university to travel to "away games" to support their college team. Although the intercollegiate football culture in Canada was always modest by US standards, it did bring together the diverse student body with an enthusiasm that has long since disappeared from the University of Toronto campus.

With the resumption of intercollegiate football after the end of the Second World War, university administrators wanted to field strong teams as a strategy to maintain alumni loyalty and assist in fundraising. The head football coaches were invariably recruited in the United States, and although there were no athletic scholarships, players were extensively scouted and recruited. There was also "unofficial" financial assistance to some players: I remember that, in 1957, a group of enthusiastic Queen's University alumni "hired" a quarterback out of the professional Ottawa Roughrider training camp, a young American from Temple University. It turned out to be a highly successful initiative, as Queen's won the intercollegiate football championship that year. However, the star left the university several days later, and the university administration was less than pleased when it learned about the activities of the "loyal" alumni.

The University of Toronto administration, disappointed with the performance of its football team, hired Bob Masterson in 1948, and he became my coach for several seasons. At the time of his hiring, he was an assistant coach of the New York Giants and had earlier been the captain of the Washington Redskins and an All-American player at the University of Miami. Although a "hard-nosed" professional who coached three intercollegiate championship teams during his eight-year career at the University of Toronto, he is still remembered with great respect and affection by his former players. He was an effective teacher with a mastery of every aspect of the game, and the training I got from him certainly prepared me for my own football coaching career during my law-school years.

As an eighteen-year-old I was overly preoccupied with my football ambitions, perhaps because I was one of the smallest players on the team. Most evenings in the fall season we practised for a couple of hours after 5:30 and then ate dinner together. Given this heavy schedule, my studies suffered during my first two years, and my academic mentor persuaded me not to play intercollegiate hockey, which had also been one of my ambitions. Still, I remember my football years at university as a happy and valuable experience. While team sports may not be relevant for many people, the discipline, teamwork, and camaraderie can add a significant dimension to anyone's education. They can produce positive competitive instincts in players while also encouraging them not to take themselves too seriously. The friendship can be important too. I played with many outstanding student athletes, such as John Evans, who went on to be a Rhodes Scholar and later president of the University of Toronto. And, during my first fall term, I was on the same football team as Bill Davis, the future premier of Ontario. Twenty-five years later the friendship we developed on the field led me into a political career – and changed my life completely.

I was honoured by my football teammates in 1953 by being elected a captain of the team. However, that same season has haunted my memories ever since because our team lost the intercollegiate championship during the last seconds of the final game with the University of Western Ontario when I failed to make a relatively easy pass interception, which would have assured our victory. The next play saw the Western Mustangs quarterback Don Getty complete a 60-yard pass and run for the winning touchdown. Getty became both a long-time quarterback for the Edmonton Eskimos and, later, the premier of Alberta. I was enormously pleased in the year 2000 when I was named a member of the Varsity Blues All-Century Football Team.

Another of my non-academic pursuits at the University of Toronto was to join the Zeta Psi fraternity in my first year. Although I was concerned about the perception of fraternities as elitist institutions, membership represented another opportunity to make friends from across the campus. Fraternities in those days, notwithstanding some silly rituals, were simply male clubs providing yet another oasis on the campus of Canada's largest university.

The male bonding at Zeta Psi was taken too seriously, as women were allowed into our fraternity house on only six occasions a year – well, officially. A more frequent female presence would no doubt have been a civilizing influence – at least with respect to beer consumption and rowdy parties. Despite the dedicated drinkers, most of the fraternity brothers were ambitious and there were many scholarly role models to emulate. Almost all the "brothers" went on to pursue successful careers in business, the professions, or academic fields. The only one I recall who did not obtain a degree was Peter Gzowski. Even then he preferred to focus on editing the daily student newspaper, the *Varsity*, and he later became a true Canadian icon as a broadcaster and journalist.

I made several friendships through the fraternity which lasted many years, some to the present time. My closest friend was Tim Armstrong, who became a respected labour lawyer, chair of the Ontario Labour Relations Board, and deputy minister of labour for the province. Like any good civil servant, he also served as a deputy minister in several other ministries during the premierships of William Davis, David Peterson, and Bob Rae – each one representing a different political stripe. And he was the Ontario agent general in Tokyo for five years. To this day, we continue to exchange views and meet on a regular basis. The president of Zeta Psi during my first year was Tom Symons, who went on to become the founding president of Trent University and a distinguished international scholar and educator. He was also active in Prince Edward Island over many years. In 2004 the trustees of the Confederation Centre for the Arts in Charlottetown created an annual lecture in his name – The State of the Canadian Confederation series – and the following year I was honoured to give the second lecture.

* * *

Another vital dimension of my education during my undergraduate years was my summer employment. My parents expected me to pay my own tuition fees, and because I lived at home, the burden was certainly not excessive. After my first year, in the early summer of 1951, I drove with two of my fraternity brothers, Clive Cameron and Peter Young, to British Columbia. We had been asked by another friend's father to take the car to Vancouver, and we chose a scenic route through the northern US states. We arrived after eight or ten days and found that Vancouver still resembled a frontier town in many ways, located in a beautiful area of mountain and sea but lacking most of its current urban elegance. We hoped to secure employment in a logging camp, where the hourly pay was generally the highest available for students.

Our first job was with a large logging operation near Alert Bay, at the northern end of Vancouver Island. We reported to a Vancouver dock area at 6:30 am and were picked up by a float plane. When we met the pilots of the small six-seat aircraft, it soon became apparent that they had enjoyed the pleasures of Vancouver without benefit of any sleep. Once they learned that we were university students, they set out to provide us with a memorable flight, and we flew through mountain passes, often not far above the tree tops. Still, the beauty of our surroundings absorbed us more than the recklessness and flying antics of the pilots – much to their disappointment. A long land journey to our logging camp followed, and we were provided with spartan but relatively comfortable accommodation. We had been hired as "chokermen," without really knowing what our jobs involved.

The next day we learned that we would be working under the direction of a supervisor who had the grand title of "rigging slinger." Because the logging operation was on the side of a mountain, the felled tree trunks had to be dragged down a steep slope. That feat was accomplished by extending thick cables up the mountain in the form of a triangle. Thinner pliable cables were attached to the large cables and wrapped around the ends of the logs. Each log in turn was then dragged down to a central stockpile for transportation to the sea. Our job was to wrap the smaller cable around one huge log after another. Once a log was secured, our boss would signal to a nearby co-worker, the "whistle punk," who sounded a loud whistle to inform the operators of machinery further down the mountainside that the log was ready to go. Every so often the logs in the stockpile were placed on trucks and transported to the coast. There they were put into the water, grouped into large "booms," and pulled by tug boats to the lumber mills.

Once we had fastened a cable around the end of a log, we had to retreat quickly to a point on the hillside well above the log. As each log accelerated downhill, it would often act as a giant battering ram, levelling anything in its way. The logs were usually clustered in several layers, and one dislodged log could result in a destructive landslide of heavy, splintering wood. It soon became clear that our seasoned rigging slinger and the whistle punk enjoyed seeing us scramble for safety, and they often blew the whistle prematurely. For us, however, it was simply part of our new adventure, and we had few worries about the potential risk for serious injury.

The camp food was good and plentiful, and we had our weekends free to explore the glorious countryside. For our fellow loggers, Saturday night was their opportunity to play bingo for beer. Management discouraged the consumption of alcohol during the week, given the dangers of the harvesting operation. The idle hours were also occupied by continuous poker games where significant sums of money were often exchanged.

Two months after our arrival, the government ordered the closing of all logging camps on Vancouver Island. The combination of hot weather and a lack of rain had created very dry forests and a significant risk of forest fires. We returned to Vancouver, where we found work in a lumber mill north of the city, and the balance of our working summer passed rather uneventfully. However, whenever I am in the Vancouver area and see the large log booms along the coast, I remember my summer as a logger. In particular, I recall the respect I developed for those men of the forests who spent their working lives in the wilderness, far from the comforts of family or urban life. Most often their holidays passed in several weeks of frantic hard drinking and frequenting brothels before necessity forced them to return to the relative loneliness of the mountains.

In late August I returned home to take part in some informal University of Toronto football practices. Most unexpectedly, I ended the summer by going on stage at Maple Leaf Gardens as an extra in the Metropolitan Opera Company's travelling performances of *Aïda* in the city. Management felt that using players from the intercollegiate football team for these roles would have definite commercial appeal. I was chosen to be one of the palace guards, all decked out in period costume, that would arrest Radames, the lead tenor, just before the intermission. The director firmly instructed me not to let my wooden spear get too close to this star – but his warning merely gave me the idea of giving my singer a prod on his derrière as he exited the stage. As the curtain closed, all hell broke loose. The tenor regarded my gentle poke as a major assault to his dignity. The stage manager was furious and, in the furore that followed, it was a wonder I was not dismissed on the spot.

More than fifty years later my friend Justice Jim Farley told this story to Richard Bradshaw, the highly respected director of the Canadian Opera Company. Shortly before I retired as chief justice of Ontario at the end of May 2007, I received a letter from Mr Bradshaw:

Dear Chief Justice,
I hear from Jim Farley that, sadly, you retire in May. Jim has asked me to persuade you to return to your cultural roots. He tells me that, in a former life, as a super, you threatened the Aida tenor at Maple Leaf Gardens with your spear. I have many tenors who deserve exactly that sort of treatment. When can you start?

With every good wish for a very happy retirement after such a distinguished career.
Yours sincerely,
Richard Bradshaw

I spent the other two summers during my undergraduate years work-ing for Frontier College. Although the college had been created in 1899, I heard about it first from Ron Watts, a fourth-year Trinity College stu-dent. He had just been awarded a Rhodes Scholarship and later be-came a distinguished academic and principal of Queen's University. He spoke of Frontier College as a tremendous life experience – and one that, in his case, had impressed the Rhodes selection committee. Curious, I took his advice and, as a nineteen-year-old second-year uni-versity student, applied to spend the following summer as a labourer-teacher at Frontier College. The work appeared to me as a unique form of public service.

Not long after, in the late winter of 1952, I was ushered into the clut-tered office of Dr Edmund W. Bradwin, the principal, on Sherbourne Street. I recall his tall, spare frame, his logger's muscular handshake, and his fine, almost aesthetic face. From the outset he instilled in me the reality of a student's humble entry into the bunkhouse, the dignity of manual labour, and the challenges of being a labourer/teacher. No one else could have made me believe that it was a privilege to have the opportunity to work the hours I did over the coming two summers – or to endure the loneliness. I remember his words from our first meeting: "McMurtry, the life of a labourer-teacher is no bed of roses, and you may not be up to it … All we can promise you is long hours, low pay, bad food, black flies [long pause], and the opportunity to help your fellow man." He had that rare ability to remove any romantic illusions without destroying the romance of the challenge. After only a few min-utes with Dr Bradwin, it was impossible not to sense the depth of his idealism. I certainly did not want him to think me inadequate, and I became even more determined to be accepted. As he had written earlier in his book *The Bunkhouse Man*, a pioneer tome in Canadian sociology: "The mines and open spaces will call her sons to the great joy of con-quest. Will opportunity find us a puny people?"

At the time Frontier College was founded, at the end of the nine-teenth century, many tens of thousands of Canadians worked in log-ging and hydro camps and on railway gangs in remote parts of the country. These men had little access to books and no real opportunities to improve their often inadequate literacy skills. Their lack of educa-tion presented significant barriers to any improvement in their employ-ment opportunities. The labourer-teachers with Frontier College were expected to join a work crew, share in the daily manual labour, and instruct the men at night. There was no set curriculum, though many books and study aids were available. In effect, the interests of each group of workers shaped the nature of the class. Not surprisingly, the majority of labourer-teachers were university students.

The founder of Frontier College was Alfred Fitzpatrick, a Queen's University graduate who had developed a deep interest in the camp workers. His initial goal had been to place books and magazines in the camps, to give the workers opportunities for reading and study during their leisure hours. He soon learned that most camps lacked any space suitable for reading or study, and his first challenge was to persuade employers to create a place for these activities. Fitzpatrick also wanted to extend community education resources to locations where no such service was available. When he discovered that literacy represented the greatest need in logging camps in Northern Ontario in particular, he founded Frontier College. His early fieldworkers learned that the best entry into a labour community was to share the work, so he developed the concept of the labourer-teacher.

Dr Bradwin joined the Reading Camp Association, as Frontier College was originally known, in 1904, and he devoted the next fifty years of his life to taking education to the hinterlands of Canada. He demonstrated a tremendous interest in the labourers on Canada's frontiers, for whom he had a deep and abiding compassion. To him, their lives possessed a dignity and purpose that few of his contemporaries recognized. In 1922 the Parliament of Canada passed the *Frontier College Act*, a charter unique among Canadian educational institutions. One clause in the act gave Frontier College the power to grant university degrees. However, the government of Ontario believed that the federal legislation infringed on its exclusive jurisdiction in the field of education, and the legislation was later amended to remove the degree-granting authority.

The list of distinguished labourer-teachers has included Prime Minister Lester Pearson; Dr Norman Bethune of China fame; Milton Gregg, VC, a war hero and Liberal Cabinet minister; Canadian diplomat Escott Reid; American pediatrician Dr Benjamin Spock; and Premier David Peterson. In recent years, the principal focus of Frontier College has been to develop more urban literacy programs for adults and young people, including prison inmates and street people. The college now has approximately two thousand student volunteers from universities in every province of Canada. My two summers as a labourer-teacher were spent on railway gangs, where I worked at hard physical labour ten hours a day, six days a week, and taught during the evenings, often for two or three hours each night. As Bradwin wrote in his book:

The man of the bunkhouse is ever found in the vanguard. He occupies the outposts. Trench by trench he assails the ramparts in nature's vastness. For the domain of the north rears hardihood, an iron dauntlessness that makes for manhood. It encourages the type of man who matches life in the struggles of the years. Such places have nursed the best in the life of the world ...

The labour of the camp man is very real. He does not write epics on sheets of paper, nor are his personal achievements recorded in the archives, but he makes of the winds and the snows a playfellow.

Such may not be phylacteries in comely virtues, nor are they always delicate of speech, but they dwell close to the verities. *These are not beaten men of a beaten race.* A knowledge of this causes one to enter a bunkhouse humbly.

And so it happened that, a few days after my spring university examinations in early May 1953, I was on my way to a railway gang. I had a day-coach pass on the CNR, and in the middle of the night, the conductor roused me just before the train stopped for a few moments in the wilderness. I still have a vivid recollection of my arrival at the railway maintenance gang, or extra gang as they were then known: first, the sense of being absolutely alone in the northern bush, but soon becoming aware of a row of railway bunk cars barely illuminated by a pale moon. Fortunately, I came equipped with a flashlight, and after looking into several boxcars, I found an unoccupied bunk. In the morning, my bunkmates were quite uninterested in my identity, and I soon learned that arrivals and departures in the middle of the night were common in the life of a railway gang. In those days, the gangs were usually made up of a few grizzled old-timers, a larger group of new immigrants to Canada, and the drifters who would wander in for several days to "dry out" and build up a small stake for another few nights on the town.

Over the succeeding weeks, I was sometimes entertained on the railway track by the sight of a new labourer, resplendent in patent leather shoes, suit, white shirt, and tie (albeit all a little worn) struggling with a pick and shovel and working for 90 cents an hour. These same men were also probably amused at the presence of a young university labourer-teacher working at a job they considered the end of the road for them. The crew soon accepted me as a labourer like the rest of them, but the supervisors, often uneducated men who had risen through the ranks, obviously resented my presence and ignored me. I had been hired by the Canadian National Railways, however, at the same hourly rate as the other men, so they couldn't do anything about it. At the end of the summer I knew I would receive an honorarium from Frontier College which would help me with my university tuition.

I was originally concerned about the shortage of potential students that first summer, but soon a contingent of new immigrants arrived from northern Italy. Their determination to learn English led to the need for two classes each evening, which made for a very long but personally rewarding day. It was depressing for the young immigrant men to arrive in Montreal or Halifax eagerly anticipating a new life in a land of opportunity and immediately be transported to a remote railway gang in the bush. However, they soon regained their sense of humour and optimism, and I well remember my fellow labourers and students serenading the setting sun and introducing the local bears to the joys of Italian opera. Even though most were enthusiastic and dedicated students, I learned as much of the Italian language as many of them learned of English. They may have been aware that immigrants from Italy could work and prosper in Toronto in the Italian language alone.

Some of them did eventually settle here, and a few remained friends for many decades. They often stated how beneficial it was to their morale that an organization in Canada had cared enough to send a university student labourer/teacher to a remote railway gang to assist them in integrating more quickly into their new country. In those days, it would have been almost unthinkable for a university student in Italy to work at a labouring job.

Inevitably there were lonely days and nights, but at these times little inspirational messages would arrive from Dr Bradwin. He had the capacity to anticipate when his young troops might need a little boost to their own morale. At the end of August 1952 I parted with some sadness from my fellow labourers and students and reported once again to the University of Toronto football training camp.

A second summer with Frontier College followed at the end of my third year, and my work the previous summer entitled me to have some choice in my location. I chose a railway gang at Red Pass Junction in British Columbia, about 40 miles west of Jasper, where I spent most of that time in the shadow of Mount Robson, Canada's highest mountain. I still recall the feeling of exhilaration after ten hours of labour and another two or three of teaching as I stumbled to my bunk-car bed, with the indescribable beauty of the moonlight on the mountain snows above me.

Dr Bradwin did not live out that year. During my Frontier College career I was privileged to receive a number of letters from him. They were always inspiring, and even excerpts reveal his greatness:

What I particularly wanted to mention is that in your letters you express interest in the men – that is the very basis and heart of a Frontier College instructor. It means so much to the labourer-teacher himself when he can find a response from the men and it is a comfort in his own life to share with them his best in hopes and aspirations.

You have had a good family training and fine education, much above the average; and it means a great deal that you are ready to go to a God-forsaken place and live your best with men. Credit to you, McMurtry! In later years, whether you go into Law or teaching, or whatever kind of professional career, may these months that you have spent so unselfishly – yes, when you did not need to do so – in order that you could share your best with men who have had lesser opportunities, count for much in the shaping of your thinking, life, and character.

I am presuming that you will be going to Banff for a few days to join a convention that is meeting there – men from various colleges in North America. If they have a general discussion on various forms of service, you could get on your feet and tell them of the humble contribution made by yourself as a Frontier College man. No matter what the different experiences offered, few if any of them will match your own; I think you have a genuine story to tell. However, be yourself. *Frontier College never got along on big talk – rather, we have sought to do a little thing in a big place and do it well.*

In his last letter to me shortly before his death, Dr Bradwin wrote:

Life does not contain a much longer span for me, but I have the satisfaction that for fifty-two years I have never varied in purpose or thought from the first camp that I went into as a labourer-teacher. Clean life and ideals backed with whatever knowledge I had to give freely to men who were my fellow labourers in a bush camp fourteen miles from Parry Sound. I look back with pride on those years that gave me incentive and purpose to carry on through the next half century and more. My only hope is that I can give to some of the young men of today some of the incentive and a realization of the need that will permeate their own lives as they go into the larger activities of their professional careers.

My summers with Frontier College taught me the great fulfilment and joy that can be obtained through public service. I shall always be grateful to Dr Bradwin for his inspiration and for his lessons taught so well.

* * *

One most unexpected result of my summer with the railway gang in British Columbia was the beginning of my interest in painting, which has been a favourite hobby all through my life. In one of my weekly letters to my parents, I attempted to describe the beauty of my mountain environment and regretted that I knew nothing about painting. Two or three weeks later a little paint box with an assortment of oil paints, brushes, and a sketch book arrived in the mail. My parents also volunteered the discouraging information that, while some of our ancestors wrote poetry, they were not aware of any family painting genes.

I soon learned that I possessed virtually no talent in drawing and was a total stranger in the use of any painting medium – whether oils, acrylics, or watercolours. I kept some of my earlier efforts, and, indeed, no self-respecting four-year-old would admit to being their creator. Still, as Winston Churchill, another amateur painter, put it, "All that is acquired to take a joy ride in a paint box is audacity."

Nevertheless, the challenge clearly interested me, and I spent a few Sunday afternoons painting in the Mount Robson area while keeping a careful watch for grizzly bears, which were very much a part of the landscape. I also managed a couple of long weekends in Jasper and Lake Louise along with my paint box, although I was careful to avoid having any spectators to my primitive efforts.

That same summer, actors Marilyn Monroe and Robert Mitchum were in Jasper filming part of the movie *River of No Return*. Monroe was accompanied by her future husband Joe DiMaggio, and their driver was a long-time friend of mine, Peter Crabtree, who was working for a local transportation company. DiMaggio was decidedly unfriendly and discouraged our attempts to any protracted conversation with his Marilyn. Robert Mitchum, who appeared to be inebriated during the one filming session I attended, was much better company. He enjoyed being the centre of attention for my college friends, and we spent a long Saturday night listening to his humorous and mostly ribald stories.

At the end of August, when I reported to the annual University of Toronto football training camp, I took my paint box and recorded some of the sunsets over Lake Couchiching. A few of the sports reporters from the three Toronto newspapers found me at work, and in one of their stories referred to me as "Van Gogh with a black eye."

* * *

During my third year at university, I had begun to think seriously about my future. I developed some romantic aspirations about a possible career in medicine, not because of any particular interest in the sciences but because of my perception of medicine as a very special helping profession engaged in healing the sick. I was also influenced by my high regard for some of the medical students I had met on the football team – John Evans, for instance; Fraser Mustard, later head of the Canadian Institute for Advanced Research; and my close friend Harry Hyde, who later became a distinguished surgeon in Alberta. My father had a good friend at the University of Toronto's Faculty of Medicine, and he introduced me to his equally supportive dean, Dr Joseph MacFarlane. It was all so different in those days, when friendly networks mattered, and university admissions or job appointments were arranged over a drink or in a phone call. As a result of this introduction, the dean agreed that I would be accepted into the medical school after I graduated in history. First, however, I had to do a "make-up" year of science courses before I could begin my core medical studies. I was also required to take a pre-medical inorganic chemistry course as an extra subject during the final year of my Honours History program. Amazingly, I passed this course, and my acceptance into the University of Toronto medical school was confirmed.

During that final year of my undergraduate studies, an unexpected offer arrived that added further confusion to my plans. In the Canadian Football League draft of Canadian university players, I was selected in the second round by the Montreal Alouettes as a linebacker. In the course of my contract discussions with the team's management, I was assured they could arrange for my acceptance into the McGill University Faculty of Medicine.

My negotiations with the Montreal Alouettes suddenly came to an end when my father suffered a serious stroke in March 1954, a few days after his fifty-third birthday. The stroke occurred on a commercial aircraft halfway home from London, England, where he had been on legal business, accompanied by our mother. I don't think she ever fully recovered from the emotional trauma of tending to a very ill husband on an aircraft many hours away from their destination.

My father had always been robust physically. He was a better-than-average tennis player and loved to join in shinny ice hockey with his four sons. Throwing a football or baseball with us was almost a daily ritual, weather permitting. The permanent disabilities resulting from his stroke included a largely useless arm and a lame leg on his left side. It was not until I became older myself that I fully appreciated the enormous courage with which he dealt with his physical challenges during the remaining nine years of his life. Initially his speech was affected, but it returned to normal after a few weeks. His mental faculties remained intact, although he suffered from ongoing depression. He never returned to his law office, but maintained an active consulting practice. His law firm, which he had headed, merged with another firm in order to maintain its client base. During the early years of his illness, Dad wrote a personal text for students and young lawyers titled *Days in Court*. It was published by Carswell in 1958 and well received in the legal profession. The book dealt with all aspects of civil and criminal litigation, and I continue to be pleased when lawyers still speak to me occasionally and enthusiastically about it.

My brothers and I will never forget the heroics of our young mother. She was only forty years old at the time of my father's stroke, and she was suddenly burdened with the challenges of a disabled husband, four sons still in school, and a dramatically reduced family income. Money was in short supply because my father had not been able to obtain any significant insurance as a result of his pre-stroke illness. The merged law firm provided my father with a modest income for a short time, but was otherwise quite ungenerous. My brother Bill was twenty and at the Royal Military College in Kingston, where tuition was low and he was enjoying a successful career as an outstanding student athlete. John, aged fourteen, was at Upper Canada College, and when our parents were unable to pay the fees for the next school year, the college granted him a full scholarship because of his record as a gifted student and athlete. It was a generous initiative, but I've always believed that, given our straitened circumstances, his remaining years at Upper Canada College with many students from wealthy families helped to nurture his radical socialist philosophy. Bob, though only twelve, was already an accomplished student, and he left Upper Canada College for the very academic University of Toronto Schools, where the fees were modest. Initially, John and Bob resented fate's apparent cruelty and, as youthful "free spirits," they were not averse to "raising a little hell." I soon realized, as I approached my twenty-second birthday, that I would have to be a surrogate father to my youngest brothers.

I remained in Toronto while trade talks continued between the Alou-ettes and the Toronto Argos for my playing rights. My father opposed my interest in playing professional football, and I did not wish to add to his anxieties at this very stressful time. Just at this point, I met Leslie Frost, the Ontario premier, who was in the Toronto General Hospital recovering from a minor operation. He had kindly arranged for some flowers to be delivered to my father's room, and after Dad wrote him a note, he asked me to deliver it. Frost politely inquired about my stud-ies and immediately commented that the Honours History program would be a useful academic background for law. He had been a law-yer himself, and I was fascinated to hear his political views. He was perplexed, however, when I told him my plans to go into medicine, especially given my father's own successful legal career. Once again the friendly network came into play, and during the next few tumultuous months I often reflected on this privileged conversation.

To complicate matters further, to help pay my tuition fees that year I had accepted a part-time job at Upper Canada College as a football and hockey coach. The option of becoming a high-school teacher still re-mained in the back of my mind, and the principal was clearly interested in converting my coaching job into a full-time teaching job. My interest in the game of football and the opportunity to coach a talented group of athletes soon became my main focus that fall. The Upper Canada Col-lege football team competed primarily in a league known as the Little Big Four – the others being Trinity College School, Ridley College, and St Andrew's College. These schools were intense rivals, and each game was usually watched by two or three thousand people – students, par-ents, friends, and graduates. I had learned a lot playing football for the Varsity Blues, and, like my coach there, I now stressed the importance of mastering the fundamental techniques of the game, along with an uncomplicated offence and defence.

The success of any football coach is closely related to the level of talent among the players. In my case there was considerable talent at Upper Canada College, led by Lionel Conacher Jr, the son of a famous athlete known as the "Big Train" who, in 1950, was selected as Cana-da's athlete of the half-century. Lionel went on to be a star running back with the University of Western Ontario Mustangs and enjoyed a brief career in the Canadian Football League. My brother John, who later played with the University of Toronto Blues and the Calgary Stamped-ers, quarterbacked the senior team during the second year of my coach-ing career. Both years the football teams were undefeated and became

Little Big Four champions. While my coaching experience at Upper Canada College was extremely pleasurable, it did not endear me to my old school, St Andrew's College.

At the conclusion of the football season that first fall, I began to confront my challenges in the Faculty of Medicine more realistically. Although I diligently attended classes and did my lab work, I continually felt out of place. My bifurcated responsibilities at home, university, and Upper Canada College all translated into a distinct failure in improving my fragile knowledge of the sciences. By the end of November I accepted the fact that the sciences and I would never be comfortable companions and that I should consider other educational or workplace options.

4

Preparing for a Career in Law at
Osgoode Hall

I was still very attracted to a career in teaching, and my first stop that
bleak November of 1954 was the Ontario College of Education, to see
if the registrar would accept my late entry into the teaching certification program. I was politely informed that I would be very welcome
– the following September. The course had commenced almost three
months earlier, and the college was not prepared to give me any special treatment.

Next I went to the Osgoode Hall Law School, which was located in
the east wing of the magnificent structure at the corner of University
Avenue and Queen Street West. I had always admired my father's legal
career, and my conversation with Premier Leslie Frost at the hospital
the previous spring also played in my mind. I was invited to meet with
Dean Charles Smalley-Baker, a most affable Englishman who, six years
earlier, had been lured to Canada from Birmingham by the Benchers
(the governors of the Law Society of Upper Canada) to head the law
school. Many years later in London, after my appointment as Canadian
high commissioner to the United Kingdom, I met some senior British
lawyers who had been associated with Smalley-Baker when he was
dean of law at the University of Birmingham. The dean was planning
his retirement when the Benchers came looking, and my new English
acquaintances boasted of their success in pawning their aging dean off
on the "colonials."

By 1954 Dean Smalley-Baker, while somewhat eccentric, had become very popular with his Osgoode Hall law students. During his first year there he had named his class his "First Roman Legion," and shortly after my meeting with him I became a member of his "Sixth Legion." Although he seemed far more interested in my father's health than in my potential as a law student, after a brief discussion he invited me to enter the law school the very next day. "Study for the two Christmas exams that are coming up in less than three weeks," he said, "and then catch up on the other first-year courses." That advice launched me suddenly into law school.

By going to law school when I did, I missed the dramatic events of the late 1940s and early 1950s when Caesar Wright, Bora Laskin, John Willis, and others engaged in a lengthy, fierce debate over who should control legal education and what should be taught. On one side was Caesar Wright, the champion for a more professional, university-controlled legal education. On the other were the Benchers of the Law Society, who thought that they, as people who actually practised law, knew best how to prepare students for a career in law. Each side had its strengths and its weaknesses, but by the time I arrived Wright and his colleagues had gone off to the University of Toronto and left the Benchers in control of the legal education I experienced at Osgoode Hall.

At that time a much lower percentage of high-school graduates went to university, and the only requirement for entrance to Osgoode Hall Law School, which had been founded in 1889, was a university degree. There was no competition for admission, and as my case showed, with the "right pedigree" you could even get in late in the term. This easy situation changed dramatically within a few years, even though there are now six law schools in Ontario. In the 1950s the law course at Osgoode Hall did not lead to a Bachelor of Laws degree but simply to a "Call to the Bar" as a barrister and solicitor. It was a four-year course – two years of lectures followed by two years of articling with a law firm. During the fourth year the students attended lectures for two hours each morning at Osgoode Hall before returning to their articling jobs. The University of Toronto Law School, in contrast, provided a three-year Honours Law Bachelor of Arts, with its graduates entering the articling program at Osgoode Hall if they wished to be called to the bar.

The law courses taught at Osgoode Hall Law School were based on the assumption that the students intended to enter the practice of law, so they covered all the core areas. They focused on a practical understanding of the law as it existed rather than on what the law might or should become. There was little criticism of the existing law, and few students thought of themselves as potential law reformers. Classes were large, with more than two hundred students except in our fourth year. More than half of our lecturers were practising lawyers, including many who were or who became leading members of the bar – G. Arthur Martin, Canada's foremost criminal defence lawyer, who later served with great distinction as a member of the Court of Appeal; William B. Howland, a future chief justice of Ontario; Sydney Robins, a future treasurer of the Law Society of Upper Canada and member of the Court of Appeal; and Walter Williston, a leading counsel who later did a major report on civil procedure at my request when I became attorney general of Ontario. This report formed the basis for a completely revised Rules of Practice, which came into force on January 1, 1984 – the first major revision since the Middleton Rules of Civil Procedure in 1912. Certainly, rapid change or procedural reform was not a significant part of the legal culture during my early years at the bar.

One of my most colourful and inspiring lecturers was Desmond Morton, an erudite, eloquent, entertaining, and hard-drinking Irishman who taught the law of evidence. A great scholar, he also had the ability to infuse life into the important issues in criminal and civil trials, where many results turn on the legal admissibility, or not, of oral testimony and physical evidence. He dramatized the legal issues in the context of actual trials so effectively that we sometimes felt we were in the courtroom. Although there are Evidence Acts both federally and provincially, the law with respect to the admissibility of evidence is largely based on common, or judge-made, law. All told, Professor Morton had considerable influence on my decision to pursue a career as a trial lawyer for seventeen years before I entered the political arena.

As law students at Osgoode Hall, we were not exposed to the broad and diverse range of scholarship that is now available in Ontario's law schools, but what we missed in academic training we more than made up for in practical experience. The location of the school provided a significant advantage to students who were interested in litigation because of the number of courtrooms in the immediate vicinity. The trial courts, including the Magistrates' Courts, County Courts, and the High Courts, were all in the Old City Hall at the intersection of Queen and Bay streets. The Ontario Court of Appeal sat as it does today in Osgoode Hall, as did the Trial High Court for the resolution of pre-trial motions. We students had the opportunity to attend the trial and appellate courts every weekday. Trials in the 1950s and for some years after were dramatically shorter than they are today, and even a brief visit to a courtroom could provide an adequate experience of most trials. The civil and criminal litigation bars were much smaller, and the leading counsel were generally well known to the student body. As a result, information quickly circulated about an interesting trial or appeal, and many law students would make almost daily visits to courtrooms after lectures were over. The leading advocates of the day – John Robinette, Cyril Carson, Arthur Martin, Joseph Sedgewick, Arthur Maloney, and Charles Dubin, to name but a few – often had a sizeable audience of students.

There were also other less law-related attractions close to Osgoode Hall. The immediate neighbourhood was deteriorating and rather seedy, and most of the buildings within a half-mile radius have since been replaced. Apart from a few down-market bars, the principal attraction was the Casino Theatre, which featured films and live entertainment. The entertainment included both accomplished musicians and celebrated strip-tease artists. These burlesque performances were more of a tease than the blatant nudity and erotica featured in stripper bars in Canada today. The musical entertainment portion of the Casino program usually began shortly after the morning lectures ended, and we frequently took a sandwich into the theatre during our lunch hour. The most prominent musician that I recall was the great Louis Armstrong – and I watched him perform on a number of occasions. In celebration of these memories, I often read, write, or paint with an Armstrong CD playing in the background.

Soon after I entered law school, I became interested in particular in the human dramas that occurred daily in the Magistrates' Criminal Courts in the east wing of City Hall. Many of the magistrates were not legally trained and, as a result, were often overly influenced by the Crown prosecutors. Although the magistrates generally attempted to discharge their duties in a conscientious fashion, I often gained the impression that, rather than the important legal presumption of innocence, there was an evidentiary onus on the accused to demonstrate innocence. The fundamental requirement that, before the accused could be convicted, the Crown must satisfy the court beyond a reasonable doubt, was not always respected. The advantages that the prosecution generally enjoyed in the Magistrates' Courts, which heard over 90 per cent of the criminal cases, were increased significantly by the fact that many of the accused were not represented by lawyers. Until a "fee for service" legal aid plan began in 1967, the only legal assistance available for the indigent was provided by a few voluntary counsel. The local

Sheriff's Office attempted to assist the unrepresented accused by administering a sporadic criminal pro bono legal aid service.

This legal assistance in criminal cases was generally available only to persons in custody. When an incarcerated accused at the Don Jail filled out an application form, officials forwarded it to the Sheriff's Office. The day-to-day management of this process in the early fifties became the responsibility of the sheriff's secretary, Helen Grinnell, an attractive, personable, and persuasive young woman. She had a list of volunteer lawyers, and she attempted to match the applications with a suitable lawyer. For the most serious cases – murder, manslaughter, and rape – she was generally able to rely on a number of experienced counsel who adhered to the best traditions of the bar by providing pro bono legal representation. The availability of these counsel was helped by the very different trial culture that existed in the 1950s and 1960s, when trials seldom took more than a week.

In criminal cases, the most experienced and successful defence and Crown counsel seldom engaged in lengthy cross-examinations. G. Arthur Martin often stated that it would be extremely rare for him to cross-examine a witness for more than forty minutes. He believed that counsel could alienate a jury by long cross-examinations and that brief questioning was more effective – at least it avoided any possibility of strengthening the evidence of an adverse witness. There was also a tradition that counsel should ask witnesses questions only when they were confident of the answers they would receive. Today a cross-examination of a single witness in criminal trials may take days, with the idea that incessant and prolonged questioning, like water torture, will shake even the most truthful witness. Another factor is the many hours of police wire taps which, under the Canadian Charter of Rights, are often subjected to searching examinations of law-enforcement investigative techniques. Police behaviour is as much on trial as is the accused.

In my first year at Osgoode Hall I learned that law students were permitted to act as defence counsel in the Magistrates' Courts. My father had always taken on a good deal of volunteer work, which he found most rewarding. Early in my second year, then, I decided to volunteer as a pro bono legal counsel. I went to the Sheriff's Office and persuaded Helen Grinnell that, because I had completed my first-year criminal law course and had spent a considerable amount of time observing criminal trials, I was ready to take on criminal defences. Every so often thereafter, when I received a copy of a particular accused's legal-aid application, I journeyed to the Don Jail to meet my potential client. The accused had little choice but to agree to my representation: he had no guarantee that another voluntary counsel would offer assistance.

My first pro bono client was destined to become a part of my life over many years. His name was John Muise and he was about my age, although, with his world-weary demeanour, he appeared older. He had an extensive criminal record, generally for non-violent offences relating to theft and fraud. He had first been incarcerated in his home province of Nova Scotia as a juvenile offender when he was only fourteen years old. A later pre-sentence report revealed that his mother was a long-time prostitute and that his father, whom he barely knew, was in the merchant marine. His parents had been only an occasional presence in his life. He had become "institutionalized" to the extent that jail terms, though not welcome, were not a great hardship to him. He appeared to be a career criminal and, in the parlance of police officers, a "rounder."

The charge that brought Muise and me into contact was assault causing bodily harm, arising from a dispute over a female acquaintance. He advised me that he had been acting in self-defence at the time and that he now wished to plead not guilty. I contacted the police officer in charge of the case, and he seemed amused that anyone would volunteer to represent this particular offender on a pro bono basis. He was happy enough to receive the overtime pay that would probably accompany his appearance in court, but he regarded me as yet another naive law student who would only waste court time.

There's an old trial lawyer's lament that runs, "I am not particularly worried about my opponent's witnesses, but God protect me from my own." *Regina v. Muise* soon taught me the truth of those words. My client obviously enjoyed being the centre of attention on the witness stand and, with a few shadow boxing moves, he seemed determined to demonstrate his prowess as a street fighter. It became clear that he had probably been the aggressor in the physical altercation that had led to the charge. The conviction that followed came as no surprise either to me or to John Muise, but the events that followed produced other revelations.

After hearing submissions on the sentence, the magistrate imposed a sentence of eighteen months – a standard term given Muise's long criminal record and the harsher sentences of that era. Muise immediately stood up and requested that his sentence be increased to two years, so it could be served in a federal penitentiary rather than a provincial reformatory. In a Kingston penitentiary he would be able to take correspondence courses from Queen's University and participate in other programs that would not be available in a reformatory. He believed that a more productive use of his time in jail would assist him in qualifying more easily for a reduction of his sentence for "good behaviour." As a veteran offender he had calculated that he would probably serve less time with a penitentiary sentence than in a reformatory. The trial judge obliged.

Over the following two or three years, I represented John Muise on other criminal charges. My continuing interest in him was encouraged by an experienced probation officer, Sophie Boyd – a truly remarkable and compassionate person. Despite Muise's criminal record, she recognized his potential, and she encouraged me to remain in contact with him and try to help him turn his life around. Ultimately he did justify her confidence, to the utter amazement of the police officers who were familiar with his career. He learned hair cutting while he was in prison and, after his release, he became a lawfully employed member of the community. When he married, I even served as best man at his wedding. I have been in contact with him occasionally ever since.

Muise moved to Prince Edward Island and, almost twenty years after our first meeting, I learned from Premier Jim Lee that he was one of Muise's customers in Charlottetown. The premier became aware of our friendship when he noticed a signed photograph of Jean Chrétien, Roy Romanow, and me (taken after the constitutional settlement of 1981) hanging on the barbershop wall. I did not tell Lee the circumstances that had led to my friendship with his barber. Soon after, I encountered Muise at the Progressive Conservative Party leadership convention in Ottawa in 1983, where he was an elected delegate from PEI. Several years later I learned from Muise that he had established a successful trans-Canada cartage business and become a millionaire businessman. He was also a public benefactor and had donated a park to the city of Charlottetown. He attended the annual Symons Lecture in 2005 that I delivered at the Charlottetown Confederation Centre. He had indeed travelled an interesting road from Kingston Penitentiary.

One of my other favourite pro bono cases also came up during my second year in law school. It involved Alfred Briggs, a member of a prominent family who were part owners of a successful road-construction firm known as Curran and Briggs. Son Alfred was regarded as the "black sheep" of the family because his alcoholism frequently brought him before the courts.

The crime that led to my meeting him was his attempted robbery of a branch of the Royal Bank on Eglinton Avenue West in Toronto. This charge was far more serious than the relatively petty offences that had made him a familiar figure in the Magistrates' Court located nearby. It was apparently the last straw for Briggs's family, and they were not prepared to provide him with any further legal assistance. Briggs was small in physique and soft spoken, and it was difficult to imagine him behaving in an aggressive manner. He instructed me that, at the time of the alleged attempted bank robbery, he was inebriated and simply had no memory of the events that led to the robbery charge. The only information that the Crown prosecutor shared with me before the trial was that Briggs had threatened a bank teller while he was demanding money from her. It occurred to me that two possible defences were available: that Briggs, as a result of his inebriation, would not have been able to form the necessary intent in law to commit the offence; and, given the bizarre circumstances, that his communication with the bank teller should not have been perceived as a threat by any reasonable person.

The case came before Magistrate Locke, an austere, experienced, and dignified lay judge. His son Hugh Locke became a successful lawyer and, later, a highly respected judge. The principal prosecution witness was a young bank teller who testified simply that Briggs had appeared with a small black-leather bag, which he placed on the counter in front of her. When she asked him what he wanted, Briggs shoved the bag towards her and stated, "Fill'er up, your life or mine." She said she believed that Briggs carried a gun, so she placed several bundles of bills in the bag and pushed it back to him. Briggs looked into the bag, replied it was "not enough," and shoved the bag back to her. At this point a policeman appeared and ended Briggs's career as a potential bank robber.

Magistrate Locke listened patiently to lengthy arguments by Crown counsel and me, without taking a note. At the conclusion of our arguments he delivered his decision succinctly: "Alfred Briggs, when it comes to alcohol you are a hardened old sinner, but you are no bank robber. Case dismissed."

I accompanied Briggs out of the courtroom, no doubt anticipating an expression of gratitude. Blinking into the afternoon sunlight, he said, "Counsellor, I sure didn't expect to hit the street today" – and asked if I could give him several dollars so he could buy a bottle of wine. After hearing my not very polite refusal, he shuffled down the street and out of my life.

Elated by this success, I regarded myself henceforth as a qualified defence counsel. During that academic year I took on other legal aid cases.

Gradually, these pro bono trial adventures convinced me that law was a helping profession and that a career as an advocate would provide both excitement and drama. In addition, I continued to coach football and hockey at Upper Canada College, and the principal made me an offer to teach full time. Although a teaching career still had some appeal, I wanted to complete law school and be called to the bar before I made any firm decisions. That meant I had two years of articling ahead, including a part-time academic year in my fourth year of law school.

* * *

Another of my activities related to law school but not to academia was the Osgoode Hall intercollegiate hockey team, which played in a league with Queen's, Guelph, and McMaster universities and Ryerson Polytechnic Institute. The team was coached by Allan "Buck" Leal, the vice dean of our law school. He later became dean, and then served as chair of the Ontario Law Reform Commission. In 1977 he accepted my invitation to serve as my deputy attorney general in Ontario.

When he graduated from McMaster with high scholastic and athletic achievements, Leal had been awarded a Rhodes Scholarship. Outside the classroom, even when coaching, he was usually attired in a dark overcoat and a bowler hat, which, together with his impressive physique, gave him a most imposing presence. The Osgoode Hall hockey team was led by Joe Kane, a future judge, who later became our playing coach. We had some excellent former Junior A and senior intercollegiate players in addition to Kane – Jack Weldrake, Gerry Fitzhenry, and Bob Dale. I played defence with Kane, who liked to bestow nicknames on most of our teammates. My favourite was "The Vulcan," for our goalkeeper John Goodwin. John had so many pucks shot at him every game, Joe explained, that he was being steadily vulcanized (rubberized).

My best anecdote about my Osgoode hockey career relates not to any hard-fought victory but to sitting in a dentist's chair in Kingston on a Saturday afternoon immediately after a game with Queen's University. Late in the game I managed to stumble head first into the opposing goal-keeper's skate, resulting in some badly damaged teeth. The Queen's hockey coach was Keith "Moon" Flanigan, a local lawyer who later became a judge. He arranged for a dentist friend to see me in his office right after the game. The emergency dental treatment turned into an informal cocktail party. Flanigan, Leal, and our keen supporter Professor Donald Spence sat themselves around the chair, sharing a bottle of whiskey. The dentist appeared to enjoy having spectators for his skills while helping himself to an occasional sip as he worked on my teeth.

When I think of Flanigan, I recall how, some years later in Ottawa, after we became friends, he shared his views on temperance with me over a drink. He explained that he had been "on the wagon" for a year, though he had never been a problem drinker, and how good he had felt as a result. However, after some time he began to enjoy his abstinence less when he realized that, after he rose each morning, he knew that he "would not feel any better for the rest of the day." A very Irish view of the world!

* * *

During my law school years, one of my most important educative adventures was the summer of 1955, when I lived in Quebec City. This experience gave me a much better understanding of the diversity within Canada resulting from the founding anglophone and francophone cultures.

After completing my first year in law school, I had hoped to obtain a well-paying construction job in northern Ontario. While waiting for a response to my employment applications, I arranged with friends to spend a weekend in Quebec City – my first visit to that beautiful old centre in the heart of French Canada. My friend Dick Wright learned of my plans and insisted that I visit Eugene-François ("Chris") Noel, the president of a major construction firm. Wright had served under Noel in the Canadian Navy during the Second World War after he became the highest-ranking francophone naval officer. Noel and Wright had both become highly successful at relatively young ages. After the war, Wright became known as an Ottawa "boy wonder" – an associate deputy minister while still in his twenties. Later he served as a vice-president of the CNR and president of a major international advertising firm.

I didn't get around to phoning Noel until the day I was scheduled to leave Quebec City. He welcomed me most warmly to visit him in his office and, during our conversation, questioned me about my interest in becoming bilingual. I had not given it much thought, really, but I replied that I would welcome the opportunity in the right circumstances. Within an hour he generously invited me to stay for the summer in his home and to work for his construction firm.

Noel knew that my friend Ian Scott, who, three decades later, followed me as the attorney general of Ontario, would be spending the summer in Quebec City with another family. Wright had made that arrangement some weeks earlier. I had first met Scott in 1951 through my close friendship with Brian Heeney, a classmate at Trinity College when we were both in the Honours Modern History program at the University of Toronto. Scott was enrolled at St Michael's College, the Catholic college on the same campus. Because of my visit with Noel, my summer plans suddenly changed. I said goodbye to my friends who had accompanied me to Quebec City and moved in with the Noel family. They lived in an attractive home at 1005 Chaumont Avenue in Sillery, a fashionable suburb close to the Plains of Abraham and Wolfe's Cove, two famous historical sites closely related to the British conquest of French Canada in 1759.

My benefactor was married to an English-speaking woman and they were raising four perfectly bilingual children. They made me feel entirely welcome, and I shall always be grateful for their remarkable hospitality. Within a couple of days, Ian Scott and I had begun work together as construction labourers, and our most interesting and educational summer had commenced.

I was almost a total stranger to francophone Quebec apart from a few of the popular ski resorts, and I was inclined to accept the concept of the "two solitudes" in relation to French and English Canada. The summer of 1955 was a few years before the Quiet Revolution of the 1960s led by Premier Jean Lesage and other Quebec francophone leaders such as René Lévesque. It was certainly a different epoch in Quebec from the dynamic and confident society that emerged only a few years later. Big business, including the major financial institutions in the province, was dominated by anglophones. The ruthless and somewhat corrupt Maurice Duplessis was the premier, and the Roman Catholic Church was the dominant institution in francophone Quebec. Many historians and other experts believe that the government of Duplessis had cynically managed partnerships with the church and the anglophone business community so that each would be supreme in its respective realm. Noel was, in fact, one of a small group of senior francophone business executives.

Notwithstanding his own personal business success, Noel never forgot the barriers francophones had faced in the late 1930s when he graduated as a bilingual engineer from Queen's University. Often when we were enjoying a drink together, his bitter recollections from that time would surface. Although job opportunities were limited during the depression years, he always remembered that advertisements for jobs in business or industry in Quebec City would invariably state that "only anglophones need apply."

As I learned about this outrageous discrimination, I was shocked, and it helped me to better understand the roots of Quebec nationalism. I believe that this knowledge had a significant influence on developing and strengthening my respect and support for the very legitimate aspirations related to language and culture not only in Quebec but in francophone communities throughout Canada. During that summer I also became aware of the hugely attractive Québécois culture. There was a sense of passion and excitement among my contemporaries in Quebec City that I had rarely encountered in the staid provincial Anglo-Saxon culture of Toronto. That summer I also managed to find a little time to paint in that historic and very beautiful city, and two or three small canvases have survived.

Ian Scott and I socialized with a number of young Québécois as we struggled to become more proficient in the French language. I began to date an attractive young woman by the name of Giselle Cloutier, who lived across the St Lawrence River from Quebec City in the town of Lévis. She usually met me, along with Scott, on the Quebec City side of the river. We enjoyed some weeks in each other's company as she encouraged me to converse in French. Unfortunately, a superficial quarrel one evening ended our relationship.

A few days later, Scott and I were moved to a construction crew working on the Lévis side. We had been given a ride to the construction site but somehow managed to miss our transport back to Quebec City. Unfortunately, neither of us had bothered to bring any money with us. At the end of the work day we walked some distance to Lévis, hoping to think of some way to return by ferry to our side of the river without any cash to pay for our fares. After wandering aimlessly for some time, Scott recalled that Giselle lived in Lévis and that I had visited her home. I had been hoping desperately that the subject would not be raised. It would be hugely embarrassing for me to borrow from my erstwhile friend the twenty-five cents for two one-way ferry tickets. Nevertheless, as dusk approached, Scott convinced me that there was really no other alternative.

We knocked on the front door of Giselle's home, and her father, whom I had met only once before, opened the door. Giselle was not at home. He did not recognize me, spoke no English, and was clearly suspicious of the two young men in grubby working clothes who were intruding on his evening. Nevertheless, we got the twenty-five

. cents from a most reluctant donor and took the ferry back to Quebec City.

I never saw Giselle again, but about a week later I met one of her friends by chance in Quebec City. She warned me to avoid Giselle at all costs because it would be a rough encounter. Apparently, when Giselle returned home the night of our visit, she was confronted by two angry parents who accused her of lying about the anglophone students from Toronto she had been meeting in the city. Her father related that two young "bums" had visited that night, claimed to know her, and "begged" for twenty-five cents. Poor Giselle was grounded by her parents during the evenings for some time. Our visit to her home had certainly not strengthened anglophone–francophone relations.

Nevertheless, the summer of 1955 was generally a positive and memorable experience. It gave me a better understanding of my country and engendered in me a huge respect for the Quebec language and culture. I even developed a modest fluency in French. It also strengthened and sensitized my understanding of the relatively small francophone minority in Ontario. No doubt my immersion during those few months influenced my decision as attorney general some twenty years later to commit the government to developing a bilingual court system in Ontario.

5

Articling Student

Although I knew more about criminal litigation than civil, I accepted my father's advice and signed on to article with Bert MacKinnon, a partner at Wright and McTaggart. The firm had around eight lawyers, and they conducted both a civil and a commercial litigation practice. MacKinnon and another partner, Joe Potts, had worked for my father, and he held them in high regard. They later became judges, MacKinnon as a member of the Court of Appeal and associate chief justice of Ontario, and Potts on the High Court Trial Division (which became the Superior Court of Justice). The senior member of the firm, Peter Wright, also later served as a member of the High Court branch of the Supreme Court of Ontario.

Wright and McTaggart was a medium-sized firm in 1956. At that time the largest law firm in Toronto would not have exceeded twenty-five lawyers – a situation radically different from the mega-size legal factories that became prevalent later in the century. It was an accomplished law firm, and I would like to believe I was a valued articling student. However, I continued to take on pro bono criminal cases and to coach football part time, so my contribution to the work inside the office was probably regarded as modest.

I was not able to continue my coaching career at Upper Canada College because of its mid-afternoon practices. However, the University of Toronto intercollegiate football teams began their football practices at 5:30 pm, so I accepted a job on the coaching staff there. That meant I had to leave my articling job shortly before 5:00 each afternoon during the autumn months. Articling students in Toronto were paid a token salary at the time, but they were often expected to work long hours. I was treated well by members of the firm, even though I was probably not regarded as the typical ambitious articling student looking for future employment there. In any event, many of the routine tasks traditionally assigned to articling students were much less attractive to me than the dramas in the courtroom and on the football field.

*　*　*

Another most happy distraction from my articling employment was my marriage in April 1957 to Ria Jean Macrae. She was named after a favourite aunt, whose full first name was Maria. We had met at the end of 1953 at a University of Toronto function and had been dating ever since. In the summer of 1955, while I was living in Quebec City, Ria was touring Europe with three of her girlfriends in a London taxi they had purchased for £100. I missed her, and I decided when I saw her again in the fall to ask her to be my lifetime companion.

Both of Ria's parents had been born in Trinidad and Tobago. My father-in-law, Harry Macrae, moved to Canada at a young age and grew up in British Columbia. He graduated in medicine from the University of Toronto and became a specialist in ophthalmology. During the Second World War he served overseas for two years, close to the battle front, as an eye surgeon.

Ria's mother, Janet Grant, was known to everyone as Jill. Her twin brother, though baptised as George, was always known as Jack. They appeared to be quite comfortable with being known throughout their lives as Jack and Jill. The Grant family had emigrated to Trinidad from Nova Scotia, where Ria's great-grandfather, Kenneth Grant, had served as an ordained Pictou County minister. Once arrived in his new island home, he created a public school system that expanded over the years to serve the large San Fernando Valley area. His son T. Geddes Grant began an importing and exporting company in his name that enjoyed major success throughout the Caribbean and became as well known there as the Eaton Company was in Canada. I was pleased to learn that the Grant family was as respected for its philanthropy as for its business success. Britain recognized this generosity and, early in her reign, Queen Elizabeth II knighted one of Ria's uncles, Lindsay Grant. After I became the attorney general of Ontario I met the chief justice of Trinidad and Tobago, Sir Isaac Hyatali, who told me that, unlike most Europeans in Trinidad, the Grants were "givers and not takers."

Two of T. Geddes Grant's sons, Jack and Rolph, were outstanding cricket players in the 1930s and both served as captains of the West Indies Cricket Team – a much admired position. Michael Manley, the former prime minister of Jamaica who wrote a history of West Indian cricket, told me that during the Grant years as captains, the positions in his view should have been held by black cricketers, "but if there were · to be white captains the Grant brothers were good people."

Rolph Grant had attended my old school, St Andrew's College, and I remember seeing a large photograph hanging outside the headmaster's office of Rolph shaking hands with King George VI. We also heard stories of the legendary cricket feats attributed to him, particularly how he had hit a cricket ball over the school chapel, which was located on a hill well above the cricket field. In later years when I referred to that feat, Rolph advised me of one problem with the story – there was no chapel when he attended the college. He assured me, though, that I had married his favourite niece.

Jack Grant moved to South Africa at a relatively young age as a teacher, from 1949 to 1956. He was the headmaster of Adams College, a school that trained black teachers – a most unpopular cause under the brutal apartheid government, which was determined to frustrate the education of blacks or South Asians in the country. In 1956 the government finally expelled Jack from South Africa. He moved on to Rhodesia (now Zimbabwe), where he ran another black school and assisted detainees and their families who were persecuted by the white government of Ian Smith.

Ria and I agreed on a small wedding because my father, disabled after his stroke, would have felt uncomfortable in the company of many people. We were married in a United Church, where my in-laws had strong ties, and soon after I decided to switch my allegiance from the Anglican to the United Church too. We invited about fifty guests to a reception in the home of Ria's parents, almost all of them relatives. Still, it was a memorable occasion and a defining moment in my life. Ria's mother was committed to temperance at that time, so we were toasted with grapefruit juice. I am confident that many of our friends who were not invited became less disappointed when they learned it was a "dry" wedding.

As a result of the inexpensive reception, my father-in-law generously offered to give us a honeymoon trip to Bermuda. Some of our friends were also honeymooning in Bermuda at the same time, and that added to the fun of our first days living together. We rented a small cottage named Sea Chest from an older St Andrew's College graduate. Our wedding trip was also most successful for a most special reason – the birth of our first child, Janet, less than ten months later.

* * *

I still had more than a year left at Osgoode Hall, so we had to rely largely on Ria's income as an elementary school teacher. A few weeks after our wedding, an articling student friend, Richard McLean, boasted to me that he was spending a great deal of time as a counsel in Small Claims Court trials. He was with a firm that had an extensive insurance company practice, particularly with automobile accident claims. McLean said his firm was so busy that his employers were interested in hiring another articling student – at the more princely sum of $30, rather than $25, a week. The opportunity for further trial experience had great appeal for me, and shortly thereafter I joined the firm of Thompson, Tooze and Muir. I expect the senior lawyers at Wright and McTaggart did not mind because they suspected I was destined to be a football coach.

My new law firm was led by Joe Thompson, one of Ontario's great civil jury lawyers. My father, who had enjoyed considerable success before juries in civil cases, had particular respect for Thompson's forensic skills. Thompson had conducted trials, usually for the defence in motor-vehicle accident cases, before juries for more than forty years and was nearing the end of his career when I became articled to his firm. Legislation requiring all Ontario drivers to be insured had not yet been enacted, so jurors could not assume that every defendant in an automobile accidence case was insured.

Thompson had grown up in a small Ontario town, and he worked hard to maintain the grass-roots persona he used effectively with juries throughout Ontario. He was determined to avoid being viewed as a "big city" lawyer. Outside Toronto, local counsel invariably followed a strategy that let members of a local jury know whenever opposing counsel came from Toronto. Their frequent references to "my learned friend from Toronto" were less effective when Thompson was the opposing counsel. He avoided complicated legal terms and forensic eloquence in favour of a more earthy "Ah shucks" approach. Whenever opposing counsel in a jury trial introduced a detailed survey or plan of an accident scene as an exhibit, for instance, he would deliberately hold the exhibit upside down while appearing to be subjecting it to intense if confused scrutiny. Inevitably some "helpful" juror would point out to him that he had the sketch the wrong way round. That remark would usually provoke a quiet chuckle from the trial judge, who no doubt had witnessed the performance on many previous occasions.

My father often stressed that jury trials were a form of theatre and that counsel, as the principal actors, were likely to be closely observed by individual jurors. In his view, counsel must attempt to demonstrate their strong belief in their client's case by their general demeanour and body language. Because they would generally know what evidence to expect from an opponent's witness, they should appear nonchalant or even indifferent to the most important and potentially damaging information as it was introduced. But they also had to remember that jurors can usually detect an insincere performance, so, to be effective, counsel had to appear natural. Joe Thompson was a fine model of the clever advocate as talented actor.

Working for Thompson, Tooze and Muir proved to be an interesting and pleasurable learning experience for me. Trial experience in the Small Claims Courts became an almost daily adventure. It was a valuable immersion in mastering effective techniques for examining and cross-examining witnesses and for making submissions to trial judges and occasionally to five-person juries – as was allowed in the court in Toronto. I also learned that there is no substitute for careful preparation for every trial. In 1957 the Small Claims Courts were known as Division Courts and were presided over by County Court judges who rotated throughout Ontario. They had a maximum jurisdiction of $200 (compared to the present $25,000) in courts presided over generally by lawyers acting as deputy judges. Cases could be held in courtrooms or in a variety of premises such as legion halls, temporarily converted into courtrooms. The Toronto court, known as the First Division Court, was the only Small Claims Court where trials were usually presided over by the same judge every day. In 1957 it was Judge Young, known to all by his nickname "Bunny," though he was actually a very cranky judge.

Young was essentially a fair-minded person whose "short fuse" could be an important training experience for young lawyers. His frequent, often irascible interruptions reminded them of the importance of not asking the wrong question during cross-examination. If counsel obtained a helpful answer from an opponent's witness, for instance, he should usually move on because further questions on the same issue might give the witness the opportunity to change his earlier evidence. Similarly, a "fishing trip" style of cross-examinations could risk strengthening evidence from an opposing witness.

I continued to take pro bono criminal cases and to coach the intercollegiate football team. These extracurricular activities clearly puzzled my employers as to my future career plans. Although by then I had decided on a career in law rather than as a high-school teacher or as a full-time football coach, I was unsure whether to specialize in civil or criminal litigation.

* * *

A further interesting distraction occurred when I worked as a volunteer during the 1957 federal election. John Diefenbaker had become leader of the Progressive Conservative Party a year earlier, and after twenty-two consecutive years in government, the federal Liberal Party was clearly in trouble. However, I had never attended a political meeting and had no particular interest in partisan politics. The major political parties had campus clubs at universities and at Osgoode Hall Law School, but politics didn't attract me during my student years.

One of my law-school classmates persuaded me to assist in the campaign of Roland Michener, the Conservative MP for St Paul's constituency in Toronto. Michener had first been elected in 1953, winning by several hundred votes over his Liberal opponent, Jim Rooney – known to his friends and supporters as "Big Jim." The Michener campaign team had obtained information that some of Rooney's supporters planned to add several fictitious names or even those of deceased persons to the lists for each polling division. These votes would add numbers they believed he needed to secure his election.

I was recruited together with other law students and young lawyers to form legal teams that would challenge anybody using suspicious names on election day. We succeeded in preventing many people from casting false ballots, though our efforts had no impact on the result of the election because this time Michener won by many thousands of votes. I don't know whether Rooney was personally aware of the deceit attempted on his behalf, but in the ensuing judicial inquiry the Honourable Chief Justice James McRuer of the Supreme Court of Ontario found that election fraud had occurred. Criminal charges were laid, and Big Jim's campaign manager served some time in jail.

Michener was a successful Toronto lawyer in a firm that still bears his name. He was a good friend of Liberal leader Lester Pearson, dating from their days at Oxford University. This connection apparently did not endear him to Diefenbaker, the new prime minister: rather than being included in the Cabinet, Michener was elected Speaker of the House of Commons. Michener served as an excellent Speaker and was later appointed as Canada's high commissioner in India. When Pearson became prime minister, he appointed his old friend to be the governor general of Canada. Michener was a distinguished Canadian, and I was privileged to have him as a friend in the later years of his life.

Notwithstanding my political adventure with Michener, it would be a few more years before I became actively involved in electoral politics. I did not volunteer in the 1958 election, and I had no compelling reason to be a member of any particular political party. I did not believe that there were any meaningful philosophical differences between the federal Liberal and Conservative parties. In fact, I knew many people in Ontario who voted for the Conservatives provincially and for the Liberals federally. Both parties had become the "natural governing political party" in their respective jurisdictions.

* * *

Our home life changed dramatically on January 26, 1958, when Janet Elizebeth arrived. It was a joyous event, and Ria and I were delighted that our first born was a daughter. There had not been a female McMurtry child for several generations. My father and I were each one of four brothers, and it had simply been assumed that our first child would be yet another male. The names Janet and Elizabeth were those of her grandmothers and, therefore, an attractive choice.

Janet was a healthy, almost ten-pound baby. I have a vivid recollection of my first visit with her a few minutes after her birth, because fathers were not then allowed in the delivery room. Ria's obstetrician, Dr Leslie Watt, who would deliver all our six children, enthusiastically introduced my new daughter to me: "Look at those strong arms and legs, Roy," he said. "What a big healthy girl." I was not sure I wanted a potential Amazon child, but it was a thrilling and memorable moment for a twenty-five-year-old dad.

The reality of becoming a father encouraged me to focus more seriously on my career. Our family income had been dramatically reduced ever since Ria was forced to resign her teaching post after it became apparent that she was pregnant. Earlier, women had been obliged to resign their positions as soon as they married, and this stricture against mothers-to-be would remain in force for many more years. We rented a small one-bedroom apartment on Erskine Avenue near North Toronto

Collegiate. Janet was a very vocal infant, and that created a few challenges for both my court preparation and my continuing legal studies.
Our rent was $95 a month and we did not own a car, so we just got by
on my weekly salary. Ria was a full-time mother, but, helped by her
savings, she was able to manage the household. When the time for my
final examinations arrived, I decided I should move back to my parents'
home so my late-night studies could take place in quiet surroundings.

My strategy was interrupted the evening before my final examination – taxation law – for me the most difficult course. The exam was
scheduled for the afternoon, and I planned to study into the early hours
of the morning, sleep in late, and awake before noon, rested and prepared for the challenge. It did not work out that way.

Shortly after retiring about 3:30 am, my mother woke me to say that
one of my clients was on the telephone and had to speak to me ur-
gently. I was puzzled because I did not have any clients other than
several pro bono criminals who were all incarcerated. Nevertheless I
picked up the phone and the voice on the line said: "Is that you, Roy
Jr? It's Sergeant Joe Holbroke, and we've got your brother John here at
the station. I don't want your father to know because of his illness, but
if you can get here perhaps we can work something out." John, though
a very accomplished student athlete, was also in his teens a true "hell
raiser." He and a friend had been celebrating the completion of their
first-year university exams, and one of their activities involved turning
street signs around in our neighbourhood. A police patrol had interrupted their pranks and taken them to the local police division, where
they were charged with public mischief and placed in a cell.

Upset as I was with this disrupting event, I hoped that this indignity
would be a useful lesson for my brother and that he would generally
"cool his act." When I arrived at the police station, however, I realized
that John regarded the whole event as something of a "lark"! He and
his friend were teasing the inmates in the adjoining cells, and already
they had created a considerable "disturbance." Sergeant Holbroke and
his fellow officers were clearly anxious to get rid of them. We agreed
that they would both plead guilty to the appropriate offence under the
Highway Traffic Act and that potential *Criminal Code* charges would not
be pursued. They appeared in a local Magistrates' Court a few hours
later, and my parents were, fortunately, not burdened with the unhappy affair. In retrospect, I must admit that this arrangement was but
one more example of the comfortable professional world in Toronto at
the time, and my father's highly respected position within it.

When I arrived exhausted for my taxation law exam later that day, I soon realized that I had been the principal victim in the affair. I was certain I had done badly and, later that same afternoon, I explained my predicament to Vice Dean Allan Leal. He was both sympathetic and amused, and he assured me that there would be no problem if I had performed well in my other exams. A few weeks later I was called to the bar.

An important footnote to this particular adventure with my brother John – and there would be many other adventures with him – is to note that he was an A student as an undergraduate while also starring on the Varsity Blues football team. Later he obtained his master's degree at the University of Toronto while playing professional football with the Calgary Stampeders and the Montreal Alouettes. He went to the University of London in England for his doctorate in philosophy and, for many years, served as a professor at the University of Guelph. In short, he turned out to be a most accomplished sibling – though with radically different political views from mine.

PART TWO

The Practice of Law

6

Early Law Career

In the spring of 1958 I met sole practitioner Philip Benson, sixteen years my senior, who represented insurance companies in casualty claims. His practice had increased dramatically, and he decided to hire a junior lawyer. I became that person once I graduated – and Phil and I went on to be partners for seventeen years. Although his practice was mostly insurance litigation, he agreed that I could continue to be involved in the criminal courts as well as in general civil litigation. It turned out to be a good working relationship because our personalities were quite different. Phil was very methodical in his work habits, and he enjoyed the administrative minutiae of a law firm. He was not interested in representing persons charged with criminal offences and was a staunch supporter of the death penalty. By contrast, I was somewhat of a free spirit, quite uninterested in law-office administration and committed to developing a criminal law practice. I was also a passionate opponent of the death penalty.

In June 1958 I was one of the 250 lawyers called to the bar in Ontario. The legal system was very different at that time. Law firms were based in a single location, and there were no national or international firms. Lawyers were more often than not generalists rather than specialists. The largest law firms in Toronto had about twenty-five lawyers. Although Osgoode Hall accepted anyone with a university degree, only seven of my graduating class were women. The legal profession was very much a male bastion, and I admired the women who were prepared to compete in that environment. It was rare to see a woman in a barrister's gown or even on a jury panel – and so it remained until the 1970s.

Ria and I were a typical professional couple – a teacher wife and a lawyer husband. The cultural change in recent years is illustrated in our own family: our eldest daughter became a lawyer and then a judge, while our eldest son is a teacher. The increased participation of women and visible minorities in the legal profession, together with the growing competition to gain entrance to law schools, has significantly increased the level of talent among lawyers – and significantly reduced the proportion of young white males in the profession.

Once at the law firm, I found it exhilarating to have my own office and secretary for the first time and to be responsible for a number of litigation files. Our young baby was developing well, and it was a very happy time at home, despite our financial constraints. I also found time for some tennis and, in the summer of 1958, with the encouragement of lawyer Alan Eagleson, played a season of indoor lacrosse with a team named the Woodbridge Dodgers, after the small town northwest of Toronto. We played in a league that included teams from similar towns such as Fergus, Brooklin, and Huntsville, where lacrosse was a popular sport. Not surprisingly, my participation was viewed with great displeasure by Ria after she witnessed her first and only lacrosse game. It is a very physical sport with frequent fights, and a major dental bill was a very real possibility. That was something we could ill afford, quite apart from the chance of even more serious injuries.

One of my teammates for the first half of the season was Bob Pulford, who had just completed his first successful season with the Toronto Maple Leafs hockey team. When his employers learned of his lacrosse activities with the Woodbridge Dodgers, he was ordered to quit the team and the game. Pulford enjoyed a very successful career with the Maple Leafs, followed by a long-time coaching and management career with the Chicago Black Hawks. My own lacrosse career ended permanently at the conclusion of the season, when we lost to the Huntsville team in the Ontario Intermediate A finals.

On the legal front, I continued to spend a great deal of time in Small Claims Court trials, usually representing insurers in automobile accident cases. However, the more compelling challenges for me were criminal defence cases, where the liberty of the accused was often at stake. I still volunteered for the majority of my criminal cases on a pro bono basis.

My first criminal jury trial came early in my first year of practice in a theft case presided over by the senior County Court judge, Robert Forsyth. Clifford Wilson, my client, was a member of a theft ring charged with stealing a great deal of merchandise, ranging from furniture to television sets. As one of several alleged thieves, Wilson seems not to have benefited well financially from this enterprise. He could not afford to hire a lawyer and ended up with me as his pro bono counsel.

The prosecution created an atmosphere extremely unfavourable to the accused by packing a segment of the large courtroom from floor to ceiling with the purported stolen goods. As the many retailers who had been victimized were called to identify the merchandise, their evidence no doubt made a strong impression on the jury. In later years, stolen property was normally identified at trial from photographs entered as exhibits.

The senior defence counsel at the trial representing another accused was a very colourful character by the name of Fred Malone. He had been a controversial Crown counsel for about thirty years before joining the defence bar. He often introduced himself to young lawyers by stating, "Malone's the name, and crime's the game." As a Crown attorney, he had attracted a lot of media controversy several years earlier when he called a defence witness a "dirty rat" during his cross-examination. The witness became so agitated in being addressed in that fashion by the Queen's representative that the trial had to be adjourned. There followed a public admonition for Malone by the attorney general of the day and highly critical editorials in the Toronto press. When the trial resumed for the completion of the cross-examination of the same witness, the courtroom was crowded. Finally, the presiding magistrate asked Malone if he had any more questions for the witness. "Your Worship, I have only one more question," Malone replied. After a long, dramatic pause, the increasingly impatient magistrate demanded, "Mr Malone, would you please ask your question." "My one question to the witness," stated Malone, "is 'Do you like cheese?'" Fred Malone was indeed one of the great characters of the defence bar in an age when colourful personalities were more appreciated than today.

During Clifford Wilson's defence, a Crown witness described how my client stopped his truck in front of a store that had a number of television sets set out for sale on the sidewalk. He watched as Wilson loaded several of the sets onto his truck, even though his name was prominently displayed on the doors. As I contemplated the challenge ahead in effectively cross-examining this Crown witness, Malone passed me a note: "Roy, the audacity of the move should speak well of its success." Obviously my cross-examination was no success at all because my client was convicted of the theft charges.

* * *

One of the questions family and friends most frequently ask young defence counsel is whether they find any moral dilemma in representing an accused who they believe is probably guilty or who may even have admitted guilt. The traditional response is that every individual charged with a criminal offence under our law is presumed to be innocent, and that the accused is entitled to be found "not guilty" unless the guilt is proven beyond a reasonable doubt. In my own experience, this response usually did not satisfy the questioner, who often seemed to find a moral ambiguity in the system which did not reflect well on the legal profession. That is unfortunate and perhaps derives from the fact that Canadians have not experienced the draconian and unjust measures that characterize criminal trials in many other societies. In later years, as miscarriages of justice have been revealed in a number of serious cases, including Donald Marshall in Nova Scotia, Guy Paul Morin in Ontario, and David Milgaard in Saskatchewan, I believe that the public has become more supportive of the heavy onus of proof that rests on the Crown in a criminal case. The entrenchment in our Constitution of a Charter of Rights has also educated Canadians to the vital importance of respecting individual rights.

The fundamental rights of accused persons can be relatively meaningless, however, if they have no access to adequate legal representation. Before 1967, many accused persons in Ontario were unrepresented, convicted, and incarcerated without having any legal assistance whatsoever. Even those who can afford some legal fees face a problem: given that the investigative resources available to law enforcement are substantial, though not unlimited, it is rare for accused persons to have the financial means to compete with those of the state. For many years, our criminal law has recognized that it is more important to prevent the conviction of innocent people than to convict every accused person who may be morally guilty. Although this principle is generally accepted by the public, it usually provides scant comfort for victims of crime or their families, particularly in serious cases.

As a student and as a young lawyer, I believed that I was serving both the justice system and the broader public interest in doing my best to ensure that accused clients were acquitted unless their guilt had been established beyond a reasonable doubt. My own views about my clients' moral turpitude were not relevant to my responsibilities. At the same time, I accepted the principle that the defence of an accused must be conducted within strict ethical principles. If an accused had admitted his "guilt" to me, for instance, I would not agree that he testify as a witness, nor would I allow anyone to be called as a witness on his behalf if I had good reason to believe that the evidence would be false.

Defence lawyers are also often asked about their personal feelings when a client who they believe is probably guilty of a serious criminal offence is acquitted. The appropriate response is that, because the law requires proof of guilt to be established beyond a reasonable doubt, it would be contrary to the public interest for any person to be convicted on a lower standard of proof. That one change could place innocent people at risk of being wrongfully convicted.

When I reflect on some of my early criminal cases, I realize that those experiences did have a significant influence on whether I would continue to take on the defence of persons accused of crime. Although the result in civil lawsuits can be serious and occasionally catastrophic for losing litigants, they do not go to jail. In criminal cases, however, an inadequate representation by counsel can result in a prison sentence that might have been avoided.

* * *

During the early years of my practice as a lawyer, the only practical ground on which a divorce could be obtained was on proof of adultery by one of the spouses. This rather narrow ground for divorce led to many abuses – in particular, perjured evidence by or on behalf of one if not both of the parties to the marriage.

I recall a criminal case during that period when I acted for a private investigator who had been charged with perjury. He had given false evidence about his "observations" of his client's wife during a purported long surveillance of her. The investigator's evidence, if true, would have established the strong likelihood that she had committed adultery. The couple involved had been long separated; in practical terms, the marriage had ceased many years before. However, the wife was apparently not prepared to allow her husband the freedom to remarry. The divorce papers were never served on the defendant wife, although a false affidavit to that effect had been filed in court. She had no knowledge of the matter, so of course did not respond to the divorce action against her.

In the 1960s, when a divorce was finalized in law by what is known as a judgment absolute, it was routine for the local newspapers to publish a list of the judgments that had recently been granted. In this way, the wife in this case learned that her husband had been granted a divorce from her. She was determined not to allow her husband to benefit from the obvious fraud. She hired a lawyer, who successfully applied to have the judgment absolute set aside. In making the appropriate order, the High Court judge recommended that the police should launch an investigation into the fraud and perjury involved in the "divorce." As a result, my client and his investigative partner were both charged with perjury. My client was acquitted, but the same jury convicted his partner – a result I could not understand.

Around the same time, I was visited by a woman from Montreal who had been separated from her husband for some years. She had been living in a common-law relationship with a man for a lengthy period. Their relationship was apparently a strong and caring one, and her children regarded him as their father.

Again, the only realistic grounds on which this woman could obtain a divorce were to prove adultery on her husband's part. My potential client and her partner were financially well off, and she wanted me to hire a private investigator, in the hope that he would obtain evidence of adultery by her legal husband. At some point I learned that this husband was a chronic alcoholic and was frequently jailed for alcohol-related offences. I explained to my client that it would be more practical and probably much less expensive if she could persuade her legal husband to commence the divorce action. The proof of adultery would not be an issue, given her long relationship with her common-law husband. The expense of a potentially lengthy and futile private investigation of her alcoholic husband could also be avoided. I had no idea whether I would hear from her again after she left my office. Her predicament demonstrated the need to reform the federal divorce legislation to allow divorce after a certain period of separation when there was no likelihood of reconciliation. That in fact happened not long after when Pierre Trudeau became justice minister and amended the *Divorce Act*.

Some weeks later my Montreal client's husband appeared at my office at her request. He did not seem particularly interested in a divorce, but I recall suggesting to him that a "good-looking" man like him might benefit from a potentially "prosperous" second marriage after regaining his single status. He replied that he would think about it. A few weeks later I received from him a financial retainer to commence an action against his wife in Montreal and her common-law husband.

The rules with respect to divorce proceedings required that the action commence in the judicial district where the plaintiff resided – in this case, in Hamilton, Ontario. Because the wife filed no statement of defence, it was set down for trial as an "undefended" divorce. When the divorce was placed on the list for hearing in the Supreme Court in Hamilton, I learned that my husband "client" was back in jail again on some offence related to alcohol. The matter became further complicated when Justice Frank Donnelly was scheduled to hear the case. I knew that this judge enjoyed a reputation of being entirely unsympathetic to the concept of divorce. It was rumoured that he had long been trapped in an unhappy marriage, but, as a devout Catholic, he simply did not believe in divorce. He was, of course, bound by the law.

It did not require much imagination for me to appreciate that Justice Donnelly would be singularly unimpressed by the fact that my "client" was in custody. That fact by itself, however, did not represent any legal impediment if the grounds of adultery were established. My real client, the wife and her common-law husband, both testified, and their long relationship was corroborated by a Montreal neighbour. Their appearance suggested that they were comfortable financially, and it was obvious to all present that they would be the principal beneficiaries of a divorce.

Justice Donnelly's remarks suggested his concern that, in these circumstances, granting a divorce would be an "abuse of process." In virtually all civil proceedings, it is the plaintiff who is seeking relief from the defendant. Justice Donnelly was clearly annoyed by the fact that this scenario was being reversed in our case. After hearing the witnesses I had called to testify, Justice Donnelly decided to recall the plaintiff husband to the witness stand. His only question was brief and to the point: "Who saw Mr McMurtry first, you or your wife?" In response, the man lied and said he had first come to my office. Justice Donnelly then turned to me and asked whether I believed his evidence. I had never heard of a trial judge asking the counsel for one of the parties such a question and, in fact, I thought it highly improper. I so advised Justice Donnelly in my response, and he did not press the question.

Instead, he launched into a long diatribe on the impropriety of defendants in the husband's position benefiting from the wife's adulterous conduct if he granted the divorce. By this time I had become quite angry and advised the judge that it was clearly not in the public interest to prevent the defendants from regularizing their relationship through a marriage, particularly given the interests of the children. A silence descended on the courtroom, and after staring at his desk for a few minutes, Justice Donnelly slammed his court-book shut, granted the divorce, and stormed out of the courtroom.

As a postscript, Justice Donnelly had, as a lawyer, earlier represented Steven Truscott at his initial trial for murder. Donnelly was then a respected lawyer in Goderich, Ontario. In any event, the Truscott case was later to occupy a great deal of my time during my last year as chief justice of Ontario.

* * *

I had been a lawyer for several years when Henry Bull, the senior Crown attorney for the Judicial District of York (Greater Toronto), asked me to serve as one of the first "fee for service" Crown prosecutors in his region. In past years, lawyers in private practice in Ontario were hired to prosecute individual trials, but this system had been discontinued because it suggested that the lawyers employed by the Ministry of the Attorney General lacked the necessary expertise within their ranks. The hiring of outside counsel for major trials was obviously not good for the morale of ministry lawyers.

As a part-time prosecutor, I would be appearing only in Magistrates' Court – "inferior courts" presided over by men who had simply worked their way through the Magistrates' Court administration or served as justices of the peace – a position that has never required any legal education. For the most part they were decent and principled men who had challenging responsibilities, though, in my early experience, they usually leaned in favour of the prosecution. Traditionally, these courts heard about 95 per cent of the criminal trials in Ontario, and over the summer in particular, there was a shortage of available prosecutors. For about five years I spent either the month of July or August in these courts, and during the balance of the year, I was also called in for an occasional week or two.

I had appeared frequently in these courts as a defence counsel, and my work as a Crown prosecutor was an interesting reversal in terms of advocacy – and an opportunity to become better known to the magistrates and police officers. Whatever role I played, defence or prosecution, these relationships were obviously useful in obtaining cooperation in the courtroom. The charges that I prosecuted in the Magistrates' Courts covered the whole broad range of non-jury criminal cases. The preparation for trials usually involved only a brief meeting with the police officer in charge of the case. There were exceptions, but the process was very much "fly by the seat of your pants." The instructing police officer would also sit beside me during the trial to brief me further, if necessary.

There was usually a degree of human drama in Magistrates' Court stemming from the common-sense magistrates, the many unrepresented accused, and a few flamboyant defence counsel, many of them volunteers. The proceedings were generally more unpredictable than those in the senior trial courts, which operated in a generally formal fashion. Some of the magistrates had obviously become bored with their routine and had consumed an alcoholic beverage or two before entering the courtroom. On one occasion I was prosecuting in a court which dealt with alcohol-related offences, and the prisoner's box was filled to overflowing. During a short lull in the proceedings, one of the accused succumbed to flatulence, and the sound reverberated through the courtroom. A moment later, a senior defence counsel stood up and stated: "Your Worship, I want you to know that there are others in this courtroom who hold you in greater respect." The presiding magistrate was clearly not amused and, later that morning, the lawyer's client paid the price.

One of the negative side effects related to the imposition of unnecessary harsh sentences, usually on the unrepresented accused. I sometimes thought these sentences resulted from a bad hangover the presiding magistrate was suffering through. As a Crown prosecutor, I felt an obligation to help ensure that everyone I came in contact with had a fair trial. I worried about the high number of guilty pleas – a result, I suspected, of Crown counsel at that time not being able, as they do now, to make submissions on sentences. In any event, I sometimes addressed the magistrate when I considered the sentence overly harsh or took the unusual step, one perhaps ethically questionable given my role as a prosecutor, of personally initiating an appeal, albeit in another lawyer's name whose permission I had sought. I agreed to do all the paperwork, and my lawyer colleague would argue the appeal pro bono. I had some success in that regard, though today such initiative would cause a great deal of controversy.

Some years ago, the Magistrates' Courts evolved into the Ontario Court of Justice, and the magistrates were replaced by legally trained judges known as sitting judges. Only members of the bar with a minimum of ten years' experience were eligible for appointment. Gradually, Crown prosecutors were given more time for trial preparation and the position became much more sought after than it had been in my early years of practice. As the opportunity for young lawyers to appear in court has become increasingly limited by the high cost of civil litigation and the competition for clients, an increasing number of young lawyers have left better-paying jobs at major law firms for positions as Crown prosecutors, in order to experience the greater excitement and fulfilment of regular criminal court advocacy.

* * *

My first criminal jury trial in the Supreme Court of Ontario took place during my first year as a lawyer. My client, Rod Rorabeck, was charged with rape – one of three accusations that, along with murder and manslaughter, were heard at that time by High Court judges. Rorabeck admitted that he had engaged in sexual intercourse with the complainant and that he had been aggressive, but he insisted the act was essentially consensual. However, I soon learned from the police officer in charge of the investigation that the victim had complained of being physically assaulted and that there was evidence of bruising about her face when she first contacted the police, approximately ten hours after the alleged assault. Although Rorabeck strongly denied the use of any violence, the bruising would be damaging evidence because it would provide corroboration of the alleged lack of consent. Such corroboration was often missing in rape prosecutions, which then turn into a "she says, he says" credibility contest.

The term "rape" is no longer found in the *Criminal Code of Canada* because it has been replaced by "sexual assault." Over time the word "rape" had attracted a great deal of mythology that was invariably unfair to the complainant. It created an unreasonable assumption that any rape should be vigorously resisted by the victim, regardless of the physical power imbalance or the presence of threats.

At the preliminary inquiry, which would determine whether there was sufficient evidence to place my client on trial, the complainant testified that Rorabeck had dropped her off at her boarding-house home at about two o'clock in the morning. She was distraught and had remained in her room until noon. After a conversation with a friend, she went the local police division and complained of the sexual assault.

In the course of my investigation, I subsequently learned from the complainant's landlady that the woman had returned to her room about two in the morning but had almost immediately left for a period of some hours. I had asked a friend with no previous experience to do the initial interview with the landlady. As a pro bono defence counsel, I had no funds for a professional investigation. As it turned out, the complainant's activities in the hours immediately following the alleged assault were critical to the case. I came to the conclusion that the bruising might well have occurred after the woman had returned to her boarding house and before she complained to the police. I also learned that the complainant's boyfriend was a member of a notoriously violent motorcycle gang, and the bruising could well have been administered by this friend in the belief that the complainant had been "unfaithful." I called the landlady as a defence witness after the complainant denied she had left her boarding house early that morning following the alleged sexual assault. I believe that the landlady's evidence significantly undermined the credibility of the complainant.

The trial came before Justice Wishart Spence, with Henry Bull as the prosecutor. Spence, like the majority of High Court trial judges at that time, was generally sympathetic to any prosecution, though Bull, tough and effective, was regarded as being fair. It was clearly going to be a challenging trial. Years before it became mandatory for prosecutors to disclose to the defence all relevant information in the Crown's possession, Bull was always forthcoming in discussing with me both the strengths and the weaknesses of the prosecution's case before trial. However, he was reluctant to concede any weaknesses in the Crown's case against Rod Rorabeck.

I learned some valuable lessons in the conduct of Rorabeck's defence, including the danger of allowing a close personal relationship to develop with any client charged with a criminal offence, particularly a serious one. Rorabeck had been allowed out on bail shortly after his arrest, and we spent a good deal of time together preparing for his trial, including meetings at my home. He was a likeable individual, about my own age, and a degree of friendship developed between us. As the date for the trial came closer, I became acutely aware that I alone stood between Rod and a jail sentence of eight to ten years. This reality, together with my lack of experience, caused me great personal stress.

An all-male jury was empanelled to try the case of *The Queen v. Rorabeck*. Although the long-time tradition of male-only juries in that era has often been described as potentially unfair to female complainants in sexual assault prosecutions, the later presence of women jurors in these trials added an unexpected dynamic to the process. In the years before jurors were prohibited by law from discussing what took place in the courtroom, the attitudes and opinions of individual jurors frequently became known at trial, and female jurors were often very critical of a complainant if they disapproved of her general lifestyle. If a complainant had shown poor judgment in the bars she frequented or in her choice of male company, for instance, her testimony might not be given the weight it deserved. On the whole, however, the credibility and strength of the jury system was strengthened significantly when women began to serve on juries.

Before Rorabeck's case commenced, I arranged for him to sit through the preceding trial, where Henry Bull was the prosecutor. I hoped, by familiarizing him with the trial process, to alleviate his understandable anxieties. This strategy proved but a mixed success: as my client witnessed Mr Bull's advocacy skills, he became very nervous about the prospect of being cross-examined by him.

All defence counsel face a difficult decision in deciding whether to recommend that clients testify at trial. In the final analysis, it must be the clients' decision, and given its importance, I always obtained instructions from them in writing. The decision is influenced by several fundamental issues. First, for those clients who have admitted guilt to their lawyers, counsel would be ethically obliged not to call them as witnesses because their testimony could only lead to perjured evidence. A second consideration is whether clients have a criminal record; if they do, the record would have to be revealed to the jury, and it could well prejudice the jury against them. Third, the clients' version of the events might appear to be so unbelievable as to guarantee rejection by the jury. As a former chief justice of Trinidad and Tobago told me, a magistrate in his country once imposed a sentence in these words: "Mr Smith, I sentence you to five years in the penitentiary; two years for your offence and three years for your defence."

Rod Rorabeck did not have a criminal record, and we assumed from the beginning that he would testify. Although he strongly believed in his own innocence, he was concerned about the probability of a very tough cross-examination by Henry Bull. I therefore decided on a *voir dire* – a tactic that would give him some experience in the witness box "under fire," but without the jury. It would determine, for instance, whether his statement to the police after his arrest had been voluntary, and so determine its admissibility. Rorabeck's statement, although not particularly damaging to his defence, came after intensive questioning; at the time, an accused did not have to be informed of his right to remain silent and to consult his legal counsel before any interrogation.

The trial judge had to be satisfied beyond a reasonable doubt that the accused's statement had been voluntary before the prosecution could admit it in evidence before the jury.

At the trial, Rorabeck did indeed seem to make a favourable impression with the jury when he testified, but Justice Spence's many interruptions clearly demonstrated his personal scepticism and a real degree of antagonism towards my client. His obvious enthusiasm for the prosecution's case did not strengthen my optimism, particularly because I was required to address the jury before the prosecution made its final submission. The order in which counsel address a jury provides a tactical advantage, and I have always believed that the prosecution is generally given an unfair advantage under the present state of the law.

About halfway through my jury address, one of the jurors fainted. I don't know whether my comments caused this surprising event, but it created much confusion. My assistant in the case was Dr Bill Jacobs, an articling student who had previously been a medical practitioner. When "Doc" Jacobs rushed to assist the stricken juror, Justice Spence angrily demanded to know why my law student was in the jury box. He was satisfied by my explanation and immediately declared a recess while an ambulance was summoned.

It soon became apparent that the ill juror would not be able to resume his duties. My client therefore had to agree whether the trial could continue with eleven jurors. At that time an accused was entitled to insist on a verdict by twelve jurors. Later, the *Criminal Code* was amended to allow the continuation and completion of a trial with as few as ten jurors. That was a sensible amendment: it avoided mistrials that could take place after many weeks or even months of a trial solely because of the illness of one or two jurors. As soon as the stricken juror left the courtroom, I was summoned to Justice Spence's chambers, where Henry Bull presented me with a typed consent for my client to sign to enable the trial to continue. Despite their annoyance, I insisted on an hour's recess so I could reflect on the advice I should give my client. The issue was simply whether my client could gain any advantage if he insisted on his right to a new trial rather than proceeding with eleven jurors. Rorabeck and I quickly agreed that the trial appeared to have gone reasonably well and that we should complete the trial with the remaining jurors.

I was determined, however, to make the jury aware of my client's right to a new trial. By continuing the present trial, I argued, he was content to place his fate in their hands. To emphasize that point, I asked that the signing of the consent be done in the jury's presence. This unusual demand clearly irritated both Justice Spence and Henry Bull, who interpreted it as "an attempt to turn the trial into a theatrical performance." There was no legal basis on which to deny my request, however, and Rorabeck was duly escorted from the prisoner's box to sign his consent on a table placed in front of the jury. I was able to make a good deal out of my client's "trust" in the jury during the balance of my closing submission to the jurors. My address to the jury was followed by very effective presentations from the experienced prosecutor and from Justice Spence, who delivered his instructions on the law to be applied in the context of the particular facts. At that point, Rorabeck's fate was placed in the hands of the eleven jurors.

The combination of Henry Bull's tough closing submissions and the judge's biased instructions favouring the prosecution placed me in a state of great anxiety while I waited for the jury's verdict. In the late afternoon the court was adjourned for two hours – oddly, to allow Justice Spence and Henry Bull to attend a birthday dinner with one of their lawyer friends. While they celebrated, I paced the corridors of the Old City Hall courthouse. Several decades later I know that even experienced trial lawyers are never free from the tension that precedes the verdict in any criminal case.

As soon as the judge and the prosecutor returned from dinner, the jury announced it had a verdict. I could not bring myself even to glance at Rod Rorabeck as the jury foreman made his announcement: "Not guilty." A moment later Henry Bull leaned over and, in a loud whisper, stated, "You son of a bitch. You scored a touchdown." "What did you say, Mr Bull?" asked Justice Spence. "Oh, nothing important," he replied, winking at me.

After a jury verdict, it was common practice back then for defence counsel to wait outside the courtroom as the jury filed out, hoping that one or more of them might want to discuss the case. It could provide a valuable learning experience. After I nodded at several of the jurors that day, two or three of them stopped to chat. "Well, you gentlemen took quite a while to arrive at a verdict," I said. "Your decision must have been a difficult one?" "Oh hell no," remarked one. "Almost as soon as we entered the jury room after the judge's instructions, we all agreed to find your client not guilty. But we decided that if we returned immediately with a 'not guilty' verdict, that 'old bastard of a judge' would be really upset, so we thought we better talk about it for a while. We also decided to order dinner, because, when eleven guys each want to give their own particular view of the trial, you use up a lot of time." So much for my hours of pacing around the courthouse, anxiously waiting for the verdict! Within several years the *Criminal Code* was amended to make it a criminal offence for a juror to discuss with anyone the deliberations in the jury room.

There is no such prohibition for a juror in the United States and, as a result, jurors are routinely questioned by members of the media after a trial. It is my view that the prohibition in Canada encourages a more frank discussion among jurors during their deliberations, knowing that these discussions will be in confidence. There is also the danger that an irresponsible juror might misrepresent the character of the jury discussions, with the result that confidence in the system is undermined.

Wishart Spence was an experienced trial judge and later became a distinguished member of the Supreme Court of Canada. In both roles he tended to express his own opinions aggressively. In a jury trial, however, that approach could be a mixed blessing for the prosecution. The presiding judge has the responsibility to instruct the jury about the applicable law, but it is the jurors who decide on the verdict. As trial judges often explain during their instructions: "Members of the jury, you are the sole judges of the facts in this case and, while I may express my opinion as to some of the facts, it is your duty to disregard my opinion if it is not in accord with your own individual views of the evidence." My general experience in jury trials has been that, if a trial judge wishes to influence a jury with respect to its fact-finding responsibility, it must be done very subtly; otherwise, jurors may feel that the judge is encroaching on their territory as the sole judges of the facts. An openly biased judge risks alienating a jury – and, in this case, Justice Spence's tactics clearly backfired.

In the prosecution of Rod Rorabeck, the jury may also have felt some sympathy for an accused represented by a young and inexperienced counsel faced with a veteran prosecutor supported by an openly biased judge. There are many subtle dimensions in any trial. In the late 1950s all the Ontario High Court criminal prosecutions in Toronto were conducted by one of the three Crown attorneys – Henry Bull, Herb Langdon, or Arthur Klein. They were all intelligent and effective advocates, though with different styles. Bull and Langdon were both aggressive, the former extremely eloquent, and the latter somewhat bombastic. Both were relentless in their cross-examinations of defence witnesses. The prosecutor I most feared, however, was Arthur Klein, who later became the chief judge of the Provincial Criminal Court.

Klein's personality and tactics with a jury were similar to those of my former boss Joe Thompson, though in the prosecutor's rather than the defence lawyer's role (see chapter 5). Both men came from rural Ontario and exuded small-town, down-to-earth charm. I have often thought that Art Klein probably embodied the famous Detective Columbo character long before actor Peter Falk made him so memorable. Klein often appeared to stumble along in front of a jury, giving the false impression that he was somewhat confused about many aspects of the case. Juries appeared to like this low-key approach, and it could be every effective.

In that era, the composition of Toronto juries was dramatically different from those in more recent years. Jury members were not only entirely male but invariably white males, men of European origin or birth. Almost the entire Toronto legal profession too were white males of Anglo-Saxon or European extraction. The Italian-Canadian population had not yet become a dominant culture in the city, and there were only a handful of lawyers of Italian origin at the time when I was called to the bar. In every respect, this total lack of diversity resulted in a much less interesting and dynamic city.

Regardless, I found my life as a young lawyer to be challenging, exciting, and invigorating. The fortunate result for my client Rod Rorabeck in the High Court of Ontario, together with the experience and confidence I gained there, provided more than adequate compensation for me in this pro bono case. The most important impact on my career, however, came indirectly. A few days after the trial, the much-respected defence counsel Arthur Maloney approached me in the barrister's robing room to explain that Henry Bull had generously made some very complimentary comments to him about my conduct of the case. And so began a close friendship and a significant professional association that was to last for the next twenty-five years.

7

Mentor, Arthur Maloney

In 1958 Arthur Maloney was the MP from Parkdale in Toronto, a respected lawyer and, for the most part, a popular figure. He had been born and educated in the Ottawa Valley, then enrolled at St Michael's College at the University of Toronto. He was passionate, charming, articulate, and generally much liked by members of the media. Maloney's large family was well known throughout Ontario. His doctor father had also been a federal MP, and his brother Jim was a long-time member of the Cabinet of Premier Leslie Frost. Jim was also well known for his alcoholic binges, which did not appear to undermine his political reputation or his effectiveness in Cabinet. One anecdote had it that, on one occasion, two of his Cabinet colleagues complained to Premier Frost about his drinking. Frost promptly replied that Maloney was more valuable to his government drunk than "both of them sober" – a nice retort, but borrowed from Abraham Lincoln and John A. Macdonald before him.

Arthur Maloney was a spellbinding orator and one of the most successful jury lawyers in Canada. There was such a demand for his services as a criminal defence lawyer that he had to delegate many cases to others. Fortunately, I soon became one of those lawyers. Our relationship was tremendously important to my career as, gradually, he became a valued legal mentor.

Maloney was responsible for my involvement in many interesting criminal and civil cases. In some trials we would work together representing co-accused or civil clients with similar interests. In the majority of cases, however, he simply referred clients to me when he was too busy to take them on. At other times I took over criminal trials from him because he had previously got into serious confrontations with the judges who were scheduled to preside over the case. Maloney was totally fearless in court and quite prepared to do battle with difficult judges, but, as he got older, he said that life was too short to spend with certain judges during a trial. In this way I became a last-minute replacement for him in some very interesting criminal cases.

These "ill-tempered judges" were a result, really, of the selection process. Many appointments at that time could be traced to political influence, where there was no adequate screening process. The system is different today, and applicants for judicial appointment both federally and provincially are subject to review by advisory committees largely independent of government. These committees are interested not only in the candidates' legal experience but also in their reputation for courtesy and patience. Although bad-tempered judges are not an endangered species, they are certainly far fewer in number than they were a few years ago. Furthermore, complaints about a particular judge's conduct can be made to judicial councils at both the federal and the provincial levels. The issue of courtesy in the courts of Ontario is now more focused on the conduct of trial counsel towards one another – a matter that has become a major priority for the governing body of the legal profession.

One such case referred to me by Maloney was the trial of Peter Colin-Jones, a young Aboriginal charged with the strangulation murder of a woman who had been involved in a sexual relationship with his sister. The trial was scheduled to proceed before Justice Ferguson and a jury in the High Court Division of the Supreme Court of Ontario. Maloney and Justice Ferguson had long been involved in an acrimonious relationship, and Maloney asked me to take over the defence. He was not in the mood, he said, to "do battle for a week with that old bastard." I had earlier acted as a junior lawyer for Maloney in a manslaughter trial presided over by Ferguson, so I was familiar with the relationship between them. After listening to Maloney's strong objections to his instructions to the jury, Justice Ferguson slammed his bench book shut and shouted, "Mr Maloney, your comments are not objections – they are insults."

In the Colin-Jones trial, Maloney's request came only one week before the trial was scheduled to begin. Along with Crown counsel, I went to Ferguson's chambers and requested an adjournment – on the reasonable ground that I required more time to prepare for the defence. The delay would also mean that the trial would proceed before another judge with less of a prosecution bias. The Crown counsel, Peter Rickaby, an old law-school classmate, objected strongly to my request. He argued that the Crown's case against my client was overwhelming: there was no issue about the identity of Colin-Jones as the killer. The only mitigating factor was Colin-Jones's intoxication and his capacity to form the necessary intent for murder – a point that might reduce a conviction for murder to that of manslaughter. "I know what you and Maloney are up to, McMurtry," Justice Ferguson intoned. "The change of counsel is simply a tactic to avoid me as the trial judge." However, he wisely recognized that the Court of Appeal might well order a new trial if the short adjournment for trial preparation was refused and the accused was convicted, so he granted my request for a week's adjournment.

The trial proceeded before Mr Justice Eric Moorhouse. I was assisted as my junior counsel by Dennis O'Connor, who had recently been called to the bar – and who went on to enjoy a most distinguished professional career as a defence lawyer, Yukon magistrate, law teacher, and commercial litigator before his appointment to the Ontario Court of Appeal and, shortly thereafter, as my associate chief justice when I was chief justice of Ontario.

Peter Colin-Jones insisted that, although he had no recollection whatsoever of the events, he knew he could not have killed the victim because "she was my friend." Earlier, Maloney had been so convinced of his client's inability to recall any of the circumstances that he arranged for a psychiatrist to question Colin-Jones after a strong injection of Sodium Pentothol – the so-called truth serum. Even in this drug-induced state, the accused was unable to recall any details. The psychiatrist, however, regarded his emotionally charged responses and profuse weeping as more consistent with guilt than with innocence and concluded that Colin-Jones had actually been able to shut his conscious memory to his probable responsibility for the death.

The defence counsel's opinion about a client's moral guilt or innocence is not particularly relevant. Counsel has a professional duty to ensure that any accused person is given the legitimate protections afforded by the criminal law. The most fundamental of these rights is the presumption of innocence and the requirement that the prosecution must establish the guilt of any accused beyond a reasonable doubt. In this particular case, I did have some doubt as to whether Colin-Jones was the actual killer, given independent evidence of his affection for the deceased. However, the circumstantial evidence implicating him in the death was strong. In the Crown's theory, under the influence of alcohol he had become enraged by the victim's resistance to his sexual advances and had caused her death by strangulation.

One of the key witnesses for the prosecution was Colin-Jones's sister, who had been involved in an intimate relationship with the deceased at the time of her death. She was no reluctant witness: every pore of her body oozed hostility towards her accused brother. I recall remarking to O'Connor that I would not want to encounter her in a dark alley. As she gave her evidence-in-chief, I sensed that her anger towards her brother was fuelled by her resentment that he had been making sexual advances towards her deceased lover – and that these advances may not have been aggressively resisted.

During this evidence, my earlier suspicions that the sister may have been the killer were somewhat strengthened. This possibility therefore became a focus of my cross-examination. I still recall her hissed responses to my questions. Certainly her body language demonstrated that, given the opportunity, she might well enthusiastically strangle me on the spot. The members of the jury appeared to be paying close attention to my cross-examination, and I decided that our strategy should not be simply to focus on Colin-Jones's alcoholic consumption, so as to reduce the charge of murder to a conviction for manslaughter, but to raise doubts as to whether he was in fact the killer.

Colin-Jones was anxious to give evidence, if only to proclaim his belief that he could not have murdered his friend, even though he had no recollection of the events immediately preceding the victim's death. Despite his strong feelings on this issue, he always spoke in an emotionless monotone. In preparing for his testimony, I tried to impress on him the importance of expressing his belief in his innocence with a real degree of conviction. Regardless, even in the witness box he could not avoid his natural taciturn manner. As his evidence-in-chief concluded, I decided to take a gamble. I suggested to him that he might well have killed his friend but had shut out that reality from his mind. That did it: he literally screamed out his response, tears streaming down his cheeks: "I could not have killed her because she was my friend."

The jury acquitted Peter Colin-Jones on his twenty-ninth birthday, and a photograph in the *Toronto Star* recorded the event in a picture of the jubilant young man flanked by O'Connor and me. Thirty years passed before the press released another photograph of O'Connor and me together – when O'Connor was sworn in as the associate chief justice of Ontario. I noted then that the aging process had been kinder to him than to me!

A year later the Crown prosecutor in *Regina v. Jones* telephoned me somewhat gleefully, I thought, reporting that Peter Colin-Jones had just been charged with another serious criminal assault. His call was followed shortly by one from the accused's newly acquired spouse asking me to represent him on this second charge. I advised her that there were many competent defence counsel in the Metropolitan Toronto area and that her husband would have to look elsewhere.

* * *

In 1972 in St Louis, Missouri, a newspaper report began: "Richard Paul Anderson, who was once one of the 10 most wanted fugitives in the country, was convicted of second-degree murder yesterday and his sentence was fixed at 60 years in prison by a St. Louis County jury." The press account made no mention of Anderson's major role in a legal drama in Toronto that had played out over several years. It included three separate judge-and-jury trials involving brothers Ronald and Gerry Shatford as a result of a single robbery on November 24, 1967. It ended with a successful application to John Turner, the federal minister of justice, to use a rarely exercised prerogative and order a second trial for Ronald Shatford after his appeals to the Ontario Court of Appeal and the Supreme Court of Canada had been denied. As part of this long saga, "commission" evidence was taken in Missouri from Anderson – a good-looking young man who was also a ruthless killer.

Anderson and the Shatford brothers were all charged with the robbery of the Sentry (GEM) department store in Thornhill, Ontario, on January 18, 1968. Anderson, a fugitive from justice from Missouri, pleaded guilty to the robbery on February 1 and, shortly after, gave a sworn affidavit to the police stating that neither of the Shatford brothers was involved. The police officers declined to give any credence to this document because Anderson refused to name his accomplices.

In the prosecution theory, three men had been involved in the robbery, even though none of the several eyewitnesses had seen more than two in the department store. Both of the Shatford brothers were committed for trial before a judge and jury after a preliminary hearing on February 21, 1968. At that time, a trial would commonly have taken place a few months later, but for reasons unexplained the Crown Attorney's Office did not schedule the trial until May 1970 – a highly unusual delay.

The jurors convicted Ronald Shatford of armed robbery, but they were unable to reach a decision with respect to his brother, Gerry. Ronald Shatford was sentenced to twenty years, a particularly harsh sentence given that his criminal record, though long, did not contain any previous convictions involving violence or the use of guns. The sentence was subsequently reduced by the Ontario Court of Appeal to fifteen years.

After the first trial, Gerry Shatford approached Arthur Maloney to take over his defence for the second trial. Maloney was too busy, and he recommended that I be retained. And so the Shatford saga began for me early in 1971. Right from the first interview, Gerry Shatford convincingly protested that he and his brother were innocent, though he could give no explanation as to why they had been arrested for the crime. Yet Ron Shatford had been identified as the robber in a police line-up by three female employees of the department store.

The investigation of the robbery involved two police departments – the Markham Police Department, in whose jurisdiction the robbery occurred, and the Metropolitan Toronto Police Hold-Up Squad, which had been asked to assist. It was not the practice of the Metro squad then to take photographs of identification line-ups, but one had been taken by the Markham Police – much to the annoyance of the hold-up squad. These line-ups are supposed to gather the suspect together with a dozen persons of generally the same age and a similar physical appearance. I still have a photograph of this particular line-up, and no one else resembled Ron Shatford. Furthermore, five of the twelve men were wearing glasses, and none of the eyewitnesses had mentioned this detail in their description of the hold-up men.

Any reluctance to take photographs of police line-ups deprives an accused person of a fundamental right to challenge the fairness of the procedure. In more recent years, judges have been highly critical of the absence of such a record. In fact, the traditional line-up has been replaced by a process of photo identification, where a witness is given a group of photos of the suspect as well as other people of similar appearance. The nature of any identification is carefully recorded, including the time the witness takes to identify a particular photograph and with what degree of certainty. In prosecutions that depend on the identification of an alleged perpetrator, the law requires that juries are warned of the inherent frailties in evidence of this kind. These frailties are particularly significant when a witness identifies someone who was previously unknown or when the suspect is pointing a gun at the witness – as occurred in the robbery for which the Shatfords were charged. Not surprisingly, hold-up victims invariably focus their eyes on the gun itself rather than the face of the person holding the gun. Juries are routinely reminded that many miscarriages of justice have occurred as a result of mistaken identification by conscientious witnesses who sincerely believed they were giving truthful and reliable evidence.

In the spring of 1971, before his second trial, Gerry Shatford advised me that a man by the name of Alexander "Buddy" Ramsdale, who was then incarcerated in the Don Jail in Toronto, was prepared to admit that he was the second robber along with Anderson in the department store. By this time, Anderson had been taken back to St Louis to face first-degree murder charges related to the killing of his former girlfriend's parents. I was sceptical about this information regarding Ramsdale because of its potential to be a jail-house "con job." If he were to be subpoenaed as a witness, he would be protected by the *Canada Evidence Act* from ever having his testimony used against him in any subsequent criminal proceedings related to the robbery. Nevertheless, I visited him at the Don Jail in the company of Frank Marrocco, one of Maloney's articling students, who became an important witness to the statements Ramsdale made during our meeting. Thirty years later, Marrocco went on to be treasurer (chair) of the Law Society of Upper Canada and, even more recently, became a judge of the Superior Court of Ontario. Ramsdale told us that he felt a genuine sense of guilt because both the Shatford brothers were innocent of the robbery, yet Ron had now been sentenced to twenty years, and Gerry was facing a second trial and a possible conviction.

Despite my initial scepticism, it soon became apparent that Ramsdale had indeed participated in the robbery. He recounted a number of details that had not been in evidence in the first trial and that he could not have gained from anyone else. Other than Anderson, he did not name his accomplices, but he did mention two men whose agreement he needed before he gave any evidence – Terry Smith and Jimmy Carroll. He insisted that only he could communicate with them if we wanted his continued cooperation.

Frank Marrocco and I both believed that Ramsdale was telling the truth, but I worried about the impact his evidence would have on a jury if we called him to testify. He had a significant criminal record, and the Crown prosecutor would be able to explain to the jury that the witness had nothing to risk by testifying other than a possible charge of perjury, which would be difficult to prove. Furthermore, he would be testifying that he had performed the role in the robbery attributed to Ron Shatford, who had been convicted and whose appeals had been dismissed. It would therefore be a huge challenge to persuade any jury to accept this new evidence. However, it would also be difficult to explain to the Shatford family our reluctance to subpoena Ramsdale as a witness. In the end, though, I was able to persuade the family that the evidence would probably do Gerry more harm than good.

There were problems too in calling Gerry Shatford as a witness. If he testified, he would be cross-examined on his own criminal record. And, when he inevitably asserted that his brother Ron had not been involved in the robbery, the jury would in effect be asked to conclude that both Ron and Gerry were innocent, notwithstanding the failure of Ron's appeals with respect to his conviction. I therefore obtained Gerry's written instructions that he did not wish to testify at his trial and that Ramsdale would not be called as a witness. I believed that dealing with the innocence of one Shatford at a time would be the best strategy.

Gerry Shatford's second trial for the armed hold-up began on June 2, 1972, and lasted for six days. The Crown's identification evidence was not strong. I emphasized to the jury that two men had already been convicted for the robbery and that all the witnesses at the scene had testified that they had seen only two robbers in the department store. I was also able to persuade the presiding judge to allow into evidence expert testimony from Professor Anthony Doob from the Centre of Criminology at the University of Toronto regarding the general frailty of identification evidence of persons not known to the witness before the crime. Professor Doob described scientific tests to the jury which had dramatically demonstrated the unreliability of such evidence. To my knowledge, such expert evidence had not been allowed before or since in Ontario because judges believe that opinion evidence of this kind could usurp the function of the jury as the sole and independent judge of the facts. Indeed, Professor Doob's testimony was not permitted at Ron Shatford's second trial, which took place in September that same year.

Gerry Shatford was acquitted by this jury, and my efforts on behalf of the Shatfords were now directed to persuading John Turner, the minister of justice, to exercise a rarely used ministerial prerogative in ordering a second trial for Ronald Shatford. His wife, Rita, and his young daughter were devoted to him, despite his lengthy criminal history. Rita was intelligent, attractive, and totally dedicated to securing her husband's release from prison. She believed that Richard Anderson was the key to Ron's release.

Rita Shatford obtained Anderson's prison address in Missouri, and she informed me that she had written to him asking for his assistance. I had difficulty imagining that a killer like Anderson would have any sympathy for Ron and Rita Shatford. And, even if she did get his co-operation, who would believe him? Nevertheless, a remarkable series of letters was exchanged between them. In her first letter to Anderson dated March 17, 1971, Rita introduced herself as Ron Shatford's wife and advised him of Ron's unsuccessful appeals. "It is my understand-ing," she continued, "that you indicated to Ron that if your partners would not come forward voluntarily, then as a last resort you would give their names. At this time, I am asking you to do this." Anderson's reply of March 20, 1971, was certainly interesting, and I reproduce it here in full, complete with spelling errors:

Your letter of March 17th arrived here yesterday. And of course, I was quite surprise to hear from you.

I decided to answer your letter because I can appreciate how anxious you are to do whatever you can to help secure your husband's release from prison. And in this day and age there are few wives who are as devoted as you are – and I greatly admire your love for your husband. .

However, I'd like to point out that at no time did I ever indicate to your hus-band that should my partners not come forward voluntarily and admit to their part in the "Gem" store robbery that as a last resort that I would name them. Your husband seems to have a tendency to mislead people in his desperation to be free. And does himself more harm than good. And the other idem I would like to point out is that their were just three of us men involved in that robbery, not four as your letter indicated!

Nevertheless, I'll come to the point, for I know you're anxious to know whether or not I'm going to assisst you in gaining your husbands release. And the answer to your request is that I will if I receive $2000.00 dollars in my ac-count. Otherwise my answer is No!

Now my reasons for putting a price on this are as follows: Number one – when I was finally arrested their in Canada I took it upon myself to tell the police that I committed the "Gem" store robbery (for which I wasn't even be-ing questioned about) because I had known for acouple of months that your husband and his brother had been arrested and charged with the robbery I committed. And I felt at the time that here was one last chance to do something decent for someone before I parted from this world. But tell me did your hus-band or his brother ever drop me a thank you note? You bet they didn't! It isn't any big thing – but a little thoughtfulness can go a long way eh?

Secondly, while I was imprisoned at Kingston I again cooperated with your husbands lawyers agreeing to come back to Toronto and testify in their behalf. And in all that time I never asked for a dime from any of you. So I came back to Toronto and sat in those high court cells day after day not seeing anyone, nor having anything to smoke or read all the time their. But again, this was just your husbands way of showing his graditude towards me. And in the end I refused to testify for him.

Later, after his conviction and transfer to Kingston I mentioned to him how stupid I thought he was and that as far as I was concerned he could rot their. However, as you know, I got soft and changed my mind again, and agreed to help him one last time – providing he do something for me which needless to say, he never did. Anyway, I gave an interview to Ron Haggart of the Toronto Star explaining everything to him and your husbands lawyers. I agreed to come back to Toronto to testify in their behalf and name my partners providing that they were given immunity – but again they choose to take me lightly and in brief ignore me. But now decide that they need my help after all.

Unfortunately, for your husband, I was returned to St. Louis before any of the above action could take place. And it is not my fault. I told both your husband and his ignorant attorney that they had better place a "Hold order" on me because I had been told that I would be deported soon. As you can note I was right and your husbands attorney was foolish.

The reason I'm explaining all this to you is fairly simple: I'm tired of always doing someone a good turn and never getting as much as a Thank You for my efforts. Never again will I help anyone unless I get something out of it.

I realize what a nitemare you must be living knowing your husband is innocent and is serving 15 years and whether you believe it or not my heart goes out to you. But you must realize I have my own problems too. And their far more serious than your husbands. And I have no one at all to help me. And if I lose in my up-coming trial I'll be going to the Gas-Chamber. Needless to say, I would like to live and if possible, see the free world again. Well the money I want now will go a long way in helping me obtain my release. If you decide to help me I assure you that I'll give your attorneys certain information which will free your husband once and for all. This is not prank, nor some kind of sick joke. I assure you I'm dead serious and I will get your husband out. Just have your attorney fly down with the money and a witness before April 10th and I'll help you. After that date I will no longer be available to assisst you in your cause, nor will I want to. For after 4 years I'm tired of being bothered with someone else's troubles – I've got my own to worry about. I'm sorry, but that's my final word.

Respectfully Yours

Richard Paul Anderson

Rita did not reply to Anderson's March 20 letter until May 28, 1971. After apologizing for her delay, she said: "As far as the $2,000.00 is concerned there is no possible way this money could be paid. I am a working woman with a small child to support and only have my salary to depend on." She concluded:

My heart goes out to you in your troubles and I only wish there was something I could do to ease your load. No one in this world deserves to be alone in time of trouble and I know from experience that this is the time you need people the most. I am sorry that you will not help my husband, but this is your decision and I must abide by it. I feel very strongly that my husband should not have to do 15 years for a crime he did not commit but it looks as though this is what it eventually will come down to.

I would like to thank you, very sincerely, for the help that you have given us in the past and if there is some small thing I can do for you in return, you only need to ask.

This reply obviously struck a compassionate chord in the psyche of the psychopathic Anderson. His reply of June 2, 1971, demonstrates a fascinating contrast between the caring side of his personality and his casual references to his regret that he had not murdered two of the men who arrived on the scene shortly after the robbery:

Dear Mrs. Shatford;
I received your letter of May 28th, and I will tell you this, that I was very happy to hear from you again. And having discussed your problem with the Warden here, "Mr. Mike Parker", I have decided to respect his advise and go ahead and help you the one and only way that I can. Enclosed you will find the statement you have endeavoured to obtain. I hope it will secure for you your husband's release.

However, before I say goodby there are just a couple of points I would like to make clear:

One, Terry Smith has indeed mislead you. He never had any part in the robbery of the "Gem store". He merely happen to be with Jimmy Carroll when I showed up in the seconded getaway car to transfer to Carroll's car. I had no knowledge that he was going to be their. In fact, I had never seen the guy before that morning. When I realized that Carroll had informed him of what was taking place I made an effort to shoot the both of them to protect my identity and my freedom. And Buddy Ramsdale could verify this point if he should choose to. Needless to say, I will always regret that I did not shoot both of them. Because it was Terry Smith and Carroll that gave the police the information with which to locate and arrest me. Had I taken those necessary steps at that time perhaps, just perhaps, I might still be free today. Nevertheless, it is obvious now that he enjoyed his role of a Judas, that he is! But a thief (my opinion of a thief) he is not! He is a swine, a back-stabbing S.O.B. and to say the least, if you will excuse my vulgarity, he is the lowest piece of shit in the world.

My second point is that your attorney's have diffenately mislead you and your husband. Because they have known all along that the police had a statement from me stating that your husband was innocent and that I committed the robbery. What do you think Ron's appeal was based on? It was that their judge in High Court wouldn't allow this statement of mine to be introduced. Furthermore, one of Stanton Hogg's assistants flew down here with a copy of the same statement several months ago for me to resign. As you mean to tell me that you and Ron had no knowledge of this? If so, do yourself a favour and dismissed those attorneys for they certainly don't seem to be trying to do their best for the money that you're paying them.

The last point I would like to make is my request for that $2,000.00 dollars. It was a very cheap thing for me to do and I greatly regret it. In fact, I'm deeply ashamed of myself. And I realize now it makes me out to be a real creep and I guess that's what I am now. But I'm sorry and I hope you'll believe me. Because I've never intentionally hurt someone in my life unless I was hurt first, or put in danger in some way. Perhaps this statement sounds utterly ridiculous considering what I previously mention about my regretting having not have killed both Carroll and Smith, oh you must remember that neither of them are what you would call upright citizens. Their both parasites and give less than a damn about anyone but themselves. I was a fugitive from Missouri, and unless I wished to give myself up (which I didn't) it was necessary for me to steal, etc. But never before have I ever tried to take advantage of a working woman like you and I'm truly sorry now.

In closing Mrs. Shatford, I would like to tell you this; that I appreciate your concern for me. It moved me deeply and I thank you from the bottom of my heart. However, there is nothing you can do for me. My trial will be coming up soon and what will be, will be. This is life, eh? But you see, I don't belong in the free world and I know it! So it doesn't bother me all that much anymore. I'm a failure and I belong here where I won't be able to hurt anyone again.

I pray that the enclosed statement will return your husband to you and your child immediately. And that he will be as devoted to you in the future as you have been to him these past years. If he isn't, he will be the biggest fool in the world.

You're one hell of a woman Mrs. Shatford. There's very few in the world like you. I hope your husband will realize this. And I wish the two of you and your child many long years of happiness. It is people like you that made me fall in love with Canada and restore my faith in making[?]. God Bless You and Good Luck to both of you.

Sincerely
Richard Anderson

P/S
Perhaps, if you have the time you could drop me a brief note to let me know if this brought your husband back to you.

Shortly after the receipt of Anderson's second letter, I prepared an application to John Turner requesting that he exercise his prerogative to order a new trial for a convicted accused person after all other avenues of appeal have been exhausted. In such cases the justice minister must be satisfied that there is a substantial possibility of a serious miscarriage of justice. The application was strengthened by the fact that the respected journalist Ron Haggart had become interested in the Shatford case and had also interviewed Anderson's accomplice Buddy Ramsdale, who admitted his role in the robbery. In addition, we had learned that one of Anderson's former girlfriends had informed the police in 1968 that Anderson had told her the Shatford brothers were not involved in the robbery.

During the investigation that followed by the Ministry of the Attorney General of Ontario, Ramsdale was again interviewed, and this time he denied his involvement in the robbery – as he would in subsequent interviews too. In his report of September 1971, the attorney general strongly opposed granting a new trial for Ron Shatford. Shortly before Christmas 1971, however, Justice Minister Turner ordered the trial, and Ron Shatford was released on bail a few days later. I still have a copy of the front page of the *Toronto Sun* of December 16, 1971, which featured a large photograph of him decorating a Christmas tree along with Sandra, his seven-year-old daughter.

The state of Missouri would not permit Anderson to come to Toronto to testify, and his evidence was heard in a St Louis courtroom in the spring of 1972. Mr Justice Lloyd Graburn (the judge assigned to the new trial), Crown attorney Robert McGee (a highly respected lawyer and a personal friend), and I travelled down for the recording of his evidence, which would be read in at Shatford's new trial in Toronto.

In this first meeting with Anderson, I was surprised by his quiet demeanour and good-looking "choir boy" appearance. I was impressed by his low-key, matter-of-fact approach and what appeared to be very credible testimony. He was an impressive witness, and I regretted that the jury presiding at the new trial would not have the benefit of observing Anderson in person. Both Graburn and McGee agreed with me in this assessment.

Anderson's recollection of the events surrounding the robbery was consistent with the letter he had written to Rita Shatford and the affidavit he had prepared with the assistance of his prison warden. Anderson obviously expected to spend the rest of his life in prison, and he had no motive to perjure himself to help Ron Shatford. McGee and I agreed that Anderson should identify the letters he had written to Rita Shatford so they could be admitted in evidence. True, the letter demanding money might undermine his credibility, but the compelling nature of the second letter would in all probability impress a jury as to his truthfulness.

In preparing for the trial, I felt that Shatford should not testify because the inevitable cross-examination on his long criminal record would in all likelihood alienate the jury. He agreed reluctantly, because that meant his widely publicized protestations of innocence would never be heard under oath in a courtroom. Even though Ramsdale and the other men implicated by Anderson in the robbery had denied their participation to police investigators, I decided to place them all under subpoena. I hoped to confuse the prosecution about my trial strategy and perhaps encourage McGee to call them as witnesses in reply to Anderson's evidence, which would be read in court to the jury. If they were called, I would have the advantage of cross-examining them.

I had formed my own theory as to why three female prosecution witnesses had mistakenly identified Ron Shatford in the police line-up. They were undoubtedly honest witnesses who had testified in a conscientious fashion at the two earlier trials. However, as I explained earlier, identification evidence is particularly weak when witnesses have not previously seen the person they are asked to identify. In this case, these witnesses worked with a police artist, James Majury, as he created a composite drawing of Anderson's accomplice – and the process apparently took two or three hours. As a result, the artist's drawing of the suspect became more entrenched in their memories than their actual recollection of the person they had observed only briefly at the robbery scene.

When I compared the artist's sketch of the suspect with the ten individuals in the line-up, Ron Shatford was the only one who looked remotely like the man in that sketch. Although it was not a good likeness of Shatford, the identification witnesses were undoubtedly looking for the individual portrayed in the artist's sketch, and that could only be Shatford. In its report to the federal minister of justice, the Ministry of the Attorney General in Ontario placed great emphasis on the fact that Shatford did not complain about the composition of the line-up. For me, that was a red herring: any innocent person would most likely be unconcerned, not expecting to be picked out.

The new trial took place in September 1972 before a judge and jury. The evidence of the identification witnesses had weakened over the years, but they still identified Ron Shatford as Richard Anderson's accomplice. When the time came for the defence to present its evidence, I began by reading Anderson's evidence-in-chief as it had been recorded in St Louis, and Crown prosecutor Bob McGee read in his cross-examination. I then announced that I would not be calling any other evidence.

McGee and his police advisers were clearly surprised. They fully expected Shatford to testify – providing them with the opportunity to grill him about his criminal record. McGee immediately asked for a recess, to reconsider his strategy and decide whether to call any reply evidence. A few minutes later he advised the court that he would call Buddy Ramsdale and his associates. As expected, they refuted Anderson's evidence about their involvement in the robbery.

The art of cross-examination is often challenging, but for perhaps the only time in my career as a trial lawyer I had the rare pleasure of knowing that my questions had the effect of "shooting fish in a barrel." Ramsdale and the other men proved to be terrible witnesses for the Crown, demonstrating one suspicious characteristic after another. Ramsdale was particularly unimpressive in denying his role. I concluded my cross-examination with the assertion that he had perjured himself because he was indeed Anderson's robber accomplice. In response, he stared at me for a long time before he uttered an almost inaudible "No, I wasn't." By that time some of the jurors were quietly laughing at the Crown's star witnesses.

It was no great surprise to anyone in the courtroom when the jury acquitted Ron Shatford of the robbery after a brief deliberation. In that era there was a higher level of collegiality between prosecution and defence counsel than there is now, so, once we were free, McGee and I retired to his office with several of the police officers who had been involved in the case to enjoy a drink as we gossiped about the Shatford saga. It had begun with a robbery almost five years earlier and included a preliminary hearing and three separate jury trials – the last one following an application for a new trial to the federal minister of justice.

When the first Shatford trial was due to begin before a jury, Judge Walter Martin, the trial judge, called Bob McGee, the Crown attorney, into his chambers to ask him why the case had taken so long to come to trial. McGee replied that Forbes Ewing and "Lumpy" Lambert, two experienced members of the Hold-Up Squad who were helping the Markham Police Department, were sceptical about the reliability of the Crown's identification evidence. The trial proceeded, and after the prosecution's identification witnesses had been heard, Martin asked McGee to arrange for Ewing and Lambert to come to his chambers the next day. The officers complied with the request, and when they entered the judge's chambers, Martin told them that they were "gutless bastards" for delaying the trial because "the identification evidence was as good as he had ever heard." This exchange was related to me years later by Bob McGee.

After the final trial, I left the University Avenue courthouse with Detective Douglas Tribbling, the police officer in charge of the prosecution. As we walked together, he confided, "Roy, now that this is all over, I can tell you that I never believed that the Shatfords were involved in the Sentry Store robbery. However, I have always believed that they owed us the time, given the fact that they were career criminals."

As a postscript, Tribbling was tragically murdered about seven years later while investigating a break-in as a member of the York Region Police Department. By that time I had become the attorney general and solicitor general for Ontario, and I attended his funeral. A little later, I read that Buddy Ramsdale was in critical condition in hospital after being set on fire by the son of one of his girlfriends. He had treated the young man's mother brutally, and the son took his revenge. As for Richard Anderson, I learned that he was spared execution and is still in prison in Missouri.

Ron Shatford worked in my unsuccessful 1973 by-election campaign in the Toronto constituency of St George. After that campaign I lost contact with him for many years, although my police contacts advised me that, much to their surprise, he was staying out of trouble. I had been reluctant to contact him directly because I did not want to risk learning that he had returned to a life of crime. In 2005, however, I contacted his now former wife, Rita, who was still living in Toronto. She told me that they had divorced some years earlier and that their daughter was now a mother. Most important to me, she said that Ron had turned his life around after his 1972 acquittal and, ever since, had pursued lawful employment. I then followed through with Ron, who was living in British Columbia with his invalid second wife, after working for many years in Florida as a gardener and cleaner for wealthy home owners.

Many Canadians would say that Ron Shatford, given his lengthy criminal record, was undeserving of the ultimate fairness with which he was treated by the justice system. It's worth remembering that Winston Churchill often expressed his opinion that a society should be judged by the fairness with which it treats alleged criminal offenders. It is essential that the Canadian criminal justice system continue to give the highest priority to the reversal of wrongful convictions, however undeserving the accused individuals may appear to be.

* * *

In 1972 the shooting of two young men in Newtonbrook Plaza in North York was to have an interesting sequence, both in my role as a trial lawyer in company with Maloney and, later, as the provincial attorney general. Joey D and his Commisso family cousin, two young Italian Canadians, decided one evening to visit the plaza to look for female company. Their visit led to a confrontation with two "Glaswegians" (born in Glasgow) who apparently regarded the plaza as a fiefdom for them personally and for their fellow gang members. They obviously did not welcome strangers.

In the course of this encounter, Joey and his cousin were shoved around, verbally abused, and escorted off the plaza. They felt that their masculinity had been challenged and vowed revenge. The next day they shared their outrage with Domenic Racco, another cousin, who enjoyed a reputation as a "real tough guy." Racco was soon to become well known in law-enforcement circles and the justice system. He agreed to accompany his two younger cousins back to the plaza the next evening to search for the duo who had abused them. Although they intended to inflict some physical revenge, my client later claimed that he did not know that Racco was carrying a concealed handgun when they returned to Newtonbrook Plaza.

Shortly after they arrived, they encountered their tormentors. They exchanged a few threats and, at that point, Racco pulled a handgun from his trousers and pointed it at the two young Glaswegians. "You don't have the parts [guts] to use that," one of them taunted. Immediately, two shots were fired, hitting both young men in the abdomen. Racco and his cousins fled the scene. The shooting victims were taken to hospital, and both survived. According to the medical evidence subsequently given in court, the bullets narrowly missed vital organs, so their recovery was miraculous. What could well have been murder charges therefore became attempted murder.

Joey D and his two cousins were arrested shortly after the shootings. I was always mystified how these early arrests came to be. Nevertheless, at the time of his arrest, Joey D gave a detailed signed statement to the police. It was apparently truthful in every respect except that he said Domenic Racco was only a casual acquaintance and he did not even know his last name. This signed statement was helpful to Joey because of its general honesty, including his insistence that he did not know Racco was carrying a handgun. However, it became a matter of some controversy within the Canadian-Italian crime community. The fact that Joey voluntarily gave a statement to the police was regarded a serious breach of *omertà*, the tradition of silence, that has long been the norm in Italian crime culture.

After the respected defence counsel David Humphrey had been retained to represent Domenic Racco, Arthur Maloney to represent Joey's Commisso cousin, and I to represent Joey De Leo, the Crown prosecutor decided to separate the indictment so that Racco would be tried separately from his two younger cousins. Undoubtedly the prosecutor had strategic reasons for doing so, though they have always eluded me. At the preliminary inquiry of Joey and his cousin, the attempted murder charges were dismissed, and both young men were committed for trial on charges of conspiring to commit an assault.

Maloney and I were pleased with this verdict, but Joey's father was clearly distressed that his son's signed statement to the police had been admitted in evidence. Shortly after the preliminary inquiry, he came to my office to emphasize his concerns about this statement having been admitted in evidence as voluntary. While I thought he should have been pleased that his son had been discharged on the much more serious charge of attempted murder, I could only conclude that he would have preferred for him to be committed for trial on the attempted murder charge than to have it established that Joey had broken the code of silence.

At his trial, Domenic Racco was convicted of attempted murder and sentenced to ten years in prison. The remaining charges of conspiracy to commit a criminal assault against Joey and his cousin, however, were dismissed. After the trials were completed, I learned more of the potential seriousness of Joey's breach of the code of silence. David

Humphrey, later a justice of the Ontario Superior Court, told me that, in order to prevent a "blood bath" in relation to Joey's family, he misled the Racco family to believe that Joey's statement had been fabricated.

I also learned that the Racco family believed that Joey had identified Domenic to the police. Domenic's father, Mike Racco, was a senior figure in the North American Mafia network and quite capable of wreaking revenge on Joey and his family. I met the senior Racco once, and while my imagination may have been fuelled by the occasion, I shall always remember him as the cruellest looking person I have ever seen. Although the appearance of organized crime figures can often be deceptive, Mike Racco was clearly "Hollywood casting." Approximately five years later he died of cancer, and his funeral in Toronto produced the last large public gathering of Mafia figures in North America. The event was recorded on film and was later featured in a well-documented CBC series, *Connections*, on organized crime in Canada.

For me, the saga related to Domenic Racco pursued me into the Office of the Attorney General because the Commisso-Racco crime family continued to be a major challenge for law enforcement. The drama also involved a police informant, Cecil Kirby, who was well known as a "biker" criminal. Fearing for his own safety after relations with his criminal colleagues deteriorated, he volunteered to give evidence against them in exchange for police protection and immunity from prosecution for any offences he had committed in the past.

My senior counsel in the Ministry of the Attorney General advised me that it would be in the public interest to enter into an immunity agreement with Kirby. The police, they said, did not have any evidence on which they could prosecute him other than his own admissions, which could not be used in court against him. With Kirby's evidence, however, serious charges could be laid against members of the Commisso-Racco crime family – and, in due course, these charges were successfully prosecuted. Kirby was apparently a very credible witness, notwithstanding his admissions about his own criminal past.

As a result of these successful prosecutions, Domenic Racco once again entered my life. Several members of the Commisso-Racco crime family entered pleas of guilty, which were later alleged to be part of a plea agreement with Crown counsel. In exchange, they claimed, the prosecutor had promised that no further charges would be laid against them for past criminal conduct. However, further charges were laid, and the Crown counsel involved denied any such agreement. His testimony was later accepted in court in a hearing to determine whether such a plea agreement had in fact been made. If found true, the charges would have been stayed by the court as an abuse of process.

The experienced legal counsel for the Commisso-Racco family had apparently come to believe, mistakenly, that there was an agreement with the Crown that no further charges would be laid. According to the Ontario Provincial Police, the Commisso-Racco family lawyer, fearing in all likelihood for his own safety, convinced his clients that the additional charges had been laid because the "crusading" attorney general had breached the agreement entered into between counsel on this matter. The OPP advised me that Domenic Racco had vowed revenge and that he planned to assassinate me. They strongly recommended around-the-clock security for me and my family – which I accepted. It ended only when Domenic Racco himself was murdered several months later, purportedly by criminal colleagues who felt personally threatened by his "rogue elephant approach." His gangster activities had clearly been influenced by the Mafia approach in Calabria and Sicily, where judges, police, and prosecutors are often murdered. This Italian Mafia strategy is very different from that in North America, which generally avoids attracting attention by targeting justice officials. Although rivals within organized crime are often assassinated, these killings do not create the same public outrage that occurs when law-enforcement officials become victims.

I was concerned with the Racco threat, but I was puzzled as to why Domenic Racco would risk putting many of his criminal colleagues from the Newtonbrook Plaza shootings again in the spotlight. At that time, the Metro police had been able to obtain search warrants for the homes and offices of many known Commisso-Racco family members, resulting in several criminal charges. The murder of Domenic Racco demonstrated that at least some of his associates were unhappy with his conduct.

Early in the weeks following the implementation of my security detail, an OPP deputy commissioner came to my office to inquire about my dinning plans the next evening. Ria and I had accepted an invitation for that time from our friends Edie and Ralph Fisher, but I did not know the name of the restaurant. The deputy commissioner then informed me that the OPP had learned the identity of the restaurant through a wire tap. I suggested that the police should stake out the restaurant and that we and the Fishers should go there as planned. "If I were in your position," my visitor replied, "I would not expose my wife to that kind of risk." So warned, we made alternative dining plans.

Some years later, Bob Rae and I were having lunch several months after his premiership ended and while he was still accompanied by OPP security. On that particular day, his security officer was Andy Hashinski, one of the men who had looked after me during the Domenic Racco threat. I greeted Andy warmly, and during our lunch Rae told me that the OPP still regarded that threat against me as the most serious it had ever dealt with involving a senior public official.

* * *

Through Arthur Maloney I also got involved in the mystery of the Coffin case, one of the most controversial murder trials in Canadian legal history. Wilbert Coffin, a mining prospector and anglophone guide in the Gaspé region of Quebec, was accused of killing three American hunters from Philadelphia in June 1953. After the bodies were found deep in the woods the following month, Coffin was discovered to have several items in his possession which were traced to the vacationing hunters' camp, along with a significant amount of US currency. He was subsequently tried for murder and convicted, even though the evidence against him was largely circumstantial. After appeals to the Quebec Court of Appeal and the Supreme Court of Canada were turned down, Coffin was hanged in Montreal in February 1956.

From the start, the case aroused controversy and strong feelings. The civil libertarian journalist Jacques Hébert, who was later appointed to the Canadian Senate, wrote two books about it, one of them titled *J'accuse les assassins de Coffin*. His basic theme was that the Duplessis government in Quebec had put political pressure on the various courts involved in order to get Coffin convicted and executed. The murders had been widely covered by the US media, and the premier wanted above all to appease criticism and increase American tourism – so important to the Quebec economy. Hébert was soon charged with criminal libel, but, represented by his lawyer friend Pierre Elliott Trudeau, he was eventually acquitted at trial.

But the controversy would not die down, and the Quebec government called a judicial inquiry into the whole affair. Maloney had been an adviser to Coffin's legal counsel from Quebec City during both the trial and the appeal to the Quebec Court of Appeal. Later, he unsuccessfully argued Coffin's appeal to the Supreme Court of Canada. Now he was asked to be a witness at the inquiry. He asked Bob Barr, a Crown attorney in Toronto, and me to accompany him, purportedly as his legal counsel but really for company in the taverns of Quebec City.

Mr Justice Brossard conducted the inquiry in 1964, and he clearly had little interest in the allegations of political influence in the Coffin case. When Maloney outlined for him in some detail his personal concerns, the commissioner assured him that his report would put the allegations to rest. Maloney responded bluntly that he personally would always be concerned by the irregularities in the case regardless of what Brossard wrote in his report. In the event, the commission heard some two hundred witnesses and concluded that Coffin had received a fair trial.

While in Quebec City, I took the opportunity to visit the Noel family – my hosts during my summer of work as a law student (chapter 4). During one of these visits I met Harry Quart, a prominent and charming Quebec anglophone businessman whose mother, Josie, had been the first female Quebec Conservative senator. When Quart heard I was in town that week for the Coffin inquiry, he told me that he had been a close friend of Coffin's trial counsel, Buddy Maher. Turning to his wife, he asked her if she remembered Maher's late-night visit to their home several days after the discovery of the murder of the Philadelphia hunters. They both vividly recalled the event: Maher, intoxicated and extremely agitated, confessed to them that he had thrown Coffin's rifle off the Quebec bridge earlier that evening. Quart clearly did not regard this encounter with Coffin's lawyer as significant. He was convinced that Coffin was guilty, and in his mind, he was simply sharing an interesting anecdote with me.

When I related the incident to Arthur Maloney and Bob Barr during our train ride home to Toronto, Maloney gave me one of his stern looks and stated firmly: "I never said Coffin was innocent, only that there was a reasonable doubt as to his guilt." He was a true champion for the "little guy," who, regardless of his moral guilt, was always entitled to a fair trial.

* * *

Maloney had long been an eloquent and persuasive advocate of the abolition of the death penalty. As an MP, his speech in the 1960 House of Commons debate on capital punishment was often referred to as the clarion call for the abolitionist movement. He had been involved in a number of capital murder cases, but the one that affected him most was his defence in 1952 of Leonard Jackson, who had been convicted of murder and executed. His co-accused, Steve Suchan, was also convicted and hanged the same evening at the Don Jail in Toronto.

Jackson and Suchan were members of the notorious Boyd gang, led by the colourful Edwin Alonzo Boyd. As Boyd told a biographer years later, he simply "enjoyed robbing banks." The robberies were reported in some detail by the local press, which added to Boyd's pleasure in his criminal activity. In subsequent years, bank robberies were seldom reported by the media because it was quite properly believed that the publicity could well encourage others to engage in similar activity, particularly if a robbery appeared to have been successful.

Boyd, Suchan, and Jackson had also managed two successful jail breaks, one after their arrest for a series of robberies and the other after the murder of Toronto police detective Edmund Tong as he and his partner were searching for the gang. When the detectives caught up with a vehicle driven by Suchan and Jackson, Suchan shot Tong as he emerged from the police car. The two robbers were soon arrested, but they escaped along with Boyd from the Don Jail before the trial. In due time they were arrested again and a new court date was set. As for Boyd, who luckily for him was elsewhere at the time of the shooting, he was convicted of robbery, served his sentence in Kingston Penitentiary, and disappeared for years into western Canada, where he lived to an old age – and was given an award for community service.

Whatever Suchan and Jackson may have earned from their participation in the robberies with Boyd, they were unable to hire lawyers to represent them at their trial. They were, however, represented pro bono by two outstanding counsel, John Robinette and Arthur Maloney. Steve Suchan's mother worked as a cleaning lady at the prestigious Toronto law firm McCarthy and McCarthy, where she knew Robinette, and he responded to her desperate plea to represent her son. Shortly before the trial was to proceed, the trial judge, Justice James McRuer, asked Maloney to represent Leonard Jackson.

Maloney never complained about the guilty verdicts in the case, but he became intimately involved with the young men during their last days before the execution and preoccupied with the value of every human life. Both he and Robinette were deeply moved by their clients' sincere repentance and acceptance of their fate. Robinette remained bitter about the verdict all his life, and Maloney became a crusader for the abolition of the death penalty.

In 1964 Maloney established the Canadian Society for the Abolition of the Death Penalty. It was a national body with local chapters, and I agreed to become the president of the Toronto chapter. I had long been convinced by him that the death penalty was immoral because it promoted a disregard for the sanctity of human life. My beliefs were strengthened when I met a young man at the Don Jail who had been convicted of capital murder for the rape and panic murder of a teenage girl when he was working as a Canada Post driver. He was nineteen years old, looked much younger, and was executed soon after. His youthful face haunted my dreams for many months.

The society's national board of directors included a number of high-profile political figures, including Ross Thatcher, the premier of Saskatchewan (whose son Colin some years later was convicted of murdering his wife). Also on the board was Senator Wallace McCutcheon, a highly respected member of the business community and close associate of E.P. Taylor of Argus Corporation, who privately became the source of major funding for the society.

Maloney was an energetic and skilful organizer, and he enlisted the support of many hundreds of people to serve on dozens of committees. Information bulletins were published at regular intervals and circulated to members and potential members. As president of the Toronto chapter, I was invited to speak on or debate the issue of the death penalty on a regular basis, generally at service clubs or church groups. I usually spoke of the penalty being imposed disproportionately on the "poor and friendless" and often quoted French philosopher Anatole France on what he called "the majestic equality of the law which equally prohibited the rich and the poor from sleeping under bridges, begging for alms on the street and stealing a loaf of bread." My regular debating opponent was Ralph Cowan, a Liberal MP and maverick who often defied the party whip, a prominent member of the United Church of Canada, and an ardent death penalty retentionist. Interestingly enough, the United Church as an institution was much more supportive of the abolitionist cause than other established churches. Maloney, for instance, was a devout Catholic, yet his church hierarchy supported the death penalty.

Although it is only human to desire some revenge following a serious crime, particularly murder, it has long been accepted in Canadian law that retribution should not be considered as a legitimate goal of the death penalty. I was further convinced in my stand by research showing that the death penalty did not possess the deterrent effect commonly attributed to it. A sentence of life imprisonment has proved to be equally effective. There are also many studies that demonstrate that the death penalty contributes to an environment that encourages violence and crime. Research in the United States, for example, has revealed a general increase in violence in communities following a highly publicized application of the death penalty. In addition, there is the bizarre and tragic phenomenon of "copy cat" murders to consider, where some individuals, many of them mentally disturbed, seek the death penalty for themselves, attracted by the huge publicity given to individuals facing execution.

In the early 1960s, however, a large majority of the Canadian public still supported the death penalty. The last executions in Canada were in 1962, when Ronald Turpin, a police killer, and Arthur Lucas, a "hit man" from Detroit, were executed at the Don Jail in Toronto the same evening.

The major event organized by the Society for the Abolition of the Death Penalty took place on Parliament Hill in June 1965, when it arranged a panel discussion in the Confederation Room of the Parliament Buildings. Almost two hundred MPs, senators, and federal justice officials attended. I was one of the moderators, and the panellists included the distinguished Toronto lawyers John Robinette and Arthur Martin; René Lévesque, the minister of natural resources in the Quebec Liberal government of Jean Lesage; Professor Thorsten Sellin, the leading American scholar on the death penalty; and Sidney Silverman, a longtime Labour MP and crusader for abolition in the United Kingdom. Although we had no supporters of the death penalty on the panel, several retentionists in the audience spoke for that side and asked questions. In any event, the evening was a success for the society and, in retrospect, a historic occasion in Canadian politics.

Perhaps the most eloquent statement supporting the abolition of the death penalty was delivered by Lévesque. In closing, he urged the parliamentarians "to show the way to a society in need of progress by ... eliminating this penalty, by taking this final step. This is one of the most important steps which must still be taken before the monkey, which one day became a man, may finally come out of his jungle, stand up on his hind legs and not fall back on his front paws and revert to his primitive state, but become truly more civilized."

As a postscript, after the discussion, I joined Lévesque and others in the bar of the National Press Club. One of our fellow drinking companions was a young MP, Richard Cashin, who was destined a few years later to become a major trade-union leader in his home province of Newfoundland. Lévesque had not then publicly revealed his support of the separatist cause, but there was already considerable speculation about his views on the subject. Cashin, a real provocateur, now set out to bait Lévesque about his suspected separatist beliefs. The increasingly heated confrontation ended abruptly when Cashin expressed the opinion that an independent Quebec "would inevitably become another Belgian Congo." Lévesque erupted, "You rotten son of a bitch," and readied himself to attack Cashin physically. Fortunately we were able to separate them before any blows were exchanged.

Another event related to the abolition debate also took place that same year, 1965, when the CBC invited Nathan Leopold of the notorious Leopold and Loeb murder case to Toronto for a television interview. Maloney and I were invited to meet with Leopold on the Saturday afternoon during his visit. In 1924 Leopold and Richard Loeb, two brilliant teenage students at the University of Chicago, pled guilty to killing fourteen-year-old Bobby Franks, a distant cousin of Loeb, in an attempt to commit the "perfect crime." For decades the murder was dramatically described as the "crime of the century" and the "greatest criminal trial in American history." The case was of particular public interest because all three principals came from very wealthy Chicago families; moreover, the legendary trial lawyer Clarence Darrow was retained to defend the accused.

Both defendants pled guilty to murder, so the only issue to be determined at the trial was whether the judge would impose the death penalty or render a sentence of life imprisonment. During the conclusion of his two-day address to the judge, Darrow focused on what he described as the barbarity of executing young people. As he put it: "I am not pleading so much for these boys as I am for the infinite numbers of others to follow, those who perhaps cannot be as well defended as these have been, those who may go down in the storm, and the tempest without aid. It is of them I am thinking and for them I am begging of this court not to turn backward toward the barbarous and cruel past ... I know that the future is on my side."

The judge sentenced Leopold and Loeb each to life plus ninety-nine years – a verdict that was almost universally denounced by the press throughout the United States. A shocked nation looked on the murderers with revulsion and horror, regarding them as monsters. They had killed and demanded ransom just for the thrill of it. Society demanded revenge. Loeb was murdered in prison in 1936, and Leopold was released in 1958, after serving thirty-three years in prison. A few months before his release, he completed the manuscript for his autobiography, *Life Plus 99 Years*.

Notwithstanding the depravity of his crime, Leopold had become somewhat of a celebrity for his positive contributions to prison society and the American military during the Second World War. In particular, he helped develop the first library system in the US federal penitentiary system, and during the war he organized a large group of prison inmates to volunteer for malaria experiments. In the Pacific war theatre, malaria was killing more US soldiers than the Japanese military succeeded in doing. The malaria experiments helped develop new vaccines, which resulted in saving many American lives. After his release from prison at the age of fifty-three, Leopold settled in Puerto Rico, where he was employed as a social worker and a laboratory technician. He appeared to be genuinely rehabilitated and was making an important contribution to society.

Before our interview, Maloney and I speculated about our likely impressions of Nathan Leopold. When we met him, we found him shy and soft-spoken, a small man, rather shabbily dressed. We were both relieved to discover that he was not interested in being a celebrity. Rather, he spoke of his distaste for people who took pleasure in exploiting their status, particularly those who were "professional ex-cons." He explained that his initial feeling on entering prison was simply regret at having been caught, but, later, he had deep remorse for what he had done. This regret dominated his life and, as he wrote in his autobiography, "it pervaded my consciousness, like a sombre shadow affecting the time of everything else; it was always in the back of my mind. The thought that I had cut off a young life haunted me. I had done an irreparable wrong." Leopold also told us that not a day passed when he would gladly end his own life if it could restore Bobby Franks.

During our time together, it became evident that Nathan Leopold did not regard himself as a crusader for the abolition of the death penalty. In fact, he rarely spoke about it in public. He simply believed in the potential of rehabilitation and in the sanctity of human life, even when it belonged to a convicted murderer.

The death penalty was not formally repealed in the Canadian Parliament until 1987, when the government of Brian Mulroney successfully introduced a resolution to abolish it and the motion carried on a free vote. Shortly before the debate, I received a call from the prime minister in London, where I was serving as the Canadian high commissioner to the United Kingdom. Mulroney explained that, when he was a law student in the early 1960s, Arthur Maloney and I had persuaded him to be an abolitionist. Because Maloney was no longer alive, he asked me if I would prepare a draft speech for his possible use in the debate. I was pleased to comply. As I recall, a few of my sentences actually made it into the prime minister's final text.

Traditionally, a fundamental concern about the death penalty has been the inequality of its application and the real possibility of error. In recent years, DNA evidence has conclusively established the innocence of individuals who have been executed in the United States or convicted of murder in Canada. For this reason, the Supreme Court of Canada reversed itself in 2005 and declared that it is contrary to our Charter of Rights to extradite an individual from Canada to an American state where the death penalty exists, unless there is an undertaking by the US state attorney general that the death penalty will not be imposed. In Canada, Arthur Maloney's dream has been achieved, as the death penalty has not been imposed here since 1962.

8

Entering the Political Arena

When I began to practise law, I never thought I would become seriously involved in politics. At the time I was called to the bar in 1958, Ria was expecting our second child, and, along with our expanding family, I was totally focused on building a successful legal career.

My father considered himself a Conservative – an attitude he inherited from his own father, William James McMurtry, who had been a passionate supporter of Sir John A. Macdonald's National Policy. He was also very proud of the political career of his maternal great-grandfather, Charles Waters, a member of the Legislature of Upper Canada and a political reform ally of William Lyon Mackenzie (chapter 1). In the smaller political community of his era, Dad knew many of the major figures, and he held diverse and not always flattering opinions of them. John Diefenbaker was in his view "half crazy," though they shared a love for courtroom drama, and he admired the Chief's political courage. I first met Diefenbaker in 1956, shortly after he became leader of the federal Progressive Conservative Party. I appreciated his concern about my father's fragile health following his stroke and also welcomed his success in the 1957 election, sharing as I did the widespread perception of arrogance in the previous Liberal government. At the same time, I admired Louis St Laurent as a francophone prime minister in the distinguished tradition of Sir Wilfrid Laurier. My summer in Quebec City two years earlier had strengthened my commitment to the essential duality of Canada – a quality he represented.

I regretted the fact that the federal Conservative Party had long been unable to establish a stable base of support in Quebec. Its reliance on the support of the Union Nationale gave it an insecure political presence and alienated many Quebeckers who had been appalled by the often ruthless premiership of Maurice Duplessis. I was also convinced that the ghost of Louis Riel would forever haunt the party. Prime Minister Macdonald's decision to execute Riel in 1887 had been influenced at least in part by political pressure from Protestant Canadians, including the infamous Orange Order. The imposition of conscription during the First World War was another problem. As a result, the Liberal Party presented itself as the only federal party truly committed to the defence of francophone and Catholic Quebec.

My friend and mentor Arthur Maloney also contributed to my general disinterest in politics. He was a natural for elected office, given his eloquence and highly developed people skills, and was dedicated to assisting the less fortunate in society – a quality I much admired. Once he was elected an MP in 1957, however, he resented the fact that Diefenbaker did not appoint him to the Cabinet. The teetotalling prime minister apparently harboured concerns about Maloney's drinking, even though it had never interfered with his performance as a brilliant trial lawyer. In the dying days of the government in 1962, Diefenbaker offered him a Cabinet post, but by then Maloney had decided not to run in the next election, so he declined the honour. Ironically, he later became Diefenbaker's most effective defender when a group within the party successfully challenged the aging Chief's leadership in 1966. A strong friendship developed between them, which endured for the remaining years of Diefenbaker's life.

Our local MP was Donald Fleming, who became Diefenbaker's first minister of finance in 1957. I voted for him in the three federal elections between 1957 and 1962, largely because he was one of my father's friends. When the next election was called in 1963, however, I mistrusted Diefenbaker's leadership for the country, particularly in the military defence of North America. Clearly Douglas Harkness, the minister of defence, was also breaking ranks with his prime minister over the issue. Harkness encouraged the Canadian Institute for International Affairs to sponsor a tour by a few Canadians to the North America Defense Command (NORAD) in Colorado Springs, including a visit to the US Strategic Air Command (SAC) headquarters in Omaha, Nebraska. Fortunately I knew one of the organizers and, when I was invited to participate, I accepted eagerly.

The four-day trip involved a number of lectures, tours, and briefings conducted by US and Canadian military personnel. When our aircraft landed in Omaha and in Colorado Springs, we were met by senior generals, including Roy Slemon, the Canadian deputy commander of NORAD. At this stage in the Cold War it was evident that the military personnel at the SAC headquarters and at NORAD were on a twenty-four-hour alert for a possible nuclear conflict with the Soviet Union. The reality of this alarm was heightened by the fact that our visit occurred only a few weeks after the end of the Cuban Missile Crisis. Although a military culture was barely discernible in most regions of Canada, we were immersed in that environment during our visit. We soon realized that our hosts were not only trained for armed conflict with the Soviet Union but would probably regard their military service as a disappointment if it did not include actual battlefield experience. In the months that followed, this attitude scared me but also helped me to understand how the US military culture shaped the tragedy of the American experience in the Vietnam War.

In any event, the missionary efforts directed towards us were successful, and we all returned to Canada convinced that greater Canadian–US military cooperation was vital to our country's national interests. My disillusionment with Diefenbaker had increased to the point that, in the 1963 spring federal election, I voted for Mitchell Sharp, the future Liberal Cabinet minister, in my local constituency of Eglinton. Shortly thereafter Lester "Mike" Pearson became the prime minister. He was widely admired in Canada because of his distinguished career in foreign policy as a career diplomat, as Canada's minister of external affairs, and as a recipient of the Nobel Peace Prize. However, Diefenbaker still retained sufficient support to deny Pearson a majority government.

My recollection of the Pearson–Diefenbaker dynamic between 1963 and 1965 is generally one of political malaise. Allegations of political scandals made by both leaders dominated the political agenda. Even the historic creation of a distinctive Canadian flag in 1965 was almost overtaken by partisan bickering. Furthermore, the assassination of John F. Kennedy created a hugely romantic political legend in the United States. In this context, most young Canadians were not at all inspired by the leadership of either Pearson or Diefenbaker.

Pearson and his colleagues regarded the growing divisions within the opposition Conservative Party as a chance to win a majority, so they called an election for the autumn of 1965 – the fifth in just eight years. There were no significant political issues at stake, so I, along with many other Canadians, saw this election simply as cynical political opportunism.

* * *

At this time I still had not become a member of any political party, nor had I ever attended a wholly partisan political event. A chance meeting with Dalton Camp, the Progressive Conservative national president, several days after the 1965 election call led to my first significant involvement in the political arena. He was the speaker at a luncheon at the downtown branch of the Kiwanis Club, and I was impressed by his rational and moderate approach to federal political issues. For me, it was a refreshing departure from the pointless partisan bickering that had for too long dominated the national political discourse. I also met Camp's brother-in-law Norman Atkins for the first time that day, beginning a forty-year close friendship. I had heard rumours that Dalton Camp might seek the federal Conservative nomination in Eglinton, and I volunteered my assistance should he decide to run. A day or two later Camp called me to confirm his candidacy for the nomination, and I became an enthusiastic worker for him. Perhaps it was my Irish ancestry that attracted me to losing causes such as the federal Progressive Conservative Party at the time. Whatever the motivation, despite my lack of any political organizational experience, I accepted responsibility for putting together a political team and went on to play a major role in the campaign.

The sitting Liberal MP was Mitchell Sharp, the candidate I had voted for two-and-a-half years earlier. He had been an effective Cabinet minister in the Pearson government, and I had not lost my respect for him. However, I believed in the principle of a strong parliamentary opposition, and I thought that Camp would be an eloquent voice in Parliament. When Camp lost his second federal election bid in 1968, Sharp confided to me that he too had always considered that Camp would be an "ornament in Parliament."

Sharp and Camp clearly respected each other, and the contest between them in 1965 was civilized and intellectually stimulating. The result was much closer than expected, and Camp lost by only eighteen hundred votes. Despite the increasing controversy within the Conservative Party with respect to Diefenbaker's leadership, many of his most outspoken critics, including former Cabinet colleagues such as George Hees, rallied to the cause, and Pearson was again denied a majority government. I still recall Camp's advice to a tearful young supporter following the defeat in Eglinton: you experience both winning and losing in life, he said, and it is important to do both well.

Once Diefenbaker was no longer prime minister, he increasingly isolated himself from his parliamentary caucus, and members often learned of their leader's policy positions through the media. He rarely attended caucus meetings, and when he did, he and his close colleagues viewed any criticism of his policy as disloyalty to the leader. As a result, a growing number of Conservative MPs and other members feared that the party was on the brink of breaking apart. As national president, Camp had progressively less contact with Diefenbaker, and the relationship between them continued to deteriorate, particularly after Diefenbaker appointed a national director for the party without any consultation with Camp. The new director promptly fired Flora MacDonald, the popular federal party secretary, who went on to be a senior Cabinet minister in both the Clark and Mulroney governments. She had been running the party's headquarters for the past decade, and Camp regarded her firing as an act of war.

Camp had played the role of peacemaker within the Progressive Conservative Party since its defeat in 1963, but in the spring of 1966 he decided to challenge Diefenbaker directly and openly. The issue at stake was an important democratic principle – the right of a political party to review its leadership at appropriate intervals. At the time, many within the federal party considered any review to be a form of political heresy, even though Diefenbaker was in his tenth year of leadership and had led the party in five election campaigns. On May 19 Camp delivered an address to 120 prominent Conservatives at Toronto's Albany Club. Although it was a private dinner, his remarks would soon send shock waves throughout the party. He did not mention Diefenbaker by name, but he spoke about the "limits to the power of political leadership which should from time to time be examined." He continued:

Leaders are fond of reminding followers of their responsibilities and duties to leadership. And followers sometimes need reminding. What is seldom heard, however, is a statement on the responsibilities of the leader to those he leads ...

The leader should give at least as much loyalty to his followers as he demands from them. This is not a personal loyalty, but rather loyalty to the party, to its continuing strength, best interests and well being. This must be shared by leader and followers alike if unity and harmony are to be enjoyed by both. While it is natural that a leader will gather about him a number of like-minded men and women, if their like-mindedness is chiefly that of loyalty to the leader, then the party system ceases to function and politics become a matter of subservience rather than service and of personality rather than purpose.

He concluded by stating that, when "the leader does not know the limits to his power, he must be taught and, when he is indifferent to the interest of his party he must be reminded." The party is "not the embodiment of the leader but rather the other way round; the leader is transient, the party permanent." No political leader in Canada has ever been sent such a message by a party president. The gauntlet had truly been thrown down.

I was enormously impressed by Camp's principled eloquence, but, given the political culture of that era, I knew that much of the grassroots of the party would regard his challenge as disloyal and unacceptable. I was therefore concerned how this speech might affect Camp's political future and was prepared to support him in his battle to establish the democratic principle of leadership review.

The next annual general meeting of the federal Progressive Conservative Party was to take place in Ottawa in November 1966. I was hardly involved in the party machinations between the May speech and the November meeting because of my own busy law practice and several criminal cases and trials I had taken over from Arthur Maloney. However, it was generally known that Diefenbaker would be facing an unprecedented challenge to his leadership at that meeting, especially as Camp decided to stand for re-election as the party president.

It was widely rumoured within the federal party that there were serious differences between Diefenbaker and Senator Wallace McCutcheon. I asked McCutcheon about those stories in 1965, but he was reluctant to admit any significant breach. I recall him taking a large sip of whisky and telling me "the major difference between Diefenbaker and me is that I usually feel a lot better than the teetotalling Chief in the evening. However, he feels a hell of a lot better than I do in the morning!"

As the AGM approached, Maloney and I would occasionally discuss the leadership issue. Although he had not been a fervent admirer of Diefenbaker, I detected that he was uncomfortable with the growing challenges to Diefenbaker's leadership. He believed that a party leader should be allowed to choose the timing of his departure. I remember joking with him that the leader should not enjoy papal-like prerogatives. A couple of weeks before the meeting, I was working on a case with him when he excused himself to meet with Michael Starr, a former federal Conservative Cabinet minister. I knew that Starr was a strong

Diefenbaker supporter and was not surprised when Maloney told me I was not invited to the meeting, given my association with Dalton Camp. Still, I was shocked two or three days later when I received an early morning telephone call from Maloney: "Brother McMurtry," he said, "get out the Maloney signs. I'm going to challenge Dalton Camp for the presidency of the federal PC Party."

Just the previous year, Maloney had been a strong Camp supporter when he was a candidate in the federal election and had even hosted a reception for him before the nomination meeting. Now, however, I knew that I faced a significant personal dilemma. I strongly supported Camp's goal of democratizing the federal party, yet Maloney was a close personal friend. Later the same day I wrote Maloney a letter explaining why I could not support his candidacy: I believed that Camp's attempt to democratize the PC Party was an important principle for all Canadian political parties as well as for the general viability of the political system; and, I continued, although I had the highest respect for him as an individual, I believed that the principle for which Camp was fighting must transcend personal friendship.

In a conversation a few days later with Brian Mulroney, I learned that he too had written a similar letter to Maloney. At the time, Mulroney was a very active young Conservative. He had worked in Ottawa for a year when Diefenbaker was prime minister and had come to know Arthur Maloney, who was then an MP. Maloney in turn had introduced him to me. Mulroney and I now arranged to connect in Ottawa two days before the opening of the AGM so we could help to push Camp's candidacy for the presidency. The vote we knew would be taken on the second day of the meeting. We thought we should meet with our old friend before the intense politicking took over, and Maloney enthusiastically agreed. He suggested that we come to his hotel suite at the Château Laurier just past midnight, when his own campaign team would have left. When we arrived, however, we found several of Diefenbaker's strongest loyalists still partying in Maloney's suite. They immediately made it clear that our presence was unwelcome, uttering pointed remarks about our lack of loyalty. An amused Maloney admonished us that, once he won the presidency, we were all welcome to come for a drink. "We will sit down together and rebuild the party," he promised.

Obviously, Maloney regarded his candidacy as similar to that of an advocate in court. Diefenbaker was his client, and the constituency delegates from across Canada made up the jury. Like any experienced trial counsel, he did not become emotionally involved in the contest, but that was not the case for the vast majority of voting delegates. I have never since experienced such a highly charged political meeting as that one. I was still a neophyte in the world of politics, but I soon learned that internal party politics can become much more bitter than those between different political parties. My most important recollection is that Maloney never appeared to regard my support for Camp as a personal affront. In any event, as a seasoned and effective campaigner he soon emerged as a formidable opponent to the essentially shy Camp. During the few days of the campaign in Ottawa, I learned that a majority of the delegates had come to accept the principle of leadership review, but many believed that Maloney would also make it happen.

The agenda provided that Diefenbaker would address the delegates during the first evening of the meeting, with speeches by Camp and Maloney the next day, preceding the vote. On day three, the newly elected or re-elected party president would chair the general meeting where the leadership review issue could be debated. It was generally assumed by the delegates that if Camp lost in his attempt to be re-elected, the leadership review issue would not come to a vote. The contest between Camp and Maloney was therefore perceived as a surrogate process with respect to the leadership review.

Before Diefenbaker spoke on the Monday evening, some of the Camp supporters decided on a strategy that backfired and provided considerable emotional ammunition for the Maloney team. Two or three hours before the evening meeting was scheduled to begin, many members of the Camp entourage occupied the first twenty rows of seats in the convention hall. They planned to remain seated when Diefenbaker entered the hall, to demonstrate to the watching national television audience the depth of the division within the party. In effect, however, this inappropriate rudeness only strengthened the support for Diefenbaker. Arthur Maloney took full advantage of the affront in his speech the following day: "Perhaps it has something to do with my Ottawa Valley upbringing," he began, "but when the Right Honourable John George Diefenbaker, sometime prime minister of Canada, leader of Her Majesty's loyal opposition, and leader of the national Progressive Conservative Party of Canada, walks into a room, Arthur Maloney stands up." These words, combined with the eloquence of his remarks that followed, proved very effective.

Dalton Camp won the election by a narrow margin, but Maloney's speech is better remembered by many who followed the political drama of the 1966 Conservative general meeting. The following day was particularly emotional as scores of delegates spoke admiringly of Diefenbaker's leadership through five elections, yet stated they would vote for a leadership convention. And, as things turned out, the resolution calling for such a convention within the next twelve months was carried overwhelmingly.

My last recollection of that meeting is of John Diefenbaker standing on a table in one of the Château Laurier's large hallways, exhorting his many loyal supporters with the words from the "Ballad of Sir Andrew Barton": "I am hurt but I am not slain. / I'll lay me down and bleed awhile, / Then I'll rise and fight again."

* * *

Arthur Maloney and I continued our close professional association and personal friendship. When we spoke occasionally about the coming Progressive Conservative leadership convention, I always reminded him that I would be pleased to support him if he decided to run. His performance at the 1966 general meeting had certainly impressed many within the party. I made my final pledge on this subject in a favourite bar one day. After kicking the idea around for a few minutes, Maloney informed me that he had decided against being a candidate. "Brother McMurtry," he said, "if I became leader of the party we would not be able to have the pleasure of sitting around in a bar like this."

My friendship with Dalton Camp also progressed, and those of us who had managed his Eglinton campaign in 1965 often got together socially. In fact, when he began his campaign for a leadership review, the *Toronto Telegram* suggested editorially that Camp and his "Eglinton Amateurs" were foolish to take on the Diefenbaker machine. Interestingly enough, after the Conservative Party voted for a leadership convention, the same newspaper began to refer to us as the "Eglinton Political Mafia." For Camp himself, though, any ambitions he might have harboured to be party leader were over. He had become a highly controversial figure for many in the federal party, given the unforgiving antagonism of Diefenbaker and his supporters.

The active rumour mill spewed out no end of potential candidates for that top position as party leader. The name most often mentioned in the opening months of 1967 was Duff Roblin, the premier of Manitoba. In fact, I have always believed that, if Roblin had announced his candidacy early enough, he would probably have won the role. Premier Robert L. Stanfield of Nova Scotia was widely reported as saying that the thought of becoming the federal Conservative leader was, for him, in the same league as taking up the sport of ski jumping. I later learned that Stanfield had told his good friend Dalton Camp that he would not be a candidate if Roblin decided to enter the race. It was only after Roblin's protracted dithering that Stanfield was persuaded to run. By that time, former Diefenbaker Cabinet ministers Davie Fulton, George Hees, and Senator Wallace McCutcheon had all announced their candidacy. Eventually, Roblin also threw his hat into the ring.

The principal drama leading up to the leadership convention in September 1967, however, was whether John Diefenbaker himself would stand. Although candidates had been campaigning for some months, the actual deadline for filing nomination papers was not until the second day of the convention. Diefenbaker clearly enjoyed the protracted drama, and it was only moments before the deadline that nomination papers were filed on behalf of the Chief.

Although I still regarded politics as but an interesting hobby, it was inevitable, given my friendship with Dalton Camp and Norman Atkins, that I would become involved in the Stanfield campaign. I had not met "Robert L.," as he was known to many of his friends, before his first press conference in Toronto in the late spring of 1967. He was clearly not prepared for the aggressive central Canada media, but I was immediately impressed by his intelligence, decency, and low-key, often self-deprecating manner. Stanfield had been the gold medallist in his graduating year at Dalhousie University and had graduated from Harvard Law School. When he became premier of Nova Scotia, he usually answered the phone himself while working during weekends. By 1967 he had held this post for eleven years, and even my Liberal friends in that province conceded that Bob Stanfield could have been premier for as long as he wished to serve.

Atkins was asked to be Stanfield's convention manager, and he and Camp assembled an experienced and dedicated campaign team. The 1967 federal Progressive Conservative leadership was the first truly modern political convention. These advertising and political campaign experts used relatively new and sophisticated polling and communication strategies, just as they produced well-designed pamphlets and prepared articulate policy statements. It was all very different from previous political conventions. I did not become involved in the campaign in any meaningful way until the convention itself, which was to take place at Maple Leaf Gardens in Toronto in September. My chief responsibility was to maintain close contact with the people I knew well in the entourages around the other candidates. As the vote progressed through the various ballots and their candidate had been eliminated, it was my job to persuade these freed-up delegates to make Stanfield their next choice. Given Stanfield's popularity, it was not a difficult task. The main challenge was to keep in touch with my friends in the other leadership camps during the inevitable confusion of political conventions. The teams supporting each candidate were spread among several hotels in the vicinity of Maple Leaf Gardens, and we developed strategies for keeping in continuing contact.

The short, focused, and meaningful speech Stanfield delivered to the convention made him a front-runner for the leadership. He called for English Canada to develop a better understanding of the aims and expectations of French Quebec. In his view, the people of Quebec sought only "that measure of authority in respect to social and economic affairs which will enable them to fulfill themselves as French Canadians." He continued, "The people of Quebec view their provincial government as the logical instrument for the execution of this authority. The desire of Quebec for these provincial responsibilities is not shared to the same extent by Canadians in other provinces." Although Stanfield made it clear that he supported the requirement for the essential authority of the federal government, he stated, "It is my firm conviction that Canada can only be strengthened if the French-speaking people of Quebec believe they have the opportunity to develop the distinctive aspects of their character." Then came the most controversial portion of his speech: "Implicitly, therefore," he said, "the requirement of Quebec is for some kind of different arrangement in the distribution of authority in respect to social and economic matters."

Stanfield emphasized that "French-speaking Canadians outside Quebec should enjoy those [language] rights that are enjoyed by the English-speaking minority within Quebec." At the same time, he rejected the term "special status" for Quebec "because it suggested that the people of that province would have rights denied to the rest of Canada." His great consuming concern was the improvement of the "quality" of Canadian life. As he memorably stated, "There are values in being a Canadian citizen beyond those reflected in the gross national product."

Stanfield's address appeared to have a galvanizing effect on the audience assembled in Maple Leaf Gardens, yet it provided additional ammunition for John Diefenbaker. He had been angered when the Conservative Party Thinkers Conference in Quebec a few weeks earlier accepted a "two-nations policy." For him, two nations meant two independent governments. The policy convention endorsed a resolution in these terms: "Canada is comprised of original inhabitants of this land, together with two founding peoples (*deux nations*) with historic rights, who have been and continue to be joined by peoples of many lands." Diefenbaker bridled at the semantic "hair splitters" who tried to assure him that the term *nation* in French meant a culturally identifiable people, not a separate political entity. In a generally effective and eloquent speech to the convention, he included a sentence stating that he "couldn't accept any policy that denies everything that I stood for throughout my life." Diefenbaker's speech failed to win the party back to support him. The majority of the delegates appeared to feel that the speech was unnecessarily divisive, creating the *deux nations* issue as a straw man in a desperate attempt to hold on to his job. On the first ballot he placed an ignominious fifth, with less than 10 per cent of the vote.

As an aside, only six months later, Pierre Trudeau's scorn for the *deux nations* principle at the Liberal leadership convention was enthusiastically applauded. I have always believed, however, that Stanfield's support for this policy demonstrated his determination to recognize the legitimate aspirations of French Quebec. It also represented the political reality that, when it comes to Quebec, the federal Conservative Party has to try a little harder.

On the day of the leadership balloting at the convention, the delegates in Maple Leaf Gardens were generally gathered in sections of the arena reserved for each candidate and his supporters. Most of the remaining seats were occupied by a large media contingent. I had agreed to serve as the floor manager of the Stanfield team. Each candidate was issued with several passes, providing a limited number of people with access to the arena and facilitating contact between the representatives of each campaign team.

By the time the convention began, many believed that the final ballot would probably include two of three candidates – Duff Roblin of Manitoba, Bob Stanfield of Nova Scotia, and Davie Fulton of British Columbia. I personally believed that Stanfield and Roblin would be on the final ballot, so Fulton's support would be critical for one or other of these candidates. Once again, Mulroney agreed with me. He was a committed Fulton supporter, but he also thought highly of Stanfield – his second choice as leader for the federal Conservative Party. Mulroney agreed that he would attempt to persuade Fulton to support Stanfield should he himself not make it to the final ballot. It was imperative, therefore, that Mulroney and I remain in close touch during the hours of the balloting.

Canadian political party leadership conventions have developed their own procedures. When candidates are eliminated from the ballot or choose to drop out after receiving few votes, for instance, they can make their support known for another candidate by certain public gestures. The most common is to join that candidate and hold his or her arm aloft. That simple act immediately communicates the message to the withdrawing candidate's supporters and encourages them to follow suit, despite the chaos in the convention hall. When Fulton was defeated on the second to last ballot, Mulroney and I immediately got together on the convention floor. Although Fulton wished to support Stanfield on the final ballot, in Mulroney's words, "Davie was hurting and was not prepared to make what would be a somewhat painful journey to Stanfield's box on the other side of the arena." Stanfield, he said, would have to make the trek to Fulton's box.

It was a reasonable suggestion, but, with only a few minutes left before the voting began again, how could we get the message to Stanfield, who was solidly surrounded by more than one hundred members of the media? I literally battled my way through the crowd so I could communicate the urgency to Stanfield himself. Fortunately, I made my point, and he walked across the crowded arena to Fulton's box to congratulate him on the quality of his campaign. Fulton responded by holding up Stanfield's arm. I have always been convinced that Fulton's support was critical to Stanfield's later success that night.

The election of Stanfield as leader gave a substantial boost to the fortunes of the Progressive Conservative Party, and in the immediate aftermath, he consistently scored high in the political polls. He was aided by Pearson's announcement in late 1967 that he was resigning as prime minister. The Liberal organizers thereupon called a leadership convention for the early spring of 1968. During his five years as prime minister, Pearson could look back on some very impressive accomplishments, including universal health care and the Canadian flag. I had met him only briefly on a few occasions but had always been impressed by his decency, civility, and obvious intelligence. In his memoirs, Pearson made one particular observation that has always remained with me. It is unfortunate, he said, that political leaders are generally remembered for their legislative and other initiatives but seldom for the evil they prevented.

In politics, the temptation to pursue short-term expediency, in order to jump forward a little, can be very divisive in the long run. In recent years, for instance, certain "wedge issues" have been used not only to polarize the public but at the same time to strengthen party support. During Stanfield's leadership, the policy of official bilingualism became a potential wedge issue. Given that many within the federal Conservative Party urged Stanfield to oppose official bilingualism, that stand would no doubt have strengthened his political support in the short run. It would, however, have been tragically divisive for the country in the longer term. To Stanfield's great credit, he not only rejected this approach but, throughout his years as leader, strongly supported the implementation of legislation for official bilingualism.

In the spring of 1968, Trudeaumania soon came to dominate the federal political scene. No sooner had Pierre Trudeau been selected as the Liberal leader and the new prime minister than he called an election for June of that same year. Dalton Camp was still president of the Progressive Conservative Party, and most people expected that he would once more be a candidate. However, it made no sense for him to run again against Mitchell Sharp in Eglinton. At the time of the surprising election call, Camp was enjoying his annual Antigua holiday. He invited Atkins and me to visit him there to discuss his political future. I recall being very pessimistic about his chance of winning in any of the available constituencies in Metropolitan Toronto, given the growing level of support for Trudeau in urban Canada. Camp decided, however, that he would be a candidate in the upcoming election. I remember him stating that, "for better or worse, I am given some degree of credit for Bob Stanfield becoming the leader of our party. In these circumstances, I cannot walk away from the fight regardless of how slim my chances are." Some weeks later, he lost to Robert Kaplan in the constituency of Don Valley West.

* * *

Pierre Trudeau became prime minister in 1968. Although a supporter of the Progressive Conservative Party both federally and provincially, I shared the fascination of most Canadians with respect to our dynamic first minister.

Trudeau's campaign message in 1968 was largely his commitment to the creation of a "just society." He had earlier been associated with the Co-operative Commonwealth Federation, the predecessor of the New Democratic Party, and was a strong advocate of the rights of labour both within and outside the union movement. Trudeau became somewhat of a public figure during the Asbestos Strike of 1949, which was based around four asbestos mines in Quebec. These mines were owned by American or English-Canadian companies, but almost all the workers were francophones. The demands of the workers, while radical at the time in Quebec, appear now to have been very reasonable. Quebec premier Maurice Duplessis sided strongly with the asbestos companies, mainly because of his hostility to all forms of socialism. The strike turned into one of the most violent and bitter disputes in Quebec and Canadian history. It was in large part led by Jean Marchand, a union leader, with strong support from journalists Gérard Pelletier and Pierre Trudeau. This four-month-long labour dispute became a major factor leading into the Quiet Revolution in Quebec in 1960, with the election of Jean Lesage as premier. It also helped to launch the careers of the "three wise men" – Marchand, Pelletier, and Trudeau – who together went to Ottawa as MPs in 1965.

As minister of justice in Lester B. Pearson's Cabinet, Trudeau earned a reputation as a progressive reformer, a strong democrat, and a social liberal. Once he became prime minister, he appointed his friends Marchand and Pelletier as key ministers in his Cabinet. Given Trudeau's commitment to a just society, I was personally shocked when he imposed the *War Measures Act* in response to the October Crisis of 1970 in Quebec – a series of events triggered by two kidnappings of government officials by the radical separatist Front de libération du Québec (FLQ). The circumstances ultimately culminated in the only peacetime use of the *War Measures Act* in Canadian history. This martial law was imposed at the request of the premier of Quebec, Robert Bourassa, and the mayor of Montreal, Jean Drapeau, and resulted in widespread deployment of Canadian Forces troops throughout Quebec and in Ottawa. The police were also given far-reaching powers, and they arrested and detained without bail 497 individuals, the vast majority of whom were later released without charges.

In my view it was most regrettable that opinion polls throughout Canada showed strong and widespread support for the use of the *War Measures Act*. It was criticized by only a handful of politicians, including Progressive Conservative David MacDonald and Tommy Douglas, who quite properly believed that the actions were excessive and that the precedent of suspending civil liberties was dangerous. The criticism, limited as it was, was supported by evidence that the police had abused their powers and had detained, without cause, prominent artists and intellectuals associated with the sovereignty movement. I was particularly disturbed by the fact that the legal profession in English-speaking Canada, except for a few prominent lawyers who supported the imposition of the *War Measures Act*, was mostly silent in the face of these civil rights abuses.

I don't want to give the impression that I believed that the October Crisis was not a serious emergency. The kidnapping of James Cross, the British trade commissioner, and the murder of Pierre Laporte, a Quebec Cabinet minister, were heinous crimes, and in the short term, Trudeau's quick response did put an end to years of terrorism in Quebec. However, in October 1970 the powers of the police under the *Criminal Code*, combined with the right of the governments of Quebec and Canada to requisition the intervention of the Canadian Army in "aid of the civil power," would have been the appropriate and effective action, without the suspension of the legal rights of hundreds of francophones, and others too. It has always been my opinion that, over the long term, the imposition of the *War Measures Act* dramatically increased the support for sovereignty in Quebec.

I was sufficiently disturbed as a young lawyer to write a letter to the editor of the *Globe and Mail* dated October 28, 1970, which was published two days later. It read:

Together with the shock, horror and revulsion that I experienced with the news of the brutal murder of Pierre Laporte, I must also confess to a deep concern about the extent to which the majority of Canadians have either docilely accepted or welcomed the War Measures Act and the suspension of liberties resulting therefrom.

In such a time of national tragedy, it is undoubtedly very unpopular for anyone to raise the banner of civil liberties for fear of being branded as one sympathetic to the perpetrators of the tragedy. For this reason I have no doubt but that many responsible voices have remained silent in the present crisis despite deep misgivings as to the conduct of our national Government. In particular as a lawyer, I am somewhat disturbed by the general reluctance of my legal colleagues to express publicly the apprehension that is felt by reason of the imposition of martial law and the known injustices that have already occurred.

By this, I do not mean that I have any quarrel with the decision (unrelated to the War Measures Act) to employ the use of our Armed Forces. I would concede that the morale of a public deeply shocked by the events of the past three weeks probably benefitted by the presence of federal troops, quite apart from the unlikely possibility of any widespread civil disorder.

However, I do believe that our federal Government should be severely censured for its almost hysterical reaction to the challenge of the FLQ, a reaction which may very well have triggered the death of Mr. Laporte and which has now led to the indiscriminate arrest of a large number of persons, including women and children. At the same time the Government of Canada has failed to reveal what, if any, beneficial effect has been accomplished by the imposition of the War Measures Regulations.

I have never been prepared to accept the Machiavellian principle that the end, i.e. the destruction of the FLQ, always justifies the means. In this instance the federal authorities have stated that the crisis required the imposition of drastic measures, quite foreign to the rule of law that is so basic to the foundation of a free society.

We are told that our Criminal Code was inadequate to cope with the emergency and yet a plain reading of the sections dealing with "sedition" in the Code would indicate otherwise.

The police are entitled by law to arrest anyone whom they believe on reasonable and probable grounds to have committed a criminal offense and this general power together with the sections of the Criminal Code dealing with sedition surely would provide our Government with the right to cause the arrest of anyone where there was any reasonable evidence to suggest that they were part of a criminal conspiracy. Nevertheless, our Prime Minister insists that our existing law was not sufficient and he has apparently been able to persuade the majority of his countrymen that it is necessary to be able to arrest anyone on the flimsiest of suspicion, to hold them without a formal charge, to deny them bail and the access to a court of law for a prolonged period of time, all in the name of protecting the people of Canada.

It is often forgotten that the hard-won civil liberties of a free society are not maintained only for those who are arrested but for everyone and when we deprive one person of this basic right then all are threatened.

If our Government continues to insist on maintaining a right to determine with an unfettered discretion when and where it may suspend the civil liberties of any of its citizens then I suggest that the FLQ terrorists will have succeeded in disturbing the essential fabric of our society to a far greater extent than what they could accomplish by any number of criminal acts.

I also wrote a letter to the Honourable Robert Stanfield, leader of the Progressive Conservative official opposition party, enclosing a copy of my letter to the *Globe and Mail* and concluding as follows: "In the present crisis I am firmly convinced that the number of indiscriminate arrests that have already occurred will produce a legacy of bitterness that can only serve to enhance the cause of the Separatists in Quebec and further alienate many young people."

Little did I know in 1970 that, less than a decade later, I would be supporting Prime Minister Trudeau and his government with respect to the patriation of the Canadian Constitution with an entrenched charter of rights. The arrest and detention without bail enabled by the *War Measures Act* and its successor legislation, the federal *Emergencies Act*, could well be challenged under the Charter of Rights. I don't recall Trudeau ever explaining his enthusiasm for both the *War Measures Act* and the Canadian Charter of Rights. However, I do remember Emerson's famous line that "a foolish consistency is the hobgoblin of little minds."

9

Family Life

Following Dalton Camp's defeat in the 1968 federal election, I focused my energies almost entirely on my busy legal practice and, of course, my now large family. For Ria and me, the arrival of our sixth child was a celebration of both our tenth wedding anniversary and Canada's 1967 Centennial. It was a joyful and a raucous household. Two years earlier we had moved to a bigger home on Lascelles Boulevard, where Ria and I still live. I often look back in awe at how Ria coped with all these small children and babies as well as a husband who was often preoccupied with his work. However, it was a very happy time with few real worries, despite the usual financial challenges facing a family of eight.

Once Ria and I announced our engagement, we told anyone who might be interested that we planned to have six children. We both came from families with four children, and the idea of an even larger family had great appeal for us. However, following the birth of our fourth child, Ria developed a serious health issue, and on our doctor's advice, we agreed that four healthy children were just fine. As things turned out, we were soon privileged to have six healthy offspring – Janet, Jim, Harry, Jeannie, Erin, and Michael (chapter 38).

Ria had been obliged to resign her position as a teacher as soon as it became evident that she was pregnant with our first child. Managing a household and six children was a major task, but she did it extremely well – and with only modest help from me. I remember adopting the unfair position that the mother was better qualified than the father to look after the children's discipline. Coming from a family of boys, I occasionally found my own daughters rather mysterious beings. The sixties and seventies were a relatively simpler age than now for family life, and Ria was able to be at home to greet the children after school. The happiest time of the day for me was coming home from the office and having time with the family. I developed a level of concentration that became useful in the years ahead. Like my father, I preferred to work at home in the evenings whenever possible, doing my trial preparation and other tasks at our dining-room table. I also invited clients to consult with me at home. Shutting out the bedlam of a young family was an almost daily challenge. My ability to assist meaningfully with the children's homework and bedtime routines, however, was limited. Too often urgent developments related to an ongoing trial interfered with my desire to be more involved in family life.

With three brothers to contend with, our daughters became accustomed to a significant degree of rough and tumble – including games of ball hockey, ice hockey, and touch football. My major hobbies were skiing with the children in the winter and playing tennis during the balance of the year. After Janet and Jim were both mobile, we began to enjoy summer vacations in the Muskoka area and ended up buying a summer property there on an island in 1968. We still go there, joined now by children and twelve grandchildren.

* * *

Fortunately for me, my painting hobby gradually established a toe-hold in my life and became more entrenched over time. When the children were young, my "joyride in a paintbox" was limited to a few afternoons a year, along with visiting art galleries whenever the opportunity arose. My library of art books also began to grow, with an emphasis on the French Impressionists, Post-Impressionists, and the Canadian Group of Seven.

Other special opportunities for painting came during family spring-break ski trips, particularly at Mont Tremblant in Quebec. At that time of the year, the weather had turned milder, so it was possible to paint outside in the afternoon. I developed the routine of bringing my paintbox up the mountain after lunch, hiding it, skiing for another hour or two, retrieving my paints and canvas, and sketching from different vantage points looking down on the village. Sometimes I encountered members of the ski patrol as I descended the mountains, and they were understandably angry with me for remaining on the mountain long after skiers were required to be off the trails.

Later, during my years in politics, I combined much of my painting with political trips to the provinces and territories of Canada. Intergovernmental meetings were usually scheduled many weeks in advance and for two or three days, invariably ending on a Friday. I was therefore able to plan weekends devoted to painting, from Newfoundland to British Columbia.

For me, landscape painting provided an opportunity for a special communion with nature, particularly when it could be pursued in seclusion. It taught me to be a close observer of nature's infinite variety of colour, cloud formations, and the range of shapes from sea coasts to mountain peaks. I was also attracted to built structures, from fishing villages to hilltop towns and villages in Europe.

* * *

My involvement with politics during the 1968 election reunited me with my old friend Frank Moores, whom I had met at St Andrew's College in 1946 (chapter 2). He had returned to Newfoundland after his graduation from school. After a brief career at Boston College, he joined the family's very successful fish-processing conglomerate, Northeast Fisheries. The general support of the family would later launch Frank Moores's successful political career. He and I kept in touch over the years, and by the time I became active with Dalton Camp in federal politics, Moores had become very curious about the political world. However, it was not until the spring of 1968, shortly after the election of Pierre Trudeau as leader of the Liberal Party, that he spoke openly about his political ambitions.

During a visit to Toronto he informed me that Northeast Fisheries was being sold and that he was considering a career in politics. His strategy appeared quite impractical to me because it involved moving to Toronto (his wife, Doty's, original hometown), learning French, and joining Camp's political entourage to learn the intricacies of modern political warfare. I knew that Moores's ultimate goal was to serve the people of Newfoundland, and I could not imagine how a detour to Toronto would advance his cause. Timing is always important in politics and, given that Trudeau had just announced the date for a late spring election, I strongly recommended that Moores return immediately to Newfoundland, where he could easily secure a nomination as a candidate for the Progressive Conservative Party in the forthcoming federal election. He was reluctant to follow that advice, pleading that he had never been a member of any political party. Fortunately, Bob Stanfield was scheduled to be in Toronto the next day, and I was able to persuade Moores at least to meet with him before he gave up this unique political opportunity.

First, I had a brief meeting with Stanfield to impress on him that Moores would be an excellent candidate. Despite his political inexperience, he was intelligent, personable, capable, and a member of a family that was well known and highly regarded in Newfoundland. Stanfield was a laid-back kind of person, often taciturn, and I thought he might have to use his influence to persuade Moores to be a candidate. When they did meet, there was indeed an initial standoff between them until Stanfield said: "Mr Moores, I think you would be a good candidate, and if you are truly interested in serving the people of Newfoundland, I believe it is time you got off the wharf and into the water." This truly Atlantic-Canadian metaphor did the trick, and Moores agreed to be a candidate. We were confident that the local party officials would welcome him eagerly.

Moores decided to seek the federal Progressive Conservative nomination in the constituency in which Premier Joey Smallwood lived. As events transpired, he had no opponents. Smallwood regarded his choice as a personal insult, particularly as the Moores family had never supported him provincially. He unleashed his rage by attacking Frank Moores personally and the Moores family in general. He clearly underestimated the popularity of this clan, and his miscalculation had an impact on his own political downfall a few years later.

Frank Moores was elected comfortably. His candidacy definitely assisted the election of four other Conservative candidates, giving the Stanfield party five of the seven Newfoundland seats. Dalton Camp's advertising agency in Toronto designed and produced Moores's election pamphlets and other materials. Moores immediately became a popular member of the federal Conservative caucus, and a year later he was elected national president of the party. I assisted him in his brief and wrote most of his speech for candidates' night at the party general meeting. Even though he clearly enjoyed this national status, in 1970 a few of us persuaded him to return to Newfoundland, where the leadership of the provincial party was his should he want it. He became the leader and, in 1971, premier of Newfoundland and Labrador.

Leaping forward to the 1972 federal election campaign, Stanfield asked me to meet with Moores to assess the progress of the Conservative campaign in Newfoundland. Unlike the situation in the larger provinces, the same individuals in Newfoundland generally ran both the provincial and the federal party organizations. As a result, Moores would be most important in influencing the federal campaign in Newfoundland. I telephoned him to make arrangements for a meeting, and he suggested that we get together in Montreal during the Labour Day weekend – which coincided with the opening Canada-Russia hockey game in the famous series that year. We met in his Montreal hotel suite for our talk about the upcoming federal election and the state of readiness of the Newfoundland Progressive Conservative political organization. Our conversation was interrupted from time to time by Moores's chief of staff, who was insisting that the deadline had come for the premier to decide on the name for a cargo ship that was scheduled to be launched in Scotland the following month. The government of Newfoundland had an interest in the ship, which would carry cargo between Newfoundland and the eastern United States.

For some reason, the ship had to have a woman's name, and because Moores was between marriages, it could not be named after his wife as the owners had anticipated. Many of his political colleagues were touting their own suggestions, and Moores was confronted that afternoon with a minor political problem. Suddenly he turned to me and said categorically, "Roy, you launched me into politics, and the name of the ship will be the *Ria Jean McMurtry*." The message was communicated immediately to the organization team in New York.

When I returned home, Ria told me her side of the story. That same Saturday, she had decided to return to Toronto from our cottage in Muskoka. The weather was bad, and after two months with several of our younger children up there, she was ready to be back in the city. As she entered the house, the phone was ringing, and she hurriedly picked up the receiver. A woman informed her she was calling from New York to arrange a date for the launch of the *Ria Jean McMurtry* in Dundee, Scotland. Ria thought it was all a prank, but when the caller mentioned Frank Moores, Ria muttered, "Well, my husband is supposed to be meeting about now with the premier in Montreal."

There was some urgency in setting a date for the launch, in late September. We were told that, according to launch protocol, a female related to Ria should perform the "christening" of the ship with the customary champagne bottle. The choice was obvious – our eldest daughter, Janet, who was fourteen years old.

The launch turned out to be an extravagant experience, with first-class travel to Scotland, the ceremony itself, and stays at luxury hotels in Scotland and in London, England. We were obviously the beneficiaries of a "boondoggle" type of tax write-off that benefited the directors in the conglomerate of companies which owned the cargo ship. Ria, Janet, and I felt a little guilty about it all, but not too much, as we looked forward to a unique family adventure.

At the launch ceremony in Dundee, the large crowd of shipbuilders surrounding the boat took great pride in their creation. And our little family took similar pride as we walked into the dockyard and saw Ria's name prominently displayed on the bow and stern of the ship. Janet, who had seen several comedy film clips of bottles bouncing off the bows of ships without breaking during launches, was very nervous about the ceremony she had to perform – and her first effort ended in that same unproductive fashion. Her second try, complete with two hands and great determination, got her the desired spectacular result. Her photograph appeared on the front page of most of Scotland's newspapers – the young daughter who had come from far-off Canada to perform her task.

As a result of the celebrations surrounding the launch, I came to know John Shaheen, an American international entrepreneur who was a director on the board of one of the companies that owned the *Ria Jean McMurtry*. He was a friend of President Richard Nixon and of Premier Joey Smallwood. He was also the moving force behind the Newfoundland Come By Chance oil refinery, which was formally dedicated by Sir Winston Churchill's grandson just over a year later. The refinery was in the immediate neighbourhood of the meeting between Churchill and President Franklin D. Roosevelt at Placentia Bay during the Second World War.

Ria and I were invited to this event, which was done in extravagant style. It involved flying all the guests to New York City, before transporting them on the *Queen Elizabeth 2* to the ceremony at Come By Chance. The cost was covered by the owners of the refinery, which was primarily financed by Japanese banks. The guest list included author James Michener and journalist William Buckley Jr. I recall that at least one Newfoundland journalist was not impressed, titling a column about the voyage "The Ship of Fools."

The sequel to these stories is depressing: the MV *Ria Jean McMurtry* sank several years later, the Come By Chance oil refinery went into bankruptcy, and after his premiership ended, Frank Moores became a political lobbyist in Ottawa as well as a close friend of Brian Mulroney. Rumours began to circulate about Moores's participation in the controversial Airbus affair involving the purchase of aircraft for Air Canada and his relationship with German businessman Karlheinz Schreiber.

Moores was a keen supporter of Mulroney in his quest to become leader of the federal Progressive Conservative Party. I was not at the 1983 federal meeting in Winnipeg which led directly to the leadership convention that Mulroney won later that year. Although I expected Mulroney to win at the convention, I supported my neighbour and close friend David Crombie, who had been a successful mayor of Toronto and a member of Joe Clark's Cabinet. After Crombie was eliminated from the ballot, I supported Mulroney, who, a year later, became prime minister of Canada. I had occasional contact with Moores during the eight years of the Mulroney government, and I attended one of his daughter's weddings.

I learned from Beth Moores that Mulroney and her husband had a personal fallout in 1993, when Mulroney believed, perhaps wrongly, that Moores had suggested to mutual colleagues that it was time for Mulroney to step down as prime minister. However, when Mulroney later learned that Moores had terminal cancer, he became quite solicitous about his old friend and offered any help he could provide. I too resumed more regular contact with Moores when I learned of his illness. I recall him dealing with his adversity with great courage and grace. Shortly before he died in 2006, he took one of his grandsons to Newfoundland to teach him how to fish. After his death, his family asked me to deliver the eulogy at a memorial service at St Andrew's College that fall.

* * *

During the spring of 1970, I enjoyed my first visit to Ireland, the home of many of my ancestors. Fortunately, Ria was able to accompany me. The occasion was a legal conference in Dublin, and I attended as a member of the Advocates' Society of Ontario. We had meetings during the day, followed by social events with members of the Irish bar. Most memorable were the two boisterous formal dinners with Irish lawyers at Dublin's Gresham Hotel. The visit also produced some unexpected political repercussions, including the resignation of the Irish minister of justice.

The first of the dinners was hosted by the Irish bar, and the second by the Advocates' Society. It was our dinner that produced the political fireworks. A senior member of the Advocates' Society, Joseph Sedgwick, proposed the toast to the Irish bar and eloquently referred to the positive influences of great Irish barristers on the legal culture of Canada. During his toast, he referred to several famous Irish advocates, such as "Serjeant" Sullivan (whose title was purely honorific).

At the mention of Sullivan, Michael O'Morain, the local justice minister, who perhaps had overindulged in the copious amounts of wine available, shouted, "What are you talking about that fellow for, he was not even a proper Irishman!" After further insults were exchanged, O'Morain stormed out of the dinner. He apparently took a wrong turn, and his entry into the adjacent kitchen was accompanied by the sound of breaking plates and glasses. That dramatic departure turned out to be the last time he appeared in public as minister of justice.

Although I recognized the name Serjeant Sullivan, I had forgotten the controversy that outlived him within some segments of the Irish public and bar. He had been a successful Dublin advocate who had moved to London to make his fortune in England. His very successful career there coincided with the First World War, when many Irish nationalists were sympathetic to the German cause, given Ireland's long struggle for independence. Sir Roger Casement, a popular Irish patriot, was accused in 1917 of bringing German guns into Ireland with the intention of supporting an uprising there against British rule. Casement was charged with treason, and Serjeant Sullivan was retained to be his counsel at trial. When Casement was convicted and executed, many Irish nationalists accused Sullivan of selling out to the English. Obviously, the accusation survived in some minds in 1970.

O'Morain's behaviour at the dinner was negatively reported in the media and served to augment other political misfortunes that had been building against him. On May 5 the *Irish Times* reported that his "resignation on the grounds of ill health had been accepted by the Taoiseach" (the prime minister). The article continued: "Mr O'Morain has been in Mount Carmel Hospital Dublin for 10 days recovering from a setback during a dinner given by the Advocates' Society of Ontario, Canada, in Dublin a fortnight ago." As for Joe Sedgwick, for the rest of his life he enjoyed recounting his role in the whole proceedings.

This incident was not the only time that a gathering of members of the Canadian bar produced a political fallout in Ireland. In 1948, when John Costello, the Irish prime minister, was a guest of the Canadian Bar Association in Ottawa, the governor general, Lord Alexander of Tunis, hosted a reception for the association, with Costello as the honoured guest. Lord Alexander was an Ulster Protestant, and apparently these two men engaged in an angry exchange over the future of Northern Ireland. Costello believed he had been seriously insulted by the representative of the British sovereign in Canada. On the day after the reception, he held a press conference in Ottawa in which he announced that, when he returned to Ireland, he would introduce a resolution in the Irish Parliament declaring Southern Ireland a republic. Costello was true to his word, and before year's end, the Republic of Ireland was created, severing that country's long ties to the British Crown.

In the spring of 2006 the Advocates' Society held yet another conference in the Irish Republic. At a reception hosted by the Canadian ambassador, I was called on to speak about the special relationship between the Irish and the Canadian legal professions. It gave me the opportunity to reflect on the sagas of 1948 and 1970 and to suggest to our ambassador that he should be vigilant when members of the Irish and Canadian bars gathered together. Fortunately, cordiality prevailed during our entire visit without a hint of any political repercussions.

After the conference, Ria and I travelled to the west coast of Ireland and the Ring of Kerry in the south, including a visit to my maternal grandfather's birthplace in the city of Bandon in County Cork. The many and rapidly changing weather patterns provided a kaleidoscope of moods throughout the Irish countryside. My lasting impression is that I gained a better understanding of my own personality during this trip.

As usual, I had my paintbox with me, and the breathtaking beauties of coastal Ireland inspired me to make several sketches. We still have a small oil painting in our dining room which I created during our trip around the Ring of Kerry. With my paintbox balanced on the hood of our rented car, I attempted in a couple of hours one day to capture the scene with a palette knife as an intermittent soft rain fell and Ria read in the car. This favourite hobby has always involved collecting memories for me.

In Bandon we were able to discover the tomb of my great-grandfather. We were amazed by the several spires of the Church of England which dominate that city. Bandon is a Protestant enclave in the heart of Catholic Ireland. As we drove out on our way, we picked up a young hitchhiker who was heading back to his police duties in another region. When he heard our comments about his hometown, he remarked, "Yes sir, there is an expression here in Bandon that even the pigs are Protestant." We never did decide whether his comment was simply a casual statement or a more pointed religious observation.

In 1970 the Republic of Ireland was a relatively poor country. Many young people were emigrating, given the shortage of employment opportunities. At the same time, many German nationals were purchasing and developing properties in some of the most picturesque areas.

Whenever I expressed my concern about the loss of the beautiful countryside, I was invariably met with the response that "our youth can't eat the scenery." Nevertheless, the warmth of the Irish people and the country's natural attractions made our first trip there a memorable experience and strengthened my determination for many return visits.

10

Member of the Kitchen Cabinet

Between 1968 and 1970 I had little time for partisan politics, and I still believed that my political activity would never be anything more than sporadic adventures. Occasionally I attended political meetings and weekend retreats to discuss strategies related to Bob Stanfield's federal leadership, but I had never been involved with the provincial Progressive Conservative Party. The Conservatives had formed the government in Ontario since 1943, with John Robarts as the successful premier from 1961 on. Bill Davis, my former University of Toronto football teammate, was the highly respected education minister – the man most likely to succeed Robarts. The opposition in the provincial legislature was hopelessly divided, and there was little prospect of a change in government in the foreseeable future. Although I respected this government, I had no particular enthusiasm to involve myself directly in either provincial or federal politics.

In the autumn of 1970 rumours began to circulate about Robarts's pending retirement. I was more concerned, however, with the ongoing pain in my lower back, the result of an old football injury. My orthopaedic specialist recommended complete bed rest. When Robarts announced his retirement late that year and Davis confirmed his candidacy to replace him, I was physically unable to participate actively in the leadership contest.

Meanwhile, my political friends from the "Eglinton Mafia" days who had remained close to Dalton Camp on a personal basis were considering whether to become involved in this provincial campaign. I had attended an early meeting where we agreed we would offer our collective support to Davis, though some in the group were friends with another provincial Cabinet minister, Allan Lawrence, and we watched him as a potential candidate too. While I remained flat on my back, a few members of our group approached representatives of the Davis team to offer our assistance to his leadership campaign. Our close association and friendship with Camp, however, led to a polite but firm no: Camp was widely disliked within the party both federally and provincially for his successful orchestration of the review of Diefenbaker's leadership. Insulted by this rejection, the Camp group turned to Lawrence and encouraged him to be a candidate. They promised support from the team that had run the truly modern and highly successful leadership campaign for Stanfield, complete with sophisticated polling techniques and other political strategies. The federal Liberal leadership convention that followed six months later used similar strategies.

Of the six competing campaigns run by ministers drawn from Robarts's Cabinet, the Lawrence leadership campaign was certainly the most professional and effective of them all. Davis's campaign was burdened by his record as a long-time progressive minister of education and the reactionary critics who branded him a "big spender." Among his many accomplishments that drew their opposition was his streamlining of the unwieldy provincial boards of education – a reform that produced more equal educational opportunities for Ontario students – and his creation of a system of community colleges throughout the province. These colleges were still at an early stage of development, and he had no shortage of critics who described them as "white elephants." Moreover, the front runner in any leadership race inevitably attracts most of the criticism, and that fact alone made Bill Davis vulnerable.

At that time, Davis was a reserved and private individual who kept his emotions under tight control. I always believed this discipline was in part related to the loss of his beautiful young wife to cancer at the age of thirty-three after the birth of their four children. However, many people regarded him as remote and aloof. In any event, by the end of 1970 predictions of a Davis "coronation" had been replaced by the realization that the Lawrence campaign was gaining in momentum and that it would probably take several ballots before a winner was declared.

By early January 1971 I had become almost totally immobile, so I was scheduled for back surgery at the Toronto East General Hospital. My brother Bob was a senior resident in orthopaedic surgery there and he directed me to the senior surgeon, Dr Edward Simmons. A myelogram revealed that I had three ruptured herniated discs in the lumbar area. At the time of my operation, I was unable to stand without tremendous pain because the "bulge" from one of the discs was impinging on spinal-cord nerves. I had to choose between a fusion of the vertebrae over the three herniated discs or a simple excision of the protruding pulp. This second procedure, known as a laminectomy and discectomy, would result in a natural fusion between the two vertebrae above and below the disc. A bone fusion over all three of the herniated discs would require several more months confined to bed. I decided to opt for the less-intrusive surgery in the hope that the two other ruptured discs would not create a significant problem later on.

While recuperating in the hospital, I had a visit from Bill Davis, who expressed his determination that I become an active participant in the Progressive Conservative Party of Ontario after he had been elected leader. I was flattered by his apparent sincerity, but also realized that he was campaigning for my vote, because I would be a delegate at the leadership convention three weeks hence. Although my friends from the Camp team were running the Lawrence campaign, I had no doubt about my intention to support Davis. For his part, Davis always maintained that he was not aware of our group's offer of support.

I recuperated sufficiently from my back surgery to attend the leadership convention at Maple Leaf Gardens, but was still physically fragile. John Robarts, who had played football in his youth at the University of Western Ontario, was solicitous about my welfare and arranged that a sofa be placed in the directors' lounge so I could rest between the ballots on the final day of the convention – a Sunday. Robarts and his two predecessors as premiers, Leslie Frost and George Drew, were sitting nearby, and I was fascinated to hear these men reflect on their days in office. All three clearly believed that Davis was the appropriate choice to lead the provincial party after almost three decades of continuous Progressive Conservative government. Drew had succeeded Liberal Mitchell Hepburn in 1943 and, five years later, had left provincial politics to become leader of the federal party. He and his successor, Frost, had provided crucial leadership in building the post-war provincial infrastructure that led to the creation of a powerful Ontario economy. Robarts had continued along the same path, and in February 1971 the province was in good shape. However, several influential political journalists had decided that no one party should hold office for so long a term, and given the largely ineffective political opposition at Queen's Park, the media took on that role.

The three retired premiers knew that the next one would face many challenges, not least an increasingly aggressive media. Although they all expected Davis to win this contest, the passing of the torch that day proved more complicated than any of them expected. The Lawrence team had gathered considerable momentum, and it would be a long and exhausting day before the new leader was chosen.

Alan Eagleson, the president of the Ontario Conservative Party, had arranged to rent voting machines that purportedly reduced the time required to count the ballots. The machines were available from a prominent member of the Liberal Party, Thomas "Windy" O'Neill, who had acquired the Canadian franchise from the US manufacturer. O'Neill was an engaging lawyer, known particularly for having played on the 1946 Toronto Maple Leaf hockey team, which won the Stanley Cup. The voting machines made sense, but they simply did not work. There were long delays between the several ballots as they were cast. Many of the delegates had travelled considerable distances and had flights or trains to catch to get them home and at work the following day. Nevertheless, the result turned out exceedingly well for the Progressive Conservative Party: the winning candidate, Bill Davis, served as premier for some fourteen years, and in 1972 Allan Lawrence ran successfully in the federal election and went on to secure a spot in the Cabinet of Joe Clark.

Almost everyone assumed that 1971 would be an election year, and Davis would obviously benefit from the assistance of the impressive Lawrence leadership campaign team. He readily agreed with my suggestion that I arrange a meeting with the key members of the team at which he would attempt to obtain the support of the Lawrence people for the coming provincial campaign. I organized a dinner at Toronto's National Club for six people from each of the two leadership teams. Coming so soon after an intense political battle, I initially found it challenging to create a respectable level of cordiality, but once Davis arrived and the diners had imbibed a few drinks, the atmosphere grew more positive. Davis made a successful effort to reach out to the Lawrence people, assuring them that he wanted them on his team.

After the dinner, Bill Davis, Norman Atkins (Lawrence's campaign chair), and I got together for a late-night drink. That in itself was an indication of Davis's determination to create an effective campaign team, as late-evening drinks were not usually part of his lifestyle. Indeed, he rarely consumed even two rums and orange juice during an entire evening – and even that rate decreased over time.

A few days later, Davis asked Atkins to chair his campaign team for the next election. While working in the Camp and Associates advertising agency, Atkins had become a highly professional political organizer throughout Canada. Davis also chose Lawrence's campaign manager, Ross DeGeer, to serve in that same capacity on his team, and other Lawrence people were given major roles too. There may have been some resentment among the Davis leadership campaign team, but I believe they generally recognized the special skills of the Lawrence group. They also appreciated the importance of focusing on the next general election and allowing memories of the leadership battle to retreat into the past.

I was asked to be involved in the early planning for the campaign and at the same time to consider being a candidate myself in the provincial election. Because of my recent absence from my law practice, it was not possible for me to try to get into politics at that time. Davis therefore asked me to serve as the general legal counsel to the Progressive Conservative Party of Ontario – an offer I eagerly accepted. This position brought me into regular contact with the premier, particularly given the determination of the media to search for political impropriety in every corner of the province.

Davis's most significant challenge was to put his personal stamp on the premiership in the few months that remained before the next election. In my view, an important opportunity presented itself over the controversial plan to extend what was known as the Spadina Expressway south of Eglinton Avenue and down through the centre of Toronto to connect with the Gardiner Expressway. Inevitably it would cut a wide swath through the heart of the city, fracturing neighbourhoods, ravines, and parks.

My brother Bill and I, together with future mayor David Crombie and city councillor Colin Vaughan, were members of the vocal and widespread opposition to the planned expressway. However, the government of Ontario had earlier agreed in principle to its construction, which could happen only with substantial provincial funding. I exploited as many opportunities as I could to persuade Davis that his government should withdraw its support. When we attended the opening of the Montreal Expos baseball season together in April 1971 as guests of the owner, Charles Bronfman, I fear that I spoiled his enjoyment by my constant lobbying against the expressway. However, he did appear to be listening.

In June 1971 Davis surprised the provincial political world by announcing to the Legislature that his government was withdrawing its support of the expressway – in effect, cancelling the project. His statement contained the memorable phrase "cities are for people and not automobiles" and emphasized the importance of maintaining the integrity of neighbourhoods. The turnabout annoyed a lot of people, including some powerful businesses that would have benefited from the new transportation corridor, but it also succeeded in giving Davis a more human face and the appearance of a decisive leader. I still believe that his choice was the correct one, even though commuter traffic into Toronto has since become a nightmare.

Davis was also developing a leadership strategy that would serve him well during his years as premier. His own experience in politics had taught him that it is easy for government leaders to become detached from unpleasant political realities. They are surrounded by the "palace guard," personal staff who act as gatekeepers to the leader's office and often enjoy their control over access to the boss. Backbenchers and even Cabinet ministers are sometimes kept at a distance, and important messages are delivered and received by a senior staff person in the premier's office. Although leaders may be comfortable with the concept of a loyal staff acting as a shield against negative political realities, it can isolate them in dangerous ways.

As the new government evolved, Davis addressed this problem effectively by creating a Tuesday breakfast gathering. It included Davis, Cabinet Secretary Dr Edward Stewart, five or six ministers, political staff, and several outside advisers who had a good sense of the political pulse of the province. As party counsel, I became one of the early members of the group, and we met almost every week in a suite at the Park Plaza Hotel. Although we always treated Davis with the appropriate level of deference, our discussions of the political challenges of the day were totally frank and unvarnished. We addressed important issues from every relevant viewpoint, without becoming unnecessarily argumentative. Despite some significant disagreements, Davis's presence in the room seemed to guarantee a high level of collegiality. The final decision on any issue always belonged to the premier, in consultation with his entire Cabinet.

Not surprisingly, these breakfast meetings were resented by Cabinet ministers who were rarely, if ever, invited to attend. The appearance of an inner circle often creates serious splits within any government, but in this case the process worked well and was never the subject of comment when Cabinet met as a whole. The key was Davis himself, who, although only forty-one, had been a Cabinet minister for years before becoming premier and was expected to be leader of the Progressive Conservative Party for a long time yet.

As we approached the September 1971 election, we believed it would be a real contest, and I never perceived any complacency within the ranks of the Davis team. The leaders of the Liberal Party and the NDP, Bob Nixon and Stephen Lewis, respectively, were both able men, and Nixon had years of experience. Nevertheless, the fact that there were two credible opposition parties at Queen's Park was an advantage to the government, simply because the opposition vote would be effectively split in the majority of constituencies.

I have always believed that being leader of an opposition party is a difficult and complex role. The party faithful expect their leaders to be highly partisan, even if they privately agree with a particular government policy. At the same time, opposition leaders, in my view, should make their criticism on a policy rather than a personal level. Most Canadians do not like personal attacks in political debate, even though these thrusts usually spring from the frustration of being in opposition. The Liberal Party of Ontario had been in opposition since 1943. Inevitably, the campaign would be somewhat bitter as well as a major political battle.

Fortunately, Davis was a master at "keeping his cool," and he rarely displayed personal anger in the Legislature or on the campaign trail. He often remarked privately that heated, impulsive retorts might suggest a lack of control, while firm, measured responses to criticism were more likely to demonstrate confidence. My duties as party legal counsel took me to the Legislature frequently, and there I had the opportunity to observe the premier's debating skills. I was always amused by the political lore that the Davis debating style was boring and bland. When confronted with this allegation, Bill Davis simply shrugged it off good naturedly, stating that "bland works." In truth, he could be a very effective debater, though he was capable of giving long, obfuscating answers simply to needle the opposition. The overall result of his performance in the Legislature was to maintain a level of civility that has not been witnessed there since he retired in 1985.

* * *

I was appointed campaign policy coordinator for the 1971 election – a responsibility that turned out to be vague and frustrating. Once the election was called, Cabinet ministers set out on the campaign trail and the policy branches they left behind in their ministries were not particularly helpful. They probably regarded me as just another backroom political operative who had to be humoured more than helped.

The one big political issue was the funding of Roman Catholic separate schools, and it did not come up until late in the campaign. It was a very divisive issue in Ontario politics, and all the parties seemed reluctant to take it on. After Davis's large majority win in the election, a political mythology developed that the premier had introduced the issue when he did as a carefully calculated political strategy. Yet I know from personal discussions with him that he was determined to avoid the issue in order to prevent any political division fuelled by religion. As a long-time minister of education, he had worked closely with the Roman Catholic bishops, and he placed great value on the friendships that had developed.

Robarts and Davis had agreed several years earlier to extend the funding of separate schools to the end of grade 10. Previously it had been accepted that the province's constitutional responsibility for separate school funding did not extend beyond elementary school. Although Catholic leaders were working to obtain provincial funding until the end of high school, this goal did not become an issue until late in the campaign, when it was raised by Bob Nixon. Davis had no alternative, then, but to affirm his opposition, as he had on many occasions, to any further fragmentation of the public school system. The response of the majority of voters indicated that Nixon had made a serious political error in raising the funding issue. Despite the electoral success this slip gave him, Davis was upset by the religious divisions that resulted in the province. Interestingly enough, almost fourteen years later, and with my strong personal support, Davis agreed that the funding for the separate schools should be extended to the end of high school. It appeared to be a dramatic U-turn, and I shall return to this issue later (chapter 28).

On election day, October 21, the Conservatives won with seventy-eight seats, followed by the Liberals with twenty and the NDP with nineteen. Now that the Conservative Party had a large majority in the Ontario Legislature, the media became even more aggressive and hostile in its attacks on the government. A vigilant media is a necessity in any democracy, but on many occasions I thought that the criticism was excessive and unfair. I agreed, however, that one area of public life – political fundraising – required urgent reform. Until 1971, there was no statutory requirement for the public disclosure of political donations.

Suspicion abounded that lucrative government contracts were granted in exchange for generous political contributions. Without doubt, this system had been well entrenched in the political culture of Canada for a very long time.

In the early years of the Davis premiership, there were two major controversies related to political contributions. In the first, it was revealed that the successful bidder for constructing a new Workmen's Compensation Board building in Toronto had made a generous contribution to the Progressive Conservative Party of Ontario. In the second, the new headquarters for Ontario Hydro in Toronto, the contract went to Gerhard Moog, one of Davis's personal friends. With allegations of favouritism swirling around him, Davis established a committee of the Ontario Legislature to conduct a public inquiry into the Hydro building. In due time the committee issued a unanimous report that exonerated Davis from having any influence in awarding the contract and found that the province had obtained very good value in this deal. In fact, Moog later sued the provincial government, claiming that he was entitled to additional compensation.

The damage had been done, however, and the fallout, I believe, contributed significantly to the loss of four by-elections in March 1973 – including my own attempt to be elected to the Legislature. As a result I became determined to push for election expenses legislation that would require the public disclosure of every contribution over one hundred dollars. Such disclosure was obviously necessary to strengthen the perception of the integrity of the political process.

* * *

In January 1972 I became involved in a judicial inquiry that was the product of Cold War politics, though in the Canadian context. It was established by the Ontario government after an unfortunate public disturbance to protest a dinner hosted by the federal government in honour of Premier Alexei Kosygin from the Soviet Union. The dinner, scheduled to take place at the Toronto Science Centre on October 25, 1971, outraged several Eastern European communities in Metropolitan Toronto and throughout Ontario. They had good reason to despise the Soviet Union for its brutal occupation of their homelands.

The key organizers came from the Canadian Ukrainian community – an important and respected part of the Canadian fabric. In arranging to hold the dinner in Toronto, the organizers demonstrated a curious insensitivity. It should have been in Ottawa, where the provocation would be less apparent. Despite warnings that huge numbers of protesters would surround the Science Centre, the federal government blundered ahead and all hell broke loose.

One of the most effective strategies in crowd control is the use of mounted police, particularly when there is potential for a major disturbance. As thousands of people gathered outside the Science Centre the day of the Kosygin dinner, they were joined by several hundred police officers, including a number on horseback. The federal government had designated the Kosygin visit a "high-risk event," and the Metropolitan Toronto Police Department had been requested to provide maximum security for his visit. When the dinner was about to begin, several senior police officers on the scene decided that the crowd intended to "storm" the building. What happened next became the subject of a great deal of conflicting testimony. The mounted unit had charged into, knocked over, trampled, and indiscriminately struck at the demonstrators with their batons, some protestors alleged, and the police had brutally treated many of those who were arrested. The confrontation was reported dramatically by the media. The *Toronto Star*, for example, headlined its account "Police on horses charge crowd 4 times."

A specially created Canadian Ukrainian committee obtained scores of affidavits describing the event, and more than a hundred of them were included in a brief submitted to the Ontario solicitor general. At that point the government announced the public inquiry, which followed several months later. Judge Anthony Vannini of Sault Ste Marie was appointed as commissioner, and I was retained by the Metropolitan Toronto Police Department to represent the police force.

Everyone agreed that a major disturbance had taken place in the immediate vicinity of the Science Centre and that it lasted for approximately half an hour. Nevertheless, the testimony included 214 witnesses over seven weeks of hearings. Many of the protesters described the mounted police riding recklessly into the crowd, trampling several people under foot, even though no evidence was presented of any significant injuries. Members of the mounted police unit testified in turn that any reckless movement of the horses was extremely limited and occurred only after the horses were jabbed with umbrellas and other sharp instruments. Under questioning by counsel, many of the demonstrators who had prepared affidavits or given accounts to the media conceded that parts of their descriptions were exaggerated and some, in fact, were retracted. A few of the witnesses even apologized to Judge Vannini about the statements they had made.

Judge Vannini concluded that the Metropolitan Toronto Police had not interfered with the rights of the public to protest, though he did find that senior members of the force should have worked in closer cooperation with the leaders of the Ukrainian Canadian community before and during the demonstration. Although he said some police officers had made errors in judgment, most of them had acted in good faith when faced with considerable provocation amid a "dangerous situation." He complimented his counsel, William J. Smith, for the "extremely thorough, completely impartial and most orderly presentation of the evidence … ably assisted in part in a most exemplary manner by M. John Laskin" – who later became a colleague of mine on the Ontario Court of Appeal. I was pleased that he concluded: "The evidence so adduced was in turn further elucidated and tested by able and responsible counsel in the person of Mr. R. Roy McMurtry Q.C. and Mr. R.J. Carter [counsel for the Ukrainian Canadian committee] who did so without emotion or rancour. From the outset, the conduct of all counsel established a seriousness of attitude and a sincerity of purpose that continued throughout the hearings."

In retrospect, I believe that inquiries should be regarded as a last resort in those circumstances where the controversy or disagreement is between members of a respected community and a respected police department. Mediation would have been a better approach, where a rational, non-confrontational dialogue could settle most of the issues and misunderstandings in a context of mutual respect. In that scenario, the end result would most likely have been apologies on both sides and a resolve to improve police communications and crowd control.

11

The By-election, Community Service, and the Law

Towards the end of 1972 Bill Davis asked me to consider running for the Progressive Conservative nomination in the St George by-election, which would likely be held in the late winter of 1973. His request presented a significant personal dilemma. I had become interested in the process for developing public policy in Ontario and was also serving as the president of my local ratepayers association. I thoroughly enjoyed the human dynamic of people working together to protect their neighbourhoods from excessive high-rise development and other problems. Certainly the opportunity to serve a broader public in the Ontario Legislature had a great deal of personal appeal.

At the same time, I harboured major concerns related to my law practice and the support of my family. If I were elected to the legislature, my practice would obviously suffer, and an appointment to the Cabinet would require me to leave my legal career. The financial realities were anything but encouraging, but I did hold strong views about the value of public service. I was, moreover, enjoying working with Davis, and the opportunity to serve with him in the Legislature might not necessarily arise in the future.

Allan Lawrence had held the St George seat since 1958, and it was generally assumed that it would be retained by a Conservative candidate. However, by-elections are traditionally challenging for any ruling political party because they allow the electorate to express disapproval of the government's performance without bringing about an actual change in administration. Furthermore, the political controversies over the contracts for the building of the Hydro and the Workmen's Compensation Board buildings were still creating waves for the Davis government. There was also the reality that any political party that had been in government for thirty consecutive years would face considerable voter opposition for that fact alone.

I was also not surprised to learn that there would be a degree of resentment if a personal friend of the premier were "parachuted" into the riding – and I did not live in the constituency of St George. Nevertheless, the majority of the executive of the constituency association urged me to be a candidate for the nomination – and I agreed. Two other long-time residents in the riding, friends of mine who were also active in the party, also expressed interest. Cren Price was a former St George riding president, a lawyer, and, like me, a graduate of St Andrew's College. He stood as a candidate for the nomination together with Jim Sintzell, another prominent lawyer. They were both personable and intelligent people who would be effective candidates.

When I announced my decision, I knew that the campaign for the nomination would be challenging. In addition, all three of us were well served by our campaign teams. Fortunately, Lawrence's 1971 campaign chairman, David Cowper, and his campaign manager, David McFadden, both agreed to serve in those same capacities on my campaign team. The principal goal for any candidate in a nomination contest is to sell the greatest number of new constituency memberships and to ensure that those members actually attend and vote at the nomination meeting. As a general rule, a candidate is doing well if 50 per cent of these new members actually show up to vote.

The by-election had been called for March 15, 1973, and the Progressive Conservative nomination meeting was scheduled for February 15. The dimensions of my challenge to become the provincial member for St George dramatically increased in mid-January when it was announced that Judge Margaret Campbell would be the candidate for the Liberal Party. She was a member of the provincial family court and had long been a popular member of Toronto City Council. She had also been a strong candidate to become the first female mayor of the City of Toronto. Curiously, she had previously been a member of the Ontario Progressive Conservative Party for many years, but resigned over what she believed was unfair treatment of the family court by the Ministry of the Attorney General. When she announced her candidacy in St George, she had to resign her seat on the family court. I later learned that she had been assured that, if she was unsuccessful in the by-election, she would be appointed a member of the county court by the federal Liberal government. Given that I was relatively unknown outside the legal profession, I realized that Campbell would be the favourite to win the by-election. I remember joking with my opponents for the Conservative nomination that we were in a contest to determine who would be "the first mate on the *Titanic*."

Nevertheless, the competition for the Conservative nomination continued to be strongly contested, with the result that, on February 15, approximately 3500 people showed up for the meeting at St Lawrence Hall. That was an extraordinarily large number of people for a provincial nomination, because all eligible voters had to live in the St George constituency. Many federal constituencies, in contrast, did not have this residency requirement, and voters at nomination meetings could be "bussed in" by the thousands. My nominator at the meeting was Lillian Roberts, the widow of Kelso Roberts, a former provincial attorney general. The Roberts family had been friends for many years. I had been her son Frank's football coach at Upper Canada College, and he later served as a Superior Court judge during my tenure as chief justice of Ontario.

I won the nomination on the first ballot, and as I woke early the next morning, I truly wondered what I had got myself into the previous night. My first commitment that day was to attend the funeral of my Liberal Party friend "Windy" O'Neill – the man with the infamous voting machines when Bill Davis won the leadership at the Ontario Progressive Conservative convention.

Even though I was heavily favoured to lose the St George by-election, the campaign proved to be an exhilarating experience. I have always enjoyed meeting people, and a political campaign provides a unique human experience for any candidate. To encounter men and women from all walks of life provides a varied daily adventure. At the same time, I had to develop a thick skin. Many people are not necessarily pleased to encounter a particular candidate, or indeed any candidate for political office.

In every campaign, the morale of the candidate depends to a large extent on the quality of the campaign team. In this respect I was very fortunate because many people rallied to the cause. Terry Clark, a former football and hockey opponent at Lakefield School from my boarding-school days, volunteered to accompany me every day from early mornings to late at night, beginning at the bus stops and subway stations and then knocking on doors. He had a tremendous sense of humour and felt comfortable talking to total strangers. The St George by-election was a winter campaign, and many people did not want to stop or even exchange a few words as they marched, grimly, to their daily employment. Many mornings, however, Terry loudly announced that we were conducting a contest for the most interesting headwear – which generally produced a chuckle from even the most stern-faced pedestrians.

My experience during the campaign was that people were mostly polite, even if not particularly receptive to my political chatter. Occasionally my approach would provoke an outburst as to why I would never receive their support – to which I responded that, obviously, they were still undecided. Although this comment often produced an even stronger denunciation of my candidacy or the political party I represented, I always tried to avoid a rude response.

My morale was somewhat bruised when, less than three weeks before election day, my good friend and Ontario campaign chair Norman Atkins advised me that a party poll had found that voter support for Margaret Campbell was more than three times greater than for me. I did not share this news with my team, and I determined that my personal efforts would continue at the maximum level. Although my prospects of winning appeared hopeless, I did not want any of my supporters to believe that I had given less than a 100 per cent effort. The by-election result actually turned out to be far closer than the earlier political poll had predicted: on election day, Campbell's victory margin was approximately sixteen hundred votes. I was very proud of my campaign team's work and felt that we had fought a good fight.

After the ballots had been counted, Ria and I, accompanied by our daughter Janet, proceeded to the Campbell campaign headquarters to congratulate the winner and her supporters. I also had the opportunity to make some complimentary comments about her to members of the media – and was rewarded by being described as "a very gracious loser" in reports the following day.

The election night party is an established tradition in most campaigns – a celebration or a lively wake, depending on the result. In my case a party had been arranged at the Cariboo Club on Church Street, a location usually frequented by transplanted Newfoundlanders. My friend Sam Sniderman (Sam the Record Man) provided the food, and there was no shortage of good eats or alcohol. A casual visitor might well have thought that our party was a victory celebration. It was an exuberant event in the best traditions of an Irish wake, a celebration of a campaign well fought. Premier Bill Davis attended along with Allan Lawrence, and they made the usual flattering comments about the candidate.

Many of my supporters, some no doubt fuelled by the alcohol on tap, were extravagant in praise throughout the evening. This enthusiasm was clearly enjoyed by Janet, who commented as we drove home, "Dad, those people at the Cariboo Club really think a lot of you." After a few moments of reflection, however, she continued. "I have never seen such a bunch of drunks in my whole life." Although unfair to most of my supporters, this comment led Terry Clark to suggest it jokingly as a suitable epitaph for the St George by-election campaign.

Despite my loss, I felt very positive about the campaign. Altogether, it had been a special adventure. At the same time, I was looking forward to returning to my law practice and continuing to be involved with Bill Davis as a member of his kitchen cabinet in developing government policy. My law partners Philip Benson, Barry Percival, and Barry Brown had been supportive of my venture into elective politics, and I was confident that our continuing association would be productive and enjoyable.

* * *

The by-election experience raised my public profile, and in the months following, I was pressured by several worthy organizations to donate more time to community service. Eventually I agreed to take over the presidency of the Big Brothers of Metropolitan Toronto, was appointed chair of the Ontario Multicultural Arts Society, and became a member of the Metropolitan Toronto Housing Commission – the coordinating body for building publicly owned residences. I also agreed to write a weekly column for the Toronto *Sunday Sun*.

My role with Big Brothers and my newspaper column both came as a result of my friendship with Douglas Creighton, the founder and publisher of the *Toronto Sun*. I had met him many years earlier when he covered the Magistrates' Courts for the *Toronto Telegram* and I was an active litigator in those courts. He rose quickly through the ranks of the *Telegram* and had become managing editor when its owner, John Bassett, folded the newspaper in 1971. The creation of the *Sun* in the wake of the *Telegram*'s demise quickly became one of Canada's great newspaper success stories. As all Creighton's legion of friends would testify, he was clearly an exceptional person. His enormous energy and success did not appear to be adversely affected by his three-martini lunches in his earlier years.

Creighton had been president of the Big Brothers of Metropolitan Toronto. When he brought me aboard, the agency was facing a strike by its seven social workers, who had been certified as a bargaining unit under the Ontario labour law. The older members of the board had become quite intransigent in their opposition to negotiating with a union: in their view, an agency that was almost entirely dependent on volunteers should not have a union within its ranks. This position was unreasonable, and Creighton hoped that someone from outside the board could bring a more objective approach to resolving the controversy.

I had long been an admirer of the work done by the Big Brothers organization and agreed to become involved. By the time I attended my first board meeting, the dispute with the social workers' bargaining unit had escalated considerably. The Toronto Labour Council had become aggressive in its support of the striking staff members. The Big Brothers depended on the United Way for its core funding, and the Labour Council threatened to boycott the United Way if it did not assert pressure on the agency to settle with the social workers. This threat was serious because trade-union support was important to the United Way.

Both the Big Brothers and the bargaining unit were represented by legal counsel, and I came to believe that a growing animosity between the legal teams was increasing the bitterness of the dispute. At this time the battle lines between management and labour lawyers were clearly apparent – to the point where it was unusual for a lawyer who had acted for a union to be retained by management, and vice versa. Fortunately, in recent years this divide between management and labour lawyers has lessened considerably and a more collegial relationship has developed. The importance of effective mediation techniques is now more recognized, particularly when a broader public interest is involved.

While I was struggling to find a resolution to the dispute, I received a call from Stephen Lewis, the leader of the Ontario New Democratic Party. He was clearly upset with the threatened boycott of the United Way by the Toronto Labour Council and concerned that undermining its financial resources would hurt the infrastructure of almost all the Metropolitan Toronto social services. The situation was "getting out of hand," he said, and he suggested that we meet to try to resolve the dispute. I immediately agreed. We met the next day, without any of the lawyers. We worked out a settlement, which was accepted by both sides to the dispute, and I remained as president until the election of September 1975. I had known Lewis only casually up to that point, but our resolution of the Big Brothers' dispute led to a friendship I have always treasured. His work internationally, particularly the struggle against the AIDS pandemic in Africa, has made him a highly respected figure around the world.

* * *

My friendship with Doug Creighton also led to another interesting adventure when he challenged me to write a weekly column for the Toronto *Sunday Sun*. The challenge came about unexpectedly as a result of one of our regular lunches. As a member of Davis's kitchen cabinet, I had become an advocate for his administration – and that included complaining to Creighton when I felt his newspaper was being unfair to the government.

During one lunch in 1973 I spoke of the partisanship of two of his major political columnists – True Davidson, a former mayor of East York, was closely associated with the Ontario Liberal Party, and Dr Morton Shulman had been an NDP member in the Ontario Legislature. The *Toronto Sun* at that time was essentially a "small C" conservative newspaper but willing to provide space for a variety of political views. Its editorial board, however, was generally unsympathetic to the "Red Tory" wing of the Davis government – those left of the political centre on social policies – and I was clearly on this side of the Progressive Conservative Party of Ontario.

In any event, towards the end of our customary high-spirited luncheon, Creighton proposed that I write a weekly column if I thought it would provide a better political balance for his newspaper. I'm not certain that he actually expected me to accept his challenge, considering the many demands on my time. However, fortified by his hospitality, I agreed to his proposal and, for the next two years, wrote a weekly Sunday column. My salary was a very modest $75 per column, but I never missed a deadline. I could write about any subject I chose, though for the most part my contributions were expected to be on legal or political themes. Deciding on the actual topic could be quite distracting, occasionally even interfering with my concentration during the course of a trial. This experience greatly increased my respect for newspaper columnists, particularly those required to produce several articles a week.

I was gratified by the fact that surveys always revealed a high level of readership for my efforts.

* * *

During this time the *Globe and Mail* was investigating allegations of brutality against members of the Metropolitan Toronto Police Department. In the spring of 1974 it published a series of front-page articles describing serious misconduct by some police officers. Most of the stories related to assaults on accused persons in custody or other individuals suspected of crime. The journalists involved in the investigation were aware that the individuals making the allegations were generally unsavoury types, people quite capable of making false allegations. Each of the purported victims of the police brutality was therefore asked to take a lie-detector test, and their allegations were published only if they had "passed." As a result of this sensational investigative journalism, there were widespread public demands for a judicial inquiry. The nature and extent of the allegations went far beyond the capacity of the governing Board of Police Commissioners to examine in a credible manner.

The Ontario government appointed Justice Donald Morand of the province's Supreme Court to conduct an inquiry into the matter – the Royal Commission into Metropolitan Toronto Police Practices. He chose as his counsel Earl Cherniak, a respected lawyer from London, Ontario, who in turn was ably assisted by Robert Armstrong of Toronto as associate counsel. Armstrong later became the treasurer (chair) of the Law Society of Upper Canada and a valued colleague on the Court of Appeal for Ontario.

Chief Harold Adamson of the Metro Police Department asked me to represent his force at the inquiry. This assignment would include representing the senior officer command team as well as the individual police officers who were the targets of the brutality allegations. At the same time, each of the policemen would have the option of being represented separately. Only a few officers made this choice, so, in practical terms, I represented almost every police officer whose evidence was deemed relevant to the Morand inquiry.

Adamson was a respected police chief – a "policeman's policeman" who had held all the tough jobs on the way to the Office of the Chief. He was fiercely loyal to the members of his force, but in no way tolerant of police officers who had "crossed the line." He often described police corruption as a form of rot that would quickly spread if it was not aggressively removed. On more than one occasion he told me that, although he was always upset by unfair criticism of his department, he was equally concerned by the sometimes blind faith of the public in the police. As an institution, the police are usually on the front line in protecting the public, and Adamson believed strongly in the principle of public accountability. His internal affairs unit was unrelenting in maintaining this accountability when there was any evidence of possible police corruption, and its activities sometimes brought it into conflict with the police union.

In recent years, relations between Toronto police chiefs and the Police Association have generally been tense at best and, at worst, distressingly confrontational. During Adamson's leadership, though there were occasional strained relations with the association, he generally enjoyed the respect and the admiration of his officers.

Shortly after being retained by Chief Adamson, I was invited to address a general meeting of the Police Association. We had a positive dialogue, and I believe I enjoyed the association's confidence throughout the many months that I participated in the Morand inquiry. Adamson assigned Staff Inspector Frank Barbetta to be my chief liaison officer with the police department – just as he had earlier during the Vannini inquiry into the performance of the Metropolitan Toronto Police Mounted Unit at the Ontario Science Centre. He was an effective comrade in arms, highly intelligent, personable, and hugely respected by his fellow police officers. This respect was invaluable to me because it ensured the cooperation of individual officers.

The Morand inquiry considered twenty-eight serious allegations of police brutality in all. In effect, each incident became the subject of an individual trial within the inquiry. As each of the purported victims had allegedly passed a lie-detector test conducted by an expert retained by the *Globe and Mail*, the reliability of these tests in general also became a focus of the inquiry. Justice Morand was from Windsor, Ontario, and had been appointed to the High Court of Ontario at the relatively young age of forty-one. He enjoyed a reputation as a fair, conscientious, and likeable jurist. At a time when the judicial landscape was still populated by more than a few ill-tempered judges, lawyers welcomed having their cases tried by Morand. Having him as the commissioner for an inquiry that was expected to last at least a year was indeed a bonus for all counsel involved.

I had not known lead counsel Earl Cherniak well before the inquiry. He enjoyed a solid reputation as an effective trial and appellate counsel, and in the years that followed, came to be regarded as one of Canada's most accomplished advocates. He and associate counsel Robert Armstrong were ably assisted by Barbara Betcherman, a law student who later gave up the law to write novels in Mexico and was tragically killed in an automobile accident there a few years later. They were a formidable team, and I expected the inquiry to be a highly adversarial process. I was not disappointed. An adversarial relationship soon developed between Earl Cherniak and me. Our examinations and cross-examinations of the majority of the witnesses can only be described as aggressive, if not competitive. The stakes were high, given the seriousness of the allegations against a major Canadian police force. Although Cherniak and I battled vigorously, by the end of the inquest we had become good friends.

I have always assumed that the major challenge facing counsel for Commissioner Morand was to persuade the complainants not to exaggerate their evidence. Most of those witnesses had previously been known to the police, and given their individual hostility to police in general, they would have been tempted to exaggerate their complaints. And that is what happened with many of them as their evidence opened rich avenues for productive cross-examinations. In describing incidents of physical abuse by police officers, for example, many witnesses alleged extensive beatings, yet their complaints were not corroborated by the medical evidence they introduced. Throughout the proceedings I often thought of the trial lawyer's traditional prayer, "I think I can deal effectively with my opponent's witnesses, but God protect me from my own."

We spent several weeks considering the evidence related to lie-detector, or polygraph, testing, and a number of experts testified on both sides of the issue. Justice Morand had to determine whether the evidence of the individual polygraph test should be heard and, if so, what weight should be attached to the tests. At the time, the major decision in Canada on the polygraph was the criminal case of *R. v. Phillion*, where Madam Justice Van Camp of the Ontario Supreme Court had refused to admit direct evidence of a polygraph test, and her decision was later upheld by the Court of Appeal. In the United States the reception of polygraph tests in evidence by trial courts was quite uneven, with some courts allowing the evidence to be introduced and others disallowing it. Commissioner Morand decided to hear the evidence of the polygraph tests, together with other evidence to determine the reliability of such tests. Never before in Canada had there been a comprehensive judicial examination of the scientific premises related to these tests.

The standard "field polygraph" is an instrument designed to monitor physiological reactions in the person taking the test, responses such as breathing patterns, blood pressure, and sweating through the skin. The machine does not measure "lying" as such but indicates variations in physiological reactions that are in theory not subject to the control of the person being tested. A number of individuals who had been recognized as experts in the United States testified before Morand. They all agreed that no single physiological response could be indicative of lying and, furthermore, that responses associated with lying might also derive from other causes. In general, the psychiatrists and physiologists who testified were critical of the reliability of the polygraph machine, explaining that any attempt to program human responses is, at best, an imperfect science.

Eventually, Justice Morand concluded that the interpretation of any individual's responses to a test on a polygraph machine was highly subjective, and as a result, the same responses could be interpreted differently, depending on the person conducting the test. "The polygraph machine is clearly crude and its operators unsophisticated in using it as a scientific instrument," he wrote. "All the test amounts to is a subjective interpretation of behaviour and conduct." He also expressed concern about the use of the polygraph in employment screening and periodic employee testing and wrote of the "dangers and abuses implicit in denying a person the right to earn a living on the basis of this test."

After hearing all this evidence, I came to share these same conclusions. To jump ahead here and complete this part of the story, when Morand released his report late in 1975, he dismissed many exaggerated allegations, but did find some instances of police brutality and of officers giving false testimony under oath. Adamson welcomed the recommendations for expanded police accountability and a more diverse police department to better reflect the growing pluralism of Metropolitan Toronto. I, in turn, after being appointed attorney general, was able to persuade my labour minister colleague to amend the *Employment Standards Act* to prohibit the use of the polygraph in the employment area.

* * *

During the late spring of 1975 I agreed to take part in another legal drama that was unfolding in London, England, where Toronto lawyer George Duchart had been charged with conspiracy to commit murder. I had known him for a few years, though he was not a particular friend.

His partner John Hamilton, later to be a Superior Court judge, had been a long-time friend, however, and he was anxious to have several Toronto lawyers, including me, called as character witnesses as part of the defence. Duchart enjoyed a positive reputation as a successful criminal defence lawyer. The events that led to the murder conspiracy charge were highly unusual and somewhat bizarre, and they came as a huge surprise to his legal colleagues.

One of Duchart's criminal law clients had a brother who was facing major fraud charges in England and was incarcerated in London's Brixton Prison. This client asked Duchart early in 1975 to visit his accused brother while he was on a holiday in London and to check on the legal representation he was receiving from his solicitors there. When Duchart made this visit, he was granted the same privileges as an English solicitor – including the right to a private consultation without the presence of a custodial officer. Duchart apparently became very interested in the details of the case and returned to Brixton for another visit or two before he returned to Canada. The case was generally referred to later as the Barclays Bank fraud.

During each of his visits to Brixton, the incarcerated brother asked Duchart to deliver information, including the names and addresses of certain individuals, to his friend "Charles." Duchart knew that Charles also visited the accused at Brixton, so he should have been suspicious why the message was not passed on directly to Charles. As events later revealed, the information he was communicating was the location of several key prosecution witnesses – details that would undoubtedly have been noted by the custodial officer during Charles's visits.

Shortly after George Duchart returned to Canada, Charles was apprehended while on the premises of one of these prosecution witnesses. At the time of his arrest he was armed with an axe, and it was alleged that he intended to murder the witness. A day or two later Duchart received a phone call from Charles, who advised him that a major development had occurred in the Barclays Bank fraud case and requested that he return to London immediately. What Charles did not tell Duchart was that he was placing the call from a police station at the request of Scotland Yard detectives.

Duchart agreed to return to London. He later related that he was initially "flattered" by the fact that the immigration officer he encountered at Heathrow Airport appeared to recognize him. "Welcome back to London, Mr. Duchart," he said as he ushered him quickly through immigration and "directly into the arms of Scotland Yard." Duchart was denied bail when he appeared in court and remained a guest of Her Majesty's government for several months before his trial commenced in the number one courtroom at the Old Bailey.

The London solicitor who represented Duchart later learned that one factor that influenced Scotland Yard to arrest him was erroneous information obtained from unidentified police circles in Canada – information that Duchart was involved in "organized crime" in Canada. Before I was prepared to agree to give "good character" evidence at Duchart's criminal trial in London, I asked my Metro Toronto Police clients to advise me whether there was any information in Canadian police circles that would indicate the possibility that Duchart might be involved in any criminal activity. I certainly did not want to embarrass myself with my client the Metropolitan Toronto Police Department. Chief Adamson's office made the appropriate inquiries to both the RCMP and the Ontario Provincial Police. Fortunately there was no such evidence, though Duchart did have a reputation for recklessness related to his occasional socializing with "clients" in his criminal law practice. Certainly in this case he had demonstrated terrible judgment.

There were some disturbing aspects of the prosecutor's case against Duchart. When he was arrested, the police seized notes he had made during his interview with his client's brother in Brixton Prison. These notes included requests to obtain certain fabricated documents in Canada that could assist in the defence of the fraud charges. Duchart later testified at his trial that, although it was his practice to record everything a client stated to him, he had no intention of obtaining false documents in Canada. In any event, the notes were filed as exhibits as part of the prosecution's case. In English courts, exhibits are generally separated into separate packages known as "bundles." Duchart's notes formed "bundle B" at his trial, and he was aggressively cross-examined about them when he testified. He made an effective witness, and judging by the body language of the jurors and the relatively supportive comments of the trial judge, he had done well in his testimony.

The last three witnesses called as part of the defence were asked to testify about his reputation in Ontario as a person of good character. Along with me, they were David Humphrey, later a judge of the Ontario Superior Court of Justice, and Arthur Maloney, Ontario's first ombudsman elect. The lead barrister for the prosecution was a very experienced counsel named Worsley, a "treasury counsel," as members of the private bar were called in the years before England and Wales adopted the Canadian model of a full-time Crown prosecutorial service. It had long been believed there that this process maintained the appropriate level of independence by prosecutors from the police and a more objective view of the merits of the specific prosecution.

In our view, Worsley's belief in his case against Duchart had already become "shaky" by the time we were scheduled to testify. I followed Humphrey on the stand, and Maloney was the last defence witness. Obviously Worsley was saving his major fire for Maloney. Towards the end of his examination, the prosecutor got into this exchange with his witness:

Worsley: Mr. Maloney, surely the members of the jury should not be surprised by your evidence and that of Mr. Humphrey and Mr. McMurtry in support of George Duchart because you are all his friends. What else would we expect to hear from witnesses who have travelled from Canada to assist a friend?
Maloney: That is exactly the point, Mr. Worsley. We all really know George Duchart. We know him professionally, we know him socially and we know his reputation in the community. This is why we have such an enormous advantage over you. We know George Duchart as a whole person. All you know about him is bundle "B."

At this point, many of the jurors smiled or chuckled quietly. The trial judge's final instructions to the jury were sympathetic to George Duchart, and his subsequent acquittal came as no surprise to anyone in the courtroom.

About a year later, Justice Donald Morand visited London to meet with senior police officials and others to assist him in the preparation of his recommendations, which would be an important part of his inquiry report into the allegations against the Metropolitan Toronto Police Department. During his visit, he met the High Court judge who had presided over the Duchart trial. I was most interested to hear from Morand later that the judge expressed his personal opinion that the "only conspiracy in the case was one carried out by Scotland Yard in order to wrongfully convict George Duchart."

A sad sequel to the Duchart trial was that, almost exactly two years after his acquittal, he was killed when his motorcycle slid off a road in Nova Scotia and collided with a tree. He was only thirty-nine years old.

* * *

As Arthur Maloney and I travelled back to Canada after the Duchart trial, we had a long conversation about my continuing involvement in politics. I explained to Maloney that although I remained an enthusiastic supporter, admirer, and friend of Premier Bill Davis, it was impractical for me to consider being a candidate in the forthcoming election. Our two oldest children, Janet and Jim, were entering independent schools – Janet for grade 13 at the Canadian Junior College in Lausanne, and Jim at my old school, St Andrew's College. That would cost money. Furthermore, the Morand inquiry would continue for some weeks after Labour Day, and I had a professional obligation to continue representing the Metropolitan Toronto Police Department. I had therefore advised the executive of the St George Riding Association that I would not seek the nomination to be their candidate in the next provincial election, expected in the autumn of 1975. I did, however, continue in my role as legal counsel to the Progressive Conservative Party of Ontario and usually attended the kitchen cabinet meetings (chapter 10).

Several weeks later, Davis called a provincial election for September 18, 1975. Shortly after, Leonard Reilly, the longtime MPP for the riding of Eglinton, where we lived, advised Davis that he would not be a candidate for re-election. His wife had cancer, and he wanted to spend more time with her. He suggested that I would be an effective candidate to replace him. As a result, a small delegation led by Hugh Macaulay, a close friend of Davis and important member of the Ontario Conservatives' "Big Blue Machine," arrived at my office to persuade me to stand as the Progressive Conservative candidate in Eglinton. Reilly would nominate me, they said, and the nomination would probably be unopposed. I declined, citing my personal problems in contesting the election and expressing the hope that my decision would be understood and accepted.

Macaulay responded by reminding me of a small private luncheon with Bill Davis I had attended the previous November. The event had been organized by two of the premier's closest friends and political allies, and much to my surprise, indeed shock, we learned that the purpose of the lunch was to persuade Davis to retire – for his own interest and his family's. Davis had been taking a fierce battering by the media but, in my opinion, most of the criticism was unfair and largely the product of his majority win in the 1971 election, even though the party at that time had been in government for twenty-eight consecutive years. Many journalists took the view that this period in office was too long for any political party – and they attacked the premier relentlessly and often personally. On one occasion John Robarts confided that the culture of negative political media coverage was increasing with every passing year and it was much tougher for Davis than it had been during his own years as premier. Yet, although I spent a great deal of time with Davis as legal counsel to the party, I had never heard him complain about the negative media coverage. In fact, the only comment he made in that context was to remark that "on some days this job is more fun than on others."

I realized that Davis's friends who were urging him to retire were motivated by their concern for his personal well-being, not the political future of the Progressive Conservative Party, but my immediate response was to state that the suggestion was totally unacceptable, given the trust that so many people had placed in the premier. I recognized that the next election would be a challenge for our party and we could well lose, I continued with some emotion, but, "if we lost, at least we would go down with our guns blazing." My reaction apparently had some influence. So far as I know, the subject of Davis retiring did not come up again for another ten years – and then only after the premier himself announced his decision.

Macaulay, having reminded me of that luncheon, repeated my exact words back to me. Then, he continued: "Now that we are facing a tough political battle, you want to stay on the sidelines." And so I somewhat reluctantly agreed to stand for nomination in the Eglinton constituency. Before my decision was formally communicated, however, I approached Commissioner Morand and his counsel to explore the possibility of delaying the continuation of his inquiry until after the September 18 election. Morand was agreeable, and I assumed that I would be able to continue to represent the Metro Toronto Police even if I was elected to the provincial legislative. Although Davis had indicated that I was a serious candidate for a Cabinet position, I fully expected I would have to spend some time as a backbencher in the legislature and, as such, I would continue my role in the Morand inquiry.

I was nominated as the Progressive Conservative Party candidate only four weeks before the election. We quickly assembled a strong team: Toronto lawyer David McFadden, who had been my campaign manager in the 1973 St George by-election, agreed to play the same role in the Eglinton riding, as did Rodney Hull, another Toronto lawyer, as fundraising chairman. Although the provincial Liberal Party had strong traditional political support in Eglinton, I was elected by a comfortable margin to the provincial Legislature.

I believe that my volunteer community service and a high public profile since the St George by-election were relevant factors in my victory. However, most important was my campaign organization, which included a large number of volunteer canvassers. As I learned in the 1973 by-election, a political campaign at the constituency level is a unique human adventure. The candidate must genuinely enjoy meeting strangers, put in long hours to motivate the team, and also possess a thick skin.

As things turned out, I did not to return to the Morand inquiry. My legal career suddenly went on hold, and I embarked on an exciting and very full public life for well over a decade.

PART THREE

Attorney General of Ontario

12

Stepping into the Attorney General's Role

On September 18, 1975, the Progressive Conservative government was returned to power in Ontario, but with a minority government of just 51 seats. The New Democratic Party led by Stephen Lewis became the official opposition, with the Liberal Party under Robert Nixon close behind in third place. Between them, however, they had 74 seats. It was the first minority government in Ontario for many years, and we didn't know how it would all work out. Obviously our government could no longer control the legislative agenda or the timing of the next election. Unless we could get the cooperation and support of the other two parties, our term in office might be only a few short months.

I was surprised but pleased when, a few days after the election, Premier Davis offered me a Cabinet post as attorney general. I had fully expected that, if I did win in Eglinton, I would as a new MPP first spend many months as a backbencher. But in making his top Cabinet appointments, Davis was primarily concerned with getting the right person (in his opinion) for the job, along with regional and cultural considerations, and he thought I had sufficient experience. I was, after all, no stranger to the world of politics. As a member of his kitchen cabinet for the previous four years, I had met weekly with Davis and his closest associates and helped to formulate government policy and strategy. Moreover, my duties as legal counsel to the Conservative Party had taken me into the Legislature quite often. As someone trained as an advocate in the courts, I initially found this assembly somewhat of a "wild-west" debating society compared with the formal decorum of the courts. However, I soon came to the conclusion that aggressive heckling across the aisle was preferable to the violence that characterizes politics for most persons on our troubled planet. In fact, as I look back on my years in government, I think it would be difficult to find a better model of collegial, decent, and civil government than the Davis years – which, over his fourteen years as premier, included both majority and minority administrations. Some of the opposition MPPs from those days still refer to that period as the "golden age of government" in Ontario (chapter 27).

My immediate problem when Davis asked me to join his Cabinet was the Morand inquiry into allegations of police brutality. The commission still had several weeks to run, and Donald Morand had postponed its resumption after the summer break to accommodate my running in the election. Even if elected, I expected to continue representing the Metropolitan Toronto Police Department at the inquiry – but that would be impossible if I became a Cabinet minister. It was a real dilemma for me – Chief Harold Adamson was a close personal friend, and the police were under enormous pressure at the inquiry. Before I made my decision, Adamson and I talked it over, and he strongly encouraged me to accept. As attorney general, he advised, I could have a huge impact on law enforcement and the criminal justice system in Ontario. My law partner Barry Percival could easily take over from me, given the nature of the commission (chapter 11). With this advice from my client, I accepted the appointment as attorney general.

The office of the attorney general is a unique example of the English genius for developing eminently practical and exportable institutions that are then patched and altered to meet new conditions in new countries. The Cabinet minister holding this position has special responsibilities to the Crown, the courts, and the legislative and executive branches of government. In Canada, he or she is charged with administering an important department of government, formulating policy, and supervising the machinery of justice – and, as such, is accountable politically. It's not often you get that kind of opportunity, and I was eager to take it on. I was confident I could do the job, and based on my previous experience as a trial lawyer, there were already many priorities I wanted to address – family law reform, official bilingualism in the courts, legal aid clinics, alcohol abuse on the roads, race relations, and violence in hockey, to name but the most urgent. As a so-called Red Tory, I had long been committed to an activist social agenda, and now I was in the position to implement many of these ideas – at least in the short term.

I was still uncertain how long our minority government might last, and I was in a hurry to begin. I privately adopted the motto of the Metropolitan Police Homicide Squad, "We are here for a good time, not a long time." As things turned out, the New Democrats considered us more left of centre than the Liberals, and we remained in power, through another election in 1977, until we once again won a majority government in the 1981 election. I enjoyed many political discussions with David Peterson, who was also elected in 1975, and he agreed that the Liberal Party was clearly to the right of us on most issues. He profited mightily ten years later from the fact that, in terms of policy, the two parties had traded places, and when he was elected as premier, he moved his party firmly to the centre. In some respects my early initiatives proved to be more popular with the opposition parties than with many of my own Conservative colleagues. I believed, however, that an attorney general should generally avoid partisan politics, given his prime responsibility to support an independent and impartial administration of justice, and I was determined that my decisions would not be influenced by any desire to seek popularity within my own party.

The attorney general's responsibilities are legion – and diverse – and at any time I was acting on myriad fronts. The chapters that follow on this decade in my life will essentially be organized around related themes, and not necessarily chronology. On taking office, I spoke out frankly on a number of the issues I wanted to implement, and the media took notice. I later learned that my predecessors for many years had demonstrated a caution in their public statements and policy initiatives. Although the responsibilities of an attorney general have important quasi-judicial dimensions that require some restraint, I believed that an elected politician is not a judge and that there is a responsibility to encourage debate about important public issues.

In my first year as attorney general, two large-circulation national magazines – *Maclean's* and the *Canadian* magazine – wrote articles about me and featured my picture on their front covers. The title of the *Canadian* article, by Earl McRae, read "The Politics of Common Sense: Tilting Off in All Directions," with the subtitle, "Roy McMurtry – stubborn crusader for you and yours." The first paragraph began with a quote from Voltaire, "Common sense is not so common," and continued: "R. Roy McMurtry would like it known that he is not (a) the new Mussolini (b) the new stalker (c) cold blooded, cunning and calculating. Nor is he a menace to the orderly flow of orderly things. What he is, he insists, is a harbinger of horse sense." McRae then referred to some of priorities I have mentioned and was generous enough to describe me as the "social conscience of the government."

On rereading McRae's article many years later, I am actually surprised by the strong language I used to express my social concerns. There were altogether too many "god damns," too many instances where I sounded self-righteous. Even a year later I had learned to express myself in more moderate terms. This evolution is probably the experience of most persons in senior political office. Whether it is necessarily positive is open to debate, because people often criticize the lack of candour they detect in many politicians. In any event, it was not unreasonable for McRae in a generally positive article to describe the forty-three-year-old attorney general as "tilting off in all directions."

The cover story in *Maclean's* was written by Robert Miller and titled "Make Way for McMurtry: Politics Newest White Knight." The subtitle stated: "The self-making of a political superstar." Miller described my purported ability to "sniff out a political story" and characterized me as a "well-bred Irish tough." In his view, my opinions on a vast array of policy issues had probably made me more enemies in my own caucus than among the opposition, and NDP leader Stephen Lewis was quoted as stating, "I like him a lot as a politician. There is a directness and candour about him that I find refreshing." Claire Hoy, my chief newspaper critic in the *Toronto Sun*, was less impressed, and thereafter he nicknamed me "Roy McHeadline."

These two profiles marked the last time that my photograph occupied the front cover of a national magazine. Although my public comments in the ensuing years may have become more temperate, I did not abandon my candour – and that, inevitably, caused a few controversies. At the same time, I enjoyed serving as attorney general, supported by an accomplished team of advisers, and I had no desire to change my portfolio, even after I was given a second portfolio as solicitor general in 1978. If I had truly been interested in the party leadership, I would probably have asked to be switched to an economic portfolio – to demonstrate my ability on a second front. As things turned out, when I retired from politics in February 1985 I was still in the office of the attorney general.

* * *

I soon discovered that my new portfolio was a heavy one, with many responsibilities, and I was determined to be an active, hands-on kind

My grandparents William and Lillian McMurtry at home with their four
sons, 1904

My mother and father during their engagement, with William Mulock,
chief justice of Ontario

The four McMurtry brothers enjoy a game of rugby

In the course of a career that encompasses the political world and the social responsibilities of a public figure, Roy McMurtry has always distinguished himself by handling both facets with equal composure and compatibility.

Studies and sports shared his academic years in almost equal proportions; the one sharpening an already quick mind, the other instilling the sense of competitiveness and teamwork that stand him in such good stead as Attorney General for Ontario.

In my Varsity Blues uniform

With Al Haig, as co-captains of the Varsity Blues, University of Toronto, 1953

With my friend and mentor, Arthur Maloney

Dennis O'Connor and I with our client Peter Colin-Jones

My daughter Janet at the launch of the *Ria Jean McMurtry*, Dundee,
Scotland, 1972

With Bill Davis at his cottage on Georgian Bay, July 1971

With my daughters Jeannie and Erin when I was nominated as the PC
candidate for the St George by-election, 1973

My children during one of our summer vacations at the cottage

With my son Michael the day I became attorney general of Ontario, 1975

A vigorous debate in the Ontario Legislature

Metro Morning Newsmaker of the Year, 1976

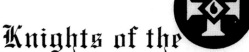

Knights of the Ku Klux Klan

Publishing Offices · Box 624 Metairie, LA 70004 · (504) 837-6528

THE HON. ROY McMURTRY
ATTORNEY GENERAL
PROVINCE OF ONTARIO

MR. McMURTRY:

This letter is in protest against your anti-White policies, which have been in direct opposition to the interests of the White Canadian population and indeed the White population of the North American continent.

Specifically, you have sought to destroy the sacred right of freedom of speech for White Canadians. Secondly, you have instructed your subordinates to apply the law unequally to White youths involved in racial incidents. Thirdly, you have betrayed your race and nation by your subservience to international Zionism and the state of Israel.

Take heed that your nefarious anti-White activities are being monitored and recorded by our international Klan movement. If you persist in your treacherous activities against the White Race, I can assure you that there can only be grave consequences.

In the Name of the White Race

DAVID DUKE

Grand Wizard

Knights of the
Ku Klux Klan

My letter from the Grand Wizard of the Ku Klux Klan, delivered by David
Duke, March 14, 1977

With my very good friend, the courageous Barbara Turnbull

Presenting a brotherhood award to Chief Justice Bora Laskin at Beth Sholom
Synagogue, 1978

Celebrating my mother's graduation from York University with the
university's chancellor, John Robarts, and president, Ian Macdonald, 1980

In the Montreal Canadien Old Timers uniform in a charity game with Maurice
and Henri Richard and referee Red Storey, 1980

With Indira Gandhi during my trip to India, 1979

Visiting a group of villagers in India

At the scene of the derailed train in Mississauga, 1979

Our family poses for a campaign photo, 1981

Arguing the Patriation case before the Supreme Court of Canada, spring 1981
(artist unknown)

During the lead-up to the patriation of the Canadian Constitution, with
Tom Wells, Bill Davis, Jean Chrétien, and Pierre Trudeau, 1982

With Bill Davis at the constitutional negotiating table

Trudeau, Romanow, Chrétien, and I pose in the famous "kitchen" after the constitutional deal

A fine panorama of the constitutional negotiating meeting, November 1981

With Prime Minister Pierre Trudeau

With Quebec premier René Lévesque

Meeting with Aboriginal leaders during my tour of Northern Ontario, 1984

Norval Morrisseau presenting me with one of his "Woodland"
paintings in 1984

of minister. Our office was at 18 King Street East, and I worked from there, not from Queen's Park, as some of my Cabinet colleagues did. I announced an open-door policy – literally leaving the door ajar – to encourage staff to drop in to talk about their problems or things they thought I might want to know. In addition to administrative assistants and advisers, I had some five hundred lawyers on staff in Toronto and throughout Ontario.

The Ministry of the Attorney General was divided into two branches, criminal and civil; interestingly, the criminal section attracted a much larger number of applicants at the time. We also supplied legal services to all the other ministries, and many of our lawyers were located elsewhere – in Toronto and in other cities and towns. There they developed expertise essential to the ministry in which they worked, so they were not rotated around very much. It was challenging, however, to keep up with all the legislation they developed in these other departments and, at times, to avoid conflicts and divided loyalties. I thought it was vital to maintain morale among our lawyers, especially given the disparity in salaries between the government and the private sector, so I always discouraged my Cabinet colleagues from seeking legal opinions from outside firms. When there were disputes with other ministries over particular issues or legislation, I tried to settle the problem before it came to the Cabinet table and the inevitable turf wars that would ensue.

To create a greater level of collegiality among all the Crown attorneys, I divided the province into regions, with a senior person as director over each one. I brought these regional directors into Toronto at regular intervals to meet with me and other key people at the ministry. This initiative improved communications considerably, lessened the resentment that had developed in the past, and gave all the regions some input into developing new policies. It became even more important as the Crown attorneys system increased in size over the years. I had two major concerns about Crown attorneys. First, it was important that they not get too friendly with the police – the attorneys, not the police, should always make the decisions about who gets prosecuted and who does not. Second, they needed to guard against the growing divide, or polarization, between the defence bar and themselves.

As for my own ministerial responsibilities, I often found the opposition parties more supportive of my legal reforms than many of my somewhat reactionary colleagues in our own caucus. To encourage their cooperation, I advised my opposition justice critics that they were welcome to meet privately with my senior policy advisers any time they wished if they wanted to learn more about our policy recommendations regarding legislation that was before the Legislature or other matters related to the administration of justice in Ontario.

I was primarily interested in policy development, not administration or details about the budget. For that side of my duties, I soon learned to rely on my senior bureaucrats. Like most people in the legal profession, I had little experience in dealing with the Ontario public service and may initially have regarded bureaucrats with some scepticism, given the frequent negative comments made about them in the media and elsewhere. James Taylor, a former member of the Ontario Legislature and briefly a member of the Davis Cabinet, was once quoted as saying, "I walked in the so-called corridors of power only to be mugged in the back rooms of bureaucracy." In legal circles, lawyers who chose a career in government service were often seen as a lesser breed than those in private practice. I quickly learned how wrong I was as I experienced the enormous talent within the Ontario public service, whether legally trained or not. There are always exceptions, but I have positive memories of my work with the staff in my ministry.

My change of heart was reinforced by attitudes throughout the government. Davis always fostered close cooperation between the political and the bureaucratic branches of government. He appointed senior government officials on the basis of ability rather than political loyalty. And, of course, the longevity of the Progressive Conservative Party in the province, in power since 1943, facilitated this spirit and endowed it with the title "Ontario's natural governing party." In the coming decade as a Cabinet minister, I had no interest in the political allegiances of my key advisers and officials. When Premier John Buchanan of Nova Scotia phoned me one day, for instance, about an official in my ministry who had applied to be Nova Scotia's first director of public prosecutions, he asked me, "Is he one of ours?" "Do you mean politically?" I asked, appalled, and quickly explained that partisan politics was not a consideration for employment in my ministry. Buchanan obviously thought I was very naive.

In my ten years as attorney general, I enjoyed a productive and close relationship with my four deputy ministers. This official, always chosen by the premier, is the chief administrative officer of the ministry, and it would be very difficult to succeed as minister without the support and advice of the deputy minister – and, indeed, the other senior officials in the ministry. Frank Callaghan was my first deputy, and he later became chief justice of the Superior Court of Ontario. I joined him on the bench as his associate chief justice in 1991. The second was Allan Leal, one of my law teachers at Osgoode Hall Law School and chair of the Ontario Law Reform Commission. Rendall Dick became the third, when he returned to the ministry after serving as deputy minister of finance. He later became deputy treasurer of the Law Society of Upper Canada, Ontario's legal governing body. My fourth deputy was Archie Campbell, a close personal friend throughout his life after he worked as a high-school student in my law office in 1958 (chapter 27).

* * *

The role of the attorney general in the provincial government represents a unique responsibility in the administration of justice. The working relationship between this minister and the judiciary is exceptionally sensitive, embracing as it does principles of judicial independence and political accountability. The independence of the judiciary is vital to a democratic society, and it is a deeply rooted value in Canada and throughout the common-law world. The description "independent" is sometimes misunderstood to mean that judges can do what they want, but it really has the meaning of "impartial": judges must not be partial with respect to any litigant before them. The philosopher John Locke asserted that the adjudication of disputes by neutral judges was the most important benefit of civilization. The independence of judges from government provides an assurance that the state will be subject to the rule of law. If a government could count on the courts to enforce legislative and executive actions unauthorized by law, the individual citizen would have no protection against tyranny.

The issue of judicial independence can, occasionally, be a source of friction between the judiciary and the executive of any government. In Canada, judges appointed by the provincial government preside over almost 95 per cent of the criminal cases heard in the province. One of the more confusing aspects of Canada's federalism, however, is found in section 96 of the *Constitution Act, 1867*, which states that the federal government "shall appoint the judges of the superior district and county courts in each province." The idea behind this seeming anomaly was that the federal appointment process would reinforce judicial independence by insulating the provincial superior court judges from local pressures. However, these judges are appointed from the bar of the particular province, so they are not necessarily immune from local pressures. They do, however, preside over only about 5 per cent of the criminal cases in Ontario. In recent decades the appointment of judges has become more independent of government, with the appointment of independent judicial advisory committees both provincially and federally.

The prosecutors in most cases heard in the province are members of the Ministry of the Attorney General. The attorney general recommends the appointment of new provincial judges to the Cabinet of the day, and it is those same judges who hear the cases presented on behalf of the ministry. The attorney general is also responsible for the courtrooms in which these cases are prosecuted and for the individuals who administer and staff them. Despite these connections, it would be a major scandal if a member of the political branch of government attempted to influence the result of a criminal prosecution. This reality is well understood by the provincial judges, and any suggestion of a lack of judicial independence seriously undermines public confidence in the administration of justice.

After my appointment as attorney general, I became aware of some tension between my ministry and the provincial court judges over the issue of salaries. Before 1982 the Ontario government established the salary levels for provincial judges. Given the protestations by some members of the judiciary, the process, both federally and provincially, then became much more independent of government. I established a tripartite committee in Ontario, with nominees suggested by both the judiciary and the government working under an independent chair. The committee's recommendations were to be accepted by government unless a sound economic and fiscal public policy reason could be established for rejecting them. Even then, the reasons for any rejection could be judicially reviewed by an appellate court and, ultimately, the Supreme Court of Canada.

Some judges alleged that there was at least a perceived conflict of interest in a system where an independent judiciary relied on the prosecuting government for salaries and court administration. They argued that, as provincially appointed judges, they were disqualified from performing their functions because of the degree of control exercised by the provincial attorney general and that this fact raised a reasonable apprehension that judges could be biased in favour of the prosecution. After the entrenchment of the Charter of Rights in the Constitution in April 1982, several provincially appointed judges even threatened to stop hearing criminal cases because they regarded themselves as not being independent of the attorney general as the chief prosecutor. In my view, the protest was chiefly a strategy to obtain higher salaries through some form of independent arbitration.

One judge in particular, Reid Scott, disappointed me by his irresponsible behaviour, which led to a very public confrontation. I had appointed him to the bench because of his long career of public service in both the federal and the Ontario parliaments as well as on the Toronto City Council. In December 1982 he announced that he would no longer preside as a judge in court because he was not independent of the attorney general. He even falsely stated in a radio interview that he had been approached by an Ontario Cabinet minister about a case he was hearing. Then he promptly left for a holiday in California.

Although I was satisfied by the Cabinet minister's strong denial, it was a serious allegation and required an independent police investigation. Already it had become a controversy in the Legislature. An OPP officer travelled to California and interviewed Judge Scott, who refused to cooperate. Instead, he telephoned the *Toronto Star* and stated that the OPP investigation was "nothing but a blatant act of intimidation. If McMurtry wants a fight, he's got one." After further investigation by the newspaper, a *Star* editorial on December 31 was headlined, "The judge wasn't harassed," and concluded that Scott's "statement and actions are not the kind of calm and sensible behaviour the people of Ontario expect from a provincial court judge." Eventually Scott returned from California and admitted that the alleged incident with the Cabinet minister had never in fact occurred. A complaint was made to the Ontario Judicial Council about his conduct, and he hired Arthur Maloney as his legal counsel. Maloney had him assessed by a psychiatrist, who diagnosed a mental disorder. As a result, Scott was allowed a disability pension and never sat again as a judge.

During my years as attorney general, the Ontario Judicial Council was presided over by the chief justice of Ontario and included the chief judges of the High Court (the former Country and District Court), the provincial criminal, family, and small-claims courts, the treasurer (chair) of the Law Society of Upper Canada, and two non-lawyer public appointees. Serious and credible allegations of improper conduct against judges are very rare. I can recall only three other complaints about provincially appointed judges that I referred to the Ontario Judicial Council during my decade as attorney general, though I admit I was reluctant to use this prerogative unless there were compelling reasons to do so in the public's interest. Two of these complaints involved judges who associated socially with individuals who had significant criminal records – a great concern to the police. Both judges resigned rather than face the Judicial Council.

The third judge was openly consorting with a known prostitute in his judicial chambers – a situation that came to the attention of the local police because of the woman's links with organized crime. When my reference to the Judicial Council became known to the local bar, I received a petition, signed by seventy-five lawyers, protesting that I was interfering in the "private life" of a judge! When he appeared before the council, the judge did not deny the nature of the complaint against him. The council decided that a public inquiry should be conducted by a High Court judge, and I named Justice Sydney Robins to perform that role. Justice Robins recommended that a resolution be put before the Ontario Legislature for the removal of this particular judge, as required by statute. At that point the judge resigned. In the speculation that followed as to why the judge would put himself through this embarrassing public process, neither he nor his lawyers offered any defence to the complaint. For some reason, the bizarre rumour spread that the judge wanted his friends to know that the prostitute was a beautiful young woman – and the only way to make that fact known was through a public inquiry!

The removal of any judge from office can be controversial: judicial security of tenure is an important foundation stone of an independent and impartial judiciary. Conduct that breaches the "good behaviour" requirement can well be a source of disagreement among judges themselves. It has long been accepted that incompetence alone does not breach the behaviour rule, although many members of the public believe it should. However, a demonstration of continuing incompetence by a judge could well be considered as crossing the threshold and used to recommend removal from office.

Early on in my tenure as attorney general, I became concerned about the apparent conflict of interest as I administered the courts in which my ministry was also a major litigant. There had been some grumbling from members of the defence bar about the potential for an employee of the ministry to list cases before judges believed to be friendly to the prosecution. In 1976 I published a discussion paper and proposed draft legislation that contemplated replacing the attorney general as administrator of the courts by the Ontario Judicial Council, which would act as of board of directors in charge of the hundreds of court administration staff employed by the government. Interestingly, the legal profession generally opposed the change. Most lawyers thought that the removal of the attorney general's responsibility for court administration would reduce the level of direct government accountability in the Legislature for the adequate funding and management of the courts. I therefore did not proceed with my proposal. Some years later the legal profession revisited the issue and approved my earlier initiative, but it has never been implemented.

The issue of the independence of the provincially appointed judges was not finally resolved legally until 1985, when the Supreme Court of Canada ruled in *Valente v. The Queen* (a case where a judge of the provincial court of Ontario questioned whether he was truly independent of the executive branch of government) that the provincially appointed criminal court judges in Ontario possessed "the essential elements of judicial independence." This decision did not preclude the attorney general from being involved in the administration of the courts, but it directed that judges should control judicial assignments related to the sittings of the courts. The Supreme Court ruled that the provincially appointed judges enjoyed security of tenure "during good behaviour" because they could only be removed by the provincial Legislature after hearings by the Ontario Judicial Council in private and, at the discretion of the council, a hearing conducted by a High Court judge.

One of the most important aspects of any attorney general's legacy is the quality of the judges appointed to the Ontario Court of Justice during his or her term in office. Approximately 150 judges were appointed during my decade in the post. In the process I followed, I encouraged the chief judges of both the family and the criminal courts to do a preliminary interview with potential appointees. If the chief judge was not enthusiastic about the candidate, consideration for that individual came to an end. Once I learned, however, that the particular chief judge was supportive and I was satisfied by other credible sources of information, I personally interviewed the candidate. If I too was impressed, I asked the candidate to appear before the Ontario Judicial Council. If all went well in that final stage, I then recommended the appointment to my Cabinet colleagues.

One of my major priorities was to make the provincial court bench more representative of the diversity of Ontario, in both culture and gender. I appointed the first African Canadian judges as well as those from other cultures and the first female criminal court judge. The relative absence of women in the provincial courts stemmed from the fact that it was only in the 1970s that women began to enter law schools in significant numbers. I am proud of having appointed Rosalie Abella to the provincial family court. She was only twenty-nine years old at the time and, as she has often reminded me, eight months pregnant. She went on to a distinguished career as chair of both the Labour Relations Board and the Law Reform Commission of Ontario, spent a decade on the Court of Appeal, and is now a member of the Supreme Court of Canada. When her two sons, now both lawyers, were young, they delighted in telling their friends that only pregnant women could become judges.

As I reflect back on my appointments to the provincial court bench, now formally titled the Ontario Court of Justice, I am generally well satisfied with the quality of the appointments as well as those known to me who have been appointed in more recent decades. Inevitably there have been some disappointments, but they are few in number. The term "judgitis," meaning judges becoming pompous and rude, has been around for a long time, but I believe it now occurs rarely. Judges appointed to the Ontario Court of Justice are always interviewed, and I know that their ability to demonstrate patience and politeness as well as knowledge of the law are all taken under consideration. The under-representation of judges from minority communities is recognized and continues to be addressed in a positive fashion.

The judges appointed by the federal government in the provinces, the "superior court judges," are removable only by resolutions passed by both the House of Commons and the Senate. Under the *Federal Judges Act*, complaints brought against judges are referred to the Canadian Judicial Council, presided over by the chief justice of Canada. The other council members are the chief justices and associate chief justices of the superior courts, in both the provinces and the federal courts centred in Ottawa. The Judicial Council must investigate and report on any complaint before a decision can be taken in relation to the removal of a judge. I was a member of the Canadian Judicial Council for sixteen years, five years in my role as associate chief justice and chief justice of the Superior Court of Ontario (Trial Division), and for eleven years in my capacity as chief justice of Ontario. In my experience the members of the Judicial Council took their responsibilities very seriously, given the importance of public accountability in a democratic society.

The great majority of the complaints are from civil litigants who are upset simply because they have lost their legal actions. As such, most complaints are rejected. Those that appear to have some merit are referred to a panel of judges who privately review the complaint, including frequently a response from the judge against whom the complaint has been made. If there appears to be real merit to a serious complaint, the reviewing panel can recommend to the full council that a public inquiry be held. The five-person panel conducting the inquiry is made up of three judges on the council and two persons appointed by the federal minister of justice.

No superior court judges have ever been removed as a result of this process. However, in recent years three such judges have resigned when they believed that recommended resolutions for removal would pass in the House of Commons and the Senate. In a number of other cases where the panel believed that the alleged misconduct was to some degree inappropriate, letters of "concern" were written to the judge involved. Though the *Judges Act* does not permit a formal reprimand, these letters were in practical terms "reprimands" in the guise of expressions of concern.

In my experience, the possibility of a formal complaint to the Canadian Judicial Council has generally ensured a high level of courtesy in court by the vast majority of superior court judges. In previous decades, we lawyers practising in Ontario courts often experienced a level of judicial rudeness that would be quite unacceptable in the twenty-first century (chapters 5, 6, and 7). Still, regulators of the legal profession are now routinely expressing concern about the lack of civility demonstrated by some litigators in the courts – a product, no doubt, of the growing numbers of the profession, particularly in large centres.

Yet another challenge for any attorney general is the building or renovation of courthouses and the proper financing of the administration of justice. Historically in Ontario, the major courthouses were centres of the communities they served. They generally represented the most attractive if not dramatic local architecture. Some years ago the Osgoode Society published a book celebrating Ontario's courthouses, *Cornerstones of Order* – an apt title given the importance of courthouses as symbols of an orderly and democratic society.

In contrast to schools, hospitals, and highways, the building of new courthouses in recent decades has faced tough political opposition. The struggle requires an attorney general to be very active in assembling political support, particularly among the legal profession, local councils, and representatives of law enforcement. During my years as attorney general I was successful in obtaining agreement for building major new courthouses in Ottawa, Newmarket, and St Catharines, and significant renovations of courthouses in other centres.

* * *

The attorney general is also the minister of justice – an extremely important responsibility. While the attorney general is the senior law officer of the Crown and chief criminal prosecutor, the minister of justice has the constitutional obligation to protect the rights of individuals and minorities from excessive state authority. This dual title has been the tradition in most, if not all, of the Canadian provinces, but in Ontario the justice title was dropped during a temporary reorganization of government and, regrettably, never restored. The attorney general's responsibilities also include relevant law reform and the provision of a properly funded legal aid system.

In 1983 the provincial attorneys general (led by Ontario) unanimously attacked the federal government for its draconian new security legislation. We were acting principally as ministers of justice concerned about the rights of individuals who could be unfairly treated under the proposed legislation. In May that year Robert Kaplan, the federal solicitor general, had introduced legislation to create a national security service – which in due time became the Canadian Security Intelligence Service (CSIS). The legislation was in response to the recommendations of the McDonald inquiry into RCMP wrongdoing – which included a number of illegal activities ranging from barn burnings to fabricated psychiatric reports intended to disrupt the activities of Quebec separatists and extreme left-wing militants.

A review of the legislation convinced me that it was extremely harsh, with the potential to interfere improperly and unfairly in the lives of many Canadians without the traditional safeguards of the criminal law. Kaplan himself admitted that the "agency would have the right to break the law in some circumstances if necessary in carrying out of its duties." For example, the legislation would allow the new force to tap telephone conversations, open mail, and break into the headquarters of political organizations and special interest groups – collectives that most Canadians would consider as legitimate advocates for equality and justice.

I arranged for my senior criminal law advisers to review the legislation, and despite their understandable bias in favour of effective law enforcement, they clearly shared my concerns and added a few of their own. In essence, they agreed that members of the new agency would have powers far exceeding those granted to any police agency, including the powers to break Canadian law without any real accountability.

The provincial attorneys general had arranged a two-day meeting months earlier in Charlottetown, and as things turned out, this get-together came soon after the introduction of the new security legislation. Although the agenda had already been agreed on, we added the new federal legislation to our discussions as an urgent matter. My colleagues had not yet found time to review the legislation in detail, but they shared Ontario's concerns. In fact, after the meeting, Quebec attorney general Marc-André Bédard was quoted in the national press as stating that the federal government had "proposed the birth of a monster."

At the conclusion of our discussion of the new security legislation, my colleagues suggested that the Ontario delegation should prepare a draft communiqué that everyone could sign. I worked with my deputy, Archie Campbell, and my communications director, David Allen, on it through the night, fortified by the favourite local beer, Moosehead Ale. Our highly critical and detailed communiqué became known in some circles as the "Moosehead Manifesto." It set a historical precedent as the only occasion when all the provincial attorneys general joined together to denounce major federal legislation. The next day the main headline in the *Globe and Mail* read, "Provinces call security force a huge threat."

The federal government was obviously concerned about this opposition, and it immediately referred the security legislation to a Senate Committee presided over by Senator Michael Pitfield, who had previously been chief of staff to Prime Minister Trudeau. I was mandated by my fellow attorneys general to present a brief to that committee on behalf of the provinces.

On August 23, 1983, I appeared before this committee. I read the sixty-one-page presentation I had prepared and then answered questions. I emphasized that my statement reflected the concerns of the other nine provinces and the territories, and began with the statement that "the legislation is very seriously flawed, to the point that it needs a complete rewriting." At the same time, I said that the attorneys general recognized that Canada required "effective machinery and power to ensure national security" and that we were "not complacent about this issue."

Our reservations were not unique, as the legislation had created widespread concern and opposition right across the country. As but one example, the highly respected Peter Russell, a professor at the University of Toronto, wrote: "The bias in drafting Bill C-157 seems to be strongly towards ensuring there are no undesirable gaps in the new agency's mandate, rather than ensuring that our citizens are protected from excessive snooping into their political activities. This, I think, is the wrong bias and gives the wrong signal to the new agency."

My statement could be summarized under five themes. The first was the vague and dangerously expansive definition of what constitutes a threat to national security and the unjustifiably wide and virtually unlimited mandate of the proposed agency. The others focused on the lack of ordinary criminal-justice safeguards associated with those powers; the lack of effective accountability; the excessive secrecy provisions; and the confusing and dangerous provision relating to the ability of members of the service to breach the law. In the context of accountability I said that, "unlike most criminal legislation, this legislation dealing with extraordinary powers will not be tested in the courts. Most of the activities of the force will take place in secret and there will be very little, if any opportunity, to test in a court of law, the true legal effect of the sanctions. This will make the service in most instances the final arbiter or judge of its own jurisdiction and powers."

Throughout my presentation I stressed that the existing provisions of the *Criminal Code* and the *Official Secrets Act* were adequate to meet any threats to the security of Canada. An example of the dangerous vagueness in the legislation was a section that would permit the spy agency to investigate anyone engaged in "activities directed toward or intended ultimately to aid in the destruction or overthrow of the constitutionally established system of government in Canada." A senior government official conceded that the definition could make it illegal to have a separatist party in Quebec. Another section made it illegal to assist in any "clandestine" manner – for example, in the fight against apartheid in South Africa. Furthermore, the legislation made it illegal to participate in activities "detrimental to any state associated with Canada" – actions that could range from opposing the use of torture, which was common in Argentina at the time, to economic competition. I concluded my comments with these words: "Governments which believe in democracy must exercise restraint in setting the ground rules for the gathering of information on individuals. It is critical in developing laws to protect individuals that we do not by those laws destroy the very freedoms they are meant to secure."

In early September 1983 I debated the legislation with Robert Kaplan at the annual meeting of the Canadian Bar Association. My debating partner was Alan Borovoy, the general counsel of the Canadian Civil

Liberties Association. Kaplan was supported by John Starnes, a former director of the RCMP's Security and Intelligence Service. That same month I appeared with former Supreme Court justice Emmett Hall at a major rally in Toronto protesting the legislation.

Finally, in December 1984 the Senate released a carefully crafted report that agreed with the majority of our concerns, with the exception of those relating to the RCMP, and recommended a major redrafting of the legislation. The end result proved to be of great benefit to individual rights in Canada.

At the outset of the controversy related to the legislation, I was also concerned about the removal of the traditional security responsibilities from the RCMP. Although the force had acted illegally and irresponsibly on occasion, I believed that this initiative was overkill. The RCMP was generally a well-trained police force, and I thought that, with proper, objective oversight, it would act within the law in security matters. I strongly believed that the Trudeau government had been negligent in not laying down stricter guidelines. When it came to security issues, there appeared to be a "nod and wink" approach with respect to the activities of the RCMP.

Furthermore, the lack of cooperation between the FBI and the CIA in the United States had been demonstrated on countless occasions. I became well aware of the bitterness within the ranks of the RCMP on losing its traditional security responsibilities. A lack of trust and confidence between the RCMP and CSIS became entrenched at the outset, and it is well documented in the report of the Air India inquiry that was released in June 2010.

The RCMP has, however, been able since its creation to avoid any effective objective oversight – something that is still an important political issue in Canada. Ottawa's political circles have come to believe that it is dangerous for any elected MP to confront the RCMP, for fear of some form of retaliation. This fear proved to be well founded when the RCMP commissioner shared with the media in the middle of the 2006 federal election information that the office of the Liberal finance minister was being investigated. It is generally believed that this event had a profound influence on the Conservative election victory, although no criminal charges were ever laid as a result of the RCMP investigation. The Arar inquiry in 2007, chaired by Associate Chief Justice Dennis O'Connor of Ontario, also recommended stricter oversight of the RCMP. At the time of writing, this recommendation has not yet been implemented.

Notwithstanding my concerns about the lack of RCMP accountability, I still question the wisdom of the separation of national security from the traditional criminal investigation role of the RCMP. Criminal and security issues obviously overlap in many critical ways, and the failure to share information between major institutions has long been deeply entrenched in the culture of large governments. In this context, in 2011 Borovoy wrote an article for the *Toronto Star* entitled "Two heads not better than one on national security file." He stated that "the interests of 'civil liberties' never required the separation of the functions of criminal and security recommended by the McDonald Commission. On the contrary, the further that intelligence gathering is separated from law enforcement, the greater the risk to civil liberties." I agree with this argument: criminal investigations are conducted in an environment where it is recognized that the tactics used may well be scrutinized by a court, but that precaution does not necessarily apply to intelligence-gathering exercises.

13

Cabinet Minister with a Law Reform Agenda

The first major decision that I made as attorney general was to create a bilingual court system in Ontario in those centres where the service was warranted. In the province of Quebec the English language had been an official language from well before Confederation, and the lack of a bilingual court system in Ontario was frequently commented on in Quebec, particularly by those who wished to fuel the fires of separatism. The general impression in Quebec was that Canada's largest province was reluctant to embrace bilingualism as a working language in its most important institutions. In truth, at that time official bilingualism remained a highly controversial issue in the rest of Canada outside Quebec. Although people in Ontario whose first language was French had never exceeded 6 per cent of the population, the bilingual issue was an extremely important one for Franco-Ontarians.

Ontario had made considerable progress in providing education in the French language, but this accomplishment received little attention. I thought that the government might have been intimidated by fear of an anti-French political backlash, particularly within the ranks of its "small C" Conservative supporters. I have also always believed that Robert Stanfield's support of Trudeau's official language policy in the federal election of 1972 may have cost him a minority government victory, though his decision avoided what would have been a tragic French-English split in Canada. Nevertheless, official bilingualism remained a divisive issue in Ontario despite Stanfield's political support and integrity. In the city of Ottawa, for instance, the Franco-Ontarian community began around this time to protest against the absence of bilingual traffic tickets and other French-language services – all of which was well publicized in the Quebec media.

A conversation with one of my Franco-Ontarian Cabinet colleagues shortly after the 1975 provincial election did much to fuel my ambitions to create a bilingual court system in Ontario. René Brunelle represented the constituency that included Kapuskasing, the local judicial centre. He said to me one day, "We have French-speaking judges, lawyers, Crowns, police officers, and other witnesses – 95 per cent of our proceedings are conducted in French – yet in our provincial court, everything has to be translated into English to create the record because only English is an official language in the courts of Ontario." In my view this process was insulting to the Franco-Ontarian community.

Soon after my discussion with Brunelle, I began to assess the political climate for official bilingualism in the courts of Ontario. I was disappointed but not surprised to learn that there was little, if any, support for such an initiative. Regrettably, the official-language initiatives currently under way by the federal government were still highly controversial in Ontario. The opposing sentiments were not simply against the use of French, but reflected a widespread paranoia within the federal public service that promotions for non-bilingual officials would be denied even if bilingualism did not appear to be necessary for a particular position. "You are not going to be able to get a job in the federal civil service unless you can speak French," people said, "or at least you won't be advanced." This fear was later confirmed by an official languages commissioner who criticized the federal government for designating an excessive number of jobs as requiring bilingual skills.

I didn't want to risk creating any formidable opposition, so I was most discreet in my political soundings with the government caucus. Although Bill Davis was a person of goodwill, moderation, and progressive instincts, I realized that the timing was difficult, given the backlash against the *Official Languages Act*. He often said he was reluctant "to test the core of the PC party too often" – in effect, recognizing that our more reactionary supporters could not be ignored. I knew that a negative response from the premier would probably put the issue of official bilingualism in the courts on the back-burner indefinitely, so I simply avoided that outcome by not consulting him about it.

Deputy Minister Frank Callaghan was supportive in principle but did not think that, in the near future, the ministry could provide the necessary financial and linguistic resources to make official bilingualism a reality. I knew, however, that General Bill Anderson, the deputy minister of the Treasury Board, believed otherwise. During his distinguished career in the Canadian military, he had become a strong supporter of bilingualism. When we found ourselves together at a bilingualism conference in Ottawa in late November 1975, I told him about my desire to create a bilingual court system in the province. Although as a deputy minister he could not provide me with the necessary political support, he was very enthusiastic in principle and informed me that he could find me the necessary funding. That assurance emboldened me: in my address to the conference soon after, I dropped all the platitudes in my speech and committed the Ministry of the Attorney General to establishing a pilot bilingual court project in Sudbury. The concept had not been discussed in Cabinet or caucus, and I realized that my promise would create considerable political controversy within our government. I was not to be disappointed.

My greatest fear was that Davis might think I had taken advantage of our close friendship in announcing an important government policy without taking it first to Cabinet. I was confident, though, that he would not obstruct my commitment. He would agree that it was the correct decision in principle, though perhaps a little premature politically given the reactionary elements in our caucus and the Progressive Conservative Party of Ontario. He informed me later that, before announcing a major new policy, I should at least have shared my intention with him. I agreed that, generally, the protocol he suggested was correct, but that I had wanted to give him the option of distancing himself from my commitment. In light of the importance of the initiative, however, that choice was probably not realistic – a fact that made his understanding even more magnanimous. It's not surprising that, thereafter, he often phoned me to ask, "What new government policy have you announced today? Would you like to share it with me?"

There were many cynics within the Franco-Ontarian community who believed that no Ontario government would ever be truly committed to the principle of official bilingualism. The official use of the French language had been controversial for a long time, and although these attitudes have now largely disappeared, that reality still existed in 1975. Some leaders in the Franco-Ontarian community even suggested that I had chosen Sudbury as the site of the pilot project because the demand for bilingual court proceedings there would be low. I did have concerns on this point: virtually all the French-speaking lawyers in Sudbury had been educated in English-speaking law schools and might well feel more comfortable conducting their trials in that language. If the pilot project was indeed underused, I might have difficulty proceeding further with the bilingual initiative.

As things turned out, the choice of bilingual trials in Sudbury was disappointingly low. I still felt, however, that the ministry had learned enough to expand the project to other parts of Ontario. I created an advisory committee of bilingual lawyers from both the anglophone and the francophone communities and provided ministerial funding to create an association – the Association des juristes d'expression française de l'Ontario (AJEFO) – to encourage the use of the French language in Ontario legal proceedings. I was proud to attend the initial banquet of the association, but mystified as the president, Robert Paris, introduced me as a UFO. After a long pause he explained that the initials stood for "Unidentified Franco Ontarian."

Early in my term as attorney general, I hired lawyer Etienne Saint-Aubin as my French-language coordinator to assist me in the creation of the bilingual court system. He was the son of a respected Sudbury judge and was totally dedicated to the project. We have remained friends ever since.

A key ingredient of French-language services in the courts was the availability of the law in the French language, particularly the Ontario statutes. In February 1978 the government made a commitment in the Speech from the Throne to ensure that more government documents, publications, and forms were available in the French language. More important, perhaps, was the establishment of a special section to begin work on translating Ontario's statutes into French. An accompanying commitment was to enhance French-language services where any unfulfilled need was identified.

A cornerstone of the ministry's French-language policy was continued funding support for teaching common law in the French language at the University of Ottawa. The records from the university state that, in March 1977, the Faculty of Law adopted a resolution to create French-language common-law programs within two years. The reason recorded in the decision referred to my commitment to create a bilingual court system in Ontario, with a pilot project established in Sudbury in 1976. The documents also record that the goal of the French-language program was to ensure that the Franco-Ontario bar was able to respond effectively to the needs of the Franco-Ontario community.

In a letter dated September 8, 1977, the Reverend Roger Guindon, the rector of the University of Ottawa, wrote to the Ontario minister of colleges and universities. "You will understand, I am sure," he said, "that as long as French has no status whatsoever in the Ontario legal system the need to educate in French, even French speaking lawyers, was not considered by our Common Law Section as a high ranking priority. Last year's pilot project in Sudbury introduced a new element in the situation and this year's extension of the project made it mandatory for us to introduce at least some French in Common Law. Recent statements by the Honorable Roy McMurtry have added a new dimension." The French Common Law Program was formally established in 1980, and three years later the University of Ottawa awarded me an honorary doctorate.

I was further pleased to be awarded the Order of Merit from the Association des juristes d'expression française de l'Ontario (AJEFO) in 1990. The citation recognized my creation of the bilingual court system in Ontario and expressed the "gratitude and the esteem" of the members of AJEFO.

For me, one of the highlights of having created a bilingual court system in Ontario was the acceptance in 2010 of my eldest grandchild, Lauren McMurtry, into the French Common Law Program at the University of Ottawa. Lauren is totally fluent in French, having received her entire formal education in French, commencing in Switzerland when her father, my son Jim, was headmaster of the Neuchâtel Junior College. I was particularly pleased that, in February 2010, Lauren received a letter from the francophone vice dean of the French Common Law Section encouraging her enrolment and referring to her grandfather's "fundamental role" in creating the program as a result of his commitment to a bilingual court system.

When I retired as the Ontario attorney general in 1985, the right to a bilingual trial, including jury trials, had been expanded through most of province, and French had been proclaimed as an official language in the *Ontario Courts of Justice Act*. The constitutional designation of Ontario as an officially bilingual province would require only that publications of the Ontario Legislature be in both French and English. I regret that this final step has not yet been taken.

The political fallout from my commitment to official bilingualism in the courts had long-lasting repercussions. The amount of hate mail I received really shocked me. Many of my colleagues in our caucus and our party never forgave me for this initiative, and in 1985, when I stood for the party leadership after Bill Davis resigned as premier, it drew support away from me (chapter 28). People still believed that, if I became premier, I would make Ontario an officially bilingual province like Quebec and New Brunswick.

My bilingual initiative also led to the creation of the Association for the Protection of the English Language in Ontario. Both opposition parties, the Liberals and the NDP, supported my efforts, however, and a few years later the French government appointed me an officer of the Award of Merit of France. I have undoubtedly sounded somewhat self-indulgent in writing about the recognition given to me. However, I simply want to emphasize that the opportunity I had to initiate a bilingual court system in Ontario is far more important to me than the often harsh criticisms I received from members of my own political party. On a personal level I shall always feel grateful that I took this opportunity to strengthen the status of the French language in the province.

* * *

My commitment to the creation of a bilingual court system without any previous consultation with my political colleagues or the public certainly challenged the standard government protocol and process. Fortunately, it did not require any initial legislation, but was clearly a course of action that could not be repeated with respect to law reform in general. I realized that, if I did not follow the long-established protocol of agreement with my Cabinet colleagues and members of the government caucus, I could not expect to remain in Cabinet.

In any event, law reform was a major priority for me. I introduced fifty-nine statutes that were passed by the Ontario Legislature during my term as attorney general. In general, enacting progressive law reform is a highly complex process. Much of the legislation required intensive consultation with members of the public and with each of the professions of accounting, engineering, architecture, and law, whose governing statutes were the responsibility of the Ministry of the Attorney General. During my years in the Legislature, however, despite having only a tiny percentage of the government budget, the ministry brought forward each year between 10 and 20 per cent of the legislation.

The policy development agenda had traditionally been an inside government exercise. Given the importance of much of the law reform, however, I was anxious to establish a consultation process with the segment of society most affected by the particular reform before we began to draft the legislation. For example, given the importance of such legislation, the legal profession and many other groups were consulted extensively on family law reforms. Interested and affected groups were brought into the policy development process early on, rather than being left to comment once a bill had been drafted and introduced in the Legislature. We also worked hard to keep the opposition critics in the loop – a very different attitude from the current parliamentary practice of secrecy and confrontation. I even invited Jim Renwick, the NDP justice critic, to do a report on group defamation – a subject of special interest to him. Similarly, we commissioned the distinguished scholar Alan Mewett to write a report on the role of justices of the peace, leading to an enlargement of their jurisdiction. And, after Justice Sam Grange reported on legal aid clinics, I increased my efforts to provide them with needed funding.

My fundamental belief was that law reform improved society and that we did not want simply to react to problems after they emerged and demanded attention. We built a culture that encouraged ministry staff to identify issues that could well become problems. As the law officers of the Crown in Ontario, we also actively encouraged and supported reform initiatives from other ministries. For example, we worked closely with Dr Bob Elgie, the minister of labour, to establish the most substantive reforms ever made to the Ontario Human Rights Code, which, today, remains relatively unchanged.

My first major reform legislation was the *Landlord and Tenant Amendment Act*, which we introduced and passed in the autumn of 1975. It provided a level of security for tenants which had never been part of Ontario's landlord and tenant law. The issue had been the focus of several reports of the Ontario Law Reform Commission (OLRC), which began studying this area of the law in 1967. In the introduction to its first report, the OLRC stated: "The concern of the commission was to redress the imbalance which existed in the law in favour of landlords, an imbalance resulting from the law's preoccupation with rigid property principles of feudal origin and the failure of the common law of landlord and tenant over the centuries to develop a legal philosophy based on a theory of vital interests."

Before 1969 the tenancies law was the same for both residential and commercial tenancies. A tenancy could be terminated by the expiry of the lease. Moreover, a landlord could often retake possession for a tenant's alleged breach of a covenant in the lease, without bothering first to obtain a court order. Our 1975 legislation provided meaningful security for the first time in Ontario. Residential tenants could no longer be evicted against their will on the expiry of a lease unless they had been in breach of a specific term of the lease and after they had the option of a judicial hearing. If no new lease agreement had been agreed on, the legislation stated that, "upon the expiration of a tenancy agreement for a fixed term, the landlord and the tenant shall be deemed to have renewed the tenancy agreement as a monthly tenancy agreement upon the same terms and conditions as are provided for in the expired agreement." The amendments also extended the tenancy protections to mobile home sites. As Jack Fleming, the author of the text *Residential Tenancies in Ontario*, described the change: "Most importantly the 1975 changes restricted termination of a tenancy to specific allowable grounds. Real security of residential tenants arrived with the 1975 reforms."

The legislation was unpopular with most landlords, including my own widowed mother, who had but one tenant. For many landlords, the requirement of a court order for eviction was seen as a heavy and often an expensive burden. Inevitably, some tenants become an unreasonable headache for their landlords in a way that falls short of an actual breach of the lease. The new legislation was therefore an example of the classic legal dilemma of one person's right (a landlord giving a lease for a specific period) and someone else's more compelling right (a tenant's fundamental need for accommodation and, essentially, a home). In 1975, however, there was a shortage of rental accommodation, and in my view the issue of security of tenure for tenants was indeed a compelling issue. In recent years, as the landlord and tenant law in Ontario has changed and evolved, the fundamental security of tenure for tenants has remained in place.

In 1978 my family law program represented the most comprehensive reform of its kind ever undertaken at one time in Canada. The legislation was introduced and passed after extensive consultations with the legal profession and the public, and we received thousands of letters from women's associations, committees of the bar, and ordinary citizens. The Ontario Law Reform Commission had produced an important report on family law reform and urged the Legislature to move towards recognizing marriage as a true partnership. The Legislative Assembly's Standing Committee on the Administration of Justice also heard submissions and made recommendations.

Marriage is the fundamental relationship in society, and the legal regulation of these unions is extremely important for the community in general. Another priority of Ontario's family law reform was the recognition of support obligations between common-law spouses who were in relationships with some degree of permanence and those where a child has been born, even if the relationship had not been a long one. In particular, the impact of family disputes or breakdowns can be very negative and disruptive, especially on the lives of children and young people. During my many years in private practice I had held the view that women were most unfairly treated by the family law regimes both in Ontario and Canada at large.

The *Murdoch v. Murdoch* case, decided in the Supreme Court of Canada in 1975, provided a major impetus for family law reform, particularly for greater respect for the rights of women. The decision involved an Alberta ranching couple who had always taken title to their farms in the husband's name – a common practice for home ownership as well in all areas of Canada when the wife took on the homemaking role and was the principal partner in raising the children. Traditionally, unless a spouse had made a specific contribution in work or money to a property owned by the other partner, the property legally belonged to the owner alone. Contributions such as homemaking or purchase of family groceries or vacations were not recognized as giving a spouse any right to a share of the property, usually the family home, should the marriage end.

Irene Murdoch argued that her labour both in running the farm while her husband was away on business and in working alongside him when he was there should entitle her to a share of the farm. At the time the couple separated, Irene Murdoch was seriously assaulted by her husband when they quarrelled over the ownership of the farm. Justice Ronald Martland of the Supreme Court of Canada understandably infuriated the women's movement when he agreed with the trial judge's finding that Irene Murdoch's contribution was "just what the average farm wife did," and so she was not entitled to a share of the farm.

Justice Bora Laskin, who later became chief justice of Canada, was the lone dissenter on the court. He held that even if no common intention to share property existed between the Murdochs, relief should be provided by finding that a "constructive trust" existed that would remedy the "unjust enrichment" that the husband would otherwise enjoy. At the same time, Laskin's decision drew a clear line between extraordinary labour, such as that performed on the farm, and ordinary housekeeping duties, which were merely a reflection of the marriage bond. The majority of wives in 1975 were homemakers and married to wage-earning men. Although Laskin's conservative dissent had little to offer most women concretely, its psychological impact was significant, and it contributed to a growing campaign to change the matrimonial law.

When I introduced the family law package in the Legislature, I stated that the traditional legal rules and concepts should be re-evaluated in light of the major social and economic changes that were occurring in our society – wider recognition of the equality of the sexes, and the participation of far more women in higher education and in the workforce outside the home. The proposed *Family Law Reform Act* provided that, when a marriage came to an end, each spouse would be entitled to an equal division of the family assets – the property ordinarily used and enjoyed by the family while the spouses were residing together. This approach reflected the belief that, in general, the spouses contribute equally to those assets which are of continuing use and benefit to the family, whether or not one spouse worked at home as the homemaker. In particular situations, however, if the court considered that it would be manifestly unfair to divide the family assets equally, it could, after considering specific statutory guidelines, divide the family assets in some other proportion or order a division of other property that was not technically a family asset. In addition, during the marriage, both spouses would have equal rights of possession in the matrimonial home, and in the absence of a court order, neither spouse would be able to sell, mortgage, or lease the home without the other spouse's consent.

In the first *Family Law Reform Act*, business assets acquired during the marriage were not subject to automatic sharing – though this exemption changed in a revised version of the Act, renamed the *Family Law Act*, enacted in 1986. Right from the start, however, contributions to a business by a spouse, directly or indirectly, were recognized. In both personal and business assets, the proposed law also allowed spouses, by mutual consent, to agree to other systems of property ownership. Existing separation agreements were recognized, or "grandfathered."

The need to revise provincial support legislation was just as pressing as reform of the matrimonial property law. Under the existing provincial support law, only husbands could be ordered to pay support for the family. Moreover, the right of a wife to support was based on evidence of her husband's adultery, cruelty, or desertion. If a wife committed even a single act of adultery, however, she lost her entitlement to support regardless of any provocation by the husband, including serial adultery.

Under our proposed new legislation, every spouse, including common-law spouses, would have an obligation to provide support for both partners, according to need and the ability to do so. Isolated instances of matrimonial misconduct would not automatically give rise to or defeat a support obligation. At the same time, repeated gross misconduct would be a factor in determining the amount of support to be awarded. Both spouses would be equally responsible for the support of children.

In the mid-seventies the proposed family law reforms were very controversial in many quarters. The concept of the ownership of property by the actual purchaser, usually the husband, had been entrenched in Canadian law since the creation of our property laws. After the first *Family Law Reform Act* had passed, I remember campaigning for re-election in my constituency. The legislation produced different results at different doors. One woman embraced me and thanked me for giving her "half of the home." At another location a woman blamed me for her boyfriend's reluctance to pursue a divorce because of the family law reforms.

Before I left government early in 1985, my officials had drafted further legislation to include in the family law reform package. These additions would lead to an equal division of all assets accumulated by a couple during their marriage, including business assets but not gifts or inheritances. The legislation was not introduced until the Liberals formed a government later that same year and I was succeeded by Ian Scott as attorney general. He told me that he would blame me for the legislation with people opposed to it but take credit with those in favour of this further package of family reform legislation.

The 1978 reform package included other legislation too: the right for dependants to sue for damages in the event of a death or injury caused to a family member by the negligence of a third party; and an obligation on adult children to provide support in accordance with the needs of parents, to the extent that the child was reasonably capable of doing so. The *Children's Law Reform Amendment Act* was also part of the package and provided a comprehensive legislation scheme to deal with custody disputes. The legislation recognized the long-standing legal principle that a custody award must be based on the best interests of the child, but, in addition, provided the presiding judge with the right to appoint a professional expert to assess the situation and give the court an opinion as to the best interests of the child or children involved. In certain circumstances the court was also allowed discretion to appoint separate legal representation for a particular child.

Allan Leal, my deputy attorney general, played a leading role in negotiating the Hague Convention, which recognized the rights of nations to enter into reciprocal agreements providing a mechanism for the return of a child to the country of its habitual residence after a parent had removed the child to another country. This international convention established a major deterrent to child abduction – an ever-growing problem in an internationally mobile society.

The *Succession Law Reform Act* was yet one more legislative enactment related to family law reform. In essence, with respect to the estates of deceased persons, it reformed the law relating to succession. The legislation equalized the treatment of children, whether a child had been born outside the marriage or not. As a result, the words "illegitimate child" disappeared from the legal lexicon. There was also the opportunity for dependants of a deceased person to make a claim against the estate where there was insufficient provision in a will or where there was no will. The legislation strengthened recognition of the actual intention of a deceased testator who had prepared a will that did not contain the traditional requirement of two witnesses. For the will to be recognized as a valid, or "holograph," will, it had to be written in the handwriting of the deceased and include the deceased's signature.

Many other statutes containing significant law reforms were passed during my decade in office and are bound in a book entitled *Law for the People*, which was presented to me by staff in my policy branch when I retired. One of my favourite reforms was the *Blind Persons Rights Act*. It prohibited anyone from denying access to facilities where the public is customarily admitted simply because the person was accompanied by a guide dog, or denying occupancy to a blind person with a guide dog in a self-contained dwelling unit.

* * *

Access to justice was another of my early priorities. The steadily rising cost of legal advice and representation has become an increasingly critical challenge for our society. Since 1967, a legal aid fee-for-service plan had been in operation, administered by the Law Society of Upper Canada and financially supported by the Ontario government. Part of this funding came from the bank-interest revenue on lawyers' mixed-trust accounts. The legal aid plan focused largely on the provision of legal counsel in criminal cases, so the greatest challenge, in my view, was to establish an adequate funding process for legal aid clinics to deal with poverty-related issues that required an understanding of the myriad social service agencies that provide financial assistance to the poor. They could only be provided from the legal aid budget administered by the Law Society.

In the previous few years a small number of community legal aid clinics had been funded by the federal Local Initiatives Program (LIP), but the grants had recently been abolished. Except for the Parkdale Legal Aid Clinic, operated by the Osgoode Hall Law School, the legal clinics began gradually to disappear. In my first address to the Advocates' Society in October 1975, I stated that access to justice was the most critical challenge facing the legal profession and society at large.

I decided to establish a system of legal aid clinics with the necessary funding mechanism in place. First we set up a clinic funding panel with representatives from the Ministry of the Attorney General and the Law Society of Upper Canada. It was soon agreed that the new clinics should be closely linked to the communities they served, with a local board of directors and an emphasis on building close relationships with social service agencies in the area. The distinguishing characteristics of these clinics are their specialization in poverty law, representing people who could not otherwise access the legal system and strengthening the fabric of the communities of which they are a part. The independence of the community governance of legal aid clinics is essential to the model, and we wanted them to address comprehensively the legal needs of the poor.

On November 13, 1976, I gave my first formal speech on these legal aid clinics, a few months after the Davis government had passed the necessary funding regulation. I stated that the clinics were "filling a void which could not be filled by other delivery models and therefore have a vital role to play in the future development of Ontario legal aid." I concluded my remarks by stating that legal aid is "perhaps the single most important mechanism that we have to make the equal rights dream a reality."

The system we developed was initially viewed with great suspicion by both the Ontario Progressive Conservative caucus and the governing body of the legal profession – the Law Society of Upper Canada. Some elected members of the Law Society believed that a system of legal aid clinics might create unfair competition for individual law firms which did not have the same access to government funding. Fortunately, wiser heads prevailed, and the Law Society came to recognize that traditional law firms generally did not contain the legal expertise for poverty-related issues. The overwhelming majority of law firms did not want to provide that type of legal assistance because it would generate little income.

Similarly, some of my caucus colleagues saw the clinics as guerrilla cells of opposition to the government. Their suspicion was fuelled by the clinics' community management boards and their commitment to what they called "poverty law" – legislation relating to financial assistance for people who qualified because of their low incomes. When NDP members David Warner became president of a clinic in his constituency in Scarborough and Jim Renwick president of another clinic in his constituency of Riverdale, this negative perception was strengthened even more.

One day during discussion in Cabinet, Agriculture Minister Lorne Henderson, who was himself a farmer and close to his rural constituents in the Sarnia area, expressed his concern about the way some of the new attorney general's policies were alienating his supporters. When asked for an example, Henderson related how the wife of his farmer neighbour had run off with the hired hand and, with the assistance of a local legal aid clinic, was suing her husband for half the farm.

Two of my senior policy advisers were particularly dedicated to the legal aid clinics and to law reform in general – Archie Campbell, my director of policy development, and his successor, Douglas Ewart. Their efforts made a strong and lasting contribution to the entrenchment of the Legal Aid Claim System in Ontario. Ewart, who recently retired from the Ministry of the Attorney General, did stellar work on the Roots of Youth Violence Report, tabled in 2008, which I co-chaired along with former Speaker Alvin Curling. I remain a special adviser to the legal aid clinics.

By the time I left office in 1985, we had expanded the system to forty-eight publicly funded and independent community clinics. Ian Scott added another nineteen clinics during his five years as attorney general in the Liberal Peterson government.

* * *

In my opinion, without a significant expansion of legal aid generally and legal aid clinics in particular, there will always be a serious problem with access to justice. Given that most citizens see this access as someone else's problem, it is difficult to be optimistic about a greater government financial commitment.

The right to choose one's lawyer with a legal aid certificate, assuming the lawyer will even accept the modest compensation, is available only to persons with very low incomes. At the same time, one of the major issues relating to access to justice under this program is that the client must be able to select a lawyer with expertise or competence in the particular area. The certificate model of legal aid was for many years administered by the Law Society of Upper Canada, the governing body of the legal profession. The Society was often complacent in deciding whether lawyers who accepted legal aid certificates were properly qualified to represent clients in particular matters – most often in the area of criminal defence.

In large cities such as Toronto, most persons charged with a crime would have little knowledge of the criminal defence bar. Early in my term as attorney general, a senior and respected defence counsel spoke to me about the lack of qualified legal representatives in many criminal cases. He suggested that many lawyers took on one criminal case a year, simply to "have something to talk about at cocktail parties."

In 1978 I shocked the Law Society by stating that I was becoming interested in the concept of a salaried defender model – in creating an office similar to the public defender office in the United States. The lawyers would be on salary and would specialize in criminal matters. Privately I had very mixed views because I did not want to weaken the defence bar. However, I did not accept the frequently advanced argument that there was some form of conflict when the prosecutors and the defence counsel were paid by the same government. My goal was simply to remind the Law Society that specialization was an important dimension of access to justice or adequate legal representation.

The matter was somewhat resolved when the Law Society established a system that enabled lawyers to qualify as specialists in criminal law and other areas of legal expertise. As part of the process, a central research bank was implemented, along with other ideas such as using social workers to help with sentencing submissions. Issues of access to justice in the Aboriginal community were also a priority, and native justices of the peace and native court-worker programs were established in the relevant areas of the province. After more than fifty years in the legal profession, I hold strongly to the view that access to adequate legal advice will always be a significant law reform issue.

The integrity of the Crown justice system was another major priority for me. In my view, it is one of the hallmarks of a democratic and civil society. One particularly controversial aspect of the criminal justice process is the negotiation of guilty pleas. More than 90 per cent of the people charged with criminal offences plead guilty to at least one charge related to the alleged offence. Often, the police lay multiple charges in relation to a single incident – a practice that frequently leads to allegations that it is all part of their strategy to encourage guilty pleas. However, the Crown prosecutor has the responsibility to determine whether the charges are appropriate and whether any plea of guilty will produce a just result.

Most criminal cases lead to plea negotiations between the Crown and the defence counsel. These discussions involve the sentence that the prosecutor will seek in the event of a plea of guilty. Although the negotiations are generally described by the media as "plea bargaining," I have always disliked that term because of its associations with the marketplace rather than the pursuit of justice. Use of that term has no doubt added to public scepticism about the criminal justice system, as many people believe that the process leads to lighter sentences than are warranted by the facts. Many Canadians also believe that the great majority of criminal cases that are resolved by guilty pleas result from overbooked courts and overly lenient Crown attorneys.

In my view, the high level of guilty pleas is related to the fact that, unlike the situation in many other countries, very few innocent people in Canada are charged with criminal offences. Some mistakes have been made, for sure, and it is important that we continue to have a vigilant defence bar as well as an adequately financed legal aid system. The high percentage of guilty pleas is, however, a result of generally reliable police investigations. Still, the outcome of a criminal trial can often be unpredictable, and the public interest can often best be served by the acceptance of a plea of guilty to a less serious charge with a lower sentence.

The traditional controversy over plea negotiations became a subject of debate in my early months in the Legislature. I decided it was time to communicate my views to all the Crown prosecutors in Ontario. I wrote a memorandum, which was later tabled in the Legislature, in which I stated that "expediency in workload" was no valid reason for not prosecuting or for agreeing that the accused be allowed to plead guilty to a lesser offence. "Expediency" in this context did not include a weakness in the Crown's case, which would be a valid reason for negotiating a plea to a lesser charge. I stressed that, in such cases, a plea negotiation "was often a better way to arrive at a just verdict than the often unpredictable results of a criminal trial." I also recommended that the Crown attorney must state in open court the reasons for accepting a plea of guilty to a lesser offence or offences. On the other side of the ledger, I was emphatic that the rights of the accused must always be respected. A prosecutor should never attempt to compel a guilty plea to an offence that could not be successfully prosecuted.

I instructed the Crown attorneys that they could give their views on a suitable sentence, but that the matter was strictly for the judge to decide. Even though the attorney general was in no way bound by the prosecution's opinion, I acknowledged, however, that my ministry would not appeal a sentence that had been suggested by the prosecutor except in exceptional circumstances. In recent years, joint recommendations by the prosecutor and the defence have been routinely made and accepted by the presiding judge.

Immediately after my statement to the Legislature, I was questioned by the media. I conceded that the procedure was "not a scientific process and was subject to human frailty" and concluded by stating that the "heavy court backlog should not be a factor in the plea negotiations and that the best interests of the community should be the paramount consideration." I regretted the often lengthy delays between the laying of a charge and the actual trial – delays caused by many reasons including, at times, the behaviour of judges and of Crown and defence attorneys. These challenges were exacerbated by the traditional underfunding of the administration of justice in Ontario. The longer I served as attorney general, the more I became aware of the huge pressures on the public treasury. Compared with health, education, transportation, and social services, the justice system was seldom regarded as a major government priority. Taxpayers are aware of the relevance of these other priorities in their own lives, but they generally never expect to be in a courthouse as a litigant in either a civil or a criminal trial.

Unfortunately, in recent years the court backlog has increased dramatically. These long delays in the criminal justice process in particular are an embarrassment for governments both provincially and federally.

* * *

Civilian oversight of the resolution of complaints against the police has, in recent years, been a major issue in police–community relations throughout the Western world. When I became attorney general, some studies had been done of this issue in Ontario, but not much action had been taken.

The first report I received soon after taking office was based on the study Arthur Maloney had prepared for the Toronto Board of Police Commissioners. In it, he recommended a civilian commissioner to handle public complaints against the police – a decidedly novel idea at the time. In 1977 the Royal Commission into Metropolitan Toronto Police

Practices under Justice Donald Morand also focused on the need for an independent civilian complaint commission.

These reports and others were in part a response to the growing violence that accompanied some racial incidents in Toronto. Unfortunately, the mistrust among visible minorities continued to escalate, and the Metro Toronto Council requested that the Roman Catholic cardinal, Emmett Carter, examine ways to improve the relationship between visible minorities and the police. By that time I had asked Sidney Linden, the counsel to the Canadian Civil Liberties Association and a future chief justice of the Ontario Court of Justice, to undertake research on behalf of the Ministry of the Attorney General. I was determined to create a pilot project in Metropolitan Toronto, and I wanted Linden to study police complaints processes in other jurisdictions and to propose a model for the province.

Although there was widespread consensus that a civilian component needed to be injected into the process, complex questions remained as to the degree of civilian involvement, how it should be organized, and how it should interact with the existing police internal systems. In our thinking, a system that combined the benefits of both the internal and the external components would be the best approach. Without doubt, a purely internal system would never satisfy the public concern that it would be biased in favour of the police. At the same time, a purely external system could become polarizing and confrontational – and impractical in many respects. Linden and I agreed that the police should be involved in the process, given their need to be directly accountable to the public. Individual police officers who were the subject of complaints had to be treated fairly and their rights protected.

The challenge was to find the right balance between civilian and police involvement. First we had to persuade law enforcement that it was in their interest to have a transparent system that would enable the police to maintain the trust of the people they were obliged to serve. Our proposal provided for initial investigations by the police, but with external oversight by a new civilian agency. The Davis government was in a minority position, and the opposition majority made it clear they would never agree to legislation that did not provide for a civilian agency to undertake the investigation from the beginning. In the United States, it's common for entirely separate institutions to provide independent investigations of citizens' complaints. Unfortunately, a very confrontational attitude develops almost immediately between the police force and the investigators, with a resulting lack of any cooperation. In other words, the police forces being investigated "invariably circle the wagons." Whatever system we decided on for Toronto was intended to be a pilot project that, if successful, would be expanded to other municipalities throughout Ontario.

When we regained our majority government in the spring of 1981, I introduced the *Metropolitan Toronto Police Force Complaints Project Act*, which passed into law later in the year. A public complaints commission was established as a three-year pilot project for Metro Toronto. However, the legislation was controversial in many quarters. Some community groups did not think it went far enough in civilian involvement, while most law-enforcement leaders felt that the new system went too far with respect to civilian oversight and that it would hinder their ability to perform their police responsibilities.

I appointed Sidney Linden to the position of complaints commissioner, but, unfortunately, there were delays in the passage of the legislation. Linden was thrown into the "deep end" without an adequate infrastructure, but he persevered and, ultimately, his intelligence and commitment produced impressive early reports. The changes he recommended to many police procedures were accepted. In my opinion, one very important aspect of the process was to allow the police to do the initial investigation, though it could be taken over at any time by the Office of the Public Complaint Commissioner. The fact that the police investigators knew that their efforts could be redone by the independent civilian complaints office was a significant incentive for a reliable initial investigation.

The newly appointed civilian investigators also performed valuable outreach to communities that were experiencing a high level of police activity. These officers attended legal aid clinics both to receive complaints and to help mediate some of the concerns between the community and the police. When the three-year pilot project was about to expire, I stated to the Legislature that "the period of time since 1981 has been marked by an unprecedented level of public acceptance of the complaints process ... and that the success of the project has led to it being copied by a number of jurisdictions throughout the world." In Britain, when Lord Scarman presented a report in the House of Lords on the major race riots that had occurred in Brixton, south of London, in 1980, he stated that the Toronto pilot project deserved serious consideration as a possible model of reform for Britain.

I shall always be grateful to Sidney Linden for his major contributions to the creation of the Metro Toronto model for complaints against the police and for his distinguished service as the first commissioner until 1985. When the Liberal Peterson government came into office that same year, the system was installed beyond the borders of Metro Toronto, and it became a province-wide agency in 1990 – the first in Canada. Ten years later, the Conservative Harris government rescinded the legislation to curry favour with police associations, which generally felt uncomfortable with the role of the independent complaints commissions. On taking office in 2003, the Liberal McGuinty government, after a report and recommendations by former chief justice Patrick LeSage of the Ontario Superior Court, restored the service in the form of the Office of the Independent Police Research Director.

14

Attorney General versus the National Hockey League

A year and a half before I became attorney general in October 1975, my lawyer brother, Bill, was asked by the government of Ontario to investigate issues related to excessive violence in hockey. The report had considerable influence during my early months in office. The fact that criminal assaults in hockey games was but one of a multitude of issues I faced at that time did not prevent massive media attention to it.

The growing public concern with violence in hockey came into sharp focus when the Bramalea Blues hockey team withdrew from the Ontario Junior B championship series with the Hamilton Red Wings ten days before my brother received his commission. The Bramalea team had forfeited the series because of management's concern about the "brutal tactics" employed by the Hamilton team. The officials felt they could not, in good conscience, expose their players to the risk of serious injury.

In 1973 the public had been shocked when a sixteen-year-old player, Paul Smithers, was charged and convicted of manslaughter after a fight that resulted in death following a house-league game. The victim had racially taunted Smithers, a young black man, during the game, and the fatal confrontation had continued in the arena parking lot. In his instructions to the jury during the trial, Judge Barry Shapiro said, "I am sure that you have been appalled as I have been, while listening to the evidence, to hear how sportsmanship has been so lost by fifteen- and sixteen-year-old participants and by some spectators as to make what was once the sport of hockey something that has practically disappeared from sight."

Everyone acknowledges that hockey is a tough physical game, but at this time the Philadelphia Flyers had institutionalized "goon violence" as a fundamental strategy. The Philadelphia team did in fact win the Stanley Cup in both 1974 and 1975. The success of the Flyers' strategy was having a growing influence on the amateur game, including the youngest players in organized hockey.

As he began his investigation, my brother emphasized that he did not condemn the application of force within the rules of the game of hockey as inappropriate violence. He then embarked on an extensive analysis and review of a number of relevant reports, studies, and research papers relating to violence not only in hockey but in athletics generally. He interviewed players, coaches, and officials involved at all levels of hockey and consulted with a number of social scientists and sport psychologists. In addition, he took advantage of Ontario's *Public Inquiries Act* to hold several days of hearings. He had already contacted Clarence Campbell, the president of the National Hockey League, who expressed his willingness to cooperate. The role of the NHL was of particular importance because, in Bill McMurtry's words, "the evidence was clear and overwhelming that the conduct and standards applied in the National Hockey League were having a profound effect on virtually every boy playing amateur hockey in every league, regardless of age or standard of competitions."

The NHL standards had been criticized for well over a decade. Eleven years earlier an experienced NHL ex-referee stated publicly that "the way they're letting hockey get out of hand, they are going to ruin the game. The big wheels of the NHL figure they have to have blood to fill the arenas." Former Toronto Maple Leaf Brian Conacher wrote in his book *Hockey in Canada* that "the growing incidents of brawling in the game, I believe, is not unconnected with the image of the game being presented to the violence-oriented American hockey fan … If there is a little blood, so much the better for the people with colour sets."

My brother also spoke with many active NHL players who were opposed to the amount of fighting that was permitted and encouraged in the league. Most of them did not wish to testify for fear of prejudicing their careers. While fighting in all other sports results in an automatic expulsion from the game, with the possibility of a significant fine too, the NHL players generally accepted the owners' views that brawling in hockey was a box-office necessity. The fact that fighting leads to expulsion from the game in international, Olympic, and college hockey had absolutely no influence on those responsible for the governance of the NHL.

In contrast to the NHL culture of brawling and intimidation, the great Russian hockey coach Anatoli Tarasov had the opposite view. He stated publicly that "courage means the ability to stay out of a fight. I know just how hard it is to contain yourself, how unfair it seems when you have to calmly take it from some over-strung athlete ... but real courage calls for self-control and patience."

My brother observed that, in European hockey, the emphasis has been to create an environment where the younger players could develop their skills without having to worry about aggression and violence. He wrote, "The professional rules and interpretations relating to boarding, interference and slashing, to name a few, are totally inappropriate if we are to create a proper environment for sports." This European culture has produced the majority of the skilled players now in the NHL. Several decades ago there were only a handful of non-Canadians in the league, whereas now they count for more than 40 per cent of the players.

When the report was tabled in the Ontario Legislature in 1974, it was praised on all sides. Stephen Lewis, the NDP leader, stated that it was the "most eloquent" government report that he had ever read. The *Globe and Mail*'s lead editorial on the report, "The McMurtry slap shot," stated that the author "had done a good, clean job and that he did not play to the gallery." The editorial went on to say in part that "there is impact and urgency in his 97-page report – enough we would hope to make most people realize that the game itself is in real jeopardy ... The skill and finesse that give it excitement are being yielded up to a crude, 'win at all costs' philosophy." The *Toronto Star* was also supportive in a lead editorial titled "Out of the game for fighting." "We share McMurtry's outrage," it began. "Fighting and stick swinging are not a necessary part of one of the world's fastest and most skillful games," and concluded that the message should be clear. "For the sake of our impressionable youngsters and for the sake of a great game, professional hockey must clean up its act."

In contrast to the overall media support, Clarence Campbell described the report as "a product of the Commissioner's imagination." He went on to state that "McMurtry has no jurisdiction to have any authority over the NHL." Campbell had testified at the inquiry hearings: in reply to my brother's suggestion that "NHL players, because of pressure inherent in a widely televised sport, are forced to fight," Campbell had said, "Your assessment of the situation may be the correct one ... but that is not what we are concerned about."

My brother summed up his feelings in a final comment in his report:

Sport, and particularly hockey, need not be a symptom of a sick society.

Hockey can be an effective instrument to improve the social conditions. Hockey can be a positive educational force, a model, to instill values such as co-operation, personal discipline, tolerance and understanding ... a celebration of speed, courage and finesse.

Rather than a divisive force, fuelled by calculated animosities, it can and should be a bond between participants, with a shared commitment to excellence and the common love of a game, hockey, which perhaps more than any other can give one a sense of physical exhilaration and sheer joy of participation.

Less than a year after the tabling of this report in the Ontario Legislature, I was sworn in as attorney general on October 7, 1975. This event coincided with the beginning of the professional hockey seasons for the National Hockey League and the former World Hockey Association, both of which had team franchises in Toronto. I was determined that these two leagues would take my brother's report seriously because I realized that the NHL, in particular, had always been a role model for young players throughout Canada. I had also learned from amateur hockey officials that many young players were dropping out of organized hockey because of the intimidation tactics increasingly being adopted by some of the most successful teams. I had even received a letter from very agitated parents complaining how, one day, they attended a team practice with their young son and witnessed the coach giving the players a boxing lesson on skates.

My fundamental concerns about the excessive violence in professional hockey, often amounting to criminal assault, stemmed largely from the negative impact that this style of hockey was having on young boys' participation in a great sport. So long as these practices were condoned and even encouraged in professional hockey, similar conduct in amateur hockey would continue and probably grow.

I knew from my own experience that hockey was a tough contact sport and, personally, in my youth I enjoyed this physical aspect of the game. However, a line had to be drawn between hard-hitting hockey, to which all players would be assumed to have consented, and the increasing level of criminal assault. I spoke to some NHL player friends,

Andy Donato, *Toronto Sun*

and although they shared my concerns, they admitted that it would be difficult for any professional player to protest publicly for fear of being regarded as chicken-livered – insufficiently tough. The exception was the great star Bobby Hull of the WHA Winnipeg Jets, who sat out a game in 1975 as a personal protest against what he described as the "mindless violence" that increasingly characterized professional hockey.

In late October 1975 I sent a letter to the chief executives of both the national hockey leagues, advising them that their games in Toronto would be closely monitored by the Metropolitan Toronto Police Department. That year, the only NHL and WHA teams in Ontario were in Toronto. I stressed that any clear infraction of the Canadian *Criminal Code* could attract a criminal charge. This warning should not have been a surprising statement from a provincial attorney general, yet for some reason the majority of the "hockey establishment" appeared to believe that the *Criminal Code* should not apply within hockey arenas.

I also made it clear that fist fights between players, which had long been accepted as part of hockey, were unlikely to attract criminal sanctions. The act of fighting generally involves an element of consent on both sides, but deliberately using a hockey stick as a "weapon" was another matter. In conclusion, I stated that this policy would apply throughout Ontario wherever the game of hockey was played. Charges would be laid only after close consultation with the local Crown Attorney's Office.

The response from both of the professional leagues was swift and predictable: I should mind my own business. Harold Ballard, the owner of the Toronto Maple Leafs, issued a statement that "the NHL had always policed itself and we do not need any help from the Attorney General. He should keep his nose out of hockey and worry about other things like crime in the streets." Ben Haskin, the president of the WHA, was quoted as saying that "McMurtry is over-reacting and has no right to suggest taking us to court, because we can run our own show." At the same time, the violent culture of the WHA was demonstrated by the advertising of the Minnesota Fighting Saints, which emphasized that potential fans "should come and watch violence on ice."

Sportswriters in Canada were divided in their comments about my statement that the application of the *Criminal Code* did not stop at the door of an arena. Many were highly critical, alleging that I was "just another politician looking for votes." I knew full well that the game of hockey had long enjoyed a "sacred cow" status in Canada, so I did not expect my initiative to be popular in all quarters. Fortunately, Jim Coleman, George Gross, and other veteran sportswriters were more supportive. Coleman wrote: "Regrettably but very predictably, Mc-

Murtry's communiqué has elicited the customary sneering cheap shots from the self-satisfied members of the professional sporting establishment who have deluded themselves into believing that the laws of the land do not apply to their athletic enterprises." Gross expressed his concern that "excessive violence in hockey does exists" and "that many young people are trying to copy the pros. This is an alarming sign as many parents are prohibiting their youngsters from playing the game, and many youngsters are themselves getting fed up with the violent style of the game."

In the Ontario Legislature, opposition leader Stephen Lewis endorsed the initiative, stating, "I'm for it completely; it is about time that something was done." In Ottawa, federal justice minister Ron Basford responded by urging all provincial attorneys general "to follow McMurtry's lead."

Conn Smythe, the former owner of the Toronto Maple Leafs and an honorary governor of the NHL, was well known for his statement, "If you can't beat 'em in the alley you can't beat 'em on the ice." Not surprisingly, he released an open letter addressed to me stating that, "with drunken drivers killing our citizens and with numerous unsolved murders, why don't you mind your own business?" Interestingly, the same day, the media reported that the governors of the WHA had "met in secret and agreed to crack down hard on violence." The *Toronto Star* reported that "Ben Haskin of the WHA said the league will be announcing stiffer sentences, including multi-game suspensions." It was, the newspaper continued, "the farthest-ranging campaign against violence that hockey has ever known."

A few weeks later, in November 1975, Dan Maloney of the Detroit Red Wings was charged with assault causing bodily harm after repeatedly banging the head of an unconscious Leaf defenceman, Brian Glennie, against the ice. The trial proceeded before Justice Patrick LeSage and a jury in the county court. Maloney was successfully defended by a senior lawyer in Toronto, George Finlayson. In acquitting Maloney, the jury released a letter to the trial judge at the same time as the verdict – an unprecedented act, to my knowledge, but one intended to send a strong double message to the NHL. First, the jurors did not want their verdict to be interpreted as condoning the violence exhibited in the Maloney-Glennie incident. Second, they believed the NHL itself should be on trial, not a single player who was simply part of the culture that was encouraged by the league. By the end of the year, however, the only reaction from Clarence Campbell's office had been to send a memoran-

The Rim, Conestoga College of Applied Arts and Technology

dum to each NHL team advising it that players should expect stricter surveillance during games in Maple Leaf Gardens.

On a more amusing level, I was in ongoing discussions with Francis "King" Clancy, an NHL Hall of Fame member and a long-time NHL referee. In 1975 he was a special assistant to Maple Leafs owner Harold Ballard. Clancy did not agree with my initiative, and he told me one day that he regretted having voted for me in the recent provincial election. "It was the first time I ever voted Conservative," he said, "and look what you do to us." To the end of his life, King Clancy believed that hockey had been tougher during his NHL career in the 1930s. This belief was largely fuelled by his memory of being "knocked cold" by Boston Bruin Eddie Shore, not on the ice but while walking to the Leaf dressing room between periods. He would not accept my view that, though hockey had always been a tough game, it was only in very recent years that professional teams had institutionalized violence as a core strategy.

The issue of criminal conduct in NHL hockey games reached a climax on April 20, 1976, when the Philadelphia Flyers played the Toronto Maple Leafs in a quarter-final playoff game in Toronto. During the game the Flyers set a playoff record by accumulating thirty penalties. I did not see the game in person or on television, but I was later advised by experienced police officers who were there that they had feared a full-scale riot in Maple Leaf Gardens, given the "hooliganism" of many of the Philadelphia players.

A few days later, Ian Macdonald, the very scholarly president of York University, informed me that he had watched the game on television and was so disturbed by what he saw that he went to his local police station to inquire whether he could lay charges as a private citizen. Macdonald, an enthusiastic recreational hockey player even in his eighties, was seriously disturbed by what he perceived as the influence the NHL was having on young players, including his own sons, as a result of the "thuggish tactics" of the Philadelphia team.

Members of the Metropolitan Toronto Police Department watched tapes of the game the next morning. They invited me to join them, but I declined: I thought it should be their decision, not that of my office, whether charges were laid. Traditionally, in Ontario, the police decide whether to lay a criminal charge, but the local Crown prosecutor makes the decision whether to proceed with the charge. In this instance the police investigators had no doubts about the justification for laying criminal charges.

When I was advised of their decision, I suggested that the arrests should be made before the Philadelphia team left Toronto, to communicate the message effectively to the governors of the NHL. Four members of the Philadelphia team were arrested and charged with various criminal assault offences. The players were photographed and fingerprinted, and the appearance of these "mug shots" in the media sent shockwaves through the ranks of the NHL. *Sports Illustrated*, which had long been critical of the NHL's acceptance of "goon style" hockey, highlighted the story, and it appeared that the NHL would, finally, have to address the issue seriously.

Clarence Campbell's initial reaction was, however, to "deplore" my actions. He attempted to defend the Flyers and, interestingly, commented that the Philadelphia team was "playing with a lot more restraint than they did two or three years ago." My own comments about Campbell at that time should, perhaps, have been moderated. On one occasion I commented that Campbell's "stubborn defence of excessive violence in hockey is nothing less than infantile." The *Toronto Sun* wrote that a "war between National Hockey League president Clarence Campbell and Ontario Attorney General Roy McMurtry is fast approaching the intensity of the on-ice battle between the Toronto Maple Leafs and the Philadelphia Flyers."

The Philadelphia district attorney general, Emmett Fitzpatrick, also got into the act. He stated that I had been involved in something that was none of my business and that my actions were a "clear perversion" of the office I held. He, in contrast, would never interfere with the operation of professional sport because "it's up to the league to look after their own operation." Again, my response should have been more restrained. I replied that Fitzpatrick "sounds like a damn fool. I pity the people of Ontario if things ever deteriorated to the point where we would have to look to officials in Philadelphia for advice."

A few of my Toronto sportswriter acquaintances told me that the charges laid against the Philadelphia players became the topic of much conversation in the bars around the Philadelphia Flyers arena. In one of them a popular new drink was concocted, the "Attorney General McTurkey."

I had few allies in the hockey establishment, but I was pleased and somewhat surprised by the degree of support I received from Scotty Morrison, the NHL's referee-in-chief, and Ralph Mellanby, the executive producer of CBC's *Hockey Night in Canada*. Morrison was quoted as saying that he was "concerned with the effect that hockey brawls are having on youngsters in Canada." As for Mellanby, he added that "we are all concerned with the violence in hockey, and I think all the media should be concerned." In a lead editorial titled "The law must do what NHL won't," the *Toronto Star* wrote on April 23, 1976: "That's why it's vitally important that hockey players … put a premium on skill and team work, rather than on violence and bullying … and that's why Ontario Attorney General Roy McMurtry is right to continue his crusade against hockey violence by the logical application of the normal laws of the land to activities in hockey arenas."

In the end all four Philadelphia players pleaded guilty to some of the assault-related criminal charges. The NHL began to create and enforce rules that were intended to eliminate or at least significantly reduce the culture of hooliganism. Whether it is a coincidence that the Philadelphia Flyers have not won a Stanley Cup since their successes in 1974 and 1975, I will leave for others to decide.

In the years that followed, the only highly publicized criminal prosecution for violence in hockey occurred in 2005, when Todd Bertuzzi of the Vancouver Canucks pleaded guilty to criminal assault in a vicious attack on Steve Moore of the Colorado Avalanche – an episode that ended Moore's hockey career. Bertuzzi received a suspended sentence, so he would still be able to travel to the United States, and the NHL suspended him for a few games. In my view, it was too gentle a penalty, given the severity of the injury to the other player.

I have often been asked whether the NHL has returned to the "goon-style" hockey that characterized the Philadelphia Flyers in the 1970s. After the player prosecutions in 1975 and 1976, the tougher penalties imposed by the NHL significantly reduced much of the criminal violence. In the intervening years, however, faster and bigger athletes have taken up the game, with the result that any bodily contact will often be violent. In recent years the concern over the issue of injuries has generally focused on the serious consequences of brain concussions – something that, earlier, was treated as a relatively routine occurrence.

In a powerful article in May 2011, *Globe and Mail* sportswriter Allan Maki described "the dirtiest job in pro sports – being a hockey heavy weight, an enforcer, a fighter." He wrote of the "bare-knuckle anguish for the men engaged in the most dangerous job in professional sports – the agony, addictions and possibly brain damage." Maki continued: "No one starts off playing hockey to break faces for a living. Somehow the opportunity finds them, then pushes them to the NHL where losing a fight could mean being sent to the minors. No more big money, maybe no job."

Dr Charles Tator, an internationally renowned neurosurgeon who is associated with Toronto Western Hospital, has provided effective leadership in alerting the public to the connection between concussion and early Alzheimer's disease and dementia. The NHL was reluctant to pay much attention to his warning until a concussion ended super-star Sidney Crosby's season in early January 2011. For me, the saddest aspect of the ongoing debate about the role of the hockey enforcer and fighter in the NHL is the total lack of leadership by the league's administration. Their priority is not the players' health but the fans' liking for fights and blood on the ice. No other professional team sport permits fighting as part of the game.

Over the years I have discussed the issue of fighting with a number of former NHL players. I have yet to encounter a single player who does not believe that fighting should lead at the very least to a game suspension. This reality was demonstrated dramatically in a 2011 article about Bill Masterton – the only NHL player to die during a game, back in 1968. It is generally believed that his death was probably caused by an earlier concussion. When he first began his career in the NHL, he wore a helmet. At that time, however, there was an idea that helmets were worn only by cowards. Masterton discarded his helmet – and, without protection, he died.

In the years since the release of my brother's report in 1974, the number of boys and young men participating in the sport of hockey has declined every year in Canada – the result of cost, no doubt, as well of the threat of injury. Unfortunately the NHL does not care about these statistics, given that its only concern is the continuing adequate supply of elite players. The concept of broad participation by young people is clearly of little interest to the moguls of the NHL, regardless of the potential benefit to thousands of young people.

Inevitably, though, NHL players become models for our youth. Allan Maki referred to this point when he wrote about retired NHL enforcer Georges Laraque:

As the NHL's most feared big man, he hated his job, hated having to live up to a reputation he never wanted. While he fought more than 130 times in 13 seasons, Laraque was quick to find solace in his charity work and religion. That was what it took for him to get past what he did on the ice.

"I always defend the job," Laraque explained. "But I never liked it. What I hated the most was that I was promoting violence to the youth. You see kids at

NHL games and they clench their fists and yell, 'Kill him,' and you're supposed to be a role model. Then they fight in minor hockey and that's my fault. That's how I felt."

The NHL, however, does not appear to have retreated one iota from its entrenched position that hockey violence is a necessary part of the game – simply in the context of selling tickets. We have only to view the ever-increasing violence on TV and in film and video games, not to mention the huge popularity of "ultimate fighting," to realize how thin is our veneer of civilization and to accept that a large number of people might well welcome a return to the spectacle of Roman gladiators fighting to the death in an arena.

On a more positive note, the concussions suffered by Sidney Crosby and many other elite NHL players seem finally to have woken up the NHL establishment to the fact that "head shots" are a serious issue.

* * *

In 2012 I became directly associated with Dr Charles Tator as a member of the advisory board of his Canadian Sports Concussion Project. I had first got to know him as the lead physician for my friend Barbara Turnbull, who became a quadriplegic when she was only seventeen as a result of being shot in a milk-store hold-up in 1983. Her immense courage, her support for spinal-cord injury research, and her work as a *Toronto Star* journalist have been an inspiration to me and many others for years (chapter 17).

Since my brother Bill's 1974 report on excessive violence in hockey and my own combative relationship with the NHL as Ontario attorney general in the 1970s, the myriad unnecessary injuries to young people playing hockey has continued to be an important issue for me. My concerns have extended to my hockey-playing children and grandchildren. Although NHL players continue to be role models for young hockey players, the league does not appear to recognize its responsibilities to those same boys and girls.

Dr Tator and I had lunch one day in 2011, a period when there were a number of suicides in professional hockey and football which were believed to be directly related to concussions. We concluded that further initiatives were long overdue and continued our conversation over another lunch with Ken Dryden, the celebrated member of the NHL Hall of Fame, a former federal Cabinet minister, and an eloquent advocate of banning "head shots" from hockey. About that same time, York University, where I serve as chancellor, arranged a symposium on sports concussions which featured the former CFL quarterback Matt Dunnigan, who had suffered significant health consequences from a number of concussions.

In the course of our discussions, Dr Tator, Dryden, and I agreed that yet another major conference was needed – one in which the highest levels of the NHL participated. The conference was tentatively scheduled for the summer of 2012, and Governor General David Johnston, a former hockey player from his days at Harvard University, agreed to host it at Rideau Hall. However, the failure of the NHL governors and the players' association to reach a collective bargaining agreement until January 2013 delayed our plans, and the conference is now planned for later in 2013 – at a time, as I write, that has not yet been agreed upon.

I believe that Dr Tator's sports concussion project will help maintain the necessary momentum. The advisory board also includes Matt Dunnigan and Leo Ezerins, the executive director of the Canadian Football League Alumni Association. One of the project's goals is to obtain more state-of-the-art diagnostic machines for accurate detection of concussions. We hope the NHL is listening.

In recent months, the issue has become a major public concern: a poll in the *Globe and Mail* reported by senior sports columnist Roy MacGregor indicates that more than 85 per cent of the parents of hockey-playing youngsters want body checking eliminated until at least the early teens. The point was reinforced in the same newspaper on March 7, 2013, reporting on a hockey game the previous night between the Toronto Maple Leafs and the Ottawa Senators. The article, written by experienced hockey reporter David Shoalts, described a fight between an Ottawa Senators player and a Maple Leafs designated fighter in which the Leaf player challenged the Ottawa player before the game even began:

The dark side of the NHL is a graphic demonstration of how ugly and pointless hockey fights can be.

By the time the game clock stopped at 26 seconds after the opening faceoff, [the Ottawa player] lay face down on the ice spread eagled and unconscious.

The knock-out was so sickening to watch …

Before the end of the first period, the Senators announced [that their player] had a concussion and would not return to the game.

Once again the NHL has demonstrated that its medieval approach to the game will prevail, even though many thousands of Canadian young people continue to turn away from a potentially wonderful sport.

15

Racism and Religion

Early in my career as attorney general I committed my ministry to making race relations a priority. The demographics were changing dramatically, particularly in southern Ontario. The South Asian community had increased significantly as a result of immigration, largely from East Africa, where tyrannical regimes had become hostile to these minority groups in their populations. Canada was also becoming a destination for immigrants from Hong Kong and South Korea, and the number of black Canadians continued to grow because of the ongoing immigration from the Caribbean.

The sad reality is that every society contains racist elements. Governments must therefore confront unfair discrimination and racist activity at every turn. Canada continues to face these challenges, though people living here have demonstrated a greater support for diversity than exists elsewhere in the world. Still, our nation has by no means been immune from the cancer of racism, as demonstrated by decades of discrimination against our own Aboriginal peoples and our long-established black population, as well as the violence at times of anti-Semitism. Furthermore, our history includes the tragic chapters of the Chinese head tax for four decades after 1885 and the incarceration of Japanese Canadians during the Second World War.

In 1975, just as I took office, the reaction of racist forces in Ontario to the growing South Asian immigration led to increasing incidents of "Paki bashing," which included hate mongering and physical assaults on member of the South Asian community generally. Although racism often occurs randomly, it was evident that many of these activities were being orchestrated by malevolent organizations. One such group, the Western Guard, led by Don Andrews, regarded itself as a local chapter of the Ku Klux Klan, and I soon learned that there was indeed a direct connection.

Many associations formed within the South Asian community in the Greater Toronto Area had already created links among themselves as well as with various public institutions. These organizations provided platforms to express their concerns – primarily the lack of adequate law-enforcement response to legitimate complaints of racist incidents. These incidents affected the Hindu, Sikh, and Pakistani communities, and they brought the South Asian associations together in a way that would probably not have happened in their home nations.

As attorney general, I received a number of individual complaints that, in many cases, appeared to demonstrate an inadequate police response. It was clearly impractical to attempt to follow up on each individual complaint, so I met collectively with the leaders of the South Asian associations and suggested that they outline their concerns in one report. The challenge was to find an individual who enjoyed sufficient credibility in that diverse community to produce a report which the majority of the organizations would support. Fortunately, I found that person in Dr Bhausaheb Ubale, an Indian-born Hindu professor who seemed well connected throughout the South Asian community.

Dr Ubale proved to be a good choice: in April 1978 he produced a well-crafted report, *Equal Opportunity and Public Policy*, that bore the signatures of thirty-two associations – Pakistani, Hindu, and Sikh. We organized a formal occasion attended by Premier Davis and several members of the Cabinet on which to demonstrate publicly the government's support for it and our commitment to act on its recommendations. In his remarks, Davis acknowledged the "many ways in which racism manifests itself in Ontario ... often including criminal acts of racism." As a result, the police forces in areas with relevant immigrant populations established effective training programs in race relations, culminating in more aggressive and sensitive responses to allegations of breaches of the *Criminal Code*.

Early in this period the Cabinet established a Race Relations Committee, which I chaired for the remainder of my decade as minister. The committee provided an important outreach vehicle for dialogue with leaders of the minority racial communities. Obviously this process could not provide the definitive answers to many issues of racism, particularly those related to employment discrimination, but it was an important initiative as racial minorities came to realize they had access to the highest levels of the provincial government. In addition, we created a special race-relations division of the Ontario Human Rights Commission, which had originally been established to help avoid racial problems, but had also to focus on many other issues of discrimination. Dr Ubale became the first chair of that new division. We also prepared an official declaration on race relations, committing the government to the promotion of tolerance and the elimination of racial discrimination. This document was circulated widely – to government offices, courts, LCBO stores, and all school boards, among other places – and officials were encouraged to post it in prominent locations.

In the 1970s the term "race relations" provoked different reactions, many of them not positive. Some people believed that it suggested the presence of racist tensions and might well encourage a self-fulfilling prophecy of racial conflict. As a result, Cabinet debated whether to use the term at all. These concerns were understandable, but our government had to be realistic in recognizing the reality of racism and in addressing it aggressively. In 1980 I encountered the same concern about this term within the ranks of the Thatcher government in Britain. During a visit to London, I met with Lord Hailsham, the Lord Chancellor, who described his responsibilities for race relations as one of community relations. In the course of our conversation about the most effective strategies to deal with racism, he stated, "In my view, the best way to deal with race relations is not to talk about it." Shortly thereafter, the Brixton race riots broke out in South London.

Personally, in speaking or writing about race relations, I have always had some difficulty with terms such as "visible minorities" and "people of colour." Although these terms are usually well understood, it's difficult to describe anyone who is a member of an "invisible minority" or who is "uncoloured."

As the chair of the Cabinet committee on race relations, I encouraged the mayors and the city councils throughout the province, where practical, to create race-relations committees. We wanted to encourage dialogue at the local level in the hope that responsible members of the community would recognize that improving race relations was a significant issue. Equally important, people who had experienced discrimination, or worse, would know that their concerns were being taken seriously. At the same time, I knew that much more was required than talk and that government had a responsibility to develop equal opportunity policies that would be reflected in government hiring. The public service, I believed, should be representative of the rich diversity of our province.

As the police forces began to target racist organizations that broke the law, the Western Guard and several of its leaders were successfully prosecuted and jailed. In due course I received a threatening letter from David Duke, the Ku Klux Klan's Grand Wizard from Louisiana, when he visited Toronto and personally delivered the envelope to my office:

This letter is in protest against your anti-White policies, which have been in direct opposition to the interests of the White Canadian population and indeed the White population of the North American continent.

Specifically, you have sought to destroy the sacred right of freedom of speech for White Canadians. Secondly, you have instructed your subordinates to apply the law unequally to White youths involved in racial incidents. Thirdly, you have betrayed your race and nation by your subservience to international Zionism and the state of Israel.

Take heed that your nefarious anti-White activities are being monitored and recorded by our international Klan movement. If you persist in your treacherous activities against the White Race, I can assure you that there can only be grave consequences.

> In the name of the White Race
> David Duke
> Grand Wizard, Knights of the Ku Klux Klan

I regarded the Klan's threats to be a distinct compliment, so I immediately had the letter framed, and I've hung it in my various offices ever since. The Ku Klux Klan is obviously still flourishing in Louisiana: Duke was nearly elected governor of the state a few years later, and his name came into prominence internationally in 2007 when he was a high-profile delegate to a Holocaust-denial conference in Iran.

Although the hate-mongering industry has always been a regrettable reality, we must be vigilant to prevent its roots from sinking deeply into Canadian soil. Many advocates of free speech question whether anti-hate propaganda laws should remain in our *Criminal Code*, but I have long believed that this code should reflect the basic values of our society. One such value is to attempt to protect minority groups from the malevolent forces that will continue to prey on the potentially vulnerable. I subscribe to the view of Dag Hammarskjöld, the former

United Nations secretary general, who stated many years ago: "The madman shouted in the market place but no one answered. Thus it was assumed that his thesis of hatred was incontrovertible. It is required that we answer the madman in order to protect every man, woman and child who may be tormented by his shouting."

The principal hate propaganda sections of the Canadian *Criminal Code* require an attorney general's personal consent before a charge can be laid – a necessary precaution to protect legitimate freedom of speech from becoming the target of criminal sanctions. It is also well known that a successful prosecution may give a hate monger sufficient publicity to counter any deterrent effect, while an unsuccessful prosecution can encourage more hate mongers to come out from under their rocks and further poison the atmosphere. Even though the phrasing of the *Criminal Code* sections provides some significant safeguards against encroachment on legitimate freedom of speech, the attorney general nevertheless treads a fine line in determining whether the public interest will be served by a hate propaganda prosecution.

Early in my career as attorney general, I learned that respected national institutions can be insensitive to the dissemination of hatred. Bell Telephone, for instance, appeared to be indifferent to the fact that hate propaganda messages could be transmitted on its system by anyone who wished to rent a phone number. These numbers would then be circulated in minority communities with an encouragement to dial the number. For many recipients, the fact that a hate message was being transmitted by a national institution added to the emotional trauma of listening to the message. When I complained personally to Bell, I received a collective shrug in response. However, my intervention with Ron Basford, the federal minister of justice, was much more successful: the federal communications legislation was amended to prohibit the use of a public communications system for the transmission of hate propaganda.

In the legal sphere, our courts did not have much experience in dealing with hate-motivated crimes. In one particularly ugly assault, a Tanzanian immigrant was pushed onto the subway tracks but fortunately survived. Although the evidence established that the assault was motivated by the colour of the victim's skin, the experienced judge who presided over the trial stated that he would not take the racist motive into account in sentencing. In my opinion, this motivation made the assault much more troubling, and I announced my intention to appeal the outcome. I wanted to convey the message publicly that cases involving hate and discrimination would be treated very seriously by our prosecutors. I was confident that the Court of Appeal would agree, and in a decision written by Chief Justice Charles Dubin, the court increased the sentence:

It is a fundamental principle of our society that every member must respect the dignity, privacy and person of the other. Crimes of violence increase when respect for the rights of others decreases, and, in that manner, assaults such as occurred in this case attack the very fabric of our society. An assault which is racially motivated renders the offence more heinous. Such assaults, unfortunately, invite imitation and repetition by others and incite retaliation. The danger is even greater in a multicultural, pluralistic urban society. The sentence imposed must be one which expresses the public abhorrence for such conduct and their refusal to countenance it.

That attitude became the law in Ontario, but it was many years before the federal government amended the *Criminal Code* to legislate specifically that any racial motive related to an assault should be regarded as an aggravating factor.

My responsibilities as chair of the Cabinet committee on race relations brought me into contact with a broad spectrum of issues that had a racial dimension. One such issue was the lack of people from minority groups appearing in magazine advertising or in television commercials. In this context I was introduced to the great Canadian jazz pianist Oscar Peterson by Lloyd Perry, the first black official guardian in Ontario. Peterson had grown up in a very small black community in Montreal and went on to perform with all the US jazz legends, including Louis Armstrong, Ella Fitzgerald, and Dizzy Gillespie. His debut at Carnegie Hall is a jazz legend. As a young man on tour in parts of the US South he was confronted by ugly discrimination, and he was not immune to racial profiling in Canada, where for many years he was routinely stopped by the police simply because he was a black man driving an expensive car. Given his illustrious career and his wonderful sense of humour, he had not previously given any attention to this advertising issue. By the mid-seventies, however, he had concluded that commercial advertising must reflect mainstream society, and he viewed the absence of people from minority groups in that medium as a form of exclusion.

I decided to host a series of luncheons to which I would invite senior executives of major advertising agencies and large retailers to meet Oscar Peterson. As a prerequisite, the Cabinet Race Relations

Committee prepared a guidebook on portraying racial diversity and persuaded the Ontario government to change its own advertisements. The lunches were well attended, and our guests learned about Peterson's concerns regarding the exclusion of members of visible minority communities from mainstream advertising. At first the executives aired a few lame excuses for their behaviour, but soon a more positive attitude prevailed, and within six months, people from minority groups began to appear in magazine and television advertising. Peterson was not only a true Canadian but much admired in many other nations, notably Japan, Austria, and the United States. He received the most meritorious honours available in Japan, including an award of merit from the emperor, and Austria issued a national stamp in his honour. When President Bill Clinton addressed the Canadian Parliament, his opening words included the statement that "it feels great to be in the land of Oscar Peterson."

Our collaboration on rectifying this racial injustice led to a close friendship over many years. I wear with great pride a beautiful Rolex watch Peterson gave me in 2006, a year before his death. On the back he had inscribed, "For Roy, my dear friend, love O.P."

* * *

A few months after becoming attorney general for Ontario, I found myself personally embroiled in the politics of Northern Ireland. In June 1976 I gave a speech outlining my concerns about the disease of hate propaganda in our diverse Canadian society. In it I referred to a number of organizations and individuals who were dedicated to racist-motivated crimes and racist propaganda – the Toronto-based Western Guard, for example, and the Reverend Ian Paisley in Northern Ireland. Paisley had recently announced his intention to open one of his Free Presbyterian churches in Toronto. For some years he had been the leader of the Democratic Unionist Party, the most extreme of the Ulster Unionist parties, and he vehemently attacked the Roman Catholic Church at every opportunity, imagining "papist plots" everywhere to facilitate a union between Northern Ireland and the Republic of Ireland. The term "unionist" in Northern Ireland politics is usually used in the context of Ulster's continuing union with Great Britain, while "republican" refers to the proponents of a united Ireland.

In my view, Paisley was a despicable individual who, in his role as both a church minister and a politician, was committed to the constant dissemination of hate propaganda. In attacking him in my speech, I was not crossing any religious divide because I was born into a Protestant family with its origins in Northern Ireland. At the same time, I had no sympathy for Paisley's antagonists, the Irish Republican Army (IRA), who had long been committed to terrorism in pursuing their political objectives. As I continued in my address:

If you want proof that the racist demagogues can be truly dangerous, look no further than Northern Ireland, where for years, innocent people have been dying for false causes they can only dimly perceive. At the heart of the vicious little war – if one human being can be held responsible – it is one man, a man called Ian Paisley. I will not dignify him with the title "Reverend." I certainly do not revere him.

Now, I understand that Paisley intends to open a branch of his so-called church here in Toronto and that he is planning a trip to Toronto this year. I, for one, hope he is not allowed into the country, and although I respect very greatly the principle of freedom of speech, I hope that the minister of immigration, Robert Andras, will bar his entry.

This province does not need this brand of bigotry. He and his followers are responsible for breathing new life into the smouldering, ancient antagonisms in Northern Ireland and for preventing the only real attempts at reconciliation between the opposing factions. They are destructive people, and we don't want them in Ontario.

Although my comments about Paisley received little attention in the Canadian media, they were widely reported in Northern Ireland. As a consequence, I became a highly publicized target of Paisley's anger, to the extent that the *Toronto Star* arranged for a journalist to attend one of Paisley's Sunday sermons in Belfast. The resulting article was titled "Paisley coming to Metro despite McMickery." It read: "Reverend Ian Paisley vowed 'by the grace of God' that he would be coming to Metro in September 'and all of the McMurtrys or McMickerys of the day can't keep me out." The writer went on to explain that "Mick is the divisive Belfast slang for Catholic," and noted that I came from Ulster Protestant stock. "But that didn't seem to bother Paisley as he bellowed out his attack on McMurtry," the article continued. "The old Attorney General has rickets," he told his flock. "I want to say God will blow upon him for putting his hand against God's public." Paisley went on to say that "horrible things happened to people who resist him." He recalled how he had once verbally crossed a senior policeman in Belfast and, soon afterwards, that same man dropped dead of a heart attack. (For the sequel to this story, see chapter 30.)

A few months later I visited Paul Martin Sr, who was then Canada's high commissioner to Britain and Northern Ireland. Not long after my request that the Canadian government keep Paisley out of Canada, Martin said, the angry reverend met with him to inquire whether he would have any difficulty in coming to open his church in Toronto. Martin advised him that there should be no problem, and the church was in fact dedicated by Paisley as scheduled. Fortunately, the event got no local media attention. I assured Martin that I had never expected the Canadian government to comply with my request. I had simply wanted to send a message to the Roman Catholic population in Ontario that to me, an elected politician of Irish Protestant origins, Paisley's conduct was unacceptable and outrageous.

For more than thirty years after my 1976 anti-hate propaganda speech, Paisley remained the leader of the Democratic Unionist Party in Northern Ireland. I have often spoken of him as a unifying force among the largely Roman Catholic Northern Ireland republican forces. In my view, those forces would have wanted to invent an Ian Paisley if he did not actually exist. In any event, Paisley can take a great deal of credit for the fact that a political stalemate continued to exist in Northern Ireland for many years. It can only be hoped that, with an elected assembly reinstated in 2007 and local government restored, the reconciliation process so long frustrated by Paisley will continue. It is encouraging that Paisley did agree to power sharing with Sinn Fein, and his Democratic Unionist Party, led by Peter Robinson, is in a coalition government with Martin McGuinness's Sinn Fein. Paisley is now retired from politics, but his old seat is held by his son of the same name, who is unfortunately also not averse to making hateful remarks.

* * *

Another race-relations challenge surfaced in 1977, when the elected council in Cavan Township attempted to prevent the francophone Cistercian Monks from Oka, Quebec, from locating in their community. Cavan Township is in the vicinity of Peterborough, approximately 160 kilometres east of Toronto. The council justified its refusal to condone a rezoning request by the monks by stating that it did not want a Roman Catholic monastery in its almost totally Protestant township.

A newspaper report at the time revealed that it was no coincidence that Catholics were outnumbered in Cavan Township nearly one thousand to one. The area had been settled by Protestants from County Cavan in Ireland who brought with them the anti-Catholic attitudes and traditions that had created an island of intolerance. In the mid-1800s a group of Protestant religious bigots known as the "Cavan Blazers" had driven Irish Catholic settlers from the area. If Catholic families did not leave when requested, they were threatened with having their homes burned down. No Catholic church had ever been built in Cavan Township, nor, in the 130 years of its history, had any Catholic·ever been elected to the Township Council.

After the council meeting that turned down the rezoning request, one of the councillors, Joe Thompson, was reported as saying that "Cavan was a Protestant Township and it will stay like this." He was responding to the fact that many local residents had contacted their councillor to object to a monastery in their township.

When the issue was raised in the Ontario Legislative, I characterized it as reprehensible and unacceptable discrimination. I stated that, if the Catholic Order wanted to proceed with the monastery, the by-law would be overturned by provincial legislation. The Cavan Township Council grudgingly responded that it would abide by my decision. The *Toronto Star* printed a tough editorial titled "Ontario's shame" that included the following statements:

No doubt the people of Cavan Township think they are good Canadians. But in their display of blatant and unashamed bigotry towards French Canadians and Catholics they are sabotaging the country's very existence …

The people of Cavan have given the separatist propaganda machine another ugly incident to blow out of proportion to support their claim that French Canadians aren't welcome as equals in the rest of Canada.

I advised the Cistercian Order that the appropriate provincial legislation would be enacted if it wished to locate in Cavan Township. However, given the availability of other suitable locations, they decided to settle elsewhere to avoid any "aggravation." And so ended a regrettable little chapter in the history of Ontario.

One of the more interesting legal sagas in Ontario was the libel suit brought by Crown counsel Casey Hill, with my personal encouragement and support, against the Church of Scientology. This action went through a jury trial in Toronto, the Court of Appeal for Ontario, and the Supreme Court of Canada. Both appeal courts upheld the highest defamation award in Canada's history – $1.6 million. A second defendant in the case was well-known lawyer Morris Manning, a former Crown counsel with the Ministry of the Attorney General.

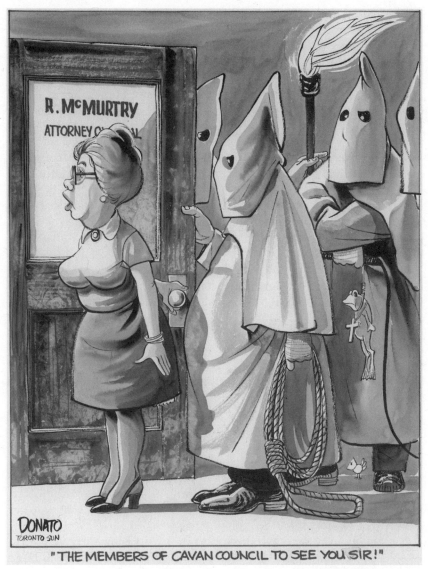

"THE MEMBERS OF CAVAN COUNCIL TO SEE YOU SIR!"

Andy Donato, *Toronto Sun*

The Church of Scientology has attracted a great deal of controversy in many countries where fraud-related allegations have been made and often upheld in the courts. The church's major ideology is related to its opposition to the practice of psychiatry and that profession's use of drugs, which is alleged to be "an evil mind-controlling exercise." This unusual denomination has attracted adherents from many segments of society, including famous film stars such as Tom Cruise and John Travolta as well as many vulnerable persons.

The Scientology movement was founded by L. Ron Hubbard in the United States in the early 1950s. It describes itself as an "applied religious philosophy" to help people "handle the problems of life" and often refers to the "technology of Scientology." According to a book written by a fervent apologist, in order "to understand fully the meaning and methods of Scientology, it is necessary to know something of Dianetics," which is essential to the denomination's approach to the modern science of mental health and the "technical foundation upon which it rests." It would seem that Hubbard, originally known as a successful writer of science fiction, adopted this technological approach to resolving mental health issues.

In books about Scientology, which I generally find unfathomable, the Dianetic technique is designed to locate hundreds of engrams (negative memories). An individual described as an "auditor" is trained to listen carefully to the individual (patient) being processed, to assist that person "back along the time track." In the course of this process, purportedly, the patient experiences curative powers that are related to mental health. The individual undergoing this form of therapy is described as a "preclear." That person's accumulated traumatic experiences are "contacted and reduced by a repetitive re-experiencing of them."

The movement has no shortage of critics throughout the world. The philosophy of Scientology and Dianetics has been described as "from Abracadabra to Zombies." (Hubbard once wrote that "a galactic emperor called Xenu brought his people to earth 75 million years ago and buried them in volcanoes.") As an organization, Scientology is very secretive, and it frequently complains about "its struggles with powerful government institutions in the nations of the world" where it has adherents or followers.

Our Scientology saga had its origins in my decision early in 1980 to establish a "Study of Mind Development Groups, Sects and Cults in Ontario" under the direction of Dr Daniel Hill (who was no relation to Casey Hill). Dr Hill, a black scholar, had been the first chair of the Ontario Human Rights Commission in the 1960s. This study investigated many accounts of the way in which various sects and cults had alienated young people in particular from their families. These groups, which were often described as religious cults, were accused of "brain-washing" fragile and sometimes disturbed individuals, to the anguish and concern not only of their loved ones but members of the public as well. The most tragic example of the extremes of such religious cults was the Jonestown community in Guyana, where hundreds of people participated in a mass suicide at the urging of their leader, Jim Jones. Some of the cults in Ontario were alleged to have been involved in mind control, financial rip-offs, mental breakdowns, alienation, hypnosis, and emotional coercion. Because "freedom of religion" has traditionally been regarded as a fundamental right in a democratic society, the issue had very sensitive dimensions. I was confident, however, that Dr Hill would approach his task wisely and well.

The Hill report was tabled in the Legislature in late 1980. Its major recommendations related to education programs to more effectively inform people about the dangers of sects and cults that often preyed on vulnerable people. In the first paragraph of his conclusions, Dr Hill wrote: "The controversy raised by new religions, cults, mind development groups and deprogramming is complex and defies simplistic solutions, posing instead questions that are basic to our democratic constitutions." The report reviewed in detail the historical evolution of rights and freedoms in the United Kingdom and Canada. It acknowledged the grave injustices in the federal government's treatment of Japanese Canadians during the Second World War and the Quebec government's mistreatment of Jehovah's Witnesses in the mid-1940s.

Dr Hill also recognized that one of the most important rights recognized in legislation applicable in Ontario was freedom of religion, which involved a broad degree of personal freedom. Attempting to curtail the activities of cults, sects, and mind-controlling activities outside the provisions of the *Criminal Code* would, in his opinion, require significant proof of necessity. Nowhere in his report did he identify any specific cult, sect, or new religion, though his concern with the activities of the Church of Scientology was apparent. Dr Hill's decision not to identify any specific organization by name was correct, given that his report was a study and not an inquiry. There was no consensus among mental health specialists as to degree of harm caused to those who become members of cults and sects, he said, and some group members spoke of improvement of their mental health as a result of their membership.

The study concluded that no new government measures were warranted. Dr Hill doubted that any of the destructive practices revealed in his report could be adequately defined for legislative purposes and observed that cult members have recourse to civil law when they feel that their mental health has been impaired through the negligence or maliciousness of leaders of the groups involved. He conceded, however, that the extent and character of financial deception and fraud practised by some groups "did generate far more serious concern for the study. In these movements, deception and fraud are endemic and carried out in a substantial scale. All energy is devoted to the pursuit of more members and, through them, more money to enrich the leader and his lieutenants ... Techniques employed by these groups include hard-sell methods, unconscionable contracts, loan frauds and falsified bookkeeping."

The Ontario Provincial Police had already received a number of complaints about alleged fraudulent transactions, and Dr Hill shared his concerns about the Church of Scientology with the OPP and with me. Casey Hill, the senior legal counsel to the Hill study, went on to become the lead counsel for the OPP in its investigation of Scientology.

The OPP engaged in an undercover police operation for many months before the issuance of a *Criminal Code* search warrant of Scientology's headquarters on Yonge Street in Toronto. The OPP's execution of that search took place over two days, on March 3 and 4, 1983, and involved more than one hundred police officers accompanied by seven accountants. The search warrant authorized by the chief judge of the provincial criminal court was over one thousand pages in length – at that time, the most detailed document of its kind ever prepared in Canada. The search and seizure was an integral part of an international police investigation that stretched out over two years.

The occupants of the Scientology headquarters had been carefully prepared for the possibility of a police search: they had conducted raid drills and developed instructions for quickly vetting and shredding documents. The third-floor Guardian's Office was fortified, and instructions had been issued to stall any search. The police recorded their search by means of video, audio recording, and still photographs, and the president of Scientology and its lawyers were provided with these records. The police also agreed to seal the files to which Scientology claimed client privilege until the court could rule on the matter.

Within a couple of days, Scientology retained Toronto lawyer Clayton Ruby to challenge the legality of the search. The months of litigation that ensued provided a significant contribution to the law of search and seizure in Ontario and Canada. In the final result, multiple court rulings, culminating in a decision by the Supreme Court of Canada, upheld the validity of the search warrant. The sealed files, however, proved to be contentious. On September 17, 1984, Scientology organized a highly publicized press conference on the front steps of Osgoode Hall. Senior Scientology officials and counsel Morris Manning had alleged that Casey Hill was guilty of criminal intent for having broken the court sealing order; his conduct, moreover, amounted to "a public depreciation of the administration of justice, tending to interfere with the due course of justice, resulting in public disparagement of justice tending to prejudice Scientology and perverting the due course of justice." He stated that these acts warranted a prison sentence and the imposition of a fine.

Not surprisingly, Casey Hill was devastated that his integrity had been challenged in such a serious and public manner. I was in the Yukon at the time, and when I spoke with him that night, I authorized him to retain the senior and much respected lawyer J.J. Robinette. In November 1989 the criminal contempt trial spread over eleven days. Justice Cromarty, the presiding judge, held that there was absolutely no evidence of the alleged contempt.

Again with my support and authorization, Hill then retained Robert Armstrong to commence a libel action against Scientology, Manning, and "print media" defendants who had published the Scientology libel. The media defendants subsequently apologized publicly and paid Hill's legal costs. A jury later awarded general damages against Manning and Scientology in the amount of $300,000, aggravated damages in the amount of $500,000, and punitive damages of $800,000 against the Church of Scientology. On its appeal, Scientology argued that the award to Hill was so exorbitant and grossly out of proportion to the libel "as to shock the court's conscience and sense of justice."

The Ontario Court of Appeal stated that the common law has long held "that in defamation cases the jury represents society and in that capacity the jury expresses society's opinion about the actions of the person who makes false statements about another." As such, "the assessment of damages by a jury should rarely be disturbed on an appeal and only in extraordinary cases." It emphasized the seriousness of the defamation and the degree of malice involved. During the protracted litigation it was learned that, from approximately 1977 on, Scientology had kept a file in which Casey Hill was labelled as an "Enemy Canadian."

I also learned that, while I was attorney general, Scientology had opened a file on me. I never saw it, but I was told it recorded that a Scientologist who was a well-known Toronto TV personality had "infiltrated" my family. Compared to the malice towards Casey Hill, this file was apparently relatively innocuous. It simply stated that this friendship might be useful in any future dealings between Scientology and the attorney general.

The Supreme Court of Canada also dismissed the appeals by Scientology and Manning. However, in light of the fact that the jury's award was the highest in Canadian history, the court first engaged in a review of libel dating back to the Roman era. In its long decision, it pointed out that the law relating to libel in the twentieth century is "essentially the product of its historical development up to the 17th Century," subject to the recognition of the defences of privilege and fair comment. It emphasized that "the central theme through the ages has been that the reputation of the individual is of fundamental importance." The Supreme Court also stressed that, for Casey Hill, special considerations had to be given to the particular significance reputation has for a lawyer: "A lawyer's practice is founded and maintained upon the basis of a good reputation for professionalism, integrity and trustworthiness ... It is the cornerstone of a lawyer's professional life." The court invoked the Canadian Charter of Rights and Freedoms, stating that "although it is not specifically mentioned in the Charter, the good reputation of the individual represents and reflects the innate dignity of the individual, a concept which underlies all the Charter rights. It follows that the protection of the good reputation of an individual is of fundamental importance to our democratic society." It also emphasized that defamatory comment "constitutes an invasion of the individual's personal privacy and an affront to that person's dignity."

In upholding the awards for aggravated and punitive damages, the Supreme Court reasoned, with respect to aggravated damages, that every aspect of the case demonstrates "the very real and persistent malice of Scientology." In relation to punitive damages, it wrote, "Punitive damages may be awarded in situations where the defendant's misconduct is so malicious, oppressive and high handed that it offends the Court's sense of decency ... However, the award is not to compensate the plaintiff but rather to punish the defendant."

Casey Hill's reputation for integrity was recognized by the government of Canada when, not long after the litigation concluded, he was appointed to the Ontario Superior Court of Justice. Scientology and a number of its executives were, however, charged with breach of trust, theft, and possession of stolen property, and various pleas of guilty were entered. Immunity agreements were made with other members of Scientology in return for their testimony on behalf of the Crown.

A further criminal trial proceeded against Scientology and a member of its Guardian's Office before Justice James Southey and a jury. The jury found the accused guilty of criminal breach of trust. Justice Southey fined Scientology $250,000, and the individual a lesser amount. Appeals to both the Ontario Court of Appeal and the Supreme Court of Canada were dismissed.

So ended Casey Hill's Scientology saga. To my knowledge the Supreme Court's decision in *Hill v. Scientology* is the most comprehensive decision ever written by the court in relation to libel and defamation. It is a mini-textbook on the development of the law in Canada and the United Kingdom, in contrast to the different approach in the United States. In my view, the US position overemphasizes the importance of freedom of speech: many reputations are unfairly attacked and defamed there because of the legal requirement and difficult onus on the aggrieved party to prove actual malice.

16

Violence on the Highways, on the Newsstands, and as Entertainment

When I became attorney general, I decided that one of my priorities would be to try to reduce the appalling loss of life on Ontario's roads. My law practice had involved a significant volume of motor-vehicle negligence litigation, including both the prosecution and the defence of impaired driving cases. I strongly believed that government could do much more to improve highway traffic safety. However, I was also aware that there was a general acceptance in society that a particular number of vehicles on a highway would produce a predictable level of accidents. A large number of police officers also shared the view that, because most drivers were law-abiding citizens, they did not want to enforce traffic laws aggressively.

During the years I was writing my weekly column for the *Toronto Sun*, I commented in 1974 on "the public's relatively calm acceptance of the annual bloodletting in automobile accidents" and set out my strong support for mandatory seat-belt legislation. The statement met with much public opposition, which seemed to suggest that, in the parlance of the time, just as the state has no business in the nation's bedrooms, it does not have any place in the nation's automobiles. Many drivers seemed to believe that they had the unalienable right to maim or kill themselves in the privacy of their automobile even if a seat belt would have prevented it.

At the time, despite the overwhelming and irrefutable evidence that seat belts dramatically reduced fatalities and serious injuries, fewer than 20 per cent of motorists in Ontario used them. Shortly after entering the Davis Cabinet, I became a noisy advocate for mandatory seat-belt legislation. Fortunately, there was sufficient support among my colleagues, and the legislation was implemented in 1976. Nevertheless, two of our government backbenchers stated that they were going to defy the law, and I received a great deal of angry mail from disgruntled constituents and others opposed to the law. Interestingly enough, I found a greater level of support from students in the high schools I visited. The younger generation appreciated the wisdom of the legislation and of the role of government in increasing highway safety.

So far as police officers were concerned, mandatory seat-belt legislation was yet another unpopular law-enforcement issue. It soon became apparent that the police throughout Ontario would benefit from focused education on the value of seat belts. I therefore organized a few symposiums to which representatives from police forces across the province were invited. We were able to obtain excellent films that demonstrated dramatically the safety dimension of seat belts: if a vehicle is involved in an accident, they showed, the people inside are twenty times safer if they are wearing seat belts. As a result of this training, a number of officers became true believers and went on to have considerable influence once they returned to their home stations.

Alcohol abuse on the highway was another challenge that had to be addressed more vigorously, even though, given the realities of human nature, it could never be eliminated. The Cabinet Committee on Highway Safety, which I chaired, proposed a two-prong strategy to deal with the issue: education and more effective law enforcement.

In an early address to the Ontario Association of Chiefs of Police, I spoke of the tough initiatives required to reduce the alarming incidence of motor vehicle fatalities. Referring to the fact that approximately 17,000 people were killed on Canada's roads each year, I reminded them that, over a three-year period, more Canadians lost their lives in motor vehicle accidents than the 45,000 Canadians who were killed in action during the six years of the Second World War. I went on to say: "I have always been astonished by the relative complacency that is demonstrated towards the appalling loss of life, maiming, and injuries that are represented by highway statistics. Perhaps for some people they represent a certain grim inevitability like death and taxes – you can't really do much about it. However, no rational or thinking society should capitulate to what is not an inevitable, unavoidable human tragedy."

We also encouraged citizen groups such as Mothers Against Drunk Driving (MADD) to sponsor grass-roots campaigns in their own communities. From an educational standpoint, it was clearly important to increase the level of sensitivity among the public. It was essential to create a culture where people were truly concerned and, indeed, very angry about alcohol abuse on the roads and highways.

Once again, I generally found high-school audiences receptive to my message, and I accepted as many invitations as I could to address them. Although there was usually a small legion of bored young people in the audience, most were interested in a dialogue with the attorney general. They also shared an awareness of the alcohol abuse on the highways that had taken the lives of some of their peers and, despite the traditional youthful feeling of immortality, a growing concern for this problem. During these years the now common practice of the "designated driver" grew dramatically.

One of the most potent obstacles to the concept of highway safety is the long North American love affair with the automobile. Vehicles are marketed in terms of design and power, and safety devices are seldom featured. Speed and power are glamorized, to the point even of violence as entertainment. This obsession is also reflected in the huge popularity of automobile racing in most countries in the Western world. We should hardly be surprised by the many tragic consequences caused by young people racing on our city streets and country roads.

Ontario Ministry of Transportation statistics reflect the positive consequences of the government initiatives between 1975 and 1985 related to highway traffic safety. In 1975, there were 1800 highway fatalities. That figure continued to decline each year to a total of 1191 in 1985, with a continuing decline thereafter. In this same decade, the number of licensed drivers in Ontario increased by one and a half million. In the latest figures available to me, those of 2009, the number of licensed drivers has increased by another two and half million, but annual fatalities have dropped to 516. The conclusion is simple: government has a major role to play in highway safety, even though many people argue that government should simply "butt out" when it comes to individuals and their automobiles.

I believe that the provincial governments continue to be reluctant to initiate safety measures that may annoy a significant segment of the voting public. An interesting illustration of this reluctance is the brief history of photo radar in Ontario. The NDP government led by Bob Rae initiated photo radar in August of 1994. Even though the Ontario Ministry of Transportation released a preliminary four-month study in January 1995 showing that photo radar had reduced speeding on highways, and Brian Patterson, the head of the Ontario Safety League, stated that photo radar was an excellent safety tool for contractor zones and high-risk areas, the program ended eleven months later when Mike Harris became premier, after campaigning on a promise to abolish it. Some municipalities have recently requested that photo radar be introduced again, but it will undoubtedly meet significant public opposition, given the traditional attraction of automobiles capable of great speed.

* * *

During my early months as attorney general I also expressed my concerns about pornography and violence: portraying women as mere sex objects would inevitably have the result of encouraging violence against them. During my own life, society had witnessed a huge escalation in the distribution of explicit pornography. I was also influenced in this view by the dismayed reaction of my eldest daughter, Janet, and her friends to the degrading depiction of women in the media. *Playboy* had become a very popular male magazine, but I was more concerned about hard-core publications such as *Hustler*.

I realized that in some quarters my concerns were regarded as tilting at windmills. As attorney general of the United States in the early 1960s, however, Bobby Kennedy had expressed similar views. I had also been influenced by many studies that found a relationship between violent sexual deviance and pornography, including the US President's Commission on Obscenity and Pornography in 1970 and the Longford Committee Report to the British House of Commons in 1972. Many police officers I have known over the years believe strongly in the relationship between pornography and criminal violence.

In my early years as attorney general, many charges were successfully laid against a number of well-established magazine distributors. For the most part they distributed mainstream magazines, but they could not resist the profits from adding pornographic magazines to their lists. I soon became unpopular with several high-profile businessmen who were directors on the boards of the distributing companies. At the same time, I had to admit in October 1976 that the prosecution of pornography was like "bailing out a flooded basement with a thimble." I therefore asked the federal government to be more vigilant at Canada's borders in preventing the importation of hard-core pornography. Magazine retailers responded to some extent by keeping these particular magazines from ready access by children.

Given the relationship between hard-core pornography and violence as entertainment, my concerns began to extend more to gratuitous violence outside the sexual content. An experienced police officer told me that one of the dimensions of violence as entertainment was the artificial or "candy coated" nature of many of these portrayals. He mentioned, for example, how often in a single TV drama an actor could be brutally beaten and then, a few minutes later, appear "attractively bandaged for the cocktail hour." In real life, such beatings often result in a death.

Prosecutions against obscenity in relation to pornography are rare, given that Canadian courts, influenced by the "freedom of expression" right in the Charter, have made such charges difficult to carry through. As Justice Potter Stewart of the US Supreme Court was reported as saying, he recognized "obscenity" when he saw it but had difficulty describing it in legal terms. Still, those who fought against violence as entertainment became better organized and, led by people such as Dr Rose Dyson of Toronto, they expressed their worries to governments at all levels. I shared many of these same concerns, and I persuaded the Davis Cabinet to establish a commission to study the issue of violence as entertainment, including violence in pornography. Late in 1975 the LaMarsh commission, led by the former federal Cabinet minister Judy LaMarsh, was appointed. She was joined by the well-known journalist Scott Young and Justice Lucien Beaulieu. Their report, released in 1978, corroborated my concerns and made many recommendations. Unfortunately, most of them were rapidly buried by the media, given its traditional opposition to any form of possible censorship.

The commission was assisted by an impressive number of researchers and scholars, and members of the public submitted many submissions for consideration. In the process, a voluminous library was created. Two years later, Ian Macdonald approached with a request to acquire this library for York University. It made a great deal of sense to house it in an academic institution, so it would be available to future scholars. I expressed my interest in the public recognition of Judy LaMarsh, who was then fighting terminal cancer. The result was the establishment of the LaMarsh Research Centre for Conflict Resolution at the university.

The issue of violence as entertainment has continued to attract a great deal of debate and ever more studies, particularly in the United States. With or without a pornographic dimension, such violence has grown dramatically in recent decades, with little effective public opposition. Although gratuitous violence has become well entrenched in film and video games, soft-core pornography is generally avoided in mainstream films. It is, however, readily available on certain cable television channels that can be accessed through subscriptions.

Andy Donato, *Toronto Sun*

More than three decades later, after I retired, I again had to think officially about violence in entertainment when I was asked to review the roots of youth violence in Ontario (chapter 37).

17

A Mixture of Challenges Involving Marijuana, Ed Ziemba, Francis Fox, and Amway Corporation

In March 1977 I found myself in some controversy as a result of statements I made about the decriminalization of marijuana during a visit to a community college in Belleville. The decriminalization had been recommended five years earlier after an inquiry into the non-medical use of drugs by Osgoode Hall Law School dean Gerald Le Dain, who later became a judge on the Supreme Court of Canada. In my talk I expressed some support for the idea, but even this limited endorsement created considerable comment both in the Legislature and among the public at large.

A day later, the editorial in the *Globe and Mail* came out in support of the decriminalization of marijuana. I was quoted as accusing the federal government of "ducking" the issue. Although the use of marijuana was a criminal offence, the courts treated it as a "trivial" one when the marijuana was for personal use and not for distribution. The editorial also referred to my belief that alcohol had caused far more anti-social behaviour than had marijuana. The newspaper cartoonist couldn't resist having some fun, and he portrayed me as the proprietor of a "Pot Shop" with a sign that stated "All Pots Legal. R. McMurtry." The pots portrayed were standard ceramic pots.

The same editorial quoted Justice Antonio Lamer, later chief justice of Canada but at the time the chair of the Law Reform Commission of Canada: "The thousands of annual prosecutions for possessing soft drugs – chiefly marijuana – are charades and it is hard to find anyone

Ed Franklin, *Globe and Mail*

involved in the cases, including often the police and the judge, who feel that they are dealing with criminals in any rational sense of that very significant word." The reality, however, was that many young people were ending up with criminal records for possession of marijuana.

The lead editorial in the *Toronto Star* that day was headlined, "Having marijuana shouldn't be a crime." It also quoted Justice Lamer and concluded with the following statement: "The time is long past for a new law making possession of a few joints no concern of the criminal courts. If society wants to impose a penalty, a fine – like a traffic ticket – would be ample."

Sadly, very little has happened to reform the law in the nearly four decades that have passed. No government, it seems, wants to address this "hot potato." A few legal changes with respect to the use of marijuana for medical purposes, particularly for the relief of chronic pain, are the only exception. And this permitted use resulted from a decision of the Ontario Court of Appeal, not the Parliament in Ottawa. The Harper government has even increased the penalties for private use of marijuana.

My close friend Barbara Turnbull, a *Toronto Star* journalist who, as a result of a senseless crime is also a quadriplegic, is a strong advocate of the use of marijuana for medical purposes. The process to obtain permission for such use appears still to be confusing and inconsistent throughout Canada, though it is now rare for anyone to be incarcerated for simple possession. Turnbull became very public about her use of marijuana in June 1999 when she wrote a powerful and convincing article for her newspaper under the heading "Here's why I smoke marijuana":

I have been a quadriplegic since 1983, when a bullet in my neck at the age of 17 put an end to my short-lived (part-time) career as a convenience store clerk.

Although I cannot move a muscle from my shoulders down, the muscles themselves can move. Shortly after my injury they began to twitch spontaneously.

I need to smoke marijuana. Simply put, the quality of my life is improved in a way that pharmaceutical medication cannot accomplish.

In the paragraphs that followed she described how cannabis for recreational use became illegal in 1923, although it could be prescribed as a medicine until 1932, when its prohibition became complete. She quoted Dr David Suzuki as saying: "It's obviously a very beneficial, useful drug. The evidence of its therapeutic value is indisputable."

Legalizing any proscribed substance will inevitably be contentious, especially if expert reports about it do not agree. Certainly, much addiction-related research suggests that an individual's personal use of marijuana often leads to the use of "harder" and more dangerous drugs. In my view, however, that is not a credible reason to incarcerate people for their personal use of cannabis. I learned from personal experience that it can be politically risky for any attorney general to become embroiled in this debate. Given its significant justice implications, however, it is a duty that must be faced.

The situation in Canada at present sounds fine in theory but falls short in application. Individuals who have a prescription from a physician can obtain a licence to use marijuana for medicinal purposes, but it is complicated to find a source of supply. The federal Department of Health apparently grows marijuana, which is then shipped from Manitoba to the United States to be radiated into a powder. According to Barbara Turnbull, that substance is not effective for pain relief. It is also possible to obtain a licence to grow a limited number of marijuana plants, but these licences are becoming ever more difficult to obtain. In light of the current federal government's reactionary approach to issues such as clean needle injection sites in Vancouver, which were unanimously approved by the Supreme Court of Canada, the medicinal use of marijuana is not likely to be encouraged by the Department of Health.

As a result of the problems related to obtaining marijuana legally, a number of "compassion clubs" have been established to distribute marijuana to persons with medical prescriptions – and probably to other users without medical authorization. These clubs are not licensed, but, given the general acceptance in Canada of legitimate medicinal needs, they are usually tolerated by local law-enforcement authorities.

In the United States, the application of drug laws has been extreme and comes at enormous social and economic cost. There the illegality of marijuana use has been employed in an outrageous manner, largely to "warehouse" thousands of black youth for years at a time. The only reality that may help reduce this scandal is the huge cost of continuing to increase the size and number of prisons across the country. In recent years, however, several states have legalized marijuana use and have moved ahead of Canada in this respect.

* * *

The challenges facing an attorney general are of infinite variety – and are often unpredictable. One such challenge landed on my desk in the spring of 1977, when a member of the Ontario Legislature was committed to jail for refusing to answer a question in a criminal preliminary hearing where he was a subpoenaed witness. The MPP was Ed Ziemba, a New Democratic Party member who represented the riding of High Park Swansea. He refused to obey a court order to disclose the source of information he had obtained relating to a criminal proceeding – the source being a constituent. The information had been ruled relevant to the defence by both the presiding judge and the Supreme Court of Ontario. Not surprisingly, the matter prompted much comment in both the Legislature and the media.

Ziemba's constituents organized protests at the Don Jail, where he was incarcerated. One placard-carrying protester was Ziemba's wife, Lois, who, curiously, appeared to have a broad smile on her face in one of the newspaper photos. Ziemba was somewhat of a maverick, and while pleasant enough to his colleagues, speculation abounded that he and Lois were not exactly close.

In a statement to the Legislature before an emergency debate on the case requested by NDP leader Stephen Lewis, I said it was a "matter of serious concern to me that a member of the Legislature is in jail." By then, Ziemba had been incarcerated for about four days, but he continued to reject legal options that were open to him to pursue. I advised the members of the Legislature that the case posed a particular dilemma for me. As attorney general, I was responsible for the prosecution of the accused in the province. To intervene on behalf of Ziemba would appear to be unfair to the defence, who had sought his evidence. I was therefore "very reluctant to take any steps that would influence or could be perceived as interfering in the proper conduct of the defence."

I also explained to the Legislature that Ziemba was using his unusual situation to mobilize public opinion behind a change in the law – to extend the privilege of MPPs to include the right to keep confidential the sources of information brought to them in the performance of their duties as members of the provincial parliament. To my knowledge, there was no precedent for this extension in any Western democracy. No law reform commission had ever dealt with the issue. In addition, it was doubtful that a province could legally pass legislation that would affect the criminal law – a federal responsibility in Canada. Finally, I questioned whether politicians should be granted rights that were not enjoyed by the general public.

In order to find a solution to Ziemba's incarceration, I announced that I would direct a reference to the Ontario Court of Appeal. I had no doubt in my own mind that this court would confirm the status quo and not extend the right of confidentiality in such circumstances to members of the Legislature. In due time, the court did indeed hand down that decision.

After my statement, I huddled with Stephen Lewis and his justice critic, Jim Renwick, on the floor of the Legislature. They were satisfied that my initiative would secure Ziemba's immediate release. But they also had a problem on their hands: "Who," Lewis asked Renwick, "is going to tell Lois?"

* * *

The most controversial case I had to handle as attorney general was the forgery allegation against the federal solicitor general, Francis Fox, in January 1978. A popular Cabinet minister from Quebec, Fox was rumoured to be a potential candidate to succeed Prime Minister Pierre Trudeau as leader of the Liberal Party.

Fox had signed a hospital consent form in the name of the husband of a woman undergoing a procedure. She wanted to have an abortion and, in keeping with a legal requirement at the time, had obtained the consent of an Ottawa hospital's therapeutic abortion committee. The evening before the procedure was to be performed, the woman, whose name has never been made public, was advised that the hospital's internal regulations required the consent of her husband.

Fox had previously had a brief liaison with the woman, who was married to one of his political colleagues. He was responsible for the pregnancy, and the therapeutic abortion was scheduled for a time when the woman's husband was out of Ottawa. When the woman was advised of the requirement for the husband's signature, she asked Fox, undoubtedly in a highly emotional state, to come to the hospital, represent himself as her husband, and sign the consent form. Fox complied with her request, and the procedure was performed. The woman apparently told several of her friends what had happened, and one of them wrote to Trudeau to complain about his solicitor general allegedly committing a criminal act of forgery.

Trudeau called Fox into his office and the beleaguered minister admitted that he had signed the form. He agreed to announce his resignation as solicitor general in the House of Commons that same day and to explain the reason for it. When Trudeau was asked whether there would be a criminal prosecution, he replied that the decision would be made by the Ontario attorney general.

My immediate reaction was that the circumstances did not warrant a criminal prosecution. Fox had been publicly humiliated and had lost his Cabinet position. Furthermore, a conviction would undoubtedly result in only a nominal penalty. My principal concern, however, was for the woman's family, who would be publicly embarrassed through no fault of their own. Nevertheless, I also believed that public confidence in the justice system required a full investigation by the Ontario Provincial Police. I admit to feeling a modest degree of relief that Fox and I were members of different political parties.

Although it was important that Fox not receive any special treatment because of his former political office, I was determined that the investigation be conducted discreetly, fully, and in an impartial manner. Once the senior OPP officers had completed their work, I met with them and we quickly came to the unanimous opinion that, in the unique circumstances of the case, prosecuting Fox for forgery would not serve any discernible public interest.

Given the significant public interest in the case, I decided to make a statement to the Ontario Legislature on our decision that there would be no prosecution. One of the frequently misunderstood principles of the criminal justice system is the inherent discretion of Crown prosecutors to determine whether to proceed with a prosecution even when a strong probability of a conviction exists. Although the vast majority of such prosecutions do proceed, the fundamental issue is whether the prosecution is in the public interest. In some cases where the accused is terminally ill, for instance, the public may generally support a decision not to proceed with a prosecution.

I read my statement in the Ontario Legislature on February 23, 1978. To begin, I said that, while "I would not normally make a public statement on the result of a police investigation ... because of the nature of the case and because of the legal principles involved," I believed that the public was entitled to an explanation to the fullest extent that it was possible for me to give one. I stressed the importance of "equality before the law" and that "justice must and will be administered evenhandedly, without regard to the position of a potential accused." Fox was therefore being treated in exactly the same manner that any member of the public would be in a similar situation.

I informed the Legislature that the principle of prosecutorial discretion in a particular case was best explained by two attorneys general of England, Sir John Simon and Sir Hartley Shawcross, both speaking in the House of Commons. Sir John Simon stated, "There is no greater nonsense talked about the Attorney General's duty than the suggestion that in all cases the Attorney General ought to prosecute merely because he thinks there is what lawyers call a case." Sir Hartley Shawcross supported Sir John's position: "It has never been the rule in this country ... that suspected criminal offences must automatically be the subject of prosecution ... The public interest ... is the dominant consideration."

I advised the members of the Legislature that the law as outlined by these two gentlemen in England was clearly the law in Canada as well. I went on to state that, to launch a prosecution in the Fox case "would be to bring disproportionally harsh consequences to a person of good character who has already suffered greatly as a result of his act." At the same time, I stressed that "the holders of public office will receive the same treatment under the law as the ordinary citizen, even though the consequences may be more injurious. My decision does not mean that I think a former cabinet minister should get any more lenient treatment because the consequences of prosecution are far more grave for him as a public figure. My decision stands for the proposition that Crown law officers in deciding whether a prosecution should be launched or should proceed must be scrupulous to treat all members of the community without any regard to their position."

At the time of the Fox incident the law required that therapeutic abortions be approved by a medical committee of the hospital. Such consent had been given for health reasons without the agreement of the husband, I reminded my colleagues, because it was considered irrelevant. The demand of the husband's consent at the last moment had not been adequately explained. I also advised the Legislature that "the woman's husband, who might be considered the most aggrieved individual in this case, has requested that criminal proceedings not be taken against Mr. Fox. It goes without saying that such a request cannot be lightly disregarded." There was another consideration too: if Fox were charged, the woman involved should also be charged because she was equally responsible for Fox signing her husband's name to the consent.

My final and very significant concern about a prosecution, as I explained to the Legislature, was that the case could not be tried without revealing the identity of the family involved. There were obviously a number of innocent parties to the case, and to reveal the woman's identity would cause irreparable harm to them all. In that context, I stated that "the embarrassment and anguish to innocent parties must be weighed against any possible advantage that might result from bringing criminal charges against Mr. Fox or the woman involved. On this consideration alone the merits of not prosecuting far outweigh those of proceeding against the parties involved." I concluded as follows:

Let me, in conclusion, reiterate what I have stated. Every day police officers and Crown attorneys decide not to prosecute potential accused. On many occasions charges are not laid, even though the police and the Crown would be fully justified in proceeding to prosecute. It is not, therefore, a question of whether the individual is rich or poor, prominent or not. Rather, it is a question of whether proceedings are appropriate, taking into account the public interest and the fair administration of justice.

Obviously, each decision must turn on the facts of each individual case. In this case, I have concluded that there is no more reason to prosecute Mr. Fox than there would be to prosecute any ordinary citizen caught up in the same circumstances. In my opinion, the public interest and the interests of the administration of justice would not be well served by a prosecution.

The response of the members of the Ontario Legislature to my statement and my decision not to prosecute was totally supportive. The response of the media was more divided: many journalists expressed their approval, but some media critics alleged that I was simply protecting a fellow politician.

Rumours abounded that the woman's family was prominent politically, and I was concerned about the pressure placed on the OPP to leak their identity. Right from the start, I secured an undertaking from the senior OPP investigators involved to keep their work totally confidential, which they did – much to the annoyance of the OPP commissioner who, personally, was very curious about this high-profile case. As a result, the identity of the family in question has never been publicly revealed.

I was pleased to learn later that my statement to the Ontario Legislature with respect to Francis Fox was being used in Ontario law schools as an example of the appropriate principles related to the exercise of prosecutorial discretion.

* * *

In 1983 Amway Canada Limited and four senior executives of both the Canadian company and its American parent company were charged with defrauding the Canadian government of $28 million. They were accused of using fabricated invoices misrepresenting the place of manufacture of many of the company's products to avoid paying many millions of dollars in import duties.

The Amway Company was and is a well-known distributor of more than 450 household products in at least one hundred countries around the world. It uses the services of over one million door-to-door salespersons. Not surprisingly, the charges attracted a great deal of international attention, and in the course of the process, Amway spent in excess of $1 million in newspaper advertising denying the allegations. Subsequently, however, Amway pleaded guilty in Toronto and paid a fine of $25 million – at that time the highest fine ever imposed in Canada.

In these years, Amway was privately owned by two prominent Republican Party members, Jay Van Andel and Richard DeVos, the chairman and president, respectively, of the company. While Amway continued its publicity campaign claiming innocence and vilifying the Ministry of the Attorney General, the real issue was whether Amway would plead guilty and we could abandon our extradition proceedings against the four officers.

This course of action was somewhat of a dilemma for me and my senior criminal law advisers because these executives were clearly complicit in the fraud. We were reluctant to abandon the charges against the officers because convictions would probably mean the imposition of jail sentences. In such circumstances it was our policy not to allow executives to achieve shelter behind the corporate veil. We felt that the sentencing process could well provide a deterrent to other executives of other companies.

Toronto lawyer David Humphrey, the counsel for Amway, would not agree to the extradition of Amway principals Van Andel and De-Vos. He did, however, say he would file a statement with the court which clearly indicated their involvement in the criminal activities of the Amway Corporation.

My deputy attorney general at the time was Archie Campbell, who later became one of Canada's most distinguished judges. My "all star" cast of criminal law advisers included future judges David Doherty of the Court of Appeal and John Takach of the Ontario Court of Justice. Paul Lindsay, the lead counsel on the case, was highly respected throughout the criminal bar. Campbell outlined the major issue in a long memorandum he wrote to me: "The possible mischief is that public confidence in the administration of justice might be lessened by a public perception that businessmen accused of a crime can by the payment of corporate fines escape liability in a manner not available to ordinary people. It is important that a criminal fine not come to be regarded as a licence fee."

My legal advisers held the view that the general deterrence principle would be served by the unprecedented amount of the fine. As the sole owners of the company, Van Andel and DeVos would be personally affected by the fine. It was also important that they publicly admit their complicity in the fraud. We were also aware that the extradition process could take many years because both men would undoubtedly fight against their extradition to the Supreme Court of the United States.

My information about the connection between the owners of Amway and President Ronald Reagan was confirmed when these two executives hired General Alexander Haig to lobby in Canada against my ministry proceeding with the charges. At the time of our pending criminal charges, the federal government had also initiated a civil action for the millions of dollars owed by the Amway companies in import duties.

General Haig had been Reagan's chief of staff and had resigned at the end of June 1982, almost a year earlier. He was obviously confused over which level of government had responsibility for the criminal case, and he first contacted federal attorney general Mark MacGuigan, a law-school classmate of mine. MacGuigan attempted to arrange a meeting between Haig and me, but I refused. He told me that Haig wanted to make the point that proceeding with the criminal charges against Amway would jeopardize the reputation of the company and threaten the livelihood of tens of thousands of Amway commission salespeople in both the United States and Canada. I was not interested in hearing Haig's argument directly, but I did contemplate the possibility that the Reagan government might be tempted to interfere with the extradition application for the surrender in Canada of two of the Republican Party's major fundraisers.

Everyone associated with the prosecution of the Amway companies in Canada, including the investigating police officers, agreed that it was clearly in the public interest to accept a plea of guilt by Amway Corporation with the understanding that the penalty would be $25 million. At the same time, the federal government would be able to continue its civil action for the millions of unpaid customs duties that were owed.

The guilty plea was heard by Chief Justice Gregory Evans of the High Court of Ontario. Immediately after he imposed the hefty fine, Amway launched a huge publicity campaign in the United States. The first line on the full-page newspaper advertisements stated: "One settlement lawyers didn't recommend." The ad continued: "Why then would Amway pay a large fine and let its lawyers submit a statement describing past company behavior in harsh terms?"

They were willing to agree to the very stiff terms demanded by the Canadians to avoid the divisions, frictions and tensions which would have incurred if the litigation continued.

This action allows us to devote our full energies to building the business on a sound and lasting foundation. Rick DeVos and Jay Van Andel had to pay a staggering price so the rest of us can go forward strongly without concern for future problems from this issue.

There was no mention of the owners' admissions about their personal involvement in the fraud. The average reader might well have asked why a wealthy company would not proceed with a defence if there had been no fraudulent behaviour, but the newspaper advertisements did not address this key issue. Clearly, the company's advisers believed that the response might at least create a smoke screen. Interestingly enough, Canadian newspapers would not accept the advertisements. I was advised that they generally believed that to do so would be unethical conduct on their part.

There is a sequel to the Amway saga of 1983 concerning defence counsel David Humphrey. A widely respected lawyer who later became a judge, he was also known for his unique and sometimes bizarre sense of humour. A couple of years after the Amway plea of guilty, he applied to be a federally appointed judge in Ontario. In his application he made reference to the fact that, at the time when he had Amway's pending $25 million fine in his trust account, he had not been tempted to leave town. Minister of Justice John Crosbie was apparently highly amused, and several months later, he appointed Humphrey as a provincial judge.

18

The Osgoode Society for the Writing of Canadian Legal History

One unexpected opportunity that came my way as attorney general was the chance to create the Osgoode Society for the Writing of Canadian Legal History. Like many lawyers, I had long been disappointed with the paucity of books about Canadian legal history. My interest in history had been my main focus during my undergraduate studies at the University of Toronto, and it has always astounded me that so few Canadians seem to enjoy reading books on this theme. Considering that our contemporary world is inevitably shaped by the past, particularly that of our own country, history should be a subject of intense interest. I don't believe we can truly understand where we are and why we do certain things unless we understand our history.

My specific interest in legal history was encouraged by my father's personal library. As both a civil and a criminal litigator, he was very fond of reading the biographies and autobiographies of the celebrated English barristers. The culture of recording legal history in England appears to be more highly developed than elsewhere in the English-speaking world.

Archie Campbell, a well-read historian himself, enthusiastically supported my wish to create an institution dedicated to the writing of Canadian legal history. I was confident that the financial resources could be found in government, particularly the Law Foundation of Ontario. I also realized that a highly qualified editor-in-chief was essential to the credibility of this venture.

I approached some university law teachers who I knew were interested in legal history. Although they supported the concept for my initiative, they were surprisingly sceptical of its practicality. Legal history would have a limited readership, they cautioned – and, over time, I did indeed learn that not all lawyers were interested in reading legal history. Nevertheless, there was enough support for the idea for me to move forward. John Honsberger, the long-time editor of the *Law Society Gazette* – a publication with speeches and brief biographies related to the law and supported by the Law Society of Upper Canada, the governing body of the legal profession in Ontario – also endorsed my project. He eventually served as a director of the Osgoode Society for more than thirty years.

Another friend with whom I discussed the project was Patrick Boyer, a lawyer who later became an MP and eventually set up his own publishing business. Through him I learned of Peter Oliver, a historian at York University. Boyer gave me two of Oliver's books – a biography of former Ontario premier Howard Ferguson and a history titled *Public Persons, Private Lives*. The timing was propitious: that same summer of 1977 my doctor prescribed several weeks of bed rest to deal with my chronic back problems, which had flared up again. Unexpectedly I had time for reading, as I explored my idea for the Osgoode Society and harassed my senior policy advisers at the Attorney General's ministry with this project and several other potential initiatives as well. In the aftermath of the provincial election in June 1977, these advisers were no doubt hoping for a little peace over the summer, but I gave them none.

Peter Oliver was not a lawyer, but his books suggested an impressive understanding of the rule of law in society. That fact, coupled with his significant reputation as a historian, led me to arrange a meeting with him. He was clearly very interested in the challenge, and I was satisfied that his scholarship would give our proposed society the necessary credibility. A graduate in history from the University of Toronto, he studied for his master's degree at Harvard University and returned to the University of Toronto for his doctorate.

The next step for me was to obtain secure funding for the initiative – and I knew where to turn first. The Law Society of Upper Canada, together with members of my ministry, administered the Law Foundation of Ontario – the recipient of bank interest payments to lawyers' mixed-trust accounts. These accounts held the trust monies deposited on behalf of clients. For years the banks had not been required to pay interest on these accounts. The lawyers were not legally entitled to the interest, and it would be just too complicated to distribute the accumulated interest among the tens of thousands of clients who owned the money deposited in the accounts. In cases involving significant amounts of money, clients could, however, ask their lawyers to open specific trust accounts in their names.

Several years before I became attorney general, the government of Ontario negotiated an agreement on this matter with the chartered banks: henceforth, interest on mixed-trust accounts would be paid to a government agency known as the Law Foundation of Ontario. These payments in good economic times could amount to many millions of dollars in a single year. The foundation's charter required that 75 per cent of the interest payments would be allocated every year to the Ontario Legal Aid Plan. The other 25 per cent would be available for initiatives in legal education, ranging from law libraries to research grants for Ontario law schools. In my view, an organization for the writing of legal history would qualify for significant grants. However, because the Law Society appointed members to the foundation's board of directors, it was essential first to obtain its agreement.

I anticipated that the Law Society would support the idea enthusiastically, but I took the precaution of speaking initially with some senior members whose endorsement would be important to the project. Brendan O'Brien, a former head of the Law Society and avid historian, was one such man, and Kenneth Jarvis, the secretary of the Law Society and a long-time friend, was another. Finally, in 1979 the Osgoode Society was formally incorporated. O'Brien served as president for the first ten years, and I was named the honorary president. The Osgoode Society's first board of directors included Archie Campbell, John Honsberger, and Martin Friedland, a former dean of law at the University of Toronto.

An Oral History Program was added soon after the incorporation of the Osgoode Society in order to record the careers of significant lawyers by means of interviews. These files remain confidential during the lives of the lawyers concerned, but they will provide a valuable source of information for historians. Early in the life of the Osgoode Society, we also inquired whether closed files from law firms might be available to us after particular clients had passed on. Not surprisingly and indeed quite properly, the Law Society of Upper Canada decided that the solicitor-client confidentiality should be maintained after the client's death. As an example, records of paternity suits could well be embarrassing to future generations if they were made public.

When I returned from the United Kingdom in 1988, after my years there as Canada's high commissioner, O'Brien and the board of directors asked me if I would take over as president of the Osgoode Society. I happily agreed and, to this day, still occupy the position.

The selection of Peter Oliver as the first Osgoode Society editor-in-chief was one of the most important decisions I ever made. A respected scholar, he encouraged a wide variety of approaches to the writing of legal history. During his twenty-seven-year tenure, from 1979 until his death from cancer in 2006, the Osgoode Society produced sixty-six books in all. Oliver was also successful in making the publication program national in scope. At the beginning, the Osgoode Society was a somewhat Ontario-centric enterprise. Over the last two decades, however, its publishing program has diversified substantially. To reflect that change, in 1993 the words "for Canadian legal history" were added to its official name.

In addition to his duties at the society, Oliver remained a professor of history at York University. In 1971 he was appointed associate editor of the Ontario Historical Study Series – a multi-volume project well subsidized by the Ontario government which aimed to produce a comprehensive history of Ontario. Over his years with the society he also researched, wrote, and published two more books himself – a magisterial account of Ontario's nineteenth-century prison system and an edition of the nineteenth-century diaries of Ontario chief justice Robert Harrison, a volume that provided remarkable detail about the legal profession and social life in general in those years.

Oliver was one of the earliest proponents of the use of oral history. At the time of his death, the society had recorded, in approximately 65,000 pages of transcripts, the oral histories of more than 450 individuals. The *University of New Brunswick Law Journal* in 1984 described the Osgoode Society's publications as the "birth of Canadian legal history, one that propelled the writing of Canadian legal history into the modern world." In Ontario, Oliver was described by a university colleague as "one of the pre-eminent historians of this great province." Although his personal politics and historical interests were very different from those of some of his authors, he supported scholarly diversity and believed in publishing good, provocative historical work whether he agreed with the author's interpretation or not. In other words, he acted in the best traditions of academic tolerance for the views of others.

The fundamental mandate of the Osgoode Society is to stimulate the study of legal history in Canada by supporting researchers, collecting oral histories, and publishing volumes that contribute to legal historical scholarship. In the years from the early 1980s through to the early 1990s, the society kept to its goal of publishing one or two books a year. In 1994, however, it released three books; in most years since, four books have been published annually. By the end of 2012, eighty-eight books had been published – on the courts, the judiciary, and the legal profession as well as on the history of crime and punishment, women and the law, law and the economy, the legal treatment of ethnic minorities, and famous trials and cases in all areas of the law. Some of our books have also been singled out for awards. One title was honoured with the John A. Macdonald Prize, awarded by the Canadian Historical Association for the best book in Canadian history for the year, and others have received different prizes from this same association.

The American Society for Legal History and the Francis Forbes Society in Australia have similar objectives to the Osgoode Society but publish fewer books. The British Selden Society for History has released a few more titles than we have, but it was established in the 1880s. Without doubt, the Osgoode Society is one of the most successful legal historical organizations in the common-law world today. Its work has been extremely valuable in establishing a basic knowledge not only of the history of the Canadian legal system but of its institutions and personnel as well. Before the society began its work, mainstream historians for the most part ignored legal history. With a few exceptions, legal history did not feature on law school agendas. My only disappointment has been that law schools, in contrast to history departments, still do not give the subject enough visibility. In fact, I have often heard comments that it is the Osgoode Society, not the legal academic community, which has put Canadian legal history "on the map."

When Peter Oliver died in 2006, the directors of the Osgoode Society and I, as president, faced another crucial decision – to choose our next editor-in-chief. We selected Professor Jim Phillips, a distinguished member of the faculty of the University of Toronto Law School since 1988 and with cross appointments to the university's Department of History and Centre of Criminology. A prolific writer and presenter at conferences, he is also the author of several books on legal history as well journal articles, essays, and reviews. In short, Phillips has become one of Canada's most highly regarded legal historians, and he is frequently invited to speak internationally.

The Osgoode Society has benefited greatly from the work of Marilyn MacFarlane, our executive administrator. She has served in that position with great dedication and effectiveness since 1979, the year the society was founded. The Law Foundation of Ontario, led by my former ministerial colleague Elizabeth Goldberg, has been another important supporter. Our annual membership hovers around the nine-hundred mark. Though not a large number, it compares very well with the American Society for Legal History, which has approximately fourteen hundred members.

The Osgoode Society has been vitally important in providing an outlet for a large group of talented historians to publish their work, and they in turn have contributed immensely to its success. It is perhaps unfair to single out only a few of the dozens of people who have written our books, but I want to mention in particular Robert Sharpe, my former colleague on the Court of Appeal, who has published four books with the society in what his friends jokingly refer to as his "spare time." They include a fine biography of former chief justice Brian Dickson. From the academic community, Professor Constance Backhouse stands out as Canada's leading scholar of the historical treatment of women and racial minorities by the law. A powerful and committed activist for human rights, she too has published four books with us. Her friends, of whom I count myself one, often refer to her as a "force of nature"!

The Osgoode Society's authors are mostly very distinguished academics, such as Professor Philip Girard, who wrote a splendid biography of Bora Laskin, and Professor Barry Wright, who has produced three volumes in our Canadian State Trials series. Martin Friedland has produced two books, including an excellent autobiography, and has been a strong member of the board of directors. William Kaplan, another legal scholar and author of the magisterial biography of Justice Ivan Rand, among several other titles, has recently joined our board. The authors also include lawyers and judges, such as Windsor lawyer Patrick Brode, whose passionate commitment to understanding our legal history allows them to do excellent scholarship on top of their full-time jobs. I like to think that the combination of academic and non-academic authors and members of the society shows that, at its best, the legal profession is indeed a learned profession.

Professor Constance Backhouse was also the driving force behind the endowment of a fellowship for young scholars to enable them to pursue research and writing projects. She announced this endowment on the occasion of my retirement from the Court of Appeal, naming it the R. Roy McMurtry Fellowship in Canadian Legal History. I was deeply moved by this gesture. The fellowship is administered by the Osgoode Society and has already helped a number of excellent young historians.

19

Solicitor General and the Mississauga Derailment

In 1978 George Kerr resigned as solicitor general for Ontario because of a phone call he made to his local Crown attorney's office on behalf of a constituent charged with a criminal offence. He had intended to be in court to give evidence of good character for this person, whom he knew well, but, when he realized he would not be free that day, he most unwisely called the office of the Crown attorney to provide his evidence. He wanted the presiding judge to consider what he had to say. Although well intentioned, Kerr's efforts could be perceived as an improper interference in the justice process. His statement to the Crown prosecutor was not made under oath, and there was no opportunity to cross-examine him. When the news broke, he offered his resignation – and Premier Davis accepted it. Davis asked me to assume the additional portfolio of solicitor general for a few weeks – and that turned out to be almost four years.

The Ministry of the Solicitor General was created only in 1971, when the areas for which it became responsible were hived off from those of the Attorney General's Ministry and the Ministry of Consumer and Commercial Relations. With an ever-increasing workload, the attorney general had too much to do. In addition, the police throughout Ontario were demanding their own ministry. The responsibilities allotted to the solicitor general related essentially to public safety in the province and included legislation in relation to policing, the Fire Marshall's Office, and the Coroner's Office.

When the new ministry was established, the government was criticized for removing the accountability of the police from the attorney general as the senior law officer of the Crown. Ironically, however, as soon as I assumed the responsibilities of both ministries, the premier was criticized for allegedly undermining the independence of the police from the prosecution arm of government. I enjoyed the opportunity of reminding the opposition parties of their inconsistency. Most of the budget for the solicitor general goes towards the operations management and support services of the Ontario Provincial Police (OPP). In 1978 it was the fourth largest police force in North America, with 184 regular detachments and 6 summer detachments.

One of my other priorities as solicitor general was to develop a more comprehensive fire code and set fire safety standards in buildings across Ontario. In the aftermath of a tragic fire at the large Inn on the Park hotel in Toronto, the inquest recommended that the provincial Fire Marshal's Office be made responsible for hotel safety inspections. This office was subsequently transferred from the Ministry of Consumer and Commercial Relations to the Solicitor General's Office. The responsibility for the Coroner's Office and the coroner's jury system became ever more challenging as the length and complexities of many inquests increased dramatically. Nevertheless, I soon learned that the centuries-old traditions of this jury system had remained effective. The results obtained generally vindicated our traditional faith in the good judgment of non-expert men and women in making recommendations that help to prevent future deaths.

One vitally important area in the Coroner's Office is the human organ donation program. Unfortunately, donations have never come close to meeting the needs of those desperate for transplants, and it is still my view that governments should be much more imaginative and aggressive in their appeals to the public. In the years while I was solicitor general, I was approached by a friend who had a child with a growth deficiency. This person told me that the very small pituitary glands that were routinely removed during autopsies from the back of human skulls were usually discarded. Yet, if preserved, these glands would provide an effective antidote to growth problems. Once I had confirmed the accuracy of this information, I began to work on a strategy for collecting available pituitary glands in a process that would not require the consent of the deceased or the family.

The issue was clearly very sensitive and delicate. The requirement for consent is an important principle, but, immediately after a death, it is difficult to approach a grieving family. I decided that the only practical strategy was to legislate a presumed consent in the absence of any objection, though I realized that this approach would be very controversial in the Orthodox Jewish community, where the religious requirement to bury all parts of a body is strictly observed. Here David Rotenberg, a Jewish MPP, became a most helpful ally. He arranged meetings with Orthodox rabbis, who eventually agreed to support the legislated presumption of consent to the donation of pituitary glands. We agreed to establish an administrative system that would inform all coroners about the Orthodox Jewish religious requirement and, where possible, ask Jewish families for their consent. This strategy proved to be quite successful and has been of great benefit to children with growth challenges.

Every year the solicitor general hosted a coroners' education program, and the lunch associated with it soon became one of my favourite functions. Many retired coroners attended, and I always enjoyed listening to their "war stories" – particularly those who admitted to "bending the rules" to be of "service" to grieving families. This service sometimes involved their attempts to avoid scandals related to the location of some deaths. One elderly retired coroner told me confidentially, "Solicitor-General, you could not imagine how many ambulances then would travel this city through the night to ensure that the deceased was found in the *right* bed." This coroner's "service" certainly had the potential to hamper police investigations, and I suspect the practice was very rare. In any event, it was abandoned many decades ago.

People in Ontario are generally well served by their police services, whether the Ontario Provincial Police or municipal police forces. There have been relatively few allegations of corruption over the years, and the number of citizen assault or abuse allegations against police officers is relatively modest when compared with our neighbours to the south, where the culture of the "wild west" has remained disturbingly intact. In my view, police accountability to the citizens they serve is an essential foundation of any civil society. The police often perform dangerous tasks that require great courage, and most citizens are prepared to give them the benefit of the doubt in most circumstances where their accountability is under scrutiny.

I particularly admired Harold Adamson, who served as the Toronto chief of police for more than a decade before he retired in 1980. During his tenure I did a lot of legal work for his police services, including the Vannini and Morand judicial inquiries (chapters 10 and 11). Adamson was a wise and tough leader, a "policeman's policeman" who was supportive of his troops but who also demanded accountability for their performance. He often reminded me that, although he was understandably upset by unfair criticism of his force, he was also concerned about what he described as the public's often "blind faith" in the police. He recognized that, without accountability, a "rot" could quickly develop within the force which would have grave consequences for the public in general and for civil society in particular.

Policing in Ontario faces significant challenges relating to the remarkable diversity within the province. Many new Canadians come from countries where the police are widely distrusted. The various police services in Ontario are therefore pursuing hiring practices that will increasingly enable members of our multicultural society to see police officers who look like themselves – a most desirable goal. As Sir Robert Peel, the founder of modern-day policing in England, famously stated, "The police are, indeed, the public."

* * *

Just before midnight on November 10, 1979, Ria and I were driving home from a legal dinner at Osgoode Hall. As we neared our house, I noticed a bright yellow glow in the western sky. It was not until several hours later that I learned the reason for that glow: a long Canadian Pacific Rail freight train had derailed in Mississauga, followed by a huge fire and the explosion of three propane rail cars. The debris, propelled through the air for hundreds of yards, caused considerable property damage. It was miraculous that no one in this urban landscape was injured or killed.

As solicitor general, I was responsible for public safety, so it became my duty to coordinate the provincial government's response to this emergency in Mississauga. At about six the following morning I received a telephone call from John Hilton, my deputy minister, who told me that at least one of the derailed tanker cars contained chlorine. Any leak could produce deadly results. "All hell has broken loose," he reported, and it was important that a senior provincial government official get there as soon as possible.

The cause of the derailment was complex but, fundamentally, the result of two of the railway car wheels overheating when a lubricator pad ceased to perform. The first derailed car – a tank car loaded with toluene – was the thirty-third in a 106-car train. It took twenty-three other cars with it off the rails, nineteen of which were carrying "dangerous commodities" (as classified by the Canadian Transport Commission). Fire spread through most, if not all, of the derailed cars, causing three that were carrying propane to explode. The seventh car in the derailment was loaded with chlorine, and it sustained a hole of almost one metre in diameter in its shell.

Fear of this deadly gas led to the evacuation of almost all the residents in the City of Mississauga and in some neighbouring communities too – at the time, the largest peacetime evacuation in North America and perhaps the entire world. Almost 250,000 people were evacuated from their homes and offices. Media everywhere covered the story, and there was general astonishment that the whole process could be accomplished in such an orderly and non-confrontational fashion. After the event, the Ministry of the Solicitor General sponsored a highly successful conference on emergency preparedness which was attended by 800 delegates from around the world and from many of Ontario's municipalities.

Following Hilton's call, I arranged for an OPP vehicle to pick me up. I arrived in Mississauga shortly before 8:00 am and found that an OPP emergency trailer had been set up. The evacuation of residences close to the derailment had already begun. The obvious strategy was one of extreme caution, given the huge risks related to any major escape of chlorine gas from the damaged car. I immediately contacted the provincial Ministry of the Environment, requesting that the appropriate experts from that ministry and the Ministry of Health be summoned to Mississauga.

I had met Mississauga mayor Hazel McCallion previously but did not know her well. She had been elected to the position only a year before, but had already earned the nickname "Hurricane Hazel" because of her aggressive and feisty character. Relations between her and the police and fire departments were obviously tense, and I sensed that my arrival on the scene was welcomed on all sides both as a mediator in disputes and as a person with the authority to engage necessary provincial government resources. As things turned out, she proved to be very cooperative.

It was agreed that I would chair a coordinating response committee that would include Mayor McCallion, Police Chief Doug Burrows, and Fire Chief James Bentley, assisted by staff and the necessary experts. We also agreed that we should meet several times a day during the emergency, both to manage the response and to keep the public informed.

By the early afternoon of day one following the explosion, 70,000 people had been evacuated from their homes. The central part of Mississauga had become a virtual ghost town, with a small army of police assisting in the evacuation. Other staff were gathering available information on air samples and wind conditions while also trying to determine the actual amount of chlorine that was still escaping from the tank. After consultation with health officials, we decided to evacuate the Mississauga General Hospital as well as all the nursing and retirement homes in the city. Ambulance crews completed the necessary evacuations within about six hours.

The area of the evacuation continued to be expanded until almost the entire population of Canada's ninth largest city had been evacuated. The level of cooperation on the part of the majority of evacuated residents was remarkable. Although many were able to move in with relatives or friends, or into hotels outside Mississauga, thousands of people accepted accommodation in nearby schools, shopping centres, and church halls. In the days and weeks following the Mississauga evacuation, many US commentators said that such an orderly evacuation would probably be impossible in any American city of a similar population.

Our committee held media briefings several times a day throughout the evacuation. We realized that the evacuees would be adequately informed through media reports on the details of the unfolding drama and the likely timing of their return home – a decision for the experts to make. We soon learned that consensus would be difficult to reach, as the various Ontario government ministries seemed reluctant to take responsibility for the health of thousands of Mississauga citizens.

The presence of senior CPR officials at our meetings further complicated matters. We soon became aware that their only real priority was to reopen their railway line, and I was appalled by their cavalier attitude towards the fundamental issue of public safety. Some of my frustration may have come through: CP Rail decided it had a public relations challenge to deal with, and early in the evacuation, William Stinson, the company president, arrived in Mississauga. We had been friends during our undergraduate years at University of Toronto.

Although Stinson hoped above all to cool down an irascible solicitor general, we had no difficulty in agreeing that the train wreckage could not be cleared and the railway line opened until our experts reached a consensus that there would be no health risks. The chlorine tank car was still leaking, and it was difficult to ascertain how much of the potentially deadly gas remained within. It had been filled at the Dow chemical plant in Sarnia, and shortly after the train derailment, an emergency crew from Dow arrived in Mississauga to work with the local fire department. I developed an enormous respect for the members of the Dow crew and the firefighters who were working in the train wreckage. Their major responsibility was to locate the leak from the chlorine tank, seal it, and maintain the seal. Within a few hours of the train derailment, we made inquiries about the availability of gas masks from the Canadian military. Regrettably, it took them more than two days to locate their supply, which was in Halifax, and despite our urgent request, no masks were made available before the emergency ended several days later. Consequently, the Dow crew and the firefighters worked without gas masks, accepting a considerable degree of personal risk. The leader of the Dow emergency response crew, who was known respectfully and affectionately as "Green Adair," died of cancer eighteen months later.

As a result of the Mississauga drama, I learned that our military and our law-enforcement agencies lived in splendid isolation from each other. During the weeks that followed, I expressed my concerns publicly in an interview with a journalist who was working on a book about the derailment. My comments made me unpopular with senior military officials, but my complaints did lead to meetings between the OPP and military representatives. They agreed to begin developing strategies and protocols whereby the Canadian military formally agreed, at least in principle, that it would have an assisting role in serious civilian emergencies.

My experience with our military and with the federal government during the Mississauga evacuation reinforced my existing bias that official Ottawa sometimes appeared to be completely out of touch with events taking place in Canada outside the nation's capital. Joe Clark was prime minister at the time, and I suggested to his office that his presence in Mississauga during the evacuation would send a positive message of his personal concern – and provide a valuable political photo-op. There was no response, and I never did learn whether Clark even received my suggestion. He had been prime minister since May 1979, but the bureaucracy and his own staff kept him tied down in Ottawa for almost the entire time between his election and his budget defeat in December of that same year. My optimism for Clark's political survival declined significantly when I learned that the largest peacetime evacuation in North American history was not significant enough for him to make a brief flight from Ottawa to communicate his personal support to the evacuees – particularly as Ontario was key to his own government's success.

The Mississauga evacuation ended after six days, once we were able to satisfy ourselves that only an insignificant amount of chlorine remained in the tanker car. Most of the liquid chlorine was probably blown far into the sky during the explosions immediately following the train derailment. The air quality had been carefully monitored throughout Mississauga for the appropriate length of time, and our health and environmental officials agreed that the evacuation could be ended on November 16.

The evacuation captured international attention. Over the next two or three years, the Mississauga emergency was examined by experts from around the world. One particular concern was the obvious danger represented by the transportation of hazardous chemicals through areas of human habitation.

Following the end of the evacuation, CPR representatives were overly aggressive in trying to settle evacuees' expense claims, mainly those related to alternative accommodations. Although a quick settlement of those claims was desirable, I was concerned that the releases should not include potential health issues related to the chlorine escape which might appear in the future. CP Rail was not prepared to concede this point, and in response to questions in the provincial Legislature, I stated that, if health issues arose, legislation would be introduced to amend the executed releases specifically to exclude health claims.

My statements in the Legislature clearly irritated Donald Sinclair, the chair and CEO of the parent company, Canadian Pacific. He telephoned Premier Davis to complain about my criticism of his company. By coincidence, I happened to be meeting with the premier when he accepted the call, and Davis invited Sinclair to convey his concerns directly to me. He declined, abruptly ending his conversation with the premier.

Following the Mississauga derailment, I conveyed to the federal minister of transport my concerns about the dangers inherent in transporting toxic and hazardous materials through populated areas of Canada. This accident could well have had tragic consequences, given the nearby human habitation. Within a month the federal government appointed Justice Samuel Grange of the High Court of Ontario to "report on the existing state of railway safety as it relates to the handling and carriage of dangerous goods," with particular reference to the Mississauga accident. Almost 150 lawyers appeared on behalf of the many international corporations that had an interest in the important issues to be reviewed. I was not called as a witness: Justice Grange explained that my evidence would not assist in determining the cause of the derailment or in his recommendations with respect to future rail transportation of dangerous substances. I was pleased, however, that he referred in his report to my role as chair of the emergency response committee: "Mr. McMurtry was (and is) also the Solicitor General and it is that capacity as Chairman of the Cabinet Committee on Emergencies he attended the scene and took command. I have no doubt whatever that he was in complete command from the moment he arrived, even though he did not conduct the matter like a military operation, his method was to discuss and obtain agreement, not to issue orders."

Under the heading in his report titled "The Decisions of the Command Team," Justice Grange wrote: "I do not consider that I have been asked to judge the validity of the teams' decisions. All I can say is that they clearly had a very difficult problem." He went on to write his conclusions with respect to the role of the Command Team: "Even in the hindsight of the 127 days of the hearing, with much of the evidence dealing exhaustively with the danger presented by the chlorine car, I am happy that the decisions were theirs, not mine." The Grange Report was delivered to the federal government in December 1980 – an impressively timely accomplishment given the mass of highly technical evidence given during the hearings. The recommendations were also very technical and, while obviously important, did not add to the drama of the Mississauga derailment as the residents and our teams experienced it at the time.

* * *

One of the controversial issues I faced when I was both attorney general and solicitor general was the Metro Toronto Police Department's raid on four gay bathhouses on February 5, 1981. About three hundred men were charged as "found" in a bawdy house, and twenty as "keepers" of a bawdy house, both of which were offences under the *Criminal Code*. Because several dozen police officers were involved, the raids seemed to invite heavy criticism for their use of excessive police force. Although I had no knowledge of the raids in advance, I was very concerned about the number of police officers who took part.

Shortly after the raids, Toronto Police Chief Jack Ackroyd came to my office to discuss the matter. He explained that the large contingent of police officers were dispatched because the department did not want to arrest anyone but simply to record each person's identity and allow him to go on his way, without being photographed and fingerprinted. That seemed a reasonable course of action to me, but not one easily explained to the public.

Although not arrested at the scene, many of those charged were later summoned to appear in court. Some of them were prominent in various Toronto communities, and they were able to obtain hundreds of signatures on a petition demanding that the attorney general not proceed with any of the prosecutions – and, moreover, establish a public inquiry into allegations of police behaviour. In the opinion of my law officers at the ministry, the police had not acted improperly and had embarked on a lawful raid. I therefore allowed the charges to proceed – and I still believe I had no legal basis on which to withdraw them.

By that time, I had been attorney general for six years and, given my profile, was an attractive target. The raids were compared with the 1969 Stonewall riot in New York, and there were mass protests and rallies. I was hanged in effigy more than once, and a group of protesters staged a "sit-in" in my office. Although I did not meet with them, they were offered coffee, tea, and doughnuts. They seemed to appreciate the polite treatment they received from my receptionist and staff, and the next day sent a thank-you note signed the "Sissy Sit-ins."

Most charges were eventually dropped or discharged, though a few bathhouse owners were fined. The issue gradually faded, but I remained upset about the continuing allegations that I was homophobic or anti-gay. Although I may have many a fault, being homophobic is not one of them. In June 2003 I presided over the *Halpern* same-sex marriage case in the Ontario Court of Appeal which made Ontario the first jurisdiction in the Western world to recognize such marriages (see chapter 34).

20

The Challenging Cases of Susan Nelles and Henry Morgentaler

When I returned to Toronto from a spring-break holiday with our family in March 1981, the news media were understandably obsessed with the arrest of a young nurse who worked at the world-renowned Hospital for Sick Children. The nurse, Susan Nelles, was charged with first-degree murder related to the deaths of four very young infants. She was alleged to have been on duty and "in charge" of the babies when they died as a result of extremely high overdoses of digoxin, a prescription drug commonly in use for children suffering from heart disease. I immediately asked for a report from Rendall Dick, my deputy attorney general.

Dick told me that the Metro Toronto Police Department had laid the charges after consulting with the downtown Toronto Crown Attorney's office. There had been no communication between that office and my legal colleagues at 18 King Street East, who included a number of very experienced criminal-law specialists. Although there was no requirement that "head office" be consulted before any charge was laid, I thought there should have been some consultation, given the high-profile nature of the case.

In any hospital, even in most critical-care wards, a number of people have access to patients. I initially assumed that one particular nurse would not have been charged unless she had made an admission of guilt or been observed administering a deliberate overdose. When Dick informed me there was no direct evidence against Susan Nelles, I was shocked. The Nelles case, I predicted, would become a major issue for the ministry – and for me as attorney general. I asked Dick to appoint senior criminal-law counsel to monitor the case and to ensure that any continuing prosecution was conducted at the highest level of professionalism.

For some months, I learned, there had been concern about the increasing number of baby deaths at the Sick Children's Hospital. Administrators there had initiated an internal probe of a number of deaths in the hospital's cardiac ward between July 1980 and March 1981, when Nelles was charged.

In serious criminal cases such as this one, Susan Nelles had the right to a preliminary inquiry to determine whether there was sufficient evidence to put her on trial. This inquiry had to show that there was sufficient evidence before the court on "which a reasonable jury properly instructed could convict." The evidence could be direct or circumstantial, or both. In recent decades, defence counsel have generally used the preliminary inquiry to obtain a full disclosure of the prosecution's case through an examination of its witnesses. They usually do not expect to obtain a discharge at this early stage of the proceedings.

The lead counsel for the prosecution and defence were, respectively, Robert McGee and Austin Cooper, both lawyers of considerable experience and established reputations. They made sure that the conduct of the preliminary inquiry was thorough and fair. The Crown produced as witnesses all the nurses who had any contact with the four babies, primarily nurses who worked in cardiac wards 4A and 4B, where the babies died. They all testified that Susan Nelles was a normal, stable person, both emotionally and mentally.

It is not usual for the defence to call evidence at a preliminary inquiry, but, in the Nelles case, Cooper produced a chart which listed all twenty-four babies who had died in mysterious circumstances, including the four babies who were the subjects of the murder charges. The list disclosed that Susan Nelles had been on duty on most, but not all, of the days when the babies died, though another nurse was on duty on all the days when the twenty-four babies died. The prosecution case rested, however, on the theory that only one person was responsible for killing all four babies. In his autobiography, David Vanek, the judge at the preliminary hearing, wrote that "the chart constituted a very important, if not critical piece of documentary evidence. It confirmed that Susan Nelles was not even on duty on the date of the death of the Baby Estrella – one of the four babies included in the charges of murder laid against [her]."

Nurse Nelles had been on duty the night before baby Estrella's death.

An US expert on the use and effects of digoxin testified that the fatal dose could have been administered the night before the baby's death. However, Judge Vanek was not impressed by this expert's evidence: "It seemed to me," he wrote, "that an inference of guilt for the number of babies could not logically be drawn against Nelles from the mere fact that the babies had been assigned to her care."

In May 1982 Judge Vanek dismissed the charges against Nelles at the end of the preliminary inquiry. He found that the basic issue was not whether murders had occurred but who had committed them. In his judgment, there was a serious lack of identification evidence, given the number of persons who had access to the infants.

The result of the preliminary inquiry had confirmed my earliest concerns about the Nelles prosecution, but it is not the role of the attorney general to second guess an experienced prosecutor unless there are compelling reasons to do so. In the months that followed, criticism began to mount in the press and among the public that Nelles had been charged at all. It was also alleged that I, as attorney general, should have personally reviewed the evidence on which she was charged. Although understandable given the high-profile circumstances of this case, the suggestion that I should interfere ignored the special role of an attorney general. Because this position is a political appointment, it is absolutely essential that there should never be even a hint of political influence in any criminal prosecution. Given the controversy and strong emotions surrounding this case, I might well have wished it simply to go away, but I knew it would be totally improper for me to interfere in any case for my own personal political comfort.

The prosecution had to be allowed to take its course under the direction of experienced prosecutors. An exception could arise if credible defence counsel complained to me about some impropriety in relation to the Crown's conduct, and I would then review the complaint with my legal counsel. Austin Cooper, however, made no complaint. In fact, when Nelles was eventually discharged, he stated in open court that all the people connected with the case had done their jobs in a professional and fair manner and that "the system worked."

During the many months of intense public interest in the issue, I personally met with the parents of many deceased infants to attempt to assure them that every possible reasonable investigation was taking place. Now, more than three decades later, however, the identity of the perpetrator of the crimes related to the deaths of babies at Toronto's Sick Children's Hospital remains an unsolved mystery. Neither the nurse who had been on duty on all the days the babies died nor any other person has ever been charged with the baby deaths.

The discharge of Susan Nelles did not end the tragic saga of the baby deaths at the Sick Children's Hospital. In September 1981 Larry Grossman, the Ontario minister of health, asked the Centers for Disease Control in Atlanta to undertake a comprehensive study into the deaths of twenty-four of the babies at the hospital between July 1980 and March 1981. Another four deaths were later added to the list. The report, released in February 1983, found that seven baby deaths were due to a deliberate overdose of digoxin and that twenty-one other deaths were consistent with overdoses.

During the criminal investigation process, it was also important to provide some assurance to the public that the Sick Children's Hospital was a safe place for infants and young children to be treated. On June 3, 1982, the Cabinet, on Grossman's recommendation, appointed a review committee, chaired by Justice Charles Dubin of the Court of Appeal, which included specialized physicians from Detroit and Vancouver and a senior nursing specialist from Montreal. The terms of reference directed the committee to investigate whether the hospital had "instituted appropriate patient care practices and procedures to protect the safety and security of its patients," especially in the vital issue of the administration of medication, and also to review the present management of the hospital. The mandate, however, did not allow an inquiry into the actual causes of death of any patients – that remained a criminal investigation. As the preface to the report stated, "Our focus was on the present and the future."

The review committee did not have the authority to examine any individual under oath – a process that could have extended its mandate for many months. To obtain the assistance of those in the hospital who had not been specifically requested to appear before it, the committee posted notices and sent out numerous letters inviting input, with full assurance of confidentiality. In its report, however, the committee wrote that it was very disappointed by the lack of response it received.

The Hospital for Sick Children in Toronto was the first in Canada to pioneer the concept of centralizing pediatric expertise and medical care for children in one facility, rather than spreading the services among all general hospitals in the community. Over the years, the hospital had earned a sterling reputation both in Canada and internationally. However, during the tragic saga triggered by the Nelles investigation, some highly qualified people communicated to me their deep concern about a growing arrogance and apathy within the hospital, stemming perhaps from the fact that this excellent reputation had never been seriously questioned. In fact, in its report, the Dubin Committee concluded one chapter, "A Patient Care Safety System," with these words: "For the reasons expressed earlier in this Report, it is our opinion the patient care system presently in place is inadequate. There have already been many changes made to the system which can be and need to be improved upon. We think that if changes are made along the lines suggested above, with the expertise available, this Hospital can establish a patient care safety system which is the equal of, if not better than, any such system in any other like institution." It was hardly a ringing endorsement of the patient-care system in place during all the mysterious baby deaths, including those that had been characterized as murders.

The committee made ninety-eight recommendations – proof, indeed, that there were a number of relevant issues that the hospital's administration had not properly focused on in the context of patient care. The report in essence could be interpreted as highly critical of the Hospital for Sick Children. Nevertheless, it concluded with this positive endorsement: "The Hospital for Sick Children has earned an international reputation for the quality of its services provided to its patients. We are all satisfied that it is still deserving of that reputation and of the complete confidence of the public. It is truly one of our indispensable institutions." In the years since, the reputation of the Sick Children's Hospital has remained intact, and the hospital and its staff still attract enormous admiration both in Canada and abroad.

I reported to the Ontario Legislature on February 21, 1983, that, of thirty-six deaths that occurred in the cardiac unit during the "epidemic period," twenty-eight were not inconsistent with digoxin overdose; in seven of the cases, "there is significant scientific evidence that death was caused by deliberate overdose of digoxin."

After the Dubin and Atlanta investigations had published their reports, I realized that, given the obvious concern of many parents, I would have to call a public judicial inquiry into the Sick Children's Hospital – once the criminal investigation was over in practical terms. Although the police investigators said it was unlikely that any further charges would be laid, the file remained technically open. Some newspapers published editorials opposing an inquiry on the grounds that the hospital's reputation might suffer unnecessarily. It was clear to me that the parents of the dead babies were entitled to full disclosure, to the extent it was possible, and the facts could only be made available through a public inquiry.

I arranged in 1983 that Justice Samuel Grange be appointed as commissioner of the Inquiry into Certain Deaths at the Hospital for Sick Children. Just three years before he had presided over the inquiry into the train derailment in Mississauga and had produced an excellent report. The hospital inquiry held 191 days of hearings, and the report was released on January 3, 1985. Justice Grange found that eight babies at the hospital were "murdered" as a result of deliberate overdoses of digoxin, that ten other deaths were suspicious, and that six babies died of natural causes. He stated that he was not able to reach a conclusion about the deaths of the remaining seven children under investigation.

Public inquiries are not criminal or civil trials, and so, as is required by legislation, Justice Grange was not permitted to attribute any civil or criminal blame in his findings. Given the controversy surrounding the criminal prosecution of Susan Nelles, however, I asked him also to inquire into the propriety of the actions of both the police and the Crown prosecutor.

In his report, Justice Grange found it "preposterous" that the digoxin might have been administered accidently. As to the actions of the police, he said: "I see nothing wrong in the arrest or in the charge related to [baby] Justin Cook. I think the police acted precipitously with the others, but I can understand and to a certain extent sympathize with their actions." In his conclusions on the actions of the prosecution, he wrote: "I come to the end attaching no great blame to anyone. I can put it no better than Mr. Cooper (lawyer for Susan Nelles) in a conversation with Mr. McGee (Crown prosecutor), You did your job. I did mine. The police did theirs, the judge did his. The system worked."

Justice Grange also expressed some concern for the mental anguish suffered by Susan Nelles and recommended that her legal costs be covered. I agreed, and in due course the Ontario government paid her $250,000.

During the period, I had conversations with several individuals who supported the principle that any important institution has to continue to earn its laurels. It is my personal view that, by July 1980, the administration at the Hospital for Sick Children had become complacent, smug, and a little arrogant. My first source was John Black Aird, the lieutenant-governor of Ontario between 1980 and 1985. Before his appointment to that office, he had been a long-time board member of the hospital. As a good friend he volunteered the information to me privately that he believed the hospital administration was not only complacent but even dysfunctional in some respects. A similar view was expressed by a senior nurse from outside Ontario who was doing a doctorate at the Sick Children's Hospital and was obviously disappointed by what she was discovering at the "world-class" institution. My third important source was none other than Justice Charles Dubin. When he learned that I was going to establish a judicial inquiry into the many unexplained and mysterious deaths at the hospital, he expressed his concern that a public inquiry could well destroy the hospital's reputation. His review of the Sick Children's Hospital had obviously disturbed him to a much greater extent than his report had revealed. By recounting this story here, I do not mean to criticize him or the members of the review committee for the stand they took. I recognize the highly sensitive balancing act they had to perform, simultaneously assessing the hospital administration and reassuring the public.

Although I am reluctant to bring up these issues thirty years after the tragic events at the hospital, I strongly support the principle that all institutions must be publicly accountable for their actions, particularly when life and death issues are involved. I am old enough to remember the age when both hospitals and the medical profession opposed the transparency that public inquests should provide. I feel that my commitment to this principle is consistent with my enormous respect for our medical institutions in general. All in all, I retain no concerns about the professional manner in which the Ministry of the Attorney General handled the tragic saga at the Hospital for Sick Children.

* * *

One of the most emotionally divisive issues in Canada and elsewhere is that of abortion. Personally, I have long believed in the right of a woman to decide whether to abort a pregnancy, though obviously it should not be a decision casually made. I came to this pro-choice position many years ago, though I can understand the strong emotions that motivate each side of the debate. I also expect that this conflict will continue indefinitely, but I hope it will not be accompanied by the violence that occasionally targets doctors who perform abortions.

My own views on abortion have been influenced by my wife, Ria, who believes strongly in the right of each woman to make her choice. For Ria, it was never an academic or philosophical issue because her own physicians had seriously recommended that her fifth and sixth pregnancies be terminated for health reasons. She had developed phlebitis, a painful swelling of the veins in her lower limbs, as a result of her earlier four pregnancies, which had occurred during our first seven years of marriage. Although her condition made her vulnerable to a stroke, she rejected the medical advice to abort. She did not, however, waiver in her belief in the fundamental right of each woman to make her independent choice.

During my tenure as attorney general, one of my more challenging decisions was whether to appeal the verdict of a Toronto jury to acquit the Montreal physician Dr Henry Morgentaler of performing an abortion in contravention of the *Criminal Code of Canada*. This verdict produced huge media coverage, and the possibility of an appeal by the attorney general led to massive newspaper headlines and other media coverage. The reason we considered an appeal was specifically related to the submission by Dr Morgentaler's defence counsel that the jury should ignore the abortion law legislated by the Parliament of Canada.

Dr Morgentaler had, for some years, been the leader in Canada of the pro-choice side. He initially opened a number of abortion clinics in Quebec and then in Ontario and Manitoba. At the time of his prosecution, a legal abortion could be obtained only if the pregnant woman had the consent of a therapeutic abortion committee established by an accredited hospital. In granting its consent, the majority of the committee had to find that the continuation of the pregnancy would be likely to endanger the woman's life and health.

When the Metropolitan Toronto Police force decided to charge Dr Morgentaler with a breach of the abortion section of the *Criminal Code*, it probably did so at the law-enforcement level. In any event, I have no recollection of any consultations with the Ministry of the Attorney General. The fundamental facts related to a *prima facie* breach of the *Criminal Code* were not in dispute, and the argument that juries in Quebec had acquitted Morgentaler on similar evidence would not prevent the Toronto police from exercising their opinion in favour of a prosecution.

During the trial, Dr Morgentaler's defence counsel, Morris Manning, a former member of the Ministry of the Attorney General, made the submission that the jury should ignore the law and acquit his client. The jury apparently accepted this suggestion, and on November 8, 1984 acquitted Morgentaler. It was highly improper for Manning to make this submission. It is not the role of the courts to consider the validity of policies underlying legislation; rather, it is a matter for Parliament and the legislatures of the provinces. In this case, however, the legislation could be challenged after 1982 on the grounds that it was inconsistent with the Canadian Charter of Rights and Freedoms.

Given all these circumstances, I was urged to consider an appeal. In response, I consulted with my senior law officers. It is essential that an appeal in any criminal prosecution never be, or appear to be, politically motivated. As I expected, given the conduct of Morgentaler's defence counsel, my legal colleagues strongly recommended an appeal. Unfortunately, the announcement was delayed for a few weeks, so the issue continued to receive extensive media attention.

In announcing my intention to appeal the jury verdict, given the importance of the issue and the enormous public interest in it, I made a lengthy statement to the Ontario Legislature to explain my reasons to the MPPs and to the public. I quote briefly from my statement, delivered on December 5, 1984:

The central principle is that decisions made by the Attorney General and his Crown law officers in criminal matters should be based purely on the law and considerations of the public interest.

The decision to appeal or not to appeal or to prosecute or not to prosecute has nothing to do with anyone's personal view on the issue of abortion.

The conduct of this case raised fundamental issues about the role of the jury in our system of criminal justice. The accused readily agreed under oath that he had decided to break the law. The jury acquitted him after being urged by the defence to use their verdict as a vehicle for the purpose of amending or nullifying the law enacted by Parliament.

If this verdict stands unchallenged, it could be open to defence counsel in any case to urge the jury that the law was wrong and that the jury should disregard the law. It might also encourage Crown counsel to suggest [that] a jury ignore traditional legal safeguards enjoyed by accused persons in order to secure a conviction. This had profound implications for our jury system and for the enforcement of the criminal law generally.

There were other legal and constitutional issues as well, and it was obvious to me that they should all be reviewed by an appellate court – first by the Ontario Court of Appeal and, possibly, by the Supreme Court of Canada.

After the acquittal was appealed, Dr Morgentaler rejected my request that he wait for the Appeal Court decision before reopening his clinic. When I appeared before the Legislature's Justice Committee, I was therefore asked whether new charges would be laid against him in relation to this recent round of abortion procedures. I replied that, although the police had an independent right to lay charges, I had a strong opinion on this matter:

Having regard to the particular circumstances of this individual case, the public interest would not be served by proceeding with a trial against the same accused on substantially the same evidence until the disputed legal issues have been resolved by the Ontario Court of Appeal.

The legal implications of this case go far beyond the complex and emotional issues of abortion. They go to the very heart of our system of criminal justice and therefore deserve the scrutiny by the highest court of law in this province.

The decision, like the appeal, provoked major criticism from both sides of the abortion debate. As often happens, the *Globe and Mail* and the *Toronto Star* took opposite positions in their editorial pages. In a lead editorial on December 6, 1984, entitled "In the public interest," the *Globe* repeated with approval the fundamental issues I had identified in my statement to the Ontario Legislature in explaining the reason for the appeal. It concluded: "The questions bear on the nature of our jury system, the role of law and the administration of justice. Irrespective of the abortion debate, their presentation to a higher court is in the public interest." On the same date the *Star* titled its lead editorial, "McMurtry's needless appeal." "Four juries in a row have refused to convict Dr Henry Morgentaler of illegally performing abortions. Under these circumstances, Attorney General Roy McMurtry's decision to appeal the latest acquittal amounts to a form of legal harassment." However, the same editorial continued that "it was not desirable for Ontario to merely follow Quebec's example of ignoring the law and not bothering to prosecute." I suspect that the average reader may have been a little confused by the *Star*'s editorial stance.

The Ontario Court of Appeal heard arguments related to both the constitutionality of the abortion provision of the *Criminal Code of Canada* and the conduct of the trial by defence counsel. The principal constitutional argument in the Court of Appeal was with respect to section 7 of the Canadian Charter of Rights:

7. Everyone has the right to life, liberty and the security of the person and the right not to be deprived thereof except in accordance with the principles of fundamental justice.

The constitutional arguments had also been heard by the trial judge, who dismissed them before the jury was selected. The trial therefore proceeded on the evidence about the abortions that had taken place. The Ontario Court of Appeal concluded that the abortion section of the *Criminal Code* was not in violation of section 7 of the Charter.

With respect to the address given by Dr Morgentaler's counsel to members of the jury, urging them to ignore the law, the Court of Appeal stated:

In our view, defence counsel was wrong in urging the jury that they had the right to decide whether to apply the law the trial judge instructed them was applicable. The defence submission was a direct attack on the role and authority of the trial judge and a serious misstatement to the jury as to its duty in carrying out its oath. In our system, the authority and duty of the judge and jury in a criminal case is well understood and followed. No further elaboration is necessary than the statement of Lord Oaksey in *Joshua v. The Queen* (1999) A.C. 121. In giving the judgment of the Judicial Committee, he said: "It is a general principle of British law that on a trial by jury it is for the judge to direct the jury on the law and in so far as he thinks necessary on the facts, but the jury whilst they must take the law from the judge are sole judges of the facts."

In conclusion, the Court of Appeal stated that "the errors at trial were so fundamental that there has been no trial according to the law." It ordered a new trial.

The Supreme Court of Canada on January 28, 1988, more than two years after the decision of the Court of Appeal, allowed the *Morgentaler* appeal on the ground that the abortion section of the *Criminal Code* breached section 7 of the Charter as it infringed on an individual's right to "life, liberty and security of the person." The decision held, regarding the the abortion section, that

[s]tate interference with bodily integrity and serious state-imposed psychological stress, at least in the criminal law context, constitutes a breach of security of the person. [The abortion section] clearly interferes with a woman's physical and bodily integrity. Forcing any woman by threat of criminal action, to carry a fetus to term unless she meets certain criteria unrelated to her own priorities and aspirations, is a profound interference with a woman's body and thus an infringement of security of the person.

The Supreme Court of Canada agreed with the Ontario Court of Appeal that counsel for Dr Morgentaler had seriously erred in urging the jury to ignore the law. That argument, in its view, "could lead to gross inequities." It "agreed with the trial judge and the Court of Appeal that Mr. Manning, Morgentaler's counsel, was quite surely wrong to say to the jury that if they did not like the law they need not enforce it. He should not have done so." In summary, the Supreme Court would have agreed with the Ontario Court of Appeal and ordered a new trial if it had not decided that the abortion law itself was unconstitutional and, therefore, unenforceable.

On a personal note, the timings of the Morgentaler appeal and the Grange report were a problem for my political career, as they both coincided with my campaign to succeed William Davis as leader of the Progressive Conservative Party and the premier of Ontario. The controversies and the emotion surrounding both cases certainly did not assist my chances of success. But to me one point was clear: My principal duty was to uphold the law, not to advance my own political ambitions.

Two days after the conclusion of my leadership campaign at the end of January 1985, the *Globe and Mail* published a feature article headlined "Late start, abortion ruling hurt McMurtry campaign." The word "ruling" referred to my decisions to appeal the jury's verdict and not to prosecute in relation to the reopening of the Morgentaler clinic. The article stated in part:

Mr. McMurtry had barely begun his campaign when a Toronto jury acquitted Dr. Henry Morgentaler on abortion charges unleashing a predictable storm of pro-choice and pro-life propaganda.

… he faced daily questions about the Morgentaler case and abortion in general both inside and outside the Legislature. His answer never varied. The Attorney General is sworn to uphold the law and his personal opinions do not matter.

It never occurred to me to resent the timing of either the Grange report on the Sick Children's Hospital or the Morgentaler case on abortion. Controversies are part of the territory for any attorney general. The challenge is simply to respond in a principled fashion in respecting the integrity of the rule of law.

21

The Constitution and the Patriation
Case in the Supreme Court
of Canada

During my years as the attorney general for Ontario, the drama surrounding the patriation of the Canadian Constitution provided an especially interesting dimension to my myriad responsibilities.

Ontario has always played a key role in Canada's evolution from
colony to nation – resulting in our present vast and diverse land with
a federal system of government. What emerges from the historical record is the changing role that Ontario has played, from the ardent defender of provincial interests to a conciliator between the provinces and
the federal government. In many respects Ontario has served as the
counterpoise against excessive views that could unbalance the equilib-
rium of federalism. Ontario's approach combines equal recognition of
a strong federal government, with full power to shape and direct the
national economy, and of the provinces, to nurture and protect local interests and priorities. In this way, Ontario helps to guard the diversity
that is the strength of Canada as a nation.

Throughout the early years, Ontario's role in Confederation was as a
champion of provincial rights, in opposition to Sir John A. Macdonald's
vision of the provinces as little more than satellites of an all-powerful
central government. Sir Oliver Mowat, who became premier of Ontario
in 1872, led the other provincial leaders in opposing Macdonald's attempts to subordinate their powers. To this end, Mowat and Honoré
Mercier, the premier of Quebec, came together in 1887 to organize the
first interprovincial conference. As attorney general as well as premier,

Mowat challenged the federal authorities several times in the courts over different issues involving the extent of provincial powers. In a series of important constitutional decisions, the Judicial Committee of the Privy Council in England held that the legislatures of the provinces are supreme within their areas of jurisdiction under the *British North America Act, 1867.*

Federal-provincial and interprovincial conferences have developed as well-publicized opportunities for each government to make its position known on important issues. They are a vital part of the power struggles that are endemic in a federal system of government. One of the most significant interprovincial meetings was the Confederation of Tomorrow Conference convened in Toronto in November 1967 by Ontario premier John Robarts. The Centennial year was seen as an appropriate symbolic moment to re-examine and evaluate Confederation and to discuss new directions. In his opening speech at the conference, Premier Robarts graphically described Ontario's sense of the meaning of our federal system:

First and foremost, the fact that Canada is a federal and not a unitary state means that the provinces were created, and they exist, in recognition of regional differences. Indeed, our triumph and our very singular achievement in this country is that we exist in spite of our differences.

A second very important implication of our federal nature is that there is only one government in Canada which can represent the interests of all Canadians. We, in Ontario, have no intention of undermining the place of primacy of the federal government. Indeed, I would say that we are and remain deeply committed to the maintenance of that place of primacy. It is our conviction that in its fullest and largest expression, it is the binding force which ensures the continued existence of the country we are proud to call Canada.

Indeed, in recent decades, Ontario has not taken the initiative in recommending constitutional change. Rather, it has generally tried to act as facilitator, compromiser, and mediator between Quebec and the other provinces and between the other provinces and Ottawa. Its focus has been on finding workable agreements, not on sweeping revision.

From 1968 to 1971, as part of the momentum generated by the Confederation of Tomorrow Conference, various governments and leaders in Canada attempted to bring about a sweeping constitutional review, and in 1971 Prime Minister Trudeau met with the provincial premiers in Victoria to try to reach an agreement on constitutional amendments.

After extensive discussions and negotiations, the participants agreed on the Victoria Charter, which included a domestic amending formula for the Constitution, allowing for a veto by Ontario or Quebec over any constitutional change. They also accepted basic individual rights, though in comparison with the Charter that was eventually entrenched in 1982 these rights lacked strength, particularly in the area of language. As things turned out, Quebec at the last moment rejected the Victoria Charter, and it was assumed that the lack of unanimity among the various governments had blocked the agreement.

It was inevitable that, as Ontario's attorney general after 1975, I would play a major role in any constitutional negotiations. Quebec and its unique situation within Canada had interested me ever since my university days and the summer I spent working in Quebec City. I felt strongly that the Constitution would soon need to be reformed in some way, particularly in the context of Quebec, and I was conscious of the historical role that Ontario had played in the evolution of the Canadian Constitution.

In my experience, there has been a great deal of confusion among Canadians and others in relations to the challenge of patriating Canada's founding Constitution, the *British North American Act, 1867*. Many people even refer to the "repatriation" of Canada's Constitution. In truth, though, the *BNA Act* was never an Act of the Canadian Parliament until it was finally patriated in 1982. People are also astounded to learn that, until that date, Canada's Constitution did not contain an amending formula.

The simple historical fact is that Canada did not become a completely independent nation in 1867. It had significant control of its domestic politics, but Britain held power over Canada's international relations for decades. Canada became largely independent of the United Kingdom as a result of its major contributions during the First World War, when it insisted on a separate signature on the Treaty of Versailles in 1919, but, formally, Britain did not relinquish control until the Statute of Westminster in 1931. In a similar vein, Canada agreed in 1867 that its Constitution could be amended only with the agreement of the British government.

Following the Statute of Westminster, several Canadian federal governments had tried for more than fifty years to reach an agreement with the provinces on a constitutional amending formula that could allow Canada to amend its own Constitution. The creation of the Parti Québécois in the early 1970s as a serious alternative to the Liberal government in Quebec was a major factor in the renewal of constitutional discussions, which had mostly been in abeyance after the unsuccessful Victoria conference. The first serious talks occurred at the annual premiers meeting in Edmonton in August 1976. It was an election year in Quebec, and the other premiers thought that progress on the constitutional front might assist the federalist forces in that province. Outside Quebec, ongoing discussions relating to the Constitution had been limited almost entirely to academic institutions and commanded little political attention. For better or for worse, constitutional reform generally had little relevance to the political fortunes of any premier outside Quebec.

As a newcomer to the politics of the Constitution and as someone who cared deeply about the separatist threat in Quebec, I was particularly enthusiastic about any initiatives that could bring about meaningful constitutional reform and, simultaneously, satisfy the legitimate aspirations of Quebec. The fact that our Constitution was an act of the British Parliament had always seemed to me to be an unnecessary irritation to the people of Quebec – a negative reminder of the British conquest of 1759. Moreover, as a lawyer and as a citizen of Canada, I was troubled by the fact that our Constitution could only be amended by an act of the British Parliament. On all counts, patriation, with an amending formula attached, appeared to be long overdue.

I quickly learned that the traditional view among political leaders in Quebec was that patriation should await the resolution of all the other constitutional issues that were important to Quebec and should be but the final step of Canada's constitutional evolution. Regardless, I still hoped for some progress on the constitutional front in the summer of 1976, particularly as the Bourassa government in Quebec was facing an election later that year. My fellow ministers from across Canada and I worked vigorously in Edmonton to achieve some degree of consensus on the Constitution in advance of the arrival of the premiers, and we were bitterly disappointed when the Quebec minister of intergovernmental affairs informed us that his government really did not want an agreement on the Constitution at that time. He stated very frankly that, strategically, it would be more helpful for his government to have the constitutional issues unresolved, simply because Quebec governments had always regarded Ottawa as a useful target on unresolved issues related to the Constitution, particularly during an election campaign.

The election of René Lévesque's Parti Québécois in November 1976 clearly surprised Ottawa and most of the other provinces. The fact that a separatist party now formed the government did not bode well for progress in the constitutional reform process. The Trudeau government decided to proceed, especially given the prospect of an upcoming Quebec secession referendum, though the other provinces were sceptical about the willingness of the Quebec government to participate seriously in constitutional discussions. Contrary to our fears, Lévesque apparently decided that he had a mandate to govern in the traditional sense and that Quebec residents expected him to participate in constitutional discussions.

Between the summer of 1978 and the end of 1979, we had no fewer than twelve major federal-provincial meetings on the Constitution. Unfortunately, the Quebec government's separatist agenda did not permit any real progress on reform of the Constitution. In addition, even though the majority of provinces recognized the importance of strengthening the federalist forces in Quebec through constitutional reform, they also had their own constitutional agendas – including a realignment of the distribution of legislative powers to give more authority to the provinces. One example of the continuing federal/provincial struggles was the legislation Ottawa introduced to give the federal government the right unilaterally to change the structure of the Senate. The provinces argued successfully in the Supreme Court of Canada that, the Senate being a federal institution, the consent of the provinces would be required before any structural changes could be made to it.

The Ontario government did not seek additional legislative authority, though we were concerned about any significant weakening of the role of the federal government. Overall, we took the view that constitutional reform was important for two reasons: to satisfy Quebec and to alleviate regional tensions generally. Although I was highly frustrated by the lack of any real progress on the issue, I enjoyed many cordial social occasions with my political colleagues from across the nation. These get-togethers forged friendships that would prove invaluable in the months ahead.

By the end of 1979 it was clear that any further discussions would have to await the Quebec referendum scheduled for the spring of 1980. Given the extent of the federal government's public commitment to "renewed federalism" during the referendum campaign, we all knew that the Constitution would once again become a priority. As things turned out, just one day after the Quebec government lost the referendum, the fiery federal justice minister Jean Chrétien, now appointed as the minister responsible for constitutional negotiations, began his cross-country tour of the provincial capitals to prepare for a hastily convened first ministers' conference on the Constitution scheduled for June. That evening, during dinner in Toronto with Bill Davis and me, an exhausted Chrétien passionately advocated the cause of constitutional renewal as a fulfilment of the commitment that had been made to the people of Quebec during the campaign and as the only way to defeat the Parti Québécois.

When the first ministers of Canada assembled for their June conference, they committed many of their own ministers to a long hot summer of constitutional discussions. They agreed on a list of twelve subjects and established a Continuing Committee of Ministers from all provinces which would meet at regular intervals at different locations across Canada. The co-chairmen were Jean Chrétien and Roy Romanow, the son of Ukrainian immigrants and deputy premier of Saskatchewan – or, as the media often dubbed them, the "Tuque and Uke Show." Because of the legal and technical complexity of most of the selected subjects, a large retinue of advisers accompanied the ministers across Canada.

The principal difficulty with the process was that most provinces had specific "wish lists" that would have to be satisfied before any real effort would be made to address the other issues. The ownership and marketing of natural resources was the overriding concern of some provinces, and the lack of support on these issues would make it very difficult for their leaders to agree to anything else. For Quebec, it was an ideal political scenario: as long as other provinces were battling with the federal government, Quebec could not be accused of sabotaging the process, even though a renewed federalism was certainly not part of its plan.

Despite these obstacles, the ministers did reach substantial agreement on a majority of the items on the agenda. In retrospect, however, I think our major achievement that summer was the understanding we gained about the concerns and aspirations of our sister provinces. Even more important, we continued to form a number of personal friendships which provided vital links among the provinces when the crucial search for a consensus was renewed in the fall of 1981.

The cautious optimism that a few of us harboured for at least some agreement at the next first ministers' conference, in September 1980, was dispelled even before the meeting had formally commenced. The governor general hosted a dinner for the prime minister, the premiers, and the attending ministers on the eve of the conference. The formal photograph had barely been taken when the first signs of ill will began to permeate the gathering. A rather silly proposal by several of the provinces led by Newfoundland – that the meeting should be jointly chaired by the prime minister and a provincial premier – provoked an icy, sarcastic response from Pierre Trudeau about *deux nations*, a comment that produced only more bickering.

The obvious animosity between some of the English-speaking premiers and Trudeau was thoroughly enjoyed by Lévesque, who, seated beside me, commented loudly several times on the theme that the prime minister, or as he called him, the "princeling," was "clearly out of sorts." Quebec was confident that the conference would not make any real progress, even without any overt effort on its part to derail the process. Somewhat downhearted, I telephoned my wife that night and remarked that the first ministers' meeting had for all practical purposes ended before it had officially begun.

It was always interesting to observe the dynamics between Pierre Trudeau and René Lévesque. They were intelligent men, well read and widely travelled. Although clearly rivals personally and in their quest for the affection of Quebeckers, they both received widespread support in Quebec at election time. In 1974 Quebec voters gave the federal Liberal Party sixty of their seventy-four seats. Two years later they elected Lévesque's Parti Québécois with a majority, and in February 1980 they gave Trudeau 68 per cent of their votes and all but one political seat. In April 1981 Quebec gave Lévesque another majority.

Both men were highly competitive, and Trudeau did not warm to people who appeared to challenge him intellectually – Allan Blakeney of Saskatchewan, to name but one. Several of his Cabinet ministers had complained to me that he was often dismissive of his more intelligent colleagues, such as John Turner, while being overly deferential to those who he thought possessed the "grass-roots" appeal he lacked – Eugene Whelan or Bryce Mackasey. Chrétien once told me that the only occasions on which he had been embarrassed by the prime minister was when Trudeau's French switched from his normal Parisian accent to imitate the *joual* often associated with the working people in Quebec. After all the meetings I attended over the years with both Lévesque and Trudeau, however, I came to the conclusion that they had a basic respect for each other which they attempted to disguise with caustic comments.

For Bill Davis, who had been at Victoria when the eleven governments had come very close to an agreement, it was particularly discouraging to witness the polarization in September 1980. Most of us who had invested a good deal of time and commitment in the project refused to acknowledge that the process was dead. We were not surprised in October, therefore, when Trudeau announced his intention unilaterally to request Britain to patriate the Canadian Constitution without the support of the provinces. The governments of Ontario and New Brunswick were both supportive, and the battle would now shift to the courts. References were made by the governments of Quebec, Manitoba, and Newfoundland to their appellate courts seeking declarations that, without the unanimous support of the provinces, the federal government's patriation request was unconstitutional.

In January 1981 I travelled to Great Britain with several of my senior ministry colleagues to review a number of justice issues with our British colleagues and support Trudeau's patriation initiative while also assessing political attitudes there concerning the Canadian constitutional controversy. My visit convinced me of two realities: first, that there was a surprisingly high level of political interest in our constitutional controversy in spite of Britain's own domestic challenges; and, second, that there would be no easy or routine passage of the Canadian constitutional patriation package by the British Parliament. At the same time, the desire of most British politicians to "do the right thing" for Canada was obvious. "Who are the Canadians?" became the question I encountered most frequently. In other words, "Are we to listen only to the federal government, or should we not also respect the views of the provincial governments who oppose the patriation proposals?"

My most important meeting was with Sir Michael Havers, the attorney general of the United Kingdom. He was obviously troubled by the Canadian constitutional issue and appeared anxious to seek my views. Although the British Cabinet wanted to accommodate the request of the Canadian federal government, Havers was clearly concerned about the court challenges in Canada. In his view, it would be acutely embarrassing to the British government if the Supreme Court of Canada were to rule the federal request unconstitutional after Westminster had passed the desired legislation. At the same time, the British government did not want to delay the legislation indefinitely in the British Parliament. I learned from Sir Michael that officials of the Canadian government had foolishly and inaccurately advised some of their British government counterparts that it would take two years or more for the court challenges to reach the Supreme Court of Canada. I informed him that the matter could be expedited by the federal government and that the case could be heard by the Supreme Court within several months.

Immediately following my return to Canada, I wrote to Sir Michael Havers reiterating my views as to the importance of the resolution of the "legality" issue by the Canadian Supreme Court. I had become convinced as a result of my meetings in London that the British Parliament would never act on our Constitution until the issue had been addressed by Canada's highest court. In part, I wrote to him as follows:

Since my return I have been reflecting very seriously on your concerns relating to the significant embarrassment that could accrue to the British Parliament should the Supreme Court of Canada render a negative judgment after the passage by your Parliament of our federal government's proposals. There is no doubt but that a cloud of uncertainty as to legality hangs over the Ottawa initiatives and my personal view is that this constitutional cloud should be lifted by an authoritative legal ruling in Canada. In my view, the best vehicle for this would be for the Governor General in Council to direct an immediate and specific reference to the Supreme Court of Canada. I communicated my views in this respect to our Federal Minister of Justice following my return from Britain although my own government has taken no official position in this regard.

As you know, constitutional challenges have been launched against the manner in which Prime Minister Trudeau is carrying forward his plans to patriate the Canadian Constitution and to legislate an amending formula and a Charter of Rights and Freedoms. The Provincial Courts of Appeal in Manitoba, Quebec and Newfoundland will be rendering judgment during 1981 on the constitutionality of the proposals. I understand that the judgment of the Manitoba Court of Appeal will be handed down in the very near future. It is very likely indeed that any decision will be appealed to the Supreme Court of Canada, whether the judgment upholds the constitutionality of the proposals of the Government of Canada or not. I should add that an appeal exists as of right.

Each day as I read the Canadian press and talk about these matters to colleagues across the country, it becomes increasingly apparent that the Federal Government's proposals are not as generally accepted by either Canadian citizens or their political representatives in Provincial Legislatures as political changes of this magnitude ought to be. This is of considerable concern to those of us who do believe that there are very many elements in Ottawa's proposals that are worthy of support.

My fear is that these worthy goals may be put in jeopardy by an approach which, in its haste, does appear insensitive to legitimate questions that others have posed as to legality, and perhaps inattentive to the need to gain the support of a broad consensus in Canada for the changes.

In an interview I gave to a *Toronto Star* reporter towards the conclusion of my January visit to Britain, I expressed the view that the UK Parliament would be reluctant to pass the patriation package before a decision was made as to its constitutionality by the Supreme Court of Canada. This interview was highly publicized and became decidedly unpopular with some members of Premier Davis's staff because they interpreted it as suggesting a shift from Ontario's strong support for Trudeau's patriation package. A provincial election was about to be announced, and an important plank in our political arsenal was our support for the federal patriation proposals. Without question, Ontario wanted an entrenched Charter of Rights in the Canadian Constitution. Furthermore, many of our fellow citizens, particularly newer Canadians, were becoming ever more irritated that the Canadian Constitution could be amended only by the British Parliament.

The federal government reluctantly agreed to an early hearing by the Supreme Court, and some weeks later, the court announced that the historic arguments would commence on April 28, 1981. The negative decision of the Newfoundland Court of Appeal, together with the vigorous opposition of the federal Progressive Conservative Party, had convinced Trudeau that his political agenda relating to the Constitution would make little progress without a decision from the Supreme Court of Canada. It was agreed that the hearing should be expedited and the House of Commons debate adjourned pending the court decision.

The provincial election campaign came to a successful conclusion in March 1981, with the Davis government winning a majority after almost six years in a minority position. It was now important that, as attorney general for Ontario, I turn the premier's mind to the upcoming patriation argument in the Supreme Court. Every province would be represented during the hearing, and I was encouraged by my ministry advisers to personally make the submissions on behalf of the government of Ontario. It turned out that I would be the only attorney general to make the oral argument as counsel for his government.

* * *

The Supreme Court of Canada was asked to determine two key questions in the Patriation reference case in the spring of 1981: first, whether the federal government's request of the British government to amend the Canadian Constitution without the consent of the provinces was constitutionally valid from a strict legal standpoint; and, second, whether there was an established constitutional convention whereby the federal government should seek the consent of the provinces before asking the British Parliament to amend the Canadian Constitution.

The question about the existence of a constitutional convention that required the consent of the provinces before any constitutional amendments could be made was in turn troubling for two reasons: many constitutional scholars regarded it as a political science question, not a legal one to be decided by the courts; and, moreover, the consequences for a breach of a constitutional convention would be political, not legal. Constitutional scholars had long assumed that provincial consent meant unanimous provincial consent, but such consent was clearly impractical in the context of a highly diverse nation, not to mention a separatist government in Quebec. To me, the difference between what is constitutionally legal and what is a constitutional convention is simple: the former has traditionally been an issue for the courts, and the latter a political issue for the electorate. In this case, however, much to the consternation of Prime Minister Trudeau, that was not to be the opinion of the majority of the members of the Supreme Court.

The day before the submissions to the Supreme Court, counsel for the federal government and the two provinces that were supporting the federal position – Ontario and New Brunswick – met in the boardroom of the Department of Justice in Ottawa. The federal government had retained two outside counsel – Toronto's John J. Robinette, who was generally regarded as Canada's most distinguished legal counsel, and Michel Robert, who later became chief justice in Quebec. The counsel representing the two provinces were startled by the large number of federal lawyers present who had worked on the case – about fifty-five in all. Jean Chrétien attended the meeting as justice minister, and he also appeared surprised. After an exchange of views and possible strategies to be used by the counsel who would be making submissions, the conversations became more theoretical and speculative, drifting away from the fundamental issues. Chrétien had not yet said anything, but, as I sat beside him, I sensed his frustration at the direction the talks were taking. Finally he slammed his fist on the table, glared around the room, and stated, "I tell you this, Roy, if we do not win this goddamn case it will be Jonestown revisited around here" – referring to the massive cult suicides in Guyana three years before.

In preparing our factum for the Supreme Court, my constitutional advisers and I agreed that we should take the "black letter" law approach. That meant we would be arguing a narrow legalistic approach, one that in my view could be justified politically only by the serious constitutional deadlock that faced our nation. At the same time, I recognized that, politically, it would be in the national interest for the federal government to have the substantial support of the provinces, rather than to proceed unilaterally. For the same reason, I thought we needed to break the constitutional logjam: the country could ill afford many more years of acrimonious debate over patriation and an amending formula. In addition, a growing number of Canadians in the English-speaking provinces were embarrassed to have a Constitution that could only be amended in a foreign country. It has always puzzled me why political leaders in Quebec were not more concerned about this "vestige of colonialism."

The legal right of any Parliament of Canada to amend the Constitution unilaterally in a manner that could directly interfere with the legislative prerogatives of the provincial governments had never before been seriously argued by any federal government. As a majority of the Supreme Court eventually did decide, this course of action would fly in the face of a long-established political convention whereby the federal government had sought the consent of the provinces for any amendment to the Constitution which affected the prerogatives of the provinces. Still, given the political gridlock of the early 1980s, the Supreme Court was now faced with an unprecedented situation – to resolve a political dilemma resulting from a historical political anomaly. The court's ultimate decision had the potential to result in many more years of bitter and divisive political debate. Surprisingly, there was relatively little grumbling about non-elected judges deciding the future course of a nation.

For me, the preparation and the five days of argument in the Supreme Court of Canada was an immensely fascinating and invigorating experience. The submissions and material presented to the court contained a great deal of Canadian history as well as law. In particular, the various counsel emphasized that the lack of an already defined process for patriation and the absence of an amending formula were constitutional anomalies resulting from the historical legacy of the evolution of Canada from a colony to a nation. In 1867, they stated, Canada became a "glorified colony" with a good deal of autonomy over its local affairs, though the new nation's constitutional development remained Britain's responsibility. As the dimensions of Canadian nationhood developed, the formal mechanisms for amendment to the *BNA Act* evolved as a matter between the federal government and the government of the United Kingdom, while internal Canadian political realities generally required consultation with the provinces. It was clearly an unhappy circumstance for the provinces that, constitutionally, they did not appear to enjoy any specific legal status with respect to amendments to the *British North America Act, 1867*.

In addition, counsel invited the Supreme Court to take judicial notice of the political stalemate. After more than fifty years of struggling for a consensus on patriation and an amending formula, it appeared that we had come to a complete impasse. As one who had participated in previous constitutional conferences, I was able personally to confirm that dismal analysis.

During the submissions to the court, counsel submitted that, even if the *Canada Act* were passed at Westminster, there was nothing to prevent a future British Parliament from rescinding the legislation. To this suggestion, Chief Justice Laskin directly replied that, in the totally unlikely event that it ever occurred, Canadians would become, in his words, "floating constitutionalists."

In the course of my own submissions, I argued that the existence of a constitutional convention is, by its very terms, a non-legal question that should not be answered by any court. Though clearly a matter of some political importance, it should be left for political scientists and the political arena to resolve. Justice Martland pressed me to admit that the logical conclusion of my argument was that the federal government had the constitutional right during the patriation process to request the United Kingdom to amend the *BNA Act* so as to abolish the provinces. I conceded this right in theory while stressing the complete political unreality of any such course of action. I learned several years later that this exchange particularly troubled Justice Brian Dickson. He expressed his concerns privately at the time that the court should recognize that the provinces must have some legal rights when it comes to amending the Constitution. I believe that this concern led directly to his embrace of the concept of a constitutional convention, which turned out to be pivotal in the political negotiations after the Supreme Court released its decision in September 1981.

Chief Justice Bora Laskin disagreed with the majority of his colleagues on the convention question. In his written dissent, he described the issue in these words: "The sanction for non-observance of a convention is political in that disregard of a convention may lead to political defeat, to loss of office or to other political consequences. It is not for the Courts to raise a convention to the status of a legal principle." He went on to express his view that no such convention existed: it would have required a very clear definition and acceptance, and that was clearly not the case. He also noted that "the degree of provincial participation in constitutional amendments has been a subject of lasting controversy in Canada for generations."

In his dissent, Chief Justice Laskin also dealt succinctly and firmly with the theoretical issue Justice Martland had raised with me. "We are not here faced with an action which in any way has the effect of transforming the federal union into a unitary state," he wrote. "The 'in terrorem' argument raising the spectre of a unitary state has no validity." In deciding that there was an existing "convention" that required "substantial" support from the provinces for an amendment to the Canadian Constitution, he also criticized the majority of the court for having "answered a question that was not before them." Indeed, the references to the three provincial appeal courts assumed that, if any convention existed in relation to provincial support, it would have to be unanimous support. Otherwise it would appear that there were two classes of provinces – the majority that agreed with an amendment, and the minority that did not.

The Patriation reference case, the most important ever heard by the Supreme Court of Canada, took only five days to argue. It was impossible to read the mood of the court during or at the end of the submissions. The most optimistic federal officials were predicting a favourable decision within a month, with the possibility of passage by both the Canadian and the British Parliaments in time for a Royal Proclamation on July 1, 1981, during a visit by Her Majesty Queen Elizabeth II to Canada. The date remained open on her calendar for some weeks, but it was not to be.

In July 1981, while still waiting for the Supreme Court decision, Jean Chrétien, Roy Romanow, and I debated the constitutional issues generally at the Canadian Institute for Advanced Legal Studies at Cambridge University. As well as touching base with some British politicians in London, we had the opportunity during the conference in that lovely university setting to discuss a few alternatives over tankards of beer with our colleagues. I believe that our debate contributed some new perspectives for the largely Canadian audience of jurists, lawyers, and law teachers. The host of the evening was the Honourable Paul Martin Sr, who, in a gracious summing up, referred to the debate as a significant historical event, particularly as it was taking place between "young political leaders not far from the Mother of Parliaments at a critical time in our nation's history." Chief Justice Bora Laskin and one of his fellow judges, Justice Willard Estey, who were both attending the conference, discreetly stayed away from our debate as the Patriation case was still under reserve by their court.

While in England, Romanow, Chrétien, and I discussed the possibility of some further political compromises, whatever the Supreme Court's decision might be. In fact, however, the manner and strategy of bringing about any compromises would be shaped by the ongoing legal and political drama. This whole issue would obviously be influenced to a major extent by the Supreme Court in particular and by the unfolding political reaction in general.

During this visit, as in my trip to London earlier that year in January, I took every opportunity to stress with British politicians the importance of a political resolution in Canada regarding the continuing constitutional controversy. Although the UK Parliament obviously had a vital role to play in the patriation process, it should, I advised, avoid the temptation to make political judgments in relation to the internal politics of Canada. Any attempt by the British government to become the arbitrator between the Canadian federal government and the provinces would, I said, represent a major assault on the sovereignty of our nation.

At the same time, I agreed, the Canadian government had placed the British parliamentarians in an excruciatingly awkward, if not untenable, position. They were being asked to "rubber stamp" legislation essentially drafted in Canada and to bury any political doubts they held. It was an extraordinary position in which to place any member of the British Parliament, and it could easily be regarded as an emasculation of the legislators' traditional role. Trudeau's advice to the British MPs that they "hold their noses" and pass the legislation provided no level of comfort for conscientious British parliamentarians.

In retrospect, I understand Trudeau's frustration with the British government, some members of which he had undoubtedly alienated by his blunt advice. At the same time, the long debate probably encouraged many British MPs to harbour a paternalistic attitude towards Canada. I believe that Prime Minister Thatcher considered the whole matter of patriation a political distraction – one she resented while not personally disagreeing with the need for patriation after many decades of debate.

Those of us who supported the federal initiative needed to convince our British colleagues that, in the circumstances, the passage of the legislation, without amendment, would in fact be the wisest application of their collective political judgment. Only that approach would reflect the reality of Canadian sovereignty. In the final analysis, the Canadian people would have to be the judge of the propriety of its government's actions. Nevertheless, the procession of Canadian politicians and interest groups to Westminster and London continued, leading to a perception in Britain that Canada's evolution from colony to nation was not yet complete. Indeed, our meetings with British politicians over the course of the year suggested that they were becoming increasingly judgmental about Canada's internal affairs. What appeared in January 1981 to be a genuine desire "to do the right thing for the Canadians" had, by July, taken on some worrisome paternalistic dimensions.

This patronizing attitude was experienced by Jean Chrétien after final agreement on the Constitution had been reached at the first ministers' conference on November 5, 1981, when he visited Westminster early in the winter of the next year during passage of the Canada Bill. He told me how, over dinner one night, a group of British MPs who had never even visited Canada volunteered their personal solutions for Canadian problems, particularly those related to Quebec and to national unity. Chrétien got the last word when, at the conclusion of the dinner, he announced that he was going to have lunch in Belfast the following day so he could provide his British colleagues there with the solution to the continuing divisions in Ulster.

In any event, the Canadian politicking in London eased off during the latter part of the summer as the Canadian and British governments waited for the Supreme Court decision. Nevertheless, the opposing provinces were gearing up for a major "last-ditch" stand in Britain should the court's decision be unfavourable. It was equally clear that very few on either side of the Atlantic regarded that prospect with any degree of enthusiasm.

When the Supreme Court of Canada assembled on September 21, 1981, to deliver the historic judgment, senior representatives from all the provinces had gathered in Ottawa. While counsel were waiting in the courtroom for the judges to arrive, I mused to those sitting around me that, when we left, there could well be some degree of uncertainty as to which side had actually won the case. My comment turned out to be much more prophetic than I wanted it to be.

The decision was a complex one, and in the first moments following Chief Justice Laskin's summary of it, both sides claimed "victory" in front of the television cameras outside the courtroom. The Supreme Court decided that, from a strictly legal standpoint, a request from the federal government for an amendment to the Canadian Constitution without the consent of the provinces was constitutionally legal. However, without the "substantial support" of the provinces, such a request would be in breach of a long-held constitutional convention that support by the provinces was needed for any constitutional amendments.

At a press conference several hours later, I stated that "the interpretation of this judgment of the Supreme Court of Canada is not a matter for debate." In distinguishing between constitutional law and constitutional convention, I noted that the court had placed "the conventions no higher than constitutional propriety for which the sanctions are political." In private, however, I realized that the court's recognition of a constitutional convention would probably make it impossible to persuade the British government to pass the necessary patriation legislation without the substantial agreement of the provinces.

I knew that "constitutional propriety" would be a matter of considerable interest to British parliamentarians. Without a written constitution in their own country, the British MPs would likely give great importance to the issue of a constitutional convention. They would therefore consider it significant that, in the opinion of the Supreme Court, the federal government had breached a constitutional convention when it acted unilaterally, without substantial provincial support, in seeking major amendments to the Canadian Constitution. Although the decision as to the legal validity of the federal government's request might encourage the British government to move ahead with the *Canada Act*, actual passage, in my opinion, was unlikely without substantial provincial support. By means of this nuanced judgment, then, the Supreme Court paved the way for the eventual settlement of November 1981.

Prime Minister Trudeau was clearly angry over the majority decision in relation to the convention question. He realized that his patriation proposals were doomed to failure in Britain without substantial support from the provinces. In a unitary state such as Britain, established political conventions are taken very seriously. Still, I have never really understood the extent of Trudeau's anger with respect to the decision of the Supreme Court of Canada on the "convention question." Scholars can well debate the issue of whether the decision of the majority of the court to elevate a constitutional convention to a judiciable issue was correct, but in my view it saved the day! To quote Trudeau in part: the majority of the court was indeed determined "to arrive at the desired result." I believe that the majority were serving the Canadian public interest when, again to quote Trudeau, they did act "as a political arbiter at a time of a political crisis."

Trudeau did not, however, publicly express his disappointment about the Supreme Court's decision until a decade later, in March 1991, seven years after his retirement as prime minister. Then, as the honoured guest at the opening of the Bora Laskin Library at the University of Toronto Law School, he referred to Laskin's dissent on the convention question: "That dissent I shall argue in this address was not only the better law, but the better common sense ... What I find most remarkable about the majority judgement is the number of times their lordships chose to turn a deaf ear and a blind eye to the legal arguments which might have led them in the opposite direction." He went on to state that conventions, being non-judiciable and therefore unsuitable for judicial determination, are enforceable only through the political process. In his strongest criticism he alleged that the majority had "blatantly manipulated the evidence so as to arrive at the desired result." He concluded, "The majority was improperly trying to act as a political arbiter at a time of a political crisis."

These remarks about the majority decision of the Supreme Court of Canada are probably the strongest criticism of that court ever made by a former prime minister. Moreover, Trudeau pronounced those words in the presence of one of the justices who had made the majority decision – Brian Dickson, who was by then the chief justice of Canada. Several of us in the audience that day were aware that Dickson was very upset by them, and we politely suggested to Trudeau that, during the reception that followed, he might perhaps say something of a more positive nature to his fellow guest. Trudeau replied: "What the hell is he upset for? I appointed him chief justice of Canada, didn't I?"

22

Negotiations over the Patriation of the Canadian Constitution

Immediately after the Supreme Court of Canada announced its decision on the patriation reference case, Roy Romanow and I went to Jean Chrétien's home in Ottawa for a post-mortem. It was obvious to us that some significant compromises would now be necessary before the continuing constitutional impasse could be resolved. We knew that certain ingredients were essential to any agreement, and we reviewed several areas where compromise would be necessary. Two items in particular were crucial: an entrenched charter of rights, despite the opposition of the majority of the provinces; and an amending formula or, as an alternative, a referendum mechanism.

By this time, it was also apparent that an amending formula with an absolute veto for any one province, as had been drafted during the Victoria conference in 1971, was no longer acceptable. On this point, Chrétien found it very difficult to surrender what Quebec regarded as its historical right to a veto. He obviously did not want to be the minister of justice in any federal government that agreed to deprive Quebec of a constitutional veto. On certain major issues, Chrétien and Trudeau had different views: I do not believe that Trudeau ever shared Chrétien's fervour for a Quebec veto, and Chrétien certainly did not share Trudeau's belief in the value of referendums as an amending, deadlock-breaking mechanism. In fact, though, after I wrote a constitutional memoir for the *Queen's University Law Journal* in 1983 about his "lack of enthusiasm" for a veto for Quebec, Trudeau sent me a note saying he "was much more supportive of the concept of a Quebec veto" than I had stated.

Supporters of the referendum concept argue that it is the most democratic of procedures because it involves direct consultation with individual citizens about important issues. In my opinion, however, it is an awkward, potentially divisive process that is inappropriate for amending a constitution (as the Charlottetown Accord demonstrated some years later). The reality is that some people dislike one item, so vote against it, while other people vote no on the basis of another item, and through such "unholy alliances" the amendment gets rejected. In addition, people might well vote for or against a charter of rights or another constitutional amendment not on the merits of the particular issue but on the relative popularity of the government making the proposal.

When the Constitution was finally patriated in 1982, several political commentators alleged that the constitutional "betrayal of Quebec" began with a conspiracy hatched that evening in Chrétien's home. This mythology, which has regrettably been given some credence, particularly in Quebec academic circles, is totally unfair to the three of us who participated in the discussion. Chrétien, though committed to ending the constitutional deadlock, remained firmly convinced that Quebec required constitutional protection to preserve its special linguistic and cultural identity in Confederation. Moreover, although Chrétien, Romanow, and I had developed a close friendship, it should not be thought that Romanow, in September 1981, had deserted the cause of the eight provinces – British Columbia, Alberta, Saskatchewan, Manitoba, Quebec, Nova Scotia, Prince Edward Island, and Newfoundland – which opposed the federal government's proposals. He remained determined to remove the sources of western alienation while, at the same time, recognizing the urgency of finding an honourable constitutional consensus – one that was desperately required in the national interest.

We were, in many ways, an unlikely team – a Liberal and francophone minister of justice; a New Democratic Party deputy premier and attorney general from the Ukrainian community of Saskatchewan; and a Conservative, Irish Protestant attorney general from Ontario. Although we represented three political parties, separate regions, and varying linguistic and cultural traditions, these differences were never an issue among us but, rather, a reflection of the Canadian mosaic. Our efforts were consistent with the Canadian tradition of working to achieve consensus and unity within our nation's diversity.

In the aftermath of the Supreme Court's decision, it was clear that the first ministers would have to make one final effort to agree on all the issues surrounding the patriation of the Canadian Constitution. The court's decision had only increased the likelihood of political opposition in the United Kingdom: although the ruling on the legality question would assist Trudeau, the adverse ruling on the convention question clouded the political horizon at Westminster. Furthermore, Canadian political leaders found it increasingly embarrassing to continue fighting a Canadian political battle on foreign soil. The Supreme Court of Canada, intentionally or not, had thrown the challenge back to the politicians: they had no choice now but to work out a political solution.

A meeting of provincial attorneys general had been scheduled in Newfoundland for the week after the Supreme Court's decision. It was an important opportunity to test the political waters with my colleagues. We had no specific mandates from our first ministers, but we did recognize that major compromises were required. The Charter of Rights was a key yet divisive issue in the constitutional debate, one often surrounded by simplistic rhetoric, so a meeting of the senior provincial law officers provided an appropriate opportunity for us to continue our dialogue on this topic. Although it was often unfairly suggested that those opposing the Charter were less interested in individual rights, the debate was actually about how best to protect such rights. The provinces that took a stand against the Charter sincerely believed that the various legislatures could provide more effective protection and, at the same time, avoid the potential in such a document for rigid judicial decisions.

A long line of distinguished constitutional experts and jurists had warned that a constitutionally entrenched charter could well upset the historic and delicate balance between Parliament and the courts. Frequently they cited the unhappy American experience in the nineteenth and early twentieth centuries when judicial interpretation of the Bill of Rights had blocked badly needed reform legislation in the areas of worker protection and child labour, and particularly in upholding the legality of racial segregation. They were also strongly opposed to any major departure from the tradition of parliamentary sovereignty, including the transfer of some of the policymaking responsibilities of elected legislators to an appointed judiciary. This opposition was not motivated by any lack of respect for our judicial institutions, but by a deeply held conviction about the role of elected parliamentarians. Premier Allan Blakeney of Saskatchewan, for one, certainly held this view.

In Ontario's view, the entrenchment of a charter of rights in our Constitution was a valid response to a widely felt need. The Charter represented a balance between the dominant English and French legal traditions and reflected the plurality of our country as a whole. Above all, it represented what Canada stood for as a nation: a basic respect for individual rights subject only to wise restraints that could be "demonstrably justified in a free and democratic society." Although each province had passed human rights legislation, Ontario also supported the idea of a charter of rights that applied equally throughout the country. We did not regard it as an American-type bill of rights that, to some extent, reflected a nation created by revolution and refined in the crucible of a long and bloody civil war. Rather, the proposed Charter took its place in the development of a nation that had evolved peacefully from colony to full independence.

At the Newfoundland meeting of the provincial attorneys general it was agreed that Canada could ill afford the indulgence of a continuing constitutional struggle. There was also the prospect of a confrontation with Great Britain which could jeopardize relations between the two nations for decades to come. Furthermore, the possibility of a patriated Canadian Constitution legislated over the objections of eight provinces would provide a dismal beginning to an important new chapter in our nation's history. While opposition to an entrenched charter of rights had become for some of the provinces almost a matter of theology, at least publicly, it was important for them to appreciate that this continuing opposition would doom any hope of compromise. The Charter was the cornerstone of the federal government's constitutional initiatives, and it had the support of all three federal political parties. By the end of the Newfoundland meeting, most of the attorneys general had agreed, at least privately, that any compromise would have to include some form of charter. At the same time, we were very much aware of the continuing opposition of some premiers who resented Trudeau's widely publicized, provocative, and basically unfair accusation that they were "bartering resources and fish for rights." Ontario generally supported Trudeau's position on resources because the National Energy Program was important to the Ontario economy. This support, although rarely stated in public, became a long-time source of some animosity between Peter Lougheed and Bill Davis.

Meanwhile, at Trudeau's suggestion, the premiers agreed to attend a first ministers' conference scheduled to begin on November 2, 1981. It was preceded by a one-day premiers' meeting in Montreal two weeks earlier. Little that happened there created any optimism for the November meeting. Premier Lévesque and his delegation remained in a combative mood, determined to maintain solidarity among the eight provinces still against the federal government's patriation proposals. This opposition remained intact during the Montreal meeting.

All through the course of the many constitutional discussions following the May 1980 Quebec referendum, Lévesque continued to be a dominant figure. His powerful and engaging personality became an effective glue helping to bind the "Gang of Eight" opposing provincial governments together. It was an unusual alliance, a separatist government surrounded by seven other provincial governments that were all committed to the Canadian federation. Lévesque and I had been drinking companions at several meetings, and on a few occasions he had invited me to join him in Quebec City or Montreal. Like many others, I was by no means immune to his considerable charm. What I particularly respected about him was his candour in private conversation. I never sensed any hidden agenda, though he was obviously committed to some form of sovereignty in Quebec. Given all the circumstances at the time, it was not difficult to understand the degree of friendship that developed between Lévesque and his fellow premiers.

The phenomenon of western alienation was an important contributing factor to the opposition of the various western premiers, fuelled considerably by the concentration of political power in central Canada and the federal government's much-hated National Energy Program. Alberta premier Peter Lougheed, as powerful and charismatic a personality as Lévesque, was generally regarded as the leader of these western premiers in the ongoing constitutional debate and confrontation. His aggressive debates with Ottawa were widely admired in the West, and all the other western premiers there were wary of the political fallout that would occur in their provinces if they disagreed with Lougheed. This potential backlash became a particular issue for Allan Blakeney, whose social-democratic government in Saskatchewan would, in more normal times, not be considered a natural ally of a Conservative government in Alberta.

The Lévesque-Lougheed axis was fascinating to observe. Both men were strong political leaders (Lévesque having founded his party and Lougheed resurrected his from oblivion) who, by the sheer force of their personalities, energy, and talent, had brought their parties to power. Although they had very different views of the ultimate evolution of Canadian federalism, they both thought that the federal Liberal government was committed to maintaining an inferior status for the regions. Their mutual dislike of the prime minister also served as a strong bond between them, and their animosity appeared to be shared to a great extent by the other premiers in the Gang of Eight.

Although the brief premiers' meeting in Montreal that October accomplished little of value in terms of a settlement, so far as I was concerned it did provide an opportunity for the provincial Cabinet ministers who had been working intensively on the constitutional file for months to canvass among ourselves possible areas for compromise. We also acknowledged that the Canadian people were increasingly fed up with the deadlock and expected us, as their political leaders, to demonstrate greater political will towards finding a consensus. By this time, we provincial ministers were a fairly collegial group. Despite our differences, as we worked and socialized together over the many months of our meetings, we became friends. Having committed so much time and energy to this issue, failure was a depressing prospect that we had, somehow, to avoid.

In contrast to our get-togethers, the meetings of the first ministers had usually been highly structured – and often broadcast on national television. They had little opportunity for informal gatherings and, unfortunately, much opportunity for public posturing. Many among our group of ministers joked privately that the only way the first ministers would achieve consensus on a new constitution would be by copying the tradition of the College of Cardinals when they met to elect a new pope: lock them up in a room and wait for the white smoke to appear, heralding success at last in their negotiations!

The opposing premiers left Montreal as strongly united as ever, but it was not long before signals began to emerge from several provinces indicating some enthusiasm for a possible compromise. As a result, a few private meetings were organized among interested individuals at both the ministerial and official levels in Toronto; athough still largely exploratory, these talks were indicative of a growing political will to reach an agreement. From Ontario's standpoint, most of the contact was at the ministerial level. Premiers Lougheed and Blakeney were the main political leaders outside Quebec, and I believed that the majority of the other dissenting provinces would follow their lead. Through Roy Romanow, I had significant access to Blakeney in Saskatchewan. The Alberta intergovernmental affairs minister was Dick Johnson, who wanted an agreement, and Lougheed was content to leave much of the "heavy lifting" to him. Premier Sterling Lyon of Manitoba, though an ardent opponent of an entrenched charter of rights, was facing an imminent election in Manitoba, and I sensed that he did not want to make the patriation proposal a major issue in the election.

As we approached the first ministers' conference scheduled to begin on November 2, it became increasingly apparent to me that Alberta would be the key to any breakthrough. The Charter of Rights was still crucial to any compromise, and Lougheed did not appear to share the same deeply held philosophical convictions that motivated Sterling Lyon and Blakeney to oppose a constitutionally entrenched charter. At the same time, it was also clear that Blakeney was becoming more prepared to accept an honourable compromise in the national interest.

For Ontario, one important compromise we thought we could potentially accept was the amending formula proposed by the Group of Eight. This formula was referred to as the Alberta formula in deference to Lougheed, who had proposed it during a meeting in Toronto in the summer of 1980. The amending formula required the agreement of seven provinces, representing at least 50 per cent of the Canadian population. That meant that neither Quebec nor Ontario would have any automatic veto. The formula also included the right for any province to opt out of a constitutional amendment, with financial guaranties in certain circumstances.

Prime Minister Trudeau made it clear that he strongly opposed the provision in the proposed Alberta formula for opting out. Part of our Ontario strategy was, therefore, for Premier William Davis to convince Trudeau not only that the formula was viable but that it was an essential prerequisite for any compromise. We also hoped that our sister provinces would view the surrender of our traditional right to a veto on constitutional amendments as a generous gesture. Despite other outstanding issues and potential areas of conflict, federal acceptance of this amending formula appeared to be fundamental to any consensus. It was also apparent that Trudeau would not accept any compromise that did not include a charter of rights.

I met with Jean Chrétien in Ottawa several days before the first ministers' conference. We both agreed that we must do everything to prevent the issues from becoming polarized during the first two days of the meeting. I told Chrétien that I believed a breakthrough was a real possibility, but that he must persuade the prime minister to avoid his provocative argumentative style. "The boss sure like to argue," he replied, slowly, "and, although he wins a lot of arguments, he can also lose the war." We agreed that a real degree of consensus was possible if a non-confrontational dialogue could be maintained during the meetings. I also stressed to Chrétien how important it was for the federal government to indicate early on in the meetings its willingness to consider a significant compromise seriously. Up to that point, both sides had revealed little about their intentions. In particular, the prime minister had not signalled that he was willing to consider any compromise whatsoever.

The week of November 2, 1981, which led to the all-important patriation accord, will undoubtedly be recorded from many different perspectives. For me, right from the start of the meeting I sensed a more positive attitude towards pursuing an agreement than I had at any earlier conference. Furthermore, Trudeau had told Davis and me privately that he was fully aware of the significant obstacles lying ahead in London if we could not achieve an agreement that included substantial provincial support. The major obstacles to overcome were the amending formula and the Charter of Rights. On the first, Trudeau was philosophically committed to a referendum mechanism as a device to go over the heads of the provincial governments if an important proposed constitutional amendment did not receive the provincial governments' support. As for the second, the Charter was the cornerstone of the federal proposals and was strongly supported by Ontario and New Brunswick. The majority of the other provinces, though recognizing privately that some form of charter was essential to any accord, were determined to water it down as the price of their agreement.

On Monday, the first day of the meeting, while the eight opposing premiers met in private, I had the opportunity to sit down alone with Trudeau to discuss a possible compromise on the Charter of Rights. After all the talks I had been involved in with others across the country, I had become convinced that incorporating a "notwithstanding clause" in the Charter had the best potential for an honourable compromise. This clause, which eventually became section 33 of the Charter of Rights, would allow Parliament or a provincial legislature to pass legislation notwithstanding a conflict with a particular section of the Charter, though any such clause would have to be renewed every five years. I was confident that the clause would rarely be used, given the strong public support I observed for a Charter of Rights. The clause would provide a balancing mechanism between the legislators and the courts in the event that elected parliamentarians believed a court decision was contrary to the public interest. Although the clause offended Trudeau's absolutist view about the role of the Charter, I was relieved when, after some consideration, he informed me that he might consider it should it become the only way to obtain agreement on a credible constitutional package.

Pierre Trudeau will always be remembered for maintaining rigid control of his emotions. It was therefore memorable during our meeting when he treated me to a prime ministerial rant about his annoyance with Margaret Thatcher because she had not provided more aggressive leadership in pushing the patriation of the Canadian Constitution. He even suggested that, if the stalemate with Britain continued, Canada should seriously consider withdrawing from the Commonwealth. I responded by advising him not to share this idea with Bill Davis if he wished to retain Ontario's support. Some four-and-a-half years later in 1985, when I became Canada's high commissioner in the United Kingdom, I learned from Thatcher that she did not miss Trudeau's presence at all during Commonwealth meetings or other important international forums following his retirement in 1984. In particular, she thought that Trudeau's peace mission in his last months of office was "grandstanding." Their dislike for each other was palpable.

As the week progressed, it continued to be evident that Quebec was not interested in any agreement. Although the other opposing premiers appeared to want some compromise, they were reluctant to isolate Quebec. The emotional undercurrents stemming from many of the provinces' continuing battles with Ottawa were still a powerful unifying force among the dissenting Group of Eight.

On the Tuesday evening I had dinner with both Blakeney and Romanow of Saskatchewan. Blakeney, a strong supporter of the principle of parliamentary supremacy and somewhat sceptical about the role of unelected judges, was still opposed to any entrenched charter of rights. His views had been well summarized in an exchange he had with Trudeau at the time of the unsuccessful first ministers' conference in September 1980:

Canadians ought not to have taken from them their fundamental rights to participate in all political choices. If we were to decide to place the Charter of Rights in the Constitution we would be taking it out of the hands of the elected representatives and giving to the Courts the power to decide some of the country's most significant political issues. The fundamental issue is what issues in our society ought to be decided by the Courts.

For his part, Prime Minister Trudeau had replied:

But when we get to protect fundamental rights of freedoms of the citizens, you say, "Don't put them in the constitution; the words are too hard to find." We say, "What is wrong with going to the courts, and why shouldn't a minority which is adversely affected be able to call us to account in front of the courts?"

I suggested to Blakeney over dinner that, if we added the notwithstanding clause to the Constitution, it would provide the balancing mechanism to allow Parliament or a legislature to override a court Charter decision for a limited but renewable period of time. Romanow believed that it was essential for an agreement to be reached on some form of entrenched Charter of Rights, and I left our dinner feeling somewhat encouraged.

To step ahead briefly, although Allan Blakeney in later years became very sceptical about the Charter of Rights, in May 2009 he sent me a note about the value of the notwithstanding clause: "The refining of the idea of a notwithstanding clause went a long way to finding a way out of the deadlock which had developed. Your championing of a notwithstanding clause and your skilful introduction of it into the mix went a long way to achieving the compromise which was reached. There can be dispute as to whether it was for good or evil, but it has worked out in a reasonable way."

The day following our dinner during the negotiations, however, a consensus appeared to be as elusive as ever, although I sensed a greater political will on the part of some of the premiers for a resolution. As the old arguments went round and round the table, it became apparent that a very frustrated prime minister was becoming more entrenched in his view that a referendum process would be the only way to break the constitutional deadlock. After yet another acerbic exchange between Trudeau and Lévesque about the democratic value of consulting the people, as demonstrated by the 1980 Quebec referendum, Lévesque told the prime minister that he would welcome any such future challenge. At this point, Trudeau suggested national referendums to decide both the amending formula and the entrenched Charter of Rights. Lévesque appeared anxious to show his support for the idea, and he embraced the referendum proposal.

Immediately I asked Davis to request a brief recess. I sensed that Lévesque's enthusiasm for the referendum process might well isolate him from the other premiers in the Gang of Eight. I knew they were strongly opposed to any federal government using referendums as a mechanism to bypass the provincial legislatures. During this recess, my brief discussions with some of our provincial colleagues suggested that the referendum proposal could indeed provide the basis for splitting the Gang of Eight and reaching a broad accord – regrettably, however, without the agreement of Quebec. In misjudging the depth of antagonism among his provincial allies to the referendum concept, Lévesque had provided the rationale for what he would bitterly describe later as a "betrayal" and the "night of the long knives." In fact, at this critical moment it was his provincial allies who felt betrayed. Ironically, the referendum procedure was the sole issue that Trudeau and Lévesque could agree on during the long constitutional battles. That agreement provided the political catalyst for the Constitutional Accord of November 5, 1981.

Later that Wednesday afternoon, Jean Chrétien, Roy Romanow, and I compared notes in a secluded food-preparation area on what we saw as the essential ingredients for an agreement. In the aftermath of the November 1981 accord, the media focused on the critical role that we three ministers played in the final negotiations. To dramatize what many journalists saw as a long-drawn-out if not dreary process, they created the impression that the final agreement was largely fashioned in a kitchen in the Ottawa Convention Centre. This view was considerably reinforced when Trudeau requested a photographer to take a picture of him with the three of us in that very kitchen and when Lévesque endorsed this view later in his memoirs. In the years since then, some of the premiers who attended that key constitutional conference have complained about an undue emphasis on the "kitchen accord."

The reality is that Chrétien, Romanow, and I had been meeting over many months and had long been determined to facilitate an agreement among the first ministers. Over that same period we had also attended several meetings with our fellow ministers who were working on the constitutional file, and because of the frequency of those get-togethers, we had developed a much greater level of collegiality and trust than the premiers had been able to achieve. This mutual trust in due course had considerable influence on the premiers. The most significant bond between the opposing premiers was their common dislike for Prime Minister Trudeau – an attitude that clearly lacked the statesmanship and objectivity required to reach an agreement in the national interest. In any event, at the critical November meeting, I detected a far greater enthusiasm for an agreement among the ministers of the eight dissenting provinces than among their premiers. In the final analysis, however, only the premiers could make an agreement.

Not surprisingly, over the three decades and more that have elapsed since the accord of November 1981, some bizarre historical revisionism has occurred. Perhaps the strangest accounting of events has come from Brian Peckford, the former Newfoundland premier, who was quoted in the *Globe and Mail* in November 2011 to the effect that the kitchen accord never happened and that the final agreement had essentially been based on a proposal made by Newfoundland. When asked why he had remained silent for thirty years, he replied that all through that time he "had other things to do." My clear recollection of Peckford was that he appeared willing to sabotage the whole constitutional process right from its beginning in the summer of 1980. At the first ministers' conference in September 1980, it was he who suggested that the prime minister could not be trusted as chairman and that a provincial premier should be appointed as co-chair. He wasted few opportunities to be insulting to Trudeau, even stating on two occasions in my presence that he preferred Lévesque's view of the future of Canada to that of the prime minister.

Coming into that conference, we all knew that Trudeau opposed the proposed Alberta amending formula, the lack of a referendum procedure, and, in particular, the notwithstanding clause, yet his acceptance of these proposals was critical to an agreement. On Thursday morning, November 5, the premiers tabled a draft agreement – based on the key items written in Wednesday's "kitchen accord" and now presented by Peckford – as the leader of Canada's youngest province. After Trudeau read the agreement quickly, he muttered something to the effect that, though he was not particularly happy with it, "I guess that's the best we can do." Even at this late stage, Peckford suggested that, if the prime minister didn't like the accord, it should be scrapped. Fortunately, his intervention was ignored, and the agreement was signed.

In the final chapter of the drama leading towards the Constitutional Accord of November 5, 1981, Ontario played a major role as broker, facilitator, compromiser, and mediator between the other provinces and Ottawa. We had focused our efforts on finding a workable agreement, not a sweeping revision. It is highly unlikely that Ottawa would have proceeded with its constitutional initiatives after September 1980 without the support of Ontario. In the final hours of the negotiations, moreover, Premier Davis played a critical role by insisting to the prime minister that he might lose Ontario's support if he did not accept the proposed compromises. Trudeau confirmed to me in writing more than once in subsequent years that he could not have proceeded with the patriation package without support from Ontario.

The euphoria many of us felt about the November 5 agreement was tempered by the absence of Quebec's signature on the deal. Although I had come to consider that outcome inevitable, I still felt very sad when Quebec's opposition became a reality. Quebec's former allies were particularly distressed about it, as was reflected in the discussion during the morning of November 5 just before the signing of the accord. Although all the English-speaking provinces were enthusiastic to adopt constitutional guarantees for French-language education in their territories, the majority refused to endorse the federal government's proposal to make such guarantees conditional on Quebec's acceptance of minority English-language education guarantees. They were reluctant, they stated, to "meddle" in Quebec politics at that sensitive time, though they expressed confidence that the Quebec people would in time resolve the issue fairly in relation to the English-speaking minority in the province.

Just as personalities shape the events that shape nations, so do events shape personalities. The *New York Times*, in an editorial analysing Canada's agreement on the Constitution a few days later, praised her leaders for their flexibility and judgment: "In a large and diverse country, few things are more difficult than forming its regions into a more perfect union. It took secession and a civil war to settle the comparable arguments in the United States. All the more credit then to a mellowed Mr. Trudeau and his reasonable opponents for settling a hard dispute in democratic fashion." High praise, indeed. However, the absence of the signature of the government of Quebec on the Constitutional Accord of 1981 was destined to haunt the Canadian political scene for years to come – as it still does to this day.

In the context of the ongoing separatist/federalist struggle in Quebec, I am often asked if I regret working for the federal/provincial accord of November 1981. I have never had any real regret, although Quebec's signature on the accord would have made the patriation of Canada's Constitution an infinitely more celebratory event. At the same time, it is worth noting the comments of Ron Graham in *The Last Act: Pierre Trudeau, the Gang of Eight, and the Fight for Canada*, his book on the constitutional patriation published in 2011: "The truth was, outside the political class and away from the media, most Quebecers remained profoundly indifferent to what had happened at the First Ministers' Conference in November [1981] ... The polls showed that 48 percent of Quebecers disagreed with Lévesque's position, 32 percent were in favour, and the rest didn't know or didn't care." He also points out that Quebec's powers and responsibilities were protected by the new amending formula, which included financial compensation should the province ever choose to opt out of any amendments affecting education and culture. Quebec also had a notwithstanding clause that it could use if the Charter affected the will of the National Assembly in any way deemed unacceptable. Francophones within and outside Quebec were assured of French-language schooling wherever the numbers warranted it.

In my view, however, we should remember that public opinion polls in Quebec were strongly in support of Canada's new and patriated Constitution. Lévesque did have a majority provincially, but Trudeau had all but one seat federally. Although the absence of the Quebec government's formal agreement will continue to be employed as a weapon by the separatists, the reasons for a divided Quebec are far more complex than the momentous events that occurred in November 1981.

The Constitutional Accord of November 5 was formalized on April 17 the following year when Queen Elizabeth II and Prime Minister Trudeau signed the *Constitution Act, 1982*, in Ottawa. It was a memorable occasion for everyone present and particularly for those who had worked for that day over many years. Ria accompanied me to Ottawa for the historic event on Parliament Hill, and the celebratory mood was in no way dampened by the rain that fell intermittently during the ceremony. The Queen and Prince Philip hosted a dinner at Rideau Hall for the prime minister and those of us involved in the process. It was the evening before our twentieth-fifth wedding anniversary, and I've never tired of telling how the Queen invited Ria and me to dine with her on the eve of this special anniversary.

In the years since, there have been many discussions about the effect on Canadians of the Charter of Rights and Freedoms. Although a large number of important Charter decisions have been made, the decided cases have had a direct impact on a relatively small minority of Canadians. At the same time, I think that the Charter has helped to eliminate many abuses with respect to criminal investigations. Most important, I believe that the Charter has significantly strengthened Canadians' respect for individual rights and their support for the remarkable diversity of our nation (chapter 35).

23

René Lévesque

When the Parti Québécois led by René Lévesque was elected as the government of Quebec in November 1976, I was not at all surprised. Moreover, although this new regime represented a serious challenge to the future of the Canadian federation, I did not regard it as an enemy of Canada. Rather, I believed it was important for the Davis government in Ontario to maintain cordial relations, to the extent possible, with the Lévesque government in the interests of a united Canada.

Shortly before the Quebec referendum, I spoke to the Empire Club on the challenges of Quebec to Canadian unity. In my remarks I said:

For Canadians, the challenge of nationhood is very real as we determine the future of our confederation. Yet there are few challenges which do not bring with them a degree of opportunity, and the challenge to our confederation is no exception.

What we do face is a rare opportunity as a civilized and pluralistic nation to build a new structural relationship in matters of government between Canada's ten provinces, our federal government and the institutions which serve all.

The people and province of Québec have a proud and traditional commitment to the maintenance, advancement and progress of their French language, culture and identity. I need not stress how important language, culture and identity are to the self-respect, pride and continuity of people.

Five million French-speaking Canadians stand rather alone and somewhat isolated in purely cultural terms on a continent of over two hundred million

English-speaking people. I therefore support the proposition that we cannot assure or even provide for reasonable cultural survival in this kind of circumstance without some particular arrangements that relate to the way in which French-speaking Québec relates both pragmatically and constitutionally with the rest of Canada.

...

The election which brought Mr. Lévesque to power in Québec brought to power a person who believed not only in good and honest government, but in Sovereignty for Québec; the voters had precious little choice – re-elect a government that had lost the confidence of the people or elect a new government with capable people and leadership who promised good government and not to pursue independence without an express mandate through a referendum.

...

I therefore believe that despite our cultural and linguistic differences, despite the rigours of climate and regional disparity, we will continue to share a common destiny. This is a destiny that has often demanded compromise, courage and tolerance from us all and that simply is the record of this nation's history.

I am therefore confident that the idea of one united country will survive any test – be it a referendum, or an election, simply because when compared to the alternatives, it is plainly and clearly a far better idea.

Regrettably, the patriation of our Constitution with an entrenched Charter did not create, as I also stated in my speech, a "new path – one based upon a compromise between the rigid federalism of our past and the regional and cultural aspirations which constitute our present." However, despite the refusal of the Quebec government to be part of the patriation agreement and its own goal of a sovereign Quebec, I shall always regard Lévesque as a true democrat.

I first met René Lévesque in 1963 through the Canadian Society for the Abolition of the Death Penalty, when he became a supporter of our cause. He was then the minister of natural resources in the Lesage government, where he played an important role in the nationalization of hydroelectric companies, though his interest in the possible separation of Quebec was becoming a matter of public knowledge. I found him immensely charming and articulate, and I immediately recognized that he was a growing political force in the province. The fact that he created the Parti Québécois was a clear indication that he was committed to pursuing power democratically, as opposed to the terrorist tactics of the Quebec separatists who had created the Front de Libération du Québec.

Marc-André Bédard, from Sherbrooke, was Lévesque's first minister of justice, and I arranged to meet with him early in the life of the new government. My lawyer friend René Dussault was his deputy minister, and he acted as an interpreter when my shaky French-language skills broke down. Bédard spoke virtually no English, but our meeting was a success, and we enjoyed a cordial relationship during his years in the justice portfolio.

The first time I encountered Lévesque in his new role was at a premiers' conference in August 1977 in Alberta. We provincial ministers with responsibilities for constitutional change had been meeting in advance of the premiers to attempt to make some progress on reform. We had not accomplished very much, although I was most interested in the comments of Lévesque's minister of intergovernmental affairs in relation to the position of the British monarch as Canada's head of state. I was curious as to whether he viewed this role as a divisive issue in Quebec. Rather to my surprise, he replied that Queen Elizabeth II and all she represented was a matter of general indifference in his province.

With little to say to the media representatives who were covering our meetings, I thought they might be interested to hear the Quebec government's views about the Queen as head of state. The Canadian public, particularly those who thought that the official role of the British monarch was an impediment to constitutional agreement, should be informed of the real situation. When Lévesque arrived at the premiers' meeting the next day, however, it became apparent that my remarks to the media had caused significant interest in Quebec and that Lévesque had faced many questions from the media there before he left for Alberta. In his first statement at the meeting he said, somewhat sarcastically but with some humour, that although he appreciated the efforts of Ontario's attorney general to explain Quebec's views on the monarchy, he thought the responsibility more properly belonged to him.

The next premiers' meeting was in Saskatchewan and included an overnight retreat in northern Saskatchewan at Lake Waskesiu. Early the next morning I went for a walk along the shore with René Lévesque and Roy Romanow. Lévesque was accompanied by an RCMP security officer, and along the way I overheard snippets of his attempts to engage in small talk:

"Great country, Officer."
"Yes, sir."
"Beautiful country, Officer."

"Yes, sir."

"Big enough for two," he opined, grinning at Romanow and me.

In January 1980, after the defeat of the Clark government just a month before, Lévesque paid a courtesy call to Queen's Park, where I was able to have a private conversation with him. He appeared interested in our dialogue and invited me to return with him on his government aircraft to Montreal, where, he suggested, we could attend a Montreal Canadiens hockey game that night. I accepted and enjoyed an interesting evening with the premier, particularly as the first referendum on sovereignty-association was expected in the spring of that year. The federal election pitting Clark against the resurgent Trudeau was also scheduled for the following month. It was clear that Lévesque hoped Joe Clark would be successful, as he admitted that Trudeau would be a much tougher opponent during the referendum campaign. At the same time, he used our flight together as an opportunity to do some "missionary" work in support of the concept of greater Quebec independence. He was clearly irritated by the perception of many Canadians that the independence movement was strongly supported by the government of France. Contrary to what he had often said publicly, he agreed that President de Gaulle's statement during Canada's Centennial Year in 1967, "Vive le Québec. Vive le Québec libre," was not helpful to the Quebec cause, given the mixed views among nationalists in the province, where many believed that Quebec had long been abandoned by its "mother country."

Lévesque went on to relate how uncomfortable he felt whenever he was in Paris. He believed that the French establishment often treated francophones from Quebec as "country bumpkins." For him, Paris was perhaps his least favourite place on earth. When I asked him why he appeared quite willing to travel to Paris to accept various awards from the French government and prestigious organizations, he replied that he did it to "piss off Trudeau." Lévesque was obviously a great admirer of American culture, undoubtedly related to his experience during the Second World War as a war correspondent attached to the US military. He told me that one of his great political experiences was addressing the Massachusetts Legislature as premier of Quebec, and he also enjoyed holidays in Florida. He was clearly confident that the United States would accept a degree of Quebec independence.

As things turned out, the Lévesque government lost the June 1980 referendum, and an emboldened Trudeau, once again the prime min-

ister, immediately instituted the serious process for constitutional renewal that he had promised Quebec during the referendum campaign.
Jean Chrétien and Roy Romanow, as I outlined earlier, co-chaired a
federal-provincial committee of ministers and senior officials who
met in different parts of Canada in an attempt to reach consensus on
twelve topics that were central to the constitutional discussions. Our
report was scheduled to be tabled at a first ministers' conference between Prime Minister Trudeau and the provincial premiers in September 1980.

As a member of the committee that met throughout most of that summer, it was obvious to me that the Quebec delegation was not interested
in an agreement, though it was prepared to participate. The people on
that team were clearly comforted by the deep divisions between the
federal government and many of the other provinces. Quebec could,
therefore, "go through the motions" without being blamed for sabotaging the discussions, and so the first ministers' conference was doomed
to failure. I have several photographs of Lévesque and me taken at that
meeting, and we were obviously enjoying a good deal of laughter and
cordiality. My view has always been that Lévesque was confident that
the talks would be unproductive, so he arrived in a relaxed mood. He
didn't allow the Ontario government's support for the federal constitutional proposals to affect our friendship.

During the long process of court challenges and negotiations on the
Constitution, Premier Lévesque established a close and very cordial relationship with the other Gang of Eight premiers, east and west (chapter 22). That association suddenly unravelled on the night of November
4, 1981, and Quebec's exclusion from the final agreement was a bitter
pill for Lévesque, leading to much rhetoric over the years in that province about the "night of the long knives." I therefore approached the
1982 annual meeting of the provincial premiers in Halifax the following August with some trepidation. I was accompanied by our oldest
child, Janet, who was to begin law school at Dalhousie University the
following month. We attended the opening reception together, where
she had a very pleasant chat with Lévesque. However, I sensed that he
was generally in a bad mood, which I attributed to the fact that this was
the first premiers' meeting since the agreement that led to the patriation
of the Canadian Constitution, with an entrenched Charter of Rights, on
April 17, 1982. I expected that Lévesque might well have mixed feelings
about his former allies, whom he claimed had betrayed him. Rather to
my surprise, Robert Normand, his deputy minister, assured me that

Lévesque was in a black mood simply because it was his sixtieth birthday that day – a milestone he did not welcome!

Lévesque resigned as leader of the Parti Québécois in the autumn of 1985. Before he retired from politics, I attended a first ministers' meeting related to Aboriginal rights as they were recognized and affirmed by Canada's new Constitution. Our relationship remained cordial, though at one stage Lévesque, somewhat tongue-in-cheek, advised the Aboriginal leaders "to post sentries during the meeting, because strange things can occur during the night in Ottawa." After his retirement, Lévesque wrote an autobiography, which was published just the year before he died, in 1987. He sent me an inscribed copy of the first French edition, suggesting in an accompanying note that reading it would be a good lesson for me in the French language. On the title page he wrote:

À Roy McMurtry
sans trop de rancoeur … le temps guérit un peu
but …
René Lévesque

Translated into English, the inscription reads, "Without too much rancour … time heals a little," with emphasis on the English word "but."

Lévesque is quite bitter in the memoir about the role of the Supreme Court of Canada in declaring that Trudeau's constitutional proposals were legal, even if they were contrary to an established constitutional convention that required substantial support of the provinces. "On hearing that," he wrote, "I was reminded of another bit of old English wisdom – the law is an ass." In describing the sudden unravelling of the Gang of Eight, Lévesque continued that, in his opinion, the "main part of the job was confided to three men, who might be regarded as three dauphins of their respective governments. Jean Chrétien was, in some respects, Trudeau's handyman. Roy McMurtry of Ontario and Roy Romanow of Saskatchewan played similar roles for their bosses." In the final result, he concluded, "all this shady dealing presided over in some kitchen apparently by the Chrétien-McMurtry-Romanow trio had resulted in a dish that was basically mediocre in which Trudeau's initial design had been considerably diluted."

In writing that Trudeau was "furious to have to put so much water in his wine," Lévesque was referring to the controversial notwithstanding clause, which, he said, he considered was absolutely essential in order to obtain the agreement of the premiers who strongly believed in the concept of parliamentary supremacy. It's certainly true that Trudeau was displeased with the compromise, but, as many of us correctly predicted, the clause would rarely be invoked outside Quebec. In fact, over the past three decades, it has been used only once in the other provinces – in Saskatchewan to introduce legislation ending a labour dispute – though in Quebec the government has employed it almost routinely as a form of protest over patriation.

I was serving as Canadian high commissioner in the United Kingdom when René Lévesque died at the age of sixty-five, a few short years after his dreaded sixtieth birthday. I was saddened by the news, as I regarded him as a man who strongly opposed violence in his pursuit of an independent Quebec. No matter how hard he fought for Quebec's independence, he always refused to embrace demagoguery. As such, during his years as premier, he led a responsible government in Quebec.

24

Israel

When I was first elected to the Ontario Legislature in 1975, I was assisted by many of my Jewish friends and others in the Jewish community. I had, of course, been interested in the State of Israel since its creation, and, not surprisingly, many of its supporters urged me to visit that nation which, in its brief life, has been at the centre of much contention in the world. As it happened, between 1976 and 1983 I made three trips to Israel in all.

In the summer of 1975 our eldest child, Janet, spent more than two months working in a kibbutz, one of the cooperative farming settlements in Israel. The experience made a lasting impression on her, and she, too, became very enthusiastic about her father visiting Israel. When, the following January, I made my first trip there, one of my hosts was Attorney General Aharon Barak. In Israel the attorney general, as an appointed rather than an elected official, is expected to be completely detached from partisan politics. There is also a minister of justice, who, as an elected member of Israel's parliament, belongs to the Cabinet appointed by the prime minister.

Barak was, and is, an impressive individual. A distinguished legal scholar, he is renowned for his integrity. When he became a judge he was entirely impartial and fair in his dealings with Israel's Arab populations – an approach that made him unpopular with members of the right wing in Israel. As attorney general, Barak was faced with the unpleasant task of deciding whether Prime Minister Yitzhak Rabin, who had been the Israeli ambassador to the United States at an earlier stage of his career, should be prosecuted for maintaining an illegal bank account in Washington. In 1977 Barak did commence a criminal prosecution against Rabin, leading to his resignation. Later, however, he returned to the office of prime minister.

The next year, Barak was appointed to the Supreme Court of Israel, and he later became its president. Although as a judge he was in theory in a non-political position, he was asked by Prime Minister Menachem Begin to become a member of Israel's negotiating team in the peace talks with Egypt which were hosted by US president Jimmy Carter in September 1978. Anwar Sadat was then president of Egypt, and while the negotiations would be difficult in any circumstances, those at the presidential retreat at Camp David were made even more challenging by the strong mutual dislike between the two Middle East leaders. Carter cleverly adopted the strategy of working continuously with the negotiation teams himself, putting in long hours each day, but keeping Begin and Sadat out of the same room as much as possible until the agreement was reached.

Shortly after this historic Camp David peace accord, I made my second visit to Israel. While there, I had the opportunity to discuss the event with Aharon Barak, but he was reluctant to take any particular credit for the settlement. When I expressed the hope that he would record his experiences at Camp David, he dismissed the idea, reluctant as ever to draw attention to himself except, inevitably, through his judicial decisions. Moshe Dayan, who was also present at Camp David as Israel's minister of defence, later wrote an article for the *Atlantic Monthly* which described the effective role Barak played on the negotiating team. On my next trip to Israel, Barak told me about his first visit to Egypt and how pleased he was, as an Israeli, to walk freely through the streets of Cairo.

I always found it interesting to go to Israel, both as a tourist and for the opportunity my days there provided for learning more about that dynamic democracy. It's a small country, so I found I could see most of the historic sites even as I was enjoying the beauty of the landscape. All these years later I still recall my first trip through the Judean hills towards Jerusalem and my first sighting of that ancient city. On all my visits there, I have been provided with a vehicle and a driver, who was also my bodyguard. I first realized that our driver was armed when, on an early trip, he mistakenly placed his revolver in Ria's purse, which was lying on the front seat beside him.

Our visit to the Golan Heights that day was unofficial because of the controversy over Israel's occupation since 1967 of the Syrian territory there. UN peacekeepers were stationed on the Heights, and down below we could see the kibbutz where Janet had worked. Before 1967, the kibbutzim below the Golan Heights were regular targets for the Syrian military. Given the continuing hatred of Israel by the Syrian government, I could well understand Israeli reluctance to release the Heights back to its arch enemy.

During my later visits to Israel, I had the privilege to meet with both Prime Minister Rabin and Prime Minister Begin. They were cordial but quite different in their personalities. Rabin was low key and not given to fiery oratory, but Begin seemed to radiate the toughness of a former leader of the Irgun Israel terrorist organization which fought the British Army in the former Palestine. I don't mean to suggest that Rabin, who was later tragically assassinated, was any less tough. Given the many violent challenges facing Israel, no one can lead that country without strength and courage.

In 1983 I saw Prime Minister Begin for a number of events during his visit to Toronto to raise money for Israeli bonds. That same year I was also honoured to receive a special Canada-Israel Friendship Award. However, my strong support of Israel was not always appreciated in Ontario and elsewhere. The Western Guard, a local chapter of the Ku Klux Klan and a white supremacist group that was also anti-Semitic and an enemy of the State of Israel, had a group in Toronto, and as I related earlier, I once received a threatening letter from David Duke, the Klan's Grand Wizard, in part because of my attitude to Israel (chapter 15).

I have given many speeches over the years which reflect my support for the State of Israel. A number of them have concluded with words to this effect:

On several occasions I have travelled to Israel to see for myself that brave nation whose brief lifetime has been spent at the centre of so much contention among the nations of the world. What I have seen was a nation, imperfect in many ways, but whose survival can never, for whatever reason or rationale, be the subject of debate. Israel must survive.

Every settlement, every house, every school, every healthy young man or woman in Israel gives testimony to the miracle of human courage, endurance, and the indomitable will to survive the most demonic fury ever unleashed by man against man. That testimony must never be silenced or put aside because, to those men and women who wish for peace with justice, whatever their race or religion, the fact of Israel is more compelling than all the rhetoric and all the logic and all the laws from the beginning of time.

Israel is the sum of a people who have endured through centuries of repression, poverty, disease, homelessness, humiliation, and murder; a people whose gaunt, ghastly survivors finally drew the line under the crushing column of inhumanity when they said, "Never again." All of humanity has a bargain to keep with those people, and with the many millions who died cruelly because the lesson had not yet been learned that it is important to answer the madman.

Jews know that the madman must be answered. They know it with a certainty and a conviction that surpasses the laboured logic of the lawmaker. They learned it in repression, torment, and death, and they will not forget it because they cannot forget it.

Because they remember, Jews, in the words of the philosopher Emil Fackenheim, "are not permitted to hand Hitler posthumous victories."

I was almost thirteen when the Second World War ended in Europe in 1945. The public revelations of the Holocaust which came shortly after seared my memory and psyche in the most powerful way imaginable. Despite the inevitable controversies that have involved Israel for many decades, I still believe that the world is collectively obliged to ensure Israel's survival.

My attitude towards Israel has been influenced by two books in particular. The first, *None Is Too Many: Canada and the Jews of Europe, 1933–1948*, by Toronto professors Irving Abella and Harold Troper, takes its title from an exchange between journalists and an anonymous Canadian government official. When the journalists asked how many Jews would be allowed into Canada after the Second World War, the official replied, "None is too many." In the authors' introductory words, the book is "a sad tale of a Canada which, faced with a humanitarian crisis of unprecedented proportions, refused to offer support let alone sanctuary to those of the greatest need. It is the tale of a Canada awash in homegrown racism and anti-semitism." The second book, *The Siege*, by Irish intellectual, diplomat, and politician Conor Cruise O'Brien, argues that Israel is under siege and, sadly, "What is not in sight is an end to the siege." I agree with O'Brien's conclusion that Israel "cannot be other than what it is."

I have my own personal memories of anti-Semitism in Canada during the 1930s and 1940s. Jews were barred from memberships in many clubs and faced barriers in entering the professions. In Quebec, the

powerful Catholic Church felt duty bound to protect the faith from
alien corruption – which, in its view, was often represented by Jews.
Canada's immigration policy tried to stream non-English-speaking immigrants onto the frontier – particularly the western agricultural, mining, lumbering, and railway sectors – but Jewish immigrants had no
experience in those areas and preferred to live in cities such as Montreal, Toronto, or Winnipeg. These examples reflected the horrific history of anti-Semitism over many centuries in Europe. Even when the
world knew that the Nazi regime was slaughtering European Jews,
immigration officials in Canada maintained their determination to
withhold entry to Jewish refugees. This attitude represented extreme
bureaucratic and political callousness in the face of human suffering.
"Canada did not stand alone," Abella and Troper write. "The nations
of the world were put to the test and were found wanting: their failure
was a failure of will, of the human spirit."

The anti-Semites' traditional pronouncement over many generations,
particularly within Europe, states that, while Jews could share a nation
with others, they were in reality "a distinct and alien people." Curiously
enough, the original Zionists apparently did not debate that view but
built on it, proclaiming that there was indeed a distinct Jewish nation
with a right to a national home in Palestine. The Balfour Declaration,
made by the British government in 1917, is generally regarded as the
first major political building block in the creation of Israel: it recognized
the right of the Jewish people to a national home. At that time, most
Jews appeared to believe that they had national homes in the countries
where they actually lived. One of the ironies of the declaration was that
Prime Minister Balfour was allegedly somewhat anti-Semitic, though
he had a strong sense of the tremendous Jewish contributions to religion, philosophy, science, and the arts. For him, the idea of a Jewish
Palestine meant a new enrichment of the world's culture.

Although anti-Semitism and anti-Zionism should probably not be
equated, it is generally accepted that the long history of anti-Semitism
in Europe turned Zionism into a political force that prepared for the
emergence of the State of Israel. The history of anti-Jewish pogroms
in Europe went back many centuries, particularly in Russia. With the
accession of Alexander III in 1881, the pogroms reverted to a level not
seen since the mid-seventeenth century. All the major Jewish communities in the Russian Empire came under attack, particularly in at least
215 areas inside Russia where most of the Jews lived, and anti-Semitism
became the established official policy. Anti-Semitism was also wide-

spread in Western Europe, so the majority of the several hundred thousands of Jews who left Russia between 1881 and 1910 emigrated to the United States.

Historians often state that the anti-Semitism of three European countries – Germany, Austria, and France – was of crucial importance in the development of Zionism. Germany was strongly affected by a nationalist/racist component encouraged by such cultural icons as the composer Richard Wagner, whose particular form of nationalism did much to make anti-Semitism respectable among cultured Germans. In all three of these countries, however, the large increase in Jewish immigration from the Russian Empire after 1881 stimulated and exacerbated anti-Semitism. It was alleged in many quarters that the Jews were taking over everything to the detriment of the particular nation.

In France following the French Revolution and the apparent triumph of liberalism, the Jews initially appeared to be secure. That changed, however, as Christian anti-Semitism grew in strength and influenced the bogus conviction for treason in 1894 of the French Jewish officer Alfred Dreyfus. Theodor Herzl, who, though not the first Zionist, is generally regarded as the founder of Zionism, later stated that the Dreyfus trial had made him a Zionist.

As the twentieth century drew near, the majority of religious Jews still believed in the concept of assimilation in the nations where they lived. However, the interest in political Zionism continued to attract converts, given the uncertainty in the minds of many Jews about their future in Europe. The first International Congress of Zionists was held in Basel, Switzerland, in 1897. This conference led to the bonding of both religious and non-religious Jews – an affiliation that was regarded as a necessity before the State of Israel could be created. After the Basel conference, Herzl noted in his diary that he "had founded the Jewish State ... perhaps in five years but certainly in fifty." The fulfilment of his prophecy took nine months longer than his projected term. On May 14, 1948, David Ben-Gurion made his historic announcement that "the State of Israel has arisen." On the wall behind him hung the portrait of Theodor Herzl.

The drama of those fifty years leading to the creation of Israel in 1948 has resulted in hundreds of historical treatises, most of which are well left to scholars. However, my reading has long convinced me that the Jewish people have suffered immensely for centuries – largely, I believe, because of the remarkable diversity of talent within what has always been a small Jewish population. That success, whether in business, the professions, or the arts, has always attracted jealousy and much worse.

The Jewish state is the embodiment and creation of Jewish nationalism, which was largely a response to the European nationalism that increasingly rejected Jews. In my opinion, Israel, by reason of its own history and that of the Jewish people, is required to remain ever vigilant. Israel is the creation of those who attacked and destroyed the Jews in Europe, and those in Europe, the United States, and Canada who quietly closed their doors.

The tragic history of the Holocaust, along with the centuries of anti-Semitism and cruel persecutions, means that all "humanity does in fact have a bargain to keep with Israel." This obligation in no way suggests that the frequent ill treatment of the Palestinians should be ignored, let along tolerated, by the international community. The peaceful resolution of the creation of an independent Palestinian State may still be seen by many as a distant dream, but it is essential before any meaningful peace can be established in the troubled and volatile Middle East.

At this moment, it is difficult to predict the future of Israeli-Palestinian relations and "the two-state solution" – the possible creation of a Palestinian state. Many of my friends living in Israel are genuinely concerned about the bellicose attitude of Israel's Prime Minister Benjamin Netanyahu, who apparently does not believe, as they do, in the two-state solution. At the same time I well remember former Israeli foreign minister Abba Eban telling me, as he often said, that "the Palestinians never miss an opportunity to miss an opportunity." Regardless, there is not the slightest doubt in my mind that the Western world and other nations will do whatever is necessary to preserve the nation of Israel. On this troubled planet, there is simply not enough justice to go around. This reality often creates intractable disputes that are extremely difficult to resolve. As I have said to law students in the context of the administration of justice, the issues are often much more complicated than simply determining right versus wrong: frequently it's a matter of one person's right versus another person's more compelling right. In the context of the Israeli-Palestinian conflict, the recognition by its neighbours of the fundamental right of Israel to exist as decided by the United Nations in 1948 would, in my view, be the appropriate manner in which to continue the dialogue.

25

Travel Abroad to India and Pakistan

My links with the South Asian communities in Ontario became close during my years as attorney general. As chair of the Cabinet Committee on Race Relations, I was invited by the governments of both India and Pakistan to visit their countries. These invitations were encouraged by the many South Asian associations in the province, which believed that a visit by a senior Ontario Cabinet minister to their homelands would acknowledge their many contributions to the economy and culture of Ontario – and, in addition, give me the opportunity to learn more about the rich culture and diversity of these nations. At that time, it was unusual for a federal or provincial minister to be a guest of these governments, and I was apparently the first in many years.

The governments of India and Pakistan had more than a benevolent interest in the well-being of their expatriates living in Canada. Although their numbers were very small compared to the huge populations of India and Pakistan, South Asian émigrés made significant financial contributions to their relatives at home – and these funds were important to the economies of both countries.

In 1978 the Indian high commissioner to Canada came to my office and extended a formal invitation to visit India as the guest of his government. Although my staff and I would be responsible for our airfare to India, our transportation and accommodation within India would be paid for by the Indian government. I had long been fascinated by the Indian subcontinent, so I accepted the invitation with enthusiasm.

Canada, like most Western nations, had followed the dramatic role of Mahatma Gandhi in the struggle for independence from Britain after the Second World War, and that interest had continued when Jawaharlal Nehru became the first prime minister in 1947. India was Canada's largest Commonwealth partner and an important ally of our federal government, though in later years, when India tilted towards the Soviet Union, the close relations between Canada and India somewhat deteriorated.

The timing of our visit to India would be my decision. I was fortunate to have two friends and colleagues who had considerable knowledge of that vast and complex nation: Bhausaheb Ubale, who had written the report on police relations with the South Asian community, had been born and educated in India and had many government contacts there; Simon Chester, a senior member of my policy branch, had married a woman from India and had a vast scholarly interest in the country. I gladly allowed them to make many of the administrative arrangements. We decided to visit India for about three weeks in January 1979, largely to avoid the excessive summer heat. The timing was satisfactory to the Indian government, and I asked Dr Ubale to check out the arrangements.

The announcement of our visit was greeted warmly by the Canadian Indian community, which had become weary of the stereotyping involved in frequent references to "poverty, turbans, and elephants" whenever India was mentioned. The reality did include large and regrettable levels of poverty, but India was also a robust democracy with a magnificently rich and diverse culture. I had often heard the expression that discovering India was like peeling the skin of an onion, given the varying layers of culture and language there.

Our final contingent included Ria; Simon Chester; Dr Ubale and his wife, Pramela; John Rowsome, my senior political assistant; Norman Stirling, my parliamentary assistant; David Allen, my director of communications; and my close friend and political ally Norman Atkins, who later became a senator. Chester soon dubbed us the "Aurangabad Irregulars" and volunteered to keep a diary in his remarkable calligraphy, which I still treasure.

Before we left, I gave many interviews to journalists in the South Asian media. We hired a film crew in India to record our journey, and as a result, we returned to Canada with several hours of raw film that were then made into a short documentary for use by school boards in Ontario. My friend Shan Chandrasekar created and hosted a popular

East Indian television program here, and he and a film crew travelled ahead to India so they could meet us at the airport in Bombay when we arrived in January 1979. Our itinerary included visiting most of the states from the Punjab in the north to Tamil Nadu in the southeast. As well as large cities, we were anxious to visit small villages, where the majority of the population lived.

The day following our long flight we travelled to the beautiful former Portuguese enclave of Goa for relaxation before we began our more formal agenda. We had meetings arranged with the prime minister of India, state governors and first ministers, the Indian chief justice, senior judges, and government officials. I had also agreed to make several speeches and grant many press conferences. With the assistance of a potent local drink known as *fendi*, we were assured a good night's sleep. Before leaving Goa, however, I managed my first oil sketch in India – of the colourful waterfront observed through my hotel window.

A day later we were in New Delhi meeting Mordecai Desai, who had replaced Indira Gandhi as prime minister eighteen months earlier. He expressed in particular his desire for closer relations with Canada. Although India was perceived in the West as pursuing closer relations with the Soviet Union than with Canada, the United States, and her NATO allies, he insisted that the country wanted to be regarded as a non-aligned nation, in the tradition of Nehru, while maintaining close friendships with all the major world powers. On a less serious note, I observed that Desai, though in his eighties, possessed a remarkably youthful skin. Later I learned that he achieved it, he said, from drinking his own urine. As I age, I have not yet been tempted to address my increasing wrinkles with either plastic surgery or urine, particularly as I also learned that Desai publicly advocated temperance as being essential for good health. His influence in this regard, I soon learned, meant that all the government receptions we attended were "dry."

I also arranged to spend an evening with Mrs Gandhi in the home of her late father, Prime Minister Jawaharlal Nehru. The government of India would not have been pleased because she was now somewhat out of favour. It was a fascinating evening, and I learned a great deal about Indian politics – particularly the politics of language, where the widespread use of English was the subject of some criticism. I had brought with me about thirty copies of the large volume on Tom Thomson, *The Silence and the Storm* by Harold Town and David Silcox, and I presented one to her. When I returned to Canada I told Harold Town that many Indian dignitaries were now proud possessors of his book. But he was not impressed: rather, he wrote to say that I was dismissed as his Indian distributor, given the small number of books I had disposed of in that vast country!

The abject poverty we observed every day was the least positive aspect of our trip to India. We saw beggars in abundance, but the most pitiful sights were the young children whose parents had crudely amputated one of their limbs or blinded an eye as a begging strategy. It has been many years since I have been in India, and I can only hope that the growing prosperity and expanding middle class there will alleviate the conditions in which hundreds of millions of desperately poor exist. This group included countless numbers of street people. As we drove through a city in the evening we would note hundreds of people sleeping under white shrouds on the sidewalks, knowing that many of them would not live to see another sunrise.

Rural poverty in India is equally real, but it was not of the same obvious kind as in the cities. In the villages and countryside generally we sensed an almost majestic rhythm of life: the people at work in the fields, the women in their colourful saris at the wells or washing clothes in the rivers, the children at their lessons in the dusty schoolyards. While the "majestic" expression may seem singularly inappropriate in the context of such widespread poverty, the seemingly timeless rhythm of life appears to allow the rural people a genuine degree of contentment.

As a member of the Ontario Legislature with a constituency of approximately fifty thousand voters, I was fascinated to discuss the challenges facing Indian MPs, who on average represent a million electors. A single constituency generally contained more than a thousand villages. They told me that their best strategy was to identify the villages that, at election time, could individually influence many others. Communication with their voters was also complicated by the high rate of illiteracy and by the absence of radios or television sets in the great majority of homes. During the evenings we often saw television sets mounted in village squares, where the people gathered to catch up with the news and local gossip.

* * *

A few months after this successful trip to India, I was invited by the Pakistan high commissioner to Canada to visit his nation as a guest of his government. Many in the Pakistani community in Ontario wanted similar recognition of the importance of their contributions to the business and cultural life of Ontario to that the Indian community had received from our visit. In addition, they saw that the film we had made during our trip to India had been well received by people of Indian origin in Canada.

There was a problem, however. The president of Pakistan at the time was General Muhammad Zia-ul-Haq, the military dictator responsible for the execution in 1979 of Prime Minister Zulfikar Ali Bhutto, the father of Benazir Bhutto, who was assassinated in 2007. The execution had followed a controversial trial in which Ali Bhutto had been convicted of conspiring in the murder of political opponents. The fairness of that trial has been a matter of debate in international legal circles ever since.

Not surprisingly, the execution of Ali Bhutto had seriously divided the Pakistan diaspora. A large percentage of the community in Canada believed that, by accepting the invitation from Zia's government, I would be giving a degree of legitimacy to the military dictatorship. I therefore politely declined the invitation – and those that followed every year after – until late 1983, when the vast majority of the Pakistan associations in Ontario encouraged me to accept. The change in attitude resulted not from any growing enthusiasm in the Pakistan Canadian community for Zia's government, but from a consensus that the key issue for them was to recognize the importance of the Canadian Pakistan community in this country.

Our April 1984 itinerary was shorter than our 1979 trip to India, partly because the Pakistan foreign ministry was disappointed by our delay in accepting the government's invitation. Furthermore, we were anxious to visit Kashmir, long a disputed territory between India and Pakistan, and to return to New Delhi to visit Indira Gandhi, who had been returned to the office of prime minister. This visit would have a dramatic and surprising twist.

First, however, our ten days in Pakistan proved to be fascinating, though it's a troubled and, according to some, a largely ungovernable country. Immediately on my arrival I sensed a missing dynamic in comparison with India, despite the similarities between the two countries. Although they shared the enormous disparity between the relatively affluent groups and the millions in poverty, there appeared to be less general vitality in Pakistan. I also felt a far greater degree of cynicism among the business, professional, and government elite than I had in India. Overall, the culture of democratic government which had developed in that country seemed to have produced a degree of optimism and energy not present in Pakistan. We visited the principal cities of Pakistan – the capital, Islamabad, then Lahore, Karachi, and Peshawar as well as many of the smaller cities, towns, and villages. During our travels we met mostly with justice officials and local business people. Because there were no democratically elected officials, our political dialogue was limited.

I was not encouraged by any conversations I had with the local judiciary because they clearly did not enjoy the independence and impartiality that is fundamental in any truly democratic society. It was obvious then, as has been demonstrated over the years, that the independence of the Pakistan judiciary was limited when cases with a political dimension came before them. Although cases in the courts of India would drag on for years, to the enormous detriment of any fair access to justice, allegations of political interference were then, and now, very rare.

During my visit to Islamabad I had a lengthy meeting with President Zia, who, like many other cruel dictators, could be immensely charming in person. Part of my discussion with him was recorded by the Pakistan State Television and was shown that evening, with an emphasis on the way my visit demonstrated a close Canadian relationship with the government of Pakistan. Zia was aware that I knew Indira Gandhi, and he used our meeting to belittle democracy in India, describing its government as little more than a Nehru dynasty. He was also critical of the closeness between the government of India and the Soviet Union. Zia spoke at some length about his friendship with the US ambassador to Pakistan, and he invited me to extend my visit so I could join them on a hunting trip. I politely declined. About four years later the US ambassador of the day and Zia both died in a "mysterious air crash," though it is widely believed that the aircraft was sabotaged.

Ria was not invited to my meeting with President Zia, but he presented me with a gift for her – several yards of beautiful sari material. She had it made into an exotically styled dress and wore it proudly when we entertained Queen Elizabeth and Prince Philip in our London high commissioner's residence several years later. She still has it – and I enjoy referring to as the "dictator's dress."

One most interesting aspect of our visit to Pakistan was an invitation to visit an Afghanistan refugee camp in the very rugged northwest frontier province of Pakistan near Peshawar. This event was arranged before we left on the trip, and the Afghan Society of Canada asked us to bring greetings to the inhabitants in the camp. The Soviet Union had invaded Afghanistan in 1979, and there were several Afghan refugee camps in that area of Pakistan. We were saddened by the wretched condition of the camps: as I made my brief remarks, I had some three thousand male refugees sitting on mats in the broiling sun and listening, through an interpreter, to this stranger from a faraway and largely unknown country. There were no women or children within view. We were also invited to visit other areas of the camp, including the school-rooms. Though primitive, they were festooned with brightly coloured children's drawings. However, the same theme carried through them all – war, with bombers in the sky, people being shot, and devastation everywhere. War had provided a tragic education for these young lives, and we still wonder years later whether they will ever enjoy peace.

When we left Pakistan our next destination was the Vale of Kashmir. Although that state has been the subject of a major dispute between India and Pakistan ever since both countries gained independence in 1947, it has remained a territory of India. While its population is almost entirely Muslim, it was where Nehru, the first Indian prime minister, was born, and he regarded it as an integral part of India despite the ongoing wars and bloodshed over its ownership.

In the spring of 1984 Kashmir was enjoying a period of peace and relative calm. The state is famous for the houseboats on Lake Dal, and we arranged to rent a comfortable vessel that had been used by Roland Michener when he was Canada's high commissioner to India. I eagerly took the opportunity to get out my paintbox and sketch the lake shortly after sunrise. I was presented with a magical scene that included fisherman, floating vegetable and fruit markets, and bordering mosques along with the natural beauty of the lake.

While ensconced on Lake Dal, I was able to host a lunch for the first minister of the state of Kashmir, a tall and charismatic figure. He had reluctantly taken over leadership of the political party long headed by his famous father, Sheikh Mohammed Abdullah, who was known as the "Lion of Kashmir" because of his aggressive leadership. Our guest had some years earlier immigrated to Britain, where he served as a physician in the East End of London before being persuaded to return to Kashmir. He was not optimistic about any peaceful settlement of the dispute over Kashmir, and his own political career ended several months later when he was arrested for reasons I have never been able to discover. What with President Zia's fate and Indira Gandhi's assassination following my visit to India, I have often thought of this trip as a negative omen for the leaders I met.

Shortly after our entourage landed in New Delhi we contacted the prime minister's office to arrange a meeting with Indira Gandhi. We learned that she was anxious to talk to me about the Sikh diaspora in Canada. In any event, our entire entourage descended on her office for a photo opportunity. She appeared to take a genuine interest in our son Harry, a science student at Queen's University, inquiring about his future aspirations. Then she indicated that she would like to meet with me in private.

What followed turned out to be one of the most memorable conversations I have ever had. Mrs Gandhi's principal concern was the amount of money coming from Sikh communities in the United Kingdom, the United States, and Canada to fund Sikh terrorism in the Punjab. The terrorism engaged in by supporters of the Khalsa movement, as it was known, was raising the stakes in the fight for an independent Punjab. Acts of terrorism were increasing, and the terrorists were apparently obtaining refuge in the Sikh Golden Temple in the Punjab capital of Amritsar, the holiest of Sikh shrines. As we spoke, a large contingent of the Indian army had surrounded the temple but had not entered its precincts.

When Mrs Gandhi asked me about the level of support for the Khalsa movement in the Sikh community in Canada, I replied that, although there was an active militant fringe group in Canada, it did not appear to have become a significant issue for the majority of Sikh Canadians. At the same time, however, I stressed that, should the Indian army enter the Golden Temple, that action would probably radicalize a significant percentage of the Sikh community in Canada. My earlier trip to India in 1979 had included a visit to the Golden Temple, and it was extensively recorded in the film made of our trip. This film had been shown to a number of Sikh groups, often in my presence, and I was well aware of the close emotional attachment that most Sikh Canadians had to the temple. I told Mrs Gandhi that, although I "could not be so presumptuous as to offer political advice to the Prime Minister of India with respect to the consequences in India of any military intrusion into the Golden Temple, the consequences in Canada would probably be very negative." In my opinion, an invasion would lead to a serious deterioration in relations between the Canadian Sikh and Hindu communities.

Mrs Gandhi was clearly very emotionally engaged by the acts of terrorism emanating from the Golden Temple. However, I believe she was sincere when she said it would be wiser to attempt to seal off the temple, given that any intrusion by her military would probably have grave consequences in India. As things turned out, the Indian military remained outside the Golden Temple for the next several weeks. In the end, though, her decision to allow her soldiers to enter the Golden Temple had tragic consequences not only for her but for thousands of Indian citizens. Mrs Gandhi was assassinated by her long-time "loyal" Sikh bodyguards several weeks after the military intrusion, the extensive violence between the Sikh and Hindu communities led to the loss of thousands of lives, and the incident precipitated the bombing in June 1985 of Air India flight 182 between Canada and New Delhi – a tragedy that, despite court cases and a commission of inquiry, continues to attract considerable controversy almost thirty years later.

26

Northern Justice, Aboriginal Art, and My Own Painting

In my years as attorney general I had come to know Judge Gerald Michel of Sudbury, who, as a provincial court judge, often presided in courts in the tiny, remote First Nations communities that cling to the banks of James Bay and Hudson Bay. The court party usually visited these communities four times a year, and Judge Michel had suggested several times that I accompany him so I could experience first-hand the special cultural justice challenges that exist in the Far North. In late 1983 I accepted the invitation. Fred Hayes and Ted Andrews, the chief judges, respectively, of the provincial criminal and family courts, wanted to come, and so, in early January 1984, we made the trip over several days. We were accompanied by my wife, Ria, my communications director, David Allen, and John Cruickshank, who at that time was a senior reporter with the *Globe and Mail*. When we arrived at our first stop, we were joined by a Crown attorney and a legal-aid defence counsel.

We visited the small communities of Fort Albany, Attawapiskat, Kashechewan, and Winisk. The people belonged to the Nishnawbe Aski Nation, and none of the villages had a population much over one thousand. These settlements are marooned in a sea of muskeg, and all the necessary supplies for stores, schools, and band councils have to be brought in by regular air flights. All the villagers rely to some extent on wild meat as a basic source of food, and in the long cold season they make the moose, caribou, and seal skins they have dried and stretched into traditional items of clothing such as mitts and mukluks. Judge Andrews told us how, one December, during the moose-hunt season, he scheduled a court date, but no one other than the visiting officials showed up.

Although Judge Michel was usually picked up at the local airstrip and driven into the community in the open back of a pick-up truck, he was always neatly dressed in his formal judicial robes by the time he was ready to preside in court. Everyone associated with the court party attempted to establish a dignified, solemn atmosphere. Judge Michel described how, on one occasion, a colleague went into a community without his proper attire; later, the court was advised that the community did not want him back because "they felt he had not shown them proper respect."

In one of the articles John Cruikshank wrote about our visit, he described Judge Michel "garbed in his august scarlet and thick boots, sitting at a rough wooden table dispensing southern justice in a community perched at the extreme edge of the northern frontier. Above him is a basketball net and before him the Attawapiskat school gymnasium, 1,100 kilometres north of Toronto, where about 60 Cree Indians gathered as subjects and observers of the Ontario judicial system." As I sat there, I realized that the shy, proud people in these villages clearly enjoyed watching the spectacle of the court from the audience, though they appeared to be most uncomfortable when they had to appear before the judge on even a minor charge or as a witness.

The band chiefs and councillors almost always attended the court hearings and sometimes sat with the presiding judge to give advice on sentencing. The great majority of the offences were related to alcohol consumption, and we heard a constant refrain from community leaders about the ravages of alcohol abuse. Most of the accused pleaded guilty – which, I was informed, was normally the case given the culture of honesty in these isolated communities. Both Crown attorney Robert Fournier and the duty counsel agreed that the basic truthfulness of the Cree made the operations of the court very different in the North. "You can almost always rely on the absolute honesty of the witnesses and the accused," Fournier told me.

Given the unique circumstances of northern justice, it was not at all surprising that our court party encountered some amusing twists and witnessed a few anomalies in the judicial procedure as we visited villages separated by hundreds of miles of frozen tundra. In one case a Cree named Mattinas was convicted of intoxication on a reserve and received a $50 fine. Shortly after another accused who spoke only Cree was called, and Judge Michel was obliged to employ the same Mattinas as a court interpreter. The fee he received enabled him to pay off his fine the very same day.

In another case a woman was put on trial for burning down most of her house. She pleaded guilty and explained that she set fire to her home because she believed her husband was having an affair with someone in the village. She reasoned that her husband would soon learn of the fire, and she would be able to see which house he emerged from and so identify her rival. The sentencing process in that case became complicated when, after Judge Michel told the woman that her offence was serious and she could be sent to prison, she told the judge, according to the interpreter, that she wanted to go to prison for a long time. At that point some members of the audience informed the court that the interpreter was a friend of the woman's husband.

In an intoxication charge, a native constable gave a brief summary of the facts, repeating the routine phrases common to these cases that the "accused's eyes were glassy, his speech was slurred, and he smelt strongly of alcohol." Judge Michel was not quite satisfied, even though there was a plea of guilty. "Did you observe the manner in which he walked, officer?" he asked. "Walk?" the obviously puzzled constable repeated. "I was carrying him."

During our final day on the northern court circuit, an accused pleaded guilty to a serious assault of his wife. His defence counsel agreed with the Crown prosecutor that the offence warranted a period of incarceration outside the community. The accused would therefore be transported to Moosonee, the nearest provincial jail facility, which was several hundred kilometres to the south. His counsel told me later that the man was aware that I would be present in the court during his trial. "I've heard about the attorney general's family violence policies," he told his lawyer. "This is going to be a bad day for me." Later that afternoon, this same accused joined our court party on the aircraft to Moosonee for his incarceration.

In meeting with the chiefs and band councillors during that trip, I emphasized the commitment of my two government ministries to extend our policy of encouraging offenders to do public service in their communities rather than being incarcerated in southern Ontario. I also stressed that we could not provide reliable and valuable rehabilitation programs without the cooperation of band councils in administering these programs well. Given the isolation of these communities, I was aware that the people on the reserves did not always wait for our itinerant court to dispense justice. When the chief and his band councillors decided that a member of the community had committed a grave infraction, the offender was usually ostracized by his neighbours – a severe punishment in small remote communities.

One of my priorities during my term as both Ontario's attorney general and solicitor general was to increase the Indian constable program on the reserves. Towards the end of my service I was pleased to learn that the program appeared to have reduced alcohol-related violence in those communities to some degree. Unfortunately, because of the high rate of unemployment on many reserves and other desperate conditions such as poor housing and cultural dislocation, the challenges related to alcohol abuse have continued to this day.

The village of Attawapiskat has been much in the news during recent months, given its impoverished circumstances. At the time of my visit, I formed the impression that the living conditions in all the communities were an embarrassment to Canadians generally – and the situation in the years since seems to have shown little improvement. At the same time, the inhabitants obviously have a profound spiritual relationship with their remote northern reserves. Although I admire their resiliency, I find it difficult to be optimistic about their futures there, given the profound lack of economic opportunities in those areas.

* * *

I was largely unaware of the rich though relatively recent heritage of Aboriginal painting until I was introduced to it by Robert McMichael – the founder of the McMichael Canadian Art Collection in Kleinburg, just outside Toronto. It was early 1976, and I was about to leave for my first trip to Israel as the guest of Attorney General Aharon Barak. Inuit stone carvings are often favourite presentation pieces for Ontario Cabinet ministers, and frequently McMichael was asked to pick out an interesting carving. On this occasion, however, he suggested a unique and more authentic Ontario gift – an Ojibway painting.

I had heard of the famous Ojibway painter Norval Morrisseau, but I don't think I had seen any of his works. He was the real founder of the Woodlands School of Art, which was inspired to some extent by his original style of painting. Morrisseau usually painted very large canvases, so McMichael suggested a smaller painting by another artist which could more easily be transported to Israel.

McMichael had established a section in his gallery dedicated to Aboriginal art, which he referred to as "Woodland Paintings." I became very interested in this Aboriginal art form, which, though gaining some prominence with the public, was still largely unknown. For generations tribal elders had generally discouraged artistic endeavours because, inspired by native spiritual legends as they often were, they challenged the taboo against giving these narratives physical form – in the Old Testament sense that "thou shalt have no graven images." Morrisseau had obviously disregarded this prohibition, and I soon learned that many native leaders were not supportive of his work for that reason. I also became aware that the "art establishment" in Canada generally lacked enthusiasm for the Morrisseau style of painting, regarding it more as a "craft" than a respected school of painting.

It is generally accepted that in traditional Aboriginal painting there was no art in the sense that non-Aboriginals view art. In the intensely practical Aboriginal society where survival was often a daily struggle, artistic talent was expressed by making useful things beautiful – for example, the quillwork on moccasins and capes among Prairie Aboriginals and, in the Northwest, the strong carvings on boxes, canoes, and ladles, the totem poles to record family lineage, or the transformation mask used for instructive storytelling during the winter months. There were, however, no paintings to hang on the walls.

McMichael told me that many of the Aboriginal artists worked on or near Manitoulin Island, Ontario. Believing that the government of Ontario should be encouraging this Aboriginal art, I arranged for McMichael and me to visit some of the artists by float plane. As a result, I met a number of them and became particularly interested in the work of a young couple, Blake Debassige, an Ojibway, and Shirley Cheechoo, a Cree from northern Quebec, who lived in West Bay on Manitoulin Island. Our meeting began a friendship of more than three decades. Debassige was only sixteen years old when McMichael purchased the first of many of his paintings for the McMichael Gallery; Cheechoo, in addition to being an accomplished painter, was also a writer, actor, and filmmaker. I was pleased to be invited a year later to participate in the formal opening of their first commercial gallery. They visited us in London when I was the Canadian high commissioner, and I arranged an exhibit of his paintings at Canada House.

My enthusiasm for Aboriginal painting led me to approach Bill Withrow, the director of the Art Gallery of Ontario, to suggest an exhibition devoted to Ontario Aboriginal paintings. He was totally negative about the idea, stating that it was gallery policy never to hold a group exhibition based on common ethnicity. There would not, for instance, be an exhibition of Ukrainian, Italian, or Greek Canadian painters – it would serve only to "ghettoize" them. I believed, on the contrary, that the Aboriginal Nations were one of Canada's founding peoples, with a distinct cultural identity. An exhibition of Aboriginal painters would form a success story in a community where there were few such narratives and would educate the public about a new and interesting style of painting. I told Withrow that he could expect further pressures from the media and others about the need for and viability of such a show. If the press reported, I concluded, that the attorney general is being disrespectful of the artistic autonomy of the AGO, I would "plead guilty."

I heard later from a mutual friend that Withrow was indeed complaining of being harassed by me. The saga continued, and certain members of the AGO board of directors recognized the wisdom of such a show. In 1984 a splendid exhibition, "Norval Morrisseau and the Emergence of the Image Makers," opened, featuring Norval Morrisseau, Blake Debassige, Daphne Odjig, and several other Aboriginal painters. A few months later Morrisseau presented me with one of his paintings – a gift I will always treasure.

That show at the AGO opened the door for Aboriginal art to move from the craft area in museums into major art galleries. In 1989, when France organized an exhibit at the Centre Georges Pompidou in Paris to mark the bicentennial of the French Revolution, Morrisseau was the only Canadian artist invited to show one of his paintings. Six years later he was elected a member of the Royal Society of Canada's Academy of Arts. In 2006 he became the first Aboriginal artist to be granted a solo exhibition, "Norval Morrisseau – Shaman Artist," at the National Gallery of Canada.

* * *

During my years in Ontario politics, I continued my painting hobby whenever I could get away for a few hours of relaxation. In 1978 I had the privilege and pleasure of getting to know A.J. Casson, the last living member of the Group of Seven and one of my constituents. Referred to as "Cass" by his friends, he had a close association with the Ontario Provincial Police, whom he assisted in art fraud investigations and prosecutions. At the time, I was both the provincial attorney general and the solicitor general; in the latter role, I was responsible for the provincial police. Casson and I became good friends, and I would often drop into his Lawrence Park home to discuss painting and his former Group of Seven colleagues. He was a gifted storyteller, and he enjoyed talking about the strengths, or otherwise, of his fellow painters. He believed, as but one example, that he had much more success with the colour green than had his talented and better-known colleague A.Y. Jackson.

Our friendship resulted in several sketching trips in and about Algonquin Park. A favourite memory for me was a beautiful autumn day when, over several hours, we focused on the fall colours. We were on a hill close to a farmyard where a dog was barking very loudly. Casson named the scene "Barking Dog Hill," a title he inscribed on the back of my canvas board along with the words, "a great place to paint if you can put up with the racket."

One of Casson's particular strengths as a painter was his superbly crafted cloud formations. In this context, I recall going to lunch with him after his return from a week-long sketching trip in Algonquin Park. "How was your week, Cass?" I inquired. "Really rotten," he replied. "Can you imagine nothing but blue sky and sunshine for seven whole days?" The absence of any clouds had clearly undermined his enjoyment.

Cass was reluctant to give me any detailed guidance with respect to my painting efforts, perhaps not knowing where to start. However, he did repeat one piece of good advice relevant to most amateur painters, who have a tendency to clutter up a painting with too much detail. "Remember," he said, "that it is often more important what you leave out of a painting than what you put in."

I was pleased that Cass was able to attend my first exhibition – a retrospective of my paintings at the US Consulate General in Toronto in 1979 – when he came in the company of Pauline McGibbon, the Ontario lieutenant governor. The exhibition was certainly more of a public relations gesture than recognition of outstanding art. Nevertheless, this event is well recorded in my memorabilia, and it provided some encouragement for me to continue with my painting hobby. A second exhibition followed two years later at the Edwards Books and Art store/gallery on Queen Street West. My one special memory of that event is that the celebrated Canadian sculptor Gerald Gladstone came to the opening, and during our conversation encouraged me to incorporate more buildings into my paintings because he thought they added strength to my canvases.

Harold Town, one of Canada's most eclectic painters, was another of my most interesting critics and, occasionally, mentors. He first came into prominence as a member of Painters Eleven in the 1950s, and over the years he used a wide range of styles – from colourful and compelling abstracts to evocative realistic drawings. At times he crafted an entire exhibition from one theme – as when Iris Nowell, his long-time companion, gave him an antique toy horse that inspired dozens of works in paint, pastel, graphite, collage, and mixed media. During most of his career, Town also enjoyed his role as an *enfant terrible* with his frequent denunciations of art critics. Not surprisingly, they replied in kind, and thus, in my view, he often failed to achieve the acclaim he deserved. He always attributed the antagonism he received from critics to the fact that his many styles of art made it impossible for them to "pigeonhole" him as an artist.

I came to know Town through Nowell when she worked as a volunteer on my political campaigns. As a result, I received invitations to many of the openings of his exhibitions. He couldn't resist a little poke on these occasions, and my invitation often included a note, such as "Roy, this is not simply an invitation to a party but, for you, a drawing lesson." He sometimes offered to give me a real lesson, but that came years later (chapter 30).

In 1978 the *Toronto Star* featured an article in its weekend magazine by Lynda Hurst, "A Portrait of the Attorney General as a Young Artist" – a title obviously inspired by James Joyce's novel *A Portrait of the Artist as a Young Man*. Shortly before publication, Hurst advised me that her editor wanted Harold Town to do a critique of my paintings. Even though he was by this time a friend, I was somewhat intimidated because I thought that any professional artist, and particularly Town, might well resent the attention being paid to an amateur painter simply because he was in politics. Nevertheless, I agreed to meet him in my home, where many of my paintings hung on the walls. I took the precaution of serving Town his favourite alcoholic beverage before he looked at my paintings. My stratagems paid off, and his review turned out to be quite generous:

When asked to evaluate the paintings of the Attorney General, I got over my contempt for amateur painting in the hope that I could arrest his development and try his patience.

To my surprise McMurtry has some very good moves … Roy has one quality unique in the Amateur. He manages within a three-dimensional format to keep his picture plane quite flat and generally there is an orderly progression of recession from the surface of the picture. McMurtry the ex-football player and jock has known violence intimately but his paintings for all their liveliness reveal him as a man reluctant to use force unnecessarily. He's obviously a sensitive man, able to arrange shapes and compose forms in an orderly manner.

McMurtry hangs nothing but his own paintings in his home. This is a thoughtful professional trait ... why give the opposition a hearing?

Town ended his critique by expressing the view that, because I was permitted to be a part-time painter, he should occasionally be allowed to be an attorney general – and went on to state the types of individuals he would target.

27

Reflections on the Davis Government and Life as a Constituency Politician

My years in the Cabinet during the government of William Davis were a unique adventure and experience for me. I had known him since our football days together at the University of Toronto in 1950 and had observed his political career with much interest. In my opinion, the Davis administration, which included both majority and minority governments between 1971 and 1985, provides an excellent model for all Ontario premiers to follow, and it's worth analysing in greater detail.

In appointing his first Cabinet, Bill Davis wisely kept his major political rivals for the PC leadership inside the tent, giving them ministerial responsibilities. The business of "Cabinet making" becomes a significant challenge for any premier. Talent was obviously the key recommendation for the senior appointments, but geographical and cultural factors were also significant considerations. In Ontario, a large and populous province, there is always some resentment towards Toronto as the centre of authority, in government, industry, and finance. It is therefore important that the rest of the province outside Toronto feel effectively represented at this centre. In Northern Ontario, in particular, strong ministers can make the local citizens feel that their voices are being heard at Queen's Park. Former Liberal premier David Peterson often used to say that resentment of Toronto made the city a unifying force in the rest of the province, just as Ontario filled the same role in the rest of Canada. Although stated half in jest, there is, regrettably, still some degree of reality to that sentiment.

As well as a geographical balance, it's also essential that the Cabinet maintain gender and multicultural balance. Occasionally, individuals would be appointed who were not as well qualified as others left out, simply because of the relevant geographical, cultural, or gender factors. In those situations, which I believe happened rarely in the Davis years, the premier would arrange that a weaker minister be well supported by a strong deputy minister and other senior officials.

When I was appointed to the Cabinet in October 1975, I discovered a great deal more about the complexities of government. For one thing, there is never sufficient revenue to meet all the legitimate public needs. The balancing act is at best a difficult process, as each ministry is determined to fight any reduction in its budget. In an attempt to rationalize the process, Premier John Robarts had created a committee that became known as the Committee on Government Productivity. He believed that the operation of individual government departments as separate and distinct entities was no longer appropriate to cope with issues that increasingly involved more than one ministry. In the course of its work, the committee identified major issues related to the size and complexity of the provincial government as well as the need for an improved system for setting budget priorities.

When Premier Davis inherited the committee's several reports, he created three separate policy fields – economic, social, and justice – each with its own senior minister and a supporting secretariat. He thought that this mechanism would help establish priorities and resolve disputes between ministries. The media called them the "super ministers," but it soon became apparent that they had minimal responsibility, given their lack of any real influence over the functioning of any one ministry. The secretariat ministers were virtually ignored in Cabinet as the other ministers brought their issues directly to the Cabinet rather than having them vetted by the three policy secretariats. I soon learned that "turf" battles were a deeply entrenched culture in any large government. In the words of Cabinet Secretary Dr Edward Stewart, "the proposals, if they were to work, required a sense of collegiality that was notably lacking. Holding on to one's turf proved to be a far stronger motivation." In any event, the creation of these policy coordinating ministries turned out to be a bad idea, and when David Peterson formed a Liberal government in Ontario soon after the Davis years, he abandoned them.

As the role of the policy fields declined in significance, however, the Davis Cabinet tried to find a workable solution. We recognized that

there were some key issues – energy planning, federal–provincial relations, native affairs, and race relations – that required attention from
special Cabinet committees that would not interfere with the independence of any one ministry. Rather than turf battles and territorial im-
peratives, cooperation would be their mandate. Again, as Dr Stewart
wrote, pragmatism took over and "what was involved … was a process
in which people were now starting to run systems rather than having
systems run them." In essence, this approach was an attempt to ensure
that the system did not get in the way of the best solutions being discovered.

In a large, complex province such as Ontario, the Cabinet has an immense range of responsibilities, including, for any new government,
a multitude of initiatives based on policies formulated by previous
Cabinets. Davis appointed a Cabinet chair for most routine matters,
but he usually led the discussions on significant policy decisions. In
recent years the trend in government, both provincial and federal, has
been to dramatically increase the growth of the authority within the
First Minister's office. This phenomenon is regularly reported in the
media, and in recent years has been the subject of complaints to me by
Cabinet ministers within the Ontario government and also in Ottawa.
Bill Davis, in contrast, was much more inclined to let his ministers run
their departments. In that sense, being a Cabinet minister in the Davis government was personally very fulfilling. Only if ministers were
unsuccessful in providing effective leadership were they replaced or
demoted.

One of the common refrains that I heard often from the business
community and others was that "government should be run more like
a business" – a comment that assumed that successful businesses were
generally operated more effectively than were government departments. Although this assumption can certainly be challenged, Davis
nevertheless arranged for two policy retreats each year to which prominent business leaders were invited. Invariably, by the end of the discussions, these leaders would concede that, given the many competing
priorities for public spending, operating a large government was much
more complicated than they had imagined.

The relationships between most of the members of the Ontario
Legislature in the Davis years were very positive. To cite my own ex-
perience, the leaders of the opposition's parties when I entered the
Legislature were Bob Nixon for the Liberals and Stephen Lewis for the
NDP. Although they often asked some tough questions, we remained

friendly on a personal level. In the succeeding years, Lewis became a close personal friend, and my relationship with Nixon was always cordial. Nixon's successor, Dr Stuart Smith, was, on a few occasions, one of my tennis partners. In general there was a fundamental civility among all members of the Legislature – a quality that appears to have diminished substantially in more recent years. Looking back I can't think of any MPP with whom I served that I could ever seriously consider as a personal enemy.

Premier Davis generally maintained a cautious but forward-looking outlook, and while he believed that government should be progressive, he did not think it should be "constantly in people's faces." In this context, Dr Stuart Smith once described the Davis approach as "government by stealth." At the same time, Davis was willing to let his ministers take strong stands on issues they thought important, just as he did himself. I knew that my particular approach to law reform, for instance, was less cautious than that of the government generally, and it certainly did not increase my popularity within the ranks of the Progressive Conservative Party. Similarly, Davis's own popularity within the party also suffered when he took on a national leadership role in relation to the patriation of the Constitution with an entrenched Charter of Rights – a position that meant strong support for Pierre Trudeau against stiff opposition from Joe Clark, the federal Progressive Conservative leader (chapter 22).

As premier, or first minister, Davis also had a profound influence on the internal workings of government. In addition, he held authority over the large public service and over the machinery of his political party. It would be nearly impossible to develop a comprehensive outline of the interests and activities in which the Ontario government is involved on a day-to-day basis. In those years, more than 90,000 people in the province were directly employed by the government or its related agencies, and each one of those staff members had specific day-to-day responsibilities.

I have often been asked whether the political and the bureaucratic arms of government can work effectively together. During the Davis years, there was close cooperation between the two branches. To a great extent, this goodwill resulted from the longevity of the PC Party in Ontario – a record of almost forty-three consecutive years by the end of the Davis era. I truly believe that talent, not political loyalty, was the major consideration in the appointment of senior government officials during those four decades. Premier Leslie Frost, for example, appointed Alex MacLeod, the last Communist member of the Legislature, as one of his official advisers simply because of the man's obvious brilliance and quite apart from his earlier personal political affiliation. After I left politics, I learned that the Liberal and NDP governments that followed the Davis era were somewhat wary of the senior officials who had served successive PC administrations, though the Ontario public service on the whole remained intact.

In my view the political success of Bill Davis was related to his basic sense of decency, which was reflected in the way he dealt with people at all levels of government and outside the government as well. His unpretentious demeanour also allowed the general public to relate to him positively and spared him from the accusations of arrogance that can easily arise when one political party has been in power for a long time. One adjustment in the "trappings" of his office, for example, was to change his title from prime minister of Ontario, as his predecessors had been called, to premier – the term used in all the other provinces. To his credit, during his time as premier, there was a level of collegiality, civility, and cooperation in the Ontario Legislature that has not been witnessed since.

Davis was particularly well served by his personal staff, led for most years during his premiership by Dr Stewart, who was not only Cabinet secretary but also his deputy minister. Stewart had previously been deputy when Davis was the minister of education and of colleges and universities. These two men made an effective team; in my view, there has never been a more distinguished public servant in the history of Ontario than Ed Stewart. He in turn was assisted by two most efficient principal secretaries – first Hugh Segal, who is now a senator, and then John Tory, who later became leader of the Ontario PC Party. After he left government, Stewart wrote that, in his opinion, "few people in public office have been as fortunate as William Davis, not only in respect of the quality of the personnel who served him, but in the dedication and loyalty which they displayed on a constant basis."

The premier's private secretary was Helen Anderson, who radiated enormous charm even as she was also very efficient. When anyone was ushered into the premier's office, Anderson immediately set a warm tone that helped to create a positive atmosphere for the meeting. Altogether, she served in the Ontario public service for a remarkable fifty-four years.

Before Davis became premier, I, like most people in the legal profession, had little experience in dealing with the Ontario public service. I may even have been somewhat sceptical of it, given the frequent negative comments made about government bureaucrats. I soon found out how wrong I was, as I worked with the enormous talent within the Ontario public service, whether legally trained or not. There are always exceptions, but, in general, I have very positive memories of my work with Ontario public servants during the Davis years.

The relationship between a Cabinet minister and the deputy minister is exceptionally important. The deputy is the chief administrative officer of the ministry. It would be very difficult for any minister to be successful without the support and advice of an experienced deputy minister and, indeed, of the other senior officials in the ministry. In my decade as attorney general from 1975 to 1985, as I have already described, I was well served by four deputy ministers: Frank Callaghan, Allan Leal, Rendall Dick, and Archie Campbell (chapter 12). In particular, Campbell's career provides a fine example of the quality and commitment of many of the senior deputy ministers. My friendship with him began when he worked as a process server in my law office for two summers during his years as a high school student at the University of Toronto Schools. With my encouragement, he served as a labourer-teacher and administrator with Frontier College for several summers during his undergraduate years at the University of Toronto, and he later articled for me as a law student before joining the Ministry of the Attorney General.

Campbell was a brilliant lawyer, judge, and historian as well as a sometimes hard-drinking companion. He became a Superior Court judge in 1986 and was the source of wise counsel to judges throughout Ontario. When, in 1994, I was appointed chief justice of what is now the Superior Court of Justice, Campbell became the regional senior justice in the Toronto area – a position that required him to administer the schedules of some ninety judges. He also undertook important problem-policy assignments, including a review into the police investigations of serial killer Paul Bernardo and a comprehensive report on the SARS epidemic of 2003. Towards the end of his life in 2007, Campbell was facing huge health problems as, simultaneously, he needed a lung transplant and battled cancer. He was an inspiration for courage in the face of calamity. And during this time, though using a wheel chair, he wrote several decisions in relation to summary judgment appeals he had heard in the court.

The approach to government in Canada is based on the British system, one that is substantially different from the American system we observe so closely. While a US president may often face a hostile Congress or Senate, here in Ontario and the other provinces a premier with a majority can assume support for most of the government's legislative proposals. What is often forgotten, however, given the general success of the fourteen years that Bill Davis served as Ontario premier, is that for almost six of those years his government was in a minority position, with the Liberal and NDP members holding the balance of power in the Legislature. As a result, careful planning became essential, as did consultation with the opposition parties on a regular basis. A sense of diplomacy became an essential characteristic of the government House leaders – first, Robert Welch and then Tom Wells. They were highly personable and intelligent men and proved to be effective diplomats in dealing with the opposition parties.

The attitude of the Davis government was dramatically different from the arrogance of Stephen Harper's minority governments in Ottawa from 2005 to 2011, with its unconcealed contempt for the institution of Parliament during those years. Harper's early years as prime minister have been marked by the undermining of the offices that exist to maintain a high level of accountability for the government of the day. These offices include those of the auditor general and the parliamentary budget office, and those responsible for overseeing the integrity of members of parliament and the freedom of information. The extreme partisanship of the Harper government, obvious in the infamous political attack ads and the general addiction to secrecy, to name but two examples, has undermined the spirit of collegiality between the various parties.

During the minority years in the Davis government, the three party House leaders worked effectively together in agreeing on the order of business in the Legislature. The result was impressive and even attracted the attention of the Social Credit government in British Columbia. Although that government enjoyed a majority, its House leader, Garde Gardom, who later was appointed BC lieutenant governor, spent several days in the Ontario Legislature. He told me how impressed he was by the cooperation among the parties – something that would never have been possible in British Columbia, he said.

The Davis minority government was also assisted by the fact that the NDP opposition, which was unlikely to form a government in that era, actually preferred a Davis government to a possible Liberal replacement. The NDP viewed the Davis government as a party of the centre, in contrast to the Liberal Party on the right on the political spectrum. David Peterson later confirmed the truth of this classification and told me that, when he became Liberal leader, his first priority was to move his party more to the centre.

As for my own ministerial responsibilities, I often found the opposition parties more supportive than many of my somewhat reactionary colleagues in my own caucus. To encourage their cooperation, I advised my opposition justice critics that they were welcome to meet privately with my senior policy advisers without my presence if they wanted to learn more about our policy recommendations on legislation before the Legislature or on other matters related to the administration of justice in Ontario.

The many friendships forged across the aisle between members of the governing and opposition parties were another of the positive results of those years of minority government in Ontario. In any event, many of the opposition MPPs from those days still refer to the Davis years as the "golden age of government" in Ontario.

* * *

I was elected in three provincial general elections in the constituency of Eglinton, as it then existed – in 1975, 1977, and 1981. While much of what I have written so far in this memoir relates to my responsibilities as a Cabinet minister in the Bill Davis government, I found my constituency work a most interesting and important part of my job as well.

In a large city like Toronto, individual MPPs generally have a much lower profile than that enjoyed by members in a smaller community. Many constituencies contain more than one community, and the member's "presence" is required in each one. This demand places a heavier burden on the MPP representing multiple groups because the member is expected at a much greater range of events – from high-school graduations to small-town fairs and charity events.

Even though I represented a Toronto constituency, I still found it essential to keep in touch with my constituents. Each MPP is entitled to an allowance to pay the rent on a constituency office and the salary of an office manager or director. I attempted to make myself available on Saturday mornings and one evening a week to meet with constituents. In addition, I welcomed the assistance of volunteers in my everyday work of helping people from my area with their problems and at election time.

The effectiveness of a constituency office is closely related to the personality of its manager. Through most of my decade as the MPP for Eglinton, my office manager was Barbara Herchimer – a thoroughly likeable and conscientious person. I have no doubt but that her efforts were a positive factor in my electoral success. We published a constituency newsletter, which was delivered to every residence. This contact was important not only for the information it provided but also because many people who lived in apartments were reluctant to open their doors during election campaigns. Amid articles and information, the newsletters also featured photographs of me with a variety of people. On one occasion I was criticized by some for including a photograph taken with the Queen during her visit to Canada. By so doing, the complaint ran, I had somehow involved her in partisan politics. Another minor controversy arose over a photo taken with my friend Cardinal Emmett Carter, the Roman Catholic archbishop of Toronto. I had a number of constituents of that faith, and I was not reluctant to publicize my relationship with the cardinal. I knew that many people were anxious to know my specific religious affiliation, though I suspect that my Irish name and six children often identified me with the Roman Catholic faith. On the whole, though, I saw no value in voluntarily clarifying that I was in fact a Protestant. I was more transparent when the issue of the death penalty was raised. During my decade at Queen's Park, from 1975 to 1985, the death penalty was still a controversial issue in the Parliament of Canada. Although it fell within the jurisdiction of the federal Parliament, many of my constituents assumed that, as attorney general, I should have an opinion about it. Moreover, given my role as the chief criminal prosecutor in Ontario, they expected that I might have some influence on the question in Ottawa.

I had been an outspoken abolitionist for many years, and when asked, I was always willing to share my views with my constituents. The subject would often arise when the public learned of a particularly nasty murder. Every murder is a horrific act, but the public seemed more aroused with some killings than with others. I became aware that some of my constituents who supported the death penalty believed that, if they were in the majority, which was probably the case, I had a duty as their elected representative to support that view. While acknowledging the electoral risks associated with my abolitionist views, I often replied that, while the views of my constituents were very important to me, "the most demanding constituency of all was that of my own conscience" – an idea borrowed from the British political philosopher Edmund Burke. My response may have been unsatisfactory to many people, but the discussions that followed were usually interesting.

Part of my education as a constituency politician was to learn that most of the electors were not much concerned about which particular jurisdictions fell within my legislative responsibilities. If a constituent was worried about squirrels damaging his eavestroughs, he might well request some personal assistance from me or from my office staff.

As my role as attorney general increased my public profile, I became aware that, in my constituency, my name was actually better known than my political party affiliation. In this context I remember an incident when I was campaigning door to door in the June 1977 provincial election. I was usually accompanied by several campaign volunteers who walked ahead of me to decide which doors would be best for me to knock on and which to avoid, because of a likely unfriendly reception or nobody being home. On this occasion I was signalled to ignore a home where a very corpulent man in his undershirt was sitting on his porch and drinking beer. As I went by I waved at him but stopped when I heard him yelling obscenities about Premier Bill Davis. My anger, no doubt stoked by the excessive heat of the day, led me to stop and respond to the man's remarks. I knew personally how hard Davis worked for the people of Ontario, I said, while he had nothing better to do than sit on his "fat ass, drinking beer in the middle of the day." When the porch sitter's wife came home she found her husband very upset about the extreme rudeness of "one of Mr. McMurtry's workers." She phoned my election headquarters to complain, stating that she and her husband were "great supporters of Mr. McMurtry." Obviously, the couple were simply not aware that I was in the Davis Cabinet. Such experiences teach political candidates to take little for granted when campaigning.

At the same time, I enjoyed the process and felt privileged to represent the electors of Eglinton in the Parliament of Ontario. As a constituency politician I attempted to keep in touch with the principal institutions of my riding: schools, churches, synagogues, senior citizen residences, and other community groups. I was always glad to welcome students and others from my area to the provincial legislature and posed for many photographs there. Constituency picnics and Christmas parties were another important part of the continuing dialogue with my electors. Fundraising was also a priority both at election time and between elections, and I was well assisted by volunteer friends.

During my three general election victories in the constituency of Eglinton, I was most fortunate to have lawyer David McFadden, now a senior partner at Gowlings, as my very effective campaign manager. The fundraising was led by another close personal friend, Bill Saunderson, a highly successful investment fund manager. Interestingly, both were to succeed me as the MPP for Eglinton, first McFadden and then Saunderson.

I realized that I was most fortunate to serve in the Davis Cabinet during my entire tenure in the Ontario Legislature. Still, becoming a minister is not everything in politics: I truly believe that the MPPs who never achieve Cabinet office can also make a vital contribution to the political process.

28

Candidate for the Leadership of the PC Party of Ontario

When I was elected to the Ontario Legislature in September 1975 and appointed attorney general two weeks later, I was delighted to have the opportunity to serve as the "senior law officer of the Crown." A trial lawyer is naturally attracted to this position, given the attorney general's broad responsibilities for the administration of justice. For nearly six years after this election, Premier Davis led a minority government. Amid all the uncertainties, I was determined to enjoy my new position for as long as it lasted. The furthest thing from my mind was the thought of ever seeking the leadership of my political party.

As my political profile increased, it was suggested, occasionally, that I prepare for a future bid to succeed Davis as premier. Although flattered, I was simply not interested. I actually felt some comfort in this attitude because I was determined never to be influenced in my decisions as attorney general by any potential leadership ambitions. I also believed that a change in government was probably inevitable under Davis's successor, given the PC Party's four decades in continuous power. Still, I was aware that several of my Cabinet colleagues were building organizations for a future leadership contest. As I stayed home to spend time with my family, they were on the move making speeches to local PC associations around the province.

Premier Davis's last year in office, 1984, was marked by a highly contentious issue: the extension of public funding to the Roman Catholic school system from grade 10 to grade 13, at that time the last year of high school. In the mid-1960s the government of Premier John Robarts had extended funding from the end of grade 8, historically regarded as the final year of elementary school, to grade 10. I had always thought it would be difficult for the Ontario government to defend the logic of providing funding for less than half the high school years. Robarts had thought this compromise would buy peace with the Roman Catholic Church, but in fact it produced the opposite result, encouraging the separate schools to continue pressuring the Ontario government for full high-school funding.

I realize that a case can be made questioning the wisdom of separating children in schools on the basis of religion. However, the funding of Roman Catholic schools was a significant part of the "bargain" that created Canada in 1867 and is part of our history. At a practical level, the cut-off of funding at the end of grade 10 meant that many children whose parents could not afford to pay fees had to switch into the public system for the final three years in high school, and I considered that disruption totally unfair.

Premier Davis announced the government's decision on the extension of funding to the separate schools in June 1984. It was immediately unpopular within certain segments of the Ontario PC Party, particularly in rural areas where the majority of the people were Protestants, and was later blamed for the party's loss of government in the election the following year. When Rosemary Speirs, a political columnist for the *Toronto Star*, wrote *Out of the Blue*, a book about the end of the PC regime in the province, she quoted a number of my Cabinet colleagues. I found it interesting that, in interviews with her, they denied they had supported the extension of funding to separate schools. In fact, the decision in our Cabinet was almost unanimous, and I, too, strongly supported it.

Certainly, by the autumn of 1984, I realized that Davis had to do some fence mending with the "party faithful." I was therefore surprised, if not shocked, when he told me privately that he intended to announce his retirement as premier within a few days. I attempted to persuade him that the political timing was bad for a number of reasons, including the need to steer his government through the heavy political weather caused by the separate-school funding decision. He did reconsider, but, over the Thanksgiving weekend, he informed the Cabinet that he had decided to step down as premier. Although very disappointed, I respected his decision: he had provided huge public service to the people of Ontario during his twenty-five years in the Ontario

Legislature, including fourteen years as premier and eight years as a Cabinet minister in the Robarts government.

Inevitably, once Davis's decision was made public, a number of thoughts tumbled through my mind. I realized that, in my own life, the opportunity to work with Bill Davis had been my most interesting professional adventure. But that did not mean I wanted to succeed him. Given that I later decided to run as a candidate, I could be accused of "protesting too much." In October 1984, however, I simply did not anticipate the pressures to which I would be exposed during the next several weeks.

Many people are attracted to a political contest, particularly when the successful candidate will automatically become the provincial premier. I also had a number of good friends who believed I could be a successful premier, despite my protestations about the overwhelming obstacles to my winning the "prize." These hurdles included the fact that there were already well-organized candidates in the field, that I had not held any economic or social portfolios in Cabinet, and that I had been perceived as a somewhat controversial law reformer within the ranks of the PC Party. In retrospect, close to three decades later, those obstacles appear equally formidable to me today as in 1984.

One of my political priorities had been to build relationships with many of Ontario's minority groups that make up our province's remarkable diversity. Chairing the Cabinet Committee on Race Relations had been an important undertaking for me, given my belief in "levelling the playing field" for those groups that did not feel part of the mainstream. These relationships had resulted in official invitations to visit the countries of origin of many of those minority groups, including India, South Korea, Pakistan, and several Caribbean nations. Although many of the leaders of these communities in Ontario may not have been supporters of the PC Party, they still appeared anxious to persuade me to try to become the next premier.

Within the Ontario PC family, a surprising number of influential people, including many past presidents of the party, also offered their support. Norman Atkins, a future senator, had been the campaign chair for all of Bill Davis's four successful elections as premier and, more recently, for Brian Mulroney's hugely successful campaign that led to his election as prime minister in September 1984. He volunteered to serve as my campaign chair if I became a candidate and also recommended lawyer Brian Armstrong, another friend, as campaign manager. I realized that, with these two people leading the team, a "long shot" might become more of a "horse race." A potential fundraising team, led by accountant Ralph Fisher and lawyers Jim McCallium and Rodney Hull, also volunteered. I therefore knew that raising the needed funds would be conducted with effectiveness and total integrity.

The potential campaign team that assembled aroused my own competitive "juices" – something that always energized my enthusiasms even though some of them were not well grounded in practicality. And so the idea took on a life force of its own. I soon realized that I was caught up in a set of circumstances that would make it difficult on a personal level to turn down so many offers of support from good friends. I also knew that, if I became a candidate, I would be supported by a strong campaign team.

The most important issue for me was how my wife, Ria, would react to this proposed new and unexpected adventure, along with my mother and our older children. Ria as always was supportive, if somewhat cautiously so, and the children viewed my candidacy as a potentially interesting adventure. My mother was the exception: she had always regarded my involvement in politics with some trepidation and was very thin skinned when it came to media criticism of her eldest son. As for my brothers, lawyer Bill was naturally highly competitive, so encouraged my candidacy from the start. My other brothers, philosophy professor John and orthopaedic surgeon Bob, lived outside Toronto. Although not supporters of the PC Party, they both adopted the attitude, "Why the hell not?"

In any event, I got caught up, if not carried away, by the enthusiasm of my supporters and friends and agreed to announce my candidacy on November 2, 1984, in the Queen's Park press studio. Ria and my mother accompanied me. Once at the podium, surrounded by a fair number of media representatives, I realized there was no turning back. I still have a copy of my statement announcing my candidacy.

To begin, in the context of my continued public service as premier of Ontario, I quoted from the famed American jurist Oliver Wendell Holmes: "It is required of a man that he should share the passion and action of his time at the peril of being judged not to have lived at all." I expressed my belief that the "most important quality in a leader is the ability to mobilize what is best in the community." I also referred to the culture of our Aboriginal people, where a leader is defined "as one who is not preoccupied with imposing his will on others but is rather someone in whose presence the truth is more likely to be found."

Next I referred to a number of practical topics, including the need to encourage entrepreneurship and nourish our multicultural heritage, to foster equality of opportunity, and to maintain competent and frugal government, but not at the expense of compassionate government. I also referred to violence in society generally, mentioning family violence, alcohol abuse on the highways, and the glorification of violent pornography. I defined myself as a Conservative who "recognized the importance of drawing a distinction between freedom and licence – the wise restraints that truly set us free." Recognizing the depressed economy around us, I emphasized my concerns about the 150,000 unemployed young people in Ontario, the tens of thousands of other young people who were seriously underemployed, and the personal tragedy for all the adults out of work in their most productive years.

In conclusion, I returned to my traditional theme that "all of us have the responsibility to continue to view the human condition with curiosity, compassion, and the conviction that we can and must help make our common lot a little better." I also could not resist taking a jab at the other three candidates – Frank Miller, Larry Grossman, and Dennis Timbrell – who had been organizing for a potential leadership bid for several years. I knew, of course, that their ambitions were more rooted in the reality of modern-day politics, where long and careful preparation for seeking higher office is fundamental to the political culture in both Canada and the United States. All three opponents were decent and committed public servants.

In the following weeks, as I prepared for the leadership convention planned for late January 1985, certain events collectively conspired to complicate my leadership campaign. First, the executive of the PC Party of Ontario decided to close off the membership of individual constituency associates on November 22, 1984. In practical terms, then, only members signed up before that date could vote for the delegate who would represent the constituency at the leadership convention. In more recent years, political parties in Ontario have allowed every party member to vote for the new leader, but in our campaign each constituency had to run a contest to choose the six or seven delegates who would vote at the convention. This decision was particularly difficult for me as the late runner in the campaign. I could not sell additional memberships to people who would support me in round one of the campaign – the local level.

Second, my decision to appeal the Toronto jury's acquittal of Dr Henry Morgentaler inevitably lost me popularity in large segments of the party. Juries in Quebec had refused to convict Dr Morgentaler for performing illegal abortions. And personally, I would have preferred not to launch the appeal. However, in the Toronto trial, Dr Morgentaler's lawyer had urged the jury simply to ignore the existing law, advice I could not condone. The Supreme Court of Canada later endorsed my stand when it stated that the trial "was not conducted according to law" because of the lawyer's statement (chapter 20). As I travelled throughout Ontario during my campaign, many potential delegates questioned me about this controversial appeal. I couldn't express any personal opinion on the issue of abortion because it was irrelevant to the legal basis for the Morgentaler appeal. I suspect many questioners interpreted my refusal to explain my own views as proof that my opinion on the issue was contrary to their own, leading to a negative political reaction.

Third, the timing of the release of Justice Samuel Grange's report, on January 3, 1985, following his inquiry into the infant deaths at the Sick Children's Hospital in Toronto was most unfortunate for me. As I described earlier, nurse Susan Nelles had originally been charged with murder but then acquitted at a preliminary inquiry (chapter 20). Understandably, there was a great deal of public sympathy for her. Neither I nor anyone at the Ministry of the Attorney General had played any role in laying these criminal charges, but, once again, a segment of the population blamed me for what had occurred. The fact that the Grange report found no fault on the part of the prosecution, including the police, and that Nelles's own defence counsel, Austin Cooper, blamed no one after the discharge simply got no media attention.

Aside from these distractions to my campaign, I realized early on that I had serious challenges quite apart from my late start in declaring my candidacy. As I had feared, I was criticized for not having held any economic or social portfolio in the Davis government. I remembered that Bill Davis himself had nearly lost his leadership bid, even though he was the obvious choice, because he had served only in educational portfolios in the Cabinet. He was also portrayed by his opponents as a "big-spending" minister because he revitalized the education system in Ontario, including the creation of the highly successful community colleges in cities and towns throughout the province. I, in contrast to Davis, was not the obvious choice for leader, but, even so, I believed I had provided leadership in a number of areas: significant law reform; traffic safety initiatives with respect to alcohol abuse on the highway and the mandatory seat-belt legislation; the successful coordination of the Mississauga derailment evacuation in 1979; and my participation in the negotiations that led to the patriation of the Canadian Constitution.

At the same time, I was well aware that many of my legal reforms had alienated not only members of the government caucus but many of the party faithful as well. In particular, my commitment to create a bilingual judicial system without Cabinet or caucus support had raised ire in certain quarters. Regrettably, our political party harboured many persons who were opposed to official bilingualism. Now my opponents suggested that I also wanted to make Ontario officially bilingual. I was quite sympathetic to the concept, I admit, because all that was needed to make it happen was for the Ontario statutes and Hansard to be published in both French and English. However, recognizing that bilingualism could be a highly divisive issue, I was not pushing for it. The "old guard" of the party also disliked my family law reforms, in particular my intention to extend the co-ownership of the matrimonial home and other family assets to all assets that had been accumulated during a marriage. Many of them resented the system of community legal clinics I had established across the province, viewing them as "guerrilla cells" for opponents of the government.

There was also a growing belief within the Ontario PC Party that it should move more to the right of the political spectrum, given the apparent success of Ronald Reagan in the United States and of Margaret Thatcher in the United Kingdom, and the recent election of Brian Mulroney in Ottawa. I understood this sentiment, but I believed that Mulroney was actually more to the centre and somewhat of a "compassionate Conservative." On the Canadian front, he was hampered by the huge budget deficit he had inherited from the previous Liberal governments, but, internationally, his real instincts were illustrated by his strong and emotional commitment to the fight against apartheid in South Africa.

There was also the Toronto phenomenon related to the leadership contest. No one born in Toronto had ever become the leader of the Ontario PC Party, but this time round Grossman, Timbrell, and I were all residents of Toronto, and Miller's home was in Bracebridge, a two-hour drive north of Toronto. Miller was an effective, folksy, small-town politician who would appeal to anyone with village or rural roots. He was also the only businessman of the candidates, and in retrospect it is not difficult to understand why he was the favoured candidate. Having worked in Montreal, he was fluent in French, although he appeared reluctant to admit it. That hesitancy alone says something about small-town Ontario more than a quarter of a century ago.

My team, nevertheless, was reasonably confident, and the campaign organization developed into a sophisticated machine under the leadership of Norman Atkins and Brian Armstrong. Atkins worked with his brother-in-law Dalton Camp in their advertising agency, Camp and Associates. Camp was a brilliant writer, and Atkins had considerable experience in all aspects of the firm. Together they had worked on dozens of provincial and federal campaigns, including leadership campaigns across Canada. I had cooperated closely with them during Robert Stanfield's successful campaign to lead the federal PC Party in 1967, and I knew they were on the cutting edge when it came to political strategy.

While the team managed my central campaign, I set out on my province-wide tour, which kept me busy for long hours at least six days a week. My tour manager was Joan Peters, a charming woman who was stern with her candidate when it came to keeping on schedule. We had rented a bus, with the McMurtry name prominently displayed in red, white, and blue. Our driver was a jubilant Yorkshireman, Freddy Watson. He was on a leave of absence from Grey Coach Lines, and our tour was apparently the first of many that he conducted for aspiring Conservative leaders. Freddy was always in a good humour, and thanks to him and Joan Peters, what could easily have been an endurance contest became a pleasurable adventure. Occasionally we used an aircraft to cover long distances, but for the most part Freddy's bus became my home away from home.

Given all the demands of the tour, I had little time to meet with my campaign leaders or my fundraising team. The financial contributions reached impressive levels as the campaign progressed, judging by the many attractive brochures being produced on a regular basis. I was continually assured by the team that the campaign expenditures would not be allowed to exceed the actual funds collected. Before I committed myself to the campaign, I arranged a dinner with John Crosbie, who had been a schoolmate of mine at St Andrew's College and later went on to be a Cabinet minister in the Mulroney government. He had also been a candidate for the federal PC leadership, so I asked him to advise me how to avoid going heavily into debt. After I related my fundraisers' assurances that the campaign would not be permitted to spend money beyond what had been raised, he warned me that financial controls were practical until the week of the convention. At that point, given all the pressures, they became very difficult to maintain. How right he was: despite the impressive fundraising success, my campaign ended about $250,000 in debt.

True enough, the campaign deficit resulted from well-intentioned supporters arranging interesting events and some lavish hospitality for the delegates and their families during the convention. The events included concerts by Rompin' Ronnie Hawkins from Arkansas and Burton Cummings. Hawkins had been a popular rock 'n' roll musician for many years in Yonge Street taverns. As a young lawyer, I had successfully represented him on a possession-of-marijuana charge, and after I became attorney general, he liked to tell people how McMurtry had "kept him on the street" in his early days. During his Arkansas days, future president Bill Clinton was one of his fans. Cummings, a very successful Canadian singer, had lived in Los Angeles for many years. While in Toronto, however, he became very enthusiastic about my leadership campaign, donned a "McMurtry jacket," and joined me in my candidate's section at the convention. He remained until the end of the voting and commiserated with me after my loss.

The leadership convention, which concluded on Saturday, June 26, was held in an auditorium at the Canadian National Exhibition. The four candidates were well supported by their volunteers, who organized a large number of signs and brochures to hand out to the delegates. The convention began with a tribute to the retiring premier, Bill Davis, followed by speeches from all the candidates. I was pleased that my remarks were favourably reported the next day by the media. The Global Television Network also did a phone-in poll, which placed me in first place in the views of the callers. On the first ballot, however, I actually came in last.

The strategy prepared by my campaign team recognized that my candidacy would be successful only if I survived to a second ballot. They assumed that most delegates had long been pledged to a particular candidate and that I could win only if I were the second choice of a majority of the delegates. A more current example would be that of former premier Dalton McGuinty, who, when he became leader of the Ontario Liberal Party in 1996, remained in fourth place for two ballots before placing third, second, and finally first as other candidates behind him dropped out of the race. Some of my "brain trust" also advocated early in the campaign that we persuade an ally to become a fifth candidate, so I would be assured of a second ballot, but I was totally uncomfortable with the suggestion and immediately rejected it.

The results on the first ballot were as follows:

Frank Miller	591
Dennis Timbrell	421
Larry Grossman	378
Roy McMurtry	300

After the first ballot, the remaining candidates lobbied me for their support. I had heard rumours of anti-Semitism in relation to Larry Grossman by some supporters of the other two candidates. Grossman and I generally held similar political views, and this fact, coupled with these allegations, led me to support him on the second ballot. On the third ballot, Frank Miller won the leadership. Although I was somewhat to the left of Miller on the political spectrum, I liked him personally – a decent and personable man.

Shortly after I was eliminated on the first ballot, I was invited to join in a panel discussion on CTV. The panel included members of all three provincial political parties, including my Cabinet colleague Tom Wells, with Fraser Kelly as host. Kelly asked me about my future political plans. I jokingly replied that I had not had time to think about them, given that, until a few minutes earlier, I had expected to be the next premier of Ontario. Wells had recently been appointed Ontario's agent general in London, England, and would be leaving to take up his post in a few weeks. I concluded by speculating that Wells might be prepared to give me a job in London. The next day Prime Minister Brian Mulroney called me to arrange a meeting in Ottawa two days later, and it was then that he asked me to be Canada's high commissioner in the United Kingdom. A few weeks later, Wells and I were both working in our different jobs in London.

Meanwhile, a day or two after the leadership convention, Miller asked me to remain in his Cabinet and was generous in offering a portfolio that could include all my major government interests. I told him I thought it was time for me to move on. He sought my advice about the upcoming provincial election campaign, including the choice of a campaign chair. I told him that my own campaign chair, Norman Atkins, would be willing to serve in that capacity. Miller was initially surprised, imagining some hostility between them, but he carried through – and Atkins accepted. Later, Miller withdrew the offer after being pressured by some of his political allies. It was a huge mistake on his part – as he would soon learn. When Bill Davis officially stepped down on February 8, 1985, Frank Miller automatically became premier. He called an election for May and won the largest number of seats, but was well short of a majority. He formed a minority government: the Liberals, led by David Peterson, formed the official opposition, followed by the NDP, with Bob Rae at the helm.

I still regard my losing campaign as a special adventure. Although I may carry some psychological bruises from my encounters with the more extreme right wing of the party, the whole experience provided good training for my later diplomatic career. I was concerned, however, about my campaign debt, especially after I accepted my new position in the United Kingdom. In any circumstances it's difficult for unsuccessful candidates to pay off campaign debts, but doubly so if that person is no longer on the scene. My team leaders assured me, however, that they would arrange events later in 1985 to raise the required funds.

Shortly after moving to London, Ria and I learned that Janet, our eldest child, planned to get married immediately after she graduated from Dalhousie Law School. Our return to Canada in June for the wedding made it possible for my supporters to arrange back-to-back fundraising events. The first took place at Frank Stronach's Magna headquarters in Aurora, just outside Toronto, and the second the following night at the Rideau Club in Ottawa. My political pals Jean Chrétien and Roy Romanow were generous in not only attending but also speaking at both events. I was flattered by the number of people who attended, including several francophone businessmen from Quebec whom I had never met. They were friends of people I knew, and they wanted to express their personal appreciation for my support of the French language in Ontario. They also cornered me in the Rideau Club bar after the dinner and insisted that they be allowed to contribute further with respect to any remaining campaign debts. The required funds had already been raised at both events, but I was deeply moved by their support and generosity. It reminded me once more of the vital importance of the relationship between Quebec and Ontario at this government level. It was also a sad reminder of the most regrettable isolation of the Quebec government during the patriation of the Canadian Constitution in 1981.

Ironically, that same June, while we were still in Ontario, Miller's minority government was defeated in a vote of confidence by a combined Liberal and NDP opposition. During the recent spring election campaign, Miller had expressed anti-union sentiments that angered Ontario's trade-union leaders. Those leaders had since persuaded Rae to join with Peterson to defeat the Miller government. Rae did not feel any particular affection for Peterson, but the union leaders' threat to withdraw their support from the NDP resulted in a legislative alliance between the two parties for an agreed period of two years. Lieutenant-Governor John Aird thereupon asked David Peterson to form the next government, and on June 26 Miller resigned, ending more than four decades of government by the Progressive Conservative Party in Ontario.

Many of my supporters urged me to run as a candidate at the fall convention to replace Miller as leader of the PC Party in the province, but I declined, particularly as I was finding my new responsibilities in the United Kingdom most interesting. As things turned out, Larry Grossman became leader of the provincial party. Ten years were to pass before the Ontario PC Party again became the government – this time under Mike Harris in 1995.

* * *

Before I leave this chapter to describe my years as high commissioner in London, I want to say something about Ian Scott, the man who became attorney general in the Liberal government of David Peterson. As I describer earlier, in 1955, during my years at Osgoode Hall, Scott and I had spent a most influential summer together working in construction in Quebec City (chapter 4). In May 1985, soon after I moved to the United Kingdom, Scott was elected to the Ontario Legislature as a Liberal. When he heard that I was back in Toronto to attend Janet's wedding, he asked me to meet with him to discuss the possibility of his appointment as attorney general in the new Liberal government. In my opinion, he was highly qualified, I said, and I was certain he would serve very effectively in that portfolio. I urged him to seek the appointment. Even though specific requests for a Cabinet appointment are not part of Ontario's political culture, and the decision is obviously one for the premier to make, I believed that Scott would be of considerable value to the new government.

The legal profession certainly favoured Scott's appointment as attorney general, but the matter was complicated by the new government's expected confrontation with the medical profession in Ontario over the issue of "extra billing" – charging patients fees above the schedule allowed by the Ontario Health Insurance Plan. Initially, Peterson believed that Scott would be the most effective advocate for the government as minister of health. By encouraging Scott to pursue the position of attorney general aggressively, however, I believe that I played some role in his appointment.

During my four years in London, I had little direct contact with Scott as he served as Ontario's attorney general. I knew, however, that he had been very successful in that role, and on his last day in office in 1990, before the new NDP government was sworn in, he invited me to join him and a number of the senior lawyers who had served under both of us in our periods as attorney general. It turned out to be a happy, nostalgic occasion, more of a celebration than a wake.

Our paths were to cross often even after his stroke in 1994, when we enjoyed frequent lunches with mutual friends. Unfortunately, Scott's chief disability as a result of the stroke was aphasia, which deprived him of much of his ability to communicate verbally. In 1996 he and I both received honorary doctorates from the University of Toronto. In June 2005 we were again honoured together when the building in which the Ministry of the Attorney General is housed, at 720 Bay Street, Toronto, was named the McMurtry-Scott Building. It was a most memorable occasion for us, attended by Premier Dalton McGuinty, Attorney General Michael Bryant, former premiers Bill Davis and David Peterson, former attorneys general, and senior members of the judiciary and the legal profession. In his speech at the opening ceremony, Peterson was generous in stating that Scott and I defined the role of the attorney general. Ian Scott spoke briefly and haltingly, saying, "I enjoyed my time as attorney general more than anything else I did in my professional life." I then had the opportunity to confirm that Scott's courageous battle against serious disability in recent years had inspired us all and gave new meaning to the concept of courage, good humour, and dignity in the face of adversity.

Ian Scott remained a good friend until his death in 2006, following another stroke, in his early seventies. He had a wide range of friends but was essentially a very private person, revealing in a memoir he published not long before he died that, because of his sexual orientation, he had led somewhat of a double life – a fact not even close family members were aware of. When he did pass on, his family asked me to deliver the eulogy at his funeral, and I was honoured to fill this role.

PART FOUR

At the Court of St James and Home Again

29

My New Life as High Commissioner in London

The possibility of a diplomatic posting had never entered my mind before I received a telephone call from Brian Mulroney on January 27, 1985, the day after my defeat at the PC leadership convention. It was a Sunday afternoon, and a friend who owned a bar on Yonge Street was hosting a post-convention party for my campaign team. Despite my loss, the mood was celebratory. I have no idea whether my supporters were impressed when it was announced that the prime minister of Canada was on the phone. I was certainly surprised, and I never did learn how Mulroney had tracked me down that particular afternoon.

The prime minister congratulated me on my campaign performance and asked me to come to Ottawa as soon as possible to discuss my future. He was not at all specific other than to say that he would like me to consider "serving the whole of Canada and not just Ontario." I agreed to meet him two days later. When I got home and discussed this brief exchange with Ria, we speculated that perhaps Mulroney might be thinking of a diplomatic posting. We had been in Pakistan the previous spring as official guests of that government and had learned recently that the Canadian ambassador there had died. Mulroney knew of my interest in South Asia, but I did not really want to serve in Pakistan, where the charming but ruthless dictator General Muhammad Zia-ul-Haq was well entrenched.

When I arrived in the prime minister's office two days later, I was informed that, because he was delayed at another meeting, I might enjoy observing Question Period in the House of Commons while I waited. Two of Mulroney's staff accompanied me to the Parliamentary Gallery, and shortly thereafter, Speaker John Bosley introduced me to the House as a "distinguished visitor." I was extremely flattered to receive a standing ovation; as things transpired, it would be my last significant political appearance in public. I noticed, however, that two or three Conservative Alberta MPs remained in their seats. As veterans of the brief Joe Clark government, they had not forgiven Bill Davis and me for supporting Trudeau's patriation package.

A few minutes later, I set off for my meeting with Mulroney at his residence, 24 Sussex Drive. After exchanging some pleasantries, he said that he wanted me to represent Canada as the high commissioner to the United Kingdom. While he was speaking, a photographer came into the room and took several pictures. One of them shows me listening intently to the prime minister in front of a large window looking out across the Ottawa River to the Gatineau Hills, the entire scene bathed in brilliant winter sunshine.

My first reaction was to ask myself why I would want to live outside Canada. It was not an option I had ever seriously contemplated. My next thought was simply, "Why not?" There would never be a better time to embark on such an interesting adventure. I knew I would not feel comfortable in the right-of-centre government of Frank Miller, so my political career at Queen's Park was probably going to end. I liked Miller on a personal level, but, as a so-called "Red Tory," I had long been committed to an activist social agenda – something that would not be a priority for the new Ontario government.

After reflecting on the prime minister's proposal for a few minutes, I responded that I was flattered and very much interested. Mulroney's fervour was such that he suggested I immediately discuss the matter with Ria. Moments later he was on the phone with her: "Ria, it is your friendly prime minister calling," he began. "Roy is with me, and I have made him an offer which I hope you will support." He handed me the phone, saying he would leave me alone for a few minutes so we could discuss the proposal in private.

Her immediate reaction was not positive. She was concerned, as I was, about leaving our six children in Canada. However, all but our youngest, Michael, were living away from home either attending university or already graduated. I suggested that it was a wonderful opportunity for us and, moreover, our children would enjoy visiting us in London. By chance, several of them were in our home at the time and, not surprisingly, their immediate reaction was one of great excitement. To have a "pad" in London would be thrilling, they said, both for them and for their friends.

The prime minister was anxious to have an early decision from me – if possible, before the end of that very day. We agreed that I would phone him after I had returned home and talked with my family. Before I left, he called Joe Clark, his external affairs minister. "Joe," he said, "I think we have a new high commissioner for London – Roy McMurtry." To this day I don't know whether there had been any consultation between them before Mulroney offered me the position, nor do I know Clark's initial reaction to this news.

Later that evening, after discussions with all six very enthusiastic children and a moderately enthusiastic wife, I phoned the prime minister, who confidently addressed me with the words, "Good evening, Mr High Commissioner." After I had formally accepted the job, he told me that I was not free to advise anyone else of his offer for ten days. According to protocol, the Canadian government had first to consult with both the Queen and the British prime minister.

Canada's first high commissioner was appointed in 1880 as a result of pressure from the Canadian government, in its formal relationship with Great Britain, to establish a more independent representation in London. There was considerable resistance from the British government, which responded that "the Queen [Victoria] could not appoint an ambassador to herself." Canada, it said, "could not, as an integral portion of the Empire, maintain relations of a strictly diplomatic character." Rather, it "wanted the Canadian representative to have a status in every way worthy of his important function." The title of high commissioner was reluctantly agreed to by the British government, and ever since has been given to all ambassadors within the Commonwealth.

The first two Canadian high commissioners in London, Sir Alexander Galt and Sir Charles Tupper, were both Fathers of Confederation and members of Sir John A. Macdonald's Cabinet. My predecessors also included two former premiers of Ontario, Howard Ferguson and George Drew. Ferguson actually resigned as premier of Ontario in 1930 to accept the appointment from Prime Minister R.B. Bennett. My own appointment as Canada's eighteenth high commissioner followed a more unusual route to London than that of my predecessors. I had been the attorney general of Ontario for almost ten years and an unsuccessful candidate for the leadership of the Progressive Conservative Party in Ontario. At a dinner in my honour shortly after my appointment, a friend offered a new definition for the position: "A high commissioner is someone who is denied a job by his political colleagues but who is given employment by the prime minister on the condition that he leave the country." It was certainly amusing and somewhat less cynical than the older definition of an ambassador as "someone who is sent abroad to lie on behalf of his country."

Prime Minister Mulroney believed that my experience in government, including my personal relationships with senior members of governments across Canada, would enable me to carry out my responsibilities effectively in the United Kingdom. In the months that followed, I became aware that, given Canada's highly professional career foreign service, those appointed from outside were regarded as political appointments. At the time of my appointment, however, the great majority of Canadian high commissioners in London had been from outside the ranks of the foreign service. Personally, I believe that there are sound policy reasons for this tradition, considering the special relationship that should exist between Canadian and British prime ministers.

My appointment made me aware of the widespread lack of understanding about the role of ambassador in the modern age. Most people know little of the varied and extensive responsibilities of Canadian diplomats. Modern communication and information technologies often divert attention from the importance of having representation "on the ground" to ensure that Canadian interests are effectively served and supported. In this context, Charles Ritchie, a most distinguished Canadian diplomat, once told me of the shock he and his colleagues within External Affairs experienced when Pierre Trudeau, shortly after he became prime minister in 1968, casually questioned him about the need for a foreign service in an era of modern communications.

In any event, I had a great deal to learn about my new responsibilities before I arrived in London in April 1985. I had several days of briefings in Ottawa relating to the broad parameters of Canada's political and economic relationships with Britain, the central importance of London as an international centre of commerce, our immigration policy, the Commonwealth Secretariat, and the many other activities carried on by our High Commission in London in support of Canadian interests. I was already well aware of the extensive and close relationship between Canada and Britain created by our shared history, family ties, and many political, legal, and cultural inheritances from Britain. Once the many ongoing government, professional, business, military, and educational contacts were added into the mix, Canada's relationship with the United Kingdom at that time was closer than with any other country, except for the United States. I soon became aware, however, that traditional and sentimental ties had to be adjusted by the reality of Britain's rapidly increasing role in Europe. In addition, our own preoccupation with the United States, our interest in strengthening our relationships with other European countries, and the growing importance of Canadian trade with Japan had also altered the Canada–UK relationship.

Nevertheless, the long letter of instructions I received from External Affairs Minister Joe Clark stressed the continuing importance of the Canada–UK relationship and referred to my responsibilities in part as follows: "Under your management and leadership, I expect the post to adapt to these conditions as well as to exploit the longstanding historical, cultural and corporate links between the two countries in order to achieve our objectives. In this effort I cannot stress too strongly the importance of your own contacts with British decision makers at the highest possible level. Nor can I impress upon you too strongly the importance of your participation in the activities of all post programs." My briefings and instructions also stressed that, in order for me to promote the interests of Canada most effectively, I must recognize Britain's position as both a major economic power and a member of the Group of 7 (G7) and take a particular interest in the British approach to the full range of global political and economic issues.

I was also urged to pay particular attention to Commonwealth affairs and to maintain close personal contact with the Commonwealth secretary general. Commonwealth affairs did become a priority for me, but I soon learned that there were very different views as to the importance of the Commonwealth within the senior ranks of the Department of External Affairs. Canada's involvement in the Commonwealth was sometimes described as a "soft option," compared to the "hard options" of the Canadian role in G7 summits, NATO, and the United Nations. I became aware that the less-enthusiastic supporters of the Commonwealth within External Affairs actually mirrored many similar attitudes within the British government.

In 1985 the United Kingdom was Canada's third largest trading partner and Canada's leading market in Europe. It was also our second largest source of foreign capital and, after the United States, the most important destination for Canadian investment abroad. Because British corporations were a major source of investment in Canada, it was important for me to communicate to the business community in London

that foreign investment was generally welcome and also very important to the Canadian economy.

Investment Canada had replaced the former Foreign Investment Review Agency (FIRA), with the goal of creating a more positive perception of Canada's attitude towards foreign investment. When I moved
to London, I became aware that negative perceptions can be enormously magnified as they cross the Atlantic. Given our long historical
and commercial relationship with Britain, I was also surprised to learn
that the majority of British business and industry leaders appeared to
know relatively little about Canada. Unfortunately, FIRA had created a
strong belief in British business circles that foreign investment was not
welcome in Canada. One of my priorities as high commissioner was
to bring the message that Canada was truly "open for business." In a
report to Joe Clark three months after my arrival in London, I wrote:

The general message that Canada "is open for business" will now require a
greater degree of focusing and specific targeting. The communications strategy will therefore be crucial. As I travel through the "City," the psychology of
investment is often of greater importance than the detailed analysis that one
would expect from "hard headed" businessmen who are often influenced by
simple "gut reactions." We are still regarded by most potential investors as an
"after-thought" when compared to the U.S. We will have to deliver a much
stronger message as to the advantages which Canada presents, including issues
related to "quality of life."

At the time I was appointed, the Honourable Don Jamieson, a long-
term Trudeau Cabinet minister from Newfoundland, held the position
of Canadian high commissioner to the United Kingdom. Despite his
enthusiasm for the post, his wife never felt comfortable in Britain and
was anxious to return to home. They actually departed some weeks before I was scheduled to take up residence in London. Jamieson wanted
to help "the new guy on the block," and he invited Ria and me to visit
him in Newfoundland before we left. However, my departure date was
moved ahead when Prime Minister Mulroney decided to make his first
official visit as prime minister to Britain in April 1985. The Newfoundland visit with the Jamiesons had to be cancelled. Sadly, Don Jamieson
died a few months later.

* * *

When Ria and I arrived in London, we soon became aware of the special status that ambassadors to the United Kingdom receive. As soon as we exited our Air Canada flight, our driver met us with the high commissioner's car and drove us to a special lounge reserved for senior diplomats while we waited for delivery of our luggage. The deputy high commissioner, accompanied by the three senior officers in charge respectively of the political, commercial, and immigration divisions at the High Commission, were our official welcoming party, together with a senior official from the British Foreign Office. I was now truly aware that a new career had begun.

We drove from Heathrow Airport to our official residence at 12 Upper Brook Street, a few yards from Grosvenor Square. There we were met by our household staff – a butler, a cook, two young maids, in addition to our driver. The maids were from Portugal, the cook came from Italy, and the butler was "very English." We soon became a happy family – and, not surprisingly, when it came time to take our leave three-and-a-half years later, we were quite emotional.

The staff of the Canadian High Commission in London were divided between two locations – Canada House on Trafalgar Square and Macdonald House at 1 Grosvenor Square, a short walk from our residence. In 1985 there were approximately 350 employees in all, a third of them Canadian citizens. The rest of the staff were British citizens or, in the jargon of the diplomatic world, "locally engaged." The majority of these people worked in Macdonald House, which for many years had been the US embassy. In 1962 the Diefenbaker government acquired a several-hundred-year lease from the United States when the US government decided to build its "fortress" directly across Grosvenor Square. Perhaps this second location would have been named Laurier House if it had been acquired by the Pearson government a year or two later. My principal working office was in Macdonald House. The elegant Canada House, while an important and long-standing symbol of Canada's presence in the United Kingdom, became the cultural and communications centre of the High Commission, with a library, a tourist office, and an exhibition and performance space. As I write, the federal government has just announced its intention to move the offices from Macdonald House to a building adjacent to Canada House.

My schedule after my arrival in London in April 1985 was very busy, particularly as the prime minister was due to arrive later that same month. I had to meet with a number of senior British officials, including Prime Minister Thatcher, before Mulroney's visit. Many of my fellow ambassadors told me that, in the circumstances, I was beginning my diplomatic career at "the deep end." A few days later I spent a day at the British Foreign Office meeting, first, with Baroness Young, the government's foreign affairs spokesperson in the House of Lords. We enjoyed a cordial chat embracing many aspects of Canadian–British relations. Her most interesting observation was that, because Canada was such a friendly and close British ally, it did not get the same attention in Whitehall that was afforded to less-important but "troublesome" nations. I also met with all the senior civil servants in the Commonwealth Office who had responsibilities that touched on Canadian interests. They professed to be delighted by what they perceived as a strengthened relationship between Canada and the United States since Mulroney's election – a closeness that they believed would benefit Britain.

My first day of talks ended with a lengthy conversation with Sir Geoffrey Howe, the foreign minister. He turned out to be congenial, relaxed, and low key. The only significant bilateral irritant at this time, he said, was the European ban related to the Canadian seal hunt. Only later did the struggle against apartheid in South Africa overtake the seal hunt as the major irritant between Canada and Britain. We also discussed the issues of defence procurement and technology at some length. Both our nations were anxious to maintain a balance between exports and imports in the defence field. Sir Geoffrey was of the view that joint ventures and cooperation in defence research were the wave of the future, though he realized that British industry was hesitant to transfer its technology without "something in return." All in all, I received a warm welcome at the Foreign Office. Two women who worked in the Canadian section greeted me wearing campaign buttons from my political leadership campaign in Ontario a few months earlier.

During that first week in London I also came into contact with the Duke of Edinburgh at Marlborough House, the home of the Commonwealth Secretariat. Sir Shridath "Sonny" Ramphal, the Commonwealth secretary general, was hosting a reception to raise funds for Commonwealth veterans of the two world wars who were living in poverty, particularly in South Asia. Prince Philip was the key speaker, and after his remarks he responded to questions from members of the media. The London press had been preoccupied for some days with revelations about the Nazi past of the father of Princess Michael, who was married to one of the Queen's cousins. The first question was directed to that subject, which had nothing to do with the plight of Commonwealth war veterans. Prince Philip was clearly irritated and responded, "Are you kidding? Who are you, anyway?" The journalist replied that he represented an American publication. "Is that the only reason that you came?" the angry prince shot back. "Your question is totally irrelevant as to why we are here." A senior officer accompanying the Duke of Edinburgh turned to me and said, "High Commissioner, that fellow just took a naval broadside, and I don't think he will ever be heard from again."

The following week, I had my first official visit with Prime Minister Thatcher. Having followed the "Iron Lady's" career, I was interested to discover that Thatcher seemed younger and more attractive than she generally appeared in newspaper photos and on television. I soon learned that she could use both a formidable demeanour and femininity with equal effectiveness. She had closely followed the recent Canadian election campaign and was clearly pleased that Pierre Trudeau had been replaced by a Conservative prime minister. As I reported back to External Affairs, Thatcher was optimistic that Canada–US relations would improve under Prime Minister Mulroney and that the United Kingdom would benefit from this friendship. "She looks forward," I reported, to "greater like-mindedness among Canada-U.K.-U.S.A. heads of government at summits in place of what she refers to as the Trudeau-Mitterrand axis."

Our conversation covered a number of political issues, with an emphasis on the upcoming Bonn G7 summit. Notwithstanding an unemployment rate of approximately 13 per cent in the United Kingdom, Thatcher was preoccupied with keeping the summit leaders focused on the need for continued caution and restraint in macro-economic policy to prevent a resurgence of inflationary pressures. She was also troubled by the US deficit and its impact on UK and European interest rates.

During this meeting, I picked up on a number of attitudes she held which helped to explain her approach to a variety of issues and personal relationships. First, she was sceptical of multilateral institutions, whether the Commonwealth, the G7, or the United Nations, all of which she often referred to as "talking shops." She clearly preferred a bilateral approach to most international issues. In relation to the Bonn summit, which was only two months away, she told me that 90 per cent of the final communiqué had already been written. As a result, she recognized that there would be little of depth in the discussions among the leaders of the industrial world. Second, while she obviously enjoyed vigorous and "no-holds-barred" debates on policy issues, she was very sensitive to any behaviour that could be interpreted as a personal slight. I felt, for example, that her antipathy towards Trudeau and Mitterrand was fuelled as much by their "rudeness" in conversing in French in her presence as by any policy differences between her and "those leftist leaders" – to repeat her own choice of words.

As Thatcher contemplated the Bonn summit, she was still very irritated by an incident that had occurred at the last G7 summit involving the French translation of the final communiqué. Apparently, after an aggressive argument, she had finally persuaded Mitterrand and Trudeau to support President Reagan's wish to include a relatively innocuous reference in the communiqué with respect to the US space program. As things turned out, the reference was included in the English version, but, she seethed, a Trudeau-Mitterrand conspiracy led to its exclusion from the French version.

Throughout our conversation, Thatcher's pro-US bias was clearly evident, notwithstanding her opposition to the size of the US deficit and her scepticism about Reagan's Star Wars initiative. Nevertheless, she was anxious for British participation in this scheme, seeing it as great opportunity for young British scientists.

During this visit, I even scored a modest diplomatic triumph – my first. Thatcher's officials had told my office that it would be impossible for the prime minister to come to Canada House during Mulroney's first official visit to Britain. I was able to persuade her, however, to attend a reception there, much to the visible irritation of her private secretary. Obviously her agreement meant that he would have to reschedule what he regarded as more important meetings. Then, when she did visit Canada House the following week, a misunderstanding created a minor diplomatic incident. Contrary to the instructions of Thatcher's security people, Mulroney met her outside Canada House – a better location for a photo op. The ensuing media scrum prevented her for a few minutes from entering the building – and this delay made her more vulnerable to a potential assassin.

On April 30, 1985, Mulroney and Thatcher had their first official meeting as prime ministers at 10 Downing Street. (They had met informally in Moscow six weeks earlier at the funeral of President Konstantin Chernenko.) I reported to Ottawa that the meeting was "characterized by palpable warmth and cordiality." It lasted more than half an hour longer than planned and ranged over a wide range of subjects. In relation to the upcoming Bonn summit, Thatcher expressed her concern that, on their arrival, the leaders would encounter a communiqué that was "all but complete." At the same time, she realized that, if there was not extensive prior agreement, the leaders would spend most of their time "haggling over words." Nevertheless, she thought that the lengthy negotiations before the meetings inhibited the chances for any spontaneous discussions. Silently, as I listened, I wondered how she could have it both ways.

Both prime ministers were clearly sensitive about their own public's perceptions of their relationship with Reagan. They believed that their respective domestic media had been excessively unfair, the UK media often referring to Thatcher as "Reagan's poodle," and the Canadian media to Mulroney as the "lackey of Reagan." At the same time, both of them agreed that the United States could often be a difficult ally, sometimes arrogant and often failing adequately to consult with its closest allies, causing them embarrassment. Thatcher was still angry that the United States had not informed her in advance of its Grenada invasion. Mulroney, in turn, was still smarting from the insult a few weeks earlier when US Secretary of Defense Caspar Weinberger, without any consultation, remarked at his Quebec summit with President Reagan that the United States wished to place cruise missiles in Canada. Both prime ministers also agreed that the large US deficit was a major problem for international growth because it contributed to high interest rates everywhere. US trade barriers were another major concern.

In addition, the two prime ministers discussed the American Star Wars initiative. They believed that a number of European countries were worried by Reagan's announced intentions to "make the world safe from nuclear weapons." This goal ran directly counter to NATO's fundamental position, which depended on nuclear weapons to deter the possibility of a conventional Soviet attack on Western Europe. South Africa was not mentioned at all during this meeting, yet, within a year, it became an issue of considerable tension between the Canadian and the UK governments.

Mulroney's visit to London included meetings with the Queen and the Queen Mother, a reception at Canada House, and a formal dinner hosted by Thatcher at 10 Downing Street. Most of the senior British Cabinet members attended, and both prime ministers performed well during the dinner. At the end of the evening Thatcher confided to me, "I hope that Brian won't be disappointed by his first summit," and once again she repeated how unimpressed she had become with the summit process. I concluded that a very cordial relationship appeared to have begun and that Thatcher was clearly anxious to be helpful to her new young colleague.

For his part, at his London press conference following his meetings with Thatcher, Mulroney was obviously sending a message to the Canadian media, which continued to be critical of his "too cozy" relationship with Reagan. People would find Canada to be loyal to its friends but "very bloody minded" over its independence and sovereignty, he stated. In reference to US suggestions that it might situate cruise missiles in Canada, Mulroney stressed that Canadian soil was free from nuclear weapons, "and we plan to keep it that way." He also expressed misgivings over Reagan's Star Wars program as well as the US policy in Central America. He emphasized that he had already expressed his views to Reagan "in a very firm and unvarnished way." Mulroney also hinted for the first time in public of the possibility of a free-trade agreement with the United States. He spoke of his concerns about the "protectionist threat in the US Congress which could seriously inhibit our commercial activities" and the need to "ensure a privileged position in Canada vis-à-vis Washington."

My first appointment with the Queen took place the same day that the Mulroneys left London. The initial meeting between a new high commissioner and the reigning monarch is a much less formal affair than the protocol required for non-Commonwealth ambassadors presenting their credentials. For them, the event involves travelling to Buckingham Palace in a horse-drawn carriage, followed by a very formal encounter that leaves no room for any real communication. High commissioners, in contrast, arrive by car and are treated to a much more informal and relaxed meeting with the Queen.

I've often been asked to explain the difference between a high commissioner and an ambassador. The simple answer is that there is no difference as to their responsibilities. Both are the senior representatives of their countries in the host nation, with the traditional responsibilities in protecting and, where possible, strengthening their nation's interests. In Britain, high commissioners and ambassadors are usually segregated at formal diplomatic receptions, often causing considerable confusion for visiting heads of state. Perhaps the best explanation for this custom was the exchange I overheard at a reception at Windsor Castle for the king of Saudi Arabia. As the king entered the salon occupied by the high commissioners, he asked the British official accompanying him why the ambassadors were in one room and the high commissioners in another. The official replied that the ambassadors "are our friends, and the high commissioners are family."

Certainly the first official visit Ria and I had with the Queen was more of a family affair than the brief and highly formal presentation of credentials by non-Commonwealth ambassadors. The Queen chatted about a number of matters, displaying considerable knowledge of current Canadian issues. Our conversation ranged from politics, including her surprise over Bill Davis's retirement as premier of Ontario, to our own family. When Ria commented that we were happy to be in London but would miss our children, the Queen volunteered that if our eldest daughter lived in Saskatoon, we might as well be in London as in Toronto.

The Queen was concerned about the BC totem pole on display in Great Windsor Park. The Haida-carved pole had been a gift to the Queen from the government and people of British Columbia to mark the centennial of the province's entry into Confederation. "I am sorry to trouble you, High Commissioner," she said, "but I do have some concern about our BC totem pole, which has deteriorated somewhat in recent years, probably as a result of acid rain." I volunteered to speak to BC premier Bill Bennett. Only weeks later, two Haida carvers, one the son of the original carver, arrived in Windsor Park. Before long the pole was returned to its original artistic beauty, and the Queen attended a ceremony we organized at the site to thank the BC carvers. For me, the most memorable aspect of the event was that the Queen arrived driving her own car – something that happened only on the royal estates. The saga of the totem pole is but a modest example of the huge variety of undertakings I could expect as high commissioner. On any given day, they might range from an early morning visit to the London Billingsgate fish market with Canadian exporters to a meeting at 10 Downing Street.

During our term in London, I had many other encounters with the Queen. Some of these meetings were brief, particularly at formal public events where a little small talk was exchanged, while others lasted for a few hours, as at dinners where there was opportunity for a more meaningful dialogue. On these occasions the Queen was often surprisingly frank and, in general, did not avoid controversial subjects. I realized at times that she expected me to deliver a message to Prime Minister Mulroney about some issue of particular concern to her. I recall her annoyance when Mulroney greeted President Reagan at the Ottawa Airport in place of Governor General Sauvé when Reagan first visited Canada as president. The actual meeting between these two leaders, both of Irish background, took place in Quebec City on St Patrick's Day, March 17, 1985, and is often referred to as the "Shamrock Summit." The Prime Minister's Office stated, rather ridiculously in my view, that it was not an official visit and therefore did not require the US president to be greeted as protocol required by the Canadian head of state. The Queen's remarks to me were made many weeks after the summit, suggesting that she had perhaps brooded over the issue for some time. Not surprisingly, the Queen was very sensitive about the treatment given to her official representatives in Commonwealth countries where she was the head of state.

As leader of the Commonwealth, the Queen was very well informed about the activities of her high commissioners. I well recall the 1987 Commonwealth Heads of State meeting in Vancouver which I attended as chair of the Commonwealth Committee monitoring South Africa. One evening there was a large reception for Her Majesty in a Vancouver hotel, with hundreds of people present. Many of the guests had lined up, hoping to shake her hand, but I did not join them, preferring to let the others express their greetings. The next time that I was with the Queen in London, however, she admonished me for not speaking to her in Vancouver. "There I was, not knowing anyone in the room, and then I saw you," she said. "I expected you to come over and say hello, but you didn't!" I felt very embarrassed but also impressed that she would recognize me amid the large crowd in the room.

Although, as protocol required, I don't recall ever expressing disagreement with the Queen, I did not feel the same inhibition with Prince Philip, whom I greatly respected. In particular I remember a somewhat heated debate with him about the seriousness of the issue of separation in Quebec. The discussion took place during a dinner at Windsor Castle in 1987, after the Queen had escorted the female guests to an adjoining salon for coffee. Prince Philip asked me to sit beside him to talk about Quebec, while the other male guests gathered around us. He had recently been to Quebec with the Queen – their first visit to that province in many years.

It seemed that Prince Philip had met only Quebec francophone federalists, who encouraged him to believe that the Quebec sovereignist movement involved only a small militant fringe of Quebec society. He therefore expressed his strong opinion that concerns about the future of Quebec in Canada were largely unfounded. Believing that the royal family should be better informed about a crucial Canadian issue, I bluntly replied that the issue would be a major concern for Canadians in the years ahead. Prince Philip was not pleased to be contradicted, particularly in the presence of a number of prominent guests, and we exchanged a few more blunt words. However, he quickly reverted to the role of a charming host and, along with the Queen, treated all the guests to a personal tour of Windsor Castle. In subsequent years I could only wonder what Prince Philip thought when Canada almost lost Quebec as a result of the 1996 referendum in that province.

The highlights of our visits with the Queen and Prince Philip included an overnight stay at Windsor Castle and the dinner we organized for them at our official residence on Grosvenor Square. For this event, both my mother and Ria's mother came from Canada. They arrived at Heathrow carrying their formal gowns as hand luggage, fearful that their checked-in suitcases might get lost.

Another member of the royal family I encountered fairly frequently in London was Prince Charles. We entertained Charles and Diana, Princess of Wales, at dinner before their 1986 visit to Canada. The evening concluded with a recital featuring the Canadian opera singer Gino Quilico accompanied by Ria, who is an accomplished pianist. Princess Diana was obviously impressed with his talent and remarked to a Canadian guest seated beside her, "I would like to chat him up, but if I don't have time, will you do that for me?" Diana seemed quite unpretentious to me, though a little frustrated with her role.

That evening, Prince Charles and I had a long chat about the media, which obviously annoyed him. The tabloid press in the United Kingdom were brutal to many people in "high places" and did not spare the prince. He knew I had been in elective politics and asked me how I dealt with the media in Canada. I replied that there were difficult moments, but that I had developed a pattern of not reading certain commentators. Prince Charles replied that at least I had chosen a public career and could therefore expect some criticism, while he did not have the luxury of making that choice.

I offered the opinion that my own prime minister, Brian Mulroney, would probably enjoy his responsibilities to a greater extent if he was not such a "news junkie." I recalled how Pierre Trudeau claimed, though not always convincingly, that he never followed the political media. As Prince Charles and Princess Diana left our residence that evening, the prince told me that, when he saw Mulroney in Canada, he would pass on my advice about paying less attention to the media. I replied simply that if I had gone from London when he returned, he would know that his remarks had not been a good idea.

Though by no means a major part of our time in London, the events related to royal occasions were always interesting. The British talent for "pomp and ceremony" is famous, and functions at Buckingham Palace or in relation to the Queen's official birthday, for instance, were magnificently staged. While often reminiscent of a world that is rapidly disappearing and perhaps already an anachronism in some quarters, the monarchy remains central to the culture of the United Kingdom. The past few years have been challenging for the royal family, containing more than one *annus horribilis*. Regardless, the institution continues to demonstrate an enormous resilience and an ability to change with the times. Today it seems appropriate for the Queen to pay taxes and give the public greater access to Buckingham Palace, but I do not expect that she or her successor will ever be seen bicycling around London.

The Queen Mother was always a delightful guest. She had a deep and abiding affection for Canada, beginning with her visit with her husband, George VI, shortly before the outbreak of the Second World War in 1939 – a tour that had a positive and significant impact on the mobilization of the Canadian war effort. She always referred to her husband as "the King." She often spoke of the warmth of the crowds that welcomed them, even if people were allowed to knock on the windows of their stationary royal train late at night. Security was relatively minimal, and she recalled acknowledging these greetings in her nightgown. The Queen Mother also referred to the "peculiar insistence" of Prime Minister Mackenzie King when he decided to accompany the royal couple to Hyde Park, New York, for their visit with President Roosevelt. Her puzzlement ended with the comment that "Mr King, of course, had become 'a little dotty by then.'" While some historians may agree with her sentiment, I did not believe it would be helpful to remind her that King had remained Canada's prime minister for almost nine more years after that royal visit.

The Queen Mother's affection for Canada was demonstrated very generously on Canada Day, July 1, 1987, when she hosted a major event at Buckingham Palace. I had arranged for two RCMP officers to stand on duty in their distinctive uniforms at Canada House during the months of June, July, and August that year. The officers borrowed horses from the Queen's stables for this special day and rode alongside the Queen Mother's carriage from her residence at Clarence House to the palace. Among the visitors were three platoons of Canadian veterans, who were probably all then living in the United Kingdom. No arrangements had been made for the Queen Mother to inspect these men, but she told me she thought she should pay her respects to those "elderly gentlemen" – who, on average, were much younger than she was. They lined up, she made her inspection in her usual gracious style, and they were delighted.

It also became apparent during my years in London that the advisers to the royal family actively pursued opportunities for the Queen and other members of her family to visit Canada and so maintain a strong relationship. The Queen as the head of state of Canada and other Commonwealth countries clearly strengthens the profile of Britain in the international community. Perhaps it even allows Britain as a middle power to exercise an influence in world affairs beyond the scope of its economic and military power. Although some of this influence is related to Britain's history of empire, to its being the mother of parliaments and the creator of the common law, and particularly to its own political stability, I believe that the monarchy also adds to Britain's international stature.

Nevertheless, when I returned home, I felt somewhat ambivalent about the future role of the monarchy in Canada. Certainly "sharing" a Queen with Britain reinforces the colonial attitude towards Canada that still pervades some segments of British society. However, this remnant is probably of little importance so long as the monarchy remains a unifying force in Canada. At the same time, the general indifference of Canada's francophone citizens towards the monarchy, and the monarchy's lack of relevance to many of our fellow citizens from other cultures, are matters of concern. The role of the monarchy will probably be the subject of more vigorous discussion in the years to come, as is happening in Australia.

30

The High Commissioner's Work

I had assumed that my responsibilities in Britain would focus almost entirely on Canada–UK relations and that there would be little time for significant meetings with other ambassadors. However, I soon learned that London provided a special listening post in relation to the broad international community and that most nations were represented by senior individuals who were very knowledgeable about important international issues relevant to Canada. Consequently, I arranged formal meetings with them to obtain their views on matters of interest to Canada. I found that ambassadors in London were more likely to be candid in expressing their personal views to a fellow ambassador than in official communications between governments. Ottawa was very interested in these meetings, and I was usually provided with a list of topics for discussion.

In South Africa, the summer of 1985 was particularly violent as anti-apartheid protests escalated, and the government lashed out with increasingly brutal responses. Before the South African government initiated a policy of censorship, much of the violence had already been reported on international television, and Prime Minister Mulroney became ever more emotionally distressed by what he saw there. As a result, the battle against the apartheid regime in South Africa soon became a foreign policy priority for him personally. Before long, Canada's aggressive policy towards South Africa became a significant irritant between the UK and Canadian governments, even to the point of threatening the future of the Commonwealth. At the same time, the British public appeared to be generally ambivalent towards apartheid in South Africa and often openly hostile towards the Commonwealth as an institution.

Every society harbours the virus of racism, and Britain was certainly no exception. The British government's generous immigration policy towards Commonwealth nations in the years after the Second World War became decidedly controversial and led directly to the infamous "Rivers of Blood" speech in 1968 by Conservative MP Enoch Powell. As the non-white population steadily increased, so did the racial tensions that, occasionally, escalated into serious violence – as, for example, in the Brixton riots that broke out shortly before my posting to London. It's not uncommon for critics to blame this changing face of British society on the country's special role in the Commonwealth.

During my years in London, the most racist institution was probably the tabloid press. Indeed, Neil Kinnock, the leader of the Labour Party at that time, advised me that any real understanding of British society unfortunately required familiarity with these newspapers. The racist tone of the tabloids was often quite virulent, and the Commonwealth as an institution invariably received negative coverage. At the same time, because the tabloids generally supported the Conservative Party, Thatcher's government was not as active as it should have been in pursuing initiatives for racial harmony.

The anti-Commonwealth stance was by no means confined to the tabloid press. The editorial policy of the reputable "broadsheet press" towards the Commonwealth, with the exception of the *Guardian*, was also quite negative. I recall a particularly scurrilous piece written about Sir Shridath "Sonny" Ramphal, the Commonwealth secretary general, which appeared in the *Sunday Telegraph*. I wrote a highly critical letter to the editor of that paper, and when I encountered him at a dinner party several weeks later, we exchanged some rude comments.

With regard to apartheid, the British business establishment in general supported the status quo in South Africa. Although business leaders probably recognized the despicable nature of the apartheid regime, they did not believe that any meaningful change could be made in that country short of a violent revolution. Given the significant British investment in South Africa and the fact that a million white South Africans held British passports, both the business sector and the Conservative government in Britain made it their priority to avoid any prospect of a bloody civil war. I soon learned that this "apocalypse view" against forcing an end to the apartheid era in South Africa was shared by the US government as well. Sir Geoffrey Howe, the British foreign secretary, advised me "in confidence" of this political assessment, though it was never expressed publicly.

Thatcher did not seem to be at all perturbed, probably because this distancing served to strengthen her political position at home. Many Britons viewed the Commonwealth's aggressive policies towards South Africa as somewhat hypocritical, given the lamentable human rights records in many of these countries. "The Blacks in South Africa were better off than the majority of Blacks elsewhere in Africa" became a common refrain in the United Kingdom. Personally I found it appalling that, because the "mad scientists" of apartheid were members of a white minority with roots largely in Europe, the collective conscience of Britain was not generally disturbed. At the same time, it was not uncommon for supporters of South Africa in Britain to criticize Canada's treatment of its own Aboriginal people.

Thatcher often spoke of the "ANC terrorists," and, indeed, refused to meet with any representative of the African National Congress. She opposed sanctions against South Africa on the grounds that she was not going to "create Black unemployment in South Africa which in turn would create unemployment in Britain." Although there have always been persuasive arguments both for and against the effectiveness of economic sanctions, I was disturbed by the level of general insensitivity to apartheid within the ranks of the British government.

There was tremendous resentment towards Thatcher's government among the non-white Commonwealth countries, which represented the overwhelming majority of that institution. The Commonwealth had for many decades been described as the British Commonwealth, and although the term "British" had long since officially disappeared from its name, the Commonwealth was still regarded in much of the world as fundamentally a British institution, particularly as the Queen is its formal head. The lack of a more aggressive strategy by Britain in the fight against apartheid caused many non-white countries to consider leaving the organization, even though the Queen was generally admired throughout the Commonwealth.

In contrast, Canada's leadership within the Commonwealth during the early Mulroney years was a major factor in strengthening the collective resolve of that organization in the fight against apartheid in South Africa, even as Britain became more and more isolated. I attended a few international gatherings largely related to the Commonwealth with

Prime Minister Mulroney and was able personally to witness his effective leadership in this battle. I strongly believe that his role, especially in his call for stronger economic sanctions against South Africa, was important in preventing the breakup of the Commonwealth, which was a distinct possibility during the mid- to late 1980s.

The Commonwealth Heads of Government had established a Committee of the Commonwealth High Commissioners in London to monitor the evolving situation in South Africa. Shortly after my arrival in Britain I was invited to chair the committee – and I accepted. This role did not endear me to Prime Minister Thatcher, particularly as our committee frequently issued public statements critical of the UK government's policy towards South Africa, with only the British Foreign Office representatives on the committee dissenting.

The most imaginative Commonwealth initiative during my London years was the creation of the Eminent Persons Group (EPG) at the Commonwealth Heads of Government Meeting in Nassau in 1985. The group, made up of highly respected people from Britain, Canada, Australia, India, Nigeria, Zimbabwe, and Barbados, was given a mandate to visit South Africa and report on its findings to the Commonwealth secretary general. Somewhat surprisingly, the South African government agreed not only to the visit but also to direct discussions between the EPG and the South African Cabinet, as well as with many other organizations and individuals. Prime Minister Mulroney provided a Canadian government aircraft to facilitate the group's travel within southern Africa.

The EPG met with many leaders of the South African black community, including Nelson Mandela in his prison cell on Robben Island near Cape Town. A meeting with the South African Cabinet followed, during which Lord Barber, a former Conservative chancellor of the exchequer whom Thatcher had appointed as the British EPG member, told President P.W. Botha and his colleagues that he had met "the true man of peace ... Nelson Mandela, and that it was most unfortunate that the South African government was continuing to keep him in prison." He also told me how Anglican Archbishop Ted Scott, Canada's EPG representative, had lectured the purportedly devout Dutch Reform Cabinet ministers on the proper interpretation of biblical texts – particular verses that had been distorted by many religious supporters of apartheid.

The South African Cabinet agreed to a second meeting with the group. However, President Botha was becoming apprehensive about the media coverage internationally and the evolving dialogue among the group, his Cabinet members, and other people. He ordered the South African Air Force to bomb the area in Lusaka, Zambia, where the ANC was believed to have its headquarters, thereby effectively ending the dialogue between the EPG and the South African Cabinet.

The EPG's unanimous report recommended an increase in the level of international sanctions against South Africa. When the British government refused to accept these recommendations, the United Kingdom became even more isolated within the Commonwealth. Several high commissioners in London spoke to me about the possibility of moving the Commonwealth Secretariat from London to Ottawa, to protest the intransigence of the British government in the fight against apartheid. Given the historical role of Britain in the Commonwealth and the crucial leadership of the Queen as head of the Commonwealth, however, the Canadian government did not encourage this development.

Thatcher had clearly expected Lord Barber to keep the process "on the rails" insofar as the British government was concerned. He turned out to be a major disappointment to her when he became a committed advocate against apartheid and signed on to the group's scathing report. Later he told me that his work on this file had made him a "non-person" to Thatcher. Clearly, the supporters of the Conservative government resented the pressure these Commonwealth partners placed on Her Majesty's Government. I recall attending the foreign policy debate at the autumn 1986 annual conference of the Conservative Party, together with the other invited members of the diplomatic corps. My Commonwealth colleagues and I were shocked by the boos and catcalls that echoed around the conference hall every time the Commonwealth was mentioned. It was also apparent that the party delegates attending the meeting included only a handful of non-white faces.

The unpopularity of the Commonwealth at this Conservative conference was also fuelled by the boycott of the 1986 Edinburgh Commonwealth Games by a number of African and Caribbean countries. Organizers of the games had spoken to me earlier in the year, hoping to obtain the assistance of the Canadian prime minister in averting the threatened boycott. I had several conversations with Mulroney about the development of a strategy, and he and Rajiv Gandhi, the Indian prime minister, almost succeeded in averting the boycott. They developed a statement for Thatcher which emphasized her opposition to the apartheid regime in South Africa without committing her to any additional specific initiatives. Such a statement would probably have averted the boycott, but she simply refused to cooperate. Her intransigence did not enhance her declining political popularity in Scotland, where many thousands of people served as volunteers before and during the Edinburgh Games.

The role of the Commonwealth in the ultimately successful struggle against apartheid was perhaps "its finest hour." Certainly Nelson Mandela acknowledged the importance of Canada's leadership when he visited Canada shortly after his release from prison. I had the privilege of hosting him in Toronto for part of his visit in June 1990. I shall always remember with great admiration his apparent lack of bitterness or recrimination despite his twenty-seven years in prison. It is still my view that Mandela was probably the only person capable of creating a democratic society in South Africa without the bloody civil war that had been feared by both the British and the US governments.

Now, in the twenty-first century, the challenge facing the Commonwealth is to find some way to ensure that it remains a relevant institution in international affairs. Given the degree of ambivalence towards the organization in the older member countries of Britain, Canada, Australia, and New Zealand, Canada's leadership role will become increasingly important if the Commonwealth is to survive in a meaningful form.

Although the role of Canada in the Commonwealth was a priority for me, I soon discovered that there are always a number of trade-related irritants that the high commissioner in London was expected to manage. In my experience, they ranged from a Canadian import tax on English tea bags to issues related to major defence procurements. During my years in London, Canada's announced intention to procure nuclear-powered submarines became a very sensitive issue because Britain was competing with France for this major defence contract. The British government clearly expected me to assist the UK submarine-building industry by doing everything I could to ensure a fair hearing by the decision-makers in Ottawa.

During this period, Lucien Bouchard was Canada's ambassador to France. He and I exchanged visits, and I soon became aware of his passionate commitment to the Canada–France relationship. In fact, he made it clear to Ottawa that, if Canada were to choose the British Trident submarine over the French product, France–Canada relations would be irreparably damaged. Thatcher, not surprisingly, also conveyed her own very strong views about British–Canadian relations to both Mulroney and me. Ultimately, despite the many millions of dollars spent by the British and the French competitors in promoting their respective submarines, the Canadian government, faced with the ferocious competition between two important allies and growing opposition in Canada to the purchase as the Cold War ended, decided to abandon the project.

* * *

Northern Ireland was also a priority for me during my years as high commissioner. My own Irish ancestry and the many family links between Ulster and Ontario undoubtedly contributed to my interest in searching for Canadian initiatives that might contribute to the process of reconciliation between the two communities in Ulster.

I learned after my arrival in London that members of the British government were reluctant to describe the "troubles" in Northern Ireland as a religious conflict between the Catholic and Protestant communities – which, of course, it was. Margaret Thatcher and her ministers preferred to use the terms "Nationalists" for Catholics and "Unionists" for Protestants. Although they conceded that the political and ethnic divisions in Northern Ireland were almost entirely along religious lines, they believed it was misleading to describe the conflict in essentially religious terms. Thatcher later wrote in her autobiography that "the IRA gunmen who murder and the hunger strikers who commit suicide are not in any proper sense Catholic, nor are loyalist sectarian killers Protestant. They are not in any meaningful sense Christians."

My first official visit to Northern Ireland took place shortly after Thatcher negotiated the Anglo-Irish agreement of 1985. It provided for a consultative role for the Republic of Ireland in the governing of Northern Ireland. The object of the agreement was to provide a forum and the needed mechanisms for discussion in order to resolve a host of issues of importance to both the Catholic and Protestant communities in Ulster. In particular, it provided for greater police cooperation between the Irish Republic and Northern Ireland in the fight against terrorism and for the monitoring of human rights issues in relation to the Catholic minority in Ulster.

A principal goal of the agreement, which was strongly encouraged by US president Ronald Reagan, was to discourage the activities of the traditionally strident and influential Irish political lobby in the United States. Among many other pursuits, they raised substantial funds for the IRA and its terrorist activities. Reagan had persuaded Thatcher that the funding would probably decline significantly if the largely Catholic Irish-American citizens were satisfied that an effective process was in place to respond to the legitimate concerns of the Northern Ireland Catholic minority – issues such as the behaviour of the largely Protestant Ulster Constabulary and discrimination against the Catholic minority with respect to business and employment opportunities.

The Protestant Ulster Unionist political leaders had not been consulted on the terms of the Anglo-Irish agreement, and not surprisingly, the Protestant majority were apoplectic when the agreement was announced, particularly when it was negotiated by a pro-Unionist British prime minister. The British government had reasoned that consultation would serve only to undermine the negotiations between Britain, the Republic of Ireland, and the United States. The Canadian government strongly supported the agreement, and I was now responsible for making this support more generally known in Northern Ireland.

During this visit to Ulster, the organizers arranged a dinner in my honour at Hillsboro Castle, an elegant stately home outside Belfast where visiting members of the Royal Family, senior government ministers, and ambassadors are lodged. For security reasons, the identity of the official dinner guest is never revealed in advance, even to the other guests, who are carefully chosen from the Protestant and Catholic communities. In my case, a false rumour had circulated that the official guest was a VIP from Dublin. An angry mob gathered outside the gates before the dinner, and several automobiles belonging to guests were damaged, though no one, fortunately, was injured. The angry protesters were readily identified as supporters of the Reverend Ian Paisley.

In my dinner speech, I emphasized the support of the Canadian government for the Anglo-Irish agreement, and my remarks were clearly not met with enthusiasm by the Protestants present in the room. As a Protestant of Irish descent myself, I was disappointed on several occasions during my time as high commissioner by Protestant political, professional, and business leaders in Northern Ireland who continually failed to work for the social and political reconciliation that was desperately required. The sad reality was that, in Ulster, most of the successful professional and business persons in both communities avoided becoming involved in politics, thereby allowing the political agenda and the public forums to be dominated by reactionaries, bigots, and demagogues on both sides. I could only hope that more of these leaders in Northern Ireland would rally to the cause of reconciliation – as they did a few years later when Tony Blair became prime minister. Finally, by the Good Friday agreement in 1998, a local government was established once again at Stormont. A peaceful future in Ulster is, however, still uncertain.

My strong personal interest in Northern Ireland led me to consider initiatives for a continuing Canadian contribution to the peace process. One idea involved the Canadian Labour Congress under the leadership of Shirley Carr. She was prepared to engage in a dialogue with the Irish Trade Union Congress in Dublin, which, interestingly, represented the labour union movement in both the Republic and Northern Ireland. To help to facilitate this initiative, I went to Dublin, where the Canadian ambassador was Dennis McDermott – Shirley Carr's predecessor as president of the CLC. McDermott arranged a meeting for me with the Irish Trade Union leaders. He was amused by the fact that I, a former Conservative politician, was anxious to work with the union movement. Unfortunately, the union leaders were reluctant to associate themselves with any reconciliation efforts in Northern Ireland. For them, it was challenging enough to maintain the trade union headquarters in Dublin without taking any moves that might be misunderstood and thereby fracture the delicate relationship between Protestant and Catholic trade unionists in Northern Ireland.

I recommended to External Affairs Minister Joe Clark that Canada open a commercial office in Belfast to try to strengthen the positive ties between Canada and Northern Ireland by creating more commercial partnerships on both sides of the Atlantic. The timing was inappropriate, however, because the federal Treasury Board had recently asked the Department of External Affairs to close some existing embassies and consulates in Europe and elsewhere.

One of my visits to Northern Ireland, in November 1987, took place two days after an IRA bombing atrocity in Enniskillen. Eleven people were killed, including a young nurse by the name of Marie Wilson. A day after the bombing her father, Gordon, gave a most courageous, moving, and remarkable media interview where he described holding his daughter's hand in the rubble and talking to her before she died. Notwithstanding the emotionally traumatic horror he had experienced, he urged forgiveness and reconciliation. His remarks had a particularly strong impact in Northern Ireland and appeared to provide some real momentum for reconciliation in both communities.

The day after this media conference, I had breakfast with Tom King, the secretary of state for Northern Ireland in the Thatcher government. We discussed how Canada and perhaps other countries might support and perpetuate the spirit of Gordon Wilson's plea for peace. Later that day, without consulting Ottawa, I announced that several young people, Catholic and Protestant, from Enniskillen would be brought to Canada every year in memory of Marie Wilson, with the object of working together in the spirit of reconciliation. In May 1988 King and I travelled to Enniskillen to announce the names of the first group chosen to visit Canada that summer. The Marie Wilson Voyage for Hope continued for twelve years, with six young people committed to working for reconciliation coming to work together with disadvantaged children in Ontario. All the participants told me that, given the religious divide, they would have little or no opportunity to become friends at home. Although a modest initiative, I hope that it made at least a small contribution to the process of reconciliation in Enniskillen. A number of people in Northern Ireland were convinced that significant progress in the reconciliation of the two communities would be unlikely as long as students were separated along religious lines in the schools.

As a sequel to my activities in Northern Ireland as the Canadian high commissioner to the United Kingdom, in the spring of 1991 the governments of Britain and the Republic of Ireland asked me to chair the political discussions in Northern Ireland scheduled for that summer. The two governments wanted a chair from outside their countries, and they recalled that, as high commissioner to the United Kingdom, I was one of the few ambassadors who even travelled to Northern Ireland on a regular basis. I had just been appointed the associate chief justice of the High Court in Ontario but readily agreed, even though I knew it would be a most challenging, if not hopeless, assignment. However, the Reverend Ian Paisley stated that his political party would boycott the discussions if I was the chair. Some fifteen years earlier as Ontario's attorney general, I had made an uncomplimentary reference to him in public – and my remarks had received considerable media attention in Ulster (chapter 15). Once again, I was reminded of the long memories that are very much a part of the Irish character and culture. In any event, Paisley continued to frustrate the process of a meaningful political agreement. The talks were scheduled to proceed in 1991 under the chairmanship of a former Australian governor general, but never got off the ground.

* * *

I was also actively involved in a number of other High Commission activities outside the mainstream political, Commonwealth, commercial, and immigration matters. To begin, I was amazed by the steady stream of Canadians who visited our High Commission – an average of three thousand on official business every year, not to mention the many more thousands of Canadian tourists.

The development of a Canadian Studies Program at various UK universities was an important Canadian initiative. The programs did much to strengthen the relationship between Canada and Britain through academic partnerships, teaching, research, and publications related to Canada. It has been long recognized that international Canadian Studies initiatives can have important economic spinoffs as people in other countries learn more about Canada. In 1987 I was honoured when Leeds University granted me an honorary doctorate for my support of its Canadian Studies Program.

Cultural exhibitions at Canada House in London and elsewhere could produce similar results. Two interesting and very different examples during my tenure were partnerships first with the British Museum, related to the culture of our northern Aboriginal and Inuit communities, and then with Liberty of London, to promote Canadian fashion designs. The British Museum exhibition was intended to educate the British public about the importance of hunting and fur-trapping traditions to our northern native peoples. The economic benefits derived from fur exports were crucial not only to their prosperity but also to their pride and self-respect. The issue of fur harvesting had long been a sensitive one for Canada–UK relations. The Liberty store initiative was originally regarded with scepticism by many people within the Canadian government. They assumed, wrongly as it turned out, that Canada could not compete effectively with the celebrated international fashion designers. As things turned out, however, Canada Nouveau, as the partnership with Liberty was called, was very successful at many levels.

In 1986 I arranged a retrospective in the Canada House gallery of the work of my friend Harold Town, who was also one of Canada's most innovative artists (chapter 26). Town, then in his early sixties, had a fear of flying and had never flown across the Atlantic before. This fear extended to driving cars, and he never learned. After his arrival in London, I encountered him sitting desolately on the front steps of Canada House looking more like a "bag lady" than an internationally renowned painter. "How was the flight?" I asked. "Like being enclosed in a vacuum cleaner for seven-and-a-half hours," he replied.

Town was our guest for a week, and with strong and often eccentric views on most issues, he was good company. During his visit we entertained Prince Andrew and his wife, Sarah Ferguson, the Duke and

Duchess of York, for dinner, not long before their official visit to Toronto. Town advised the duchess that she could ensure a favourable reception for herself if she pronounced the name of the host city "Tronta"
rather than "To-ron-to."

Many times before, Town had offered to give me a painting lesson,
but I had never had the time to arrange it. I agreed to have one now,
and we met in the north London home of Canadian journalists Richard
and Sandra Gwyn, who for some years had been there on European
assignments. Their attractive flat overlooked a canal with several colourful river-house barges. The area, a popular location for artists, was
known locally as "Little Venice." During my lesson, Town stood over
me for more than two hours, offering me interesting advice as I worked
on the canvas. At the end of the session he said that my main challenge
related to the fact that I was in too much of a hurry, attempting to finish
the painting before it had properly begun. Rather than adding highlights prematurely, he continued, I should layer the painting gradually,
ensuring always that the overall composition "worked." He summed
up his advice pungently by stating: "To explain it in terms that you
might better understand, Roy, there should be more foreplay in your
painting, and the highlights should be delayed. Your principal problem
as a painter is 'premature ejaculation.'"

In addition to several trips organized for Prime Minister Mulroney, I
also greeted Cabinet ministers, senior public servants, military officers,
educators, and many business executives. These visits were all related
to Canada–UK relations, and I found that the British counterparts to
these Canadians were usually delighted by an invitation to our official
residence. As a result, I soon realized that I, in turn, had more easy access to British officialdom.

I was expected, through commercial, cultural, and media promotions, to make every reasonable effort to raise the Canadian profile and
strengthen an awareness and understanding of Canada in the United
Kingdom. To that end, I encouraged members of my staff to maintain
constant contact with British officials and with all the international organizations that included Canada and Britain. We also supported provincial initiatives in areas of trade, investment tourism, and culture.
During my time in London, six provinces were represented by commercial agents general, but today only Quebec maintains such an office
in Britain.

As high commissioner, I attended lunches in "the City," London's
business and commercial centre, almost every week. These occasions

were intended to promote British investment in Canada and the export of Canadian products to the United Kingdom. Never did I see even one woman at these lunches with senior British executives. The "glass ceiling" may still be an unfortunate reality in Canada, but twenty-five years ago it was much more pronounced in the United Kingdom. I recall the bitterness that frustrated middle-level female executives occasionally shared with me, so I can only hope that the situation has improved in the intervening years. The fact that both the monarch and the prime minister at the time were women appeared to have had little or no influence in advancing this particular women's cause. I also learned that Thatcher was little interested in the principle of promoting equal opportunities for women. Indeed, I heard her exclaiming in a loud whisper at a business dinner one day that women should be twice as tough as men.

The issue of women's equality in Britain became a personal cause for me in relation to the then 175-year-old Canada Club. The club had originally been created by English businessmen who had dealings in Canada. Over the years, however, it assumed a semi-official status and provided an important platform for politicians and businessmen from both countries. The dinners took place in elegant London hotels, and the Canadian high commissioner was expected to act as the honorary chair. When I arrived in London, I was shocked to learn that women were not only barred as members but not even allowed to attend the dinners.

I asked what had happened when Jean Casselman Wadds, the only female high commissioner to the United Kingdom in Canada's history, served in that capacity. I was further shocked to learn that the executive of the Canada Club merely proclaimed her to be an "honorary male" for the dinners. I advised these men that I would have no relationship with the club until they reversed the discrimination against women. Moreover, no members of the High Commission would be permitted to attend the dinners while the status quo existed. The resulting stalemate between the Canada Club and me lasted for most of my term in London. Just before I returned to Canada in the summer of 1988, the club changed its policy, and women were made more or less welcome. I presided over one dinner in the company of many new female members.

Regrettably, the male-only rule also applied to many clubs in Toronto and other cities until the 1970s. I nominated one of our female Cabinet colleagues to be the first woman member of the Albany Club. Before she was admitted, there was an acrimonious debate among the

With my painting buddy A.J. Casson

A portrait by me of the Parliament Buildings in early winter as viewed from
the Ottawa River

With President Zia in Pakistan, 1984

British prime minister Margaret Thatcher leading Brian Mulroney and me into
10 Downing Street in London, 1985

With Ria, Queen Elizabeth II, and Prince Philip at the high commissioner's
residence at 3 Grosvenor Square in London

With Prince Charles and Diana, Princess of Wales, before their visit to Canada in 1986

The Queen Mother hosting a Canada Day event at Buckingham Palace,
July 1, 1987

Riding in a carriage with John Rowsome accompanying the RCMP Musical
Ride in London, 1986

As chair of the Commonwealth Committee on South Africa, 1986

With Nelson and Winnie Mandela in Toronto, 1990

With Charlie Francis, coach of Ben Johnson (The Canadian Press)

With Bill Baker, presenting the Grey Cup to the Saskatchewan Roughriders
in the SkyDome, Toronto, 1989

With "Pinball" Clemons, the popular Toronto Argonauts star player, when he received the Order of Ontario

With Oscar and Kelly Peterson, Ria, Bill and Kathy Davis, Bob and
Arlene Perly Rae

During my visit to Cuba in 1999, with Fidel Castro

As chief justice of the Trial Division, with my associate Patrick LeSage and the
regional justices, 1995

Justice Archie Campbell in his favourite suit and hat

The judges of the Ontario Court of Appeal, 2005

With Dennis O'Connor during his swearing in as associate chief justice of
Ontario, 2001

SECTION F THE GLOBE AND MAIL ■ CANADA'S NATIONAL NEWSPAPER ■ GLOBEANDMAIL.COM ■ SATURDAY, DECEMBER 13, 200

Globe
Focus

INSIDE: THE HUSTLER WHO MAY MAKE THAILAND'S SEX TRADE LEGAL, F3; STEPHEN LEWIS' NEW AFRICAN STRATEGY; CALL IN OPRAH! F6; AND WHY WENDY DENNIS HATES YOUR KIDS, F8

'This case is ultimately about the recognition and protection of human dignity and equality.' From left, Madam Justice Eileen Gillese, Chief Justice Roy McMurtry and Mr. Justice James MacPherson in the lobby of Osgoode Hall, Toronto

NATION BUILDERS OF 2003

After weeks of nominations from readers, The Globe and Mail selects the Canadians who did the most this year to shape their country: The authors of the same-sex marriage decision at the Ontario Court of Appeal.

Globe and Mail "Nation Builders of the Year," 2003, Eileen Gillese, Roy McMurtry, and James MacPherson, in relation to the same-sex marriage case

Cutting the ribbon at the ceremony opening the McMurtry Gardens of Justice,
2007

With my colleague and friend of many years, Stephen Lewis, 2009

With Ria and our six children, 2012

With my granddaughter Lauren McMurtry, LLB

members, but fortunately common sense prevailed. I had many critics, both male and female, for the position I took in relation to the Canada Club in London, but the key difference between private men's clubs in Toronto and the Canada Club was the official status the London club enjoyed in relation to government and the business community.

* * *

In the spring of 1988 Prime Minister Mulroney was in London to attend a Commonwealth conference as well as a bilateral meeting with Prime Minister Thatcher. The issue of apartheid in South Africa and the release of Nelson Mandela dominated the agenda. Although the British government had very reluctantly agreed to strengthen the Commonwealth sanctions against South Africa, Thatcher remained a hesitant warrior in the battle against apartheid. She seemed to express her concern even more frequently that trade sanctions against South Africa would cause unemployment both in that country and in the United Kingdom.

Her opposition to sanctions was also shared by several progressive leaders in South Africa, notably Helen Sussman, a member of the South African Parliament and a consistent foe of the government. However, most black leaders in South Africa strongly believed in the importance of sanctions in the struggle against apartheid, even if these measures led to increased black unemployment there. They felt that democratic change would occur in South Africa only if the nation suffered economically and if the international community regarded it as a pariah.

Although Thatcher and Mulroney took opposite and at times acrimonious positions on the appropriate strategy to apply to South Africa, they still enjoyed cordial relations on a personal level. This friendship was particularly important to Mulroney that spring after she accepted his invitation to visit Canada in June and to address our nation's Parliament. It was assumed that the Canadian media would be interested in Prime Minister Thatcher's views on the Canada–US free-trade negotiations. It was widely believed that Mulroney would call a federal election before the end of the year, with the proposed bilateral trade agreement becoming the major issue. At the time, Mulroney was well behind in the opinion polls. Thatcher, in contrast, was a respected figure in Canada, and any favourable comments she made about the agreement would probably be of significant political assistance to Mulroney. I was asked to brief her on the Canadian political scene before her departure and then travel to Ottawa for the duration of her visit.

Spring 1988 was for me a very busy period. I had long decided not to stay in the United Kingdom beyond the summer of 1988, and there were a number of High Commission initiatives I wished to advance or strengthen before my departure. The average term is about three years, and I had already exceeded it. I had enjoyed myself thoroughly in the post, but my desire to be closer to my family and to return to the practice of law were priorities at that time. Perhaps my most pressing task was to prepare for Prime Minister Thatcher's visit to Ottawa in June. One of the sensitive trade issues between Canada and the United Kingdom was the export of Canadian furs, particularly when the animals had been caught in traps of some kind. "Leg-hold" traps were controversial because British animal rights groups and others branded them as inhumane. There was considerable substance to their concerns, and Canadian governments at various levels strongly encouraged hunters and trappers to use more humane methods. That said, it was very difficult for fur exporters to know the specific methods of trapping when the furs were purchased from Aboriginal communities. I don't wish to trivialize the issue, but on occasion the criticism was made that the English were hypocritical: they took their pets on holiday yet placed their young children in boarding schools. They also "hounded" foxes and other animals and birds on their hunting forays.

The controversy was further exacerbated by the long-standing international opposition to the Newfoundland seal-pup hunt – criticism that only added to the perception of animal-rights groups that Canadians were cruel or at least insensitive when it came to these issues. In any event, there was considerable pressure on the British government, both from within and outside Cabinet, and in due course regulations were passed to eliminate fur exports from Canada. This example was expected to encourage the European community to adopt similar restrictions. I spoke about Canadian concerns to Sir Geoffrey Howe, but I soon learned that he was not prepared to take on the British animal-rights lobby, which had significant support within the British Cabinet.

In one of my discussions with Prime Minister Thatcher about her upcoming Canadian visit, I included the Aboriginal trapping issue on my list. I explained that, while the revenue from Canadian fur exports did not appear to be large in commercial terms, the trapping of fur-bearing animals was an important aspect of Aboriginal culture. My words caught Thatcher's attention, and she expressed considerable sympathy for our Canadian native people and their many challenges in the modern world. Soon after, she unilaterally rescinded the anti–fur export regulations, much to the annoyance of the animal-rights lobby in the United Kingdom. When the news reached northern Canada, the Aboriginal communities celebrated with joy. They had won a victory for a culture whose history had been nothing short of discouraging in recent decades. Over the following weeks, some beautifully made Aboriginal crafts arrived at my door.

The Ottawa visit of Prime Minister Thatcher was a political success for Brian Mulroney. In her address to the Canadian Parliament, Thatcher strongly supported the proposed free-trade agreement with United States. Her remarks infuriated the opposition, and several MPs left the chamber during her address. The private meetings between the two prime ministers were less successful. I attended their principal meeting – a very small luncheon at 24 Sussex Drive – where the main topic of conversation focused on the battle against apartheid in South Africa and the release of Nelson Mandela. Thatcher opposed any strengthening of the sanctions against South Africa simply because she believed that the African National Congress was essentially a terrorist organization and that Nelson Mandel was in all probability a Communist.

Following this visit to Canada, I did not have any significant meetings with Thatcher other than a very friendly farewell chat. As I prepared for my return to Canada, I often reflected on the "Iron Lady's" highly complex nature. She had become the first female prime minister of Britain, yet in the two decades and more that have followed, no other woman has been seriously considered as a potential leader of any major political party in the United Kingdom. Though often a controversial prime minister, she will come down in history, I expect, as not only a formidable leader but a highly successful prime minister as well.

Personally, I was very disappointed in her lack of leadership in the fight against apartheid in South Africa. Furthermore, her financial policies allowed much of Britain's infrastructure to deteriorate. Her opposition to government regulation created public safety hazards, as demonstrated by a disastrous car-ferry sinking and a tragic fire in the London underground. As a supporter, generally speaking, of the trade-union movement, I nevertheless believed that the more radical and reactionary union leaders had damaged the British economy through unnecessary strikes and other unreasonable demands in industrial relations. The "winter of discontent" in 1979 under Prime Minister Callaghan had convinced the majority of the British public that changes were required – and that feeling led directly to the election of Margaret Thatcher later that year.

While serving as high commissioner in London, I frequently heard from British business and industrial leaders about their ongoing concerns regarding the huge political divide between the two major parties – Conservative and Labour. In their view, this division made long-term planning decisions very difficult because a change from a Conservative to a Labour government would result in radically different economic policies that would have a negative impact in the marketplace. In Canada, in contrast, there have been relatively few major differences in economic policies between the Liberal and the Conservative parties.

In retrospect, I believe that one of Margaret Thatcher's most significant contributions was that her success, followed by the short-term regime of John Major, led to the creation of Tony Blair's New Labour Party. In this way, most of the radical political differences between the two parties were eliminated as both parties came closer to the centre of the political spectrum. As a result, Britain has experienced a greater degree of political and economic stability in recent years.

On a personal level, Thatcher was usually charming and considerate. For example, whenever she learned of a personal problem that affected her Cabinet colleagues or her large bloc of backbenchers, she sent them a personal note expressing her concern or sympathy. She obviously believed that there was a significant distinction between personal relations and policy differences. Although she could be aggressive in advancing her views, she did not regard policy differences as personal affronts. As the Queen remarked to me on one occasion, Prime Minister Thatcher always enjoyed a good "argy-bargy" on political matters.

Never, however, was there any doubt in Thatcher's Cabinet about who was in charge. On several occasions as I left the prime minister's office at 10 Downing Street, I noticed several of her senior ministers sitting like schoolboys as they waited to see her. Lord Hailsham, the Lord Chancellor, once aptly described Thatcher as the "headmistress." After her third election victory in 1987, however, she was becoming just too imperious for some of her Cabinet colleagues, and finally, in 1990, she was rejected by the majority in her own party caucus.

In my view, Dennis Thatcher, the prime minister's husband, was totally underestimated by the British public. He exercised considerable self-discipline in not commenting on government policy in public during his wife's premiership. The media often made unfair caricatures of him at public functions, describing him on all occasions as having a gin and tonic in hand. In my own experience, I found him a perceptive observer, and he provided me with helpful insights regarding the cultural diversity in the United Kingdom. His wife obviously considered him an important adviser, and with the exception of South Africa, where he had personal investments, I believe he was an objective and valued ally. I have no doubt that Margaret Thatcher was absolutely devastated by his death.

* * *

After I took up my duties in London, I became aware that my performance would be appraised on an annual basis by Canada's Department of External Affairs. Such a review was standard practice for all senior officials in the public service. My first appraisal read, in part: "Mr. McMurtry has provided strong leadership ... And this combined with his great enthusiasm for his assignment has resulted in very good morale in the High Commission ... Mr. McMurtry's extensive experience in public life has given him a practical, result-oriented approach to problem solving and an ease of communication with both the public and his staff which have enabled him to begin functioning quickly and at a high level of efficiency in his new assignment." The review concluded: "Mr. McMurtry has demonstrated the ability to discharge effectively one of the most demanding positions in the Canadian diplomatic service."

The following annual appraisals were in a similar vein, and the final report of June 1988 ended with these words: "Under Mr. McMurtry's stewardship, trade, investment, cultural and academic activities have all intensified. Morale at the mission is good and the Team Canada approach has brought concrete results ... Highly motivated, be it in the pursuit of Northern Irish, South African or commercial objectives, Mr. McMurtry has moved programs ahead in accordance with Canadian governmental objectives and, in some areas, particularly Northern Ireland, private sector funding for the arts and academic relations, developed remarkably innovative ideas." I realize that repeating these positive comments may well appear to be self-indulgent. However, given the scepticism that often follows the appointment of former politicians to senior diplomatic posts, I believe that these reviews are essential in completing the record of my years as high commissioner.

To me, my diplomatic experience serving in the United Kingdom was a grand and interesting adventure. I shall always be grateful for the support and friendship of my colleagues at the mission. I was permitted to take John Rowsome, my senior assistant from the Ministry of the Attorney General, with me, and he and his wife, Mary Anne, became an important part of my team. My deputy high commissioner, Louis Delvoie, a bilingual Canadian born in Belgium, was an experienced international diplomat, and many years after his retirement, he was still sought out as a speaker on international affairs.

* * *

Before Mulroney returned to Canada from London in the spring of 1988, he and I had a brief conversation about my potential future involvement in federal politics. He said that he would like me to be one of his candidates in the next election and, once elected, he would appoint me as minister of justice. This offer, assuming another Mulroney victory, was certainly a compliment. However, I strongly believed that being attorney general for Ontario, with its overall responsibility for the administration of justice in the province, was more interesting than being minister of justice for Canada. I had also been spoiled by living close to the Ontario Legislature when I served as attorney general and had little interest in commuting between Toronto and Ottawa. Above all, after a fourteen-year absence, I wanted to return to the practice of law. I replied simply to Mulroney that I was flattered by his interest but would need time to consult my family before discussing his proposal further with him. This future conversation never took place, but Mulroney apparently assumed, mistakenly, that I had agreed in London to be a candidate in the expected 1988 fall election. In due course, this misunderstanding placed considerable stress on our more than twenty-year friendship.

Very shortly after my return to Canada in July 1988, I received a phone call from Derek Burney, who, as Mulroney's chief of staff, had extensive political duties. "Roy, it's all settled," he began. "We've got a very good seat for you as a candidate in the forthcoming election, namely Don Valley. John Bosley [the incumbent] will nominate you, and he will be appointed our consul general in Boston." I was completely taken aback: I had not had any further communication with Mulroney since our very brief conversation three months earlier in London.

I explained to Burney that I had dismissed the thought of being a candidate, particularly as I had not heard further from the prime minister. Burney appeared to be stunned. "Roy," he said, "I am not going to mention our conversation to the prime minister. You will have to tell him personally."

I immediately drafted a letter to Mulroney and sent it by special courier to Ottawa. In it, I explained why my family responsibilities would not permit me to be a Progressive Conservative candidate in the 1988 election. I later heard from Marjory LeBreton, Mulroney's deputy chief of staff and a future senator, that she had never seen the prime minister so angry as when he read my letter. It was to be two-and-a-half years before any further words were exchanged between us. In September 1988 I attended an early election luncheon in Canada associated with Frontier College – perhaps my most influential outside interest during my undergraduate student days (see chapter 3). In the forthcoming election, the pledge to reduce illiteracy in Canada became one of the major issues in the Progressive Conservative platform. That day I was seated at the prime minister's table beside Lucien Bouchard, the minister of state responsible for the literacy file. I quickly became aware that I had become a non-person in Mulroney's eyes, and we exchanged not a word. I knew that Brian Mulroney was a deeply emotional person, and I have no doubt that he sincerely felt that my refusal of his invitation to become a candidate in the 1988 federal election was a betrayal of our personal friendship. His annoyance with me, however, in no way reduced my considerable respect and affection for my long-time friend.

31

My Years with Blaney, McMurtry and the Canadian Football League

As my term as high commissioner in London was coming to an end, friends often asked me what I planned to do after I went back to Canada. When I explained that I simply wanted to return to the private bar, many of my lawyer friends responded that I would probably not enjoy the role as much as I had in my earlier years. The practice of law, they cautioned, had become more a business than the profession it had traditionally been. Expensive overhead costs had made "bottom-line" considerations dominant, opportunities for pro bono work had diminished, and the concept of a helping profession was under siege. These warnings did not change my mind, however. I felt sure there would be interesting legal work for me to do.

When Ria and I settled back into our home in Toronto in September 1988, I received expressions of interest for my services from a number of law firms. I decided, however, that I would like to practise law with my brother Bill at the firm of Blaney, McMurtry. At that time it was a "full-service" firm with between seventy-five and eighty lawyers. I was referred to as a "partner," but preferred to accept a salary without any management responsibilities. Bill and I had never worked in the same law office before – a decision partly influenced by our father, who did not think that families should mix blood and business. He had never forgotten the acrimonious disputes when his three brothers joined their father's successful furniture manufacturing company (chapter 1). As things turned out, my colleagues at Blaney, McMurtry treated me very well and somewhat as an "elder statesman," but I expected that, over time, I would have to conform more to the business of the law.

One of the disciplines I had generally been able to avoid in my earlier practice was docketing my time into ten-minute segments – a custom that had since become a fundamental aspect of the new legal culture. My preference had been to review the file, reflect on the result I had obtained for my client, and value my legal services accordingly. When I had not been able to obtain a favourable result, there often would be no fee at all. Many of my clients were individuals, not corporations, and because legal fees could not be written off as part of the cost of doing business, they were not tax deductible. My flexible approach to billing had therefore suited them well.

Several of my earlier corporate clients had been major liability insurance companies. When I returned to the practice of law, I soon learned that several claim managers, although good friends, did not believe that I would long remain in this role, given the many interesting challenges I had obviously enjoyed in public service. They had a better sense of my future than I had. In any event, they were reluctant to ask me to take on a major case when I might return to the public sector in the middle of litigation. Regardless, in my two-and-a-half years at Blaney, McMurtry I worked on a number of very different cases, a few of which I'll describe here.

One of my first clients was Charlie Francis, the coach for sprinter Ben Johnson before and during the 1988 Summer Olympic Games. When Johnson won the 100-metre sprint in the world-record time of 9.79 seconds in Seoul, Korea, that year, I was in Calgary speaking at a conference for Aboriginal lawyers. I watched the historic race at the home of my brother Bob, who was then chair of surgery at the University of Calgary medical school and chief of surgery at the Foothills General Hospital. Like most Canadians, we celebrated our new hero's dramatic accomplishment with pride and joy. A few days later we were devastated when he failed his drug test. Little did I expect to become a part of the Johnson saga as it unfolded before the Dubin Commission of Inquiry, which the federal government established soon after to investigate drug use in sports.

Once the commission was announced, Charlie Francis contacted me and asked me to represent him. My lawyer friend Mike Wadsworth, who worked with Charlie's brother, Barry Francis, had recommended me to him. To digress briefly from my main story here, Wadsworth soon after was appointed as the Canadian ambassador to Ireland, where he served with distinction for five years. After he returned, he became the director of athletics at Notre Dame University, where, as an undergraduate, he had starred on the Fighting Irish football team. He was one of the finest people I have known, and his tragic death at sixty was a devastating loss to his legion of friends. His widow, Bernadette, remains a very close friend. Not long before Wadsworth's death, she had donated a kidney to her beloved husband.

Francis was a brilliant coach, a man with a computer-like mind. He could recall in detail the precise results of every 100-metre elite international sprint run of the past several years. He was also familiar with the facial structures of all the leading sprinters and had observed subtle changes of this kind among Johnson's major competitors. Those alterations could, he concluded, only be consistent with the use of steroids – those performance-enhancing drugs which were banned in international track and field competitions. He decided to put Ben Johnson on a similar steroid program simply because he believed that, given the pervasive use of these drugs, it was now impossible to win without them. He was determined to create "a level playing field" for his young athletes. He attributed the dramatic drop in world record times for women in the 100-metre event to anabolic steroids – and his analysis of these statistics became one of the many highlights of his evidence before the Dubin commission.

Essentially, Francis was a very human guy, absolutely devoted to his athletes and their welfare. He was the kind of person who, literally, would give them the shirt off his back. Many of his athletes were poor black kids from the Caribbean – and they worshipped the ground he walked on. Every spring before the snow had melted in Ontario he took them in a rented van to the southern states, where they trained on an outdoor track at a local university to get an early start on the season.

During my first conversation with him in my office, I advised him that I would be pleased to represent him but only on the condition that he would reveal the entire truth both to me and before the inquiry. Francis agreed without hesitation and readily admitted that Johnson had been on a steroid program for some time. Not knowing very much about steroids, I was curious to learn the extent to which a "safe" program would enhance a sprinter's performance. Francis told me that it would probably have improved Johnson's performance by one stride in the 100-metre run. Weightlifters, who are at the other end of the user spectrum, would have considerably more steroids administered to them – to the point where they risked severely damaging their health and undergoing changes in personality – becoming, for instance, susceptible to "roid rage." The widespread use of steroids in other sports has been well documented: as but one example, an Oakland Raider NFL football star died shortly after his retirement from football as a result of excessive steroid use.

The Commission of Inquiry into the Use of Drugs and Banned Practices Intended to Increase Athletic Performance was presided over by the Honourable Charles Dubin, at that time the associate chief justice of Ontario. A brilliant judge, Dubin had been highly respected in the legal community as a lawyer for many years. The inquiry ran from January 11 to October 3, 1989, heard from 119 witnesses, and provided riveting testimony on television.

As the various counsel prepared for the Dubin inquiry, they learned that, before the Seoul games, a great deal of information had been coming out of Eastern Europe in particular about drug programs being administered to high-performance athletes. Most commonly this information came from former senior sport officials who had defected to the West and who were willing to share their secrets with the media. The Dubin inquiry was most interested in learning why the Medical Commission of the International Olympic Committee – the body responsible for the IOC's anti-doping program – had apparently ignored this readily available documentation. The head of the IOC Medical Commission, Dr Arne Ljungqvist, a respected Swedish physician and former Olympic high-jump athlete, was therefore invited to give evidence at the inquiry. He agreed to appear, even though, because he lived outside Canada, he was not a compellable witness.

Dubin and his lead counsel Robert Armstrong, later a colleague of mine on the Court of Appeal, requested that I be present for Dr Ljungqvist's evidence so I could put him through a tough cross-examination. They felt that Armstrong would have to be gentle with this witness because he had come voluntarily and was a "guest" of the inquiry. I had always intended to be present for his evidence because, like many other observers, I was not convinced that the IOC truly wanted to assist us in breaking the conspiracy of silence. This concern was confirmed dramatically during Dr Ljungqvist's evidence, when he appeared to be a true member of the "see no evil, hear no evil, speak no evil" club.

During my cross-examination, I asked the good doctor why there appeared to be no attempt whatsoever to follow through on the information provided by former sport officials from Eastern Europe who had defected to the West and had spoken to the media about drug use in sports in their home countries. Every time I returned to this theme, Dr Ljungqvist replied that the IOC did not regard this "hearsay" information as convincing proof of the serious allegations. He seemed to indicate that, before IOC officials pursued these tips, they would actually have to witness one of the drug programs first hand.

Somewhat frustrated, I concluded my cross-examination by stating sarcastically that it was fortunate for Dr Ljungqvist's community that he had decided to become a doctor rather than a police officer. Otherwise, he would never have investigated a crime unless he had personally witnessed it. Commissioner Dubin at that point interrupted me to state facetiously that I was being unfair to the witness.

Charlie Francis also had a good deal of information about the drug-related strategies of Eastern European countries in international track-and-field competitions. He testified that, during the Seoul Olympic Games, a laboratory ship from the Soviet Union moored off the Korean coast. Its purpose was to test athletes shortly before their competition to ensure that they would pass any drug tests after their performances. As a result of their findings, Francis noted that some of the Soviet Eastern Bloc athletes withdrew at the last moment from their competitions to avoid detection. The Soviet Embassy in Ottawa was so outraged by his testimony that it made a formal complaint to the government of Canada for allowing the Dubin inquiry to provide a platform for anti-Soviet propaganda. Interestingly, within two years, as a result of greater press freedom, reports about the presence of the lab ship at the Seoul games were reported by Russian journalists writing in Russian magazines and newspapers.

I should also make some mention of Francis's knowledge of the use of steroids by American athletes. Before the Dubin inquiry, most people assumed that the principal offenders were Eastern Europeans and the Chinese. The Americans, however, were also heavily involved in steroid use and, thanks to Francis's testimony, the inquiry compiled a lot of information about activities south of the border. These leads led, in turn, to the evidence provided by Dr Robert Kerr about the extent to which steroids were a significant factor in the 1984 Olympic Games in Los Angeles. In this way we learned the interesting story of how the Americans used the IOC Olympic laboratory in Los Angeles to establish their own foolproof clearance times.

One of our many concerns before the inquiry began was that Ben Johnson's lawyer, Edward Futerman, had stated publicly that his client had been put on his steroid program without his personal knowledge.

If true, this claim would have been devastating to his coach's reputation – which I, as Francis's lawyer, already knew was very fragile. Futerman had, moreover, arranged for Johnson to undergo a psychological assessment, and the testing demonstrated that his client's intelligence, or lack thereof, would have made it relatively easy for him to be deceived by his coach. Fortunately, this theory was abandoned before Johnson gave his evidence at the inquiry. There, on the stand, he clearly acknowledged that he knew about his steroid program.

Johnson's admission that, while using steroids, he had participated in a large number of 100-metre competitions without being detected inevitably raised the question of why his steroid use had finally been detected at the Seoul Olympics. It seemed that the strategy he and his coach followed had been to ensure that, to avoid detection while still enjoying the benefits of the steroid use, a sufficient time should lapse between the final steroid injection and the actual race. Obviously, enormous effort had been spent in calculating the necessary clearance times for Francis's athletes. In general, they operated on the basis that twenty-eight days were required for the drug to clear an athlete's system. Although Johnson never volunteered any plausible explanation for his failed test at Seoul, Francis believed that his star athlete had probably administered a "booster shot" closer to the race without advising him of what he had done.

Charlie Francis's cooperation with the various counsel at the inquiry and his testimony there assisted Commissioner Dubin significantly in making the process a successful search for the truth. Armstrong has, in the years since the commission report was released in June 1990, frequently referred to the importance of Francis's testimony not only in breaking the conspiracy of silence that prevailed in international sport circles at the time, but also in sharing his comprehensive knowledge of the often opaque world of high-level sprinters. Without doubt, his evidence played a huge role in the general international acclaim Commissioner Dubin received for his report.

After the release of this report, Charlie Francis received a lifetime ban by the International Track and Field Association. Some years later, because of the valuable contribution Francis had made to the inquiry through his honest and informative testimony, Dubin and Armstrong went out of their way to support his reinstatement. In 2008, for example, in an article related to the twentieth anniversary of Johnson's performance at the Seoul games, Armstrong stated that Francis "in his own way became a bit of a heroic figure." Fortunately, Francis prospered in later years as a highly sought-after personal trainer. In October 2008, when Charles Dubin, my predecessor as chief justice of Ontario, died at the age of eighty-seven, Ben Johnson and Charlie Francis both attended his funeral. Bob Armstrong and I delivered the eulogies to celebrate his distinguished legal career. Very sadly, less than two years later, on May 10, 2010, Charlie Francis died of cancer at the age of sixty-four.

* * *

Shortly after joining Blaney, McMurtry, I was approached by several directors of the Canadian Football League to become the league's new commissioner. The current commissioner, Doug Mitchell, who had earlier played in the league and is now a prominent lawyer in Calgary, had announced that, after five years in the office, he intended to leave at the end of 1988. I was and remain a strong supporter of the CFL. I believe it has been an important national institution for more than one hundred years as well as a very entertaining football league. For some time, it had been facing significant financial problems, and it had not been able to compete financially with the National Football League for players for many years.

Because I wanted to return to the law, I could not agree to be a full-time commissioner. I had been away from the practice of law since 1975, and it was time for me to return to my professional roots. When approached by the CFL, however, I replied that I would like to help out on a part-time basis if I could assist the league in any significant way.

I was quite surprised when the league governors decided on a new administrative structure to accommodate my involvement. They agreed that, in addition to a full-time president and chief operating officer, they would create the position of chair and CEO for me to fill on a part-time basis. My brother Bill had been an accomplished athlete and, in particular, a hugely enthusiastic football and hockey fan. He and his partners encouraged me to accept the CFL job, and Bill negotiated the annual salary I would receive. It would be paid directly into the Blaney, McMurtry account. My CFL responsibilities, combined with my law practice, provided me with a most demanding but enjoyable adventure for the next two years.

Bill Baker, a former aggressive CFL all-star defensive end, was appointed the league's president and chief operating officer. Initially, he was not at all sure whether he wanted to take direction from a part-time CEO, one who, moreover, was a lawyer and previously a politician. He himself had enjoyed senior executive experience with SaskEnergy, and in addition was intelligent and unpredictable. He sometimes spoke to me about his theory of "management by chaos." As things progressed, there was certainly a degree of chaos in our relationship, but, on the whole, we proved to be effective partners.

We often played the "good cop, bad cop" strategy in dealing with particular disputes. Bill was the "bad cop," given his size and the assertiveness that had made him such a feared opponent on the football field. Having come recently from the Court of St James, I was more the diplomat and the "good cop." In any event, our joint efforts and strategies enjoyed a good deal of success.

I have to admit that I underwent a profound culture shock in my move from diplomatic circles in London to the CFL. In the relatively rarefied world of ambassadors, forceful confrontations were rare. When Sir Geoffrey Howe, the British foreign minister, advised me that his government was "concerned" about a particular Canadian policy, for instance, I understood him to mean that his government was really "pissed off" with Canada. When I chaired my first meeting of the CFL Board of Governors, I soon discovered that the "F" word and even more pungent expressions punctuated much of the dialogue. The governors and general managers who were present did not mean to insult anyone, but they seemed to believe that tough language would convey the emphasis they intended.

My first meeting as chair of the CFL was in Edmonton, the home of many great Grey Cup teams. It soon became obvious to me that the league was more fragile than I had thought. The Montreal franchise had folded two or three years earlier, and Harold Ballard, the owner of the Hamilton Tiger Cats, had simply walked away from the franchise. The BC Lions, a community-owned team, were facing a financial crisis, as were the Ottawa Rough Riders. Harry Ornest, a former NHL team owner, had recently bought the Toronto Argonauts and would become a particularly aggressive member of the CFL Board of Governors.

The Edmonton football organization was well managed by Hugh Campbell, a former Saskatchewan pass-receiving star, and the team was strongly supported by the local community. Edmonton's Commonwealth Stadium could accommodate more than 50,000 people, and the games were well attended. Norm Kwong, the CFL Hall of Fame running back who later became Alberta's lieutenant governor, was the governor representing the Calgary Stampeders.

Notwithstanding the many financial challenges facing the CFL, the league governors and general managers had not lost confidence in the resilience of the organization – and, in subsequent years, they proved to be right. The Grey Cup Championship game has for many years been the major single sporting event in Canada. In a vast and relatively underpopulated country, the CFL has been an important unifying factor.

Early in 1989, Bill Baker and I recognized an opportunity that enabled us to increase the league's television revenues. Paul Godfrey, who had recently become chairman of the *Toronto Sun*, had long embraced the idea of bringing a National Football League team to Toronto. He was supported by Douglas Creighton, the newspaper's founding publisher, and the successful developer Rudy Bratty. All three of them were friends of mine. The O'Keefe Brewery, which had the television advertising contract for CFL games at the time, was also behind this goal. In our view, O'Keefe's support for an NFL team in Toronto was a breach of its agreement with the CFL. I did not believe that a lawsuit would be practical, but, fortuitously, around this time Molson Brewery purchased O'Keefe, subject to the consent of the federal Competition Bureau.

The Competition Bureau was expected to approve the acquisition, but the process provided a modest window of opportunity for the CFL. I contacted the offices of the premiers of the provinces in which there were CFL teams and encouraged them to raise a "little hell" with the federal government about the agreement between O'Keefe and Molson. This strategy, coupled with the threat of a lawsuit against O'Keefe for its breach of the television agreement with the CFL, ended in the settlement we wanted with Molson. By the terms of this new television contract, Molson agreed to double the previous fee for the next two years, thereby producing an additional stream of desperately needed revenue for the CFL.

One of my earlier challenges as chair and CEO of the league was to find a new owner for the Hamilton team. In all probability this purchaser would need to sustain losses for the foreseeable future, and so, in effect, the Hamilton Tiger Cats had no real market value. The challenge was to find an owner who was willing to underwrite these future losses. I enlisted the assistance of Bob Morrow, the Hamilton mayor, who was very helpful. He knew that David Braley, a successful Hamilton businessman, was interested in the franchise, and because of his auto-parts and real-estate development interests, he was known to be wealthy. Braley agreed to pay the munificent sum of one dollar for the franchise, and he paid by cheque so he could frame it later. However, as chair of the CFL, I was required to do a "due diligence," or audit, of

Braley before the sale was approved. To satisfy the governors that he could meet all future financial obligations connected to his ownership of the team, I requested a letter from his bank outlining his financial assets.

Braley produced a one-line letter from the bank confirming that he was capable of meeting his financial obligations. He informed me that he did not feel obliged to provide any further details because he had not requested financial due diligence from the CFL – a statement that he knew would look precarious. Braley had impressed me with his clear passion for football, but with no real financial statements for him to give to the governors when they met in Hamilton, I asked Mayor Morrow to assure them that Braley would be a reliable owner. The governors accepted his word – and in subsequent years Braley became the senior statesman of the CFL. He not only purchased the Hamilton Tiger Cats and underwrote the team's losses for a number of years but went on to buy the BC Lions and the Toronto Argos as well, both of which he still owns as I write.

The next major crisis for Bill Baker and me occurred when the executive of the BC Lions advised us in September 1989 that they would not be able to meet their payroll beyond the next two or three weeks. We were not surprised – we had been urging them, without success, to search for a buyer before the football season began. I arranged immediately to travel to British Columbia to meet with both Premier Bill Vander Zalm and Gordon Campbell, the Vancouver mayor. David Braley, representing the CFL governors, accompanied me. Campbell, who later became BC premier, suggested Jimmy Pattison, the hugely successful BC businessman, as a possible purchaser, so I arranged a meeting with him. He confirmed that he had been interested earlier, but the deal had fallen through because he wanted a particularly generous agreement in regard to the government-owned stadium – something that would have been very difficult politically for the Vander Zalm government. He told me, however, that the flamboyant Vancouver stock promoter Murray Pezim was interested in buying the team. Pezim had a somewhat controversial reputation, but Pattison assured me that, although Pezim "could be a little crazy at times," he believed that we could trust his word and that he would be a financially responsible owner.

I respected Pattison, and his advice turned out to be very helpful. During my meeting with Premier Vander Zalm and one or two of his Cabinet ministers in Victoria, I advised them that the BC Lions were about to fold for financial reasons. The CFL was paying the team's payroll, but we couldn't afford to do so for more than two weeks. After convincing them that our attempts to come up with a purchaser had failed, Vander Zalm turned to one of his ministers and said, "It's time to bring in the Pez." We had not attempted to contact Pezim for strategic sessions, believing that the senior government members would be more influential, given his many requests over the years for government assistance in building roads related to mining exploration.

One of the BC ministers called Pezim and arranged a dinner with him that night in a Vancouver hotel. As we waited, he arrived with several former BC Lions football players as his "advisers." We consumed a great deal of wine, and our discussions were interrupted on several occasions by the arrival of TV crews, who had been tipped off by Pezim that he was going to buy the Lions team. The Pez thoroughly enjoyed the attention.

The terms of sale for the team, which by then had been legally acquired by the CFL, were relatively simple. Ownership would be transferred to Pezim when he agreed to pay the team's debts, including the loans from the CFL. About midnight the terms were verbally agreed to, with an understanding that Pezim's personal "good faith" deposit cheque in the amount of $100,000 payable to the CFL would be delivered to us in the morning before we returned to Toronto. He came through as promised.

On our arrival in Toronto, we were shocked to learn that Pezim, in one of his many statements to the media, had said that his acquisition of the BC Lions would facilitate the acquisition of a National Football League team for Vancouver. A competing team would not be welcome in any Canadian city with a CFL team. I firmly advised Pezim that, if we heard another word from him about the NFL, the sale of the BC Lions to him would be cancelled and his $100,000 deposit forfeited.

Murray Pezim did turn out to be a reliable, if somewhat colourful, owner of the BC Lions. He absorbed the losses of his football team until his death a few years later. Whether or not the Vander Zalm government helped him with another mining road is something I don't expect ever to know.

Although the balance of the 1989 CFL season continued to present interesting financial challenges for Baker and me, the competition on the field was extremely entertaining. The Grey Cup game was played that year in Toronto in the SkyDome, the extraordinary new facility now known as the Rogers Centre. It was a huge success, with a full stadium and a most thrilling game, as the green-uniformed Saskatchewan Roughriders defeated the Hamilton Tiger Cats 43 to 40 with a last-minute field goal.

As the game was coming to an end, I was standing on the sideline with Bill Baker, waiting to present the Grey Cup. We agreed that "someone up there" loves the CFL, given the large crowd and incredibly exciting game. For Saskatchewan it was its first Grey Cup win in some years, and there must have been well over 10,000 fans from that province in the stadium. They had come by air, train, bus, and car, and after the game hundreds of them remained on the playing field mingling with the Saskatchewan players for a couple of hours. It was once again a reminder of the importance of "Saskatchewan Green Pride" to the province. The CFL team, the only professional sports franchise in Saskatchewan, is a great unifying force for the province, and its thousands of supporters travel long distances to attend both the home and the "away" games. The team is community owned, and members of its board of directors donate their services.

Bill Baker had a number of confrontations with individual governors of the CFL, and on several occasions tendered his resignation. Each time I talked him out of it, but by this point I had come to the conclusion that it would be better for the league not to have both a full-time president and part-time CEO. Rather, it should revert to its tradition of just one CEO – namely, a commissioner. Baker was certainly intelligent and knew the CFL well, but his aggressive management style did not sit well with most of the league governors. When he once again tendered his resignation several weeks after the 1989 season had ended, I accepted it, and we parted on good terms. To my knowledge he has since enjoyed a successful business career in Calgary. The search for a new commissioner then became a high priority.

Before the next commissioner had been selected, the CFL had to make a decision on the location of the 1991 Grey Cup game. Harry Ornest, the combative owner of the Argonauts, wanted the game in Toronto, but I favoured a bid from Winnipeg, which had never hosted a Grey Cup game. Incredibly, some of the sports media there ridiculed the idea because of the city's early winters and the absence of a covered stadium in the city. The decision required a meeting of the Board of Governors in Toronto, and I was somewhat pessimistic about Winnipeg's chances, given the lobbying carried on by Ornest and his respected general manager, Ralph Sazio, a former Hamilton player and coach. Fortunately, a high-level delegation arrived from Manitoba led by Premier Gary Filmon and the province's lieutenant governor. An informal vote before lunch appeared negative for the Winnipeg bid, but I delayed the final decision until the afternoon. Over lunch, I was able to persuade a majority of the governors that turning down the bid would be a significant political embarrassment for the Manitoba premier. Such a decision could also alienate other provincial premiers whose support was important to the CFL. In the final vote, Winnipeg was chosen for the 1991 Grey Cup, and the game itself was a huge success. Ornest was furious and did not speak to me for some weeks – a silence I regarded as something of a bonus.

The search for a new league commissioner turned out to be a protracted and complex process. Several excellent candidates initially came forward, but, for a variety of reasons, they later withdrew their names from consideration. Eventually Donald Crump, the chief financial officer of Maple Leaf Gardens, was chosen. The fact that Harold Ballard, his employer and friend, had walked away from the CFL eighteen months earlier did not prove to be a problem for his candidacy because of Braley's strong support. Crump turned out to be a competent financial manager – an attribute that was certainly important for the CFL.

Once Crump had taken up his new position, I decided to withdraw more into the background because I planned to leave the league at the end of the following season. Given the roller-coaster history of the CFL, I wanted to end my position there in good times rather than bad, when I might be accused of deserting a beleaguered organization.

During the following year, I made it my priority to find owners for a renewed franchise in Montreal. It was obvious to me that the relatively small but spectator-friendly McGill University stadium would be a fine home field. The Montreal Olympic Stadium was simply too large for most games, and empty seats there would again create a negative image for a team, as they had already for the former Montreal Alouettes. My various attempts to bring just the right group of businessmen together to make this move happen were not successful. Several years later, however, the Montreal franchise was revived at the McGill stadium, and it has been a huge success.

I was also not successful in persuading the league governors and the general managers to initiate a strategy for developing Canadian quarterbacks. Not since the era of the highly talented Russ Jackson with the Ottawa Rough Riders had Canada had any outstanding talent in that position. The majority of the CFL coaches and general managers were Americans, and they simply believed that US college experience was essential, given the special demands on any professional quarterback. My friend Hugh Campbell, the general manager in Edmonton, often mentioned the experience of a particular promising Canadian quarterback with the Montreal Alouettes. He believed that the understandable fan enthusiasm about having a Canadian CFL quarterback once again forced the Alouettes to "bring the Canadian quarterback along too quickly," and that, in turn, led not only to his failure but also influenced the demise of the franchise. My enthusiasm for the initiative remained, but I was unable to obtain a league consensus.

The 1990 CFL season passed without any memorable crises and with a successful Grey Cup finale in Vancouver. The league's future looked decidedly promising, and Harry Ornest was able to sell his Toronto Argonaut team to a consortium in the spring of 1991 for $5 million. The new ownership was led by Wayne Gretzky, John Candy, and Bruce McNall, the owner of the NHL Los Angeles Kings. I was still the league's chair and CEO when the sale was approved, and knowing as I did that the team was having difficulty breaking even, I was very surprised that Ornest had been able to extract this purchase price.

I was even more surprised when, a few weeks later, the Toronto team announced that it had signed Rocket Ismail, the All-American pass receiver from Notre Dame, to a multi-million-dollar contract. This signing shocked the NFL, which expected him to be their number-one draft pick from the US college teams. I felt sorry for Gretzky and Candy – I thought that McNall had given them very bad advice. Indeed, McNall later went to prison after being convicted of criminal fraud in relation to his antique coin business.

In my farewell letter to the CFL governors in April 1991, I stressed the importance of maintaining a strict salary cap in order to maintain an economically viable league – one that is so important to Canadian sporting culture. More than twenty years later the CFL is relatively strong, though far from the money-making machine of the NFL. I shall always have positive memories of my two-year stint with the league.

* * *

In addition to sports-related work, I also got involved in several very different legal cases during my years with Blaney, McMurtry. One, for instance, was a lengthy hearing before a new Competition Bureau in Ottawa. The hearing was the first under the new federal *Competition Act*, and the members of the tribunal included two Federal Court judges and an economist. Our client was Tosoh Incorporated, a Japanese-

Dutch partnership engaged in the production of an artificial sweetener similar to aspartame – an ingredient found most notably in Diet Coke. Another company, NutraSweet, owned the aspartame patent that had protection in the United States, Canada, and Western Europe. Nutra-Sweet was anxious to maintain its dominance of the marketplace by locking in its customers long after its patents expired. Our clients had therefore complained to the Competition Bureau in light of a new concept in the legislation that prohibited the "abuse of a dominant position in the market place."

The hearings extended over several weeks of evidence, including expert testimony from economists giving their views as to what would be considered an "abuse." The NutraSweet aspartame patent was a most valuable asset, given the wide demand for artificial sweeteners. The company's power was such that the name NutraSweet was displayed prominently on all the Diet Coke containers. Ultimately, the Competition Bureau found that NutraSweet had abused its dominant position in the Canadian market and ordered appropriate sanctions.

Tosoh was very pleased with this outcome, though I never found out whether its sweeteners succeeded in the Canadian market after the expiration of the NutraSweet patents. What I did learn during this long-drawn-out case is that I would never have succeeded as an economist. As I sat through the complex testimony of the experts in this area, I often thought of Harry Truman's comment after he left the US presidency about the mixed and often conflicting advice he had received from economists. If he had the opportunity of serving as president again, he said, he would hire only one-armed economists. Never again did he want to hear "on the one hand, but then on the other" explanations.

I also became involved in an inquiry into the strategies employed by police emergency response teams, known generally as Emergency Task Forces (ETFs). In recent years there had been several tragic shooting deaths in Ontario involving innocent individuals, sometimes when police officers simply arrived at the wrong address.

I was retained by a prominent plastic surgeon whose son had been shot dead by a member of the York Township Police Emergency Task Force. In this case, the young man presented a serious risk to the safety of people around him when, after a dispute with his girlfriend, he went berserk, got hold of a rifle, and began to fire shots at random from a balcony in his home. When the police arrived, they made no attempt to communicate with this teenage boy. They simply shot and killed him at the first opportunity.

Although many people would not criticize the police in these circumstances, the current practice for law-enforcement officers responding to that type of emergency is to try first to communicate with distressed individuals and to use those skills to diffuse the fraught situation. Officers are trained in a variety of psychological strategies to make verbal contact with aggressors and, it is hoped, to talk them out of the dangerous threats they pose. This strategy had been used frequently and usually with success in hostage-taking incidents both in Canada and internationally.

In this case, the doctor asked me to obtain "standing" at the public inquiry called by the provincial government into his son's death. This legal term simply means having the right to call witnesses if we chose and to cross-examine other witnesses. We retained a well-known emergency response expert from the United States who had worked with police forces across that country.

It soon became apparent that the different police cultures south of the border resulted in a variety of different approaches to this particular problem. A dramatic difference in strategy existed, for example, between the police departments in Los Angeles and in New York. According to our expert in his testimony, the response of the Los Angeles Police Department to a gun emergency or hostage taking was simply to "bring out the cannons and blast away." By contrast, the New York Police Department had carefully trained emergency response teams that were very successful in their verbal communications and usually defused the crisis. Until the date of our inquiry at least, he said, the New York teams, if they were able to reach the crisis scene in time, had never had to shoot at anyone.

Sadly for my client's son, the crisis he created was just outside the jurisdiction of the boundaries of Metropolitan Toronto. There the Metro Police Force had a highly trained emergency task force which also had a successful record in negotiating peaceful resolutions to crises. Had the incident occurred within the boundary of the former Metropolitan Toronto, the young man would probably have survived the deadly police confrontation.

32

Sport as a Development Tool in the Commonwealth

In 1989 Joe Clark, Canada's external affairs minister, asked me to chair the Commonwealth Heads of Government Committee on Sport Relations to review and report on the future of sports relationships among Commonwealth countries. This committee was intended to be one of several similar bodies tasked with recommending initiatives to strengthen the Commonwealth as it went into the twenty-first century. Sports events such as the Commonwealth Games, held every four years, were obviously an important link among the almost fifty nations (at the time) that made up the Commonwealth. Just three years before, the boycott of the 1986 Edinburgh Commonwealth Games by many African and Caribbean countries had created a great deal of stress and division within the institution (see chapter 30).

I served as chair of the committee for a dozen years and, during that time, I visited many different countries in the Commonwealth and thought deeply about the role of sport in society. I believe that sport, particularly for young people, is a very cost-effective tool for individual development. In my own experience, team sports helped me to develop valuable social skills and competitive instincts, without taking myself too seriously. However, within the Commonwealth, the lack of funds often means that basic sports equipment is not available.

My committee was mandated to report to the Commonwealth Heads of Government Meeting (CHOGM), which is held every other year. The Commonwealth Games Federation was represented on the committee by its chair and its secretary, together with members from six Commonwealth countries representing different geographical areas – Britain, Nigeria, Australia, India, the Caribbean, and Canada. I was assisted by Anne Hillmer, a Canadian public servant who was hugely dedicated to the project but who died tragically young of cancer a decade later. The committee generally met formally twice a year in both Ottawa and London, England. Because many of our members also sat on their national Olympics committees, we also met in the particular city hosting the summer Olympic Games just before the event began. In addition, I received valuable information from an advisory committee that included former Canadian Olympian and Commonwealth athletes Richard Pound, a senior officer of the International Olympic Committee, and Bruce Kidd, dean of the Faculty of Physical Health and Education at the University of Toronto.

Early in our mandate, our committee prepared a blueprint for future Commonwealth Games which was intended to make the athletic competitions more representative of the cultural diversity of the Commonwealth – particularly in the addition of sports for women. Early on, because I had long believed that sport is a very cost-effective strategy for encouraging positive development in young people, I persuaded my colleagues to focus also on creating sports opportunities for disadvantaged youth. With only a few exceptions, governments in both the developed and the developing worlds have never truly appreciated the enormous role sport can play in getting young people off on the right track in life. Most nations support their elite athletes, because of the national pride that accompanies winning medals in international competitions, but they often fail to encourage and provide funding for other athletes – and particularly for disadvantaged youth.

After a great deal of advocacy, we were able to obtain additional government funding for sport development among youth in certain disadvantaged areas of the Commonwealth. We also established a centre in Barbados for the development of sport curriculums and the training of coaches in the Caribbean.

As a result of my work in Commonwealth sports relationships, I became intimately aware of the enormous disparities in the opportunities available for youth not only between the developed and the developing worlds but even within the developed world. I also learned that international aid agencies gave low priority to youth development through sport, regarding it as a frill that might be addressed after they had met other more basic needs such as housing or clean water. Hundreds of millions of young people in the developing world have no access to any sporting infrastructures whatsoever: the cost of a soccer ball is beyond the means of tens of thousands of communities in Africa and Asia. The perception of sport only in the context of professional and elite athletes is a major hindrance to developing the broader social purposes it could provide, and there will always be vigorous debate about the extent to which sport should be the business of government. Professional sport generally creates huge commercial profit, and many argue that the private sector should be responsible for the development of professional athletes. However, not all sports are commercially viable, and without some community support, they would cease to exist.

The extent of the challenge in persuading governments and international aid agencies about the importance of sport was well articulated by Richard Pound in an article he wrote some years ago, "Sport Development Assistance: A Challenge for the 1990s":

Unfortunately, the potential and the reality today are far apart. Sport has not generally been regarded as part of the cultural framework of society, but, instead, as something completely apart from culture, a veritable frill, which should only be considered after all the other pressing needs of society have been met. Indeed, so pervasive is this type of mental set that the equivalent word for "sport" may not exist in some languages, in which it becomes a subcategory of the concept of "play," an activity which is engaged in only after everything else important has been done.

Political leaders and policy-makers have often been drawn into the same misconception and tend to regard sport as something to be put at the bottom of the political and economic agenda. The result is that funding, if it exists at all, is erratic and inadequate.

Fundamental to our committee's efforts was the recognition that sport lies at the heart of the Commonwealth association and is an integral part of individual growth and community development. Sport and physical activity are essential to a healthy, creative, and productive society, touching on a great many aspects of the activities, aspirations, and interests of the young and helping to develop individual confidence, social skills, and leadership. Prime Minister Manley of Jamaica often told me that, in his view, sport represented the best hope of weaning young people from the horrific cycle of drugs and crime and providing a bridge back to the world of education. Nelson Mandela made the same point when he said, "Sport is a right, not a privilege for every child." To me, sport provides an excellent medium through which social and health issues such as racism, delinquency, hygiene, nutrition, and gender equity can be addressed.

Many people have drawn inspiration from the work and legacy of Arthur Ashe – a champion not only in the sport of tennis but also in the battle for human rights and opportunities for disadvantaged youth. Some years ago, Ashe founded a program in the United States which promoted social development through his chosen sport. As he explained: "Our idea was to use tennis as a way to gain and hold the attention of young people in the inner cities and other poor environments so that we could then teach them about matters more important than tennis. To start our program, we deliberately chose some tough neighbourhoods, the kind of places as far removed as possible from the genteel world of tennis." Many thousands of disadvantaged children have benefited from this program and, shortly before his death, Ashe commented that his goal was "to help poor young people, especially poor, young black people, make the transition from youth to adulthood without a crippling loss of faith in society and in themselves." The program, he continued, "can hardly solve the problems of poverty, racism, juvenile delinquency, cynicism, sexual promiscuity, crime, and drug addiction that plague the youth of this country, but .... We have an obligation to try to do something to counter this social and spiritual plague. Too many people have simply given up."

Street Kids International (SKI), a non-profit organization with headquarters in Toronto, is dedicated to promoting independence and self-respect among the estimated 40 million street children worldwide. It has mounted innovative community-based health, educational, and small-business projects in the Commonwealth, Asia, Oceania, and Africa. Peter Dalglish, its former executive director, was also an adviser to our Commonwealth Heads of Government working party. SKI projects take direct aim at delinquency, unemployment, substance abuse, street crime, illiteracy, and health issues among homeless and out-of-school youth. Sport remains an integral part of SKI projects: in an interview survey, project managers identified basic sports equipment as one of their top three priorities. The Lusaka drop-in centre in Zambia, for example, began with sport. Organizers there used soccer and net ball to open a dialogue with the street youth, first building rapport and confidence, and finally the trust and mutual respect essential to the program's success.

The potential for positive youth development through sport is illustrated by the Mathare Youth Sports Association (MYSA) project in Kenya, which began in 1987 as a small self-help program to improve the quality of life in the community. Situated just outside Nairobi, the Mathare Valley and neighbouring estates are home to some of the most destitute people in the world. In the MYSA program, organizers made an arrangement with local authorities to provide the young people with access to soccer balls, net balls, and playing fields. In return, the sports teams tackled major causes of disease and death on the estates by clearing away garbage, cleaning clogged drainage ditches, and engaging in education about HIV and AIDS. At the time of my first visit in 1992, the Mathare program had expanded to six leagues, 225 teams, and more than 4000 players. Some members of the teams have gone on to compete at the national and international levels.

Today the MYSA program is recognized for the success it has had in improving health, living conditions, skills, and job prospects for people in the area. Plans are now under way to expand the sport, health, and environment program to include drop-in centres, study halls, library facilities, and leadership and vocational training. The *New York Times* became interested in the project and noted that, in the last few years, "organized soccer as opposed to chaotic pick-up games played with balls of paper tied together with string has become a useful antidote to the gasoline sniffing, drinking and violence that overwhelm the youth. For young drop-outs, sports win out over crime and getting high."

In addition to all these programs, MYSA has also organized cultural activities, particularly in music, writing, and photography. In one initiative, the young people were loaned cameras and encouraged to keep daily journals. The photographs illustrated the journals and helped to make them into interesting and sometimes beautiful records. As time went on, the quality of the photographs reached the point where they were exhibited internationally. Most important, MYSA brought a sense of pride to a poor and underprivileged community, and most young people are no longer embarrassed to admit that they live in Mathare.

While on a lecture tour of South Africa in 1991, I had the opportunity to visit a successful sports program located in a very poor township outside of Cape Town which, again, had been funded internationally. The program brought in young coaches from Europe and North America to organize a variety of athletic activities, mostly in team sports. The program was extremely popular and was open to teenagers who attended school regularly. Teachers reported that, rather than distracting students from their studies, the program supported their education goals. They were also enthusiastic about the program's contribution to gender equality: for the first time, they said, males saw females excelling in athletics. The sporting program also allowed for positive contact between black youth and white youth.

The Australian Sports Commission's study of delinquency among Aborigines recommended that sport should be used to provide a healthy alternative to crime and to empower young people with a sense that they can control their own destiny. The study reported, "The provision of sport as an antidote to boredom would appear to be a key factor in the prevention of aboriginal juvenile crime." The Australian commission's recommendations were put to the test in the Geraldton region of Western Australia, where a full-time sports officer was employed to introduce a community sports program designed to encourage leadership and initiative. Subsequent studies showed that the crime rate in Geraldton had dropped by 24 per cent.

I have spoken with Canadian volunteers who have worked with youth in some of the most impoverished communities of the world – street children in Khartoum, indentured children in Karachi, refugee children in the Sudan, and children in the black townships of South Africa. These workers are unanimous in their view that sport programs, when they are available, play a vital role in developing educational opportunities, a spirit of cooperation, and a sense of self-worth and purpose. Sport can, and does, discourage young people from drugs, criminal activity, and anti-social activity in general.

In my experience, it is not just the potential international donors who must be persuaded that the development and encouragement of sports is a worthy and cost-effective investment. Potential recipients must also be convinced that a genuine benefit will result from such assistance to their countries. In a world where most countries face many different major challenges, it can be very difficult to list sports among the priorities for government. As a result, there has been surprisingly little demand for sport-development assistance, especially from developing countries and international aid agencies.

It is obviously necessary to develop an effective strategy that will persuade governments to pay more than lip service to the value of youth development through sport. The Commonwealth Heads of Government some years ago unanimously accepted my committee's recommendation that governments should "recognize the crucial role of sport in national development" and that they should impress on "national and international aid agencies the importance and value of including sport in aid programmes." Unfortunately, recognition is still poles apart from any real commitment.

One article on sports development assistance to the disadvantaged which impressed me appeared in an international sports magazine. Entitled "A Father's Lament: A Dad's Joy over His Kids' Swimming Is Tempered by Thoughts of the Many Children Kept from Play," the article concluded:

We must remember that sport is not a luxury to a child. Play is a child's business. It is what teaches him about cooperation, achievement and the pursuit of happiness. It shows him that the world cares enough about him to let him play.

"Unless somebody begins to pay attention [to children in poverty] ... we can expect our culture to fall apart," the eminent paediatrician T. Berry Brazelton said recently; "I think we've already seen it." I don't know about that last sentence, but I do know that if we're not careful, children who have never played games will inherit the earth. That would be a joyless day indeed.

The cause of youth development through sport remained a major interest after I resigned as chair of the Committee on Sport Relations. My focus on this issue became more local when Mayor David Miller asked me, in 2004, to chair an advisory committee on disadvantaged youth in Toronto. The value of youth development through sport was also the subject of broader geographical focus in Ontario during a review and report for the Ontario government, after Premier McGuinty requested Alvin Curling and me in June 2007 to undertake a review of the roots of youth violence in Ontario (see chapter 37).

PART FIVE

Sixteen Years as a Judge

33

Appointment to the Bench, 1991

The combination of my legal practice at Blaney, McMurtry and my responsibilities with the CFL provided a full, interesting, and demanding working life and, as I approached my fifty-eighth birthday in May 1990, I was generally very content. That same spring Frank Callaghan, my first deputy attorney general from my years in the Ontario Cabinet, was appointed chief justice of the Ontario High Court of Justice, shortly after Ian Scott, the attorney general in David Peterson's Liberal administration, announced that the government intended to merge the County and District Courts with the High Court. The reorganization had been recommended in 1987 by Thomas Zuber, a Court of Appeal judge, in his Report on the Ontario Courts Inquiry. Initially this newly blended court was known as the Ontario Court of Justice (General Division), and nine years later it became the Superior Court of Justice, though it was commonly called the Trial Court. When the merger was first announced, however, it was very controversial.

The High Court judges, who numbered somewhere between fifty and sixty in all, had previously tried all the homicide cases and the major civil law claims. Given that the County and District Courts had four times that number, the High Court judges believed that the quality of their work would be significantly diluted by the merger – and, certainly, there was a hierarchical element in their opposition. In previous years, the federal government had paid far more attention to appointments to the High Court. Some of the County and District Court judges, in turn, resented the thought of having to leave their little fiefdoms and travel around on a circuit court within one of the eight regions in Ontario. No provision was made for any judicial education during this blending of the courts, though, as Callaghan had often joked with me, the High Court judges tried the amateur criminals (the murderers) while the County and District Court judges tried the true professional criminals, so it should not be difficult for competent judges to move from one jurisdiction to the other. Inevitably, within a few years, attrition would take care of the minority of weaker judges in the Trial Court.

The merger of the two courts had already occurred in most other Canadian provinces, and I felt it was inevitable that it would occur in Ontario too. However, Chief Justice Callaghan, new to his post and undoubtedly under pressure from his fellow High Court judges, initially believed that he might be able to prevent it. As the debate continued, the relationship between the judges on both courts deteriorated further. The strain on Callaghan was exacerbated by the fact that he had recently been diagnosed with cancer – a disease that would take his life four years later.

With the merger planned for September 1990, Callaghan began to consider who should become his associate chief justice of the blended court. He had held the associate position on the High Court before being appointed as chief justice, and his successor had not yet been named. The appointment was the personal responsibility of the prime minister, and Callaghan had convinced Kim Campbell, the minister of justice, to ask Brian Mulroney to delay the appointment pending the merger. Callaghan wanted an associate who had not been a member of either of the merged courts and who could play a peacemaking role in reducing the antagonisms between the two groups of judges.

During the summer and early fall of 1990 I had several long conversations with Callaghan and, with his encouragement, for the first time began to think of becoming a judge. I liked the idea that I could work in that capacity until I turned seventy-five, and after my long period in politics and diplomacy, I found some of the new features in the practice of law disturbing – particularly the very high cost of civil litigation. Overall, I thought that a return to public service would be fulfilling – even though, once again, it would mean a severe cut in my earnings. As associate chief justice, I knew I would have the opportunity to make a significant contribution to the administration of justice in Ontario – and that thought was a decided attraction. Before the appointment could happen, however, I would first be required to make a formal written application to be a judge, and my appointment would have to be recommended by a federal judicial appointments advisory committee made up of judges, lawyers, and representatives of the general public. The next step in the process would be for the minister of justice to recommend me as associate chief justice to the prime minister, who would have the ultimate decision.

My appointment as a judge was apparently strongly recommended by the advisory committee, and Kim Campbell phoned me to say that she would immediately follow through. After several months of silence had passed, Campbell advised me that her recommendation was still sitting in the prime minister's office and that she had not been able to learn the reason for the delay. Eventually I heard from Bill Davis and John Tory, who were friends with both Mulroney and me, that the prime minister was reluctant to appoint me because he had never made a senior judicial appointment that could be viewed as politically partisan. Soon after, I learned the real reason for the delay: Mulroney had not forgiven me for my refusal to be a candidate in the 1988 federal election. I was well aware that he was annoyed with me on that count, but more than two years had passed, during which he had won a second majority. The logjam was broken only after Bob Rae, the new Ontario premier, learned of the issue and telephoned Mulroney to say that his NDP government strongly supported my appointment. That put the purported partisan issue to bed. Shortly thereafter, in March 1991, Mulroney phoned me to say that I would be appointed. It was a very cordial conversation, even though we had not spoken to each other in over two years.

I have never felt any resentment towards Brian Mulroney for delaying my appointment as associate chief justice for many months. I have some understanding of his emotional psyche, and I can accept the fact that he may have mistakenly convinced himself that I had agreed to be a candidate in the federal 1988 election. Moreover, because he had appointed me as the Canadian high commissioner in the United Kingdom, he may have thought I had an obligation to him politically. That misunderstanding aside, in my view Mulroney was an effective and highly successful prime minister, particularly for negotiating the free-trade agreement with the United States and for his political courage in introducing the goods and services tax (GST), which was unpopular but necessary given Canada's fiscal deficit. It is most unfortunate that, by accepting payments in cash from Karlheinz Schreiber soon after he left Ottawa, as outlined by William Kaplan in *A Secret Trial* and reviewed later in Justice Jeffrey Oliphant's commission of inquiry report,

Mulroney severely tarnished his reputation and significantly damaged his legacy. I expect that his important public service as prime minister will, however, be better appreciated by future historians. Abroad, as I explained earlier, Mulroney's leadership in the struggle against apartheid in the mid- to late 1980s was a major factor in maintaining the unity of the Commonwealth (see chapter 30). Once Nelson Mandela was released in February 1990 after twenty-seven years in prison in South Africa, he went out of his way to thank Mulroney publicly during his first visit to Canada in June 1990.

* * *

I had a personal relationship with almost every one of the judges on the newly merged court, and I was able to encourage them to believe that the new court made a lot of sense. Frank Callaghan was a brilliant judge but could occasionally be overly brusque in his dealings with our fellow judges. I recall that I became somewhat of an antidote to his "hard edges."

The sheer size of the court provided a variety of administrative challenges. The assignment of judges to particular cases was often a delicate responsibility because many judges believed they were capable of presiding over any type of case while, obviously, special skills had to be recognized. A complicated murder case, for instance, might best be presided over by a judge with particular talents, while a complex commercial case would generally require judges who had previous extensive commercial experience in the practice of law. Commercial cases, whether corporate disputes or insolvencies, usually demand a timely decision. Frequently, large numbers of jobs are at risk, and a quick resolution of the issues is important for thousands of workers. To this end, Callaghan created the first specialized commercial civil court in Ontario, and I believe also in Canada. Over the past two decades it has become an international model by reason of its effectiveness.

A large court is essentially a very human institution with a broad range of frailties, many of which must be solved by the chief justices. In my view, even with a very large Trial Court, it was essential for the chief justice to establish personal contact with every member of the court. I sensed early on in the discharge of my judicial responsibilities that, because they were all important members of the team, the vast majority of judges wanted some form of relationship with their chief justice – even if it was no more than the occasional friendly chat. If members of the public had complaints, they could take them to the

Canadian Judicial Council (CJC), a valuable forum to share information about the operations of the provincial trial and appellate courts.
First, however, many issues had to get at least some attention within
a particular court. Being a judge is essentially a lonely responsibility.
While seeking the advice of a fellow judge is very common, judges for
the most part work in isolation. The parties who appear before them
are generally not in a position to express their appreciation for a judge's
performance, as would be the case with a client in private practice, so
judges must be confident and self-reliant. If cracks appear, they need
the support of their superiors.

When the courts were merged in 1990, the province was divided into
eight judicial districts or regions. Each region was headed by a regional
senior justice, appointed by the federal government, who was responsible for assigning judges in the region. Chief Justice Callaghan chaired
the Council of Regional Senior Justices, and I assisted him in this role.
It was customary for the regional senior justices to consult with the
chief justice over the assignment of judges in major cases, particularly
in high-profile murder cases.

Our court was also responsible for the administration of the Small
Claims Courts, which were scattered throughout Ontario. When I was
appointed associate chief justice, the jurisdiction of the Small Claims
Courts covered disputes up to $10,000, as compared to $200 when I was
called to the bar and $25,000 today. Although half-a-dozen full-time
Small Claims Court judges dating from my years as attorney general
were still in place, the vast majority of the courts were presided over
by practising lawyers, appointed as "deputy judges" through the office
of the regional senior justice on a per diem basis. This assignment was
much sought after by local lawyers, not because of the modest remu-
neration it gave but because of the prestige associated with it. Some
lawyers also listed their role as part-time deputy judges on their business cards and professional letterheads.

Callaghan put me in charge of the overall administration of the Small
Claims Courts. I regarded it as a significant assignment, given that
thousands of people appeared before these courts, often unrepresented
by counsel. Because of the importance of these courts to the administration of justice in Ontario, I initiated regular educational sessions for
the judges.

As the associate chief justice of the General Division, I enjoyed sitting
in various courthouses throughout Ontario. It provided an interesting
diversity and allowed me to "show the flag" among the local judges

even as I learned more about their particular regional challenges. I was particularly attracted to sitting in Bracebridge in the spring and fall. Our island cottage was only about eight miles from the courthouse, and I could combine work with some much-needed leisure time.

I recall two murder cases in particular which contained significant emotional dimensions. The first involved a young man from a well-known local family – a family so prominent, in fact, that a road just to the south of Bracebridge is named in the family's honour. The victim – the brother of the accused's girlfriend – had been understandably upset by his sister's allegation that she had been beaten by the accused. After a night of drinking, the brother and a friend arrived at the accused's home, trashed it and attacked the accused. Soon after, the accused sought revenge.

The accused had loaned his hunting rifle to a friend. Unfortunately, the friend was at home when the accused visited him to retrieve the rifle. He was then able to locate the victim and his sister, who were staying with friends in downtown Bracebridge. The accused immediately went to that location and shot the victim dead. The police laid the charge of first-degree murder. Under the *Criminal Code of Canada*, murder in the first degree is a killing that is both "planned and deliberate," while second-degree murder is unplanned, spontaneous, but deliberate. A conviction for first-degree murder brings an automatic life sentence of twenty-five years without eligibility for parole. The conviction for second-degree murder also carries a life sentence, but with eligibility for parole after ten years.

In this case, the issue of the identification of the killer was raised at the trial, but, after the evidence had been introduced by the Crown, it was not seriously pursued. For reasons I will never really understand, counsel for the accused would not consider a plea of guilty to second-degree murder notwithstanding my views of the prosecution's very strong case of first-degree murder. One provision in the *Criminal Code* will reduce murder to manslaughter "if the person who committed it did so in the heat of passion caused by sudden provocation." The relevant sections go on to state in part that, in order for the defence of provocation to apply, the accused must have acted "on the sudden and before there was time for his passions to cool."

In my view, the evidence did not justify my instructing members of the jury that the defence of provocation could be considered in their verdict. Obviously, provocation was involved in the killing, but it was not the spontaneous type required by the *Criminal Code*. In any event, the accused was convicted of first-degree murder. After he appealed the conviction, my opinion on the inadmissibility of the defence of provocation was upheld by the Ontario Court of Appeal some months later. It has long been my opinion, however, that the facts of this case illustrated the potential danger and indeed unfairness of mandatory penalties. There was a form of provocation in the deceased's behaviour, and if some judicial discretion had been allowed, the penalty would probably have been something less than the mandatory twenty-five-year sentence.

Many of the statutory imposed sentences in the United States have been extremely unfair and much criticized – as but one example, the automatic "three strikes and you are out" sentence of life imprisonment in California has created huge injustices. The move towards legislatively imposed sentences by the Harper government is simply catering to the worst instincts of the tough-on-all-criminals crowd. Most convictions usually have unique facts which should be considered by the trial judge on an individual basis.

In another criminal jury case I presided over in the Bracebridge courthouse, the accused was charged with second-degree murder in the death of the son of an OPP sergeant following a fight fuelled by alcohol. The victim's father, who was seated in the courtroom, was so emotionally distraught and fragile that additional court security had to be provided during the trial.

The role of a trial judge in any discussion of a plea of guilty has to be handled carefully, particularly when a jury is involved. Because the accused is entitled by law to a jury verdict, the judge must not apply significant pressure in the decision. After hearing two days of evidence, two conclusions were clear to me: the alleged self-defence claimed by the accused would not succeed, but neither would the charge of murder. I discussed the possibility of the accused pleading guilty to a charge of manslaughter with counsel for the Crown and the defence, and both seemed open to the idea, though the prosecution was understandably concerned about an eruption from the victim's OPP father. In the end, though, the accused did plead guilty to manslaughter, and the victim's father managed to remain silent in court.

As a result of the high tensions in these two criminal cases, I began to rethink the advisability of my position as a criminal Trial Court judge in this area while I owned an unprotected island cottage nearby. From that point on, I decided it might be wise for me to hear only civil cases in Bracebridge.

* * *

In 1994 I was appointed chief justice of the General Division, now known as the Superior Court of Justice. This appointment was much less complicated than the earlier one as associate chief justice of that trial court. When Frank Callaghan advised the federal minister of justice of his intention to retire because of his illness, he strongly recommended me as his replacement to Jean Chrétien, whose government had been elected a few months earlier. Given my long positive relationship with the new prime minister and the support of his justice minister, Allan Rock, the appointment went through quickly. I thoroughly enjoyed the challenges associated with being chief justice of the largest trial court in Canada, numbering some 240 judges. The administrative challenges were significant and interesting. They required the full-time assistance of a senior executive legal counsel as well as many court administrators throughout the province. John McMahon, my executive legal officer, was excellent in this role. He was an experienced Crown prosecutor and was later appointed to the Superior Court of Justice, where he serves with great distinction.

Given the large number of trial judges, a great many new appointments had to be made every year. That required considerable dialogue with the federal Department of Justice. Every appointee had already been approved by an independent judicial advisory committee, but, to secure the most-qualified appointments, I had first to be constantly on the lookout and get involved in a lot of advocacy and persuasion. Despite the understandable political pressures that existed in Ottawa, I was well satisfied with the quality of the appointments made during my term of office.

I also enjoyed sitting as a trial judge, and the only court I did not sit in regularly was the commercial court, given my lack of experience in that area. The human drama associated with most trials, both criminal and civil, could often be compelling. The actual course of a trial can be quite unpredictable and usually involves a wide range of emotions. Because I did not want to take too much time away from my administrative duties, I assigned myself to cases that I believed would not last more than three or four weeks. I arranged for Patrick LeSage, my associate chief justice, to preside over the high-profile Bernardo/Homolka trials. These emotionally demanding trials were very challenging, and LeSage handled them with consummate skill.

The responsibilities associated with a jury trial are particularly interesting because it is the judge's duty to assist the jury to reach a fair result while also avoiding any personal bias. The members of all juries are instructed that they are the sole judges of the facts, and strong opinions expressed by a trial judge can often work to the disadvantage of a litigant whom the judge appears to favour.

I played a significant role as chief justice of the Trial Court in forcing the government of Mike Harris to back down from major cuts it had announced in the administration budgets of the courts in Ontario. With regard to the role of judges in speaking out on political matters, I believed that my responsibility was largely restricted to the adequate resourcing of the courts, except in exceptional instances. In this case, as a former Progressive Conservative attorney general in the province, I publicly attacked the proposed budget cuts, which would have done great damage to the effective administration of the courts. Given my previous political association with Premier Harris, my criticism had a non-partisan political dimension – and was successful: in the end, the budget cuts proposed by the Harris government were almost entirely eliminated.

* * *

During my five years on the senior Trial Court in Ontario, I continued to be involved with the Commonwealth, particularly in regard to the momentous developments taking place in South Africa. In the late 1980s, in expectation that Mandela would soon be released, Foreign Minister Joe Clark, acting on behalf of the Mulroney administration, had established the South African Education Trust Fund, a non-government organization to finance the training of non-white citizens in South Africa for major roles in government administration, the media, and the law. I was appointed to the board of the fund and, in that capacity, I hosted Nelson Mandela for part of a day in Toronto during his 1990 visit. I regard Mandela as one of the greatest twentieth-century figures, so this opportunity was a memorable experience for me. In my view, he was probably the only person who could prevent a bloody civil war in South Africa – one that Great Britain and the United States feared was inevitable – and lead the country to a democratic election (as did happen in 1994).

Mandela was particularly interested in the Canadian banking system, which he had identified through research as a possible model for South Africa. I agreed to host a meeting of senior bankers with the future South African president, though I was able to arrange only for senior executives to attend, not bank chairmen. One very senior chairman told me he was puzzled about my invitation because, in his opinion, "Mandela was a communist." Given the complex history from which his country was emerging, it is true that Mandela never denounced the earlier association between his African National Congress and the Communist Party in South Africa. His reluctance was straightforward in that, for a lengthy period, communist parties internationally had been engaged in the fight against apartheid in South Africa to a much greater extent than most of the democratic political parties. In any event, before long, bank chairs and other senior business executives were lining up simply to shake Nelson Mandela's hand.

I remained a member of the board of the South African Education Trust Fund after I became associate chief justice of the Superior Court of Ontario. In that capacity, in 1992 the trust fund arranged for me to do a two-week lecture tour of South Africa to speak to largely black and South Asian lawyers about the creation of the Canadian Charter of Rights and Freedoms and the Canadian experience with the Charter. After Nelson Mandela became president in 1995, the new South African government decided to create a Constitutional Bill of Rights modelled to a great extent on the Canadian Charter – as indeed happened. Mandela's minister of constitutional affairs visited Canada, and, on several occasions, I participated in meetings between him and former Canadian premiers and federal officials to discuss the role of a Charter of Rights in a federal state.

* * *

Until the summer of 1987 I had never taken a holiday committed to painting. The opportunity arose that year when Ria and I agreed that, for the month of August, we would swap our Muskoka Island cottage with Adrienne Clarkson and John Ralston Saul for their villa in Provence. It turned out to be a very successful arrangement for all concerned. The picturesque villa is situated in the small village of Eygalières, which is constructed largely on Roman ruins and surrounded by beautiful landscapes. It is only about 12 kilometres from Saint-Rémy-de-Provence, where Vincent van Gogh was hospitalized for several months towards the end of his life. I painted for many hours every day and returned to my post in London with about three dozen canvases.

In early 1992, after my appointment as associate chief justice of Ontario, I was flattered to be invited by the Whitten Gallery in King City to mount a one-person exhibition. I would need at least fifty paintings to fill the room and was initially reluctant, realizing I might well be parting with some of my favourite works. At the same time, given the relatively high prices dictated of the gallery, I thought there might be embarrassingly few sales. The gallery would receive 40 per cent of the revenue from the sales, and I planned to donate my share to Camp Awakening, a camp for physically challenged children that had been established by my son Harry (chapter 38). The fact that the camp was the principal beneficiary undoubtedly helped to make the exhibition a success. Ria's mother, Jill Macrae, also generously agreed to make a contribution to the Camp Awakening Foundation equal to my share of the sales. As things turned out, this exhibition is the only major sale I ever had for my paintings, though I've donated many dozens to be sold individually at charity auctions. My day job simply has not allowed the significant time required to prepare for another commercial exhibition.

The next year the Koffler Gallery arranged to borrow a number of my paintings for a major retrospective to raise money in support of the gallery. Toronto philanthropists Murray and Marvelle Koffler had built their gallery as part of the North York Jewish Centre, and I was honoured to have my paintings recognized in this fashion. When Lieutenant Governor Hal Jackman opened the exhibition, he referred to his artist friend as "Red Roy," as he has done since my political days at Queen's Park. The organizers invited Canadian art historian Joan Murray, the director of the Robert McLaughlin Gallery in Oshawa, to prepare an introduction for the exhibition brochure. She wrote:

McMurtry has remained the same essential personality: enthusiastic, full of delight over the scene before him, putting it down with a firm no-nonsense hand. Somehow the *joie de vivre* of his painting affects the fluffy Kleenex-like clouds, the idiosyncratic tree forms, the high-keyed colour effects, the careful textures ... It is the zest that he brings to painting that is invaluable. Famed for his desire to learn, it impelled Roy McMurtry to tackle the world before him, and it remained a vital source of energy in his art.

For me, landscape painting has always been a special form of collecting memories. Although a photograph can help, nothing compares with a canvas painted on site. My travels, or "joy rides in a sketch box," have taken me to every province and territory in Canada and, during my years in London, to spots throughout Britain and Ireland. More recently, I've enjoyed painting abroad – including trips to Kranjska Gora in Slovenia, Dubrovnik in Croatia, and Prague in the Czech Republic.

34

Chief Justice of Ontario

I had never had any particular ambition to be appointed chief justice of Ontario, even though two of my recent predecessors in that role – George "Bill" Gale and Willard "Bud" Estey – had also served as chief justice of the Trial Court. In Canada, the chief justice in every province is also by law the chief justice of the Court of Appeal. A provincial chief justice has but one specific statutory authority: to administer the Court of Appeal, including the assignment of judges and the scheduling of court sittings. As the senior judge in each province, however, the chief justice also wields considerable moral authority – for instance, through advocacy for the courts with both the government and the public.

I was reluctant to be a candidate for appointment as chief justice of Ontario for two major reasons. First, I enjoyed my role as chief justice of the Trial Court – in both its administrative and its trial-judge responsibilities (see chapter 33). I knew that, in contrast, there would be far less drama on the Court of Appeal for Ontario (as is its official name): in that court, all the evidence in the overwhelming majority of cases has already been recorded, and written arguments based on the evidence and the law have been filed. As a result, there are few surprises, although the variety of cases heard in any one week is most stimulating. Judges sit in panels of three and hear ten to twelve appeals during the average week (or more than a thousand appeals every year for the court as a whole), though some appeals may require several days of hearings. It is also, for practical purposes, the court of last resort in the province because, of the approximately sixty cases heard each year by the Supreme Court of Canada, fewer than twenty come from Ontario. Fortunately, the record is good: the Court of Appeal for Ontario has in recent decades been highly regarded throughout Canada for the quality of its judgments.

The second reason I hesitated to become chief justice of Ontario was that, at the time Charles Dubin retired, his associate chief justice was John Morden, a brilliant judge and one of my long-time personal friends. I thought it would be very awkward to be appointed over his head, given his obvious qualifications as a judge and the respect his colleagues had for him.

After Dubin announced his retirement in January 1996, a few weeks before his mandatory retirement age of seventy-five, I was approached by a senior trial counsel who was well connected with the federal Liberal government. He advised me that many senior members of the bar were concerned about Dubin's successor, given the apparent antagonistic attitude towards the administration of justice exhibited by the provincial government of Mike Harris. As a result of my successful intervention when Harris tried to implement significant cuts to the administrative budgets for Ontario's courts, many lawyers supporting the federal Liberal government argued that the new chief justice of Ontario should be someone with political as well as judicial experience (chapter 33).

The one mitigating issue for me when I was asked informally whether I would be prepared to serve as the province's chief justice was that Patrick LeSage, another friend of long standing, was my associate chief justice on the Trial Court. I knew that he would be an excellent chief justice on that court, given his many years of judicial service and highly developed people skills. Just at this point I had lunch with two close colleagues, John McMahon and Archie Campbell, and they persuaded me that, because my service as chief justice of Ontario would be important for the administration of justice, it would be inappropriate for me to turn down the opportunity. I was both flattered and influenced by their advocacy, and so when Allan Rock, the minister of justice, called me in February 1996, I advised him that I would be honoured to serve. I was delighted when Rock also said during the same conversation that he would recommend to Prime Minister Chrétien that Patrick LeSage replace me as chief justice of the Trial Court.

I knew Jean Chrétien well from my days as Ontario's attorney general (chapters 21 and 22), and I was aware that, coming as he did from a small city and a non-establishment background in Quebec, he was somewhat sceptical of judicial appointments. Such appointments were, unfortunately, often regarded as a form of sinecure in that province. When Chrétien called me one evening a few days later, he was sitting with his wife, Aline, enjoying a quiet evening at 24 Sussex Drive. We had a brief chat, and he told me that Aline was pleased with my appointment because she believed it would give me more time for my hobby of oil painting. I bit my tongue and simply conveyed my very best wishes to the gracious Mme Chrétien.

After my appointment was announced publicly the following day, I arranged to meet with the members of the Court of Appeal. I was somewhat apprehensive because I recognized the strong feeling of loyalty to John Morden and realized there could well be some resentment about my appointment. In my opening remarks, I therefore referred to my long friendship with Morden and my high regard for him. I assured my new colleagues that Morden would continue to have a major role in the administration of the court. As things turned out, he served as my associate chief justice of Ontario for more than three years, and I never for a moment doubted his loyalty and support.

* * *

My major challenge in taking over the reins of the Court of Appeal was the unacceptable backlog in the hearing of appeals. A well-established oral tradition in the court made it difficult to establish time limits for oral arguments in each appeal. Still, it was obvious that, if the large backlog was to be reduced, more appeals had to be heard every week. After a little acrimonious debate, I managed to implement time limits on arguments, more appeals were heard, and, over the next two or three years, the backlog was eliminated – from a three-year wait to an acceptable five or six months. Ultimately these reforms were carried out with the strong support of the legal profession.

The assignment of judges to specific appeals is a sensitive human issue: it is essential that the members of the court believe that the chief justice is not assigning "favourites" to the more interesting cases. I established a system in which cases were assigned randomly, with some exceptions in complex cases to provide the appropriate expertise. This decision was more common sense than science: a chief justice has to be constantly aware of individual egos when dealing with highly competent judges. In addition, I scheduled monthly court meetings to discuss relevant issues relating to the work of the court and as a way of keeping in constant contact with the individual judges.

There are no specific guidelines with respect to the general role of a provincial chief justice. John Cartwright, the chief justice of the Supreme Court of Canada for six years after 1964, referred to the judiciary as the "silent service," meaning that judges should communicate to the public through their decisions and not from public platforms. In the seventeenth century Francis Bacon, the English Lord Chancellor, memorably described "much-talking judges" as "ill-tuned cymbals." Another traditional, well-established principle holds that judges never publicly discuss a decision after it has been delivered. Because judge-made law is based on precedent, the integrity of the process would become chaotic if a judge's decision was reviewed in the context of any explanation given by the judge outside the actual words in the decision.

In Canada, it is also generally understood that judges should never express publicly any views relating to politically partisan issues. Such commentary could seriously undermine the appearance of judicial impartiality – the core principle of judicial conduct. There is one exception, however: a chief justice may be required to express concerns about the underfunding of the administration of justice by the government of the day. In all other respects, judges not serving as chief justices are generally reluctant to agree to media interviews. Although I rarely gave interviews to journalists, simply because they were usually interested in some controversy in which a chief justice should not become involved, I did give a number of public addresses every year with respect to issues of more general importance to the administration of justice. I believed that the judiciary as an institution should not appear to be too remote from the public.

When I became the provincial chief justice, I revived a tradition instituted by Chief Justice William Howland, but abandoned by his successor Charles Dubin, and chaired a formal opening of the courts every year. These openings were attended by the majority of the judges, many justices of the peace and masters, and many members of the legal profession. I was joined on the court dais by the chief justice of the Superior Court and the chief justice of the Ontario Court of Justice. First I gave a brief report on the work of the Court of Appeal, including some observations about the administration of justice in Ontario in general. The other chief justices followed with their own reports.

Although I retain the greatest of respect for my predecessors as chief justice, I believed that the office could be used more effectively to advocate issues within the legal profession, such as pro bono work, that would serve both the members of the profession in particular and the community in general. The actual ceremony to mark the opening of the Ontario courts was preceded by a morning press conference that was open to any member of the media. There, journalists could ask each of the chief justices searching and tough questions – a process that, in my view, added greatly to the transparency of the courts. Their questions covered a wide range and were often influenced by current controversies related to the justice system. The reporters usually addressed funding issues as well as trial delays, both legitimate issues of public interest, and, in general, stirred up controversies, particularly if they involved government action or inaction. In my eleven years as chief justice of the province, I never cancelled one of these news conferences. My successor as chief justice continued the annual formal opening of the courts, but discontinued the press conference. An editorial in the *Toronto Star* in September 2009 commented as follows:

In previous years McMurtry not only delivered his verdict on the state of the courts, he also invited journalists to pose questions to him and the other leading judges.

It was a refreshing departure from the customary remoteness of senior judges. McMurtry descended from the mount, as it were, to take questions and expound on the strengths and the weaknesses of the justice system.

In doing so McMurtry added transparency, accountability and credibility to his position by shedding light on the workings of this very important branch of government.

An important responsibility for provincial and federal chief justices is membership on the Canadian Judicial Council, which meets twice a year. The council's many committees, which meet more often, cover most of the issues related to the administration of justice in Canada, including the important task of dealing with complaints from the public with respect to the conduct of federally appointed judges. In the committees on which I sat, I found that ethical issues relating to the role of judges in their communities were frequent topics of discussion. Judges cannot, for instance, be members of political parties or contribute financially to them, and their role with respect to charities is quite complicated. We agreed that, in the interests of maintaining the essential appearance of judicial impartiality, judges should not attempt to raise money, especially for political candidates. As an amateur artist, however, I felt free to contribute paintings to charity auctions, just as I also continued to make personal donations to charities of my choosing.

The size of the community in which judges live becomes relevant to their personal activities. In larger cities, judges are usually anonymous, but in smaller centres they are usually well-known local citizens. As such, their behaviour is carefully scrutinized. The level of public confidence in the administration of justice is very much related to judicial accountability. The great majority of complaints against individual judges come from unsuccessful litigants. However, occasionally there are serious complaints, which are closely analysed by members of the Canadian Judicial Council.

Fortunately, during my lifetime, these complaints have never been related to an allegation of judicial dishonesty in the conduct of a case. Rather, most of them result from a judge's significant lack of courtesy or simply plain rudeness.

The legal profession has experienced tremendous growth since I became a lawyer, with almost 45,000 licensed lawyers in Ontario at present. These greater numbers have made it a less collegial profession, as it becomes impossible to maintain the same degree of familiarity among lawyers that existed before. One result has been that the Law Society of Upper Canada, the governing branch of the legal profession, has become concerned about the increasing lack of civility among many lawyers, particularly among those representing different interests. When I became the province's chief justice, I was approached by the head of the Law Society, Robert Armstrong, later a colleague on the Court of Appeal, and other senior members of the profession to discuss how best to strengthen the concept of professionalism. I agreed with one suggestion in particular – to establish a Chief Justice of Ontario Advisory Committee on Professionalism – and in due course the committee was implemented. The Law Society began to deliver education programs to stress the importance of civility as a core element of professionalism.

Public respect for the law, particularly among young people, was also a personal concern for me. As chief justice, I wished to create a greater educational component for young people as they visited courthouses throughout Ontario. For some years, for instance, students had been attending courts with their teachers and spending short periods of time in courtrooms. I felt that this experience was essentially superficial because no one was present to explain to the students the relevance of what they witnessed, particularly given the slow pace of most trials. I therefore instituted the Courtrooms and Classrooms project, in which judges and lawyers met with the students before the court proceedings began. We soon discovered that these legal professionals were anxious to volunteer and that their interaction with our visitors provided a much more meaningful experience. Before long, the project was extended to courtrooms throughout Ontario.

Buoyed by this success, in 2001 I created and chaired the Ontario Justice Education Network (OJEN). We established a summer institute to assist teachers who taught law courses in high schools and met in major cities throughout the province for several days every August. Judges and lawyers delivered lectures on the law and we provided written materials to assist the teachers in their classrooms. In addition to the courtroom visits, we expanded the mock-trials program throughout the province. Realizing that many young people do not take law courses in school, OJEN partnered with many youth centres, boys and girls clubs, and after-school programs. The network has also identified a need to provide youth workers with basic information about the operation of the justice system. These programs are of particular importance to young people who are disadvantaged or from visible minorities and who harbour negative images of the justice system. They often have a deep mistrust of authority and believe that the system is biased, racist, or exclusionary.

It has long been my view that our society should not take public support of the justice system for granted. It is the bedrock of any democracy, and continuing public education is essential for its strength. I find it encouraging that many hundreds of lawyers, judges, and others who volunteer for participation in OJEN's programs share this same opinion.

Another priority for me outside my responsibilities for the Court of Appeal was to participate in the creation of Pro Bono Law Ontario in 2002. Although many lawyers have traditionally provided legal assistance without a fee, it has always occurred on an ad hoc basis. Initiatives here have also lagged behind similar programs in the United States because Canadian fee-for-service legal aid services have traditionally been more generously funded than those in place south of the border. Although the legal aid clinics movement is reasonably well entrenched in Ontario, access to justice in the future can only be improved if this model is dramatically expanded (chapter 38). The Canadian Bar Association (CBA) has passed resolutions encouraging lawyers to contribute a percentage of their time to pro bono work, an initiative I wholeheartedly and publicly supported, but they have had little impact in Ontario. My support was not endorsed by some members of the bar, who suggested that, in promoting pro bono work, I was indirectly encouraging the Ontario government to underfund the legal aid fee-for-service program.

Unfortunately, no provincial government will ever be able adequately to fund an aid plan that is able to address all the legal needs of the poor and disadvantaged. It was therefore essential, in my view, that a formal pro bono program be created that would have the support of the legal profession. And, to attract lawyers to pro bono projects, it was essential that law firms give them financial credit for the hours they spent on these initiatives – that those hours be counted as part of their annual billable hours. As part of my strategy, I encouraged law-school deans to advocate the value of pro bono work to their students. The result over time has been that many law firms did come to realize that pro bono initiatives could help them to recruit the most outstanding students.

As chief justice, I was invited to a number of breakfasts attended by the managing partners of the larger law firms. These events provided a platform for "missionary work" on behalf of Pro Bono Law Ontario. Many Ontario law firms are now supporting this program, though there is still some distance to go. For many lawyers, legal practice has become more of a business than a profession, but for others, and for me, assisting the most vulnerable in society is very much related to the soul of our profession. After retiring as chief justice, I remained active in the affairs of Pro Bono Law Ontario and the Ontario Justice Education Network. I believe that both initiatives have become important aspects of the Ontario legal landscape and will remain so. Obviously it is important to the credibility of the legal profession for the public to know of lawyers' voluntary work in the community.

Another aspect of my role as chief justice that I particularly enjoyed was my relationship with my fellow judges on all the courts of the province. I do not recall any particularly challenging personal issues on the Court of Appeal – in my years there the judges on the court were highly intelligent and well motivated, and the occasional antagonisms that surfaced were resolved or at least ameliorated through civil discussion. The quality of the court collectively created a natural and dynamic peer pressure simply because all its members wished to have the respect of their colleagues. Although there were some disputes, as can be expected in any human institution, they never disrupted the work or the quality of our decision making.

I was also blessed with the succession of three very fine associate chief justices – John Morden, Coulter Osborne, and Dennis O'Connor –

all of whom shared the administrative burden. They enjoyed my total confidence and contributed greatly to maintaining the court as the most respected provincial appellate court in Canada.

The major priority for me was to have some influence in the quality of appointments to our court. In this context, I was most fortunate to have a positive personal relationship with each of the four Liberal ministers of justice who were in office during my years as chief justice – Allan Rock, Anne McLellan, Martin Cauchon, and Irwin Cotler. All those ministers were committed to the principle of high-quality appointments rather than political supporters of the government. In the course of these eleven years there were fifteen appointments to the twenty-four-member Ontario Court of Appeal. Three of them had been law-school deans, six were women, and two were the first from their particular racial group to be appointed to an appellate court in Canada – the first Aboriginal and the first South Asian.

The high degree of collegiality on the Ontario Court of Appeal was somewhat related to its size. Decisions are made by three-member panels, and the decision binds all other members of the court. Occasionally the court will revisit a decision when there may be a credible issue about the correctness of the case, and a five-person panel is appointed to review the particular law that has been engaged. The composition of the panels varies every week. As a result, when every member of the court generally sits on each panel hearing appeals, as in the Supreme Court of Canada, tensions are less likely. Sitting together regularly on the same panel can, of course, produce a degree of stress given the disagreements that are a natural dimension of the decision-making process.

* * *

Occasionally I received requests at the Court of Appeal to televise the arguments of a case that had wide public interest, and I always agreed. One such case related to French-language resources in an Ottawa hospital that served a large Franco-Ontarian population. The court ruled in favour of requiring French-language services.

As a trial chief justice, however, I had very different views about the presence of TV cameras in a trial courtroom. I believed then and still do that cameras can be an unnecessary distraction for the participants, and particularly for witnesses testifying in the proceedings. In the United States there have been instances where irresponsible television coverage has led to riots, particularly in race-related cases where a jury's decision appears to conflict with the evidence seen and heard on television. Although such incidents have been uncommon, the US federal trial courts disallow the presence of TV cameras in its courts, but state trial courts may permit the televising of proceedings. Over the years, this issue has been the subject of many debates in Canada, but, generally, the exclusion of TV cameras in the trial courts has been maintained.

* * *

I had the privilege of sitting on many interesting and important cases during the more than eleven years that I was a member of the Court of Appeal. For the purposes of this memoir, I would make reference to only two of those major cases, *Halpern v. The Attorney-General of Canada* (the same-sex marriage case) and the Steven Truscott case. The *Halpern* case involved many parties and interveners who had a legitimate point of view to argue before the court. The conviction of Steven Truscott for murder in 1959 had been a matter of public controversy for many decades, including its treatment in published books and in television documentaries.

In the *Halpern* appeal, the attorney general of Canada opposed same-sex marriage as a constitutional entitlement, and the attorney general of Ontario took no position. The federal Canadian Human Rights Commission supported same-sex marriage. I heard several motions brought by organizations wanting to participate in the appeal on both sides, and I gave them all intervener status, even though the federal government argued vociferously against granting status to groups who supported same-sex marriage.

Our decision in *Halpern* noted that the definition of marriage in Canada had been based on the classic formulation by Lord Penzance in the English case of *Hyde v. Hyde* in 1866: "I conceive that marriage, as understood in Christendom, may for this purpose be defined as the voluntary union for life of one man and one woman to the exclusion of all others." Two important facts should be noted in this definition: it is judge-made law in the United Kingdom and not reflected in any Canadian statute; and the reference to "Christendom" defines "marriage" essentially as a tenet of the Christian faith. The central issue in the *Halpern* appeal was whether the exclusion of same-sex couples from the common-law definition of marriage breached the equality section 15(1) of the Canadian Charter of Rights and Freedoms in a manner, under section 1 of the Charter, "that is not justified in a free and democratic society."

In our thirty-nine-page decision, although we recognized that the appeal raised significant constitutional issues, we wrote that "this case is ultimately about the recognition and protection of human dignity and equality in the context of social structure available to conjugal couples in Canada." In the case of *Law v. Canada* (1999), Justice Iacobucci, writing for a unanimous Supreme Court of Canada, stated: "Human dignity means that an individual or group feels self-respect and self-worth … Human dignity is harmed when individuals and groups are marginalized, ignored or devalued and is enhanced when laws recognize the full place of all individuals and groups within Canadian society." Our court also noted that the Ontario Human Rights Code stated that "it is public policy in Ontario to recognize the dignity and worth of every person."

In response, many of the critics of the *Halpern* decision state that it undermined or denigrated the importance of heterosexual marriage in Canada. In this context, however, our decision noted:

Marriage is, without dispute, one of the most significant forms of personal relationship and for centuries marriage has been an element of social organization in societies around the world.

Through the institution of marriage, individuals can publicly express their love and commitment to each other. Through this institution, society publicly recognizes expressions of love and commitment between individuals, granting them respect and legitimacy as a couple. This public recognition and sanction of marital relationships reflect society's approbations of the personal hopes, desires and aspirations that underlie loving, committed conjugal relationships that can only enhance an individual's sense of self-worth and dignity.

The ability to marry, and to thereby participate in this fundamental societal institution, is something that most Canadians take for granted. Same-sex couples do not; they are denied access to this institution simply on the basis of their sexual orientation.

A law that prohibits same-sex couples from marrying does not accord with the needs, capacities and circumstance of same-sex couples. While it is true that, due to biological realities, only opposite-sex couples can "naturally" procreate, same-sex couples can choose to have children by other means, such as adoption, surrogacy and donor insemination. An increasing percentage of children are being conceived and raised by same-sex couples.

In our view, the critical question to be asked was whether opposite-sex couples were in a more advantaged position than same-sex couples.

We noted that, historically, same-sex couples as a group had experienced a great deal of discrimination and many disadvantages and that, without question, opposite-sex couples are the more advantaged group. The existing legal definition of marriage was clearly discriminatory in relation to same-sex couples because it restricted their access to a fundamental social institution. Exclusion only perpetuated the view that same-sex marriages are less worthy of recognition than opposite-sex relationships. In this way the existing legal definition of marriage offended the dignity of persons in same-sex relationships and therefore offended the equality section 15(1) of the Charter.

The attorney general of Canada argued that, if its submissions were rejected and the common-law definition of marriage was found by our court to be unconstitutional, our declaration should be suspended for two years to give the Canadian Parliament the opportunity to consider the issue. Our court did in fact declare the existing definition of marriage to be invalid, to the extent that it referred only to "one man and one woman." We reformulated the definition of marriage as "the voluntary union for life of two persons to the exclusion of all others." Our decision was released on June 10, 2003, and was to take effect immediately. Later the same morning, a same-sex male couple were married at Toronto's City Hall. The federal government of Jean Chrétien was placed under considerable pressure to appeal our decision to the Supreme Court of Canada, but it did not take that step. In the following months and years when Chrétien and I were together at some function, he would often say, "I appoint McMurtry chief justice of Ontario and he bring me the same-sex marriage decision."

The *Halpern* decision was roundly condemned by Stephen Harper, who at that time was leader of the official opposition in Ottawa, and continues to provoke controversy. Harper criticized the Liberal government for having appointed a series of liberal judges who, in turn, produced the *Halpern* decision. When a member of the media reminded him that I had been a Cabinet minister in the Ontario Progressive Conservative government of Bill Davis, he replied that I was not a true conservative. When it comes to small "c" conservative political philosophy, he is probably correct. I have always been uncomfortable with political labels and think of myself as a political pragmatist and a "Red Tory" with a particular interest in social justice. I can only speculate as to whether my role in the *Halpern* decision helped to influence him when he removed the word "Progressive" from the name of the federal party.

No major newspapers opposed our decision in their editorials, though the *Globe and Mail* criticized us strongly for not suspending implementation for a time to allow the issue to be debated in the federal Parliament. This major national newspaper did not disagree with the actual reformulation of the definition of marriage, but on at least two occasions it did editorialize that our decision was "reckless." In taking this course, we followed a decision, *Schacter v. Canada* (1992), of Chief Justice Lamer in the Supreme Court of Canada in which he outlined three steps to be followed in determining the remedy for a Charter breach, including a temporary suspension of the remedy. Our decision not to suspend the remedy clearly fell within Lamer's suggested approach, particularly as the Charter challenge was to a common-law judge-made law and *not* to a legislative provision. Chief Justice Lamer also stated that suspending a declaration of invalidity is warranted only in limited instances, such as where striking down the law poses a potential danger to the public, threatens the rule of law, or has the effect of denying deserving persons of benefits of the impugned law. The *Halpern* case clearly did not fall within the limited instances outlined by Chief Justice Lamer. For that reason, the members of our court wrote that "an immediate declaration will simply ensure that opposite sex couples and same sex couples immediately receive equal treatment in law in accordance with s.15 (1) of the Charter."

I have never understood the alleged value of a parliamentary debate on the issue: Parliament cannot invalidate constitutional decisions of the courts except for a limited period. For me and my colleagues, it was simply time for Canadian society to get beyond the issue of same-sex marriage and to see that the "sky wasn't falling." Certainly it was a non-issue to the great majority of younger people, and the rest of society would come to appreciate its fundamental fairness for same-sex couples.

A few months later, the Supreme Court of Massachusetts legalized same-sex marriage, quoting our decision with approval. A noted columnist in the *New Yorker* magazine also wrote that our decision in *Halpern* "made him proud to be a North American." Most surprisingly of all, at the end of 2003 the *Globe and Mail* editorial board named our panel of judges on the *Halpern* appeal – Eileen Gillese, Jim MacPherson, and me – as the newspaper's "Nation Builders of the Year."

Most encouraging of all, in the years that have elapsed since the *Halpern* decision, I have met many same-sex couples who have chosen to be married and many who have not, but who equally value the decision for validating their relationship in the context of their dignity and self-respect. Although hostility and discrimination towards the gay and lesbian community has diminished considerably in recent years in the West, it is still a reality in much of the rest of the world. In Canada it has only been in recent years that the opposition to discriminatory practices related to our gay and lesbian populations has become a real part of our mainstream dialogue. Legislation to prohibit discrimination on the basis of sexual orientation was regrettably delayed for many years.

During my decade as attorney general between 1975 and 1985, for instance, I don't recall any debate or questions with respect to discrimination on the basis of sexual orientation. The issue simply did not appear on the political radar screen. One possible reason was suggested by Professor Miriam Smith in her seminal article "Lesbian and Gay Rights in Canada: Social Movement and Equality Seeking, 1971–1995": "In the wake of the murder of Toronto Shoe Shine boy Emmanuel Jacques in 1977," she wrote, "the city was gripped by Homophobia, stirred up by the mainstream press which depicted the murder as the result of homosexual depravity." If this explanation is correct, the public attitude that related the activities of a few violent pedophiles directly to the gay community was clearly irrational. The crimes of the brutal serial killer Paul Bernardo were never described as "the result of heterosexual depravity."

Progress in relation to gay and lesbian rights in the political and legal arenas was painfully slow in Canada in the pre-Charter years. In fact, Quebec was the only province that had listed sexual orientation as a prohibited ground of discrimination in its Human Rights Code before the entrenchment of the Charter in 1982. But even after the Charter, there was no progress on the issue of sexual orientation in the rest of Canada. Indeed, when a proposed amendment to include sexual orientation within the Charter as a prohibited ground of discrimination came before the Justice Committee of Parliament in 1981, it was overwhelmingly defeated, with little public reaction. It was not until 1998 that the Supreme Court of Canada read in sexual orientation as an analogous ground similar to race, religion, and sex in the Charter equality section 15(1). This decision meant that section 15 would be interpreted, applied, and administered as though it contained sexual orientation as a prohibited ground of discrimination. Discrimination on the basis of sexual orientation had already been included in most provincial Human Rights Codes, but it was not until 1996 that a similar amendment was made to the Canadian Human Rights Code.

The decision in *Halpern* that ensured that opposite-sex couples and same-sex couples receive equal treatment in relation to marriage provoked further strident debate about the role of judges in policymaking in a democratic society. In my view, however, Canada has a responsibility to be more aggressive internationally in advocating for equal rights for gays and lesbians. There are many international forums, including the Commonwealth, where Canada should be heard on this issue – one that is of critical importance to the lives of millions of people.

* * *

For my colleagues and I, the *Halpern* decision was an obvious one given the jurisprudence developed under the Charter of Rights. Soon after, as I usually did, I attended the annual Law Society reception for gay lawyers. The combination of the decision and the reception proved too much for some members of the anti-gay community, and I received several items of hate mail from people who saw our decision as an attack on the institution of marriage. This hostility brought back unwelcome memories of the homophobic allegations that had been made against me more than twenty years earlier after the bathhouse raids (see chapter 19).

About the time of my retirement as chief justice of Ontario I was contacted by Gerald Hannon, a well-known gay journalist who was also an instructor in journalism at Ryerson University. He wanted to do an interview with me about my relationship with the gay and lesbian community over the years, beginning with my time as attorney general. Somewhat to Hannon's surprise, I agreed to what turned out to be a very long interview, resulting in his five-page article in *XTRA*, Toronto's lesbian and gay bi-weekly, on October 11, 2007. The opening page began with several headlines: "In June the Gay Community Paid Tribute to Retiring Chief Justice Roy McMurtry ... 25 years ago we burned him in effigy ... How did the most despised politician in the Legislature come to bask in our standing ovations? ... Roy's Resurrection."

The background to the "standing ovations" was that, when I retired as a judge, my relationship with the lesbian and gay community had improved to the extent that they arranged a reception to raise money for the McMurtry Gardens of Justice – a sculpture garden created by the legal profession in my honour. My eminent lawyer friend Clayton Ruby was quoted at length in the article. His first comment was not flattering: "McMurtry enthusiastically supported the bath-house raids prosecutors ... I don't think he initiated the raids but he prosecuted and it was horrible and mean and nasty for a lot of people." He then went on to state more positively: "He's changed, and not many of us change. He's turned into a Red Tory saint, he's done wonderful stuff, he's tough minded and is radical as you can get." Senior lawyer Howard Morton, who in the 1980s was in charge of criminal appeals, reflected in the article that many of the lawyers in the Ministry of the Attorney General reflected "a general homophobic state of mind." He also stated that "if Roy McMurtry hadn't been Attorney General you would have seen a much greater homophobic push coming from the Ministry. If anything, he was a tempering force."

In 2009 the Sexual Orientation and Gender Identity Section of the Canadian Bar Association presented me with its Ally Award. It all goes to prove that public life is indeed unpredictable.

* * *

One of the most complex criminal appeals that I and four of my colleagues heard during my years on the Court of Appeal for Ontario was that concerning the murder conviction of Steven Truscott. This case was referred to our court by Irwin Cotler, the federal minister of justice, in October 2004. The *Truscott* decision is undoubtedly the best known and most controversial murder case in Canada's history.

In 1959, fourteen-year-old Steven Truscott was charged with the murder of his twelve-year-old classmate Lynne Harper on June 9 of that year in Clinton, Ontario. He maintained his innocence from the outset, though he did not testify at his trial. After a two-day preliminary hearing the following month, Truscott was committed for trial. The trial began on September 16 at the Goderich courthouse before Mr Justice Ferguson and a jury. On September 30 the jury returned a verdict of guilty, with a recommendation for mercy. The trial judge sentenced the appellant to death by hanging, as was then required by the *Criminal Code*. An appeal of the verdict to the Court of Appeal for Ontario was unanimously dismissed. On January 21, 1960, the federal Cabinet ordered that the appellant's death sentence be commuted to life imprisonment.

An interesting comment on the different style of advocacy in place in 1959 is the speed with which the trial proceeded and the fact that it lasted only twelve days – both factors that were not at all unusual at the time. The Crown prosecutor called some sixty witnesses, and Frank Donnelly, the counsel for Truscott, called fourteen in all. Truscott himself did not testify at his trial. Donnelly was the most highly respected defence counsel in the Goderich area and later became a High Court judge.

On February 9, 1960, the appellant applied to the Supreme Court of Canada for leave to appeal the conviction, but his request was refused. There is no automatic right of appeal, even in a capital murder case.

Six years after the conviction, Isabel LeBourdais, a journalist, published *The Trial of Steven Truscott*, a book that sparked widespread debate about the propriety of Truscott's conviction. Given the extent of the controversy, the federal government made a special reference to the Supreme Court of Canada with the question: "What disposition would the court have made of such an appeal on a consideration of the existing record and such further evidence as the court in its discretion may receive and consider?"

In October 1966 the Supreme Court heard the testimony of sixteen witnesses called by counsel on behalf of Truscott and nine witnesses on behalf of the Crown. The testimonies of those witnesses were in addition to the written record of the trial. Truscott testified publicly for the first time at this hearing. In a decision released on May 4, 1967, the majority of the court (Justice Emmett Hall dissenting) concluded that had a formal appeal of the case been heard by the court, it would have dismissed the appeal.

Steven Truscott served most of his sentence while a minor at the Ontario Training School for Boys in Guelph. At the age of eighteen he was transferred to Collins Bay Penitentiary, where he remained until he was released on parole in October 1969. On November 12, 1974, he was granted relief from the conditions of his parole for good behaviour and has not had any other involvement with the law since his release from prison at the age of twenty-four. By all accounts, he has been a responsible and productive member of the community.

On November 28, 2001, counsel on behalf of Truscott applied to the federal minister of justice in relation to a provision of the *Criminal Code* that allowed for review of a conviction to determine if there was a reasonable basis to conclude that a miscarriage of justice had likely occurred. On January 24, 2002, the minister retained Fred Kaufman, a retired member of the Quebec Court of Appeal, to carry out the review. Kaufman and his counsel, Mark Sandler, interviewed a number of witnesses, some of whom had testified for the prosecution at the trial. His detailed report, which was provided to the minister in April 2004, concluded that "there is clearly a reasonable basis for concluding that a miscarriage of justice … likely occurred."

On October 28, 2004, the minister referred the *Truscott* case to the Court of Appeal for Ontario to determine a decision, based on the existing evidentiary record and any other evidence we felt fit to consider, as though it were an appeal on the issue of fresh evidence. In December of that same year our court decided that the Kaufman report would not be part of the court record before us because his investigation and report were not subject to the rules of evidence and admissibility that apply on an appeal. However, the transcripts of some of the witnesses who testified before Kaufman were admitted, as were other statements agreed to by counsel for both Truscott and the Crown. The parties also tendered as fresh evidence a vast amount of material, including hundreds of documents from the Archives of Ontario, the archives of the Ontario Provincial Police, the original court files, and the files of others involved in the case, including those of Dr John Peniston, the man who performed the autopsy on Lynne Harper's body.

The bald facts of the case could be summarized briefly. Between approximately 7:00 pm and 7:30 pm on June 9, 1959, Steven Truscott was seen riding with Lynne Harper on his bicycle. Close to midnight that evening, Lynne was reported missing. Two days later her partially nude body was found in a wooded area known locally as Lawson's Bush. She had been sexually assaulted.

The Crown's case at trial, in the view of our court, rested on four main evidentiary pillars. The first consisted of the pathologist's evidence that Lynne had died between 7:00 pm and 7:45 pm on June 9. Dr Peniston's evidence depended on his observations of the stomach contents of the body. This evidence was extremely crucial for the prosecution.

The second pillar involved witnesses who had seen Lynne riding with Truscott on his bicycle shortly after 7:00 pm in the location of Lawson's Bush, where Lynne's body was discovered. This area was a short distance away from the school grounds, where several children testified that Truscott had returned about 8:00 pm. The prosecution urged the jury to find that Truscott had remained in the bush for some three-quarters of an hour, giving him ample time to commit the crime.

The third pillar was the evidence called to demonstrate the physical impossibility of Truscott being able to see Lynne getting into a late-model Chevrolet with a yellow licence plate, shortly before 8:00 pm, as claimed by him. The fourth pillar related to medical evidence of two large lesions on the sides of Truscott's penis which, in the opinion of the prosecution, were between two and four days old and could have been caused by the sexual assault of a young girl.

As we reviewed all this information, we found there was conflicting evidence at trial about the sightings of Truscott by various witnesses between 7:00 pm and 8:00 pm on June 9, 1959. However, my brief review here does not attempt to outline the evidence at trial in a comprehensive fashion, nor do I think it necessary to outline the evidence adduced at the reference to the Supreme Court of Canada in 1966. In referring the matter to our court in 2004, the minister of justice stated that he was "satisfied that there is a reasonable basis to conclude a miscarriage of justice likely occurred in this case." In our decision, we wrote that the minister's assessment of the new evidence could not influence our ultimate decision of whether there had been a miscarriage of justice. Furthermore, the reference was limited to "the issue of fresh evidence," and we were not asked to opine on the reasonableness of the results in the earlier proceedings. However, the fresh evidence had to be considered in the context of the entire record of the proceedings.

Three highly qualified medical experts gave evidence, supported by recent scientific research, before us. In our view, in light of the scientific evidence, Dr Peniston's crucial evidence at trial, providing a forty-five-minute window during which the death occurred, had to be rejected as scientifically unsupportable. We also emphasized that it was the Crown's theory, presented at trial, that Truscott would have had to murder Lynne before he returned to the school grounds no later than 8:15 pm. Truscott's lawyers also discovered two unofficial versions of Dr Peniston's autopsy report which contained statements to the effect that Lynne's death could have occurred at a much later time than that he testified to at trial.

It's not necessary here to review the other evidence heard or reviewed by us. Suffice it to say that it cast some doubt on the other three pillars of the Crown's case. Our reasons ran to over 300 pages in our decision, and our analysis of the evidence was highly detailed and somewhat complex.

The appeal was heard over ten days in early 2007, and we released our decision on August 28 of that year. In our opinion, the key pillar of the prosecution's case was the expert evidence that Lynne must have died before 8:00 pm on June 9, and our finding that this evidence was scientifically untenable removed that key pillar. We concluded that, "while it cannot be said that no jury acting judicially could reasonably convict," we felt that, "if a new trial were possible, an acquittal would clearly be the more likely result." We therefore decided that, "having

regard to the highly unusual circumstances of the reference ... we have
determined that the most appropriate remedy is to enter an acquittal."

* * *

The acquittal by the Court of Appeal for Ontario led to the final public
chapter in the Truscott saga – his application made immediately after
our decision to the Ontario government for compensation. In Canada
there is no legal entitlement to compensation for a wrongful conviction unless a wrongfully convicted person can establish a civil cause of
action – as for malicious prosecution, negligent investigation, or other
prosecution misconduct. The Court of Appeal did not attribute blame
to anyone responsible for the investigation and prosecution of Stephen
Truscott.

Immediately following our decision, Michael Bryant, the Ontario attorney general, retained the Honourable Sydney Robins to provide advice and recommendations on whether compensation ought to be paid
to Truscott and his family – and, if so, in what amount. Robins was a
much respected lawyer and judge on both the Trial Court and Court of
Appeal for Ontario. We served together on the Appeal Court for five
years and, in my view, Bryant made an excellent choice in appointing
Robins for this review.

In his report, Robins noted that "in recent years there has been a
growing recognition in Canada and elsewhere that persons who have
been wrongfully convicted and imprisoned should receive compensation from the state." However, given that there is no legal entitlement
in Canada to compensation except through a civil action, it can be obtained only by a voluntary payment by the state. Although many international bodies and legal scholars have expressed opinions on the
appropriate criteria for compensation, no legislation has been passed
in Canada.

In his report, Robins referred to our Court of Appeal decision where
we declined to issue a declaration of Truscott's innocence while stating
that proof of innocence as a practical matter would be impossible for
him to establish. He was also clearly concerned that the lapse of time
made a new trial impossible and that Truscott would never "have the
opportunity to seek factual vindication and will never be able to establish conclusively that he did not commit the offence." The reality is that,
in the absence of conclusive DNA evidence, very few persons charged
with a criminal offence will ever have the opportunity of conclusively
establishing their innocence. Robins decided that, "given the very un-

usual circumstances of the case," and in the context of our decision, "if a hearing could be held to determine Mr. Truscott's innocence, it would be more likely than not that he would be found, on a balance of probabilities, to be innocent in fact." Not surprisingly, he placed great importance on our court's statement in paragraph 3 of our decision that, "if a new trial were possible, an acquittal would clearly be the likely result."

Robins recommended to the attorney general that Truscott be granted compensation. In determining the amount, he wrote: "In short Mr. Truscott and his family have lived their lives for almost 50 years in the shadow of his murder conviction. There is no question but that Mr. Truscott's conviction, incarceration and parole forever altered his life. For nearly 50 years he bore the stigma of being a convicted rapist and murderer of a 12 year old girl. I would not presume to minimize his suffering." In his view, "the aim of such an award is to provide Mr. Truscott with the amount needed for him to live the rest of his life in financial security." He did not attempt to separate various heads of damages, as would occur in a traditional civil lawsuit, but simply chose a figure for a global award that "reflects and provides a measure of compensation for the hardship caused by the wrongful conviction and the public recognition of the seriousness of the wrong suffered by Mr. Truscott."

At the same time, Robins "recognized that no amount of money can erase the ordeal Mr. Truscott has suffered … or turn the clock back and give Mr. Truscott his life to live over … Any attempt to place a dollar value on such suffering is quixotic at best … and … no money can provide time restitution." He also acknowledged the "mental terror for a 14 year old boy being sentenced to death and being denied the normal opportunities for emotional and social development through his adolescence and young adulthood. He was also affectively denied a secondary and post secondary education; and a family life over the years … His very personality was changed by his years in incarceration."

In concluding his report, Robins recommended compensation to Steven Truscott of $6.5 million, to be paid by the provincial and federal governments in equal amounts.

* * *

Shortly before my retirement as chief justice of Ontario, I agreed to what turned out to be long interviews with two journalists who specialized in legal matters – Tracey Tyler of the *Toronto Star* and Kirk Makin of the *Globe and Mail*. (Sadly, Tracey Tyler, a fine journalist with a comprehensive understanding of the administration of justice, died of cancer during the summer of 2012.) Both of them asked me to talk about who, in my opinion, should succeed me in the role of chief justice. Given what happened, it might have been better not to have responded to the questions at all.

The other members of the Court of Appeal and I all thought that my successor should be Associate Chief Justice Dennis O'Connor – and I gave his name in answer to the reporters' questions. He was not appointed. O'Connor is widely respected as one of Canada's finest lawyers and judges. He enjoyed a most interesting and eclectic career as a lawyer in Toronto, magistrate in the Yukon, law teacher, senior counsel, and litigator before his appointment to the Court of Appeal. The great irony related to his rejection as chief justice of Ontario was his enormous success as the commissioner appointed in June 2000 to inquire into the deaths of seven local residents in Walkerton, Ontario, caused by contamination in the town's water supply. His involvement in the Walkerton inquiry came at the request of Jim Flaherty, the attorney general in the Ontario government of Mike Harris. O'Connor was very enthusiastic about undertaking the assignment, and I gladly agreed to his appointment.

Given the undisputed facts of the process in place at the Walkerton water-treatment plant, it was inevitable that the O'Connor Report would be critical of the provincial government for not regulating water quality sufficiently and not enforcing the existing guidelines. In addition, the Premier's Office was annoyed that Harris himself was called as a witness at the inquiry. When the two-volume O'Connor Report, published in 2002, led to some negative political fallout for the provincial government, Flaherty was, according to reports, angered by this outcome.

As things happened, the Ontario government had been represented at the inquiry by members of the Gowlings law firm, which some years later I joined after I retired as chief justice. Once there, I learned that the Gowlings legal counsel had always thought that the O'Connor inquiry was conducted in a very fair and balanced manner. Unfortunately, Flaherty's resentment seemed to linger, and in 2007, when he was minister of finance in the Harper government in Ottawa, I was advised that he persuaded Cabinet to block the appointment of Dennis O'Connor as my successor as chief justice of Ontario. Flaherty told some of his former political colleagues in Ontario of his strong opposition to O'Connor's appointment, and they in turn revealed the information to me. I also learned from other former political colleagues about the "cover story" – that the Harper government believed I had no right to state my views publicly about my successor.

In relating this story, I do not want to appear critical of my actual successor, Warren Winkler, who was a brilliant and widely respected trial judge. The issue for me will always be the mean-spiritedness of Flaherty and his federal colleagues. Nevertheless, Associate Chief Justice Dennis O'Connor accepted the decision of the federal Cabinet with grace and a continuing deep commitment to the work of the Court of Appeal until his retirement in December 2012.

35

The Role of Judges in Relation to the Rule of Law, Independence, and the Charter of Rights

The public interest in the appointment of members of the judiciary has increased dramatically in Canada since the entrenchment of the Charter of Rights and Freedoms in our Constitution in 1982. As a result, there have been frequent and sometimes overheated arguments about whether certain judicial decisions should in fact be reserved for elected politicians to make. One of the ironies of the ongoing debate is that the momentum for an entrenched Charter of Rights was created by elected politicians and a few legal scholars, but not by members of the judiciary. Indeed, Bora Laskin, the future distinguished chief justice of Canada, wrote while he was still a law professor of his concern that an entrenched Charter might well interfere negatively with the sensitive balance that had long existed between the parliaments and the courts.

The principal protagonist for an entrenched Charter was Prime Minister Trudeau. At the same time, I well recall his ambiguous views of the role of the courts, particularly the Supreme Court of Canada, before 1982. Trudeau was very upset when the Supreme Court struck down his attempt to unilaterally alter the structure of the Senate in 1979. He was also reluctant to expedite the hearing by the Supreme Court in 1981 of the lower-court challenges to his patriation package. When the Supreme Court announced its decision that a political convention did exist that required substantial provincial support for any constitutional amendments, Trudeau was furious. For me it has always seemed contradictory that the leading advocate of an entrenched

Charter of Rights had long harboured mixed views on the role of the courts in a democracy.

The debate on the role of unelected judges in relation to that of elected legislators will continue indefinitely, but, as a strong supporter of an entrenched Charter of Rights, I am encouraged by the high level of continuing public support for our Charter. The maintenance or otherwise of this support will undoubtedly continue to shape attitudes about the role of unelected judges in shaping political policy.

For me, one of the most interesting political and public reactions to a court decision occurred in 1998 when the Supreme Court of Canada announced its decision on the *Vriend* case – one that involved the dismissal of a teacher at a private religious college because of his sexual orientation. At issue was the failure of the Alberta Legislature to enact sexual orientation as a prohibited ground of discrimination in the province's Human Rights Code. The opposition to such an enactment appeared to be supported by the majority of the citizens of Alberta. The principal issue in the Supreme Court was the proper interpretation of section 15 of the Canadian Charter of Rights – the equality-of-rights section – which did not directly prohibit discrimination on the basis of "sexual orientation." In a controversial decision, the Supreme Court of Canada ruled that discrimination on the basis of sexual orientation was clearly an analogous ground of discrimination which should be prohibited by section 15. The effect of the decision in *Vriend* was to amend by judicial fiat the Human Rights Code of Alberta to include discrimination on the basis of sexual orientation as a prohibited ground of discrimination.

The public reaction in Alberta was fuelled considerably by the strong indignation expressed by the premier, Ralph Klein. In his initial response he declared that the provincial Legislature would use the notwithstanding, or override, clause of the Constitution to override the Supreme Court's decision. However, the political winds that blew over Alberta during the days that followed suggested that the use of the notwithstanding clause might well be politically unpopular, and the premier's promise to override the decision by provincial legislation was quietly abandoned. As I explained earlier, the notwithstanding clause was a political device included in the Canadian Charter of Rights to allow parliaments to suspend the operation of court decisions in relation to the individual-rights sections of the Charter (chapter 22). The override would automatically expire after five years unless it was renewed by the particular parliament or legislature involved. As Professor Peter

W. Hogg, a distinguished Canadian constitutional scholar, has written: "[The notwithstanding clause] was the crucial element of the federal/ provincial agreement of November 5, 1981 that secured the consent of those provinces (other than Quebec) that had until then been opposed to the Charter on the ground that it limited the sovereignty of their legislatures. Section 33 preserved that sovereignty provided the legislature satisfied the requirements of the section."

Those of us who supported the inclusion of the override clause in the constitutional negotiations predicted that the section would be resorted to rarely. And so it has proved to be: outside Quebec, the clause has been invoked rarely, and neither its existence in the Constitution nor its use has proved to be controversial. This history is, in my view, directly related to a high level of public support for the Charter. There is, moreover, no particular tension between Charter adjudication and democratic values. A democracy is more than simply majority rule and, in this context, the Supreme Court of Canada has noted that democracy requires that legislators "take into account the interests of majorities and minorities alike ... and where the interests of a minority have been denied consideration, especially where that group has historically experienced prejudice and discrimination ... judicial intervention is warranted."

The independence of the judiciary is generally viewed quite differently in Canada and in the United States. Although our US colleagues pay lip service to the importance of an impartial judiciary, the reality in my view is often the opposite. Most state judges are elected and usually campaign for judicial office as members of a political party. Furthermore, these campaigns often stress the judicial candidate's "tough on crime" approach. Moreover, appointed judges at both the state and federal level are usually selected on the basis of their political allegiances, while the members of the US Supreme Court in particular are invariably appointed because of their perceived personal political philosophies in the context of "conservative" or "liberal" views. Given the enormous influence of US culture in Canada, we are fortunate as a nation that our principles of judicial independence reflect traditions developed in the United Kingdom rather than in the United States.

I am not suggesting that political-party affiliations do not sometimes play a role in the process of judicial appointment in Canada. Those who apply to be judges, however, must be recommended by independent advisory committees for both provincial and federal appointments, with the exception of appointments to the Supreme Court of Canada.

Those committees in my experience are interested in the candidates' knowledge of the law and personality – in relation to treating litigants and lawyers in their courts with impartiality and courtesy. They are not concerned about whether the candidates' legal philosophy is liberal or conservative. The government of Stephen Harper, however, has frequently signalled its distrust of liberal judges who fail to demonstrate a high level of deference to elected politicians. When I presided over the Ontario Court of Appeal in the *Halpern* decision, which ruled in favour of same-sex marriages, for instance, Harper publicly complained about the "Liberal judges" who wrote the decision (see chapter 34). More recently his government demonstrated its wish to create a "law and order" judiciary federally when it amended the composition of the federal advisory committee to require that at least one member of each committee be a representative of law enforcement. In practice, this change appears to have had little impact on federal judicial appointments, and the Harper government has generally maintained a high standard in this area.

In Canada, the judicial appointment process has not had the degree of political transparency that occurs in the United States. When a nomination to the Supreme Court is made by the US president, the confirmation process before the Senate can be protracted, personally intrusive, and unlimited with respect to a candidate's past history. In recent decades, the individuals nominated invariably shared the same political philosophy of the president in office. If he or she is a Democrat, the nominee will be expected to hold liberal views; if a Republican, the nominee will hold conservative views. There are no guarantees, however, and members of the US Supreme Court have sometimes surprised their nominators with the unexpected judicial philosophies reflected in their decisions.

Perhaps the most dramatic example was Earl Warren, the former Republican governor of California who was nominated as chief justice by the Republican president Dwight Eisenhower in 1953. During his sixteen years in the office, Warren was a far more liberal justice than had been anticipated. Eisenhower is said to have stated that nominating Warren as chief justice was "the biggest damned fool mistake that I ever made." Warren orchestrated a long series of landmark decisions, including *Brown v. Board of Education* (1954), which banned segregation in public schools; *Miranda v. Arizona* (1966), which required that, during interrogation while in police custody, individuals must have certain rights clearly explained, including the right to have their own lawyers present; and *Loving v. Virginia* (1967), which overturned the *Racial Integrity Act of 1924* that had banned interracial marriage in Virginia. He was on the court for *Gideon v. Wainwright* (1963), which held that all indigent criminal defendants should receive publicly funded counsel. As a result, Warren became a villain in the eyes of the majority of Republicans, many of whom publicly advocated his impeachment.

In Canada, the appointment of judges to our Supreme Court has followed a much less partisan path. Although many of the judges have previously had some links with a political party, it is my firm conviction that the appointments have had no connection with any particular political or legal philosophy. The judges were all very well known to the legal community generally, and I cannot recall anyone in the Canadian legal community commenting seriously on an appointee's liberal or conservative views. Rather, the overriding concerns have always related to a judge's legal qualifications and impartiality with respect to the issues under consideration. Given this history, I do not believe that the majority of the Canadian public would support judicial appointments clearly made to reflect the political and legal philosophies of the government of the day.

The US Senate confirmation process for Supreme Court nominees has also created enormous damage to the reputations of some candidates. The most controversial example perhaps was the hearing involving Clarence Thomas, whose nomination was approved by the very narrow vote of 52–48 in the Senate. The key dispute related to allegations of sexual impropriety by Anita Hill, a former junior lawyer assistant. Although Thomas has been a member of the US Supreme Court for more than two decades now, he has reportedly remained very bitter about his experience, which, because the hearings were televised, he describes as a "high-tech lynching."

In recent years the federal government has experimented in various ways with the appointment of Supreme Court judges. Lists of candidates have been drawn up by advisory committees, although there has been no consistent method used to appoint the advisory committees. In 2005 the then new Harper government decided that once the nominee had been appointed (in that case Justice Marshall Rothstein), there ought also to be a parliamentary hearing. Justice Rothstein, an excellent choice whose performance as a Federal Appeal Court judge was highly respected, was the first Supreme Court judge to go through such a hearing, and they were also held for two other equally admired judges from the Ontario Court of Appeal, Andromache Karakatsanis and Michael Moldaver, and one from the Quebec Court of Appeal, Richard Wagner. The process for all was really pro forma, with the judges making opening statements and members of the House of Commons Committee asking generally polite questions, though it did give Canadians the opportunity to hear directly from the new Supreme Court justices. That said, I strongly believe that if a government seeks to extend this process into a real "confirmation" process, it will probably evolve into a highly partisan proceeding, with opposition MPs wanting to embarrass the government through its nominee. Because such questioning would inevitably involve criticism of the qualifications of the nominees, it is widely believed in legal circles that many highly qualified candidates would be reluctant to participate in a politically partisan process.

The debate about unelected judges making major decisions with respect to issues that have major religious and moral dimensions is one that will continue indefinitely on both sides of the border. One of the prime examples of dispute is the debate over abortion. The decision of the US Supreme Court in *Roe v. Wade* in 1973 was a landmark case and, by any measure, is one of the most controversial and politically significant cases in the court's history. The court held that a woman may abort her pregnancy for any reason up until the "point at which the fetus becomes viable" – and it went on to define viability as the potential "to live outside the mother's womb, albeit with artificial aid." After viability, an abortion may be available to protect a woman's health as protected by her constitutional rights to "due process," which included the concept of a woman's personal liberty.

In disallowing many state and federal restrictions on abortion in the United States, *Roe v. Wade* promoted a national debate that continues today, particularly in relation to the role of religious and moral views in the political sphere. *Roe v. Wade* reshaped national politics, dividing much of the nation into pro-choice and pro-life camps. If a political candidate is seeking a Republican Party nomination, an anti-abortion platform is almost always essential, and the reverse is generally true for someone seeking a Democratic Party nomination. Candidates for the US Supreme Court are routinely asked their views about *Roe v. Wade* in any confirmation proceeding in the Senate. The issue of abortion is an immensely emotional issue, with conflicting rights that are worthy of respect on both sides. One of the dissenting judges in *Roe v. Wade*, Justice Byron White, although a former Democrat, spoke for many when he wrote that the court had created "a constitutional barrier to state efforts to protect human life and by investing mothers and doctors with the constitutionally protected wrath to exterminate it." In any event, the abortion issue will continue to be revisited by the US Supreme Court, and the public debate will never be exhausted.

In contrast, abortion, while still a major controversy in Canada, has never become the huge issue it is in the United States. Most Canadians have strong views on one side or the other, but it has not gained the political profile it has south of our border. The controversy here has not had a significant influence on election results or on the appointment of judges. The Roman Catholic Church, the largest established church in Canada, is extremely vocal in its opposition to abortion. However, during federal election campaigns, there is little abortion-related rhetoric about the enactment of amendments to the federal *Criminal Code*. Indeed, the sections related to abortion in the code were struck down by the Supreme Court of Canada in 1988 in the case of *R. v. Morgentaler*, largely on the basis of unequal access throughout Canada to the legal process required for performing abortions (see chapter 20). After the *Morgentaler* decision, the federal government of Brian Mulroney introduced legislation to place some restrictions on performing abortions, but the legislation was not passed in the Senate because of a tie vote. No federal government has since revisited the issue.

Even as the debate continues about the role of judges in making decisions that relate to moral issues, judges in constitutional democracies such as Canada and the United States are responsible for making major policy decisions. This responsibility has become particularly relevant in an age of international terrorism. In recent years in Canada, and in particular following the 9/11 atrocity in the United States, there has been an intense debate over whether we can maintain our traditional commitment to individual rights in the face of this escalating threat. In the United States, the issue has been characterized by the *New York Times* as "Civil Liberty vs Security: Finding a Wartime Balance." During the administration of George W. Bush, the great majority of Americans believed that the United States was fighting acts of war and not mere crimes on American soil. That attitude led to government proposals to establish military tribunals to try non-US citizens accused of terrorism, to track down and question thousands of immigrants who have entered the United States in recent years from Middle Eastern and some other countries, and to monitor conversations between individuals in federal custody and their lawyers.

In the United Kingdom, the British home secretary has stated that "we can live in a world with airy fairy civil liberties and believe the best in everybody, and they then destroy us." Shortly after 9/11, Britain moved quickly to introduce emergency legislation allowing, in certain circumstances, detention without trial for renewable six-month periods, the jailing of uncooperative witnesses in terrorist investigations, and the right to search and take into custody airline passengers who have aroused suspicion. In France, marines and police officers patrolling the Paris subways have been given the right to intercept travellers and search their baggage without any specific cause for suspicion.

It has often been acknowledged that, in times of fear, the majority of people place security above all else and are quite willing to cede to their governments extraordinary authority. As one US law professor expressed it, "We love security more than we love liberty." This reaction was dramatically and tragically illustrated by the jailing of Japanese Americans and Japanese Canadians during the Second World War and by the imposition of the *War Measures Act* in Quebec in 1970 (see chapter 8).

In the context of the rule of law, I am often reminded of a scene from Robert Bolt's play *A Man for All Seasons*, which was made into a successful film of the same name. The play revolves around the life of Sir Thomas More, the Lord Chancellor of England, who found himself in a fatal clash with King Henry VIII over the monarch's desire to divorce Queen Katherine. In one memorable scene, William Roper, More's future son-in-law, argues that the end justifies the means and that the villain of the play should be arrested not because he has broken any particular law but because he is clearly evil and offends the law of God. "Then let God arrest him," Sir Thomas replies. He goes on to say that he would let the devil himself go free until he had broken the law of man. Roper is shocked: to get the devil, he responds, he would be prepared to cut down every law in England. "And when the law was down and the devil turned round on you, where would you hide?" Sir Thomas replies. "I'd give the devil benefit of law for my own safety's sake."

Sir Thomas More's reply represents a traditional commitment to the rule of law: even when faced with significant evil, there must be a respect for basic rights and values. In Canada, our rights and values are entrenched in the Charter of Rights and Freedoms. The Canadian security proposals will continue to raise many concerns as we debate how best to defend our model of a diverse and tolerant society in the face of international terrorism.

The Canadian government has a duty to take measures to protect Canadians against terrorism internationally or locally. The federal security legislation will continue to be tested in our courtrooms and, as a result, the role of judges is being subjected to closer scrutiny than at any other time in our nation's history. While the accountability of any important institution is essential in a democratic society, it is appropriate that it occur with an understanding of the basic principles of judicial interpretation of our Constitution.

The *Constitution Act, 1982* provided that our Constitution, which includes the Charter of Rights, "is the supreme law of Canada and any law that is inconsistent with the constitution is invalid." Since the creation of the Charter, some Canadian commentators have argued that it has given the courts too much power to enforce the rights of minorities and criminals. They further state that courts have generally become too activist and give too liberal a meaning to the expression of the rights and freedoms in the Charter. At the time the Constitution was enacted, however, the Parliament of Canada clearly intended that the courts should play a very activist role in the interpretation of the Charter of Rights. At a first ministers' conference I attended as attorney general for Ontario in 1980, Premier Blakeney of Saskatchewan and Prime Minister Trudeau had this exchange:

Blakeney: Canadians ought not to have taken from them their fundamental right to participate in all political choices. If we were to decide to place the Charter of Rights in the constitution, we would be taking out of the hands of the elected representatives and giving to the courts the power to decide some of the country's most significant political issues ...
Trudeau: Well, I say, What is wrong with going to the courts, or why shouldn't a minority which is adversely affected be able to call us to account in front of the courts?

Some of the criticism also ignores the judicial interpretation process. People often assume that, in every case that comes before the courts, the Constitution holds a simple right answer that merely awaits discovery by the judges. There is no truth in this assumption. The key words and expressions in the Charter of Rights are very general, such as "freedoms of thought, belief, opinion and expression," the "right to liberty and security of the person," the "principles of fundamental justice," "unreasonable search and seizure." They are inherently indeterminate in that they are often capable of more than one reasonable meaning. This word choice was, moreover, deliberate because the drafters wanted the Constitution to evolve in response to new challenges and conditions. It was intended to endure without having to be reinvented by an endless series of constitutional amendments.

When I worked with Jean Chrétien and Roy Romanow on developing the Charter in the early 1980s, we knew that, to secure public support for the Charter, it had to include a balance between the role of elected governments and the sober second thoughts of judicial review. The interpretation of the Charter requires balancing and judicial neutrality. If there is a dispute as to the constitutionality of any legislation, the conflict should be viewed as one between Parliament and the Constitution, not between the court and Parliament.

Although judges have the task of interpreting the often uncertain provisions of the Canadian Charter, they recognize that their task must be exercised in a principled fashion. They know that any suggestion of judicial imperialism will serve to undermine the public confidence that is essential to the discharge of judicial responsibilities. My former Appeal Court of Ontario and other appellate courts have stated in many decisions that, without public confidence, the courts cannot effectively fulfil their role in society. Any uncertainty in a law is a reflection of the reality that law is not mathematics. The uncertainty derives from human limitations, the nature of society, and the unpredictability of the future. There is simply no one single legal answer to every legal problem. Judicial creativity is part of legal existence, and law without discretion has been compared to a body without a spirit.

Courts are not representative bodies – they do not represent specific or special interests. Rather, they are impartial bodies that must reflect the basic values of our society. Furthermore, because courts are not bound by the majority of public opinion, they are not necessarily democratic institutions. In my view, when the majority takes away the rights of a minority, democracy dies. Democracy is, therefore, a delicate balance between majority rule and individual rights. Judges should be directed by basic and fundamental values, not by public opinion surveys or the transient fashions of the day. They must reflect history rather than hysteria. When a society is not faithful to its basic values, judges may be required to intervene.

In many cases, judges are told that the solution to the conflict lies in a balance between the conflicting values. However, there is no legislation or legal precedent that adequately indicates what weight should be attached to each value and how judges should balance between values that conflict. That said, it does not follow that judges can decide whatever they wish. There is no absolute judicial discretion; indeed, any absolute discretion for judges or any other public official would be the beginning of the end for democracy.

The history of our legal system has been gradual development and evolution, not revolution. While a judge should often be guided by public consensus, there are times when a court should lead and be the crusader for a new consensus. In the United States, *Brown v. Board of Education* was one such landmark.

Judges must be impartial, neutral, and objective, but they should not be cut off from their surroundings. They must make use of their life experiences as they try to reflect the fundamental values of the nation. If they are to maintain public confidence in the administration of justice, they must be seen to exercise their judicial discretion by means of a neutral application of the laws.

As the process now stands, there appears to be very little if any provincial or professional input with respect to the selection of members for Canada's highest court. At the same time, I repeat what I wrote earlier about my concern that the confirmation process not become a demonstration of political partisanship.

36

Visits to Cuba

The same year that I was appointed chief justice of Ontario, 1996, I made my first visit to Cuba – and, in the years since, it has been one of my favourite destinations. In particular I like Havana, the picturesque old colonial city of Trinidad, Pinar del Rio, and the Valle de Viñales, where much of the Cuban tobacco is grown. The initial invitation –to address an international legal conference – came from the University of Havana Law School. I was asked to speak about the Canadian legal system and, specifically, the Canadian Charter of Rights and Freedoms. The conference included lawyers from some South American nations and a number of African countries.

As a matter of protocol, I advised Mark Entwistle, the Canadian ambassador in Cuba, that I would be attending this conference. He in turn told Lloyd Axworthy, the minister of external affairs in Ottawa, who asked me if I would spend a few additional days in Havana so I could meet several Cuban officials of his choosing. I replied that I would be pleased to cooperate. At the time, the Canadian government was trying to persuade authorities in Cuba to show greater respect for the individual rights of citizens there, and Axworthy hoped I could help Entwistle in strengthening those contacts. As a secondary goal, the Canadian government wanted to demonstrate to the United States that Canada's "constructive engagement" with Cuba could contribute to the well-being of the Cuban people and to international stability – in contrast to US policy, which, ever since the Missile Crisis of 1962, had tried to prevent economic and political contact with its island neighbour. The Cuban government, meanwhile, tolerated the presence of a US "special interest section" in the Swedish embassy in Havana.

Before I prepared my remarks for the Cuban legal conference, I inquired whether simultaneous translation would be available. If not, I would need to shorten my speech to allow time for an interpreter standing beside me to translate sentence by sentence as I spoke. I was assured that voice-over translation would be in place, but, when I arrived in the lecture hall, I found that it wasn't, much to my personal embarrassment. My address took place in the principal chamber of the elegant Capitol building in Havana. Both the minister of justice and the attorney general were sitting in the front row, and I sensed they were annoyed by the length of my speech. The next day when I made a courtesy call on the justice minister, he got his revenge with a lengthy monologue – again translated sentence by sentence.

During this visit, I also hosted a lunch, which the Cuban chief justice and the attorney general attended. The chief justice was not very informative, but the attorney general, who spoke a little English, was outspoken about Cuba's many challenges. In particular, he was emotional about the substantial decline in Russia's financial and economic support following the breakup of the Soviet empire. "The dream is over, and the nightmare has begun," he said, referring to the already augmenting problems on the island.

In 1997–8 I made two vacation trips to Cuba that were relatively uneventful. Then, in 1999, Axworthy again asked me to go for an important meeting, this time with President Fidel Castro. Axworthy, who was generally an optimist with regard to his international responsibilities, had decided that the time was right to convince Castro that he should, in Cuba's best interests, demonstrate a greater sensitivity to human rights, including a degree of tolerance for political dissent and some support for individual entrepreneurship. Our meeting took place over a four-hour luncheon at the Canadian ambassador's residence on February 12, 1999. When I was introduced as the chief justice of Ontario, Castro responded, "I don't trust judges. They have too much power, and in some countries have even been involved in political coups." I replied that I could not imagine that any members of the Cuban judiciary would create problems for his government.

It is common for totalitarian leaders to oppose the concept of an independent judiciary. However, from what I have been able to learn about the Cuban administration of justice, it seems that it functions quite fairly by Latin American standards, unless the accused is a political dissident. In criminal cases, the few Cubans I have come to know are critical of what they believe to be overly lenient sentences. Because there are no private businesses of any significance on the island, there is no commercial litigation. Most of the civil litigation is related to family disputes, given the high rate of divorce. However, the splitting of family assets is difficult because houses can only be exchanged, not sold. Nevertheless, assets are sold or bartered "under the table."

At the luncheon, Axworthy was accompanied by Michael Kergin, his deputy minister, a career foreign service officer I knew from my days as high commissioner in London. Before the meeting, we shared a few thoughts about whether anything significant could be accomplished. I had few expectations, given my earlier meetings with senior Cuban government officials, but Kergin was blunt: "I can't understand why we are even here," he said. His remarks were prophetic.

Castro, trim and looking younger than his seventy-three years, demonstrated considerable personal charm throughout our meeting. He was also very well informed about Canadian domestic affairs and, at one point when Axworthy was trying to poke a little fun at my Conservative Party political roots, Castro commented on the largely conservative path being pursued by the government of Jean Chrétien. Axworthy also told Castro that I had been a "distinguished Conservative Cabinet minister" – to which I quickly added, "*progressivo* conservative." At this point, Castro chided Axworthy about the Liberal government's privatizing of Canada's international airports. "What are you going to leave for the Conservatives?" he asked.

We soon found that Castro was equally knowledgeable about the relationship between Canada and the United States, as well as US domestic politics. At several points in our discussion, Axworthy pursued the issue of Cuba joining the Western world in allowing the development of a free-enterprise business sector. Each time, Castro asked whether Russia was a good model for the transition from a socialist regime to a free-enterprise culture. He did not have to be more specific because we all knew how the transition had inflicted huge corruption on the Russian people. Essentially, Castro had two refrains throughout the luncheon: the essential corruption of capitalist systems and the ongoing "war" between Cuba and the United States.

Axworthy was anxious for something positive to emerge as a result of the meeting. As it lurched towards a conclusion, he said to Castro, "El Commandante, I am confident that, for humanitarian reasons, you will agree to support Canada with respect to its leadership in the creation of an international ban on the use of land mines." "Certainly not," replied Castro. "Land mines are poor countries' weapons. We can't afford tanks or nuclear armaments." He clearly harboured no personal remorse whatsoever about the maiming, or worse, of thousands of Angolans after Cuba used land mines in its support for the Communist side during Angola's civil war. At the same time, the other side in the civil war was South Africa's brutal apartheid regime.

As a result of this long meeting, Castro entered into but one agreement: the Cuban government would allow its judges to participate in any judicial symposiums proposed by the Canadian government. Even this achievement was bittersweet because he also stated that he didn't believe that Cuban judges had anything to learn from Canadian judges. Axworthy was obviously disappointed, and his dream of Canada's "constructive engagement" with Cuba producing a degree of democratization in Cuban society quickly evaporated. In the decade and more that has followed, Cuba has remained a totalitarian society under the presidencies of Fidel Castro and his brother Raoul Castro. At the same time, however, Cuba has remained a major tourist attraction for Canadians.

Immediately after the luncheon, I made notes on several topics we discussed that day, including uncorroborated information we received from Castro:

Democracy
The Cuban government consults its citizens with respect to all important issues. Government is decentralized, and Cuban citizens vote for local and state members of the councils. The important concept is "government by consensus ... everything else is theoretical," Castro said.

There are no "sultans" in Cuba or anyone with Swiss bank accounts. Castro said that, as he looked at so-called democracies around the world, he saw societies characterized by poverty, crime, and corruption. In this context he frequently mentioned Russia as a good example of what happens when a Communist state makes the transition to Western-style democracy.

The adoption of international norms
There can be nothing normal, Castro stated, about a country that has been under siege by the United States for about forty years. When Axworthy suggested that the United States was not the world and that there were many other important political groupings independent of the United States, Castro questioned

the relevance and strength of these political groups. For many years, he said, the United States had been able to ignore almost unanimous UN resolutions calling for the end of the US boycott against Cuba.

Capitalism

Castro did not believe that capitalism served the interests of ordinary people – they invariably became the pawns of the international capitalist elite. However, he admitted that he was not rejecting capitalism totally, adding with a chuckle that he had become a member of the capitalist elite to the extent that he had been given one share of Sherritt Mines of Canada by Pat Sheridan, the president and controlling shareholder. Because of the extensive business Sherritt Mines does in Cuba, the company is not allowed into the United States.

Cuban accomplishments

Castro stressed at every opportunity the accomplishments of the revolution in education and health and in eliminating economic disparity in Cuba. The rate of literacy in Cuba was now about 90 percent, as compared to less than 40 percent at the time of the revolution. Health care was free to all Cubans. Cuba has the highest per capita number of doctors and teachers anywhere in the world, with the result that doctors and teachers were volunteering their services in many other countries. Furthermore, many children who were victims of the Chernobyl disaster were being treated with success in Cuban hospitals.

Shooting down of Cuban exiles' aircraft

The shooting down by the Cuban air force of the two aircraft flown by Cuban expatriates from Miami gave great impetus to anti-Cuban feeling in the US Congress. Although Castro has never expressed any public regret, he brought up the subject with us, blaming President Clinton for allowing the "illegal overflights of Cuba." He maintained that an agreement had been reached with the United States, through a third party, to the effect that the United States would prevent the "highly provocative" invasion of Cuban air space. The Cuban vice-president, Carlos Lage, "expressed concern" to me last April about the downing of the aircraft, which our ambassador told me was the first and only expression of regret by the Cubans he was aware of.

On another topic, Castro expressed some sympathy for Clinton, "whom they just won't let alone," referring to the problems with Paula Jones et al.

As Castro left the luncheon table, he wrapped up the flowers from the table centrepiece in his napkin and made an elaborate and amusing presentation to Axworthy's female chief of staff. After very friendly farewells all around, he stood outside our ambassador's residence chatting in Spanish with reporters camped there while young women standing across the street excitedly waved, calling "Fidel, Fidel."

Lloyd Axworthy asked me to attend the press conference later at the international press centre hosted by the Cuban foreign minister and himself. The Cuban foreign minister was pretty tough, making it clear that Cuba was not looking for a "certification of good behaviour" from Canada or anyone else. "The trouble," he said at one point, was that "too many people talked about Cuba rather than talking to Cubans." Although the Cubans were careful not to make any specific commitments whatever with respect to international protocols in relation to human rights and democracy, a modest commitment to continue our dialogue was, in my view, an important step.

As a result of my several visits to Cuba, I also came to know Carlos Lage very well during the period when he was a vice-president of the Council of State of Cuba and executive secretary to the Council of Ministers. He was generally described as Castro's de facto prime minister and his "primary economic fixer." Lage, who trained as a pediatrician before entering the Cuban government, is a most intelligent and charming individual. Although our conversations took place through an interpreter, I thought of him as an effective spokesperson for Cuba. I was convinced that, even with translation on US television, he would be a fine representative of Cuba's future leaders. In the 1990s he initiated a series of economic reforms that allowed for limited land holdings and small business ventures.

When President Fidel Castro resigned in early 2008, Lage was mentioned as a possible successor. However, on February 28 that year, Fidel's brother Raoul was elected president. Although Lage was unanimously re-elected to his old post on the Council of State, he was removed one week later. Fidel Castro apparently stated that Lage had become too attracted to "the honey of power." The Associated Press, on March 5, 2009, reported that Lage, in a letter published that day, had accepted Castro's criticism and admitted he had committed errors.

I was back in Cuba in April 2009 and tried unsuccessfully to contact Lage. It appeared that he had become a non-person, and the current rumour holds that he is now in jail. The treatment of Lage is a strong indication that, despite the very modest free-enterprise reforms he initiated in the 1990s, doctrinaire Communist ideology has been restored and even strengthened in Cuba.

On several of my visits to Cuba I was hosted by Navin Chandaria, a close friend and a successful businessman who has long had an importing business in Cuba for products that are sold in Cuban "dollar" stores. Through him, I came to meet a number of his Cuban employees, and they provided me with a special window into their society. It seems that support for the Communist regime is very much a generational phenomenon. The older generation generally appears to favour the regime, praising its health and educational systems and the absence of obvious gaps between the wealthy and the poor such as exist in most Western societies and in Russia. Members of the younger generation, however, have more information about the greater economic opportunities available in free-enterprise societies, and their frustration with the Communist regime is often expressed in private. In my view, significant economic free enterprise will come to Cuba in the years ahead, but very slowly. And, despite Axworthy's hopes, I do not believe that Cuba will be a foreign-policy priority for Canada in the foreseeable future.

PART SIX

Retirement

37

Life after Judicial Retirement

Before I retired as chief justice of Ontario on May 31, 2007, I was approached by two successful litigators and close friends – Glenn Hainey, a future Superior Court justice, and John Callaghan, the youngest son of the late Chief Justice Frank Callaghan – who invited me to join the advocacy department in the Gowlings law firm. They stressed in particular that the firm would be happy for me to remain active in community service and did not expect me to become a major profit centre. Patrick LeSage, my former associate chief justice and my successor as chief justice of the Superior Court of Justice, had already joined Gowlings, and he concluded an agreement with me some weeks later. I did not pursue any negotiations with other firms because I respected Gowlings's commitment to pro bono legal work and felt confident that my comfort level there would serve me well. My decision to join Gowlings was the right one, and in the years since, I have enjoyed a stimulating and happy adventure with the firm, which is well led by Scott Joliffe at the national and international level and by Peter Lukasiewicz in Toronto.

As the date for my actual judicial retirement approached, I was treated generously by the legal profession with a number of events organized in my honour. The year 2007 was the twenty-fifth anniversary of the entrenchment of the Canadian Charter of Rights, and the Ontario Advocates' Society organized a conference dedicated to the Charter. Jean Chrétien, Roy Romanow, and I opened the conference with a lengthy panel discussion. We described the events that led to the historic federal-provincial agreement of November 5, 1981, which resulted in both the patriation of the Constitution and an entrenched Charter of Rights (chapter 22).

The conference was followed by a dinner to mark my retirement, and I was delighted when some two thousand people attended. I received tributes from a host of speakers, including Premier Dalton McGuinty, Lieutenant Governor James Bartleman, Chief Justice Beverley McLachlin, Minister of Justice Robert Nicholson, former Ontario premier Bill Davis, and from Chrétien and Romanow as well. The tributes were flattering, but my actor son, Michael, put everything in perspective with a hugely amusing roast of his father. His vivid portrayal of me struggling to open a cereal box was particularly memorable, as I have learned in talking to people since then. It all goes to show that parents should always be grateful to their children for not allowing them to take themselves too seriously.

My judicial retirement was also marked by the opening of the McMurtry Gardens of Justice, a sculpture garden between Osgoode Hall and the large trial courthouse on the east side of University Avenue just north of Queen Street in Toronto. The initiative was led by Justice Gloria Epstein, now on the Ontario Court of Appeal; Seymour Epstein, her husband; and Clifford Lax, a respected Toronto litigator. The first sculpture to be unveiled was *Pillars of Justice*, a large steel structure dedicated to the important contributions of jurors to the administration of justice. It was designed by Edwina Sandys, a granddaughter of Sir Winston Churchill. On my eightieth birthday, five years later, several other large sculptures related to the theme of justice were added to the garden.

* * *

Immediately after I joined Gowlings in 2007 I was asked by Stephen Lewis to join the board of his eponymous foundation, which plays a major role in the struggle against HIV/AIDS, particularly on the African continent. I have known him since 1972, the year he became leader of the Ontario NDP at the young age of thirty-five. He rapidly gained a reputation as one of the most effective speakers in Canada. David Lewis, his father and a long-time trade union lawyer, was the leader of the federal NDP. Together, they created perhaps the most unique father-and-son political team in the history of Canada.

Since 2003, the Stephen Lewis Foundation (SLF) has raised tens of millions of dollars for the cause and has distributed this money to more than three hundred organizations that are accountable to it in fifteen countries. Every organization with which the SLF works has a strong connection with the local community. They recognize that gender inequality drives the AIDS pandemic in Africa and that it is essential to have dedicated programs that support grandmothers, women, and girls.

Some 68 per cent of the people living with HIV worldwide are in sub-Saharan Africa, and 72 per cent of the deaths from AIDS occur there. Although great progress has been made in recent years, only 37 per cent of those who need anti-retroviral drugs are receiving them, and the number of orphaned children is continuing to rise. Regrettably, just as advances are beginning to make a difference, Western governments have flatlined or cut back their funding of AIDS assistance.

One of my initiatives during my time on the SLF board was to introduce Lewis to CEOs of banks – people he did not think were part of his socialist constituency. Even though I was unsuccessful in persuading him not to focus on his socialist roots during meetings with senior members of the financial community, he is always an effective advocate for causes in which he believes. As such, the bankers recognized the vital importance of the foundation's work and offered significant financial support.

It was a privilege to serve on the Stephen Lewis Foundation board for four years. In a generous letter to me after my retirement from it, Lewis wrote in part, "It's fascinating how political ideologies fall into inconsequence in the face of friendship."

* * *

My post-judicial retirement career also began with a commitment I had given to Michael Bryant, the attorney general, some weeks before my actual retirement as chief justice of Ontario. Bryant had received a "blistering" report, *Adding Insult to Injury,* from the office of the Ontario Ombudsman in relation to the Criminal Injuries Compensation Board, which was administered by the Ministry of the Attorney General. He asked me, once I was free, to conduct a review of the board, and I agreed. Ombudsman André Marin approved of Bryant's initiative, and the issue quickly disappeared from the political radar screen.

The report concluded that the Criminal Injuries Compensation Board was in "deplorable shape." It found that the root of the board's "colossal failure" could be found in the lack of consistent and adequate funding by successive Ontario governments over many years. It also alleged that the board's bureaucratic and insensitive attitudes and processes exacerbated the funding difficulties. The ombudsman's report traced the slow and onerous journey that some victims of violent crime experienced at the board, beginning with the lengthy time it took to obtain an application form and ending on average about three years later. During this period, victims could expect to fill out "an avalanche of documentation." In addition, the report continued, application forms were routinely returned for minor corrections, and applications sat for months while claims analysts prepared reports. Victims attempting to obtain information about their applications were frequently met with "suspicion and a lack of sensitivity and compassion."

Jill Arthur, the wife of Toronto mayor David Miller, had been a lawyer with the Ontario Court of Appeal during much of my judicial term and had recently returned to work for the Ministry of the Attorney General. When my appointment to review the Criminal Injuries Compensation Board was announced, she wrote to wish me well. I thereupon asked her to act as my principal legal counsel for the review, and she agreed.

My many years of experience with the criminal justice system had convinced me that crime victims are more often than not the forgotten people in the whole process. Traditionally, they are often treated with less attention, respect, and sensitivity than they deserve. Because 90 per cent of criminal charges in Ontario are resolved with pleas of guilty, the overwhelming majority of victims of violent crime never have an opportunity to describe their experiences in court. Frequently, they don't even learn of the results following a guilty plea. During my early years as attorney general I attempted to provide a process in which victims of crime would be informed of these results, but I was told that there were not enough prosecutors and police to make sure that adequate communication with victims had actually occurred.

Later amendments to Canada's *Criminal Code* attempted to strengthen the rights of victims by stipulating that victim impact statements be provided to the courts, either in writing or by oral testimony, as part of the sentencing process. However, this process has been encouraged only in the most serious criminal cases.

Several decades ago, the passage of legislation that provided compensation to victims of violent crime was a significant response to the issue of victim's rights in both Ontario and other provinces. The importance of providing similar financial assistance has also been recognized by the international community through the United Nations Declaration of Basic Principles of Justice for Victims of Crime and Abuse of Power. Under the Ontario legislation, an order for compensation may be made whether or not anyone is actually prosecuted or convicted of an offence. The Ontario board has the discretion to refuse to make an order for compensation or to award a reduced amount if the victim applicant has refused to cooperate reasonably with the police investigation. The legislation also provides for limits on awards, with a maximum for very serious injuries of $365,000, paid in instalments.

Over a number of months, Jill Arthur and I met with dozens of victims and victim service workers, and we received many written submissions. We also met with the senior staff and adjudicators at the Criminal Injuries Compensation Board as well as senior administrators at the Ministry of the Attorney General. In addition, we hosted a seminar with senior academics who had studied and written about victims of criminal injuries.

Curiously enough, the Ministry of the Attorney General never made any formal submissions to me, even though I was given the distinct impression that the government wanted to change the system from adjudication to one that could be managed entirely through administration: the hearings would be eliminated, the injuries would be categorized in schedules, and financial assistance would be awarded accordingly. In my view, such changes would not be consistent with a timely, compassionate, appropriate, and responsive approach to the victims of violent crime.

As part of my review, I attended hearings before panels of the Criminal Injuries Compensation Board. They convinced me of the value of oral hearings as an option for victims. Some victims clearly wanted the opportunity to speak of their victimization to some official body, and their testimony had therapeutic value for them quite apart from the compensation. Other victims, for understandably emotional reasons, did not want to testify. I therefore emphasized in my report that the option of oral testimony should be preserved.

During our meetings I heard many reports about the emotional suffering of victims, including feelings of fear, shame, isolation, and humiliation. As the Canadian Resource Centre for Victims of Crime in Ottawa has written: "Criminal victimization is a frightening and unsettling experience for many Canadians. It is unpredictable, largely unpreventable, and usually unexpected. Unlike normal life experiences, victimization is obviously not sought out. It is debilitating and demeaning, and it effects can often be long term and difficult to overcome."

There are many other dimensions of criminal victimization as well, and my report was largely intended to prevent the issue becoming a declining priority for the Ontario government. Victims are not part of any visible political constituency, and statements about their needs are seldom heard in Parliament or in the various provincial legislatures.

I delivered my report to the Ministry of the Attorney General in May 2008. At the time of my review, the ministry operated a pilot project – the Victim Quick Response Program – that provided immediate financial assistance for emergency expenses, funeral costs, and short-term counselling. I recommended in my report that this program should become a permanent part of victim compensation in Ontario – and the suggestion was accepted.

In my report, I expressed the view that the term "compensation" should be replaced by "financial assistance." "Compensation" wrongly suggests that the board's awards were intended to replicate civil damages, but that is not the case.

One of my principal recommendations was to create a victims' advocate independent of government. Although this recommendation has not yet been implemented, the Criminal Inquires Compensation Board remains intact. In the years since my report, significant administrative improvements have been made.

* * *

In June 2007 Premier Dalton McGuinty called to ask if I would do a review of the roots of youth violence in Ontario. The request was directly related to the shooting death of fifteen-year-old Jordan Manners, a young black male who was killed in a corridor of C.W. Jeffreys High School in Toronto. For several years there had been an increasing number of young black-on-black killings, and the black community in the Greater Toronto Area was understandably very concerned. They were demanding a response from all three orders of government, and particularly from the Ontario government. Because I had enjoyed a long relationship with the black community in Toronto, McGuinty's advisers told him that my appointment to review the deteriorating situation would be highly acceptable to that group. The premier also asked me about appointing Alvin Curling, the former Speaker of the Legislature, as co-chair for the review. I had known Curling ever since his appointment to the Peterson Cabinet in the late 1980s, and I readily agreed. The perception of the review would be well served with a Jamaican-born co-chair.

The background to my appointment to this review went back many years over several different initiatives, and youth issues had become a particular interest of mine – as I will describe in the next few paragraphs. After his election as mayor in 2003, David Miller asked me to chair an Advisory Committee on Safety and Youth Issues for the City of Toronto. I had long held the opinion, influenced by leading Canadian criminologists, that the justice system had little deterrent effect with respect to crime in general and violent crime in particular. It would be far more effective, I argued, for the municipal, provincial, and federal governments to collaborate on initiatives for crime prevention. As a result, the mayor's advisory committee included elected representatives from both the federal and the provincial levels and received some additional funding for youth-related issues.

With my encouragement, the University of Toronto organized an important conference on practical options for preventing youth crime. After the expert speakers had delivered their papers, the essays were published as a book, *Research on Community Safety: From Enforcement and Prevention to Civic Engagement*, edited by Bruce Kidd, a former Olympic runner who was dean of physical health and education at the university, and his colleague Jim Phillips, the director of the Centre of Criminology. The research behind these essays, mainly by criminologists and sociologists, is comprehensive, and to my knowledge the book is the major study of its kind in Canada. It is of particular interest to scholars and those responsible for community safety and for improving the social fabric of our cities.

The focus of our deliberations on the mayor's advisory committee related to young offenders – those legally defined in the *Young Offenders Act* (1984) as persons between the age of twelve and eighteen. This definition is obviously rigid because the term "youthful" can apply to people well into their twenties. However, a different legal system for youth has been part of the Canadian justice system since 1908, though it has varied over the years. For many decades, the youth justice legislation was enshrined in the *Juvenile Delinquents Act*. In Ontario, until 1985, any person over the age of sixteen was treated as an adult offender. That same year the wise decision by the federal government to create a uniform maximum age of eighteen for young offenders in all provinces came into effect, after considerable debate among Canada's justice ministers.

Many studies have concluded that, because of lack of maturity and more vulnerability to peer pressure, adolescents differ significantly

from adults in their capacity to make sound decisions. These young offenders benefit more from a systemic focus on treatment than from incarceration, and a youth justice system, because of the greater number
of social services it can provide, is better able to redirect youth behaviour. Most Canadian provinces in my opinion have overly criminalized
their youth – certainly, the rate of youth incarcerations in Canada for
relatively minor crimes has been higher than in most European countries. Even conviction without incarceration can have a very negative
impact on young people's future. They often self-stigmatize themselves
as bad – a label that then becomes a self-fulfilling prophecy.

In 2003 the federal government proclaimed a new *Youth Criminal
Justice Act*. The legislation sought to achieve a better balance, in the
sense that serious youth crime would attract tougher penalties, while
relatively minor criminal behaviour could be treated by community
sanctions outside the criminal justice system. Where a young person is
convicted of a criminal offence, the youth justice court is directed not
to impose a custodial sentence unless the court has considered all the
alternatives raised in the sentencing hearing that are reasonable in the
circumstances. In addition, four "gateways" to custody are provided in
the act, and if a case does not meet one or more of those criteria, a community sanction must be imposed.

The development of community programs has indeed resulted in
the diversion of young persons from the criminal justice system. These
programs vary greatly, but the emphasis is generally on different forms
of community service. In Canada the charity run by the Duke of Edinburgh Awards provides some of these community programs. A few
months after the proclamation of the new *Youth Criminal Justice Act*, I
was present at a fundraising event in London, England, for the awards.
In a conversation with Prince Philip, I made reference to the important
programs his awards funded, particularly for young people who, having committed a crime, were kept out of the criminal justice system.
The prince, clearly of the "old school," replied that he hoped "they
would at least get a good beating."

Being chair of the mayor's advisory committee increased my interest
in the realities of the youth justice system. Very few issues related to
youth justice ever reached the Court of Appeal, and I had, at least since
my attorney general days, become somewhat detached from the day-
to-day operations of the youth courts in Ontario. I had known about
problems related to delays in the youth courts, and my concerns in that
context led to a series of meetings with provincial judges and Crown
attorneys who I knew were particularly interested in the challenges

related to youth justice. As a result of those meetings, I learned that there was consensus that the youth courts in Ontario were generally treated by the Ministry of the Attorney General simply as "add-ons" to the adult system. Delays in the youth justice system were simply not regarded as a serious problem. The reality is, however, that young people's lives and personalities usually change dramatically within a relatively short period. The judges and Crown attorneys I consulted generally thought that the public interest would be much better served by a more timely disposition of cases involving youth.

Youth courts, in my view, require both judges and counsel to have a high degree of specialization. However, I found that the opposite was often the reality: the courts were described as "kiddie courts," and the Crown prosecutors as "baby Crowns." An attitude had developed that the youth courts did not involve the prosecutions of "real criminals." To me, youth criminal prosecutions should be reserved for the more serious cases. When youth offenders were prosecuted, the way in which it was done had the potential to turn the accuseds' lives around in a positive fashion.

Unfortunately, youth justice did not become a priority for the provincial government generally. It was a priority for Mary Ann Chambers, the first minister of children and youth services in 2003, but I don't believe she received the necessary support from many of her political colleagues. In all probability, they did not want to be perceived as being "too soft" on youthful offenders. On a more positive note, Chambers oversaw the planning and building of a new "state-of-the-art" youth incarceration facility in Brampton, which was designed to emphasize that its principal role was to rehabilitate and educate its residents. It opened in 2009 and received international praise, although proper staffing remained a challenge for a time. Premier McGuinty, with Chambers's encouragement, honoured me just before my retirement as chief justice in 2007 by naming the not-yet-opened youth facility "The Roy McMurtry Youth Centre." They presented me with a commemorative plaque that stated: "In tribute to the Honourable Roy McMurtry. In appreciation of your many years of dedicated support for the rehabilitation and just treatment of the youth of Ontario. The Ministry of Children and Youth Services, by order of the Premier of Ontario, hereby proclaims that the new youth centre to be opened in Brampton in 2009 be named in your honour."

And so it was, because of all these various links with the youth justice system I had made over the years, that Premier McGuinty asked me and Alvin Curling in 2007 to chair a review of the roots of youth violence in Ontario – a significant challenge, to say the least. To begin, the government set up a secretariat to assist us with our mandate. We met with many people in the community, young people as well as representatives from a number of professions. We appointed Scot Wortley, a senior criminologist at the University of Toronto, as our research director, and Doug Ewart, my former policy adviser in the Ministry of the Attorney General, as our policy coordinator.

Curling was clearly sensitive about the possibility of the Jamaican community being unfairly stigmatized, given that young Jamaicans had been involved in much of the violence that led to the review. I shared his concerns because I knew that Jamaican Canadians were a respected and generally law-abiding community. Even though a small number of young Jamaican males were caught up in a culture of gangs and violence, that connection was only part of the issue. Poverty and racism had also contributed to the roots of violence in many communities.

We knew that racism, largely directed at non-white youth, had long been an issue in Ontario's diverse society. A feeling of being outside mainstream society can be a toxic cause of alienation and violent behaviour. In our report, we tried to place the evil of racism in the appropriate context, as we wrote: "Racism is morally wrong. However, at the community level, it is also the evil fertilizer that nourishes the other roots we have identified: poverty, especially concentration of poverty, inadequate housing, unfair practices in schools, and lack of employment opportunities." Although racism continues to be an important issue in Canadian society, we did not want it to "hijack" the report, given the many recommendations we wanted to make in relation to other important problems. In my experience, many people feel acutely uncomfortable when the topic of race relations is mentioned. In this context I still remember an English Lord Chancellor who had responsibility for community relations telling me many years ago that the best way to deal with race relations was not to talk about it. Within a year, the very ugly race riots occurred in Brixton, a community near London.

In the late 1970s the Cabinet of Bill Davis had created a Cabinet Committee on Race Relations which I chaired. Subsequent Ontario governments have been reluctant to give the issue priority or any kind of high profile – the McGuinty government, for instance, largely buried racial problems in a Cabinet Committee on Poverty Reduction. The fact of racism did, however, obtain a high profile in the spring of 1992 in Toronto, when young people of colour grouped together to protest the serious lack of equal job opportunities. For some decades, the level of unemployment for black youth had been significantly higher than that for white youth in Toronto and the surrounding area. Bob Rae, the premier at the time, asked Stephen Lewis to investigate the problem immediately, and his report eloquently and strongly supported the allegations behind the protest. Rae followed through by establishing a study committee on which the four orders of government were represented: the Metro Toronto government, the City of Toronto, and the provincial and federal governments. These officials worked through the summer and, by the end the year, produced a comprehensive report, *Towards a New Beginning*, with many useful recommendations and timelines for implementation. The NDP government also established the Commission on Systemic Racism in the Criminal Justice System, but, by the time it reported, the Harris government was in power, and the report had no influence.

When Curling and I began our review of the roots of youth violence in the summer of 2007, we inquired about this report and its implementation. No one within the senior levels of the Ontario government was able to tell us whether any of the recommendations had been pursued. We were simply advised that no records were available and that, regrettably, governments often have "short institutional memories." I was discouraged by this information because it provided a negative precedent for our very ambitious undertaking. However, I strongly believed in the importance of our mission and was prepared to accept the apparent sincerity of the McGuinty government with respect to our mandate.

We met with hundreds of individuals in different parts of Ontario and made a special effort to contact youth in their own neighbourhoods. We talked to young people individually and through their grass-roots associations, including consultations with Aboriginal youth. Young people were also encouraged to complete our online survey or voice their opinions through our toll-free telephone line. We also commissioned several experts to write research essays as well as review the relevant literature.

Alvin Curling and I delivered our five-volume report to Premier McGuinty in November 2008. McGuinty responded with a flattering letter about the quality and value of the report. In the years since, we have been assured that it has attracted a great deal of attention in communities throughout Ontario. Volume 3 of the report was dedicated specifically to recording what we had heard during our communications with people all over the province. We wanted to satisfy our contacts that they had truly been listened to and that they had significantly influenced our report. Volumes 4 and 5 contained the research essays and the review of the literature.

In our review, we emphasized that, historically, the focus had been on the specific problems rather than the roots of those problems, and on interventions once the roots had taken hold rather than on actions to prevent the problems from happening. The most common intervention is law enforcement, although most senior officers agree that the problems of youth violence "cannot simply be arrested away." To succeed in creating prevention strategies, it is essential that governments, schools, law enforcement, and communities in general address entrenched social problems in a collaborative way, one that involves working in neighbourhood partnerships in the most disadvantaged areas. The trends identified in our report, although largely masked by the overall stability of the crime figures, suggest that Ontario is actually incubating an increase not only in youth violence but in more serious violence. These trends are deeply troubling. They include the growing concentration of violent crime among young people, the frequency with which guns and knives are being used in disputes that might previously have been settled with fists, the public nature of extreme violence, and the prevalence of both guns and gangs.

We encountered many young people who have a deep sense of alienation and low self-esteem. Many believe that they are oppressed, discriminated against, and neither "belong to nor have a stake in the broader society," with a resulting loss of hope for their futures. The first paragraph of our report stated:

Ontario is at a crossroads. While it is a safe place for most, our review identified deeply troubling trends in the nature of serious violent crime involving youth in Ontario and the impacts it is having on many communities. Those trends suggest that, unless the roots of this violence are identified and addressed in a coordinated, collaborative and sustained way, violence will get worse. More people will be killed, communities will become increasingly isolated and disadvantaged, an ever-accelerating downward cycle will ensue for far too many, and our social fabric as a province could be seriously damaged.

The public response to youth violence is often very simplistic – "Just get tough!" Youth justice is one of those policy issues that never seem to lose their ability to ignite debate in Canada, particularly when they are exploited for partisan political ends. My many years in the justice system have taught me, however, that the law and the criminal justice system are very blunt instruments for problems caused by a tangled web of social and other factors. When used to over-criminalize youth, rather than in a strategic and balanced way, the criminal justice system needlessly generates even greater feelings of alienation in already disadvantaged youth. This reaction can in some cases lead to increasing, rather than reducing, the kinds of violence that ignite public concern.

In general, our report calls on the province to be more strategic in the way it deploys expensive criminal-justice resources and more realistic about the limited capacity of the justice system to effectively address deep-seated social issues. In this context, President Obama's description of inner-city youth in his book *Dreams from My Father* is relevant:

I know I have seen the desperation and disorder of the powerless: how it twists the lives of children ... how narrow the path is for them between humiliation and untrammelled fury, how easily they slip into violence and despair. I know that the response of the powerful to this disorder, alternating as it does between a dull complacency and, when the disorder spills out of its proscribed confines, a steady, unthinking application of force, of longer prison sentences and more sophisticated military hardware, is inadequate to the task. I know that the hardening of lines ... dooms us all.

In our report, we organized our thinking around four pillars, and then proposed a series of mechanisms to promote effective and integrated responses and solutions at the neighbourhood level. As a foundation, we recommended that both the province and individual communities adopt a place-based approach in which the roots of violence are addressed by working within and with the neighbourhoods in areas where there are downward cycles of disadvantage and violence. We urged the province to use an index of relative disadvantage in order to identify those areas.

The first pillar we described as a "repaired social context." It brings together strategies to address the level, concentration, and circumstances of poverty along with closely related issues, including racism, housing, education, mental health, family and community support, transportation, and the justice system. Among many other ideas, we recommended a major investment in and coordination of youth mental-health services; employment initiatives involving meaningful work; a voice for youth; arts and sports initiatives; the provision of effective mentors; and strengthening the network of youth workers.

The second pillar we described as a "youth policy" – in particular, the need to bring youth-led organizations into policymaking and delivery roles. Young people must have key roles in the design and delivery of the strategy because they will pay the heaviest price if it does not succeed.

The third pillar we described as a "neighbourhood capacity and empowerment focus." This pillar is intended to create local centres, often based around schools, in which opportunities and services for youth and their families can be maximized and community cohesion fostered. These centres will not only provide space and services, but will form hubs in which communities can anchor ever-increasing local public policymaking, priority setting, and program delivery. If the most disadvantaged neighbourhoods are not strengthened, they will become even more fragmented and isolated, leading in all probability to an entrenched underclass.

The fourth pillar we described as "integrated governance." It is essential that the provincial government organize itself to provide an effective and coordinated approach to the broad range of issues affecting youth violence. This pillar calls for a community-based approach through which the province's own more integrated approach can develop strategic partnerships with other orders of government to set priorities, develop policies, and deliver services. This integrated governance simply will not happen without mechanisms to cut across the many silos that exist in provincial and local government and the facilitation of aligned engagement in communities.

Once the disadvantaged neighbourhoods have been identified, our report calls for a structural approach that fully involves the community and, at the same time, creates a viable platform for all orders of government to work together. In essence, we call for neighbourhood strategic partnerships in each of the most disadvantaged neighbourhoods across Ontario. The partnerships will bring together, in a formal, ongoing structure, the participating government, schools, community residents, and agencies that serve the community. They reflect and respect the highly local nature of what has to be done and build on the knowledge that municipalities have about their communities and what works on the ground.

Through these partnerships, the neighbourhoods can become the place where the provincial–municipal relationship on root issues is built. In this approach, residents and local service providers are inside the governance model at the outset and integral to how it is built and operated. Government, in turn, can engage with residents and service providers in ways that build community strengths and a culture of collaboration. Once a plan has been prepared, it would be incumbent on the service providers and governments, as partners in the neighbourhood strategic partnerships, to work together to prioritize and align their programs and funding to make that plan work. Whether to support and plan hubs, align services, advance progress towards outcome goals, or promote other community priorities, the essence of this approach is that neighbourhoods develop plans with governments and agencies which they then all work together to achieve.

As we expected, we received submissions from individuals and organizations that identified graphic violence in the entertainment industry as a major factor in the increase of youth violence. Although we generally shared their views, Curling and I relied for the most part on the research conducted by Scot Wortley, who advised us that the professional research on both sides of the border was severely divided on whether violence as entertainment influenced or encouraged youth violence in the community. As a result, we did not write anything of significance on this issue in our long report. Although I have my own gut feeling about its negative impact, I was also aware that any recommendations we might make against violence as entertainment would have little, if any, practical influence on government. We decided, therefore, to focus in the report on the many recommendations that could be implemented by government. We did not want the violence as entertainment issue to become a major and controversial distraction that might undermine the credibility of our report in general.

As things turned out, our *Review of the Roots of Youth Violence* remained buried to some extent in the Cabinet Committee on Poverty Reduction. It did, however, encourage some government initiatives, including a significant increase in the funding of mental health for children. We had learned from credible mental-health advocates that one in five children begins school with some kind of mental issue, ranging from minor to significant problems. More often than not the schools are not informed because parents are often reluctant to report their concerns for fear of stigmatizing the child.

The *Roots* report was elevated to a higher priority for the McGuinty government in July 2012, when there was a barrage of shootings during a barbeque on a single street in a Scarborough neighbourhood. The shootings, believed to be related to gang rivalry, resulted in the death of two innocent bystanders and injuries to twenty others. McGuinty immediately asked Eric Hoskins, the minister of children and youth services, and Madeleine Meilleur, the minister of community safety, to provide a report on Ontario's Youth Action Plan. Their report, which was published on August 22, 2012, once again adapted our basic recommendations, stating that they are "and will remain the blueprint and foundation for action on youth violence in Ontario."

Although we are disappointed that progress towards the goals we envisioned has been painfully slow, we do believe that the report is a useful road map for the future. I have learned over the years, however, that the success of preventative initiatives is difficult to measure or quantify and that they therefore have mixed appeal for governments. When we add to these challenges the traditional silos and rivalries within governments in particular and society in general, one has to struggle against being somewhat pessimistic on occasion.

* * *

In September 2010, in the wake of the Group of Twenty (G20) Summit in Toronto the previous June, I was retained by James Bradley, the minister of community safety and correctional services, to do a review of the *Public Works Protection Act* (*PWPA*). This act had been used by the Toronto Police Service to enhance police authority during the summit. The *PWPA* had originally been passed by the Ontario Legislature in September 1939 at the outbreak of the Second World War. It was clearly emergency legislation intended to give the provincial government and others very broad powers to protect important municipal structures from potential sabotage. In preparing for the G20 meetings, the Toronto Police Service had requested that a regulation be passed under the *PWPA* that would give the police additional powers that might be necessary to protect the security perimeter established to protect the delegates – the finance ministers and central bank governors from the world's major economies. The provincial regulation was passed, leading to considerable confusion related to its effect and lack of information about it given to the public.

The McGuinty government was initially reluctant to be associated with the G20 summit, regarding it as a federal responsibility. However, the passage of the regulation shifted some of the political controversy to the provincial government. Minister Bradley asked me to take into account the historical context of the *PWPA*, to examine its current uses by the interested parties, and to review the other reports that had been made on the G20 disturbances. Moreover, although the G20 summit security was primarily the responsibility of Toronto Police Service, it also involved members of the RCMP, the Ontario Provincial Police, and police services from other areas in Canada.

Prime Minister Harper had, on June 19, 2008, announced that Huntsville, Ontario, would host the smaller Group of Eight (G8) Summit for government leaders from the world's major economies, scheduled for June 25–26, 2010. It was not until December 7, 2009, that he announced that Toronto would host the larger G20 summit scheduled for June 26–27, 2010. On February 19, 2010, the Metro Toronto Convention Centre was finally named as the specific site for the meetings.

In my view, given the level of public protests that usually accompany these international meetings, the choice of downtown Toronto was a colossal blunder on the part of the federal government. The protestors were expected to include anarchists who were committed to creating as much havoc as possible. The time to plan for security around the convention centre was just over four months – clearly insufficient for an adequate planning process.

The G8 and G20 meetings proved to be very expensive, including a security cost of more than $1.2 billion and serious damage to the reputation of the Toronto Police Service, generally a highly regarded police force. The many legal proceedings arising out of the G20 in Toronto guarantee that the cloud over the Toronto Police Service will remain for several years. Immediately following the summit, a public opinion survey revealed that 73 per cent of the public approved of the actions of the Toronto Police Service. However, in polls taken a year later, as more information became available, the support for the actions of the police declined dramatically. The public's "blind faith" in the police, as Police Chief Harold Adamson used to say, had obviously been shaken.

My review was one of several related to the G20 events. A watching brief by the Canadian Civil Liberties Association (CCLA), organized by president Nathalie Des Rosiers before the G20 took place, was most effective. The CCLA clearly anticipated problems with the law-enforcement agencies assigned to provide security for the Toronto summit. As a result, it organized a voluntary team of monitors to observe the events of the summit weekend, and their published reports make an important contribution to our knowledge of the major law-enforcement overreaction at the G20. Three other reports – by Ontario ombudsman André Marin, by the Office of the Independent Police Review Director (Gerry McNeilly), and by former associate chief justice John Morden – are also highly critical of the police response. Both the federal and the provincial governments have, however, rejected numerous media and political demands for a full and comprehensive public inquiry with the power to summon and cross-examine witnesses – an important aspect that was not part of the mandate of any of the other inquiries, including my own review.

With respect to security for the G8 and G20 summits, an Integrated Security Unit (ISU) was established in 2008 under the direction of the RCMP – the institution with the overall legislative responsibility for protecting "internationally protected persons" such as those who would be attending the summits. The RCMP was responsible for protecting three defined security zones – the controlled access zone, the restricted access zone, and the interdiction zone – as well as the perimeters around these areas and the hotels in which the protected persons would be staying. For the G8 summit in Huntsville, the Ontario Provincial Police became the designated partner; and for the G20 summit in Toronto, it was the Toronto Police Service.

The Ontario Provincial Police did not request any regulation giving the force additional authority under the *PWPA*, simply because it did not think any increase was necessary. However, the Toronto Police Service thought that it did require additional legal authority to protect the interdiction zones for the G20. The Toronto police therefore requested that the Ontario government enact a regulation pursuant to the *PWPA* which would designate the interdiction zone near the conference centre as a "public work," thereby triggering the extraordinary powers granted by that legislation.

The passage of the *PWPA* in September 1939, according to reports of the legislative debates at the time, indicated that protecting the province's vital public works from sabotage, particularly the hydro-electric facilities, was of particular concern. The Ontario government had asked the federal government to provide members of the Canadian military to guard these facilities. When that request was refused, the *PWPA* was passed. The debates reveal that the new legislation would allow the province to establish "private armies," and that virtually every municipality in Ontario could be declared a "public work." The powers of the "guards," as defined in the legislation, are far-reaching and draconian. They allow guards to search, without a warrant, any person approaching, entering, or attempting to enter a public work and to deny entry by force. The limits or perimeters of an "approach" are not defined. These guards could be appointed by a broad range of public officials, who could thereby create their own private armies. Curiously, in reviewing the *PWPA*, I was unable to find any historical record of its actual use during the Second World War.

Before the G20 in June 2010, the *PWPA* had been relied on only in very limited circumstances – to conduct searches at courthouses, in the context of providing security, and to permit the Ontario Power Generation to empower guards at its nuclear and non-nuclear power-generating facilities, again for reasons of security. As the attorney general of Ontario from 1975 to 1985, I had never been aware that the *PWPA* existed. The only judicial reference to the legislation was in the context of courthouse security between 2002 and 2005. No other province in Canada had ever passed legislation similar to it.

There was no mention of the possible use of the *PWPA* until fairly late in the planning process for the security of the G20 summit. The federal *Foreign Missions and International Organizations Act* gave the RCMP primary responsibility to ensure the security for any international intergovernmental meeting in Canada. This legislation allowed the RCMP to take any reasonable action, "including controlling or limiting or prohibiting access to any area." Neither the RCMP nor the Ontario Provincial Police believed that the *PWPA* was required for the G8 summit in Huntsville.

On May 12, 2010, a few weeks before the G20 summit in Toronto, Chief William Blair of the Toronto Police Service wrote to the provincial minister of community safety requesting a regulation under the *PWPA*. It would, he said, "offer legal support for the extraordinary security measures" that he thought were necessary. Chief Blair wanted the province to designate a specific area within the intended security perimeter as a "public work" for the period June 21–27, 2010. I learned during my review that the letter had been prepared on the advice of a lawyer in the City of Toronto legal department. However, before the provincial minister of community safety could reply, an assistant commissioner of the RCMP sent a letter to Chief Blair advising him that, in his view, the police had the necessary authority to fully secure the G8 and G20 summits. He made no mention of the *PWPA*.

It was obvious to me that, by this stage in the planning, pressures of time did not allow the provincial government to reflect adequately on the possible consequences of resorting to the *PWPA*. Although the regulation may have been seen by members of the Ministry of the Attorney General, I received no documents to suggest that anyone there had made a careful review of the *PWPA* in the context of the Canadian Charter of Rights and Freedoms. The Charter provides Canadian citizens and others within Canada with certain fundamental freedoms, including freedom of expression and peaceful assembly, the right of security of the person, the right not to be arbitrarily detained, and the right to be secure against unreasonable search and seizure. In my opinion, many of the draconian provisions of the *PWPA* were vulnerable to constitutional challenge. Furthermore, the provisions of the *PWPA* were not adequately communicated to the public, and some of what was communicated was inaccurate or difficult to understand. In summary, the use of the *PWPA*, together with the general security hysteria that permeated the G20 summit in Toronto, provided all the ingredients for a "perfect storm." The *PWPA*, as the product of emergency Second World War concerns, was clearly not tailored for international summits, even in an age of terrorism.

More than 1100 individuals were arrested during the weekend of the G20 on June 26 and 27, 2010. They were detained in very cramped and unsanitary conditions. Only a small number of the people arrested were charged with any criminal offence. Hundreds of other people were "kettled," or detained, for long periods on streets a significant distance from the G20 meetings, at one time during a heavy storm and well on into the evening. The Toronto Police Service later admitted that it had no reason to suspect any wrongdoing by the vast majority of people detained in that manner.

Notwithstanding the excessive actions of some police officers, including members of many other police forces in Ontario and beyond, the media's coverage largely focused on the activities of the small number of hooligans who set fire to two police cruisers and damaged many business premises. The hooligan element also included a number of anarchists known to the police as the "Black Bloc."

I presented my report on the *PWPA* to the Ontario government in April 2011. By that date, the Canadian Civil Liberties Association and the Ontario ombudsman had already prepared reports that were highly critical of the legislation. In my report I stated that I agreed with the observations made by the Civil Liberties Association that the provisions of the *PWPA* led to a "lack of clarity as to the scope of the search and seizure powers" – a situation that created many unnecessary confrontations between the police and members of the public. In addition, I strongly supported the comment in the conclusion that "it is the duty of police officers to act with fairness and equanimity towards all citizens in accordance with the law of the country. The presumption of innocence and protection against arbitrary arrest and detention are at the core of a commitment to justice." The ombudsman's report accurately described the *PWPA* as unique in Canada in terms of the breadth of its reach and the power it confers. No other Canadian statute defining "public works" contains provisions similar to those found in Ontario's act.

In my report, I recommended the repeal of the *PWPA*. "The vagueness of the *PWPA*," I wrote, "permits it to be used in situations when it is arguably not necessary and potentially abusive. The *PWPA* has been used for programs beyond its original intent." At the same time, I recognized that, before the *PWPA* is repealed, substitute legislation would be required to provide for security for courthouses and power-generating infrastructures. Within twenty-four hours of receiving my report, the government announced its intention to accept my recommendations.

In 2007 the Supreme Court of Canada wrote in *R. v. Clayton* that "in determining the boundaries of police powers, caution is required to ensure the proper balance between preventing excessive intrusions on an individual's liberty and privacy and enabling the police to do what is reasonably necessary to perform their duties in protecting the public." I believe that Canadians are entitled to demand the best public-order policing possible from their governments. There is no question that we live in a different world after 9/11. With constant terrorist threats both domestically and from abroad, the police clearly require adequate powers to carry out their duties. They use their expertise and discretion on a daily basis to assess the extent of the authority they require. In instances when they take action that exceeds their legal authority powers, their actions can be reviewed by various public bodies. This process, I believe, generally results in the proper balance between police powers and individual rights and freedoms. Therefore, any legislation that purports to grant special police powers must be specific, understandable, and developed in consultation with the public, then tested through debate in our transparent democratic system.

* * *

Another important part of my post-retirement activities was to sit for six years on the board of directors of Just Energy Group Inc. – the only for-profit corporation I joined among the many not-for-profit community boards I have served over the years. The company is led by our family friend Rebecca MacDonald, who is also our frequent host on her large estate in the Dominican Republic. She came to Canada from the former Yugoslavia more than thirty years ago and presents a fine example of the success many immigrants achieve after arriving in Canada with but modest financial means. She and her late husband, Pearson MacDonald, gradually built up a large sales force marketing products door to door. In recent years she has been recognized in Canada and the United States as an outstanding corporate leader. MacDonald is also a dedicated philanthropist who has made generous gifts to Mount Sinai Hospital in Toronto and to a variety of causes in the Dominican Republic.

Established in 1997, Just Energy is primarily a competitive retailer of natural gas and electricity. With offices located across the United States, Canada, and the United Kingdom, it serves close to 2 million residential and commercial customers through a wide range of energy programs and home-comfort services, including fixed-price or price-protected energy program contracts, the rental of water heaters, furnaces, and air conditioners, and the installation of solar panels. The company's Just Green products enable consumers to reduce the environmental impact of their everyday energy use.

During my years on the Just Energy board, I learned how difficult it is to achieve success in the business world. It requires a great deal of knowledge about finances along with sound judgment in selecting senior management. My fellow board members included an impressive group of Canadians and Americans: Senator Hugh Segal as the lead director; former Senator Michael Kirby; Brian Smith, a former BC Cabinet minister and chairman of both BC Hydro and the CNR; John Brussa, a knowledgeable energy lawyer in Calgary from Canada; and, from the United States, Gordon Giffin, the former US ambassador to Canada, and Bill Weld, the former governor of Massachusetts.

In 2011 my friend Tim Armstrong asked me to join the board of governors of the Radiation Safety Institute of Canada – created in 1980 after concerns about radiation became a major and tragic issue in relation to the Elliott Lake uranium mines in Ontario. As I write, I am still very much on a learning curve in this area, though I am highly committed to the institute's goals.

The institute's mandate is to promote radiation safety in the workplace, the home, and the environment in order to prevent injuries and cancers resulting from unacceptable levels of exposure to radiation. The institute is a self-governing, national, not-for-profit organization with an independent board of governors – whose members serve pro bono. Funding is provided by governments and the private sector. Both the federal and the provincial governments are responsible for overseeing the protection of workers from radiation, though safety concerns extend well beyond uranium mines and nuclear power plants and can be an issue wherever X-ray machines are used. In particular, the radioactive gas radon can be found in homes, schools, and workplaces. Radon forms naturally, and its concentration can increase within buildings and present a real health threat.

Previously Armstrong was the long-time deputy minister of labour in the Davis and Peterson governments, as well as a deputy ministry of industry, trade, and technology in the government of Bob Rae. All his life he has been committed to the rights of workers, and it is very difficult to refuse a request from him. The institute's first CEO was Fergal Nolan, who served until 2012 and has been succeeded by Steve Mahoney, a former head of the Ontario Workplace Safety and Insurance Board and member of both the Ontario and the federal parliaments.

* * *

In 2008 I was asked to become chancellor of York University. The invitation came from the president of the university, Mamdouh Shoukri, and the board chair, Marshall "Micky" Cohen, a former federal deputy minister of finance, with the approval of the York Board of Governors. I regarded it as a compliment that I was invited by an Egyptian-born president and a Jewish board chair, yet on the day of our meeting I committed the embarrassing faux-pas of wearing my University of Toronto tie!

My main connection with York University came through its Osgoode Hall Law School, from which I graduated in 1958. At that time the school was still located in the venerable Osgoode Hall on Queen Street West, where it had been since its founding in 1889. The law school moved into a new building at York in 1969. I was particularly interested in York's student diversity and its commitment to social justice. In any given year, the university comprises more than 50,000 students with ancestral origins in some seventy countries. A significant percentage of the graduates are the first in their families to attend university – a fact that makes the convocations particularly happy events.

A chancellor's duties are largely ceremonial, but it is possible to have some influence on the priorities the university sets for itself. York University is located in the northwest York-Finch area of Toronto. I suggested that members of the university's faculty and student body could assist many of the disadvantaged people in that part of Toronto by pro-

viding mentoring, for instance, or legal assistance and vocational guidance. Part-way into my chancellorship, I was delighted when the York
University TD Bank Community Engagement Centre was established
at the Yorkgate Mall, a "user friendly" location near the university.

During my career at Gowlings, the firm has been very supportive of
my volunteering in community projects, including a number of initiatives related to youth: community legal clinics, legal education, pov-
erty-reduction initiatives, and scholarships for young people who have
been in conflict with the law but have turned their lives around. When
combined with my arbitration and legal mediation work, my professional life continues to be challenging and enjoyable.

38

Reflections on My Life

My life has had no master plan. Not until I became a judge at the age of fifty-nine and realized I could stay in that role for sixteen years did I ever think seriously about what I might be doing ten years hence. Nor did I ever envision that I would have so many different careers. My life is a result not so much of good management as of good luck, and a willingness to accept new challenges and opportunities when they arose.

I was fortunate in my parents, who were devoted to their sons. We were encouraged always to do our best, whether in school, sports, or summer jobs. They never mentioned success in any specific area, so it was difficult to feel a failure. Many people have spoken generously about the careers of the four McMurtry brothers, occasionally describing us as a "Kennedy family without money." Our father never allowed himself to appear overly ambitious for his sons, but his own competitive instincts certainly had an influence. This fact, coupled with his integrity and our mother's humanity and sensitivity, provided us with an important and positive home environment, despite our father's own health and financial challenges during the last decade of his life (chapter 2).

Sport has been one of the few continuing threads throughout my life. I believe that my success in football, combined with our father's enthusiasm for all things athletic, encouraged my brothers to become successful in football and other sports. I have long believed that team sports teach social skills, such as teamwork and not taking oneself too seriously, which can be useful in human interaction in every context.

My years as a football coach also taught me a great deal about motivating people. Art has been another thread in my life – a solitary endeavour, but one that has provided endless satisfaction and relaxation as I've carried my paintbox with me in all my various careers.

These careers, in turn, have been influenced significantly by individuals who provided guidance and encouragement. My belief in the value of public service was shaped by Dr Edmund Bradwin as I spent my university summers as a labourer/teacher with Frontier College under his leadership (chapter 3). Once I moved into law, Arthur Maloney became a mentor in criminal law and in supporting important causes such as the abolition of the death penalty (chapter 7). Later, Bill Davis and Dalton Camp awakened my interest in electoral politics (chapter 8). In my ten years as attorney general of Ontario, Davis gave me the support and independence I needed to implement no fewer than fifty-nine law-reform statutes even as I was responsible for the administration of justice as well as criminal prosecutions in the province (chapter 13). The highlight of these years was the patriation of the Canadian Constitution with an entrenched Charter of Rights after more than fifty years of debate between the federal and provincial governments (chapter 22). Later still, a strong recommendation from Davis led to yet another totally unexpected adventure – as part-time chair and CEO of the Canadian Football League (chapter 31).

My political career led Prime Minister Brian Mulroney to appoint me as high commissioner to the United Kingdom (chapters 29 and 30). To represent Canada in the mother of democracies was truly an exciting adventure, particularly given the issues I encountered related to apartheid in South Africa and the troubles in Northern Ireland. I have often wondered since whether I would have enjoyed a foreign-service career, but I think not. As an ambassador, I was a visitor in a foreign county, and my activities and policymaking were limited. Moreover, the many moves involved in such a career would not have worked well for my large family.

Curiously, perhaps, I never thought seriously about becoming a judge. My first judicial appointment as associate chief justice of Ontario in 1991 occurred largely because of a close friendship with Chief Justice Frank Callaghan, who had earlier been my first deputy attorney general. Then, in an unusual twist of events, my actual judicial appointment was facilitated by the support of Bob Rae, the new NDP premier of Ontario (chapter 33). In that role, I focused on strengthening the collegiality of the court following the stresses caused by the merger of the former County and High courts. I was appointed chief justice of the High Court, which later became the Superior Court of Justice, in 1994 and chief justice of Ontario in 1996 (chapter 34). I soon realized I had moral influence beyond my own court in relation to other courts and to the broader public. I tried to use that "bully pulpit" to speak publicly about social justice, to open up the justice system to all, and to advocate a transformation of the judiciary by appointing the first visible-minority judges to the Court of Appeal for Ontario.

* * *

Before we were married, Ria and I spoke of having six children, and that did happen despite the health risks she faced with her last two pregnancies. Our children have remained close to us and to each other, along with most of our extended family of grandchildren, nieces, nephews, and cousins.

Our eldest child, Janet, now fifty-five years old, has served as a Superior Court judge in Regina since 2006, having earlier been a member of the Provincial Court for eleven years, including a term as associate chief justice of that court. Her husband, Ross Macnab, a long-time lawyer with the Saskatchewan Ministry of Justice, has taken early retirement to write, including blogs for the *Huffington Post* in Canada. They have three sons – Aidan, Caillen, and Tynan – who have not yet decided on their future careers.

Our eldest son, Jim, age fifty-four, has been a career high-school teacher for the most part in Surrey, BC, after serving as the headmaster of the Canadian Neuchâtel Junior College in Switzerland for six years. He is also a community activist, particularly in environmental issues. He ran unsuccessfully as a federal candidate for the Liberal Party under Paul Martin in 2006. His wife, Laurie, whom he met while they were both undergraduates at Queen's University in Kingston, is vice-principal of an elementary school in Surrey. Their oldest child, Lauren, graduated from the French common-law program at the University of Ottawa in June 2013. Their second daughter, Marlena, who graduated on the Dean's Honour List at the University of British Columbia, is also planning to pursue a degree in law. Their son, Devin, who stands six-foot-four, has so far majored in basketball at a small BC community college, though he is now focusing more seriously on his studies and may perhaps follow his sisters into law.

Our third child, Harry, now fifty-one, practised commercial litigation until 2011, when he was forced to retire because of Parkinson's disease.

This diagnosis is sadly ironic, given his dedication to assisting physically challenged children for more than a decade. In 1977, when he was fifteen years old, he wanted to go to a twelve-day basketball camp. Somewhat to his annoyance, I said I would be pleased to pay for the camp if he did a few weeks of volunteer work during the summer. He reluctantly agreed to volunteer at the insensitively named Blue Mountain Crippled Children's Camp in Collingwood, Ontario. After just one day there, Harry was dedicated to these children, and he returned to the camp for the three following summers. He then spent two more summers at the again misnamed Ontario Crippled Children's Centre, which is now the Holland Bloorview Kids Rehabilitation Hospital.

Harry became convinced that the children wanted more real challenges, including canoeing and camping, and he was determined to create the appropriate facility. He asked a family friend, John Latimer, the owner of the long-established Kilcoo Camp for boys in Minden, Ontario, if he would accept a few of the physically challenged children for two-week programs in his camp. They would simply share the facilities with the mainstream campers – a special camp within a camp that became known as Camp Awakening. Several years later a female version was established at a girls' camp nearby. Harry spent six summers as the director of Camp Awakening and sat on the board for many years. As a very positive result, he found that the mainstream campers developed a great deal of respect for their physically challenged friends. And, on a personal note more recently, he has found that his involvement with these children has helped place his own serious illness in perspective and reinforced his courage. Certainly, his eight-year struggle with Parkinson's has been characterized by grace, good humour, and a complete lack of self-pity.

Harry has had a complex marital career. His first wife, Valerie, now the chair of the Canadian Olympic Foundation, is the mother of their three sons, David, Thomas, and Matthew. David is studying engineering at McGill University, Thomas is in the Arts Faculty at Queen's University, and Matthew will begin a business course in the fall of 2013. Julie, his second wife, is, like Valerie, a truly wonderful woman, as is his fiancée, Deborah, who lives in New York City. All three enjoy close relations with our family and have contributed a great deal to our happiness.

Our fourth child, Jeannie, a yoga instructor by training, is the momma to her partner Patty's daughter, Kaia, who in a few short years has become a centrepiece of our family. It is widely known that Jeannie has had her same-sex partner for a long time, and sometimes people suggest that her relationship influenced me in the *Halpern* decision in 2003. Jeannie's involvement in the gay community has probably been an important part of my education. However, despite this couple's devotion to each other, they have never expressed any interest in getting married.

Our youngest children, Erin and Michael, chose to be actors. Notwithstanding excellent training and early acclaim, they have found this most difficult profession to be an emotional rollercoaster, although, to their credit, the glass is usually more half full than half empty. Erin lives with her partner, Lisa, who is the principal of a French elementary school in Toronto, and Michael and his wife, Chris, have two daughters, Callie and Zoey.

Our children are members of a Canadian society that has changed hugely during my lifetime. As a result, Canada has become a far more diverse and interesting society, but one with increasing challenges for young people, many of whom face uncertain economic futures.

* * *

I was also very fortunate to grow up with my talented younger brothers, Bill, John, and Robert. Bill, a lawyer and excellent mediator, died in February 2007, three months before my retirement, after a two-year struggle with lung cancer. He faced his personal tragedy with tremendous courage. He appeared to have an ambivalent or perhaps agnostic view when it came to the worship of a God, in that he embraced the general principles of Christianity but not the Holy Trinity. He arranged for Douglas Stout, the Anglican dean of St James Cathedral, who is married to his good friend Justice Mary Lou Benotto, to conduct a service that did not contain "too much religion."

When the day arrived, the well-known blues singer Salome Bey and her daughter performed, along with a small blues orchestra. Bill had a host of friends in the black community in Toronto, dating from his university student summers as a railway sleeping-car porter. He was much loved and respected in that group, and I shall always remember the pride of being able to work with him in the continuing battle against racism. Bill was a great athlete and a devoted sports fan, so I was not surprised when I found that he had arranged for a TV set displaying tapes of Maple Leaf hockey games to be on view at the reception following the funeral service. For several years before his death, Bill had been writing a musical about one of our heroes, Paul Robeson, the great American baritone and athlete. Sadly, when an accomplished black singer friend, Val Pringle, who had agreed to play the lead role, was murdered in Botswana, the project went into limbo.

Around this same time our younger brothers John and Bob were also contemplating retirement from their professions – respectively as a philosophy professor and an orthopaedic surgeon/teacher. For some years John, who taught at Guelph University, had railed against the sixty-five-year-old retirement age for university professors in contrast to the seventy-five-year age limit for federally appointed judges. As his own retirement age approached, the university asked him to continue his teaching indefinitely. Instead, he decided to retire and devote his time to his academic writing. An internationally renowned socialist philosopher, his best-known book, *The Cancer Stage of Capitalism*, written more than a decade ago, has proved to be remarkably prescient, given the international depression that began in 2008. Among his current projects is a daunting request from UNESCO to "construct, author and edit *Philosophy and World Problems* as a multi-volume study of world philosophy." John was named a Fellow of the Royal Society of Canada in June 2001 for his outstanding contributions to the study of humanities.

My youngest brother, Bob, nine years my junior, enjoyed an eclectic and successful career in medicine until his retirement in 2012. During his medical residency he spent two years in Africa, first in a mission hospital in South Africa and then with the Canadian International Development Agency, teaching in Uganda. Following his orthopaedic residency, he did a fellowship in hand surgery at the University of Iowa. Bob began his practice at Sunnybrook Hospital in Toronto, where he founded and directed Canada's first trauma unit, helicoptering patients from distant accident scenes to the hospital. In 1987 Bob was appointed chair of surgery at both the University of Calgary and at the Foothills Hospital in Calgary, and from 1992 to 1999 he served as dean of medicine at the University of Western Ontario. He then became the first "Cameron" Visiting Chair at Health Canada, where he was responsible for providing advice to Health Minister Allan Rock and his deputy minister, David Dodge. Bob has served in a number of other prestigious government posts – as a member of the Health Council of Canada, for example, and as a special adviser to former Saskatchewan premier Roy Romanow during his inquiry into the Future of Health Care in Canada. In 2011 Bob was appointed to the Order of Canada.

One of my favourite photographs on my desk shows the four Mc-Murtry brothers as teammates on a rugby team many years ago. John played in the Canadian Football League for two years, and, together, we created a bit of havoc with our opposing teams. Throughout our lives, we have all remained close. Although we've had academic disagreements, right versus left, with very few exceptions we've maintained a united front to the outside world. Any success we have enjoyed we attribute to the encouragement and expectations of our parents.

* * *

As I write this final chapter, I am nearing my eighty-first birthday. In conclusion, I would like to share with my readers a few thoughts in relation to politics and the law – the two careers that have occupied most of my life.

I have not been a member of any political party since I was appointed a judge in 1991. I do, however, exercise my franchise, usually voting for the candidate who I believe has the most potential to contribute to the betterment of society. The candidate's political party can also be very relevant to my choice. Political ideology has little interest or appeal to me, except for my deep concerns about its extreme forms. In this context, the move by the US Republican Party to the extreme right and the rise of the "Tea Party" have alarmed me greatly. I believe these developments represent the rejection of the social contract – the commitment of the individual to assist the most oppressed and vulnerable in society. In my view, this commitment can generally be met outside charitable giving by supporting a political party that demonstrates a level of compassion for the most disadvantaged.

I have been publicly critical of the intense lack of compassion in the federal government led by Stephen Harper. This trait, combined with the government's obvious political partisanship, has deeply divided Canadian society. The term "wedge issue" was not in common parlance when I served in electoral politics, but, in its simplest terms, it encourages political parties to look for issues that will drive a wedge between their traditional supporters and the majority of the electorate, knowing that a minority of voter support can guarantee a majority government in a three- or four-party system, especially in an era of low voter turnout. In the years when Mike Harris was premier in Ontario, for example, he found that demonizing people on welfare and members of the teaching profession were successful political strategies. By these means he attracted the right-wing vote and won a majority government, even when a majority of eligible voters were opposed to his policies.

The Harper government has used this strategy in a number of contexts, specifically in its false claim of an increase in crime rates even when Statistics Canada maintains the reverse. The government's response has simply been that it does not believe in statistics – and it has dealt harshly with the traditional role of Statistics Canada. Traditionally, a tough-on-crime rhetoric has influenced the voting public, whether supported by statistics or not. As a result, the federal government has committed to building more prisons, legislating tougher sentences, and reducing financial resources to assist our vulnerable youth.

One of the many ironies in this approach to crime is that it is being rejected by Harper's Republican allies in the United States. The Republicans now publicly recognize that the tough-on-crime policy, particularly in the period from 1980 to 2010, has been a failure. Even the well-known conservative pastor Pat Robertson has been critical of the earlier policy, pointing out that, during those years, twenty-one prisons, but only one university, were built in California. Millions of young males, particularly black men, are warehoused in US prisons, often for minor drug offences, while resources for public education are starved. The Harper government has also appeared to be hostile to the world of science: the cutting of many scientific grants will have negative consequences for decades to come.

At the end of 2012 I received a card from Senator Marjory LeBreton, the Harper government's leader in the Senate. I had been out of touch with her for some time, except for the annual exchange of Christmas cards. However, I shall always be grateful for her hard work when I ran unsuccessfully for the leadership of the provincial Progressive Conservative Party in 1985. In the note in her card, Senator LeBreton took me to task about some of my public criticisms of the Harper government, particularly those related to the criminal justice system. Given our long friendship, I deemed it appropriate to reply:

I do admit to some considerable concerns about the federal government. I do not intend to be exhaustive, but my concerns began with the decision not to appoint Dennis O'Connor, my associate chief justice, as my successor as chief justice of Ontario. Dennis is one of the most respected legal figures in Canada …

My other comments will be briefer and are as follows:

The P.M. has done a great deal to undermine the accountability of Parliament as well as fuelling a poisonous partisan atmosphere.

I have long been an advocate for youth justice and am very disturbed by the repeated false comments about increases in youth crime. When Mulroney was P.M., his government advocated less youth incarceration.

I am concerned about the lack of federal government initiatives to encourage and assist provincial governments in increasing programs for vulnerable youth. Similarly, by the cancellation of the federal correctional farms, which according to criminologists have been quite successful.

There are many additional concerns that I harbour, but in summary there appears to be almost a complete lack of compassion in the federal government for the less fortunate, beginning with our Aboriginal peoples. Winning elections is not in my view the only test!

Some will regard my complaints as those of a grumpy old man, but grumpy or not I still retain a great deal of appreciation and affection for you!

I am deeply concerned about the large percentage of Canadians who have become cynical about the ability of the political system to resolve or even ameliorate our social challenges. In particular, I worry that young people have lost faith in the political process and are becoming more and more disengaged. There is already considerable evidence of this apathy, which, if allowed to continue, could have disastrous consequences for our democracy. At the same time, I remain committed to the fundamental, indeed crucial, importance of electoral politics.

When I first ran for political office in 1973, I strongly believed that politics was a most honourable profession. Although there has always been a degree of scepticism about politics, I was satisfied that it provided an opportunity to make a unique contribution to the betterment of society.

* * *

The fifty-fifth anniversary of my call to the Ontario bar is fast approaching. I entered law school with the idea that the legal profession was essentially a helping profession. My lawyer father embraced that view, and he passed it on to me and my brother Bill. In my view, the legal profession has been struggling for some years now to determine whether it is fundamentally a business or a helping profession. The reality is that it is both, and the challenge is whether it can maintain the helping tradition as a significant and meaningful element of the profession.

It is in the context of the law as a helping profession that the many challenges relating to access to justice generally arise. The issue undoubtedly dates back to the beginning of recorded history, but there is at present a consensus that the challenges increase with every successive decade. I dwelt on this topic in my first speech as attorney general in October 1975, and the Right Honourable Beverley McLachlin, the current chief justice of Canada, addresses it frequently in her remarks.

Many pilot projects have been attempted over the years in search of a remedy, but the challenge remains and, unfortunately, continues to increase. When lawyer Malcolm Heins retired in early 2012 after ten years as the chief executive officer of the Law Society of Upper Canada, the governing body of Ontario's lawyers, he made some interesting comments about the issue of access to justice: "The complexity of our laws and the importance of excessive processes have pushed up costs," he said, "making our justice system, good as it is, inaccessible to most and therefore maybe unsustainable in the longer term. There's really no one in overall charge of the justice system, so between two levels of government and an independent judiciary, it is difficult to effect meaningful reform. I think personally that the legal profession needs to push government and the judiciary to reform. That's the most significant challenge the justice system faces."

Having been an attorney general, chief justice of the Trial Court, and chief justice of Ontario, I strongly believe that governments and the judiciary would welcome changes that increased the public's access to justice. The traditional difficulty has been to obtain a reform consensus within the legal profession. Major corporations can usually afford adequate access to the courts because legal fees are tax deductible. For most individuals, however, the cost is prohibitive unless the person is a plaintiff with a strong cause of action. In those cases, particularly personal-injury cases, lawyers are usually willing to enter into a contingency-fee arrangement. However, court records demonstrate an increasing percentage of self-represented litigants. Although the issue grows in importance with each successive year, it is not yet a serious priority for any government in Canada. The great majority of the public do not expect to face the problem and, therefore, government focus lies elsewhere.

The January 2013 edition of the *Canadian Lawyer* contains an article entitled "The Scourge of Unrepresented Litigants," which states that record numbers of Canadians with legal cases looming no longer turn to lawyers to represent them in civil matters. The availability of fee-for-service legal-aid lawyers in criminal cases is somewhat greater. According to the author, the associate chief justice of the Alberta Court of Queen's Bench in a highly publicized decision "issued a call to arms against self-represented litigants," referring to their arguments as usually "contemptibly stupid." The article also refers to Professor Julie McFarlane of the University of Windsor Law School, who is conducting a national research project on the subject of unrepresented litigants and is quoted as saying that she "has found as many as 80 per cent of family disputes involve self-represented litigants." She concludes by making the astute observation that the vast majority of self-represented litigants "are simply people who can't afford good legal representation."

Most people wrongly assume that provincial legal-aid plans provide a great deal more legal assistance than actually is the case. At some point in the not too distant future, the lack of adequate access to legal assistance could well create a real degree of social unrest and, in the worst-case scenario, lead to a form of vigilante justice in the context of violence between opposing litigants. That has already happened in Russia, where an inadequate legal system has led to physical violence and destruction of property.

In Canada it is ironic that, at least in the large centres, where most cases are settled out of court, fewer and fewer young lawyers have the opportunity to appear in court. The growing phenomenon referred to as the "disappearing civil trial" has been the subject of much comment in Canada and the United States. In Canada some younger lawyers are leaving large law firms to accept lower salaries as assistant Crown prosecutors in order to gain court experience, the flush of adrenalin, and the greater satisfaction that generally accompanies trial advocacy.

Many lawyers are willing and even anxious to do pro bono advocacy, and many do. However, identifying cases that are worthy in a credible sense of pro bono assistance can present complex administrative challenges. An effective program requires a process that can identify both the appropriate case and the appropriate volunteer lawyer. That was the reason for establishing, just over a decade ago, Pro Bono Law Ontario, the administrators of which develop programs to identify both the appropriate recipients and the volunteer lawyers.

There is also an understandable degree of tension between pro bono lawyers and the staff lawyers who work in the eighty community legal clinics in Ontario. When I became Ontario's attorney general, legal clinics were a priority for me. They remain so as I chair an advisory group known as the Friends of Legal Aid Clinics. As chief justice of Ontario I also assisted in the creation of Pro Bono Law Ontario, so I have long been aware of the tension between the legal clinics and PBLO (chapter 34). In my view, the tension is probably related to staff lawyers' job-security concerns in the sense of their possibly being replaced by volunteer lawyers at some point in the future. Understandably enough, my personal assurances that this will not occur have not eliminated the tension.

Access to justice by means of adequate legal advice will continue to be an issue, probably indefinitely. It is my view that more resources will have to be found for legal aid and pro bono volunteers with respect to duty counsel and other needed legal advice. In 2013 the Canadian Bar Association announced the creation of an inquiry into the future of legal practice, and I expect that the issue of access will be high on the agenda.

Throughout the long history of the legal profession, lawyers have been expected to perform services essential for both the individual and the collective welfare of society. It is this ideal that I have sought to serve. All along I have been inspired by the words of the poet Emerson: "Do not go where the path may lead; go instead where there is no path and leave a trail."

In all my careers in law, diplomacy, and politics, I hope I did just that.

Index

2013   Roy McMurtry, *Memoirs and Reflections*
        Charlotte Gray, *The Massey Murder: A Maid, Her Master, and the Trial that Shocked a Nation*
        C. Ian Kyer, *Lawyers, Families, and Businesses: The Shaping of a Bay Street Law Firm, 1863–1963*
        G. Blaine Baker and Donald Fyson, eds., *Essays in the History of Canadian Law, Volume XI: Quebec and the Canadas*
2012   R. Blake Brown, *Arming and Disarming: A History of Gun Control in Canada*
        Eric Tucker, James Muir, and Bruce Ziff, eds., *Property on Trial: Canadian Cases in Context*
        Shelley Gavigan, *Hunger, Horses, and Government Men: Criminal Law on the Aboriginal Plains, 1870–1905*
        Barrington Walker, ed., *The African Canadian Legal Odyssey: Historical Essays*
2011   Robert J. Sharpe, *The Lazier Murder: Prince Edward County, 1884*
        Philip Girard, *Lawyers and Legal Culture in British North America: Beamish Murdoch of Halifax*
        John McLaren, *Dewigged, Bothered, and Bewildered: British Colonial Judges on Trial, 1800–1900*
        Lesley Erickson, *Westward Bound: Sex, Violence, the Law, and the Making of a Settler Society*
2010   Judy Fudge and Eric Tucker, eds., *Work on Trial: Canadian Labour Law Struggles*
        Christopher Moore, *The British Columbia Court of Appeal: The First Hundred Years*
        Frederick Vaughan, *Viscount Haldane: 'The Wicked Step-father of the Canadian Constitution'*
        Barrington Walker, *Race on Trial: Black Defendants in Ontario's Criminal Courts, 1858–1958*
2009   William Kaplan, *Canadian Maverick: The Life and Times of Ivan C. Rand*
        R. Blake Brown, *A Trying Question: The Jury in Nineteenth-Century Canada*
        Barry Wright and Susan Binnie, eds., *Canadian State Trials, Volume III: Political Trials and Security Measures, 1840–1914*
        Robert J. Sharpe, *The Last Day, the Last Hour: The Currie Libel Trial* (paperback edition with a new preface)

David Murray, *Colonial Justice: Justice, Morality, and Crime in the Niagara District, 1791–1849*

F. Murray Greenwood and Barry Wright, eds., *Canadian State Trials, Volume II: Rebellion and Invasion in the Canadas, 1837–1839*

2001   Ellen Anderson, *Judging Bertha Wilson: Law as Large as Life*

Judy Fudge and Eric Tucker, *Labour before the Law: The Regulation of Workers' Collective Action in Canada, 1900–1948*

Laurel Sefton MacDowell, *Renegade Lawyer: The Life of J.L. Cohen*

2000   Barry Cahill, *'The Thousandth Man': A Biography of James McGregor Stewart*

A.B. McKillop, *The Spinster and the Prophet: Florence Deeks, H.G. Wells, and the Mystery of the Purloined Past*

Beverley Boissery and F. Murray Greenwood, *Uncertain Justice: Canadian Women and Capital Punishment*

Bruce Ziff, *Unforeseen Legacies: Reuben Wells Leonard and the Leonard Foundation Trust*

1999   Constance Backhouse, *Colour-Coded: A Legal History of Racism in Canada, 1900–1950*

G. Blaine Baker and Jim Phillips, eds., *Essays in the History of Canadian Law: Volume VIII – In Honour of R.C.B. Risk*

Richard W. Pound, *Chief Justice W.R. Jackett: By the Law of the Land*

David Vanek, *Fulfilment: Memoirs of a Criminal Court Judge*

1998   Sidney Harring, *White Man's Law: Native People in Nineteenth-Century Canadian Jurisprudence*

Peter Oliver, *'Terror to Evil-Doers': Prisons and Punishments in Nineteenth-Century Ontario*

1997   James W.St.G. Walker, *'Race,' Rights and the Law in the Supreme Court of Canada: Historical Case Studies*

Lori Chambers, *Married Women and Property Law in Victorian Ontario*

Patrick Brode, *Casual Slaughters and Accidental Judgments: Canadian War Crimes and Prosecutions, 1944–1948*

Ian Bushnell, *The Federal Court of Canada: A History, 1875–1992*

1996   Carol Wilton, ed., *Essays in the History of Canadian Law: Volume VII – Inside the Law: Canadian Law Firms in Historical Perspective*

William Kaplan, *Bad Judgment: The Case of Mr Justice Leo A. Landreville*

Murray Greenwood and Barry Wright, eds., *Canadian State Trials: Volume I – Law, Politics, and Security Measures, 1608–1837*

1995   David Williams, *Just Lawyers: Seven Portraits*

Hamar Foster and John McLaren, eds., *Essays in the History of Canadian Law: Volume VI – British Columbia and the Yukon*

W.H. Morrow, ed., *Northern Justice: The Memoirs of Mr Justice William G. Morrow*

Beverley Boissery, *A Deep Sense of Wrong: The Treason, Trials, and Transportation to New South Wales of Lower Canadian Rebels after the 1838 Rebellion*

1994   Patrick Boyer, *A Passion for Justice: The Legacy of James Chalmers McRuer*

Charles Pullen, *The Life and Times of Arthur Maloney: The Last of the Tribunes*

Jim Phillips, Tina Loo, and Susan Lewthwaite, eds., *Essays in the History of Canadian Law: Volume V – Crime and Criminal Justice*

Brian Young, *The Politics of Codification: The Lower Canadian Civil Code of 1866*

1993   Greg Marquis, *Policing Canada's Century: A History of the Canadian Association of Chiefs of Police*

Murray Greenwood, *Legacies of Fear: Law and Politics in Quebec in the Era of the French Revolution*

1992   Brendan O'Brien, *Speedy Justice: The Tragic Last Voyage of His Majesty's Vessel Speedy*

Robert Fraser, ed., *Provincial Justice: Upper Canadian Legal Portraits from the Dictionary of Canadian Biography*

1991   Constance Backhouse, *Petticoats and Prejudice: Women and Law in Nineteenth-Century Canada*

1990   Philip Girard and Jim Phillips, eds., *Essays in the History of Canadian Law: Volume III – Nova Scotia*

Carol Wilton, ed., *Essays in the History of Canadian Law: Volume IV – Beyond the Law: Lawyers and Business in Canada, 1830–1930*

1989   Desmond Brown, *The Genesis of the Canadian Criminal Code of 1892*

Patrick Brode, *The Odyssey of John Anderson*

1988   Robert Sharpe, *The Last Day, the Last Hour: The Currie Libel Trial*

John D. Arnup, *Middleton: The Beloved Judge*

1987   C. Ian Kyer and Jerome Bickenbach, *The Fiercest Debate: Cecil A. Wright, the Benchers, and Legal Education in Ontario, 1923–1957*

1986   Paul Romney, *Mr Attorney: The Attorney General for Ontario in Court, Cabinet, and Legislature, 1791–1899*

Martin Friedland, *The Case of Valentine Shortis: A True Story of Crime and Politics in Canada*

1985   James Snell and Frederick Vaughan, *The Supreme Court of Canada: History of the Institution*

1984   Patrick Brode, *Sir John Beverley Robinson: Bone and Sinew of the Compact*

David Williams, *Duff: A Life in the Law*

1983   David H. Flaherty, ed., *Essays in the History of Canadian Law: Volume II*
1982   Marion MacRae and Anthony Adamson, *Cornerstones of Order: Court-houses and Town Halls of Ontario, 1784–1914*
1981   David H. Flaherty, ed., *Essays in the History of Canadian Law: Volume I*